# Redrawing the Boundaries

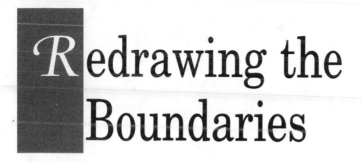

# Redrawing the Boundaries

## THE TRANSFORMATION OF ENGLISH AND AMERICAN LITERARY STUDIES

Edited by
STEPHEN GREENBLATT
AND GILES GUNN

The Modern Language Association of America
New York   1992

© 1992 by The Modern Language Association of America. All rights reserved

**Library of Congress Cataloging-in-Publication Data**

Redrawing the boundaries : the transformation of English and American
  literary studies / edited by Stephen Greenblatt and Giles Gunn.
      p.    cm.
    Includes bibliographical references and index.
    ISBN 0-87352-395-4 (cloth)   ISBN 0-87352-396-2 (pbk.)
    1. English literature—History and criticism—Theory, etc.
  2. American literature—History and criticism—Theory, etc.
  3. Criticism—Great Britain—History—20th century.   4. Criticism—
  United States—History—20th century.   5. Canon (Literature)
  I. Greenblatt, Stephen Jay.   II. Gunn, Giles B.
  PR21.R43   1992
  820.9'0001—dc20          92-24416


Published by The Modern Language Association of America
10 Astor Place, New York, New York 10003-6981

Printed on recycled paper

# $C$ ontents

# $\mathcal{A}$cknowledgments

In addition to expressing our gratitude to the contributors, for whose patience and perseverance during a long and demanding editorial process we are very grateful, we would like to thank several people at the Modern Language Association: Walter Achtert, without whose initial encouragement this project would never have seen the light of day; Phyllis Franklin, who was quick to appreciate its importance and generous in her show of support; Joseph Gibaldi, who took over its supervision early on and, in addition to lending some invaluable editorial assistance, has seen it through each stage of production with an admirable professionalism; and Rebecca Lanning, for removing almost everything onerous from a copyediting process that was nothing if not exacting. To Robin Craig we owe special thanks for checking citations and assisting with proofreading. The preparation of this manuscript was supported in part by a grant from General Research Fund of the Academic Senate of the University of California, Santa Barbara.

SG and GG

ntroduction

## STEPHEN GREENBLATT AND GILES GUNN

Literary studies in English are in a period of rapid and sometimes disorienting change. In addition to the configuration of new areas of teaching and research, from medieval studies and postmodernist studies to African American literary studies and subaltern studies, the last several decades have witnessed the development of a variety of methodological and interdisciplinary initiatives: deconstruction, cultural materialism, gender studies, new historicism. At least one historical field, namely, Renaissance studies, is under pressure to change its name; others, like American literary studies before and after the Civil War, eighteenth-century studies, and modernist studies, have experienced a series of challenges to their constitutive interpretive paradigms. And virtually every field has been altered, sometimes radically, by the recovery of lost or marginalized texts of women writers. Just as none of the critical approaches that antedate this period, from psychological and Marxist criticism to reader-response theory and cultural criticism, has remained stable, so none of the historical fields and subfields that constitute English and American literary studies has been left untouched by revisionist energies.

Not surprisingly, such developments have met with a varied reception. For some readers, as the favorable response to a book like Allan Bloom's *Closing of the American Mind* revealed, these changes have seemed to pose a threat to humanistic education. For others, they have been welcomed as evidence of a profession in the process of renewing itself. Many members of our profession, however, find themselves situated uncertainly between condemnation and celebration. Convinced neither that some rough beast is slouching toward Bethlehem to be born nor that we are witnessing again the rise of a phoenix, they find themselves vacillating uneasily between the belief that received opinions and procedures have for too long gone unchallenged and the view that much revisionist activity may be motivated more by modishness or political posturing than by critical insight. That English and American literary studies have undergone a series of transformations in the last several decades is obvious; what to make of them in one's own teaching and research is less clear.

It is quite possible, of course, to exaggerate the stability of English and American literary studies in earlier periods; there have always been change, conflict, and diversity in our profession. But until quite recently, professional

1

differences rarely called into question the cohesiveness of the field as a whole. Most graduate programs, for example, fostered the conviction that it was still possible to grasp the whole picture. Doctoral oral and written examinations in the 1960s typically expected candidates to answer questions on English and American literature from *Beowulf* to T. S. Eliot's *Four Quartets*; if there was no similar breadth in theoretical expectations, this was only because there was very little sense of a range of competing theories. While the difference between critical reading and historical scholarship (and hence between the interpretation and the contextualization of works of art) was strongly felt, this difference could largely be set aside in the interest of close study of the great works themselves.

English and American literary studies were held together by an uneasy alliance of older historicists and New Critics who were willing to suspend some of their disagreements for the sake of creating graduate programs that combined historical "coverage" with training in close reading. The object of close reading was to train students in the analysis of the principal works of the literary canon, which were assumed, in turn, to reflect the relations between, as the title of Eliot's famous essay described it, "tradition and the individual talent." Graduate courses were typically designed to display the interaction between these two basic coordinates, and academic requirements for advanced degrees were established to ensure that specialization in the humanities was not purchased, as it often appeared to be in the sciences, at the expense of a general familiarity with the materials of the entire field.

Now, however, even in those graduate and undergraduate programs where this consensus is still honored, there is an uneasy feeling that these requirements, and the assumptions on which they are premised, belong to a vanishing order of things. In part this feeling may arise simply from changing patterns of reading—older members of the profession now often lament that their brightest students are more interested in becoming theoretically sophisticated than widely read—but in greater measure it derives from changes in the underlying organization of knowledge that defines the discipline. As the parameters of individual historical fields have been redrawn and new theoretical and methodological orientations have been devised, the possibility of a unifying, totalizing grasp of our subject has, for all but the very few, receded. And the technique of close reading that was yoked to the service of the larger enterprise has also begun to recede. In the face of new pressures of professionalization, the global generalities and disciplinary distinctions that once held departments together are coming to seem less meaningful. We are fast becoming a profession of specialties and subspecialties whose rapid formation and re-formation prevent many members of the profession (and especially those burdened with heavy teaching loads who work at some distance from major centers of research activity) from keeping abreast of significant developments even in their own areas of expertise.

    *Redrawing the Boundaries* attempts to remedy this situation without pretending that the field can be comprehended within a single, cohesive frame. What confronts us at the present time in English and American literary studies is not a unified field at all but diverse historical projects and critical idioms that are not organized around a single center but originate from a variety of sources, some of which lie outside the realm of literary study altogether and intersect one another often at strange angles. To provide an adequate sense of the way the field has been reconstituted, we have thus been obliged to place a disproportionate emphasis on significant departures rather than important continuities. This emphasis has given to all the essays prepared for this volume a selective focus: they were written not to furnish a full account of the state of scholarship in any given area but to disclose some of those places where scholarship has responded to contemporary pressures. These responses have raised far-reaching questions about disciplinary mapping. Why are such maps made? On what principles are they based? Who makes and maintains them? What institutions and practices do they serve? How does one go about examining, challenging, or replacing them?

    As American higher education has become more accessible to people of different backgrounds—ethnic, racial, social, cultural, sexual, and religious— teachers of literature have found that the traditional humanistic curriculum seems less representative. This perception has aroused interest in revising and expanding the literary canon; it has also forced into the open long-neglected questions about the assumptions on which that curriculum was based, the process by which it was created, the public constituencies it was designed to serve, the social and educational problems it was perceived to address, and the intellectual and heuristic purposes it was intended to fulfill.

    Another development that has focused fresh attention on the map-making practices of literary studies has been the reconception of its object. What was once conceived as a "work" is now, in most fields of literary scholarship, construed as a "text," and this critical shift of focus from forms of the signified to processes of signification has raised serious questions about a number of other widely accepted interpretive conventions. Chief among them may be the "scene of writing" itself, which posits, as the archetypal "literary" situation, an individual author toiling in isolation from history and society to bring into being a work of personal artistic authenticity. But now that this "scene" has been repeatedly depicted as a hermeneutic "fiction"—that is, a critical construct designed in part to legitimate certain ways of reading modern works and to delegitimate others—other interpretive assumptions have been called into question as well: that works of art can be securely isolated from all other texts; that reading, interpretation, and criticism are primarily reflective, passive, and secondary activities; that the modes of analysis appropriate to literary study cannot be applied to the interpretation of nonliterary cultural forms; and that the distinctions between text and context can always be maintained to protect the integrity of "literary" understanding.

English and American literary studies, along with composition studies, have now become much more self-conscious about the shifting conditions of their own making and remaking, as well as about the comparable conditions that govern the making and remaking of the objects they study. Realizing that the objects of study are largely constituted by the terms in which we study them, our profession has become increasingly concerned with the problem of boundaries. Indeed, reflection on the meaning and function of boundaries has become a kind of "revolving Drummond light," in the language of Herman Melville's *Confidence-Man*, "raying away from itself all around it" (278).

The boundaries to be reckoned with in literary studies range from national, linguistic, historical, generational, and geographical to racial, ethnic, social, sexual, political, ethical, and religious. Moreover, literary studies have many demarcation lines that are less visible but no less determinative, boundaries that differentiate reading from writing, print cultures from oral, canonical traditions from heretical, elite cultures from vernacular, high art from popular. These boundaries can be crossed, confused, consolidated, and collapsed; they can also be revised, reconceived, redesigned, or replaced. The one thing they cannot be in literary studies is entirely abolished.

Appreciating the diverse roles that boundaries play is no easy task. It involves figuring out what boundaries enclose and what they exclude; whether they are drawn in bold, unbroken strokes or as a series of intermittent, irregular dashes; what functions in literary studies beyond the purely heuristic they actually serve; where one must stand conceptually either to accept or to redraw them; what sorts of obstacles are confronted by those who desire to challenge, nullify, or abolish them; how to define the places where boundaries cross, overlap, or converge; and what to say about the activities that seem to go on at the points where they intersect.

This determination is further complicated because boundaries are being breached all the time in literary studies. The breaching of boundaries occurs on the comparatively basic level of puns and tropes, where language solicits the mind to resist the movement of its own inherited associations, as well as on the more elevated level of disciplines themselves, where kinds of knowledge are constantly being restructured by interpretive paradigms that were never designed to make sense of them. It is tempting to believe that every time borders are crossed at the level of disciplines one automatically enters the domain of the interdisciplinary, but this assumption confuses the desire to see from different sides of the same border with the desire to reconceive the relation between various borders. The disciplinary gives way to the interdisciplinary only when changes in interpretive frames actually manage to produce changes in what can be seen with their assistance and only when reconceptions of the question also change what can be represented as an answer.

Foregrounding the issue of boundaries has reminded us that literature is not something given once and for all but something constructed and reconstructed, the product of shifting conceptual entitlements and limits. Not only is the canon of literary works in any genre fashioned by a simultaneous perambulation and transgression of boundaries but the very concept of the literary is itself continually renegotiated. Any study of literature, then, is necessarily bound up implicitly or explicitly with an interrogation of imaginary boundaries: their identification or definition, the regulation of what may cross them and at what times and under what circumstances, the alarms that go off when unauthorized crossings occur, and so forth. There are no transcendent or absolute rules about what belongs in the zone of the literary and in the zone of the nonliterary. On the contrary, the lines can be drastically redrawn, and the consequences of this redrawing can be considerable: merely contemplate, for example, what is at stake in conceiving of the Hebrew scriptures or the Christian Bible as literature.

A comparable mapping and remapping characterizes the field of literary criticism: research projects that would in one generation have resulted in ostracism are in the next rewarded with tenure; questions that at first seemed absurd come in time to be accepted as routine; a technical vocabulary that initially appeared to belong to a different discipline altogether is relocated at the very center of the enterprise of literary analysis. Conversely, practices that were formerly taken as givens are latterly almost completely given up; that which once passed for a satisfactory and even brilliant answer comes to seem woefully inadequate; and texts that did not seem to qualify as "literature" at all are celebrated as major achievements. It is easy to dismiss these transformations as "mere" changes in intellectual fashion, as if fashion were not—or at least should not be—important to literary intellectuals. But in fact continual refashioning is at the center of the profession of literary study: it is both a characteristic of the texts we study and a crucial means to keep those texts and our own critical practices from exhaustion and sterility.

But what, more particularly, is the status of the terms we have been using to describe the shifting, unstable category of literary study (and, for that matter, of "literature")? In an illuminating study of the geographical idea of frontiers in France, the historian Peter Sahlins remarks that these frontiers reflect "neither an 'interest' nor an 'ideology' but a belief that gave shape to an imagined national space, bounded and unified" (1425). We can perhaps say something comparable for the notion of literature: literature is not entirely separable from either interest or ideology, but it is not reducible to those either. Indeed, in certain circumstances literature may pull quite sharply against both interest and ideology, may even function precisely as their opposite. A "belief [in] an imagined . . . space" seems closer to a sense of what literature is, though it is not clear that this space is always "national" or "unified." The odd thing, in fact, about literature as an imagined territory is that there are apparently no natural limits—and hence, it would seem, there are apparently no natural limits to the field of literary criticism.

But if there are no natural limits—conceptual equivalents of impassable rivers or mountains—there are for literary critical studies at any given moment distinct boundaries that delineate not only the field as a whole but the provinces within it. One notion of such a boundary is that it marks, as an atlas in the time of Richelieu noted of the frontiers of a prince's realm, "the limits of his ambition" (P. Sahlins 1425). Each branch of literary study is inherently ambitious, eager to extend its sphere of influence. But this ambition has its limits—due either to some inherent restraint (for example, some limit to the resources of energy, intelligence, and time) or to some feature in the larger organization of knowledge that presents an insurmountable resistance. The sign of the limit here is a recognition that the advantage of expanding the sphere of influence would be outweighed by the cost. It is better to pull back or to profess a lack of interest or to look elsewhere.

This notion of limit can be set against the quite different implications of *frontier*. "The frontier," Sahlins writes, "was that which, etymologically and politically, 'stood face to [face to]' an enemy. This military frontier, implying bellicose expansion and zonal defense, stood opposed to the linear boundary or line of demarcation—the *limites*—of two jurisdictions or territories" (1425–26). Here there is little notion of an inner restraint in the face of obstacles and still less of a principle of indifference, a garnering up of energy for more important ends or more appropriate concerns. Now, what lies beyond the existing boundary is an enemy—whose forces are feared, whose territory is regarded with a hostile gaze. That gaze may have within it desire, envy, the wish to appropriate, or, alternatively, the wish to eradicate, tear down, reconstruct on a better pattern. In any case, what is meant here by *frontier* is not a fixed line but the furthest point to which you can push your forces, extend your influence.[1] Often, though not always, the frontier is the point beyond which they speak languages, eat foods, and worship gods that are simply not your own.[2]

The notion of the frontier as the zone between antagonists raises another issue of importance to the demarcation of the fields of literary criticism. The frontier is often not an abstract demarcation line but a place. The word *fins* in French, from which comes *confine*, implied in the Middle Ages "a strip of land and the border region of a country" (Febvre 208). As this border zone—

the marches—becomes bureaucratized, it becomes the place where you have to show papers, display documents authenticating your identity and authorizing your presence. Without these signs of identity and right, you are not allowed to pass; indeed, you risk being shot. One might add that documents, such as a passport, are characteristically *stamped*, and this stamp can perform one of several functions. In some instances, the stamp finds its analogue profession-ally in the permission it grants its bearer to travel through territory where he or she does not possess permanent institutional standing. In others it confers the equivalent of rights of citizenship by constituting a certification of competence implied by the various institutional structures of the profession, from the impri-matur of certain academic journals to panels at the annual convention of the Mod-ern Language Association to interdisciplinary research and teaching programs.

In general, we might think of the ways in which the frontiers are places of highest tension, vigilance, delay. But we should add that all talk of boundaries sits in a complex relation to a recognition of the larger whole within which most of the profession operates. We do not generally identify ourselves as occupying only one of the subgroups with which our volume is concerned. Each of those subgroups functions in a coordinated, if not exactly an integrated, system in which we may occupy more than one position. Within this system there are tensions, but these tensions are themselves part of the way the larger whole functions. The frontiers in our profession seem to exist only to be endlessly crossed, violated, renegotiated.

As we have seen, there is very little evidence that these frontiers are natural or stable. We can always imagine alternative ways of practicing our profession; indeed, we are continually called on to explore such alternatives. How then are frontiers established at all?

One of the ways in which historical claims of territory are established is through continuous possession, inheritance, ancient titles. A simple example in literature (as distinct from criticism) is rhyme. There is no reason in nature (including the nature of social life) why nonliterary discourse should not rhyme—we may notice, in fact, that rhyme is a frequent feature of the nonliter-ary. But literature has an ancient title to systematic, self-consciously sustained rhyme. The title could be challenged—one could imagine a phone book orga-nized by rhyme that would not be widely regarded as literature—but such a challenge is unlikely to occur precisely because it seems natural to associate rhyme with the literary. We might also argue that certain complex emotions, certain patterns of perception, are claimed by continuous possession or indis-putable title—so much so that when nonliterary discourse wishes to speak of certain phenomena it uses words like *quixotic, Kafkaesque, Rabelaisian*, or, for that matter, *tragic* and *comic*.

This last point shades into a slightly different conception of the histori-cal formation of boundaries: not through inheritance or lineage but through procedure, specific rights, jurisdiction. Now the territory is bounded not in a linear sense at all—even on the metaphorical level on which we have been speaking—but through more or less recognized rights. The root idea in this case is not space or territory but procedure: the limits we are speaking of here are procedural limits (though these limits are not necessarily distinct from a vague sense of territory). When someone practices the new historicism, or psychoanalytic criticism, or deconstruction, he or she is appealing not to an imaginary space but to a more or less established set of procedures, distinct from other procedures. The notion of jurisdiction thus seems quite useful in conceiving of the professional discriminations within which literary studies operate, since we can easily conceive of an identical set of expressions being judged differently according to the jurisdiction in which they find themselves.

Jurisdictional boundaries are generally settled by treaty. Criticism, for example, possesses written and unwritten treaties—subject, as all treaties are, to challenge, rupture, and abrogation but for a while at least understood by all parties as binding. The sense of solidarity that builds up around something like deconstruction, the new historicism, or cultural criticism, or around early modern, eighteenth-century, or modernist studies, is largely an illusion. Yet the illusory feeling is important, even if it is the result not of natural limits—there are none—but only of arbitrary regulations that have become naturalized in the imagination.

In some periods these regulations seem so powerful that they are almost entirely dehistoricized. One such period occurred during the consensus of the 1950s and early 1960s, when the terms of analysis associated with the New Criticism, and formalism generally, seemed to many in the profession almost universally applicable. Another may have just passed (or may be passing) when, though no one critical ideology has achieved similar dominance, many of the leading candidates, from deconstruction to post-Marxism, have shared a "hermeneutics of suspicion" that seemed entirely natural, indeed inevitable. But just as the New Criticism never succeeded in establishing complete hegemony in the profession (nor, for that matter, intended to), so the various critical orientations associated with the poststructuralist moment have failed to place all things in doubt. Were such practices or regulations ever to secure complete imaginative naturalization, they would effectively close off the realm of the frontier altogether. But even if this were theoretically conceivable, it would be intellectually and professionally disastrous. For the goal in literary studies is not to seal off the frontier completely but to keep it conceptually alive; what is sought are not closed boundaries but regulated thresholds, controlled passageways.

Where twenty-five or thirty years ago the profession was organized almost everywhere around the close reading of a stable, determinate set of masterworks, literary studies are now being reorganized in many institutions around an open series of inquiries about what constitutes literary interest in the first place. How is such interest produced, disseminated, assimilated? What forms best represent it in any given period? With what sorts of material are those forms linked? How are those forms to be explored and evaluated? And what purposes do the study of those forms serve in the societies where such study is still encouraged? Our hope is that by exploring these inquiries our book will reveal what gives contemporary English and American literary studies much of their intensity and consequence.

Yet we by no means wish to suggest that the only work in contemporary literary studies that commands attention or respect is configured around these issues alone. As various of our contributors attest, exemplary traditional scholarship is being produced in virtually all the historical fields, often with the help of insights derived from some of the newer critical movements. But we have asked our contributors to concentrate on what is most challenging and, at the same time, disquieting about this present period in English and American literary studies, and we have invited them to comment on such additional questions as these: How are significant changes in literary study generated? Where and how have these changes met resistance either within the institutions of literary study in America or in the wider society? Which alterations have produced (and continue to produce) the most resistance and conflict? Which seem to have been most easily absorbed and why? What effect have these changes had on the concept of "field" itself, or on the notion of professionalism associated with various fields, or even on the concept of literature associated with any given field's notion of literary professionalism?

This book's table of contents is a map that could easily have been drawn some other way. The study of American literature does not, for example, divide itself neatly in half, with the Civil War serving as the point of rupture or differentiation. Romantic studies is for many scholars no longer readily distinguishable either from studies of the late Augustan Age or from Victorian studies; and, for that matter, Victorian studies is no more easily differentiated from modernist studies than modernist studies is from postmodernist studies. Early modern studies encompasses much of what we have here isolated as seventeenth-century studies, and the latest phase of seventeenth-century studies blurs into eighteenth-century studies. African American studies at some points overlaps with ethnic studies; at others, it intersects with the boundary redrawing that is going on in American literary and cultural studies generally. Medieval studies now finds some of its deepest communities of interest with fields as remote as ethnic studies and postcolonial criticism, while a significant segment of postmodernist studies may well in time dissolve into a form of popular culture studies.

A similar fluidity and selectivity is evident when one considers our list of critical theories and methods. A number of critical dispositions—archetypal criticism, interpretation theory, reader-response criticism, semiotics, and linguistics—have long since made significant contributions to literary study and could easily have been assigned separate chapters in this book. Instead, for reasons of space, their importance is to some extent assessed in the course of other discussions. We have also had to forego extended treatment of various highly visible critical options that either, like ideological criticism, subsume several different critical orientations within themselves, such as Marxism, feminism, ethnic studies, and the new historicism, or, like cultural materialism and the new pragmatism, intersect and extend critical dispositions already included. To this list of omissions we must add as well a variety of more specialized critical enterprises—for example, the speech-act theory of John Searle or the ritual action studies associated with Victor Turner—that have done much to enrich contemporary critical discussion. Finally, we regret the lack of any extended treatment of such cognate areas as film theory, the study of photography, architectural criticism, the study of dance, art criticism, contemporary music criticism, and the sociology of taste and manners, all of which have entered into important conversational relations with the study of literature as a whole.

Still more complex are the serious issues to be reckoned with in treating as one critical method among others several of the intellectual enterprises taken up in the second half of this volume. This problem occurs most notably with respect to deconstruction, which, according to Jacques Derrida, can only be reduced to a technique of literary analysis by being distorted and trivialized. But a similar problem can be cited with the new historicisms, psychoanalytic criticism, gender studies, various forms of rhetorical and compositional criticism, and, above all, feminist studies. As central as these insurgent undertakings have become to the recent reconfiguration of literary studies in various fields and areas, their influence has had far less to do with their respective ability to generate techniques for interrogating individual works of literature than with their capacity to resituate all the interrogatory operations of criticism within new constellations of force and tension.[3]

All of this should forewarn the reader that if this map is redrawn—as it should be in another decade or so—it will undoubtedly possess a noticeably different appearance. Just as some of the critical orientations we have accentuated here will surely have been replaced by others, so various periods we have delineated will have formed new associations not only with the neighbors on their borders but possibly with quite distant friends. The provisionality, pragmatism, and occasional capriciousness of disciplinary distinctions should also remind us that there will always be something about literature that resists the language of boundary, limit, jurisdiction. The power of literature, and of literary study, lies in its ability to infiltrate any speech and writing, transforming what seems outside itself into something else, into its own odd being.

## Notes

[1]Lucien Febvre cites a letter written in 1558 by the French Ambassador in Constantinople to his colleague in Venice: "Alas! How very blind we have been up till now in not realizing that the true and surest way of expanding and living in peace and tranquillity in the realm is to continue to push the *frontières* as far forward as we can and continue to drive the enemy far away before us!" (209–10). Frontier here is not something in the ground, as it were; it is the line of advance against an adversary.

[2]A military frontier implies hostility to difference, though we can imagine other attitudes. For example, the forces of one territory may wish to occupy the other, without substantially challenging or eradicating its otherness. We are still dealing with hostile foes (that is, we are not in an alternative model, where the territories are distinct but basically friendly, like Canada and the United States, or closely conjoined members of the same whole, like California and Oregon). But the other may in some sense survive the occupation, either through the policy of the occupying force or through the ruses of the occupied. Hence there may be powerful, if obscure, currents of literary criticism running through a work of history, while the assumptions that govern history writing may shape a formalist work of literary criticism ostensibly indifferent to history.

[3]This is particularly true of an emergent field like postcolonial studies, which, if defined in methodological terms, almost immediately risks the hypostatization of those very hierarchies of significance that its strategies are intended to undermine.

# edieval Studies

ANNE MIDDLETON

## *Secession*

Twenty-five years ago is a good reference point for assaying the current state and relations of what is now commonly called medieval studies: at that very moment this field was in the process of being invented. Moreover, as a new division within English literary studies, its founding may be seen as something of an avant-garde action and as an anomaly. Its fortunes since then may therefore offer a test case for other specialists seeking to renew their disciplines and renegotiate the boundaries of their enterprises, especially inso-far as these involve the revision of institutional as well as intellectual models.

These general assertions are of course intentionally perverse and dis-orienting. Far from seeming a field fraught with innovation, medieval studies now appears to many literary scholars outside this field (and few cross its borders regularly) as not only the most steeped in traditional research agendas and critical practices but also the most isolated from, and unchanged by, recent developments within a radically revised and expanded definition of what con-stitutes literary studies. In twenty-five years, its projects and critical languages have reflected almost none of the theoretical considerations that have produced broader ferment in the discipline, nor has it thus far exported any of its own to challenge those generated in other specialties within literary-critical discourse. While these impressions are not mistaken—indeed, many medievalists have themselves of late begun to notice, and lament, their truth—neither are they incommensurate with my intentionally startling, and equally truthful, claims of the newness of this field.[1] On the contrary, these apparently contradictory truths are mutually implicated, and it is their implications that are the focus of this essay.

The new professional self-identification of literary scholars of medieval texts as medievalists, and of their discipline as medieval studies, marks a secession with important historical and theoretical consequences for literary studies generally. It not only allows an assessment of the liabilities and advan-tages of literary inquiries that self-consciously proclaim their extradisciplinary or cross-disciplinary character; it also invites renewed attention to the histori-cal function of such claims. If the Middle Ages was, as Brian Stock has said, "invented long before it was studied," as an enabling historiographical premise in the construction of a distinctive character and destiny for Western Europe, then medieval studies also required invention, and it came into existence at an interesting historical juncture: at the moment when the Middle Ages largely ceased to exist as the ideological construct it had been for European self-definition for half a millennium (Stock, "Middle Ages" 536–37). Before we examine the circumstances, both intellectual and institutional, that warrant our regarding the fortunes of medieval studies during this generation, and its promise for the next, as primarily a function of its professed discontinuities with its historical role and intellectual heritage in modern language studies, we should notice the problematic situation of this field over a slightly longer *durée*, at the intersection of historically contradictory expectations latent in the enterprises still broadly encompassed by English literary studies. Some of the unique difficulties that the latter, as a category of inquiry, presents to medievalists are not new, but they have been multiplied manyfold by developments of the last generation.

Apart from the works of Chaucer, which have had a more or less continuous presence in the literary culture of English speakers and writers since the fourteenth century—as, in a more limited and special sense that has proved especially important recently, has *Piers Plowman*—there is virtually no curricular or critical canon of works of the Middle Ages continuously subjected to literary-critical analysis and judgment.[2] The texts that have long comprised the matter of inquiry for students and scholars of Old and Middle English literature were printed (most of them for the first time in the nineteenth century) and for decades were objects of study and scholarship, for two reasons that stood almost entirely apart from the constitution of literature as a disciplinary object or civilizing objective. For one, these works exemplified the vocabulary and grammar of early states of the language; as K. M. Elizabeth Murray has shown, the production of the *Oxford English Dictionary* was fed by the growing list of texts published by the Early English Text Society (87–100). For another, as purportedly unmediated representations, they attested to what the indefatigable EETS general editor F. J. Furnivall called the "customs and beliefs of our ancestors." It was this documentary information— which was imagined to lie "behind" or "within" the text that unproblematically recorded it, and was valued by nineteenth-century scholars especially insofar as it was thought to attest to universally held sentiments and nondivisive social relations in the early English—rather than the forms and genres through which it was inflected that constituted the ultimately civilizing objects of the reader's attention.[3]

Both purposes are intimately bound to the constitution of literary scholarship and pedagogy as the study of modern national languages, for both presuppose that the continuities of the language as such, and of national character, are the binding principles of the curriculum, if not of scholarly

scholarship in art history, a discipline that, as Erwin Panofsky notes, "came into its own" in the United States in the early postwar years (327). This expansion of intellectual horizons was further inspired by the impressive personal examples of several Continental scholars who were exiled or who escaped from the European holocaust and found academic homes and new publication venues in the United States and England. But as Panofsky observes of this *translatio studii* in art history, Continental medieval scholarship underwent further changes in migration. In transatlantic perspective, national boundaries tended to dissolve. His characterization of what seemed to him the intellectual promise of this *translatio* in the early 1950s succinctly identifies the terms of a perceived new dispensation for medieval scholarship, outlining what might well serve our purposes as a founding charter for literary medieval studies while it simultaneously suggests the forces that would quickly dissipate their idealist consensus:

> Where the European art historians were conditioned to think in terms of national and regional boundaries, no such limitations existed for the Americans. . . . Seen from the other side of the Atlantic, the whole of Europe from Spain to the Eastern Mediterranean merged into one panorama the planes of which appeared at proper intervals and in equally sharp focus. And as the American art historians were able to see the past in a perspective picture undistorted by national and regional bias, so were they able to see the present in a perspective picture undistorted by personal or institutional *parti pris*. . . . "Historical distance" (we normally require from sixty to eighty years) proved to be replaceable by cultural and geographical distance.          (328–29)

To the "spiritual blessings" of a synoptic and almost Olympian transatlantic distance, Panofsky adds what he considered a salutary new local ingredient: "contact—and occasionally conflict—with an Anglo-Saxon positivism which is, in principle, distrustful of abstract speculation" (329). Liberated by this "wholesome" encounter, which included new exposure to academic institutions that forced scholars to address nonspecialist audiences, "we suddenly found the courage to write books on whole masters or whole periods instead of—or besides—writing a dozen specialized articles, and dared to deal with, say, the problem of classical mythology in medieval art in its entirety instead of—or besides—investigating only the transformations of Hercules or Venus." These were exhilarating times. If at this distance nearly every one of these "blessings" appears to have a double edge—as well as sociopolitical implications of which Panofsky here seems largely unaware—the excitement of such ambitions is nevertheless audible in every page of the major publications on English medieval literature that between about 1957 and 1963 seemed to warrant the belief that literary medievalists had attained a new transdisciplinary reach.[8]

While the landmark studies of English medieval literature published during this era do not represent anything like unanimity in interpretive results or in critical methods, they suggest the sense of both a break with the past and an agenda for future work that invigorated younger scholars entering advanced literary study—of whom there were a great many, at least in the United States. The best work in this field showed a marked increase in methodological explicitness and a general internationalization of critical ambitions, at least in principle. Despite the differences that framed the well-publicized debate between New Criticism and exegetics, these enterprises nevertheless concur in several implicit aims that help to explain why such works as these, and this brief moment, continue to represent to many nonmedievalists the last occasion on which they took any notice of discourse in this field, and to many medievalists the ideals of cultural address and intellectual scope that sustain them still, even (perhaps especially) in acts of scholarship that are now chiefly devoted to dismantling the idealist and monolithic notions of the medieval on which most of these postwar endeavors were variously predicated. Three features warrant mention: the then-prevailing art-historical model of critical analysis; the implicit positioning of these critical projects, and of medieval artistic practice, in relation to the canons of "high modernism"; and the pedagogical imperatives of these revisionary enterprises. All contributed key premises to the founding moment of medieval studies, and each has undergone significant alteration since.

Both Charles Muscatine and D. W. Robertson prominently adduced the synthetic work of art historians, as well as sociologists and philosophers of the visual arts, in support of their chief projects, which were to identify the characteristics of medieval styles as expressive resources; it was through these, and not through the opinions of authors or the customs of groups seen by earlier criticism as directly depicted in medieval literature, that one could arrive at what still remained the ultimate intellectual goal, a grasp of the spirit of an age—now seen as provocatively discontinuous with the naturalistic notions of representation according to which medieval literature had previously been read. Philological naturalism was succeeded by variant forms of philosophical idealism, as style for both critics supplanted both "the man" and "the nation" as categories of explanatory continuity. This is not to say that style had the same meaning as an analytic category, or the same expressive effects, for all these scholars. But what New Criticism and exegetics had in common, and what both shared with the renewal of interest in the rhetorical dimension of medieval composition and canons of interpretation, was the enabling premise that principles of artifice, not laws of nature, were the central objects of critical analysis and explanation. The new literary medieval studies of the postwar years implicitly articulate the distinctive character of the human as against the natural sciences, eschewing the alleged determinism of the latter and asserting the active role of representative choices in constituting, rather than reflecting, the "real." A concomitant change in the writing of literary history was a general abandonment of evolutionary or progressive models of cultural change.

In these enterprises, the visual arts and architecture were everywhere the chief reference points for anchoring the meaning of verbal representation: Robertson's "Gothic realism," copiously illustrated by plates of manuscript pages and Gothic architecture and sculpture, Robert Jordan's "inorganic form," and, more recently, V. A. Kolve's reading of Chaucer in terms of an iconographical lexicon. One hazard of these analogies had to do with the cultural status of the representative exemplars and touchstones of meaning they invoked. The surviving monuments that provided the lexicon by which vernacular expressive intention was interpreted were usually drawn from the most decisively regulatory and prescriptive discourses of the culture, and those artifacts that had endured longest and in most widely or multiply attested forms: the cathedral, the summa, the curricular materials of clerical education.[9] What was persistently explained by reference to such official discourses were the romances, dream visions, "secular lyrics," and other vernacular texts deemed "literary" chiefly because of their imagined or self-proclaimed position, in respect to the social groups for which they were made, as nugatory objects for the beguilement of leisure time, as entertainment. The medieval practices against which the deployment of this increasingly elaborate rhetorical and classificatory armature was implicitly directed remained for the scholars of the 1960s silent, unaccounted for—indeed, unproblematic. There was no attempt to question how the discursive relations between the cultural realms of work and play were disposed in various segments of medieval societies, to attend to the signifying systems within which various classes of artifacts functioned, or to understand the syntax within which "earnest" was supposed to be superimposed on "game" or the ways in which "game," in turn, served to activate, or contest, the "earnest" meanings of the culture. These questions now appear to be major items of unfinished business on the agenda of medieval literary scholarship in the next generation. For several recent scholars, the allegedly transparent disclosures of design and "universal" opinion that emerged largely from the center of governing cultural agencies have become provocative opacities, themselves in need of decoding by some of the same strategies to be applied to the literary text itself: the "figure-ground" relation implicit in this distinction has itself been called into question, as it has been elsewhere in literary studies.

A second problem in using art-historical analogies in general, and in particular in referring literary "symbolism" to a supposedly secure and universal iconographical language to ground verbal meaning, was that differences between the syntax and genres of each medium and representative mode, and the special circumstances of each distinct occasion or performance, were usually ignored. As Michael Camille has suggested, the verbal and visual representations on a manuscript page have rich, varied, and locally negotiated spatial and often punning relations that may comment on each other with more precision and complexity than, for example, a column-capital sculpture, made in the same century but hundreds of miles away, comments on either.[10] Indeed, in recent medieval studies, "commentary" has become a more fruitful term than "meaning" as the ultimate interest of literary or art-historical interpreters: the interplay between several simultaneous systems of significance, rather than the superimposition of a unifying system on culturally disparate phenomena, is the implicit model for the interpreter's object.

The styles that these scholars of the later postwar era found in medieval art deployed chiefly conceptual, abstract, nonnaturalistic, and disjunctive techniques of representation. These were also, not coincidentally, considered the chief representational techniques of high modernist art. Midcentury formalist critical enterprise in general had the cultural effect, if not the explicit purpose, of providing the terms that would enable the assimilation of high modernist practice in earlier twentieth-century literature and the visual arts to midcentury critical and scholarly institutions. From the perspective of formalist literary history, the disjunctive and abstracting techniques of artistic modernism are recurrent phenomena, periodic estrangements that implicitly function within cultures as strategies for bringing perceptual artifice and convention to conscious attention and control. The founding syntheses of literary medieval studies also represented an effort both to situate medieval representative techniques in relation to the values of modernist artistic practice and to position its critical approaches in relation to a formalist model of literary history. It was these moves that tended to underwrite claims, which now became more frequent in the critical analysis of medieval writing, of the hitherto undiscovered modernity of the Middle Ages.[11]

The broadly formalist notion that "baring the device," the technique or practice of calling attention to the expressive medium itself, was the constitutive gesture of artistic production seems to have underwritten efforts by some medievalists of the 1960s to undertake studies of medieval philosophies of language, as grammatical system, as system of "signs," and as systematic analogue to divine forms of signification (Colish; Carruthers). The ultimate objective of these studies for literary scholars seems to have been to discover the outlines of medieval theories of literature that they assumed would be implicit in theories of language and meaning and correlative to systematic accounts of imagination and cognition.[12] Interesting as these studies have been as intellectual history, they have not as yet successfully demonstrated that medieval thinkers made such connections between theories of language or cognition and the theory or practice of writing. Composition and writing, though often implicated in metaphors—such as the world as book or divine creation as an act of writing, figurative topics that have been at the center of efforts to connect theories of linguistic signification, writing practice, and textual interpretation—tend more often to be discussed in medieval texts not as modes of expression or cognition but as cultural technologies. Medieval classifications of textual genres and modes of writing have, rather, been emerging steadily, if unspectacularly, from more recent studies of medieval traditions of commentary on both biblical and classical texts. Yet Robertson's evident hope that investigations of these commentary traditions would yield support for his notion that all medieval literary meaning was allegorical or figurative has not on the whole been borne out: "allegory" as the chief term of art and of scholarly controversy that most deeply characterized the founding moment of modern medieval studies has largely receded from contemporary medievalists' discourse.[13]

Although Robertson's well-known moral revulsion from the "modern solipsism" that he traced to the Romantic era opposes the positive New Critical reading (exemplified in both Donaldson's and Muscatine's account of "character" in Chaucer) of modern literary practice as a liberation of the individual from a determining historical context, these different judgments on the modern were, in retrospect, less important than the shared ambitions implicit in such bold critical judgments. The common project of both New Critical and exegetical scholars in depicting medieval artistic practice as conscious and rational within explicable canons of purposive behavior, as the product of representative choices of artisans in confrontation with their cultural matter, and hence as critical rather than determined, implicitly assigned an equally critical power to the modern scholar in interpreting such phenomena to his contemporaries. By this route, these midcentury medievalists implicitly positioned their own enterprises as forms of cultural critique, as means of assuming a perspective on preexisting "philological" inquiry in its narrower and more positivistic forms, which at that time dominated literary scholarship and the teaching of medieval literature.

It is in the two senses I have described here—as an analytic regimen that would yield a unitary meaning in the object and disclose the formal operations by which the cultural background became conscious representation, and as a critical program that would appropriate medieval "otherness" in a revision of prevailing critical values and cultural assumptions—that Robertsonian exegetics discloses the formalist mediation of its professed historicist ambitions. The Middle Ages as revealed by exegetical methods was no less an ideal and unitary construct than the poem as projected by formalist analysis. The founding moment of medieval studies soon after midcentury coincides with the increased prominence of the New Criticism within universities in the United States, and in Britain with the increased academic influence of Leavisite paradigms of literary analysis. Recent association of formalist intellectual enterprises with a massive dehistoricizing and dematerialization of texts, and with subsequent poststructural reductions of all historical phenomena to purely linguistic events, tends now to obscure from our view the pedagogic passions and commitments that underwrote these earlier formalist endeavors.[14] As applied literary theory, these midcentury formalisms were perhaps more fundamentally pedagogies, and not in the first instance imagined as merely for university classrooms but rather for renewing and extending the cultural accessibility of literary texts. As Edward Said has noted, on both sides of the Atlantic these critical formations were *au fond* "strangely populist in intention."[15]

It is the pedagogic ambition and passion that attended both the New Critics' and the exegetical interpreters' regimens for reading medieval writings that helps to explain, perhaps better than the durability or persuasiveness of their readings, or their accounts of medieval thought or culture (still imagined by both camps as monolithic), why the deep debate, and the still deeper agreement, between these two models of critical and investigative practice seemed to define, especially for those in United States universities, the promise of important and illuminating cultural work for the young medievalists (as they were already beginning to be called) repopulating advanced study in American universities. It is therefore the cultural sites and political situation, as well as the intellectual antecedents, of literary-critical enterprise generally in the postwar years that in part account for both the sense of excitement and ferment in this field at midcentury and its rapid deflation and (to its practitioners) unexpected marginalization soon thereafter. The project proposed by both New Criticism and exegetics, and by medieval studies generally at midcentury, was a massive intellectual program of redefined solidarity with a deep European past. The United States had fought, and helped to win, the Last Good War; now its scholars would explain what had been won. Medieval studies was for the first time a broadly institutionalized American academic enterprise, one of the accoutrements of the coming of age of the United States as a world power and hence as a producer of world-historical signification.

## *Medieval Studies Institutionalized*

These were, for the United States, the years of the GI Bill and the Marshall Plan; in Great Britain, they eventually produced the Open University. To an Anglo-American public perspective, these were years of new beginnings: of almost boundless educational optimism and expenditure, of reformulated political alliances of the "Western" powers, of civilian reindustrialization marshaled against a redefined and now non-European "threat."[16] Having received its intellectual charter and pedagogic impetus by these postwar circumstances, medieval studies gradually assumed the institutional forms that furthered a withdrawal of medievalists from the developing disciplinary discourses that its very cross-disciplinary claims and organization ought logically to have facilitated. We can better understand this paradoxical result, and the almost immediate turn away from its critical founding agendas to a comparatively uncritical historicism, if we recognize that the institutionalization of medieval studies is broadly analogous to another academic innovation contemporary with it, the founding of "area studies" programs in universities.

Both are distinctive institutional products of the era and thought structures of the Cold War. Implicit in the existence of, for example, Soviet, East Asian, and Latin American area studies programs, most of which were founded in universities in the United States after World War II, is a definition of these geographical regions chiefly in terms of current international political relations rather than distinctive historical affinities and coherence. This definition conceives of these entities as, for investigative purposes, culturally more homogeneous than diverse, and as irretrievably "other." Combining teaching and applied-research enterprises within a single institutional center, the activities of area studies programs were ultimately less concerned with the philosophical implications and historical affinities of their methods of inquiry, as they drew their investigators freely from diverse disciplinary backgrounds, than with the integrative and pragmatic results achieved, in terms of applicable "professional" knowledge of the aggregated "others" that were the focus of their interest. As teaching organizations, these centers produced specialized "training" for those "educated" by other means, and normally within disciplines.[17] By a similar process the academic invention of medieval studies as a chronological rather than geographical alien terrain rendered the Middle Ages philosophically inert by fiat: while, institutionally, medieval studies became from the mid-1960s increasingly diverse, prosperous, and industrious, it also became intellectually impoverished and underconceptualized.[18] Now accessible to kinds of study that could be seen as dispassionate, objective, because its objects were viewed as without immediate intersubjective and historical relations with the investigators, the European Middle Ages could be researched almost indefinitely in increasingly minute particulars, but they could no longer be understood.[19] It may therefore be the organs and signs of the apparent prosperity of medieval studies at present that also assure and perpetuate its diminished or constrained trade relations with other cultural and chronological areas of literary study, and a reduced philosophical and practical relevance to literary studies generally.

Since the mid-1960s, there has been a rapid proliferation of groups, journals, and venues for regular intellectual exchange between medievalists from a wide spectrum of disciplines. Included in this widened field of vision are scholarly specialties distinctive to work on medieval artifacts but otherwise without traditional homes in any single academic department or discipline:

paleography, codicology, and liturgy, for example. While scholars in most of these subject fields belong to college or university faculties organized according to older disciplinary divisions—English, French, history, and the like—they have during this generation achieved regularly available institutional means of becoming acquainted with work in progress across departmental boundaries. To some degree, of course, these developments exemplify a much wider institutional tendency in recent literary studies, particularly in North America, to topical and interest-group fragmentation. What is distinctive about the institutionalization of medieval studies, however, is that it almost always cuts across, and for a high proportion of scholars has wholly replaced, disciplinary affiliation. It is not simply that medievalists, like many others in literary studies, are taking more notice of publications beyond literary journals, but that they encounter such work in the making, while they are at the same time less and less likely to engage in the same way, and at the same stage of conceptualization, research, and production, with the work of colleagues in their own departments. This marked change in patterns of their professional socialization and production, and in venues for exchange, helps to explain—perhaps more forcefully and concretely than the persistence of belief structures, even in unconscious and unexamined form, since the founding years of medieval studies, or the still longer persistence of positivism—the major changes in vocabularies and expository objectives that now differentiate literary medievalists' work not only from recent theoretical discourses within literary studies but from the practices of their early-1960s founders.

Counting the blessings that have followed from these arrangements is itself likely to become a burgeoning practice in the next few years, as the several organizations that owe their existence to that era celebrate their twenty-fifth anniversaries through the 1990s. These blessings are genuine, and considerable: in addition to new venues for cross-disciplinary intellectual exchange, they include a specificity of focus and a strong suspicion of monolithic and universalizing arguments about "the middle ages." To realize the full value of the past generation of changes, however, medievalists of the next will also have to overcome some of the liabilities that have attended these altered institutional forms. These are evident thus far in an aversion to critical engagement with theory in any form, a disinclination to examine traditionally accepted skills and practices in historical perspective, and a comparative deficiency in the ordinary competences possessed by their peers in constitutive disciplines to confront major claims analytically rather than merely anecdotally or empirically. Moreover, in another paradoxical reversal, it is precisely the regular encounter of literary scholars with historical work in other disciplines that reframes the need and renews the possibilities for writing a kind of literary history that has its own distinctive objectives, standing apart from mere instantiation of the conclusions of social or intellectual historians and differing from the interpretive methods and objectives of the history of other nonverbal arts.

## *Toward a New Literary History of the Middle Ages*

During the century preceding this generation, and still in the work of the formative scholars of medieval studies, literary scholarship always bought its history secondhand, with its social texture smoothed, its local specificity subordinated, and its documentary evidence submerged by paraphrase, into broad studies of such narratable (if spectral) abstractions as the "waning of the Middle Ages." Events and texts were used to illustrate such constructs as the differentiation of "popular" and "courtly" art, "oral" and "written" composition, "religious" and "secular" motives, "heretical" and "orthodox" beliefs— oppositions largely drawn from semantic fields that surrounded contentious interpretations of broader cultural circumstances and the competing *grands récits* of English and European history generally.[20] The polemical antecedents and agendas implicit in such vocabularies were largely overlooked by literary scholars, who used such categories uncritically to frame their own interpretive questions.[21] In this way, the literary scholar's "history" often unwittingly retailed the discarded master narratives of preceding generations of historians who—to multiply the unfortunate consequences of such unconscious recirculation of "knowledge"—may in turn have derived them in part from the attestation of literary texts, without regard for their local discursive or contextual purpose, or their generic inflection, within the literary work.

Signs of revised practical relations of literary interpretation to the work of historians are legible in several ways. One is evident in the scale and kind of reference of nearly any work of recent critical scholarship on a medieval English literary text. Articles are cited more frequently than books, and the work of social historians far more frequently than the interpretive discussions of other literary scholars, which figure very little, and anecdotally rather than systematically, in framing the terms of the argument. Current historiographical disputes—for example, the "Brenner debate" over the process and chronology of the capitalization of European agriculture—are likely to be taken into account as such in the interpretation of a text by the literary scholar who adverts to the documents and practices at issue in them.[22] Similarly, historical narratives contemporary with the medieval phenomena they register, such as monastic, royal, or dynastic chronicles, are far less likely now than a generation ago to be cited uncritically as mere documentary descriptions of current events, or examples of typical beliefs and attitudes; they are now treated as writings with their own generic designs and specific local positioning and relations to governance and record making.[23] In short, good literary-critical scholarship is becoming more indistinguishable from good historical scholarship on the page, not only in the interpretations both kinds of scholars offer but in the kind of evidence they adduce and what they do with it and, more fundamentally, in the kind of texts that invite their attention.

Another major effect of this rapprochement between the practices of historians and literary scholars is discernible in the latter's thoroughgoing terminological ascesis, their general retreat from the organizing vocabularies and concepts that at midcentury were all that was left to mark the sites of debates over the interpretation of the Middle Ages in the *grands récits* of European history. From these ancient historiographical debates there had arisen two competing ideological requirements: if medieval phenomena were irretrievably "other" in relation to the organs of political rationality and progress, and the canons of critical inquiry, by which modern Europe reappropriated Western antiquity, at the same time they constituted the primary site of origin for all manner of equally treasured local practices that produced the vernacular distinctiveness of modern nations and regions. Later European society had therefore both to arise from and to repudiate this millennium, which was its cradle, mirror, and abyss. These contrary explanatory pressures support the two major narrative forms of most efforts to interpret medieval literature historically: on the one hand, the pervasive search for origins and sources and the concomitant effort to identify a text's meaning with its antecedence; and, on the other, the interpretation of perceived fissures or inconsistencies in the text in relation to polarized forces in contest for the future of Europe: illiterate-literate, popular-learned, oral-written, lay-clerical, heathen-Christian, sacred-profane, heretical-orthodox, magical-scientific, secular-religious, urban-agrarian, feudal-commercial (or capitalistic), traditional-modern (or rational). These pairs of terms, which for decades figured in debate largely along vertical axes of value, as high-low, could also be disposed along a temporal axis (which usually reduced to the same thing) to describe rising or declining, progressive or obsolescent, mobile or moribund phenomena. While the lines of value imposed in such accounts did not always run one way—one historian's "decline" was another's apex or "origin"—in general, the literary history and criticism mapped between these polar terms implied stories with direction and outcomes, winners and losers. The function of such critical exposition for its readers and writers as cultural narrative differed little from those that Georg Lukács and M. M. Bakhtin attribute to the epic, and literary works stood within this global process as exemplary or illustrative instances, simulacra or reflections of the operation of more comprehensive cultural forces but not constitutive of them.

Though many of these polarized terms still occur in scholarship and criticism of the past twenty-five years, they have undergone two kinds of changes that suggest that they have rapidly become vestigial, even without the application of much conscious attention to method by many practitioners within the field. One is a general purgation: such terms are rarer, and when they appear, it is often within actual or implicit quotation marks, indicating that they function as a point of departure, not an expository goal. The second change is a repositioning of these binary terms into horizontal rather than vertical relations, with the result that the expository and explanatory discourses in which they operate have become not only more local and specific but, in Giambattista Vico's sense of the term, markedly more "secular"—that is, without an insistent rhetorical investment in determining a dominant design or direction of events on the temporal, social, or textual field described.[24] Counterpoised terms now more often name forces that act on and modify each other through sustained engagement, while the literary work has come to be seen as a site of actions, a locus of complex agencies, rather than an illustrative or exemplary artifact in a sweeping narrative of progress and decline. That the making of literature is itself a specific and highly contested form of action in this period has only lately begun to attract systematic attention. Recent work suggests further opportunities for differentiating a specifically literary history and criticism of medieval texts from the practices and goals of cultural studies, into which literary scholarship in general has lately been widely subsumed.

As Lee Patterson has noted, "literature" as a category of verbal production and reception is itself a historical construction, and in various medieval situations an assertion of its problematic distinctiveness is not always—as has been widely assumed elsewhere in current literary studies—an "agency for authoritarian and conservative forces, . . . devised in order to enforce hegemonic interests" (*Negotiating* 74). The question of the social legitimacy and formal intelligibility of the enterprise of making a text, and the problem of its form, genre, and utility among other modes of material and social production, and among other possible genres of artifice and performance, is in one way or another a site of major conflict in the Middle Ages—a conflict from which nearly all the others enacted by the text radiate. During most of the medieval centuries, writing itself is the chief technology for the production of distinctive forms of subjectivity and community: in Said's terms, text production and the form of texts constitute an "exemplary uncertainty" around which the other conflicts of these cultures revolve.[25] It is at this point that specifically literary-historical scholarship must insist on—and is uniquely able to provide—a finer grid for describing and understanding the nature of these social negotiations than cultural studies more broadly considered can offer. Its concerns are not in the first instance the material interests that are discursively contested, but rather the specifically textual processes, and the cognitive structures they foster in individuals and societies, through which these material interests are mediated.[26] The focus of a revised literary history would be the formal factors and cognitive practices that make human beings, individually and in groups, intervene in their societies by defining themselves as makers, users, and possessors of texts, to examine how such formal concerns generate conflict rather than merely serve as a displacement for conflicts supposedly produced elsewhere, in "material" interests.[27]

As Michel Foucault observes, the author is an ideological product and acts as a "principle of thrift in the proliferation of meaning." Literary scholars must now engage some of the fundamental questions to which social and cultural historians have led them, while attempting to understand why the latter have fallen short of providing sufficiently nuanced answers—questions such as Foucault's in "What Is an Author?": "How, under what conditions, and in what forms can something like a subject appear in the order of discourse?" (118–19). Such questions might lead to a refiguring of the expository shape of historical literary criticism, which thus far has remained argumentatively centered on a relatively small number of canonized texts and authors.[28] As long as inquiry into specifically literary operations and conflicts is construed as a flight from the socially and historically "real," rather than the critical pursuit of distinctive medieval modes for shaping it, literary historians can have nothing of substance to offer to a cultural criticism that has for the most part been strangely obtuse about the formal properties and social dispositions of the medium in which its objects are given to inquiry—a medium of almost infinite variety before the age of print.

## *Returning from the Margins*

The refocusing of literary studies on textuality itself as central to any possible adequate literary history of the Middle Ages appears to be the chief contribution that studies in medieval literature might offer to literary studies generally in the coming generation. A "new philology"—an interpretive practice grounded in the manuscript matrix of texts, as a cultural place of "radical contingencies" that contrasts sharply with the rationalized and codified textual forms that were the imaginative objective of early humanist philological endeavor and were in turn sustained by print culture—has been proposed as a model of medievalists' critical practice. Some believe that such an enterprise would answer both to the distinctive material and cultural character of medieval writings and to a perceived need to call into question certain universalizing tendencies in contemporary critical theory.[29] It might also articulate the long-deferred response of medieval literary studies to the implicit challenge of the "new historicism," which, though issued from within a traditional field to which it has long been critically allied, has thus far failed to stir medievalists' emulation.

New historicism in Renaissance studies is, according to some recent retrospectives, scarcely intelligible solely as a theoretical position and an interpretive practice, but gains its salutary critical force from the felt need of scholars at a specific moment in their own cultural history to expose and dismantle the ideological maneuvers that had historically defined this chronological period. The traditional acceptance of Renaissance culture at its own face value as a rebirth of ideals of civil society and a cradle of modern Western European identity had also implicitly assigned to critical scholarship the unwelcome role of apologist for many of the less-than-humane enterprises carried out in the service of these assertions. As new-historicist scholarship on the Renaissance has sought to make explicit and to resist this rhetorical posture, so a "new philology," proposed from within medieval literary studies at the end of the twentieth century, may be seen as emerging from the internal logic of the generation-long self-marginalization of the field, to insist on the multiplicity and contingency of the processes by which communities become textual communities and individuals constitute themselves as literate.

Whether or not such a new philology might have a paradigmatic value for future literary studies, comparable to the effects of new historicism in the 1980s, one can already discern prospects emerging within a few major areas of discontent with earlier terms of investigation. Even though some of the landmark studies that thus far suggest new directions have not necessarily been produced by literary scholars, the terrain still to be explored by a new philology lies in fact along the horizontal expanse of middle ground bracketed between the old polarities of traditional medieval literary history.

Changes are evident in three main areas, each framed by sets of oppositions that scholars have been laboring to dissolve. The first of these, the study of medieval literacy itself, includes redefined ways of thinking about differences between oral and written discourse, as well as the opposition of popular to learned practice, and the forms within which these modes allow an individual or a community to shape memory, history, and biography.[30] The second, studies in medieval religion as practice rather than as doctrine and as defined within a variety of textual communities, allows new emphasis on the continuities rather than oppositions between heresy, dissent, heterodoxy, and orthodoxy; on a range of communal practices, including civic and court ceremony as well as ecclesiastical ritual; on the interactions of sacred and secular space and discourse more generally; and on the framing of individual subjectivity within the terms of paradigmatic texts and symbolic performances.[31] A third area of substantial rethinking enacts what, from a midcentury perspective, could only seem a return of the repressed: a renewed attention to what might be termed the material and institutional base of medieval literature, to the kinds of information about production, reception, and generic definition that are often legible in the physical form of the manuscript book, and the circumstance of production, dissemination, and reception that can be inferred from it.

Of these developments, the last—which in a sense underwrites all the others—marks the most radical turning away from the kind of interpretive operations proposed at the founding moment of medieval studies. It is also, to those outside the field, least likely to seem at first glance a change with implications that could influence work anywhere else in literary studies. Yet it is the most radical ascesis of all, though it complicates rather than simplifies all that follows from it. A renewed awareness of the mediated form in which all edited texts represent medieval writings has led to a conceptual remapping of what sort of scholarly activity can produce major rethinking in the field. As Patterson has observed of the Athlone edition of *Piers Plowman*[32]—the text that, perhaps more than any other, has forced renewed attention to textual studies for English literary medievalists:

> The plethora of brackets and the thick band of variants at the foot of the page continually remind the reader that he is dealing with an *edited* text; the false security of unmarred print, such as we find in virtually every edition of Chaucer, is here denied us. No longer can the interpreter in the executive suite blandly assume that his job starts when the editors in the basement have finished theirs. *(Negotiating* 108)

What has lately come to be called the "return" to the manuscript text may be something of a misnomer, for the concerns of recent scholars do not greatly resemble those that motivated the editing and textual study of medieval writings a century ago. The current turn to manuscript textuality, both within and beyond English medieval studies, has been driven most fundamentally by theoretical and critical interests, not simply a positivistic insistence on the ineffably unique instance or a resistance to comparative or synthetic statement. Its force and effect has been to discern in medieval textual practices the indigenous systems of order, and terminological distinctions, that supported generic systems and denoted practical criteria of literary form. Its emergent objective has been to map medieval literary theory, as a base for future dialogue with contemporary theoretical concerns.[33]

It is thus only one more of several paradoxical reversals within this field that an interest in the materiality and diverse circumstantialities of medieval texts also discloses a need, and some possible sites, for theoretical reflection. It is this ultimate reversal that gives this field a possible paradigmatic interest to literary studies in English generally at the end of the twentieth century.

## Lessons of Marginality

After a generation of increased isolation from some of the major currents of literary studies, the double identity of medieval studies as one of the oldest and one of the newest subfields of English literary scholarship confers on its practitioners a Tiresias-like double vision of the larger enterprise with which they have been, if distantly, historically associated. Medieval studies may now once again be distinctively equipped not merely to rejoin but to contribute to the disciplinary discourses from which it has for a generation largely seceded. Patterson has argued ("On the Margin" 104–07) that such a move would be salutary for medieval literary scholarship; the foregoing account argues that it would be equally salutary for the larger field it rejoins, particularly if medievalists are able to identify, on the transformed terrain in which they stake a claim, some partners and allies in their newly defined ventures. A generation's experience reveals both the immediate rewards and the ultimate intellectual impoverishment of self-proclaimed withdrawal from historically constituted disciplinary discourses. Collectivities as well as individuals have their life stories, and, as Alasdair MacIntyre has argued, the specific acts of both gain their intelligibility from their place in a continuity of articulated intentions.

Marginality, however, has its perspectival and tactical advantages, and it prompts alliances and partnerships, as well as conversions, that might never have been imagined in other circumstances. If, as I have argued, one of the most fertile areas of recent rethinking concerns the constantly renegotiated relations of popular and learned, local and official verbal cultures, written and oral cultural modes and verbal genres for remembering and recording and constituting truth—if, in short, a central issue in medieval studies is the processes of the vernacular transformations of authority, and the reciprocal redefinition of authority by this process, then there is every reason to expect that medieval scholars and critics will perceive and develop their important community of intellectual interest with scholars of ethnic and colonial literatures. Their common grounds lie not only in the possible homology of cultural circumstances within which texts are conceived and composed but in the exuberant and unclassifiable verbal and formal results that such conditions for mediation produce—that is, in precisely the rich and resourceful literary character of such performances. Multilinguicity as a fact of medieval as well as modern colonial life, literacy, and text production, and the strategic reformation of canonized written genres and forms, are common concerns of criticism and scholarship in all these areas. A comparative cultural poetics of such exchanges would be well worth striving for, even though the way there is not yet on any map.

Finally, the marginalization of medieval studies, and its consequent critical immersion in the distinctive material and institutional forms in which writing occurs within the historical period that is its concern, suggests that the articulation of a specifically literary history differentiated from, if still contributing to, cultural history is not only possible but necessary, and not only for medieval studies. What is now urgently needed both within and beyond this once-marginal terrain is a restoration of the possibility of literary history, grounded not in the traditional organic analogies, or in the cultural apologetics that produced the Middle Ages as either alien or as origin, but in the multiple material and institutional forms of literacy and textuality, and in the individual and communal varieties of creative responses to, and assertions of, the power to possess and deploy texts. It is only by striving to understand social forces as articulated in textual forms that cultural history can become literary history, and by this process become fully and precisely answerable to the political and material constitution of both medieval society and our own. Anything short of that makes literary studies merely, in Bacon's phrase, a "serving science," a form of tendentious illustration, and would demonstrate that we have learned nothing since the foundation of modern language studies over a century ago.

### Notes

[1] Lee Patterson, *Negotiating the Past*, offers an indispensable guide to the issues posed by this essay, and I am everywhere heavily indebted to its insights. It is perhaps the fullest of many recent instances of stocktaking in this field. Another provocative statement of current issues was provided by a special issue of the journal *Speculum* entitled "The New Philology" (1990), under the editorship of Nichols. The essays of Patterson ("On the Margin") and Spiegel and the introductory essay by Nichols ("Philology") provide especially helpful orientation to readers of this volume. Zumthor, in *Speaking of the Middle Ages*, offers a longer, less specific, and more speculative view.

[2] Possibly the last important book organized around the premise of a critical canon of Middle English works was also the first to indicate the disappearing charter of expectations on which it was based, and to point the way to a different kind of literary historical work: Burrow's *Ricardian Poetry*.

[3] See Bloch, "Naturalism, Nationalism, Medievalism"; Baldick 59–85; Middleton 3–4.

[4] In Spiegel's terms (74–76), Anglo-American medievalists have tended to stand with historians as investigative practitioners, rather than with historicism in its idealizing and essentializing modes, which includes, ironically, Robertson's critical project. In an issue of *New Literary History* entitled "Medieval Literature and Contemporary Theory," in which the work of medievalists in French and German traditions of scholarship predominates, Burrow, commenting on the essays, notes that "all the contributors . . . seem to feel considerably further from their Middle Ages than I feel from mine" ("Alterity" 385). See also Patterson, "On the Margin" 101n51, and *Negotiating* 4, on the empirical resistance to exegetical criticism. There are exceptions, notably the work of Eugene

Vance, but in general one cannot count on medievalists in Anglo-American literary studies to possess a working vocabulary of common critical terms of more recent vintage than the 1960s. Lately, however, there have been signs of retrenchment about the power of much current theory to illuminate medieval texts and cultural circumstances; see, for example, Zumthor.

[5]Stock, *The Implications of Literacy*, offers new accounts of the complex and shaded relations between "oral" and "literate" culture. He proposes these to replace the more sharply contrastive formulations typical of scholarship on the subject in the 1960s, which he terms the "golden age" of "strong theses" about the oral and the written. His remarks on the redefinition of this field of investigation, which develop those of the book, were offered in a series of lectures at Berkeley in 1990.

[6]See Aers, *Community, Gender, and Individual Identity* 17 and n51, and "Rewriting the Middle Ages"; Patterson, "On the Margin" 92–101.

[7]See Patterson, ch. 1, "Historical Criticism and the Development of Chaucer Studies," *Negotiating* 3–39. First presented to a special session of the MLA Chaucer Division in 1983 as "New Criticism and Exegetics: Sibling Rivalry in the Academic Family," this essay in its earlier form emphasized more strongly the totalizing historicist agenda to which, in different ways, both critical regimens were committed. Rather than rehearse either the complementarities in their opposition, or the deeper intellectual history of their premises—both of which Patterson addresses thoroughly and unsparingly—I shall attempt here only to indicate those institutional and practical forces that figured in this well-known debate, to suggest both why it appeared so promising at midcentury and why it seems superseded by more than a generation now.

[8]The landmark publications that may best indicate these new horizons to literary scholars in the Anglo-American critical tradition include Muscatine, *Chaucer and the French Tradition* and "The Locus of Action in Medieval Narrative"; Bloomfield, *Piers Plowman as Fourteenth-Century Apocalypse* and "Symbolism in Medieval Literature"; Robertson, *A Preface to Chaucer*; *Critical Approaches to Medieval Literature*, ed. Bethurum; *Chaucer's Poetry*, ed. Donaldson; Lawlor, "The Imaginative Unity of *Piers Plowman*"; Payne, *The Key of Remembrance*. While these examples emphasize Chaucer criticism, there are in this period studies of other Old and Middle English texts with comparable methods and premises; a comprehensive bibliography is beyond the scope of this essay.

[9]One example of a regulatory discourse taken by critics simply as an element in a monolithic and causeless medieval worldview is the often-cited "three estates" model by which many medieval writers represented the functional structural relations of their societies. Duby has discussed in detail the polemical occasions and formation of this model in Capetian France, and his analysis suggests what interests were served and which ones were occluded by its promulgation in each of several successive local circumstances.

[10]These are distillations of Camille's remarks in a discussion of a paper he presented at a conference entitled Commentary as Cultural Artifact, at the University of California Humanities Research Institute at Irvine, 1–3 June 1990. The presentation was drawn from a portion of a book manuscript in progress.

[11]On the modernizing impulse in theorizing enterprises in medieval literature, see Patterson, "On the Margin" 106.

[12]Some extremely interesting intellectual history emerged from these endeavors, of which one of the immediate fruits for literary scholars was the recognition of the pervasiveness of and rationale for grammatical analogy as an explanatory figure, a medieval practice that scholars a century ago found perverse and inexplicable—as W. W. Skeat dismissed one such analogy in *Piers Plowman*, "barely intelligible and very dull" (see Alford). Tuve's inquiry into the logics of figurative representation, particularly in her posthumous book *Allegorical Imagery*, is also germane here.

[13]A useful indication of the changes in approach over a generation, even within the work of those who are broadly committed to the critical importance of medieval exegetical materials for literary interpretation, is exemplified by the work of Judson Allen and Minnis: both, but particularly the latter, take sharp issue with Robertson's arguments and methods, even while demonstrating the appositeness of specific exegetical texts to literary forms and terms.

[14]Aers's *Community, Gender, and Individual Identity*, an exemplary instance of what a cultural studies approach to major Middle English literary texts has to offer, nevertheless counterpoises to his own work the analytic efforts of both formalist and poststructuralist critical endeavors, assigning to them an almost parodically nugatory disregard of the socially "real." It is possible that in another generation the currently imputed opposition between formalist-inspired and cultural-materialist accounts of medieval literary works will seem as false a dichotomy as that between exegetics and New Criticism appears now.

[15]See "Opponents, Audiences, Constituencies, and Community" 4–6. Said sees a similar impulse in the early writings of Roland Barthes and the French *nouvelle critique* of this era: "For about four decades, then, in both France and the United States, the schools of 'new' critics were committed to prying literature and writing loose from confining institutions. However much it was to depend upon carefully learned technical skills, reading was in very large measure to become an act of public depossession. Texts were to be unlocked or decoded, then handed on to anyone who was interested. The resources of symbolic language were placed at the disposal of readers who it was assumed suffered the debilitations of either irrelevant 'professional' information or the accumulated habits of lazy inattention" (5).

[16]It was during these years that European scholars who had survived the war, many now resettled in academic institutions in the United States, began to publish their obituaries of the world they had lost—and hence of the explanatory agendas deeply implicated in their methods. Some of the finest of these took the form of awe-inspiring books and articles of medieval literary history and critical scholarship. That the genre of these monumental performances went largely unrecognized at the time is one of the many ironies of these years. Nor is it any accident that their elegiac aspect became more apparent, at least to American scholars, as the United States began to face the debacle of its postwar prosperity and certainties in the late 1960s, as it began to seem possible that some cultural losses were irrecoverable, inconvertible. See Bloomfield's review of *On Four Modern Humanists*; and Stock, "The Middle Ages as Subject and Object": "Ideas

that had lost their creative vigor and which clung to the educational system like parasites were destroyed along with their benefactors. Erich Auerbach typified those whom political circumstances forced to articulate positions that in more stable times might have remained unexamined" (543–44). Idealist historical study thus received a new agenda in the United States at exactly the point of its most decisive practical defeat in Europe.

[17]Patterson notes the current prevalence of *training* rather than *education* as the term for the preparation of a medievalist; see his introduction to *Literary Practice and Social Change in Britain, 1380–1530* 3.

[18]Stock, "*Antiqui* or *Moderni?*" notes that the training of most medievalists in philosophy and the social sciences is "notoriously weak" (392). Whether area studies programs have lately experienced similar intellectual fortunes is likely to be discussed more widely in the 1990s, as the international arrangements that gave them their rationale dissolve.

[19]On the bifurcation between research and conceptualization in this field, see Stock, "The Middle Ages as Subject and Object" 543, and Coletti 265. Coletti's argument, a thoughtful and thorough survey of the fortunes of medieval drama scholarship over the generation since the early 1960s, is also more broadly applicable as a description of the current state of medieval studies. (On "understanding" as intended here, see Skinner 24.)

[20]Stock, in "The Middle Ages as Subject and Object," describes Charles Homer Haskins's construction of the twelfth-century "Renaissance" in a form certain to make it palatable to current American political convictions about what constituted progress (545).

[21]The debate over Chaucer's class and class allegiances, as expressed in his representation of character and of his own persona, in which George Lyman Kittredge and Robert K. Root's interpretations participated, is, for example, scarcely intelligible as a critical issue apart from the debates over the origins of parliament and the distinctive character of English political liberties in which its terms were unconsciously embedded. In a different way the question of the date of composition of *Beowulf*, and of the oral or lettered mode of that composition, inherits, for the most part unwittingly, Romantic historiographies of the origins and function of legendary and historical narration in early societies. Questions of the orthodoxy or consistency of the religious ideas of *Piers Plowman*, or of the tonality and purpose of the staged representation of sacred history in the English cyclical drama, were likewise implicated, not only in the pervasive organic metaphors of growth and decline in which most grand historical processes were conceived but more specifically in contention over the "beginnings of English nonconformity" (see, e.g., McFarlane), and, hence, in the competing notions of revolution and reform as formative processes in the British religious and political establishment.

[22]See, for example, Patterson, " 'No man his reson herde' "; Aers, "*Piers Plowman*: Poverty, Work, and Community"; *The Brenner Debate*, ed. Aston and Philpin; Macfarlane, *The Origins of English Individualism*. Aers offers a brief guide to the controversy over the latter's approach to individualism (184, n46).

[23]Recent examples are Fradenburg, "Narrative and Capital in Late-Medieval Scotland," and the work of Spiegel and others on the form of genealogical history (for citations, see Spiegel 78).

[24]Said, in "Opponents, Audiences, Constituencies, and Community," discusses Vico's sense of "secular interpretation" (9–11).

[25]Said discusses this difficulty of positioning an authorial identity and enterprise as a feature of "certain moments in the history of literature" that require particularly careful critical study (*Beginnings* 224).

[26]Literary scholars ought to be better prepared than most social historians to offer an analysis of the matrix of texts and forms, literary as well as social, through which, for example, Margery Kempe became in her own eyes the possible subject of a book she undertook to have made. Literary scholars are uniquely equipped to investigate the conflict, not merely of material and political interests *but of textual genres*, that made Carlo Ginzburg's miller of Friuli a target of inquisition and that constituted inquisitorial procedure as a specific form of discourse, with a logic and syntactic decorum that the miller's own style violated at least as persistently as his "beliefs," if indeed it is possible to distinguish the latter from the language and forms in which they were proposed. Or, to take an instance from a more recent venture into literary history, what kinds of writing subject and differentiated literary purpose are asserted in medieval society by the choice of prose? On the latter question, see Spiegel 82; Godzich and Kittay, *The Emergence of Prose*.

[27]In several ways Aers's recent work illustrates the distinctive achievement and continued promise of cultural criticism paradigms for releasing medieval writings from various monologizing impositions on them; see his *Community, Gender, and Individual Identity*. Yet Aers's analysis also discloses, though it does not engage, opportunities for differentiating a specifically *literary* history and criticism from the broader practices and goals of cultural studies with which he largely identifies it; most of Aers's admirable analyses of texts stop at the point where a literary-historical analysis would begin. As a result, there is a certain sameness to the conclusions in all these splendidly illuminating analytic essays: each writer is shown to have encountered intolerable conflicts and contradictions in social action that he or she valiantly made the best of or elegantly suppressed, with the discursive instruments available, but could scarcely have resolved because these tensions resided somehow in another fashion in the society itself—which in his usage appears to mean the network of its material interests, and not, in the first instance, its textual and generic forms for talking about them. Patterson, in *Negotiating the Past*, helpfully discusses these interpretive difficulties for current medieval studies (52–74); see also Spiegel 72–84.

[28]Patterson, in "On the Margin," points to the "history of the medieval subject" as a central desideratum of *literary*-critical study, while he also indicates the contemporary social and scholarly formations that have so far kept it from realization (100). Similarly, Spiegel proposes that historical analysis be focused on "the moment of inscription" (84–85).

[29]See Nichols, "Philology" 2–9, and Patterson, "On the Margin" 106.

[30]The scholarship that traces a generation's changes in these debates is vast, and several surveys are now available; a convenient guide to some of the main points of dispute is D. H. Green, "Orality and Reading." In *The Implications of Literacy*, Stock offers a prospectus of issues now facing medievalists that differs radically from the one framed by critical discourse of the early 1960s. His emphasis is on the organization of

social cognition and the modes of its replication within textual communities; heresy, for example, becomes in his account an epiphenomenon of the textualization of truth claims. Bold syntheses of these newer approaches to literacy as cultural and political technology, in which literary texts are interpreted within a field that also includes legal performatives, have been offered by several literary scholars, although scholarship on French literature has theorized such endeavors far more pervasively than any work thus far on English culture and literature; see Bloch, *Medieval French Literature and Law* and *Etymologies and Genealogies*.

[31]The fortunes of the provocative term *play* in the medieval scholarship of this generation neatly illustrates what is at stake. *Play* entered the lexicon of medieval literary studies from the work of Johan Huizinga, though it has only been during the past several decades that it engaged the attention of scholars of medieval English literature, chiefly through Kolve's deployment of it in his deservedly acclaimed study of cyclical dramatic texts, *The Play Called Corpus Christi*. What Huizinga saw as a culturally exempt space filled by various forms of art and artifice that offered instruction as entertainment is now treated as the place and occasion of constitutive rituals, a scene of cultural work, often designed with an eye to current political objectives. Studies of chivalric ritual and ceremony, of the court as a social institution, and of the ceremonial life of late medieval English towns, have all transformed the terms in which the meanings of literary texts and their performance were debated a generation ago. For examples, see M. Vale; J. Vale; R. F. Green; M. James; Pythian-Adams, "Ceremony and the Citizen" and *Desolation of a City*. Coletti's survey article is particularly astute at assessing the force of these developments for current scholarly and critical agendas.

Two examples may indicate the transformations in the way religion is defined and studied as a social and imaginative force. Beginning in the early 1970s, the work of Anne Hudson has not only revised certain widely accepted assumptions about the history of the Lollard movement but, more fundamentally, altered the terms in which *heresy* and *orthodoxy* are understood and the role that texts play in these differentiations.

The work of Caroline Walker Bynum offers a valuable anchor point for understanding the shifts in criticism of what might be called spiritual subjectivity. In revised accounts of individual and communal forms of religious observance that previous generations of scholars often relegated to categories of individual abnormal psychology or collective decline in the ethical fabric and credal consensus of a supposedly unitary age of faith, the varieties of feminist scholarship have had some of their deepest and most salutary effects. See Bynum, *Jesus as Mother* and *Holy Feast and Holy Fast*. An exemplary account of various anthropological analyses of medieval religious practices, and hence also a fine introduction to some of the critical issues at stake in interpreting medieval subjectivity, is her article "Women's Stories, Women's Symbols," reprinted in *Fragmentation and Redemption*, a collection of Bynum's essays written between 1982 and 1989 that touches on many of the interpretive revisions I have indicated here.

[32]Patterson's chapter on the premises of this "experimental" edition, and the controversies surrounding it, provides an excellent account of its historical and paradigmatic importance, and suggests the broader significance of the return to textuality that it exemplifies (*Negotiating* 77–113). The importance of this edition is not chiefly in its status as a model for other editorial enterprises: its austerely "classicizing"

account and representation of the text belongs, as Patterson has shown, to the high-humanist tradition of editorial practice and inherits some of the major interpretive self-divisions of such enterprise, as not only Patterson but Nichols has outlined them. Its significance lies, rather, in its having caused within English medieval studies a broad "coming to consciousness" of editorial intervention as a practice with specific representative objectives, many of which are quite different from the textual operations and goals of medieval users of texts. (The phrase is that of Ralph Hanna III, in a paper presented at a meeting of the Medieval Academy: "The Mark of Kane[-Donaldson]: Textual Criticism in Disarray.")

[33] A brief but telling example of the connection between material and conceptual presentation is the influential article by Parkes on the terminology of text making, which identifies a differentiated vocabulary for kinds and degrees of intervention in a text by various kinds of writers. More recently, Minnis has discerned in the vocabularies of late-scholastic scriptural commentary a nuanced language for defining and positioning authorial agency in a text.

## Selected Bibliography

The following list offers a sampling of changed terms for framing major conceptual problems in the study of medieval literature and literary culture. Some are not the work of literary scholars, and do not prominently feature application to specific texts or classes of texts. The reader who has not attended to criticism or scholarship of any kind in this field in a generation, however, will find in this selection several of the main concerns that both differentiate current work from that of a generation ago and are likely to frame new work in the next few years; many of their introductions and bibliographies also form valuable points of entry for those seeking a reintroduction to the field. The list is ordered chronologically, to indicate the stages and relations through which thought on these issues developed.

Kolve, V. A. *The Play Called Corpus Christi*. Stanford: Stanford UP, 1966.
The book that for Anglo-American literary scholarship defined revised terms for discussion of the relations of sacred and secular motives in medieval vernacular performance and of re-creative designs in the representation of doctrinally and affectively edifying works and, in the longer term, set the terms of debate for the discernment of medieval literary theory and its application to questions of pragmatic cultural meaning. For a valuable account of its effects and importance, see Coletti.

Colish, Marcia. *The Mirror of Language: A Study in the Medieval Theory of Language*. New Haven: Yale UP, 1968.
One of the seminal efforts to investigate the philosophies of language and cognitive and semantic theory in the voluminous medieval academic writ-

ings of grammarians and speculative theologians. Such writings had been for centuries a chief target of humanist scorn and now became a substantial alternative to the practical rhetorical traditions that had heretofore been the chief site of modern inquiry into the sources of medieval thought about verbal forms and linguistic effects. Complemented since then by voluminous publication of many of the primary texts, this work both indicates the variety and innovation in medieval speculative discussion of language and mind and illustrates the radical difference between medieval and later European classifications of the disciplines to which thought on these matters belonged.

Parkes, Malcolm B. "The Influence of the Concepts of *Ordinatio* and *Compilatio* on the Development of the Book." *Medieval Learning and Literature: Essays Presented to R. W. Hunt*. Ed. J. J. G. Alexander and M. T. Gibson. Oxford: Oxford UP, 1975. 115–41.

An important example of the derivation of medieval critical terms and categories, and of operative formal distinctions for kinds of writing and modes of authorial responsibility, from the physical disposition and social arrangements for text making. This article has had the effect of reframing the terms of debate about the authorship and integrity or "unity" of medieval texts.

Kane, George, and E. Talbot Donaldson, eds. Piers Plowman: *The B Version*. London: Athlone, 1975.

A controverted landmark in medieval vernacular textual study and editing. This edition focused for many Anglo-American literary scholars a renewed awareness of, and dispute about, the problems that the manuscript forms of medieval literary works present to interpretation, and to modern representation of these works to "current critical interests and to the institutions of literary consumption" (L. Patterson, *Negotiating* 108).

Stock, Brian. *The Implications of Literacy*. Princeton: Princeton UP, 1983.

Valuable in indicating how discussions of literacy and its forms of interaction with medieval oral culture have been reframed since what Stock calls the "heroic age" of "strong theses" about these matters, exemplified for the early 1960s by the work of Milman Parry, Albert Lord, the earlier studies by Eric Havelock and Walter Ong, and, on a different scale of speculation, Marshall McLuhan.

Bloch, R. Howard. *Etymologies and Genealogies: A Literary Anthropology of the French Middle Ages*. Chicago: U of Chicago P, 1983.

A broadly speculative view of the thesis first proposed for a more limited range of materials and problems in Bloch's earlier *Medieval French Literature and Law*, concerning the homologous relations between the practice of the text and high-medieval social formations. Although in its synthetic ambitions and broad scope this book has no counterpart in the Anglo-

American critical tradition, and its conclusions are not easily transferable to other regional vernacular literatures of the Middle Ages, it offers an instructive instance of the intersection of French historical study of the *Annales* tradition with social theory and contemporary critical theory in the interpretation of medieval writings.

Minnis, A. J. *Medieval Theory of Authorship: Scholastic Literary Attitudes in the Later Middle Ages.* London: Scolar, 1984.

A learned illustration of changed approaches to defining the relations of medieval traditions of biblical interpretation and commentary to literary practice and theory.

Bynum, Caroline Walker. *Holy Feast and Holy Fast: The Religious Significance of Food to Medieval Women.* Berkeley: U of California P, 1987.

Exemplifies, like Bynum's preceding book, *Jesus as Mother*, current approaches to the investigation of medieval religious subjectivity and spiritual practice, and to the constitution of gender as a critical category. Her work has two kinds of value to literary scholars: it offers a nuanced introduction to the application (and limits) of anthropological and psychological models in the study of early texts and their societies, and it radically questions an interpretive habit still deeply rooted in many medievalists' practice, despite the general revolt during the past generation against the express premises of the "naturalism" that provided its rationale—namely, the assumption that metaphors and analogies are direct reflections of the practices, values, and life situations of the persons and communities that use them, rather than (as both books powerfully and painstakingly demonstrate) strategic defamiliarizations.

Patterson, Lee. *Negotiating the Past: The Historical Understanding of Medieval Literature.* Madison: U of Wisconsin P, 1987.

An indispensable critical survey of the development of the field and its position in current literary studies.

Hudson, Anne. *The Premature Reformation: Wycliffite Texts and Lollard History.* Oxford: Clarendon–Oxford UP, 1988.

A thoroughgoing revision of the defining program and history of the Lollard movement, written against the broad consensus represented by K. B. McFarlane in both his posthumously published *Lancastrian Kings and Lollard Knights* (Oxford: Clarendon, 1972) and *John Wycliffe and the Beginnings of English Nonconformity*. Hudson demonstrates the ways in which the movement constituted a continuous textual community; an early article setting forth her research methods and arguments—"A Lollard Sermon-Cycle and Its Implications" (*Medium Aevum* 40 [1971]: 142–56)—also brilliantly exemplifies the process of making social and institutional inference from the physical form and textual disposition of a group of medieval writings, an enterprise that has since come to greater prominence in the critical study of medieval texts.

Aers, David. *Community, Gender, and Individual Identity: English Writing, 1360–1430.* London: Routledge, 1988.

Exemplary in its well-researched and carefully argued historical accounts of major late-medieval texts and in its explicit self-awareness about its own historical and critical position in advocating and practicing a cultural studies approach to medieval literary texts. The book illustrates the strengths of its perspective—chiefly an intense specificity in situating literary texts among other contemporary discourses, and a well-documented account of the kind of interests embedded in medieval attitudes or themes long considered monolithic—and what has thus far proved to be a largely self-imposed rather than necessary limitation: the positioning of its methods and goals in an oppositional rather than complementary relation to formal and generic analysis, expressed in the form of a manifesto against formalist and poststructuralist literary theory. Its approach offers a telling contrast to the earlier landmark work of John Burrow in this field: where the "literary" was a largely unquestioned presence as a category of thought in Burrow's *Ricardian Poetry*, it is a provocative absence in the work of Aers.

Patterson, Lee, ed. *Literary Practice and Social Change in Britain, 1380–1530.* The New Historicism: Studies in Cultural Poetics 8. Berkeley: U of California P, 1990.

A collection of new essays by various hands, illustrating various modes of historical criticism of British medieval texts.

# enaissance/Early Modern Studies

## LEAH S. MARCUS

What manner of beast is early modern studies? The scholarly area here characterized under that rubric covers a terrain that is, despite some differences, quite similar to what is often still termed Renaissance studies. The new, or supplementary, nomenclature "early modern" is far more than a mere relabeling, however. To explore the implications of the terminological shift is to encounter an important set of conceptual reconfigurations by which scholars in the area of Renaissance/early modern studies are remapping the field itself. We are moving away from interpreting the period as a time of re-naissance, cultural rebirth, the reawakening of an earlier era conceived of as (in some sense) classic; we are coming to view the period more in terms of elements repeated thereafter, those features of the age that appear to us precursors of our own twentieth century, the modern, the postmodern.

In my survey here of new directions implied by the change in nomenclature, I unquestionably oversimplify and cannot hope to be exhaustive; because of the limits of my own training, my evidence is heavily weighted toward English and American as opposed to Continental works of scholarship, even though many of the trends I discuss had their origins in Continental European thought. But solipsism sometimes facilitates self-diagnosis. I hope to suggest through this discussion that the scholarly tropes we use as favorite tools in interpreting the Renaissance and/or early modern era are themselves signs of the change encapsulated in the nomenclature: we need to examine the functions of the intellectual and rhetorical baggage we bring to our enterprise, by whatever name we call it. To single out for the moment only terms I have used in composing these introductory paragraphs, we need to ask why we think of our subject in terms of such pervasively geographic metaphors: as a "terrain," an "area," a "field" that is being "remapped" or "explored," or as an "enterprise" that, like travel across a space that is not our accustomed terrain, requires us to take along "baggage."

The idea of the Renaissance goes back to the Renaissance itself, though the name was adopted in English only in the ninteenth century; the term *early modern* is much more recent, associated in particular with the *Annales* school of historians since the 1940s in France, somewhat later in England. *Early modern* carries a distinct agenda for historians, who have adopted the name quite consciously as a sign of disaffiliation from what they perceive as the elitism and cultural myopia of an older "Renaissance" history. Some of that same attitude has carried over to the term as adopted by literary scholars. The revised label points to a weakening of disciplinary boundaries not only in the sense that early modern literary scholars borrow from history or art history or anthropology (Renaissance studies has often been interdisciplinary in that way) but in the sense that, through the new label, the distinctness, the particularized structure of literary study itself is brought into question. Roland Barthes has asserted that "interdisciplinary work is not a peaceful operation: it begins *effectively* when the solidarity of the old disciplines breaks down" ("From Work" 73). If Barthes is right, and I think he is in this case, it is not surprising that the shift from *Renaissance* to *early modern* has aroused resistance and even outrage among many literary scholars. The category *early modern* not only erodes the traditional segment of literary studies called *Renaissance*; it appears to dissolve literary studies as an autonomous category of intellectual activity. Or, to put the matter more precisely, it dissolves the *appearance* of autonomy that literary studies has long prided itself on having.

That is not to suggest that the term *Renaissance*, any more than *early modern*, is solidly fixed in meaning. Neither set of nomenclature enjoys complete scholarly consensus even in terms of the precise time period it designates. Both *Renaissance* and *early modern* are chronologically shifty, the former term sometimes applied to European cultural phenomena occurring as early as the twelfth century; the latter, to phenomena as recent as the last quarter of the eighteenth century. But it is worth noting that the more hotly contested boundary in each case is that which is closer in time to the period privileged by the nomenclature. Scholars of the Renaissance have generally been less concerned about when the Renaissance ends and much more concerned about how to date its beginnings—the magical moment, or set of moments, or epoch(s), in which European culture, or at least an elite segment of it, developed the capacity for objective consideration of other historical epochs, perceived itself as markedly different from its own immediate past, and identified itself more passionately and pervasively with the classical era than with the more recent past. Renaissance studies, as it has been traditionally practiced, opens itself out toward the past in numerous other ways as well: it is concerned with questions of origin, influence, and filiation, producing a number of books with titles like *Classical Influence upon the Tribe of Ben* (McEuen).

While the boundaries of the Renaissance tend to push toward earlier and earlier chronological beginnings, early modern tends to creep up on the present. Scholars of the early modern period have devoted relatively little energy to the contestation of points of origin, much more to the issue of defining a terminus. At what point does the early modern become the modern, and, assuming pronounced elements of continuity between one and the other, how are scholars to define the relation between the two? In the field of history, the early modern leads directly into the modern era. Early modern history ends with the close of the eighteenth century; modern history begins roughly with the start of the nineteenth. When adopted by literary scholars, however, the term *early modern* designates a time period that usually ends in the late seventeenth century or the first half of the eighteenth—more than a century before the beginnings of literary modernism, in the twentieth century. What is termed *early modern* seems almost inevitably to take on some of the aura of twentieth-century modernism to the eclipse of temporal and intellectual categories in between (the Age of Enlightenment, the Romantics, and, in England, the Victorians). To look at the Renaissance through a lens called early modern is to see the concerns of modernism and postmodernism in embryo—alienation, a disjunction from origins, profound skepticism about the possibility for objectivity (in literary studies or anywhere else), an emphasis on textual indeterminacy as opposed to textual closure and stability, and an interest in intertextuality instead of filiation.

The term *Renaissance* is optimistic, upbeat—rebirth and renewal are marvelous ideas. One of the reasons many historians have become suspicious of the term is that it buys its optimism at too great a price—the neglect of other cultural currents and forms of cultural production, of a vast sea of human activity and misery that *Renaissance* either failed to include or included only marginally. The term *Renaissance* implicitly calls for a perception of historical rupture (in order to be reborn, a culture must previously have died) and, along with that, a subtle hierarchical valuation of disparate cultures. In *The Civilization of the Renaissance in Italy*, the book that, more than any other, encouraged subsequent generations of scholars to think in terms of "the Renaissance," Jacob Burckhardt could write of humanism's rediscovery of a capacity for individualism and independent thought, a dedication to the freedom and dignity of humankind that he associated, as did the Renaissance humanists themselves (at least in his reading of them), with the intellectual flowering of classical Greece and Rome. The Middle Ages, by comparison, was a time of monkish servitude and darkness, as were those elements of Renaissance culture untouched by its spirit of new quickening, *naissance*. By concentrating on a small ruling elite who controlled artistic production through patronage, traditional scholars of the Renaissance were able to paint glowing, idealized pictures of cultural life during the period. In such a hierarchical schema, high culture is set on a pedestal and given almost worshipful attention while lower cultures are perceived, much in the manner of Renaissance humanists themselves, as representing a lack of culture, lumpish chaos, the many-headed monster of the pit. Early modern approaches to the period set aside the implicitly hierarchical agenda of "Renaissance" in its traditional sense for a more prosaic, level mode of analysis that strives for greater cultural inclusiveness. It is perhaps symptomatic of the altered emphasis that *Renaissance* is regularly capitalized even in recent work while *early modern* is not. Historians of the early modern period typically use quantitative methods and/or local research to get at the commonplace lives of common people, economic trends, commercial practices, forms of popular entertainment and popular "mentality"—either strands of culture that cut across class divisions or strands identified as nonculture by Renaissance humanism in its most purely elitist form.

It is easy to find reasons why the term *early modern*, with its lower and more egalitarian connotations, might appeal to recent literary scholars: fewer of us who teach in universities come from (or, at least, are willing to identify with) a social elite than was the case, say, before the Second World War. The university itself, particularly with the expansion of public education, has become a more inclusive body, drawing students from a broader cross-section of society than it did forty or fifty years ago. Yet the term *Renaissance* has by no means been discarded, even by scholars whose interests align them squarely with the set of values I have here associated with the category *early modern*. It is quite common to find *early modern* and *Renaissance* used together in the work of even very recent literary scholars (and I cannot claim to be an exception), on the grounds that each term has its own special purpose, one of which appears to be the preservation of literature as a separate category (our own turf!) despite our declared interest in breaking down disciplinary boundaries.

Interdisciplinary violence à la Barthes is rather invigorating when imagined against disciplines other than our own, less attractive when imagined as depradation on literary studies itself. In the introduction to the superb collection of essays entitled *Rewriting the Renaissance* (ed. Ferguson, Quilligan, and Vickers), for example, the editors repeatedly refer to historical developments as "early modern" and literature of the same period as "Renaissance," even though their project is to rewrite what *Renaissance* means in order to "break down such barriers" (xxxi). This way of parceling out terminology is typical of work in the field at present. We are in a state of creative turmoil and indecision, feeling both a strong pull toward interdisciplinary approaches in our study of the past and a proprietary desire to preserve our own scholarly domain; experiencing a strong need to move the discipline toward greater egalitarianism and cultural inclusiveness but also a reluctance to give up the charismatic idea of rebirth, the aura of elitism carried by the idea of the Renaissance (for a medievalist's view, see Wallace). Given the lingering éclat of the term *Renaissance* among scholars whose articulated aims place them in the camp of the early modern, at least as I have defined those polarities here, I shall in what follows use the term *early modern* for recent scholarly work that conforms to the summary profile I have suggested, whether or not such work itself gives prominence to the term.

We might suppose, since the Renaissance tends to push back into the past while the early modern period creeps up on the present, that study of the Renaissance would imply a sense of greater cultural distance than suggested by the more recent term. The reverse is usually the case. The idea of rebirth implies the perception of cultural disjunction, but also the possibility of renewed identity and therefore of essential similarity between two periods separated in time. The famous letter from Machiavelli describing his communion in his study with Greek and Roman authors may be taken as paradigmatic of a Renaissance view of the ancients:

> On the threshold I slip off my day's clothes with their mud and dirt, put on my royal and curial robes, and enter, decently accoutred, the ancient courts of men of old, where I am welcomed kindly and fed on that fare which is mine alone, and for which I was born: where I am not ashamed to address them and ask them the reasons for their action, and they reply considerately; and for two hours I forget all my cares, I know no more trouble, death loses its terrors: I am utterly translated in their company.                                   (xxix)

This poignant scene of conversation associates the classics with freedom, dignity, transcendence, a separation from the sordid aspects of life, and a confirmation of selfhood: as he dons his gorgeous robes and wills himself into their presence, Machiavelli appears to assume an intrinsic bonding and continuity between his own intellect and that of ancient authors. He will understand them and they, him. That assertion of essential similarity is characteristic of traditional Renaissance scholarship as well but is called into question by more recent work of an early modern bent, work that posits identity not as innate and unchanging but as culturally constructed and therefore unstable, never more than partly recoverable across time.

Instead of interpreting the scene of Machiavelli's communion with the ancients as a confirmation (in the manner of Burckhardt) of the "freedom and dignity of man," more recent scholars like Stephen Greenblatt and Wayne Rebhorn might reembed it in the immediate cultural contingencies that Machiavelli himself seeks to transcend. They might, for example, call attention to the manufactured and performative quality of the scene, its "self-fashioning" function of creating a scenario of prestige and continuing "courtiership" for Machiavelli amid the ignominy of exile, its oblique assertion, to a friend who was also a potential advocate with the Florentine state, of Machiavelli's worthiness for public office: anyone welcome in the courts of the ancients was obviously worthy of employment in the courts of the Medici. One reading of the scene would emphasize its elements of universality, intellectual continuity, and transcendence; the other, its elements of strangeness and provisionality, its inseparability from a specific cultural situation. A striking effect of early modern historical and literary research has been the defamiliarization of such

seemingly universal categories as childhood, the family, carnival, war, or courtiership in a way that disrupts our perception of identity with the past and
therefore defamiliarizes the major literature as well (Ariès; Stone; Le Roy
Ladurie; Bakhtin, *Rabelais*; Whigham; see also Montrose's essay in the present
volume on the new historicism).

Like identity in general, that peculiar offshoot of identity that we term
literary authorship is also being called into question in the work of early
modern scholars. Traditional work in the Renaissance assumes that literary
works have authors in the sense of finite historical personages whose identities
can be discovered, whose intentions toward their own work can be, to a significant degree, understood and reconstructed—much in the way that Machiavelli
asks his classical companions "the reasons for their action" and receives their
courteous reply. One of the key ideas of postmodernism is the "death of the
author": the perception of an essential, comprehensible authorial presence
behind the literature we read registers to many of us as a fond or even
dangerous illusion. Michel Foucault's essay "What Is an Author?" has been
enormously useful in its assertion that the idea of "the author" is not a transhistorical category but a cultural construct associated with the beginnings of
authorial accountability and censorship in the early modern era.

Thus understood, scholars' traditional ways of understanding authorial control and intentionality can be reinterpreted as a product of Renaissance
humanism itself, a continuation of one possible way of conducting interpretation to the neglect of other possible ways. The demotion of authorship and
intention as the controlling center of meaning has created a sense of loss, as
scholars find themselves bereft of the trusty methodological tools they have
had since graduate school, but it also produces many gains. Traditionally, the
canon of Renaissance literature overwhelmingly emphasized works by humanists that looked like what we have been taught "literature" looks like—works
that showed signs of participation in the heady developing enterprise of authorship, with its high seriousness about the dignity of the task, its emphasis on
classical learning as a prerequisite, its revival of classical forms, its exaltation
of literature as a transcendent, "golden" achievement of the human spirit, and
its concomitant denigration of any writing that did not conform to its own
exacting standards. Now, with the reinterpretation of such claims as historically conditioned and limited rather than as universally true, we are freed to
explore the circumstances during the period that helped bring self-conscious
literary authorship into being; we are also freed to explore a vast panorama of
"nonauthorial" writings as part of our study of literature.

One such new area is writing by women, which in the early modern
period was usually highly pragmatic in function—diaries, advice to children,
letters, speeches (as in those of Queen Elizabeth I, for example)—and which
therefore has not been traditionally included as part of "literature." Older

scholarship simply assumed that women in the Renaissance for the most part failed to write high literature because they lacked the interest or ability; more recent scholarship is asking, "Did women have a Renaissance?" and discovering that women did write much more and much more effectively than earlier scholars had thought; to the extent that early modern women failed to write, they were conforming to and showing the effects of overwhelming cultural constraints advocating silence as a sign of chastity and obedience (Kelly-Gadol; S. W. Hull; Hannay; Woodbridge; Lamb; Beilin). The discovery of a hitherto dimly perceived culture of women's reading, writing, and allied intellectual activity has helped to stimulate a recognition that gender itself (as opposed to biological sexual identity) is culturally produced—a factor that must be integrated into our study of the period as a whole if we are to redress the narrowness and overselectivity of traditional Renaissance scholarship (Kahn; Boose; Callaghan; McLuskie; K. Newman). The same recognition is generating new investigation of homoeroticism during the period: we are discovering that the early modern era had vastly different, usually less rigid, ways of defining sexual deviance than our society does; that sense of difference cannot but alter our interpretation of what constitutes normative sexual behavior in the literature (Orgel, "Nobody's Perfect"; Pequigney; Bruce Smith).

The unexplored or underdeveloped territory within early modern studies also includes a vast array of writings whose form and apparent function disqualified it as serious literature—pamphlets, romances, ballads, even popular drama, and, at the other end of the cultural spectrum, ephemeral forms like the court masque, which was disparaged by its learned authors as the mere illusion of a night. The traditional canon of the Renaissance is opening little by little to admit such authorially heterodox works. Writings by women like Elizabeth Carey, Queen Elizabeth I, and Mary Wroth (to take recent English examples) are being published in scholarly editions (Ferguson and Weller; Heisch; Roberts). Traditionally suspect forms like the Stuart court masque and London Lord Mayor's shows have been made available in collected, separate editions that posit such hybrid creations as worthy of study in their own right rather than as minor addenda to the works of canonical authors (Orgel and Strong; Bergeron). In addition, popular polemical literature of the period is increasingly accessible. Within the last fifteen years, for example, it has become possible to read, in paperback, the writings of the English social revolutionaries known as Levellers (Morton).

Simultaneously, critics who continue to concentrate on canonical texts are turning their attention from "high" to "lower" forms of writing within the period. Thirty years ago, the lyric poem was generally regarded by scholars of seventeenth-century English literature as the most distinguished and intellectually intriguing achievement of the age. To have composed a *Well Wrought Urn* was the pinnacle. The phrase is borrowed from Cleanth Brooks's famous book, the title of which was itself borrowed from a lyric by John Donne asserting, in admirable humanist fashion, the lyric poem's capacity to communicate greatness despite its limited scale ("As well a well wrought urn becomes / The greatest ashes, as half acre tombs"). Now, pace T. S. Eliot and the New Critics, the lyric has lost its centrality in seventeenth-century studies and been replaced by less elitist genres such as the drama. To the extent that traditionally prestigious poets like the English Cavaliers are still being taught in the classroom, their graceful, often misogynist lyrics are frequently supplemented by newly available countervoices in the form of women poets and diarists or puritan controversialists writing at the same time. These expansions and alterations in the canon can be measured by the availability of convenient textbook collections. Twenty years ago, there were several handsome paperback collections of seventeenth-century lyrics to choose from; now there are almost none. Years ago, there were no textbook anthologies of work by women writers of the period. Now there are several, among them Katharina M. Wilson's *Women Writers of the Renaissance and Reformation*, as well as others in preparation.

Such changes in the canon are by no means exclusive to the area of Renaissance/early modern studies; however, because of their implicit assault on the very idea of re-naissance, their impact there has been more intense than in many other literary fields. A snowball effect has been created whereby the study of noncanonical writings precipitates a rereading and revaluation of canonical figures and an increasing erosion of modes of interpretation based on elitist assumptions about literature and its superiority to more workaday forms of writing; that rereading brings about, even as it is facilitated by, a leveling of hierarchical modes of thought and evaluation so that even the "greatest" authors (like Shakespeare) lose their patina of transcendence and cultural privilege and come to look rather more like what we used to call their lesser contemporaries.

Twenty-five years ago, Shakespeare was regularly read and taught as an upholder of state and religious orthodoxies—a proponent of order along the lines of E. M. W. Tillyard's *Elizabethan World Picture*. In newer critical work, Tillyard has become a standard whipping boy, and Shakespeare is reinterpreted as less comfortably orthodox, estranged from the elitist values of his own era or uneasily complicitous with Elizabethan doctrines of state (Dollimore, *Radical Tragedy*; Dollimore and Sinfield, *Political Shakespeare*; Drakakis; Howard and O'Connor; Greenblatt, *Shakespearean Negotiations*). Instead of taking Shakespeare's greatness for granted or giving it worshipful admiration, scholars of an early modern and postmodernist bent are arguing that Shakespeare was not an "author" at all in the exalted Renaissance sense but a playwright who functioned in much the same way as others we call hack dramatists—who produced for his company a steady supply of material over which he exerted none of the rights of ownership. Rather than assume that the bard was born great, scholars are investigating the social, economic, and intellectual factors that worked together to *make* Shakespeare canonical, the high point of civilized value, exponent par excellence of the freedom and dignity of humankind (Bentley; Hawkes; Orgel, "Authentic Shakespeare"; L. Marcus; Garber, *Shakespeare's Ghost Writers*).

Not all the "classic authors" of the period have been so readily adaptable to the new ideas. John Milton, with his strong, brooding, and, to some readers, overbearing authorial presence over his own work, has been tougher for critics to assimilate to the antiauthorial bent of postmodernism; partly for that reason, the study of Milton has been slowly losing the centrality it used to have during the 1950s and 1960s. There are other reasons for the decline. In postfeminist scholarly writing and in the classroom, the "Milton bogey" is harder than it once was to overcome: lines like "He for God only, she for God in him" now often come as a shock even for seasoned Milton scholar-teachers, and certainly for their students. As Christian humanism in the manner of Douglas Bush no longer plays *the* key role in literary scholarship, Milton has been reinterpreted as a less genial, more rigidly doctrinaire Protestant, but that image has also hurt his case with many readers. By far the most influential Milton book of the last couple of decades has been Stanley Fish's brilliant *Surprised by Sin*, a study that has intrigued a whole generation of scholars but has also, as John Rumrich, in *Uninventing Milton*, points out, solidified Milton's reputation as a crabbed, inflexible figure whose chief interest is to trap the reader into seeing the world as the author insists we must. The new malleability of the canon has caused more than one scholar to advocate even that Milton be formally decanonized—dropped from the lists of required authors by which we define our discipline. If new critical trends have led to a partial eclipse of Milton, however, there are strong signs that those same trends are beginning to effect a revival and reinterpretation: increasingly, scholars are exploring the ways in which Milton's poetry undermines its own seemingly ironclad author-ity, interpreting his misogyny as a site for conflict about gender roles, and revising his Protestantism away from its traditional Christian humanist or rigidly Calvinist construction and in the direction of political radicalism and doctrinal experimentalism (B. Rajan; Froula; Shoaf; J. M. Walker; J. G. Turner; Nyquist and Ferguson; C. Hill; Rumrich, *Uninventing Milton*; Armstrong and Tennenhouse, *Imaginary Puritan*). If the authorial Milton has refused to die in properly postmodernist fashion, he has at least become divided against himself.

To scholars of a more traditionalist frame of mind, the imposition of late modernist or postmodernist notions about the "death of the author" on a period like the Renaissance is an act of flagrant historical irresponsibility— the fact that the complex of ideas associated with authorship is now under eclipse is no reason to assume it never existed. To such an objection, postmodernists might take one or more lines of defense. First of all, they might attack the assumption that there is such a thing as critical or historical transparency: all interpretation is generated at least as much by the culture that has produced the critic as by the culture under scrutiny. Postmodernist readers of the early modern period cannot claim, as could their forebears who believed in scientific and critical objectivity, to be disinterested; they are obliged to strive for an awareness of where their own interests lie, instead of assuming, in the style of Burckhardt, an objectivity that, to postmodernist scholars, appears to be the product of a specific flowering of nineteenth-century optimism and haut-bourgeois individualism rather than a transhistorical contribution to universal truth.

Second, postmodernists (or late modernists) might assert that recent emphasis on nonauthorial forms of authorship allows us not less but more access to a culture in which such forms were just beginning to develop. One of the milestones of the Renaissance/early modern age, however we define it, was the invention of printing and a massive, if gradual, shift in the ways ideas were presented and disseminated as the technology became widespread (Eisenstein). However, scholars of different generations interpret the onset of print culture very differently: more traditional scholarship tends to read the assumptions of later and more highly developed print culture back into the Renaissance, while newer work in the field generally emphasizes the ways in which the first centuries of printing *failed* to conform to our received notions about what a world of letters has to be like. One reason for the shift in emphasis is the development of new technologies of writing. The fact that our computerized age has produced an alternative to the book is causing the idea of the book to lose its aura of universality. By looking at a period when books were a fresh invention from a time in which they are gradually becoming outmoded (strange and painful though such an idea may be), we get quite a different perspective on Renaissance/early modern print culture itself and begin to associate the production of literature with what D. F. McKenzie has termed the "sociology of texts"—a complex of economic and social trends along with related changes in institutions like patronage, the Stationer's Company, the printing house, and the bookstall that exerted strong pressures on the form and function of literature (McKenzie; Blayney; Helgerson; Loewenstein; Brink; Mark Rose, *Author*; Oliphant and Bradford). For our period at least, the printing house was not organized to allow for flexibility in dealing with the authors of books in production; the final shape of a printed book might have precious little or nothing to do with the "author's intent." As we factor the history of printing into our view of literary production, we are, once again, confronted with a development in the field that challenges assumptions about authorial autonomy, individuality, and artistic control inherited from the nineteenth century.

A new fascination with the instability of literary texts is characteristic at present of literary studies across the spectrum, not only in the area of Renaissance/early modern. Indeed, in Barthes's influential definition, a text is always unstable ("From Work"). It is not a fixed entity, like the physical book that may serve as its vehicle; not something that can be specified, objectified, held in the hand, and interpreted according to rational, linear categories of interpretation. It is instead a "field" of force, in the scientific sense of the term, that, in interplay with the consciousness with the reader, sets in motion a volatile, indeterminate, and open-ended process, always resisting the rational-izing and codifying thrust of interpretation as it is traditionally understood. According to Barthes's formulation, the idea of the Renaissance would be asso-ciated with the idea of the "work" of literature—a fixed entity bound between covers, having an author and clearly defined purposes, a specifiable set of historical parameters and an identifiable meaning arrived at through rational, lucid, usually linear modes of interpretation. The idea of the early modern is more easily assimilable to the idea of the "text" in Barthes's formulation, in that the text operates independently of, even in subversion of, traditional assumptions about the universality and orderliness of literature—the goal of interpretation is not to get the story straight but "to get the story crooked," understanding the ways it goes against the grain of received authorial modes of interpretation (Kellner; see also Esch, in this volume, for a discussion of deconstruction). Despite its attractiveness and utility, however, the notion of text as it is used in Barthes and other poststructuralist theorists has been questioned by a number of recent critics who find the idea of textual indetermi-nacy exhilarating and indispensable but are unwilling to abandon the study of a given text's "sociology"—its embeddedness in specific historical circum-stances, its shifts in morphology and function over time, and the relations between those shifts and other forms of cultural transformation (McGann, *Beauty* and *Critique*; Said, *World*). Increasingly, literary scholars are adopting a "tool box" approach to poststructuralist ideas about the text, basing their interpretation not on one single theoretical paradigm but on an eclectic blend of ideas and techniques.

One of the most interesting recent developments in the field of Renais-sance/early modern studies has been an adaptation of postmodernist ideas about textual indeterminacy that cuts across the Barthian distinction between "text" and "work" to explore forms of textual instability related to modes of textual production specific to the period. Deconstructive readings of Renais-sance/early modern language theory and rhetoric document the age's own ob-session with the "doubtfulness of words" (P. Parker; Goldberg, *Voice*). What we are discovering is the extent to which our sense of the stability of Renaissance texts has been created by the codifying practices of generations of editors. In the past, instability and unreliability were routinely attributed not to the author but to elements of the process of transmission: quarto A was bungled in the printing house; quarto B was defaced by scribal error; quarto C was a "memorial reconstruction," maimed by the inadequate memories of actors who were (improperly) stealing the text. Now such arguments are beginning to look dated—like yet another encoding of Renaissance elitism: the author and his (never her) production are exalted, pristine in themselves, but marred by the low jostling exigencies of the marketplace.

This implicitly hierarchical thinking saves the idea of the author and the interpretive strategies associated with the positing of authorial rationality and control by excoriating some other element of the process by which the author came (or was forced) into print. But what if authors themselves destabilized their texts, or never made them stable in the first place, or sat by passively and approvingly—as Shakespeare may have at rehearsals of his plays—as their manuscripts were jostled and reshaped in the process of transmission? By asking such questions about the milieu of writing and reception during the period, scholars are moving toward a disconcerting, fascinating set of questions not only about interpretation itself but about the kinds of interpretation that are enabled and blocked by our modern editions. What have been the cultural assumptions behind our "standard editions" of the canonical authors? How might reading Renaissance classics in a dark blue cover marked with the imprimatur "Clarendon" differ from reading as it was experienced at the time that the texts first became available to readers in the form of a circulated manuscript, or perhaps in a cheap quarto edition competing in the bookstalls with hundreds of other books? How has editorial practice since the eighteenth century formed and re-formed Renaissance authors rather than merely bringing them to us in some "original" and uncontaminated form (de Grazia, *Shakespeare*)?

Not surprisingly, this interrogation of standard editorial practice began with the texts of Shakespeare, with the seemingly modest suggestion by Steven Urkowitz, Michael Warren, and Gary Taylor that *King Lear* is not one play but two. They have argued that the quarto and folio texts of *King Lear* are not partially garbled simulacra of a single lost original (Shakespeare's own manuscript of the play) but independent texts each with its own form, content, and dramatic logic, its own wording of key speeches, its own presentation of key characters like Goneril and the Duke of Albany, its own claim to the cohesiveness and clarity traditionally attributed to works of literary art (Urkowitz; Taylor and Warren). For poststructuralist critics, the new claims about *King Lear* do not go nearly far enough, because they depend on outmoded assumptions about the essential rationality and orderliness of literary texts in order to establish the differences between the two versions of the play (Trousdale; Goldberg, "Properties"). For more conservative scholars, the new claims go much too far, in that they bring into doubt and confusion a key assumption not only of Shakespearean interpretation as they envision it but also of Renaissance editorial practice in general—the idea that there was an "original" version of *King Lear*, or of any other literary work for that matter, and that the goal of scholarship is either to recover or to reconstruct that original as a way of coming as close as possible to the author's intent.

Until fairly recently, literary interpretation and the editing of literary texts were divided and distinguished worlds: editors produced standard editions of the major authors; scholars accepted these editions as reliable and used them to generate interpretation. Part of the reason for the division was that early printed versions of early modern texts were unavailable outside a few major research institutions: only scholars already affiliated with such institutions or blessed with the leisure to visit them could presume to edit texts. But as in so many other elements of Renaissance scholarship, the implicit elitism of traditional textual editing has broken down. For standard authors such as Shakespeare, not only have early texts been dispersed, particularly to American libraries, but they have been reproduced in handsome, affordable facsimile editions that give the average Shakespearean almost the same access to the raw material as editors themselves have had (Hinman; Allen and Muir). Now the average scholar can second-guess editors and override their judgment, with the result that the standard editions of the plays are losing much of their authority. Like the Bible in early Reformation times, the hitherto unreachable "sacred" texts have suddenly become available to nearly everyone (although the price of recent facsimile editions is rising alarmingly). As during the early Reformation, the effect of this dissemination of materials has been to demystify the traditional guardians of the text and its meaning and to create a new "priesthood of all believers." Shakespeareans are beginning to question traditional editorial assumptions about other plays beyond *King Lear*, with the effect that standard editions are themselves changing—the new Oxford Shakespeare, with its strong attention to variant versions of the plays in the *Textual Companion* volume that accompanies the edition, conveys a much less solid and magisterial sense of the text than most older editions marked "Clarendon" and bound in dark blue, even though the new Oxford continues in some ways to protect the integrity of the idea of the Shakespearean "original" (Wells and Taylor). In a similar spirit, Jill Levenson's Oxford edition of *Romeo and Juliet* will use the second quarto as its copytext and give the first quarto version complete in the back. Margreta de Grazia is planning a new edition of Shakespeare's sonnets that will break the editorial molds in which readers have encountered the poems since the eighteenth century. Shakespeare is coming "un-edited," in Randall McLeod's provocative phrase, even as new editions are being produced.

The authority of other standard editions is also coming into question—not only for the non-Shakespearean drama but for the lyric as well. Like the drama, the lyric in early modern society was markedly unstable in terms of form and authorship. Just as more than one playwright might collaborate on the creation or revision of a playtext, with the attribution of authorship either casual and imprecise or nonexistent, so, as Arthur Marotti and other scholars are suggesting, lyric poems were typically written in a social setting rather than some solitary garret; they were circulated among a coterie of friends and acquaintances, recopied with variations by any number of readers, perhaps also by the author to incorporate felicitous variations introduced by someone else, so that a very popular poem might exist in dozens of different forms, none of them definitively authorial (Marotti; Pebworth and Sullivan). It is arguable that the new work on the cultural construction of the lyric will stimulate a revival of critical and pedagogical interest in the genre, but the lyric will not be the same transcendent, serenely aloof artifact it was for earlier generations of scholars. And it will be harder to perceive as "authored" in the traditional sense.

The recognition that textual indeterminacy was more the rule than the exception for many types of written materials during the period is causing the same kind of shift in our expectations of the texts themselves that we have earlier discussed in terms of the shift in terminology from *Renaissance* to *early modern*. The idea of origination loses much of its energy once a single original can no longer credibly be posited. Machiavelli's fantasy of instant communication with the past through the texts of its major authors is necessarily giving way to a sense of greater distance and opacity. Our critical editions cannot easily replicate the period's association with rebirth by bringing a highly valued "original" back to life for the use of the modern reader; to the extent that they continue to do so, as in the new Oxford Shakespeare, there is an increasing sense of strain between the acknowledgment of variability and the desire to reconstruct a reliable authorial text. Michael Warren's *Complete* King Lear, *1608–1623* goes beyond the new Oxford Shakespeare in that it allows readers to assemble their own preferred version of the play from separate facsimile texts: the edition is "complete" in the sense that it gives readers all the early versions of the play that the editor considers significantly different, but it is forever incapable of completeness in that it generates not a single "reliable" text but a variety of potential texts limited only by the ingenuity of its readers. Warren views *The Complete* King Lear, in its many separable, interfolded parts, as a stage in the dissolution of the standard literary edition. A recognition of textual indeterminacy, or even a preference for it, is making its way into other new scholarly editions as well—as these appear in print, we can expect an erosion of the traditional editorial task of creating a single authoritative text and an increasing interest in variant versions of a text and the ways in which the variations are significant.

For a text that exists in many different versions, the printed book may no longer be the most felicitous format for an edition. Particularly with the introduction of computerized *hypertext*, with its potential for displaying two or three or even more versions of a given passage in parallel on the screen, for ranging easily through several layers of editorial notes of different degrees of complexity, and for instantly calling up on the screen one or another variant version of a text in its entirety, editions of early modern literature need not be limited to the capacities of the book. If the scholarly edition in book form, with its emphasis on sequence and on a permanent fixity of elements on the page, may be said to lend itself well to Renaissance modes of interpretation, then the computerized edition in hypertext, with its greater capacity to display a text as a live thing—fluid and dynamic rather than immutable and static— lends itself to postmodernist modes of interpretation and may allow us increased access to the more mercurial, unstable elements of early modern literature that the book, with its physical solidity and durability, has tended to suppress (Slatin; see also Delany and Landow; Oliphant and Bradford). Proponents of computerized editions are even talking about the new editions as a renewal of manuscript culture, at least insofar as such editions will allow each owner to customize a work as he or she wishes. We are approaching a time like the Renaissance/early modern period itself, when alternative technologies for promulgating written material will exist alongside, and in competition with, the printed book.

My discussion thus far has used the terms *modernist* and *postmodernist* as though they were interchangeable. To some extent, this imprecision reflects our uncertainty over the definition of the terms: some critics would argue that postmodernism is merely the latest phase of modernism, while others would emphasize a disjunction between the two. However we may choose to label ourselves, we can be sure that future generations of scholar-critics will reserve the right to relabel us at will. Nevertheless, there has been a significant slippage in my use of terminology in that I have assigned the term *Renaissance* and the traditionalist assumptions associated therewith to generations of twentieth-century critics associated with literary modernism—T. S. Eliot and the New Critics in particular; I have assigned the term *early modern* and the attitudes associated with that choice of nomenclature to more recent critics who might label themselves postmodernist and who, whether correctly or not, perceive themselves as conducting a thoroughgoing critique of the isolate stance of literary modernism. The slippage is historically significant. Twentieth-century modernist writer-critics have, to a significant degree, hung on to the idea of the Renaissance as solace against their own feeling of alienation and fragmentation, a way of retaining a sense of connectedness with a time, again to use Eliot, before the "dissociation of sensibility" and other symptoms of a lost wholeness and integrity (*Selected Essays* 247). For more recent generations of scholars, Eliot's notion of a sensibility that was once *not* dissociated is a cultural myth—the blanket imposition of notions of individual self-sufficiency and autonomy on a period when such ideas were only beginning to emerge. The set of attitudes I have associated with the nomenclature *early modern* can be described in summary as a refiguration of the period that abandons the modernist "scene of writing"—its imaging of the writer as a figure in splendid solitude, locked away from history and social process in a garret of some kind where he (since the writer, according to this paradigm, is almost by definition male) will be sufficiently unfettered from the world to generate authentic art (Brodkey).

This image of the writer as an essentially private figure may be re-garded as an invention—in part a fantasy—dating back to the early modern era itself: we may think of Machiavelli in his splendid robes of state, in a space apart from the "cares" and "trouble" of his ordinary life, or of Montaigne up in his tower, or of the poet in Milton's *Il Penseroso*, watching out the lonely night in lofty, silent communion with Hermes, Plato, and the mysterious powers of "immortal mind" (74). For more recent critics, the issue is not so much whether these private "scenes of writing" ever existed during the early modern era; the issue is rather that such scenes are themselves culturally produced—part of a developing desire for privacy that accompanied the rise of individualism and the decline of corporate forms of social organization in the early modern age (Ariès; Alpers; Stone; F. Barker; Wayne, *Penshurst*). The shift from Renais-sance to early modern does not mean the utter effacement of the modernist "scene of writing" but, instead, a questioning of its aura of special privilege, a demotion of its implicit status as a touchstone for true literary creativity in favor of less familiar, more collective alternative scenes.

A disestablishing of the modernist image of the writer-thinker is also characteristic of other disciplines that have made a strong mark on our field in recent decades. The history of science provides a good example. Newtonian physics posits the individual mind as capable of reaching a realm of abstract truth in which human contingency is replaced by immutable laws of motion. Histories of science during the Renaissance shaped their subject to emphasize the rise of modern science in the Newtonian and experimental sense and to downplay or even ridicule the superstitious animism that preceded and accom-panied "true science" during the period. But post-Einsteinian science is more and more challenging the myth of abstract individualism as the basis for scientific thinking and replacing the Newtonian model of the universe as a precisely functioning machine with the idea of a "cosmic web"—a less orderly model that posits the interdependence of "objects, events, and observer as belonging inextricably to the same field," so that objective study and measure-ment are no longer possible and science loses its capacity to posit abstract models and conduct precise measurements (Hayles 10). The new developments in the conceptualization of science have been called a latter-day Copernican revolution surging through late twentieth-century culture: we are living through a paradigm shift in cosmology rather like that of the seventeenth century, but operating to some degree in reverse, giving us renewed access to Renaissance/early modern scientific models that even forty years ago would have been confidently branded as merely occult, heterodox, prescientific. According to one writer on the subject, Galileo would be completely at home at MIT, except that even Galileo would have to abandon his belief in strict causality and the discreteness and particularity of objects in order to participate imaginatively in the new post-Einsteinian "cosmic web" (Hayles 18; Eichner). The importance of this shift for Renaissance/early modern studies is vast and only beginning to be felt: the relations between science and literature will have to be massively reconceptualized and rewritten as we recognize the rich spectrum of scientific activities during the period and learn to think beyond our own inherited, linear models of scientific progress. Already it has been suggested that Kepler and his *anima motrix* are more important for John Donne than Copernicus was, and that Newton's secret dedication to alchemical mysteries should carry as much significance for scholars as his interest in gravity and optics (Gossin; Vickers; Hedrick; Wojciehowski).

In psychoanalytic approaches to Renaissance/early modern literature, there has been a similar shift away from the valorization of autonomous selfhood. The classic Freudian "scene of analysis" is much like the modernist "scene of writing" in that it centers on an image of a small room dominated by the patient on the couch in (near) solitary reflection and separation from the world; the achievement of normal functioning within this scenario means the development of a personal autonomy that will allow the patient increased self-mastery and effectiveness in the tasks of life. To the extent that Freudian approaches have been applied to Renaissance literature in the past, they have usually involved the psychoanalytic reading of an author or text in isolation, with the at least implicit assumption that Freudian theory is as applicable to the sixteenth or seventeenth century as to the late nineteenth and twentieth. Now an array of post-Freudian theories are challenging the assumption that psychic individuation is always necessary for healthy functioning and pointing to the gender- and culture-bound assumptions behind the view that psychic structure is essentially similar from one period to another.

Heinz Kohut, for example, has suggested that different forms of psychopathology can be correlated with different forms of social organization and social malaise. He notes that while sexual neurosis was the dominant form of pathology observed clinically in Freud's own time, more recently, the dominant symptomatology is not sexual neurosis but a broader, vaguer fragmentation and anomie; he ties the shift to a number of significant cultural alterations, among them the decline of the nuclear family in its closely knit, intimate, sexually repressive late nineteenth-century form (Kohut, *How Does Analysis*

*Cure?* 55–61). Speculative work of this kind from the field of psychoanalysis, along with similar work from anthropologists with a like-minded interest in the culturally specific aspects of psychic functioning, is providing literary scholars with a set of new tools for identifying just what it is that we mean when we brand older psychoanalytic approaches as anachronistic. The early modern era was a time when the nuclear family as we are accustomed to think of it was in process of formation but still associated with fairly marginal social groups and existing alongside other patterns of family life and other forms of psychic organization, some of which more closely resemble the late twentieth-century fragmentation of self observed by Kohut and others than the late nineteenth-century psychoneurosis described by Freud. Instead of reading Freudian assumptions back into the early modern era, critics are coming to regard the period as a vast laboratory for generating different forms of social organization and different models of mind, and to interpret the literature of the period as enacting frictions and transformations among the different models (this inquiry is only beginning to be made in Kohutian terms; for similar work in a Foucauldian vein, see Barber; F. Barker; Foucault, *Madness*; Stallybrass and White; Armstrong and Tennenhouse). As part of the same shift, new feminist readings of the Renaissance/early modern period regularly place emphasis on the gender-coding of psychosocial development, then as now: on the relationships between women's reading and writing, specifically female "scenes of writing," which were often communal rather than individual, and on the gender-specific psychic work that women's writing had to accomplish, given the culture's expectations for women (Ferguson, Quilligan, and Vickers; Mary Beth Rose; Lamb).

     Post-Freudian psychoanalysis has also given us models for conceptualizing some of the methodological splits between generations of scholars that I have been discussing under the rubrics *Renaissance* and *early modern*. If, as reader-response critics have emphasized, the act of reading normally involves various kinds of transference mechanisms, then there has been a basic shift in the types of transference mobilized in the study of Renaissance/early modern literature. An older generation of modernist critics of the Renaissance, as I have already suggested, tended to idealize it and/or emphasize its own idealizing currents of thought. For them, the idea of the Renaissance was powerful in part because it was a psychic refuge against the perception of twentieth-century cultural fragmentation and the stress that went along with it; academic institutions, similarly, were a repository for values either threatened or abandoned by the culture at large. More recent critics of a postmodern stamp tend to take that fragmentation more as a given, something to be applauded and played with rather than regretted; either they never experienced the cultural cohesion perceived by their elders as lost, or, having experienced it and found it incongenial, they regard its vestiges as imprisoning. Their dominant transference mechanisms as readers have more to do with reaction formation against idealization and against "high culture" and with what Kohut might term the maintenance of a healthy grandiosity. In this transference mode, the literature of the past is placed in the service of self-enhancement rather than the other way around; interpretation becomes a means for self-empowerment and, beyond that, for reengagement with communal structures and social problems outside the narrow confines of the academy. Although this rough sketch of differences is much too brief and generalized, it will at least indicate some of the ways in which recent psychoanalytic theory and psychohistory can be placed in the service of postmodernist self-reflection and speculation about the hidden agendas behind our interpretive practice.

Like psychoanalysis, anthropology has traditionally been important to scholars in our period but has recently become significant in more inward-looking ways. The most obvious sign of its impact during the past two or three decades is an increased interest on the part of literary scholars in cross-cultural forms like witchcraft, festival, shaming rituals, patterns of gift-giving, scapegoating, kinship systems, and patterns of incest avoidance. While scholars of a Renaissance bent regularly mined the field of anthropology for essentially static models of particular cultural forms, in more recent work of an early modern cast—work strongly influenced by historical writing that has also become anthropological in orientation—the emphasis is instead on dynamics: the kinds of transformation associated with various cross-cultural forms, the degree to which a work of literature with obvious ties to some ritual structure may be taken as functioning for its culture in a similar way (N. Z. Davis; Underdown; Bakhtin, *Rabelais*; Thomas; Garber, *Cannibals*; Barber; Girard; Stallybrass and White; Tennenhouse; Greenblatt, *Shakespearean*; Fumerton; Mallin; Montrose). Some of the most interesting recent literary analysis in an anthropological vein has gone further still, modeling its discursive stance toward its early modern materials on that of an ethnographer in the manner of Clifford Geertz, who strives, in mingled respect and puzzlement, to piece together a "cultural poetics" from observations in the field (Geertz, *Interpretation*; Greenblatt; Mullaney, *Place*). But there is a postmodernist anthropology just as there is postmodernist literary analysis: the two fields have developed a parallel skepticism about the hermeneutic circle of interpretation. Like the modernist "scene of writing," the classic picture of the ethnographer in the field, watching and taking notes with patience, impassivity, and objectivity, is coming to appear more an enabling fiction than a valid portrayal of research in that it effaces the network of culture-bound assumptions that shapes even the most responsible attempts at observation. The new anthropology is calling Geertz's work into question along with more traditional ethnography; it can be expected to provoke a greater hesitancy, or at least a greater wariness, on the part of literary scholars who take an ethnographic stance toward elements of early modern culture.

For the new postmodernist anthropologists, ethnographic research is the last gasp of colonialism. As earlier generations of Western Europeans and Americans penetrated the wilds of "darkest Africa" or South America to bring enlightenment and take away monetary rewards, so modern ethnographers alter by their presence the fragile culture they come to observe and subtly exploit it in the name of objectivity (Clifford and Marcus). Literary scholars of the early modern period have also become markedly more interested in the historical phenomenon of colonialism, in terms not only of its impact on writing and other cultural forms during the Age of Discovery itself but also (and this brings us back to the question I asked, at the beginning of this essay, about our pet scholarly tropes) of its formative influence on our ways of conceptualizing our own scholarly pursuits. Like printing, the discovery of the New World is a key feature of the Renaissance/early modern period by whichever name we call it; however, there is a pronounced difference in geographical emphasis. Renaissance approaches are oriented toward the Mediterranean, concentrating on Europe's debt to the earlier Mediterranean-centered cultures of Greece and Rome and on cultural interchange within the area bounded by mare nostrum, as the ancient Romans termed it. To the extent that Renaissance approaches take cognizance of the voyages of discovery, they have tended to emphasize their positive impact on the colonizing countries in terms of enhanced wealth and cultural diversity, broadened horizons, and a liberation from earlier limits. Early modern approaches are more oriented toward the Atlantic and the Pacific, more interested in analyzing the Age of Discovery from the viewpoint of the colonized than from that of the colonizers; they are paying new attention to the literature of discovery—the diaries of Columbus, for example, or contemporary accounts of the conquistadores—and using postcolonialist and ethnographic methods to place such work within the nascent early modern drive toward domination and exploitation of non-Western societies (Greenblatt, *Marvelous Possessions*; Quint; R. Adorno; Todorov, *Conquest*).

To some extent, this altered emphasis reflects the demise of colonialism itself—the sun really has set on the British Empire, and the dessicated remains are more accessible to analysis than during empire's heyday. The new emphasis also reflects a westward migration of the discipline at large, as scholars from New World and commonwealth nations gain increased visibility and dominance. In early modern studies, however, the critique of colonialism is almost invariably accompanied by a continuation of some of its guiding metaphors: like New World travelers, we envision our subject as a field to be mapped out, as a territory to be explored, or a contested terrain to be conquered from some opposing critical camp. We filter our analysis through a set of geographic metaphors that can be interpreted in various ways but that suggest our continuing engagement on one level with a cast of mind we have rejected on another (P. Parker; Said, *World*). The contradiction is particularly marked in critical work of an early modern persuasion because of that work's simultaneous engagement of postcolonial modes of interpretation: once again, as in our use of the term *Renaissance*, we can uncover a lingering dependence on methodology we believe ourselves to have discarded. Through our "colonizing" tropes, we align our activity with shimmering visions of New World discovery, with a new richness and complexity, with the tantalizing promise of vast new areas to bring under our intellectual domination. By spatializing our discipline so insistently, it has been suggested, we are hanging on to vestiges of modernism—its tendency to elide history and contingency by conceiving of texts synchronically, its simultaneous disavowal and transmission of a distinct ideological agenda (Grady; Brodkey; Aronowitz). The goal of our quest to explore and map new worlds out of the past is intellectual stimulation, of course, but also, increasingly, financial well-being and prestige: professorships at major universities in the United States have become more remunerative than at any time before, or at least within living memory, and much of the largesse has gone to scholars in the area of Renaissance/early modern studies. Renaissance dreams of glory still haunt us as we open up vast new territories for conquest within the early modern.

As the twentieth century draws to a close, we seem to sense that we are at the end of an era: we call ourselves postmodern; we are devoting increasing energy to collections like this one, which seek to assess and explain the plenitude of contemporary critical approaches but which also serve, whether we like it or not, as a mechanism of classification and codification (see also Kelsall et al.). We are defining a methodological terminus, turning inward on ourselves and our motives as scholar-critics in recognition of the idea that the major critical movements of our century are finally winding down. But the present moment of postmodernist self-reflection is likely to be brief: self-analysis is not necessarily comfortable, and can become tiresomely repetitive over time. My survey here of disciplinary shifts has of necessity been rapid and fragmentary, but suggests that we are moving toward a period of great and fecund methodological instability, even anarchy, as our own discipline interpermeates with others that once appeared remote from it and as even the book as we know it is challenged by other technologies of writing. But we must not underestimate the human capacity to find new (or old) methods of closure and restabilization. There are inklings of a new interest on the part of early modern scholars in idealization and in the aesthetic as important categories for (and elements of) analysis (Eagleton, *Ideology of the Aesthetic*; Fumerton). As we move beyond the critique of modernism, we may lose some of our persistent tendency (as amply represented in this essay as in other recent work) to polarize the discipline in generational terms and to exclude from our own intellectual endeavor those elements of early modern culture that were the most significant for earlier modernist critics. In theory, recent work has moved away from the synchronic, "mapping" style of analysis associated with modernism; in practice, we continue to make use of it as our dominant conceptual model, despite strong signs of uneasiness with it. Renaissance/early modern literary studies may already be on its way to becoming linear and diachronic again, as it was a few generations back. It may be on its way to becoming a self-contained and highly structured field once more, perhaps along lines that are familiar to us from the past, but perhaps in ways we cannot begin to imagine.[1]

### Note

[1]The works I have cited in this essay are representative of recent critical trends but far from inclusive. I owe special thanks to the many authors who shared their work with me before publication.

## Selected Bibliography

Ariès, Philippe. *Centuries of Childhood: A Social History of Family Life*. Trans. Robert Baldick. New York: Vintage, 1962.
This is one of the earliest works of social history to show Renaissance scholars the degree to which accepted cultural categories like childhood and the family are socially constructed.

Bakhtin, Mikhail. *Rabelais and His World*. Trans. Helene Iswolsky. Cambridge: MIT P, 1968.
This work has, more than any other, influenced literary scholars to reexamine Renaissance texts from the bottom up—in terms of their indebtedness to popular rather than high culture.

Dollimore, Jonathan, and Alan Sinfield, eds. *Political Shakespeare: New Essays in Cultural Materialism*. Ithaca: Cornell UP, 1985.
Along with John Drakakis's *Alternative Shakespeares*, this enormously influential collection brought cultural materialist approaches to the forefront of Shakespeare studies.

Eisenstein, Elizabeth. *The Printing Press as an Agent of Change*. 2 vols. Cambridge: Cambridge UP, 1979.
This study has significantly altered our notions about literary transmission and the meaning of the book by demonstrating the centrality of print technology to the vast cultural changes we associated with the idea of the Renaissance.

Ferguson, Margaret W., Maureen Quilligan, and Nancy J. Vickers, eds. *Rewriting the Renaissance: The Discourses of Sexual Difference in Early Modern Europe*. Chicago: U of Chicago P, 1986.
   Representing a wide variety of topics and approaches, this influential collection encapsulates much of the best recent work in feminist and gender studies.

Foucault, Michel. "What Is an Author?" Trans. Josué V. Harari. *Foucault Reader*. Ed. Paul Rabinow. New York: Pantheon, 1979. 101–20.
   Foucault's influence on the field of Renaissance/early modern studies has been vast. This essay is worthy of special emphasis because, through its discussion of the rise (and fall) of the author function, it has significantly altered our sense of the range of possibilities open to interpretation in dealing with preauthorial texts.

Greenblatt, Stephen. *Renaissance Self-Fashioning from More to Shakespeare*. Chicago: U of Chicago P, 1980.
   More than any other single volume, this book sparked a renewal of interest in historical method on the part of recent scholars in the field.

McKenzie, D. F. *Bibliography and the Sociology of Texts*. London: British Lib., 1986.
   This volume, which deserves to become better known, is exemplary of the best new revisionist work in textual studies.

Orgel, Stephen, and Roy Strong, eds. *Inigo Jones: The Theatre of the Stuart Court*. 2 vols. Berkeley: U of California P, 1973.
   With its de-emphasis on the writers of the masques included and its emphasis on spectacle and social context, this atypical scholarly edition exemplifies a new, less stringently writerly, way of conceptualizing literature that can be extended to genres less dependent on performance than the masque.

Taylor, Gary, and Michael Warren, eds. *The Division of the Kingdoms: Shakespeare's Two Versions of* King Lear. Oxford: Clarendon–Oxford UP, 1983.
   This volume, along with Steven Urkowitz's *Shakespeare's Revision of* King Lear, revolutionized Shakespeare studies by opening up the prospect of multiple authorial versions of the canonical plays.

# $\mathcal{S}$eventeenth-Century Studies

## WILLIAM KERRIGAN

How does change occur in literary criticism? There is no good nonmetaphysical way of answering such a question in the abstract, but the changes that have inspired this volume occurred like so: In the 1960s some American academics began reading structuralism, the first import of the Theory Industry. There was much confusion over what structuralism was and what it meant. Then a certain number of clichés about what it was and what it meant began to circulate, most of them issuing from introductions to anthologies and special issues of literary journals; Jonathan Culler and Robert Scholes produced their handbooks; the wary agreed on the failings of the new movement, primarily its emphasis on the synchronic and the communal, its preoccupation with binarism, and its consequent weakness in dealing with historical process.

At Johns Hopkins in 1966, Jacques Derrida attacked the metaphysical dichotomies living on in the structure of structuralism, and poststructuralism, later called postmodernism, came on the American scene. There was much confusion over what it was and what it meant, compounded by the fact that most American academics possessed only a clichéd, handbook knowledge of structuralism. Then a new series of clichés about what it was and what it meant began to circulate, most of them issuing from introductions to anthologies and special issues of literary journals; Culler and Scholes produced their handbooks; the wary agreed on the failings of the new movement, primarily its ahistorical, Nietzschean-Heideggerian attack on the metaphysics of presence (really Husserl), and its consequent weakness in dealing with historical process. Both of these movements sometimes combined with older creeds, such as psychoanalysis, and both of them have left sediments of jargon and cliché in contemporary literary discourse. Some of their spawn (demonstrations that culture has been mistaken for nature, exposures of the metaphysical subject, attacks on truth and logic in the name of rhetoric) continue to thrive.

Then, early in the 1980s, Stephen Greenblatt began referring to his work and that of other (mostly) West Coast Renaissance scholars as a new historicism. Greenblatt was less an inventor than a namer; he was not to new historicism what Lévi-Strauss was to structuralism or Derrida and Foucault were to postmodernism. His desire to fuse the study of literature with the study of culture in its entirety was already common in the profession, was already an option possible in structuralism and, via Foucault, in postmodernism, which must be one reason why his term caught on so rapidly outside Renaissance studies. The name suggested that at last the common resistance to structuralism and postmodernism would be taken seriously and that literary theorists would now discard the philosophical aspects of those movements in order to come to grips with historical process. Again, much confusion; again, new clichés from the usual sources; again, Culler and Scholes. The wary, their satirical energies depleted from two decades of trying to respond sensibly to Lacanians and Derrideans, are just now regrouping.

Here are some recent clichés from the wary. The new historicism is not really a methodology, but (this cliché does not fit the work of Greenblatt himself) a contentious description of Western culture by a new academic left wing apparently too unhappy in Western democracy to venture a concept of utopia, tricked out in jargons and clichés drawn from the various layers of contemporary theory—yet another new way of mistrusting one's education. Its effects on the memory of Renaissance studies have been devastating, especially in conveying the notion that the old historicism was the likes of E. M. W. Tillyard and Douglas Bush; one gets a rather different fix on the inheritance of this discipline by treating Tillyard's *Elizabethan World Picture* as the Culler-Scholes of its day and reserving serious attention for Jacob Burckhardt's *Civilization of the Renaissance in Italy* or L. C. Knights's *Drama and Society in the Age of Jonson*. The new historicism oscillates between Foucault's accounts of ubiquitous repressive power and some of the fancier Marxisms born of the Theory Explosion; one result is a peculiarly unsuspicious attitude toward the pretensions of absolute monarchy, which seem to be welcomed virtually at face value by the new historicists as a literal incarnation of Foucault's view of power. The movement has generated little or nothing in the way of new historical data; it has not assembled overlooked traditions or isolated new genres but rather reinterprets the discoveries of the old historicism as instances of ideology, usually of exclusion and control. Far from being an antidote to the sins of structuralism and postmodernism, it continues their attacks on the mythology of individualism, continues their polemical skepticism toward the intellectual, cultural, and institutional achievements of Western civilization, and has arranged bizarre liaisons with some of their most dubious authorities, such as Lacan. With its preference for grand totalizing designs ("the ideology of pastoral") and essentialist constructs ("the liberal humanist subject"), the new historicism, like its predecessors in the Theory Explosion, is relatively feeble on the matter of historical process. Streamlined history, history molded to fit theories, is its preoccupation.

These developments have changed the face of seventeenth-century studies. A new set of expository conventions, featuring long allegorical anecdotes and cascades of rhetorical questions, has seated itself in the discipline. Centers and origins are bad. Any practice described with the adjective *proper*, such as an attempt to adduce the "proper interpretation" or to discuss "literature proper," is a practice under attack. Closure is ominous. Boundaries are harmful; the notion of a distinct aesthetic realm is especially loathsome. Abhorrent criticism is described as "hegemonic," "disingenuous," "elitist," "neoconservative," or "reductive." The supposed fait accompli of fundamental change is in fact one of the distinctive claims of the new work, which is expressly self-canonizing and anxiously wants to have made a difference.

It is certainly true that previous generations of Renaissance scholars felt, more or less explicitly, that their own work was renewing and preserving the very traditions of early modern humanism they were studying, while the new work sees itself in a deconstructive opposition to the pedagogical aims of Renaissance humanists. A recurrent enemy in the new work is "liberal humanism," a loose label for residents of contemporary humanities departments whose ideals belong in some fashion to the line of Montaigne, Erasmus, Bacon, Hooker, Herbert, Marvell, and Milton. Squeezed between the new theorists on the academic left and the William Bennetts and Allan Blooms on the Straussian right, liberal humanists are getting harder to find. But one of them is writing this essay, comforted, like Sir Thomas Browne before him, that he has no sins that want a name.

How does change occur in literary criticism? There is another kind of answer to this question—the utopian answer. For surely change is not just quantitative. Does the new work deserve to make a difference? Is it good enough? I remember being impressed some years ago by a philosopher's description of Heidegger's *Being and Time* to the effect that Heidegger wanted to destroy the metaphysical tradition, but in a manner, and at a level of rigor, commensurate with the energy and dedication of that tradition. I now recognize this to be a cliché of the older Heidegger commentaries, based, in fact, on one of Heidegger's favorite passages, the madman's announcement in Nietzsche's *Gay Science* of the death of God:

> All of us are his murderers. But how have we done this? How were we able to drink up the sea? Who gave us the sponge to wipe away the entire horizon? What did we do when we unchained this earth from its sun? Whither is it moving now? Whither are we moving now? Away from all suns? Are we not plunging continually? Backward, sideward, forward, in all directions? Is there any down left? . . . God is dead. God remains dead. And we have killed him. How shall we, the murderers of all murderers, comfort ourselves? What was holiest and most powerful of all that the world has yet owned has bled to death under our knives. Who will wipe this blood off us? What water is there for us to clean ourselves? What festivals of atonement, what sacred games shall we have to invent? Is not the greatness of this deed too great for us? Must now we ourselves become gods simply to seem worthy of it?    (qtd. in Heidegger 59)

The truth in this finely hysterical passage, with its uncanny echoes of *Macbeth* and *Paradise Lost*, is that movements dedicated to changing history fail in nerve, fail to achieve the highest pitch of usurping ambition, if they do not want to convince their fathers and mothers, both living and dead, of the justice of their cause.

After all, as the best of the theorists have taught us, there is nothing in the datum of history that requires it to be described in terms of power, ideology, or material production—or in any other terms, including those used by Burckhardt or Knights. I make this obvious point because moral and political attacks on the traditional procedures of literary interpretation often behave as if there *were* arguments, rationally unanswerable arguments, against the inherited notion of "literary values." But nothing counts prima facie against writing a book on Renaissance poetry that ignores most of the volumes of verse in the *Short-Title Catalogue* on the grounds that they are not good enough, or for that matter excludes Donne's verse letters and Marvell's satires because *they* are not good enough. Such a book could be said to ignore the bad verse of women, the illiterate doggerel of popular ballads and broadsides, and the misfired conceits of university wits. But its author is not on that score an enemy of these folk—just a student of distinguished verse, which the newer styles of criticism marginalize. Marginalization is not itself a crime; everything marginalizes something. There is as always an element of willfulness in the new work, and the only thing that can prevent that work from looking like mere willfulness is an honest desire to fold itself into the traditions of Renaissance studies, carefully weighing the new against the old, seeing through differences in jargon and disposition to the matter of what, in all likelihood, Renaissance words and conventions mean. When self-canonizing scholars simply forget or glibly vilify previous scholarship, they have no way of becoming worthy of their crimes.

To put the point psychoanalytically, contemporary theoretical criticism in this field, perhaps in other fields, suffers from a shallow engagement with the dynamics of generational transmission. The slaying of the parental gods has been mimed repeatedly, and the news of their demise spread throughout the profession. Then again, they have not really been killed at all. The difference modern theory wants always already to have made keeps being deferred.[1]

In this respect, the only sector of the Theory Industry to have earned its spurs in seventeenth-century studies is one I have thus far left out of account: feminism. Varieties and combinations of the new theoretical options appear in feminist versions, and some of the stuff is as empty and forgetful as other pastiches of Derrida and Foucault. However, the subdisciplines of contemporary literary theory do not entail each other in a rational fashion.

Feminism need not, and indeed does not always, fall in with psychoanalysis, Marxism, or new historicism. That the subdisciplines of theory seem to some practitioners to entail each other is an effect of current political alliances in American English departments, the collegial feeling of new arrivals sharing strategies of empowerment with each other. Feminism alone, it seems to me, has earned its rhetoric of self-canonization. Feminist scholars have rescued, in annotated editions, the poems, diaries, domestic treatises, and religious writings of Renaissance women largely ignored by previous generations of scholars. They have found and mapped new genres. They have demonstrated in telling ways, ways that impinge on literary form, genre, and characterization, the masculine bias of canonical authors. Because of their work, familiar lines in famous poems don't seem the same anymore. They have revealed mere facts to be potential areas of inquiry. How much new and interesting might now be said, for example, about the behavior of female beloveds called "coy" in Caroline love poetry? Linda Woodbridge's *Women and the English Renaissance* is a helpful synthesis of feminist contributions to old-fashioned historical knowledge.

But there is no single book produced by a structuralist, postmodernist, or new historicist that has enough evidence, accurately represented, to justify in seventeenth-century studies the more extravagant claims of revolutionary success. Nothing of great importance has been published on Suckling, Lovelace, and the minor Royalist lyricists in recent years—save, if I may be forgiven my pride, the history of English Petrarchism in the third section of William Kerrigan and Gordon Braden, *The Idea of the Renaissance* (157–218). More surprisingly, there has been no groundbreaking work on Marvell. By far the best recent discussion of Herrick is Braden's theoretically unprogrammatic chapter in *The Classics and English Renaissance Poetry*. We have had a few worthy books on Herbert, Stanley Fish's *Living Temple: George Herbert and Catechizing* and Richard Strier's *Love Known: Theology and Experience in George Herbert's Poetry* in particular, but they are only lightly tinged with theory's palette and clearly take their central inspiration from older ideas of what constitutes convincing interpretation—in the case of Fish, a prose genre brought to bear for the first time on puzzling aspects of well-known poems; in the case of Strier, the familiar alliance of intellectual history and literary explication. The theorists appear to be getting nowhere with the metaphysical poets—favorites, of course, of the much-maligned New Criticism.

One might have supposed that Donne, with his lavish delight in defying the world, his exploration of metaphors of death, absence, and writing, would inspire vigorous attention from contemporary theorists. But in fact the theory-based contributions of the last decade seem rather minor in relation to the vast body of detailed explication produced by the New Criticism. Arthur

Marotti's *John Donne, Coterie Poet* places the early lyrics in an interesting context of semiprivate "answer" poems circulated among the resentful younger sons shunted off to the Inns of Court, but much of the book is an elaborate theoretical justification for letting this context restrictively determine Donne's meaning, thus refusing the imaginative invitation of those arresting metaphors for the sake of (poetry lovers are nodding off throughout the auditorium!) "social transaction," the literary concept that has driven out imagination, wit, and beauty.

John Carey's *John Donne: Life, Mind, and Art*, though not in the least bit theoretical, catches the wave of the zeitgeist nonetheless. This study gives us a breezily contemptuous view of Donne, who is represented as a disingenuous creature of obstructed ambitions, projecting his frustration onto female victims—and a Catholic turncoat to boot. Explicating the psychopolitical subtext of Elegy 19 ("On His Mistress Going to Bed") has become a minor contemporary genre, and a brief look at this nascent tradition may help to explain my assertion that no theoretical book has enough evidence, accurately represented, to warrant delimiting a new era in seventeenth-century studies. Carey writes: "The despotic lover here, ordering his submissive girl-victim to strip, and drawing attention to his massive erection (the point of Donne's jokes about 'standing'), is of course a perennial dweller in the shadow-land of pornography, particularly attractive as a fantasy role to males who, through shyness or social circumstance, find relations with women difficult" (105). Certainly Donne's "The foe oft-times, having the foe in sight, / Is tir'd with standing, though they never fight" alludes to his erection. But whence "massive"? (I cannot think of an English poet of the period who *does* mention the size of his penis except for Campion, and the point of his epigram is that he would have been more successful with a smaller one.) No size is stipulated, and "tir'd with standing" seems to convey, if anything, a fear that the erection, whatever its current size, will lapse if they do not proceed with the standard forms of foreplay. And what of these silly generalizations about the enjoyment of pornography? Isn't the poem in part about the foolishness of merely looking, the frustration of seeing as opposed to the joys of touching and doing? Does one address a "girl-victim" as "Madame"?

It is a small measure of the wantonness in literary studies these days that Carey's discussion of the poem seems to have been influential. Marotti— though in all fairness he might have arrived at the view independently—refers to each of the few scattered references to the penis in Donne's poetry as "phallic narcissism." Donne's elegies, Thomas Greene concurs, "can be described as aggressively phallocentric and cheerfully sexist" (133). What pressing desire is the male writer of a love elegy to register without calling down postmodern reproach? His tumescent quill? Yes, but even that will occasion indictments of literary violation. The postmodern author of *John Donne Undone*, influenced by Carey, sees in Donne's "girdle, like heavens Zone glittering, / But a far fairer world incompassing" defilements of the signifier:

> The *girdle* "contains" the *girl*, and the breach made in this girdle to "produce" the girl becomes tantamount to a breach in the body of the girl herself, tantamount to the opening of the girl's legs, her "compass." The linguistic suggestion here, in the play between "girdle" and "girl" is meant to suggest that the word "girl," the supposedly pure and naked "girl" produced in the rupturing of the "girdle" is already, in a sense, at least linguistically impure, mixed up promiscuously, anagrammatically, in another word or object. The opening of this "compass" or world, and the subsequent re-encompassing not of the girl herself but of the male in the circle described by the embrace of the girl's legs, constitutes the enactment of the rupture of the "girl" [both word and person] in the breaking of her hymeneal boundary.                                     (Docherty 78–79)

But "Madame" is not a virgin, and Donne nowhere addresses a "girl." What we have here is a critic fantasizing about Carey's fantasies about the poem, admonishing Donne for covering over his "discovered" woman with leering tropes when in fact the poem is itself, for the critic, disastrously covered over by Carey. This sort of thing (sometimes called "intertextuality") may have its champions, but it appears to me that elucidating Donne awaits an age less troubled about sexual thoughts and, therefore, I would hope, less prone to project massiveness onto tired erections and less intoxicated by the gratuitous act of spinning symptomatic scenarios out of unintended anagrams.

I am happy to report that M. Thomas Hester's *Kinde Pitty and Brave Scorn* is a reliable guide to the satires. Achsah Guibbory's *Map of Time: Seventeenth-Century English Literature and Ideas of Pattern in History* deals with several major authors, but an especially fine chapter on Donne indicates that the traditional alliance between this author and intellectual history remains strong. Work on the vexed problem of the symbolic meaning of "shee" in Donne's *Anniversaries*, once a thriving enterprise, seems to have fallen off without achieving an altogether satisfactory conclusion. One predicts it will come back, since the most exciting mysteries, the venerable ones that struck even our grandparents, are impossible to replace.

Jonson was not a favorite of the New Critics, and the theorists deserve credit for recovering sympathetically the urgencies of his social verse. One must note first of all the appearance of a noble biography by David Riggs; its psychoanalytic passages are among the finest ever written about a Renaissance figure and in no way compromise the historical acuity of the author. Don E. Wayne's *Penshurst: The Semiotics of Place and the Poetics of History* is an exception to the grim ambience of ideological studies in its welcome indulgence of utopian speculation. It even pauses to record the joys of ownership, marriage, and wage slavery. "And it is not too much of an exaggeration," Wayne writes, "to say that the referent for a poem like 'To Penshurst' is an archetype (and an origin) of the image which the twentieth-century mortgager of a cottage in Surrey, a *petit pavillon* on the outskirts of Paris, or a suburban tract house in Southern California is likely to have of himself, his family, his home" (26)— one can only guess at how much enthusiasm for historicizing had to be put to sleep before the critic could pass on this charmingly incredible sentence! Wayne makes interesting points about the semiotics of place and architecture, but much of the structuralism is heavy going, and the thesis (that Jonson was gesturing in aristocratic terms toward a bourgeois notion of virtuous dwelling) rather predictable. Wayne's book might be compared with Fish's superb article "Authors-Readers: Jonson's Community of the Same." Both critics note the monumental abstractness of Jonson's definitions of virtue; both realize that Jonson is using real people and real places to furnish an imaginary community with imaginary values. But whereas Wayne, who wants to praise Jonson, concludes with his author's prescient contribution to the modern mythology of alienation, Fish is struck by the person, by the audacious strength of the individuality Jonson forged: "for the present I am content to marvel at the controlled power of a poetry that manages to convince itself—and on occasion manages to convince us—that to owe money is already to have repaid it, that to ask a favor is to have granted one, that to praise kings is to exercise majesty, and that in the very posture of supplication and dependence one can nevertheless be perfectly free" (57). In Wayne an effect of history acknowledges its early modern roots. In Fish one redoubtable individual salutes another.

Most of the new historicists have concentrated on the Elizabethan period, but there have been several notable attempts to extend the new mannerism into the seventeenth century. Jonathan Goldberg's *James I and the Politics of Literature: Jonson, Donne, and Their Contemporaries* measures the fallout of the romanizing political ideology of the Basilicon Doron in the pageantry, portraiture, coins, sermons, plays, and poems of James's reign. Here the commanded's search for kinds of autonomy (or pseudoautonomy) that can be won in a theater of deference, long a theme in discussions of the court masque, gets generalized to the whole of Jacobean culture. The book resembles Foucault's work in its combination of historical detail with operatic evocations of an impersonal and imageless power that, rather like the One of the neo-Platonists, leaves traces of its determining but unknowable essence in all cultural particulars.

Graham Parry's *Golden Age Restor'd: The Culture of the Stuart Court, 1603–42* covers much of the same ground, and in some ways more informatively. Still more informative, and not much else, is David Norbrook's sober *Poetry and Politics in the English Renaissance*. The facts in this book, the extensive literary interpretations launched from these facts, and the overall view of literary history are hardly novel. Authors are categorized on the basis of their presumed attitudes toward masquing, court morality, foreign policy, and Protestant apocalyptism; Jonson invents poetic conservatism; Milton recovers the prophetic strain in Spenser. Although Norbrook makes some weak efforts to assess poetic form (against the closed couplets of Jonson, for the broken verse paragraphs of "Lycidas"), his usual technique is not to read poems but to circle them with rings of political associations:

> In "To Penshurst" Jonson contrasts the relative modesty of Sidney's country seat with the "proud ambitious heaps" of the "prodigy-houses" which other members of the nobility were building to display their wealth. Some of these houses, such as Sir Robert Cecil's, were built with the aid of large pensions from the Spanish; Sir Robert Sidney, true to Elizabethan tradition, had refused a Spanish pension. Sir Robert Wroth came from a family with strong Puritan traditions. The Earl of Pembroke became a leader of the anti-Spanish group at court; he has been described as the head of a Parliamentary and Puritan "opposition."                                                                 (184)

But in history there are always more facts—more houses, more associates, more European connections, more family traditions, more descriptions. Norbrook strikes out on expository drifts that might go on forever, achieving conclusions only because he arbitrarily decides to stop.

The major literary figure in Goldberg, Parry, and Norbrook is perforce Jonson. In *Ben Jonson and the Roman Frame of Mind* Katharine Maus shows that the romanizing aspects of Jonson's social imagination treated ideologically by these authors can be illuminated in traditional terms as adaptive assimilations of classical precedent—moves within the psychology of stoicism. There is still a lot of gold in the oldest mines.

Annabel Patterson's *Censorship and Interpretation: The Conditions of Writing and Reading in Early Modern England* ranges from Sidney to Jean-Jacques Rousseau in developing the thesis that literature as we know it evolves dialectically with the pressures of state censorship. Power for Patterson is not impersonal and imageless, but the policies of individuals with their self-interested axes to grind. The polemical side of the book wants to convince us that the true depth of topical allusion in Renaissance literature has been obscured by the conscious distortions of authors hoping to circumvent the long arm of the censor; this, she thinks, is the true untold story of modern literary invention. While allowing for the fact that this thesis confines us to an unsteady universe of hermeneutic speculation, the merely conceivable—where finding no overt support in the text may itself be support—many of Patterson's readings seem rushed, sketchy, and highly conjectural. With its attempt to justify its own recourse to innuendo and insinuation, this book resembles the hurried, unrelievedly suggestive accounts of the "secret history" of Renaissance occultism written by Frances Yates toward the end of her life. Patterson clearly wants students of literature to leave their gardens of imagination and turn instead to that hodgepodge of event, rumor, gossip, and fantasy known as the "topical." Maybe it is a matter of whether one has an ear for literature or an ear for ideology. Those who feel that *King Lear* contains all an interpreter really needs to know about Renaissance indigence will not be persuaded by Patterson's contention that an ear for literature *is* an ear for reconstructing political situations from the scattered topical details of an age that had not yet found the good sense to invent the daily newspaper or, better yet, the weekly newsmagazine. Politics in this sense is, Michael Oakeshott reminded us memorably, "a second-rate form of human activity, neither an art nor a science, at once corrupting to the soul and fatiguing to the mind, the activity either of those who cannot live without the illusion of affairs or of those so fearful of being ruled by others that they will pay away their lives to prevent it" (lxiv).

The main roads in seventeenth-century studies lead to Milton. That new historicism enjoys its greatest prestige in Shakespeare studies, and can claim scant impact on Milton studies, may reflect longstanding differences between the two disciplines. Every intellectual fashion of the last 250 years has left its mark on Shakespeare studies. New historicism has been able to absorb the more congenial achievements of thriving traditions of psychoanalytic, Marxist, Christian, and feminist interpretation. Yet during my professional lifetime, and no doubt before, the study of Shakespeare has seemed gloriously out of control. The deep and irresolvable uncertainties that beset both the author and his texts turn out to inspire rather than restrain the critical imagination. Major new editions, or the updating of completed editions, seem a yearly event. The sheer volume of the contemporary output is such that no one scholar could possibly keep up with it, or for that matter would want to keep up with it; the discipline lacks arbiters of sense—accomplished senior scholars who read the work of young critics, noting the books and articles that have been overlooked, separating the lively from the screwy, praising genuine advances. Milton studies, by contrast, is more disciplined, more unanimous, just as Milton himself, unlike Shakespeare, was so careful to correct his texts and so abidingly conscious of recording his own development.

The pioneer Miltonists of the twentieth century (Denis Saurat, E. M. W. Tillyard, James Holly Hanford, and others) synthesized the annotational alertness of the eighteenth century, the visionary agonistics of the Romantics, and the historical contextualism of David Masson to generate a fairly coherent discipline, capable of producing and recognizing progress. Few living Miltonists would deny that they now understand the last two books of *Paradise Lost*, the epic invocations, the characterizations of Satan and Eve, the heresies of the *Christian Doctrine*, the implications of the divorce pamphlets, the ironies of *Samson Agonistes*, the climax of *Paradise Regained*, and hundreds of other things, great and small, better than the pioneers did. Milton got a lot of himself into print in his self-mythologizing way; we also have his family Bible, his commonplace book, his horoscope, his marginalia, his drafts, his treatise on theology, some correspondence, and a cache of state papers. The major attention devoted to his ample remains by generations of scholars makes it unlikely that a general disposition to tear down the boundaries between literary and nonliterary texts will produce radical change. A new historicist with a thick knowledge of the history of medicine may be able to transform the conventional understanding of certain writers, texts, and literary cruxes. But contemporary Miltonists inherit a fund of medical learning from their forebears—Kester Svendsen's *Milton and Science*, plus a great deal of commentary about Milton's blindness and other medical conditions. Milton himself was a main participant in the pamphlet wars of the revolutionary decades, and the subject of his political ideology began receiving extensive treatment a couple of generations ago in William Haller's *Rise of Puritanism*, Don M. Wolfe's *Milton in the Puritan Revolution*, and Arthur Barker's *Milton and the Puritan Dilemma*. For all the intellectual history, and the many classical, patristic, and Reformation traditions that have been applied to his verse, politics have by no means been ignored. Miltonists have longer, better-organized memories than Shakespeareans, and the character of their discipline makes it harder to bring them news.

Christopher Hill's *Milton and the English Revolution*, dedicated to Wolfe, does what it can to associate Milton with the radical sects of the period, offering a genial and undoctrinaire charter to political interpreters of the verse. At one point Hill calls attention to "the crucial question—why Milton could not let go of God, even though some of his contemporaries could. This seems to me the starting point for an enquiry into Milton's beliefs which could perhaps be fruitful" (242). The most theoretical effort to address this "crucial question" has been Christopher Kendrick's Marxist work *Milton: A Study in Ideology and Form*. The basic thesis is that the concept of predestination in *Paradise Lost* represents an effort to include all of life within the sphere of religion, yet proliferating aporias eventually shake loose a relatively unreligious domain of ethical and psychological individualism in Milton's epic that in turn resists the emergence of authentic politics, an understanding of the class struggle: the poem is a series of contortions to avoid the fate of Marxism. Kendrick's abstract analysis dramatizes some of the problems facing the new theoretical consciousness in the presence of this author. Milton wants to talk about politics in a religious framework. While critics have become accustomed to setting aside the question of Shakespeare's religion, ignoring Milton's religion appears at once either irresponsible or foolish. Kendrick's solution is to talk about Milton's religion in a political framework. But in doing so he drifts away from the emotions, values, and conflicts of the poem, staging a pyrrhic victory of the critic's language over the language of Milton. It is easy enough to observe that if God had enjoined an action rather than forbidden one, conditions in Milton's universe would be "less neurotic and more permissive than those deriving from the narrative of prohibition" (199). Yet the obvious rejoinder is that a narrative of permission would also be less profound.

Postmodernism is still beating on the door in Milton studies. R. A. Shoaf's *Milton, Poet of Duality: A Study in Semiosis in the Poetry and Prose* contains some nifty wordplay, but does not grip Milton's text with the sustained power necessary to change anyone's mind. John Guillory's *Poetic Authority: Spenser, Milton, and Literary History* is a more impressive work, combining Harold Bloom, Louis Althusser, Derrida, and Paul de Man; though its obscurity discourages quick assimilation, Guillory may yet find a wide audience. My own *The Sacred Complex: On the Psychogenesis of* Paradise Lost remains the one book-length study of Milton from a Freudian point of view. But psychoanalysis has become common coin as a result of the Theory Explosion, and many of the recent books and articles on Milton have Freudian episodes.

Grant McColley once took note of the "defensive psychology which has permeated and influenced" much of Milton criticism (326). A decade ago many Miltonists must have been girding themselves for another major battle. They had defended Milton's style, his Puritanism, his character, and now they would have to arm against forthcoming feminist attacks on his attitudes toward women. Sandra M. Gilbert and Susan Gubar paved the way in a chapter of *The Madwoman in the Attic* entitled "Milton's Bogey: Patriarchal Poetry and Women Readers," which casually assumes that Milton has always been a repressive figure to independent female intellectuals: "To such women the unholy trinity of Satan, Sin, and Eve, diabolically mimicking the holy trinity of God, Christ, and Adam, must have seemed even in the eighteenth and nineteenth centuries to illustrate that historical disposition and degradation of the female principle that was to be imaginatively analyzed in the twentieth century by Robert Graves, among others" (199). But the historical sections of Joseph Wittreich's *Feminist Milton* suggest that, on the contrary, the portrait of Eve has often intrigued and inspired his female readership. The tradition lives.

Gender has turned out to be not an embarrassment but Milton's best claim to contemporary cachet. If Milton reflected the ideology of his century, no other writer did so less passively. He deliberately set out to activate and redesign the mythologies of gender difference, and modern female intellectuals are discovering that *Paradise Lost* provides an opportunity to engage the strategies, possibilities, and contradictions of patriarchy more fully and rigorously than any other English poem. One of the editors of *Re-membering Milton: Essays on the Texts and Traditions* remarks that Eve has taken the position once occupied by Satan: "For the Romantics it was Satan who was oppressed by the author's consciously held beliefs. In our own time it tends to be Eve" (Nyquist and Ferguson xiv). But the degree of that oppression remains in doubt. Almost everyone who surveys the problem of Eve finds that in the course of the poem something interesting and indeterminate happens to the strong gender differences defined at the introduction of Adam and Eve. Milton begins with apparent clarity on the sexes but leaves us in complexity and confusion; the initial God-given gender differences become, as it were, no more than a theory.

It would appear that feminism has a real use for Milton, that he helps to clarify its internal variety. Left-wing feminists such as Mary Nyquist (see her contribution to *Re-membering Milton*) emphasize the bourgeois trap of Milton's appeal for the alliance of the genders. Liberal feminists discern that Milton, in his complexity and confusion, offers women exactly what they needed at his historical juncture—a blank check for creating an individualism of their own. A Christian scholar like Diane Kelsey McColley, whose *Milton's Eve* is one of the finest books of the last decade, can defy the radicals and liberals with a powerful reactionary sting:

> Curiously, some people object to Eve's derivation from Adam, in spite of her original splendour in truth, beauty, wisdom, and sanctitude, who are un-alarmed by the news that we are all derived from hairy bipeds called *Australo-pithecus afarensis*. Some resent her service of "God in him" who recommend the narrower confines of "self-servience" and have no interest in service of God at all. Some censure the slight imparity of perfections of Eve and Adam without lamenting our general inferiority to them both. Some think Eve unfree who do not protest the massive oppression of psychological theories that put each person and all action and affection into a few sexual categories and locate the genesis of all creativity in the vicinity of that portion of the male body on which "Adam sat." Some denounce Milton's fidelity to the scriptural idea of the family who accept the stupendous repression of spirit with which much criticism ignores the wellspring of holiness from which all value issues in *Paradise Lost*.
> ("Milton and the Sexes" 163)

One of feminism's liveliest conversations is now taking place in Milton studies.

The best recent books on Milton are well within the traditions of the discipline. The question of how to regard Milton's theological heresies, which I tried to reopen in *The Sacred Complex*, has been further advanced by John Peter Rumrich in *Matter of Glory: A New Preface to* Paradise Lost and, with Derridean touches, by Regina M. Schwartz in *Remembering and Repeating: Biblical Creation in* Paradise Lost. Sanford Budick's *Dividing Muse: Images of Sacred Disjunction in Milton's Poetry* treats the poetic world emanating from Milton's Godhead in terms of his ambivalence toward images. In *One Flesh: Paradisal Marriage and Sexual Relations in the Age of Milton* James Grantham

Turner assembles little-studied materials from the history of representing Eden to reveal with new precision the unusually ample and forthright treatment of sexuality in *Paradise Lost*. These books orbit within the friendly, familiar skies of biblical poetics, classical imitation, and intellectual history. Nor have they forgotten, in seeking answers to modern questions, the perennial lessons of the Old Philology.

### Note

[1]This paragraph is indebted to Murray M. Schwartz.

### Selected Bibliography

Braden, Gordon. *The Classics and English Renaissance Poetry*. New Haven: Yale UP, 1978.
A fine chapter on Herrick and the classical lyric explores *imitatio* as an aesthetics of decoration.

Carey, John. *John Donne: Life, Mind, and Art*. New York: Oxford UP, 1981.
The work addresses in a racy style the linked themes of blocked ambition and Catholic "apostasy"—sometimes trenchant, sometimes impertinent.

Fish, Stanley E. "Authors-Readers: Jonson's Community of the Same." *Representations* 7 (1984): 26–58.
Jonson, master of denial and defiance, presides over an imaginary community in his social verse. Since virtue is its own reward and needs no praise, there is always a happy surplus of the laudatory. Compare with Wayne.

Goldberg, Jonathan. *James I and the Politics of Literature: Jonson, Donne, and Their Contemporaries*. Baltimore: Johns Hopkins UP, 1983.
Goldberg generalizes the edgy theatrics of the court masque to Jacobean culture as a whole. Derrida and Foucault are much in evidence.

Guillory, John. *Poetic Authority: Spenser, Milton, and Literary History*. New York: Columbia UP, 1983.
The volume provides a postmodernist account of how the two authors translated their desire for literary preeminence into more than just literary modes of self-presentation.

Kendrick, Christopher. *Milton: A Study in Ideology and Form*. London: Methuen, 1986.
Kendrick's work is a highly abstract, Marxist study of Milton's elaborate resistance to the possibility of politics as an autonomous discipline.

Kerrigan, William. *The Sacred Complex: On the Psychogenesis of* Paradise Lost. Cambridge: Harvard UP, 1983.

This Freudian study is focused mainly on *Paradise Lost* but has chapters on *Comus* and *Paradise Regained* and contains a lengthy consideration of Milton's theological heresies.

Marotti, Arthur. *John Donne, Coterie Poet*. Madison: U of Wisconsin P, 1986.
Although the work is a programmatic nonstarter when it comes to interpreting Donne, the contexts supplied for many of the poems are valuable.

McColley, Diane Kelsey. *Milton's Eve*. Urbana: U of Illinois P, 1983.
McColley offers a Christian defense of Milton's characterization of Eve.

Norbrook, David. *Poetry and Politics in the English Renaissance*. London: Routledge, 1984.
This sober survey of the politics of verse from More to Milton is useful for its nests of facts.

Nyquist, Mary, and Margaret W. Ferguson. *Re-membering Milton: Essays on the Texts and Traditions*. New York: Methuen, 1987.
This anthology presents itself as a revolutionary replacement of Frank Kermode's *Living Milton*; the most interesting contributions are feminist.

Patterson, Annabel. *Censorship and Interpretation: The Conditions of Writing and Reading in Early Modern England*. Madison: U of Wisconsin P, 1984.
Censorship, by encouraging authors to invent metaphorical displacements of political themes, helped create imaginative literature in the Renaissance; some of the readings look doubtful.

Riggs, David. *Ben Jonson: A Life*. Cambridge: Harvard UP, 1989.
This superb biography combines psychoanalytic with historical acumen.

Schwartz, Regina M. *Remembering and Repeating: Biblical Creation in Paradise Lost*. Cambridge: Cambridge UP, 1988.
Schwartz distinguishes among the kinds of repetition in *Paradise Lost*, setting satanic obsession against Milton's religious desire to reassert "the beginning."

Turner, James Grantham. *One Flesh: Paradisal Marriage and Sexual Relations in the Age of Milton*. Oxford: Clarendon–Oxford UP, 1987.
Accounts of sexuality in the Genesis tradition, from Augustine to Agrippa, Jan Baptista Van Helmont, Robert Fludd, and others, set the stage for Milton's representation of "wedded love." There is a good discussion of the rage and pain in the divorce tracts.

# $\mathcal{E}$ighteenth-Century Studies

## JOHN BENDER

Locke asserts in the introduction to *An Essay Concerning Human Understanding* that he wants to find the "horizon . . . which sets the bounds between the enlightened and dark parts of things" (sec. 7). Social theory at least since Durkheim—not to mention contemporary critical movements—has found the quest for such a division to be as delusionary as Locke considered metaphysical and religious speculation to be. And the Enlightenment, thanks to Max Horkheimer and Theodor W. Adorno's *Dialectic of Enlightenment*, has long been seen to have its own dark side: that is, the instrumental use of reason to control and dominate rather than to emancipate.

The revelation that the neutral inquirer's reasonable stance is not only historically and ideologically constituted but potentially threatening to human society can be traced through Horkheimer and Adorno back to Nietzsche and Marx. This genealogy's venerable antiquity, when viewed from any number of late twentieth-century vantage points, may mark the central contention of this essay as surprising but not, I believe, as historically inaccurate: until recent revisions of critical method by feminism, new historicism, and cultural materialism, Anglo-American investigation of eighteenth-century literature proceeded largely within deep-rooted postulates—within a frame of reference—that fundamentally reproduced Enlightenment assumptions themselves and therefore yielded recapitulation rather than the knowledge produced by critical analysis.[1]

Anthony Giddens has remarked that knowledge cannot situate itself within the same framework as its object of study because the result is nothing more than recapitulation.[2] I understand this to mean that if knowledge is to escape tautology, it must conserve its own systems of reference and its own contemporaneity. Equally inadequate, on this understanding, are the fiction of positivist historicism that the specificity of ages past can be immanent to the inquirer as if to a divinely comprehending eye and the Hegelian fiction that the spirit of each age, comprehended philosophically, participates in a teleologically directed causal order. In the positivist case, abstractive analysis is delimited because the minutiae of the past are recapitulated ideologically within the historian's tacit assumptions. In the Hegelian, a theoretical system overwhelms the particular and eradicates dissonant facts or subsumes them into abstract dialectical patterns.

These observations need not call forth an excursus on historiography. Rather, Gidden's notion is useful here to frame some reflections on the reception that certain historically observant, theoretically alert modes of inquiry have received in American eighteenth-century studies. I shall focus, as suggested above, on the related if loosely defined, and sometimes overlapping, movements usually known as new historicism and cultural materialism, as well as on the feminist rewriting of eighteenth-century literary history. I shall concentrate more on the affinities among the new movements than on their manifold differences, though I recognize the imperfect coherence of any categorization that attempts to contain their diversity. I aim to move away from content-specific consideration of these movements toward the question of systemic function. For this reason, the argument is intentionally broad, aiming at more general points than a survey of current research could accommodate (see the bibliography for a sample of some of the innovative scholarly projects that mark eighteenth-century literary studies today).

The early parts of this essay lay the groundwork for a central section reviewing four indicative Enlightenment categories that have underlain the critical enterprise: the categories of aesthetic autonomy, authorship, disinterestedness, and gendered sexuality. Along the way, I offer some conjectures about why the new movements have arrived belatedly in eighteenth-century studies. I close with some speculations about the new historicism as a symptomatic feature of the legitimation crisis under way in academic literary studies at large, a crisis especially germane to the eighteenth-century field because this period, more than any other, produced the assumptions that have structured modern literary study.

None of this will be to urge that anyone discard the findings of previous—or present-day—scholarship: the project of recapitulation has immense value in preserving, ordering, and systematizing the traces of the past, selective though the transcription may be. Nor do I wish to imply that attempted recapitulation—or even seeming repetition—can ever be neutral. The old historicist ideal of value-free scholarship seems increasingly a delusion even in the case of works like catalogs, much less editions and biographies. Choices grounded in various interests and assumptions must be made even in simple listings or topologies, and, to this extent, the most anatomical scholarship is ideologically conditioned. But whereas editions or catalogs arguably might benefit from an unself-conscious subsistence within the framework of the objects they preserve, critical knowledge, as Giddens defines it, must pay the price of ceasing to be knowledge at all.

# I

New historicism in the United States, cultural materialism in Britain, and feminism in both have provoked so much notice—and hostility—because they have changed the frame of reference. They have denaturalized and transformed into historical phenomena a range of assumptions fundamental to mid-twentieth-century Anglo-American literary study. Retreat to the previous status quo now seems unlikely, though reassertions of the old values are bound to continue. It will be a long time before inaudibility overtakes the graciously phrased echoes of that orderly, well-reasoned, fundamentally hierarchical vision of Augustan England so brilliantly epitomized in Maynard Mack's 1950 introduction to the Twickenham Edition of Pope's *An Essay on Man* and, during the same period, in his essays entitled " 'Wit and Poetry and Pope': Some Observations on His Imagery" and "The Muse of Satire." Secure in its vision and at peace with its classical and Renaissance heritage, this "eighteenth century" held the bastions against modernity through the wit, common sense, and good taste of gentlemen like Swift, Pope, Fielding, and Johnson. To be sure, these men sometimes gave way to rage, spite, despair, or even to madness or obscenity, but only on extreme provocation. And even their outbursts occurred in finely wrought styles that yielded riches when assayed with the precision instruments of disciplined formal and rhetorical analysis. Irony, the master trope in New Criticism's lexicon, chimed loud and clear in this Augustan eighteenth century. Whatever injury the others may have done through its brilliant misuse, Johnson more than counterpoised by refining their techniques and turning them to the service of high moral seriousness.[3]

Having myself been trained in graduate school during the 1960s on the combination—uneasy to be sure, but then customary in American English departments—of historical philology and formalist poetics (chiefly those of the New Criticism), I have personally undergone the change of referential framework that I am describing. And so it may be useful, though risking the appearance of self-regard, to illustrate the shift by serving as my own witness: by portraying the contrasting methods and operative premises of my own work about the relationship between the eighteenth-century realist novel and the technology of reformative imprisonment. Probably no single book could display every vital sign of the new framework, but several indicators are indeed present in *Imagining the Penitentiary*[4]: the dissolution of boundaries between venerated aesthetic objects like novels or paintings and tracts, pamphlets, or legislation; the reading of institutions as "texts"; the treatment of subjectivity as a socially constructed—and therefore historically changing—phenomenon rather than as a permanent feature of human nature; and, perhaps above all, the view that manifestly fictional texts like plays and novels are culturally constitutive—not mere reflections of a "reality" that exists prior to and outside them.

Questions about the formulation and maintenance of power would have to figure in any work on prisons. And, broadly speaking, I join Michel Foucault in viewing transgression and lawlessness as structural positions—as necessary elements—in the fluid and contestatory scene within which power is defined and arrayed. Power cannot exist merely as a possession of governmental authorities. Instead, it lives in reciprocation with—and partially shared by—the alien, resistive, disorderly, and criminal elements that seem to define otherness in any given society. I argue, for example, that when Henry Fielding became a judge at midcentury, he adopted systems for controlling information about crime that were devised in the 1720s by the underworld figure Jonathan Wild. Power is all too often treated as if it were a fixed commodity rather than a range of complex discursive practices which alter so radically over time that they are scarcely recognizable from one era to another. The constant is not power but rather discourse as the structuring principle of human social formation.

It is worth contemplating, in this last regard, the immense changes in governmental, social, and cultural forms that occurred between the reigns of Elizabeth and the first two Georges (often, and significantly enough, called the reign of Walpole). The revolutions of 1641 and 1688 altered fundamental assumptions about the monarchy. The settlement of 1689, in particular, not only established a succession that brought foreigners to the throne; it reinscribed the monarchy as a contract with Parliament. Rule by party—a practice unthinkable to Elizabeth I—became ever more central to both the theory and the exercise of English government. On the social front, a vociferous critique of traditional aristocratic display and arbitrary authority accompanied the increasing appropriation of aristocratic forms by commercial magnates seeking broader social and political power than commerce alone could sustain. Meanwhile, the management even of long-held landed estates was breaking with conventional patterns and laying more stress on commodified production. Finally, in matters of religion, the settlement of 1689 definitively institutionalized the Protestant hegemony in England and worked both to diminish sectarian differences among non-Catholics and to broaden the reach of the Anglican establishment. Religious concerns remained vital but would become less urgently political with each passing decade of the eighteenth century. Whether or not by reason of the dominant Protestant consensus, cultural arenas opened within which questions about ethics, morality, psychology, and human institutions that previously had had to be considered within highly overdetermined religious-political contexts could be viewed in a secular light.

If Foucault taught us anything, it is that power is never a fixed object but a multiplicity of relationships and techniques that have continuously to be reproduced, and therefore changed, in order to maintain themselves. Power and authority often are conceived as transhistorical abstractions, but their nature in fact alters according to social and cultural structuration. A fully historicized, fully theorized practice of eighteenth-century studies, therefore, must have a distinctive profile because of the necessarily dialectical relationship between an object of study and its apprehension by criticism.

## II

I return now to the earlier assertion that criticism before the new movements was tacitly founded on Enlightenment premises—first adding a disclaimer that the term *Enlightenment* is used here not to define a strict historical period but rather as a marker to signify a large, somewhat rough-edged phase in European culture. *Webster's New Collegiate Dictionary* singles out the usual attributes when it observes that the movement is marked "by questioning of traditional doctrines and values, a tendency toward individualism, and an emphasis on the idea of universal human progress, the empirical method in science, and the free use of reason." A longer essay might encompass a more subtle definition of the Enlightenment not as a monolith in which certain categories of thought emerge or become definitive but as a period structured by its production of and operation within certain characteristic dyadic oppositions, such as reason versus sentiment, practical versus aesthetic, public versus private, the masculine versus the feminine, and so forth. Such an account also would accommodate resisting individuals and even institutions at variance with prevailing forms. I have in mind a writer like Swift or, if one may call it an institution, the amazingly persistent and powerful coalition of Loyalists supporting the Pretender.

Peter Gay echoed Kant when, some years ago, he dubbed the Enlightenment the "age of criticism." Gay sees the period's thought as fundamentally unified by the informality of its social and literary forms, by its stress on utility, and by its confidence in critical method. He sums up his view by quoting Gibbon's encomium to criticism: "All that genius has created, all that reason has weighed, all that labor has gathered up—all this is the business of criticism. Intellectual precision, ingenuity, penetration, are all necessary to exercise it properly."[5]

Although Peter Hohendahl speaks out of a tradition very different from Gay's—the Frankfurt school—and stresses institutions rather than individuals, he too marks the Enlightenment as the founding era of criticism as we know it:

> Seen historically, the modern concept of literary criticism is closely tied to the rise of the liberal, bourgeois, public sphere in the early eighteenth century. Literature served the emancipation movement of the middle class as an instrument to gain self-esteem and to articulate its human demands against the absolutist state and a hierarchical society.    (52)

Both Gay and Hohendahl refer to the eighteenth-century formulation of an independent—seemingly autonomous—intellectuality of the kind typified by Addison's *Spectator* and by coffee houses, clubs, and societies where, in contrast to literate exchange within the traditional courtly milieu, external marks of rank were laid aside and aristocratic patronage was displaced by a paying literate public. Especially in the earlier phases, aristocratic privilege everywhere penetrated the new intellectual institutions, nor was the kind of education necessary for entry into the realm of critical discussion available to anyone beneath what were called the "middling sort," if indeed to many of them. But this was not the point. A powerful convention had come into being: the convention that ideas are equally accessible to educated men and that, in the realm of public discussion, men are judged by the degree of their information and the quality of their ideas, not by rank, office, or wealth. I refer advisedly to "men" here, for the Enlightenment, though a source in the long term of powerful arguments and institutional formations supporting educational and social equality for women, not only was a male possession but worked to efface the question of gender in the public sphere by idealizing impartial neutrality.[6]

Criticism framed in this way presumes a whole stance toward reality that became coherent during the earlier eighteenth century and that increasingly was naturalized as the truth of reality itself. Romanticism and various later movements would challenge Enlightenment culture, the early phase of which Addison exemplified and promulgated. Over time, this culture would be reproduced within a broad range of institutions that at once deeply held its values and in many ways altered their nature. Still, these values and the reality they postulated—this sense of the nature of things—endured as foundational presumptions. I single out four of these postulates because of their specific relevance to literary study. But more broadly, this naturalized reality presumed above all the existence of an integral subjectivity expressing personal individuality. This subjectivity was validated in any number of ways, including a revised conception of the imagination that also was broached by Addison in his influential papers on "the pleasures of the imagination" (Bond 3: 535–82).[7] Other naturalized presumptions included the division of social life into private and public realms; the division of labor along lines of class, profession, and gender; and the construction of middle-class ideology in general, and of sexuality in particular, as self-reproducing social forms that enforced these divisions.

Perhaps I may digress to give just one example of the perdurance of

Enlightenment presumptions through various periods and institutionaliza-
tions. Friedrich Schlegel redirected attention away from the evaluative obsession of Enlightenment aesthetics when he argued that criticism should reveal
the immanent nature of the work of art, whose attributes "one can learn to
understand only from itself" (qtd. in Hohendahl 59).[8] The critic assists, indeed
guides, art in its move toward fulfillment through contemplation of specific
works and through empirical study of their attributes. The various institutions
that reproduced such thinking across the nineteenth and twentieth centuries
stressed different features within it. The organicist aspect flowered into *l'art
pour l'art*, informed writing in literary periodicals, and then flowed into aestheticism—ultimately to be lodged, in the mid-twentieth-century academic
establishment, as the New Criticism. The historicist aspect, having joined in
an entente cordiale with nationalist Romantic philology, much earlier found
its path into universities in the disciplinary shape of literary history conceived
as an account of forms and types derived not from classical or conventional
generic concepts but deduced from art itself—from the productions of genius.

The afterlife of ideas of the kind we identify with Schlegel might be
cast into a different story. Obviously I have told it a certain way to suit my
purposes here. But any account would have to observe the endurance of an
Enlightenment presumption that individual subjectivity can be willfully suspended and reconstituted, according to certain rules, as disinterested objectivity in service of purposive ends—be they the ends of literary criticism, of justice,
of education, of scholarship, or of any other constructive order. Even in the
domain of imaginative literature, the category of disinterestedness, which
might seem to have sunk in the Sturm und Drang of Romantic subjectivism,
lives on as the everyday groundwork—the contextually normative other—in
opposition to which Romantic and post-Romantic creative aestheticism defines
itself. Aestheticism reconstitutes disinterestedness and puts it in the service
of art but preserves it still. All of the categorical assumptions I shall shortly
treat in fact are strengthened by fuller articulation and institutionalization
during the Romantic period, though usually with some distinctive reorientation. The persistence of the Enlightenment framework is scarcely surprising
in view of the institutionalization—delineated by Hohendahl—of the critical
stance as a defining feature of middle-class consciousness. This institutionalization has been especially potent in the United States, where a liberal arts
education in colleges and universities has long been central to the middle-class
definition of success and where this education in itself has worked to preserve
among faculties as well as among the general public the very Addisonian ideals
to which Hohendahl refers.

Such is the general background. But when it comes to academic inquiry, I would observe, further, that eighteenth-century studies have worked
under a kind of double jeopardy. Let me clarify. It seems to me that students

of each historical period—be it the Renaissance, the eighteenth century, or Romanticism—have tended quite strongly to adopt the terms of reference and points of view within which their respective periods beheld themselves. Earlier Renaissance critics joined the Elizabethans in glorifying Elizabeth I or Renaissance humanism, and, as Jerome J. McGann and Clifford Siskin have shown, study of the Romantics has worked largely within that period's epistemology and terminology.[9] But since, as Hohendahl argues, the whole institution of criticism has been built on Enlightenment foundations, at least critics of the Renaissance or the Romantic period could benefit from a certain cognitive dissonance that provided openings for genuine analysis. In eighteenth-century studies, however, the institution of criticism and the object of study are far more congruent. The field's often remarked conservatism reappears, in this light, as a historically determined systemic function.

Recently, however, we are seeing scholarly books that explicitly analyze—even attack—the Enlightenment framework. I have in mind, for example, Jerome Christensen's *Practicing Enlightenment*, in which the author specifically says that he is approaching Hume's literary career from a Romantic perspective, or Nancy Armstrong's *Desire and Domestic Fiction*, which opens with a chapter on the need to denaturalize the eighteenth-century constitution of gender in order to arrive at an unblinkered history of the novel. Interestingly enough, in view of my suggestion that some kind of double jeopardy or over-determination may have been at work in eighteenth-century studies, several of the books that operate within the new framework, including Christensen's and Armstrong's, are by authors with marked affiliations to periods other than the eighteenth century. Christensen started as a Romanticist, and Armstrong has strong scholarly interests in the Victorian period. Cathy N. Davidson, whose *Revolution and the Word* deals in substantial part with the eighteenth century, is an Americanist based largely in nineteenth-century studies. I also think of Peter Stallybrass and Allon White's cultural materialist work *The Politics and Poetics of Transgression*, even though it deals only in part with the eighteenth century, because their other writings have attended, respectively, to the Renaissance and to fiction in the two following centuries.[10]

## III

There is space here to describe just four assumptions characteristic of the Enlightenment framework within which criticism has proceeded. The new historicism, cultural materialism, feminism, and, to a lesser extent, deconstruction (or at least deconstruction's original impetus in Derrida) have challenged and largely denaturalized this framework.[11] Although I lay stress on those assumptions that most obviously concern literary criticism, the elements I identify are in fact interdependent parts of a large cultural system and should not be thought of hierarchically or teleologically.

First let us take up the Enlightenment invention of the aesthetic as an autonomous discursive realm. Literature, along with the other arts, became in this construction a disclosure of sensate experience produced and arranged according to principles entirely different from those governing other forms of knowledge. Now it was a specialized department in a system, conveniently epitomized by d'Alembert's *Preliminary Discourse to the Encyclopedia of Diderot*, a system that categorized human endeavor by correlating it with the physiological and psychological faculties. Literature was ideologically, if not actually, confined to the realms of sense, intuition, and imagination, where previously it had comprehended virtually everything written. The new late twentieth-century movements work, at least tacitly, to reestablish the previous state of affairs by challenging the autonomy of the aesthetic domain and reconstituting it as a historical phenomenon subject to critical analysis.

The Enlightenment constitution of the aesthetic delineated one major axis in a complex geometry—a division of knowledge into disciplines that not only separated the arts from the historical, scientific, and argumentative discourses but led to sharp distinctions among the arts themselves such as we find in Lessing's *Laocoön* and its English predecessors. This division of knowledge had large material consequences as it was institutionalized over time and yielded, for example, not merely the various professions with which we are familiar but the concept of professionalism itself. In universities, where, to be sure, learning had for centuries been parceled into broad areas, the ultimate repercussion of the new division of knowledge by faculties was the emergence of separate departments not only of philosophy, history, political theory, and economics but of music, the visual arts, and literature.[12]

The new movements under discussion here often are described as innovative because they reach across the customary boundaries between literary study and the visual arts, history, anthropology, sociology, law, and so forth. Certainly, interdisciplinary criticism existed and was thought desirable well before the new historicism, cultural materialism, or feminist literary history. In fact, the American Society for Eighteenth-Century Studies originated under a banner of interdisciplinarity that it continues proudly to fly.[13] But the word itself implies the preservation of traditional disciplinary boundaries and provokes one to think of the critic either as a fugitive living dangerously in limbo between nations or operating as a kind of extraordinary ambassador moving without portfolio from one sovereignty to another. Interdisciplinarity in itself does nothing to denaturalize the category of the aesthetic.

It is one thing to compare literature with the other arts or with—shall we say—philosophy, conceived as uniquely structured disciplines, and quite another to treat novels, paintings, buildings, logical treatises, legislation, and

institutional regulations all as texts participating in the complex and contestatory processes through which societies define and maintain the structure not
only of their institutions but of human entities. (We usually call the human
entities that live within and largely constitute society "persons," though we
might more properly use some analytical nomenclature like that of narratology
and label them "actants.") The new approaches might better be called "transdisciplinary" because they work to erode presumptions on which the existing
disciplines are founded. They are so disturbing, I believe, because they challenge not merely ways of thinking about the aesthetic but ways of disciplinary
existence that are deeply ingrained within the schools, museums, universities,
and other educational establishments of our own society. The discourse of the
aesthetic disguises the constitutive role that symbolism plays in social life at
large and founds institutions that segregate the arts both physically and men-
tally from other social processes. Professors of literature have been earning a
fair living perpetuating this segregation.

Authorship is a second category of Enlightenment belief at once central to orthodox criticism and challenged by the new historicism and other
movements. Here, again, Foucault helped us to understand the historicity of a
phenomenon that had been taken for granted ("What Is an Author?"). He
describes the "author function" as a culturally variable designation used at
times to affiliate certain texts and to lend them authority by attributing their
production to a historical person like Vergil or to an imagined individual like
"Homer." An "author" in the modern era is, above all, a simulacrum to which
are assigned traits that allows its interpretive construction as a personal subject who creates a unique world of thought in a manner that usually has been
considered to be universal but is in fact confined to the post-Cartesian West.
An author's uniqueness is manifest in the "work" and confers identity on it.
Once the category of creative authorship exists, it influences not only scholarship and criticism but literary production itself. The anchoring of discourse
in sponsoring subjectivity that began in the seventeenth century and was
naturalized in the eighteenth is noticeable, for instance, in works like the
Ossian forgeries or in the emergent construction of Shakespeare as an artistic
personality. The category of authorship was consolidated in the Romantic era,
when it was sanctified as an attribute of the creative personality and written
definitively into copyright laws throughout Europe.[14] Authorship was progressively institutionalized in the nineteenth century, when the study of literature
was gaining its place among the university disciplines. It is hard to think of
even one major canonical English work after the early Tudor period that is
*now* designated as anonymous. Of course what Foucault called the "author
function" can be assigned to anonymous works (as has routinely happened in
medieval and Renaissance art history), but it says much about the strength

of our presumptions about writing that such has seldom been the case in literature.

Although the new historicism and, to a large extent, cultural materialism have been strongly affixed to the authorial canon—most especially to Shakespeare—in practice they also have challenged the centrality of the canon by placing an enormous array of anonymous or collective social texts on an equal footing with acknowledged masterpieces. Legislation, legal documents, press reports, and conduct books, for instance, now have standing as texts, not just as background or underpinnings. Feminist scholarship has gone very much further in altering the canon despite—or possibly even because of—the preservation of sponsoring subjectivity in some versions of feminism. The point here is not so much the imperfect execution of theory: after all, we still live in a culture that places enormous value on the category of subjectivity, a culture in which biography is about the only type of academic writing on literature that trade publishers or the general public will touch. The point is, rather, that the comfortable and repetitious gentlemanly discussion of a few masterpieces that typified the New Criticism is almost over. Certainly in its early years the New Criticism had to struggle against the old orthodoxies of philology and literary history, and, perhaps as a way of vaccinating my own essay against the charge of Whiggishness, I note that the astounding speed with which the new movements seem to have become standard in Renaissance and Romantic studies causes me to be curious about what new "isms" may overtake them. In any case, feminism, new historicism, and cultural materialism have forced the up-to-date critic—like Marvell's lover—to contemplate a vast eternity of primary texts. Indeed, while the frequent accusation that the new historicism takes an anecdotal view of the past puts a negative spin on the question, it may well be true that the issue of selection poses any method's single biggest theoretical quandary.[15]

A third definitive category of Enlightenment belief within which subsequent criticism has operated is faith in transparency, neutrality, and disinterestedness as ideals of critical discourse. Related to and produced by this category is the definition—epitomized by a work like Dr. Johnson's *Dictionary*—of a public language against which all others may be judged. Kant is the eighteenth-century figure who most fully theorized the already existent ideal of critical communication in a public sphere free of special interests—whether personal, political, or religious.[16] In this ideal sphere only the spirit of impartial, rational inquiry is supposed to guide research, the findings of which are examined by an equally impartial audience, improved by further analysis, and eventually perfected not merely into knowledge but into truth. This disinterested dialogue is technically ungendered, but it of course turns out to be presumptively male.

New historicists have not been as thoroughgoing in their challenge to the category of disinterested inquiry as to those of the aesthetic and of authorship. They have consistently treated history as a narrative function relative to the historicity of the historian. And certainly they have broken with the idea of history or any other form of knowledge as empirical representation. But self-reflexive introductions and conclusions notwithstanding, new historicism on the whole has preserved the *voice* of disinterested inquiry and, despite the fascination with Elizabeth as a woman exercising the power of monarchy, all too often has treated humanity as if it were ungendered.[17] More explicit have been the cultural materialists in Britain: the temporal, geographical, and political position of their historical criticism has been extraordinarily precise. For them, the stress on Shakespeare goes beyond any question of residual aesthetic admiration to become a contest with established ideology (and especially with Thatcherism) over the significance of a playwright at once deeply embedded in the British system of education and central to an outworn and delusionary nationalism. More explicit still have been feminists who find that the canons of disinterestedness and impartiality cloak the old male patriarchy in a new garb that is part of its adaptation to emergent capitalism.

This brings us to the fourth and final category I discuss here, that of gendered sexuality. Foucault's late work *The History of Sexuality* presents a conveniently available, eloquently argued case for the general proposition that while the biological traits of the sexes remain constant over long periods of time, sexuality is constructed socially and operates differently in each historical period. He maintains, specifically, that the delineation of sexuality as at once constitutive of personality and subject to scientific mapping, surveillance, and social consciousness is an attribute of modern existence that took initial shape as its features emerged across the eighteenth century and that became fully operational in the nineteenth. Feminist literary scholars, already having built on historical studies of the family that draw, however generally, on Marxist categories, have taken further impetus from Foucault. They have retold the story of the eighteenth century to disclose the ideological implications of writing for and by women. They have stressed above all the operative place of narrative writing in an emergent system of gendered sexuality within which the male moves as wage earner and speaker in the open realm of a public sphere, where disinterested discourse reigns, while the female is confined to the closed realm of the family, working without wages to reproduce the moral, educational, and psychological orders that enable capitalism at once to function and ideologically to disguise its exploitation of labor through the maintenance of the categories of class, race, and gender. Nancy Armstrong's *Desire and Domestic Fiction* and Felicity Nussbaum's *Autobiographical Subject* present forceful versions of this feminist critique of eighteenth-century gender construction as it works through literature. Their arguments exhibit attributes of the new historicism and cultural materialism as well.[18] Ludmilla Jordanova's *Sexual Visions*, a book that displays affinities with cultural materialism despite its authorship by a professional historian, is one of a growing number of historical studies that document the social construction of gender in the eighteenth century. Such work in the history of gender makes it seem increasingly artificial to discuss literary study as a separate discipline. (See also other writings by Jordanova in the Works Cited.)

## *IV*

My observations thus far have deemphasized the differences that separate the new historicism from cultural materialism and feminism by grouping them together. Now, in conclusion, I want to suggest one way in which the new historicism may be different—not rhetorically or as a method but functionally, in today's academy. This difference does not imply superiority on the part of new historicism. On the contrary, I consider the long-range significance of feminism to be far greater. I simply want to engage in an episode of systemic thinking in order to consider the force of recent debates about the new historicism. The catalytic role the following analysis assigns to new historicism in the discipline of English at large can work with my description of eighteenth-century studies—as a field operating under double jeopardy because of the resonance of its assumptions with those of its objects of study—to explain in systemic terms the field's belated acceptance of the new historicism and other new movements. On the account that follows, the Enlightenment framework's legitimating force simply endured somewhat longer in eighteenth-century English literary studies than in the early modern, Romantic, nineteenth-century, and modern-period specialties.

The role of the new historicism in the American academy of the 1980s can be understood with reference to Jürgen Habermas's discussion of legitimation crises, which depends in turn on his theory of communicative competence. The theory goes like this in the convenient summary offered by Habermas's translator, Thomas McCarthy[19]:

> [A] smoothly functioning language game rests on a background consensus formed from ... different types of validity claims that are involved in the exchange of speech acts: claims that the utterance is understandable, that its propositional content is true, and that the speaker is sincere in uttering it, and that it is right or appropriate for the speaker to be performing the speech act. In normal interaction, these implicitly raised validity claims are naively accepted. But ... situations arise in which one or more of them becomes problematic in a fundamental way. In such cases ... specific forms of problem

resolution are required to remove the disturbance and restore the original, or a new, background consensus. Different forms are needed for each type of claim. But the validity of problematic truth claims or of problematic norms can be redeemed . . . only . . . by entering into a discourse whose sole purpose is to judge the truth of the problematic opinion or the correctness of the problematic norm. . . . The speech situation of [such] discourse represents a break with the normal context of interaction in that, ideally, it requires [the suspension] of all motives except that of a willingness to come to an understanding.

("Translator's Introduction" xiii–xiv)

The purpose of this special form of interest-free discourse is to reestablish the working fiction under which normal communication proceeds: namely, the fiction that speakers understand the beliefs and norms under which they operate and can, if called upon, justify them in good faith. Of course this fiction of accountability is counterfactual and can be stabilized, to quote Habermas, "only through legitimation of the ruling systems of norms" and through systematic barriers to bad-faith communication. These barriers have contradictory effects because they both "make a fiction . . . of the reciprocal imputation of accountability, [and] support at the same time the belief in legitimacy that sustains the fiction and prevents its being found out." This, says Habermas, "is the paradoxical achievement of ideologies" (*Legitimation* xv). Legitimacy is, thus, an effect of ideology. The specialized, interest-free discourse Habermas describes allows escape from ideology through entry into what he calls a "reciprocal supposition" that enables the critique of systematically distorted communication (ideology) and provides guidelines for rational institutions— in short, and returning in another form to the proposition from Giddens with which I began, to genuine knowledge.

How does this apply to the new historicism? I think it does whether or not one rejects as impossible the ideal of interest-free discussion. Ever since the 1960s, and possibly before, the academic literary disciplines in the United States have responded to challenges to their prevailing norms by entering into discourse and by attempting to assimilate representative dissenters. For a time this strategy worked to sustain the disciplines and their communicative norms, but the very process of taking in dissenters, as well as the emergence of challenge by converts from within, broadened and varied the community that had to reach consensus in order to maintain legitimacy and thereby energized the crisis anew.

It is tempting to view the new historicism as another challenge to disciplinary ideology. This is how I have described it in this essay, and this is one of the ways in which it has functioned. Tempting also is to view its odd amalgam of various theories and methods as a new orthodoxy. My introduction of Habermas lends plausibility to this interpretation. The new historicism seems in many ways to bear the marks of a new groundwork of norms, a new consensus within which communication can proceed. If the movement indeed has the makings of a new ground of assumptions working to legitimate the discipline, this situation can explain its having become an object of attack by other challengers because, in fact, the discourse used to reestablish a new ground of legitimacy for speech acts can never really be interest-free.

Yet the very quality of the new historicism that has been most attacked by feminists—its tendency to slide into a neutral, authoritative, putatively interest-free voice—may be a mark of the actual role it is playing in a legitimation crisis underway in the literary disciplines, because such a voice, on Habermas's reading, would be a feature of the discursive mechanism the system of communication produces to confront crises in legitimation whether or not new consensus actually emerges. In this light, I consider the new historicism not as a recently legitimated consensus—not really a new orthodoxy or even a prototype of one. Rather, it is a discourse produced by a discipline in crisis, with a view to finding a new ground that may or may not resemble it. This, I believe, explains the overwhelming volume of commentary about new historicism. By one count the 1988 Modern Language Association meetings alone included thirty papers on the subject.[20] This, too, is why some of the movement's leading practitioners have attained such high profiles. They are not merely standard-bearers of a new orthodoxy. Through no premeditation of their own they have become the visible signs of a sweeping and profound process in which whole institutions are at stake. By the logic of this process, new historicists, feminists, and cultural materialists alike become necessary players and find themselves to be commodities in demand. Whether this process leads to new forms of disciplinary legitimacy, which is to say to a new ideology of literary study, or to a sustained critical discourse yielding genuine knowledge in Habermas's or Giddens's sense, remains to be seen.

In a sense, Anglo-American literary criticism is just catching up with the rest of the world, a world in which not only the Frankfurt school but, for example, the *Annales* group in France stretch back for generations. The opening to literature and to what we may call cultural studies came, however, with the revelation, which arrived in this country under the rubrics of structuralism and poststructuralism, that human endeavor is discursively constituted— whether this endeavor happens, like literature, to lie under the discredited rubric of the aesthetic or in some other disciplinary domain like history, philosophy, or politics—and that this discursive constitution is historical. These, I believe, are the basic insights within which the new movements—including new historicism, cultural materialism, and feminist literary history—work and that not merely eighteenth-century studies but the whole discipline of English must confront.[21]

### Notes

[1]Criticism of eighteenth-century English literature by Raymond Williams is a conspicuous exception; see, for example, *The Country and the City*. See also Kettle, *An Introduction to the English Novel*. Williams, Kettle, and such other Marxist literary critics in England as Christopher Hill have operated as a minority, largely outside the dominant trends I am describing in this essay.

[2]West Memorial Lectures, Stanford Univ., Apr. 1988. A written version of these extempore lectures has appeared as *The Consequences of Modernity*. The basic idea to which I refer here is developed, much less explicitly than in the lectures themselves, on 10–17 and 36–45.

[3]These works are conveniently gathered in Mack's *Collected in Himself*. Mack says, for instance: "Against this Renaissance background, a number of important elements in the *Essay on Man* stand out in their full significance. In fact, it may not be unfair to say that while Pope's poem is in all its surface aspects a work of the Augustan period, its underlying themes have much in common with the kinds of meaning Renaissance poets constructed. . . . Readers of Shakespeare, for example, have long sensed in several of the plays a structural pattern that asserts some form of equilibrium or order, usually with reference to the universal order, which is then violated in one or several ways, and reestablished at the close. . . . It is also, of course, and particularly, the theme of Milton in *Paradise Lost*. As every one knows, the central conflict in Milton's epic is that between the hierarchical order, coherence, law, love, harmony, unity, and happiness of a world created and sustained according to God's purposes, and the chaos, rebellion, dissension, hatred, and misery brought into it by man's and Satan's unwillingness to be contented with these purposes and their part in them" (221).

In an essay from the same time, Bredvold's "Gloom of the Tory Satirists," one reads: "Good satire may be withering, it may be dark anger, it may be painfully bitter; but it cannot be great satire without having at its core a moral idealism expressing itself in righteous indignation. The *saeva indignatio* which Swift suffered from is radically different in quality from a morbid *Schadenfreude*. Once that distinction is admitted we have the essential justification for our pleasure in satire, as well as an understanding of the fellow feeling with which the satirists sustained one another" (11).

For a survey, from a contemporary theoretical perspective, of postwar eighteenth-century literary study in English, see Nussbaum and Brown 1–22. W. H. Epstein's "Counter-intelligence: Cold-War Criticism and Eighteenth-Century Studies" appeared after this essay was written. Epstein connects the tacit collaboration of the New Criticism and positivist literary history with strategies of concealment and personal effacement characteristic of counterintelligence as practiced during World War II and during the cold war by several members of the Yale school of eighteenth-century studies.

[4]See also "Prison Reform and the Sentence of Narration in *The Vicar of Wakefield*," in Nussbaum and Brown 168–88.

[5]*The Enlightenment* 16–18. Gay quotes Gibbon's *Essai sur l'étude de la littérature* from *Miscellaneous Works* 4: 38.

[6]Even the French Revolution refused women an active political role. Indeed,

as Joan Landes argues, in *Women and the Public Sphere in the Age of the French Revolution*, in many ways women had more influence under the old regime. Addison does welcome female readers in paper number 10 on the *Spectator*'s desired audience. Having condemned "ordinary" women as engaged in trivial and irrational amusements, he welcomes the "Multitudes . . . that join all the Beauties of the Mind to the Ornaments of Dress" and hopes to increase their number "by publishing this daily Paper, which I shall always endeavour to make an innocent if not an improving Entertainment, and by that Means at least divert the Minds of my female Readers from greater Trifles." In context, the hyperbole of "multitudes" and the characterization of the *Spectator* as a trifle seem to me to take back at least as much as they grant. See also the treatment in numbers 37 and 92 of a lady named Leonora, who possesses a remarkable library. (See Bond 1: 46–47, 152–59, 389–93.)

[7]The papers appeared between 21 June and 3 July 1712 as numbers 411–21; the conventional title comes from Addison's announcement in number 409 of an impending "essay on the pleasures of the imagination."

[8]My discussion of Schlegel is inspired by Hohendahl, though it moves in somewhat different directions.

[9]See McGann, *Romantic Ideology* and *Beauty of Inflections* 135–72, and Siskin.

[10]I too run in this pack of interlopers since my own first book was *Spenser and Literary Pictorialism*.

[11]Although Rousseau, in particular, figures importantly in the writings of Derrida and de Man, the movement did not have a widespread impact in the field of English eighteenth-century studies. See Derrida, *Of Grammatology*, and de Man, *Blindness and Insight*. Important among the exceptions are Warner, *Reading* Clarissa, and W. Dowling, *Language and Logos in Boswell's* Life of Johnson. I mention deconstruction here because certain of its features and procedures have been absorbed by other new movements.

[12]On the historical constitution of the aesthetic and on its ideological significance, see Wellbery, *Lessing's* Laocoön, especially ch. 2, and Eagleton, *The Ideology of the Aesthetic*.

[13]On the ASECS and its reinforcement of the traditional relationship between literary and historical study, see Nussbaum and Brown 7–9.

[14]See Bosse 8–9. David Wellbery called this work to my attention and summarized its chief points. See also Mark Rose, "The Author as Proprietor."

[15]On the intrinsically anecdotal character of history writing, see Fineman's brilliant, posthumously published essay, "The History of the Anecdote."

[16]See Kant, "What is Enlightenment?" On reason as a regulative principle in Kant, see also Scruton 54–55.

[17]An important exception is Greenblatt's chapter "Fiction and Friction" in *Shakespearean Negotiations* 66–93.

[18]See Armstrong's "Introduction: Literature as Women's History."

[19]See also McCarthy's *Critical Theory of Jürgen Habermas*. My discussion of a legitimation crisis in literary studies is broadly inspired by Lyotard's application of Habermas's term to the entire system of intellectual production in *The Postmodern Condition*. After this essay was written, I became aware of McGann's rather different use of Habermas on the question of legitimation in *Social Values and Poetic Acts*.

[20]The flood of publications is comparable. For comprehensive bibliographical references on the subject, see the annotations to the essays in Veeser; since this book's publication a substantial, exhaustively annotated essay by Liu has appeared: "The Power of Formalism." In addition, New Literary History devoted an entire issue, entitled *History and . . .* , to the subject. See also D. Simpson, "Literary Criticism and the Return to 'History.' "

[21]Portions of this essay have appeared in the book *Professing the Eighteenth Century*, edited by Leopold Damrosch, Jr., published by the University of Wisconsin Press in 1992.

## Selected Bibliography

Armstrong, Nancy. *Desire and Domestic Fiction: A Political History of the Novel*. New York: Oxford UP, 1987.
    Studies the role of the novel in the formation of culture and gender during the eighteenth and nineteenth centuries.

Barrell, John. *The Political Theory of Painting from Reynolds to Hazlitt*. New Haven: Yale UP, 1986.
    Considers the interaction of aesthetic and political theory during the late eighteenth and early nineteenth centuries.

Bender, John. *Imagining the Penitentiary: Fiction and the Architecture of Mind in Eighteenth-Century England*. Chicago: U of Chicago P, 1987.
    Argues that the novel played a role in the eighteenth-century invention of the penitentiary and the forms of consciousness it implies.

Brown, Marshall. *Preromanticism*. Stanford: Stanford UP, 1991.
    A broad study of the "crisis of expression" in aesthetics and literature during the last half of the eighteenth century.

Carnochan, W. B. *Gibbon's Solitude: The Inward World of the Historian*. Stanford: Stanford UP, 1987.
    A phenomenological study of Gibbon's life and authorship in relation to his historical subjects.

Castle, Terry. *Masquerade and Civilization in Eighteenth-Century English Culture and Fiction*. Stanford: Stanford UP, 1986.
    Views masquerade and the novel as genres exploring the margins of hegemonic social and gender formations.

Christensen, Jerome. *Practicing Enlightenment: Hume and the Formation of a Literary Career*. Madison: U of Wisconsin P, 1987.
    Uncovers the subversive, counter-Enlightenment currents in Hume's life and thought.

Damrosch, Leo. *Fictions of Reality in the Age of Hume and Johnson*. Madison: U of Wisconsin, 1989.

Considers the uncertain boundaries between fiction and reality in eighteenth-century thought and literature.

Davidson, Cathy N. *Revolution and the Word: The Rise of the Novel in America*. New York: Oxford UP, 1986.
Relates the rise of the novel in America to developments in colonial print culture.

De Bolla, Peter. *The Discourse of the Sublime: Readings in History, Aesthetics, and the Subject*. New York: Blackwell, 1989.
Rereads the sublime as a discourse having to do, among other things, with the imponderability of the national debt.

Doody, Margaret Anne. *The Daring Muse: Augustan Poetry Reconsidered*. Cambridge: Cambridge UP, 1985.
A broad account that views early eighteenth-century poetry as fundamentally unorthodox, even subversive.

Eagleton, Terry. *The Ideology of the Aesthetic*. Oxford: Blackwell, 1990.
Treats the emergence of the idea of the aesthetic in England and Germany as a necessary segment of the development of bourgeois culture.

Epstein, Julia. *The Iron Pen: Frances Burney and the Politics of Women's Writing*. Madison: U of Wisconsin P, 1989.
Relates Burney's sociopolitical situation to her bodily life and writings.

Erickson, Robert A. *Mother Midnight: Birth, Sex, and Fate in the Eighteenth-Century Novel*. New York: AMS, 1987.
Relates the novel—especially Defoe, Richardson, Sterne—to the discourses of midwife, madam, and marriage.

Hunter, J. Paul. *Before Novels: The Cultural Contexts of Eighteenth-Century English Fiction*. New York: Norton, 1990.
Explores the numerous prototypes of the modern novel in late seventeenth- and early eighteenth-century England.

Landry, Donna. *The Muses of Resistance: Laboring-Class Women's Poetry in Britain, 1739–1796*. Cambridge: Cambridge UP, 1990.
A political and ideological study of the production and reception of verse by eighteenth-century women of the underclasses.

Marshall, David. *The Figure of the Theater: Shaftesbury, Defoe, Adam Smith, and George Eliot*. New York: Columbia UP, 1986.
Maintains that a fundamentally theatrical mode of self-absorbed consciousness emerged during the eighteenth century.

McKeon, Michael. *The Origins of the English Novel, 1600–1740*. Baltimore: Johns Hopkins UP, 1987.
Argues that the crystallization of the novel as a recognizable genre during

the 1740s is part of a long cultural struggle concerning the roles of opposing narrative forms and moral values.

Mullan, John. *Sentiment and Sociability: The Language of Feeling in the Eighteenth Century*. Oxford: Clarendon–Oxford UP, 1988.
Explores connections between changing eighteenth-century literary genres and the period's thought about the origins and functions of social and emotional bonds.

Nussbaum, Felicity. *The Autobiographical Subject: Gender and Ideology in Eighteenth-Century England*. Baltimore: Johns Hopkins UP, 1989.
Analyzes private, often unpublished, writing to examine the cultural, political, and economic construction of subjective individuality.

Nussbaum, Felicity, and Laura Brown, eds. *The New Eighteenth Century: Theory, Politics, English Literature*. New York: Methuen, 1987.
A representative, though not complete, sample of work by specialist practitioners of new methods of inquiry.

Paulson, Ronald. *Breaking and Remaking: Aesthetic Practice in England, 1700–1820*. New Brunswick: Rutgers UP, 1989.
Departs from the emphasis on affect both in eighteenth-century aesthetics and in later scholarship. The work stresses ideas and practices of the period that treat works of art not as abstractions or emotions but as material objects that are made, broken, destroyed, remade.

Pollak, Ellen. *The Poetics of Sexual Myth: Gender and Ideology in the Verse of Swift and Pope*. Chicago: U of Chicago P, 1985.
Places the poetry of Swift and Pope in context with the emergence of modern ideas of the feminine.

Richetti, John. *Philosophical Writing: Locke, Berkeley, Hume*. Cambridge: Harvard UP, 1983.
Shows, through close analysis, the artificiality of the modern distinction between literature and philosophy as applied to texts of the eighteenth century.

Rousseau, G. S., and Roy Porter. *Exoticism in the Enlightenment*. Manchester: Manchester UP, 1990.
Contains essays on the relationship of eighteenth-century Europe to its non-Western colonies and counterparts.

———. *Sexual Underworlds of the Enlightenment*. Chapel Hill: U of North Carolina P, 1988.
A selection of essays, broadly inspired by Foucault, on the delineation of modern categories of gender and deviation during the eighteenth century.

Stallybrass, Peter, and Allon White. *The Politics and Poetics of Transgression*. Ithaca: Cornell UP, 1986.

A broad study of social underworlds and legal marginality from the Renaissance through the eighteenth century.

Todd, Janet M. *The Sign of Angellica: Women, Writing, and Fiction, 1660–1800*. London: Virago, 1989.
A survey of women in the profession of writing.

# $\mathcal{R}$omantic Studies

## FRANCES FERGUSON

I should begin by indicating what the following essay does not include—a survey of recent criticism that exhaustively names positions and exponents, parties and partisans. There are two distinct, if related, reasons why it does not. In the first place, students of the Romantic period are especially fortunate in having, in addition to essays like the annual reviews of scholarship in *Studies in English Literature*, MLA volumes that provide effective and informative reviews of scholarly writing in the field. To try to compete, in such a brief compass as this, with the accomplishment of *The English Romantic Poets: A Review of Research and Criticism* (ed. F. Jordan) would be foolhardy as well as redundant. In the second place, I have felt that the most useful way into the issues of Romanticism and its criticism is through the arguments that underlie the disputes. It seemed to me, in other words, that the narrative most readily available—one that traced the rise of a deconstructive, language-oriented, and rhetorical account of literature and its recent replacement by a more historically and politically oriented model—would be perfectly true, on the one hand, and a significant misrepresentation, on the other. It would be true in that the summary of recent Romantic criticism does involve that plot. What that plot line misses, however, is Romantic criticism's continuing engagements with the arguments of Romanticism—about what literary works might be, about the relation between aesthetic experience and individual experience, about the place of aesthetic experience in relation to society.

In the effort to honor some of the arguments of Romantic aesthetics, I have broadened the time frame of this essay beyond the last quarter-century and condensed the list of names of contemporary critics. I have used the selected bibliography at the end of the essay as a vehicle for identifying persons and positions that have not been named in the essay, so that readers will be able to employ it to suit their needs.

Jerome McGann, in his *Romantic Ideology*, has renewed a debate about how many Romanticisms there are—which is, of course, tantamount to asking how we know what Romanticism is. The original debate, in which the central position papers were Arthur O. Lovejoy's "On the Discrimination of Romanticisms" (first published in *PMLA* in 1924) and René Wellek's "Concept of Romanticism in Literary History" (first published in *Comparative Literature* in 1949), set out to determine whether the kinds of generalizations made about the literary historical field of Romanticism had any use at all. Lovejoy, firing the opening salvo, asserted that "the word 'romantic' has come to mean so many things that, by itself, it means nothing. It has ceased to perform the function of a verbal sign" (66). His anxiety about the all-inclusiveness of the term might, he suggested, merely reflect the personal tic of professional specialization: ". . . for one of the philosopher's trade, at least, the situation is embarrassing and exasperating; for philosophers, in spite of a popular belief to the contrary, are persons who suffer from a morbid solicitude to know precisely what they are talking about" (67). Having converted the apparent confession into a display of professionalism, he went on to argue for the importance of discriminating Romanticisms, to distinguish between "possibly quite distinct thought-complexes" (68) in various manifestations of Romanticism and to identify, as examples of such distinctions, a Romantic naturalism that conceived the "natural" as "a thing you reached by going back and by leaving out" (72) and that "was associated with primitivism of some mode or degree" (73); a Romantic aestheticism that saw itself as "in its very essence a denial of the older naturalist presuppositions" (73); and a Romanticism that specifically identified an aesthetic perception of infinitude with Christianity.

Wellek's response, some years later, was to shift the terms of the debate rather fundamentally, from a consideration of the modes of Romanticism to a discussion of what people expect when they hear or use a word like *Romanticism*. Building on his argument from "Periods and Movements in Literary History," Wellek affirmed that he had

> concluded that one must conceive of [period terms] not as arbitrary linguistic labels nor as metaphysical entities, but as names for systems of norms which dominate literature at a specific time of the historical process. The term "norms" is a convenient term for conventions, themes, philosophies, styles, and the like, while the word "domination" means the prevalence of one set of norms compared with the prevalence of another set in the past.       ("Concept" 182)

After surveying the major poets and critics of the Romantic period, he averred that " 'On the Discrimination of Romanticisms' proves, it seems to me, only that Joseph Warton was an early naturalist preromanticist, that Friedrich Schlegel was a highly sophisticated, self-conscious intellectual, and that Chateaubriand held many classicist views of literary criticism and on Shakespeare" (203).

Where Lovejoy had continually seen conflicts as generating a need for new categories, Wellek viewed the exception only as proving the rule. "The fact that Chateaubriand was conservative and Hugo ended in liberalism does not disrupt the continuity of French romanticism as a literary movement" (204).

Instead of Lovejoy's divergence, that is, Wellek saw "complete agreement" among English, French, and German Romantic writers on "all essential points": "imagination for the view of poetry, nature for the view of the world, and symbol and myth for poetic style" (193).

As gestures that represent what it means to conceive of oneself as a professional literary historian, both Lovejoy's and Wellek's are supremely interesting, in themselves and in their fundamental opposition to each other. Lovejoy seizes on a popularly available word like *Romanticism* and takes the job of the professional literary historian to be one of supplying distinctions. The need for these distinctions, moreover, is particularly pressing not just because it will produce greater specificity (as a diagnosis of "cancer" as opposed to "illness," or "lymphoma" as opposed to "cancer," would be). Rather, Lovejoy's desire to demonstrate what's in a name develops from his perception that one is not moving from the particular to the less particular to the most general in describing Romanticisms but instead that one encounters absolute contradiction in the very process of trying to move from one level of generality to another. Romanticism may be one, but *Romanticism* includes, for Lovejoy, not merely an embrace of primitivism but also a repudiation of it. Once a term has come to mean both one thing and its opposite, Lovejoy argues, has it not come to lose meaning?

The very question of how one discusses a literary historical period becomes a question about the unity of the object under study. It is on those grounds, and not because of any presumedly positivistic desire for clarity (which is, at any rate, impossible to attain), that Lovejoy's position has its significance. The question of periodization, in other words, becomes a critical version of the question of unity so prominent and so vexed in Romantic aesthetic theory. Unity can be preserved because the differences, from Wellek's perspective, do not represent contradictions at all but merely variations that, when combined, produce historical irony. Wellek responds to Lovejoy by suggesting that the only way of achieving unity is to look to "systems of norms" and to look to reception as demonstrating the unity of those systems. If Lovejoy is preoccupied by the differences between Thomas Warton's primitivism and Schiller's equally Romantic but diametrically opposed insistence on the unavailability of such primitivism, Wellek performs the high New Critical gesture of finding a reader who will reconcile the contradictions that Warton and Schiller would have avowed themselves to have.

Thomas Babington Macaulay, for Wellek, exemplifies the reader who recognizes that Romanticism has altered what counts as difference, what counts as unity. What had seemed to Lovejoy like substantive differences between Byron and Wordsworth had earlier, to Macaulay (writing in the *Edinburgh Review* in June 1831), appeared merely as the public and private faces of the same movement, Romanticism: "Lord Byron founded what may be called an exoteric Lake School—what Mr. Wordsworth had said like a recluse, Lord Byron said like a man of the world." As Wellek declares, with a sense of triumph, "Macaulay thus long before he knew a term for it, recognized the unity of the English romantic movement" (189). Macaulay's recognition of the unity of the movement, in anticipation of the existence of the term *Romantic*, reveals that the term does not, as Lovejoy suggests, create a mistaken impression; rather, its emergence was, as Wellek suggests, an effort to supply a name for a perception, to register the existence of the shared "systems of norms which dominate literature" in this particular period. "Systems of norms which dominate literature" approaches near enough to the sound of common sense so that one is in danger of passing over the internal fault line in the phrase, especially in the light of Macaulay's testimony *avant la lettre* of the critical doctrine it supposedly supports. Systematicity and normativeness, that is, continually compete with each other. While the empirical standard of the norm and of the comparison (the dominant) operates to make the period classification look like a matter of plausible comparative judgments (Byron is more like Wordsworth than he is like Dryden), the systematic account does not really rely on such an empirical procedure at all. Instead, the system occasions the production of the units that compose it. Even though the norms appear to be discernible by way of contrast with other periods with their different sets of norms, the unity of Romanticism involves its taking its place in a sequence of periods, the "total process of literature" rather than "the usual odd mixture of biography, bibliography, anthology, and disconnected emotive criticism." Wellek concludes with the reassurance that "we can then go on speaking of romanticism as one European movement" with a dominant "system of ideas" with "their anticipations and their survivals" (205), but that reassurance is based on the need for something like Romanticism to occupy a place in a systematic unity. Literary history here relies on a notion of organic form exactly analogous to the one that kept literary works whole (for the New Criticism in particular). The task of the professional literary historian is, from this standpoint, not to discriminate among Romanticisms but rather to insist on a body of professional knowledge that enables one to see literary history as systematic. One needs period categories not because they correspond to inductive classes, wholes composed out of units of similar works, but rather because they are themselves units that can be arrived at only through having postulated an all-subsuming unit—in the form of a systematic, holistic account of literature.

Now for McGann the ultimate point of rehearsing the debate is to take Lovejoy's side and to extend it, so that one ultimately sacrifices the notion of periodization to that of pluralism. One must create new critical distinctions to account not merely for certain general tendencies but for individual authors. To do anything less—or else—is, in McGann's view, to fall into the fatally self-incriminating disclosure of one's own critical ideology. Thus, M. H. Abrams does not, for McGann, merely "elide the problematic cases of Keats and Byron" in his model of English Romanticism (*Romantic Ideology* 26). Rather, Abrams provides evidence of his own ideology when he argues, in "English Romanticism: The Spirit of the Age," that "the militancy of overt political action [that had appeared available in the example of the French Revolution] has been transformed into the paradox of spiritual quietism" (58). To see Romanticism in Abrams's terms is, for McGann, to express ideas that "are clearly drawn from a Wordsworthian and, more generally, a Christian (Protestant) model." For Abrams to see the Romantics as having such ideas is, in this view, tantamount to his holding them himself. It is, from McGann's standpoint, to endorse as well as to summarize, because it is to accept (some) Romantics' self-definitions rather than to critique them. Abrams thus becomes not merely a historian of Romanticism who depicts "a transcendental displacement of human desires from the political arena to the spiritual" (*Romantic Ideology* 26). The choice of scholarly objects constitutes, in McGann's view, an endorsement. It is, moreover, an endorsement of political views that are seen to be inherently conservative because they align poetic formalism with poetic politics.

McGann seems willing to credit the first part of Abrams's literary historical argument about the Romantic period—namely, that the poetry's "relations to the revolutionary climate of the time" (Abrams "English Romanticism" 29) are definitive of it. The historicity of the period would thus be guaranteed, as it were, by the existence of a historical event—the revolution—to underwrite it. The second part of Abrams's argument is what, presumably, causes McGann his misgivings; although the revolution may function to provide unity to the intellectual field, Abrams dissolves that apparent unity by treating that event not merely as a central term but as a line of division. The view of the revolution as "the most glorious event" of the time gave way to despair over the possibility of realizing meaningful—that is, millennial—change in the historical arena. If, as in a quotation from Southey that Abrams features, the Romantics began in a spirit of optimism, in which "old things seemed passing away, and nothing was dreamt of but the regeneration of the human race" (316; see also M. R. Adams), this exultation yielded to "the later mood of revolutionary disillusionment or despair" (Abrams 324).

Here the most interesting aspect of Abrams's account is that it enables him to read "many seemingly apolitical poems of the later romantic period" as, basically, political poems (325). Having, that is, argued that hope and disillusionment are ultimately references to hope and disillusionment about the French Revolution, Abrams would thus provide a formal version of politics, the political waged through implicit, aesthetic means. The first move in Abrams's argument is straightforward. He cites the paradigmatic instance of political cycles of expectation and disappointment finding echoes in analogous personal alternations—namely, Wordsworth's discussion of his travels in

France immediately after the fall of the Bastille, where social hopes and disappointments correspond to the individual emotions that Wordsworth describes himself as feeling as he crosses the Alps. Were the argument limited to book 6 of *The Prelude*, where both elements of Abrams's discussion appear juxtaposed but not always directly related, it would be not only convincing but almost self-evident. Yet Abrams pursues this line of argument, in a form that Geoffrey Hartman will brilliantly extend in his "Poem and Ideology: A Study of Keats's 'To Autumn' " (*Fate* 124–46), to argue that mood comes increasingly to perform the function of theme. Where mood was once a response to theme, it increasingly becomes a self-sufficient formal substitute for it. Optimism and pessimism, once immediate responses to the French Revolution, ultimately lose their direct relationship to that political event. The formal association of optimism and pessimism with the event, however, means that Abrams can identify the "spirit" of the Romantic age with reactions to the French Revolution even when dealing with "seemingly apolitical poems." For the very notion of a genuinely apolitical poem becomes invalid for any poem that expresses sentiments that can be sorted into exultation and/or despair; Romantic poems can, according to Abrams's reasoning, be at most "seemingly apolitical poems."

It therefore seems implausible, to say the least, to accept McGann's assessment of Abrams's political quietism. For what has Abrams done other than to claim that the French Revolution has become so deeply implicated in Romantic structures of emotion that it must remain as implicit referent even when Romantic poets apparently take themselves to be writing a lyric of the most personal nature, or expressing the most individual sentiments? McGann imagines a political valence for emotion that has detached itself from one referent (the world of political and historical event) and attached itself to another (the analysis of mood per se). And if Abrams's point is that politics gets sustained by form, McGann's point ought to be that politics can never be conducted by formal means (since, presumably, the formal version of politics continually tends toward the political masquerading as the apolitical).

A question of the relationship between form and content is at stake here, and one could plausibly say that any analysis that uses form to mount an argument at odds with a poem's content has extended the notion of form into a notion of self-contradiction. That extension is equivalent, for McGann, to a transcendental gesture, a substitution of the unrealizable for the immediacy of the world of practical politics. He thus feels "obliged to observe, of course, that such a transcendental displacement of human desires is the basis of the (formerly) common view that Romanticism was (and is) a reactionary movement" (*Romantic Ideology* 26).

The improbability of that "of course" is instructive. For McGann has done nothing less than to criticize Abrams's account of the dissemination of radical political emotions into the seemingly apolitical and to criticize it not for seeing politics everywhere but rather for suppressing politics and, in the process, becoming an apologist for reactionary politics. McGann, that is, recapitulates a formalist reading of Abrams's formalist reading, in which he not so much challenges the conflation of form and politics as encodes some forms as more politically conservative or radical than others (as when he suggests that Byron's poetry, on formal grounds, is more politically correct than Wordsworth's). And it does not help matters when he concludes this portion of his discussion by averring that "Abrams' historical characterizations, then, are a function of a certain ideology, and their persuasive force waxes and wanes to the degree that we can agree to *accept* that ideology" (26; emphasis mine).

In that account of the relationship between persuasion and ideology, McGann makes an extraordinary if sketchy pair of claims. The first is that "historical characterization" and ideology are so thoroughly productive of each other that literary critics' description of literary materials is always a version of self-description in which their immersion in the values of what they describe is always to be assumed. Literary history, in this view, is involved in a process of primary idealism, seeing only what one wishes, because of one's acceptance of ideology, to see. The second is that agreeing or not agreeing to accept that ideology becomes an idealist's way of fighting idealism. This secondary idealism (as I call it for want of a better term) would rectify the errors that an individual commits on behalf of the culture. It would restore the individual's franchise, in the form of a celebration of "a critical consciousness, whose first obligation is to resist incorporation, and whose weapon is analysis" (2). In short, the notion of persuasive ideology functions first as if it were identical to individual perception, secondly as if it were the mere subject matter on which a critical subject might work. Persuasion is persuasion by virtue of never having to persuade anyone of anything, never having to alter a view; it merely rehearses the identity of the individual with his or her culture. Resistance thus, in this pluralist scheme, comes to occupy the formal and formulaic place of virtue by its assertion of the importance of individuality per se.

With the emergence of the critique of Abrams, that is, the implicit logic of McGann's initial return to the Lovejoy-Wellek debate becomes clear. While McGann frequently chides critics for their scholarly lapses, the issue is not critical ignorance or willful injustice at all, but rather a willingness in both Wellek and Abrams to imagine a spirit of the age that functions to conscript individual writers. To recast McGann's discussion, Lovejoy and Wellek are at odds over the relationship between an individual literary work and an individual author, on the one hand, and his or her age and its spirit, on the other. Lovejoy serves as a hero precisely by refusing to allow a contradiction to enter into any grouping that he accepts as a unity. The very idea of a "spirit of the age" uniting disparate writers (however much they imagine themselves to differ from one another) becomes anathema because it suppresses a notion of individual agency, the ability to discriminate not just Romanticisms from Romanticism but oneself from others. Even irony, in the form of Anne Mellor's discussion of it in *English Romantic Irony*, comes in for a drubbing because McGann quite rightly recognizes it as a literary accommodation of differences in unity. For irony represents a literary incorporation of distinctions so that contradiction no longer suffices to establish a new unit.

Thus, however improbable it may at first seem to stake any kind of political argument on distinguishing one kind of Romanticism from another, McGann manages to install politics as the central concern of the apparently innocent operation of literary taxonomy. Any gesture that can be identified with unification or collectivization assimilates itself to retrograde politics (so that Abrams's dissemination of the impact of the French Revolution over the entire field comes to look politically reactionary, as would, even more strangely, Fredric Jameson's account, in modernism, of a political unconscious that can unite psychology and politics on the basis of the argument that individuality is impossible and that the psyche, like the political, is always collective). Ideology for McGann is of necessity false consciousness, because the very notion of a collective culture or idea acting through an individual is what he attacks in addressing the Romantic ideology.

Pluralism, the critique of and escape from generalization and collectivization, becomes for McGann both a scholarly method and a political program. Yet it is easier to recount the narrative stages of this position than to supply the rationale behind it. For even though McGann is usually identified as a new historicist in Romantic criticism, the problem of naming that arises with new historicism has become just as acute as that of Romanticism once was. Because McGann is uninterested in history as event or as the kind of "cultural poetics" that concerns Stephen Greenblatt with his version of new historicism, McGann's version of new historicism commits itself to history as the ongoing proliferation of more minimal units, be they literary periods, aspects of periods, authors, poems, or drafts of poems. Having made the formal process of differentiation and individuation a virtue in itself, this version of new historicism produces distinctions that make no difference at all, because the only version of history that it can recognize is one that homologizes history and texts by making them continually about the relationship between parts and wholes, the individual and some collective, generalized term that functions as an oppressive rather than expressive name. For all his insistence on particularization, that is, McGann relies on a procedure that essentially analogizes and equates the relationship between an individual perceiver and an object of perception with the relationship between an individual and society.

In suggesting that there is something inherently political about recognizing the independence of an ever-growing number of categories, McGann's work is symptomatic in revealing how urgent the problems of Romantic formalism continue to be. For though it has become almost routine for critics to dismiss formalism as synonymous with the formulaic drawing of boundary lines around "the text," McGann's work demonstrates, by contrast, the complexities that Kantian formalism establishes for the ideas of aesthetic and political unity.[1] The recent renewal of interest in Kantian aesthetics (in the work of Weiskel; S. Knapp; F. Ferguson [*Solitude*]; and Eagleton [*Ideology of the Aesthetic*], for example) has involved precisely an attempt to locate the relationship between literary works and social and political structures. From their various positions, these critics have been attempting to determine to what extent Romantic formalism involves an intrinsic politics so implicit as to be masked. For although critics continually and repeatedly claim to move beyond formalism, the formal idealist account that Kant offered in *Critique of Judgment* (1790) continues to set the questions even of the deconstructive and historicist criticism that would reveal its limitations. Kant's aesthetics fundamentally reconfigures the terms of the relationship between the individual and the collective. First, it makes the reaction of the individual perceiver important not for providing testimony about an object but for making aesthetic experience not rely on taking an object as already given, already established as meaningful, as made. In Kant's famous formulation, the existence of the object becomes irrelevant. This is to say that Kant's account of the aesthetic judgment makes human intention, in the form of what an individual perceiver attends to, a new object of attention.[2] While a problematic relationship between pleasure and instruction had dogged earlier discussions of aesthetic experience, the Kantian emphasis on the indifference of the aesthetic judgment to communication and content dissolves that problem. Aesthetic reception may not create its objects, but neither does it emphasize their messages. This point becomes particularly clear as Kant divides his analysis of the aesthetic into two parts—the Analytic of the Beautiful and the Analytic of the Sublime. The sublime Kant—unlike most commentators—limited strictly to the experience of natural, as opposed to human-made, objects. By means of this restriction, he established the term *sublime* as a counter and opposite number to a concern with objects as vehicles for someone else's intentions (conceived as mental states or mental contents, feelings or information). By confining the term *sublime* to the natural world and by explicitly excluding the social, artifactual world, Kant indicated that his questions lay with what one can think of as the fundamental improbability that comes to constitute the possibility of aesthetic experience—the fact of human beings finding enjoyment in objects that were never produced "designedly" and for their pleasure. Once the aesthetic occupies itself with a rock, a stone, a tree, that is, the fundamental question of aesthetics conspicuously shifts. Artistic productions had, throughout the Western tradition, looked at best like a relatively inefficient way of communicating information. They had looked at worst like a prime vehicle for deception, so that they continually could be assimilated to versions of lying. Kant's identification of the sublime absolutely dispatched this account of aesthetic objects, not by stressing accuracy but by making it irrelevant—by making it clear that any deception in the experience of sublime natural objects had to count as a version of self-robbery on the part of the perceiver. Trees never try to pass themselves off as rocks.

If the deception that individuals might work on one another ceases to be a focus in Kant's account of the sublime, understanding the connections between persons becomes a more difficult project than it had seemed when one was concerned with communicating reliably or unreliably about determinable and existing things. First, the sense that objects, in and of themselves, represent the world that human beings share with one another no longer has the same force. For objects cease to be guarantees of anything other than their own substantial nature, and become instead occasions for demonstrating how the structures of human understanding continually supplement those objects and make the material count. An idea of an object, a *Ding an sich*, becomes the transcendental version of an object, understood less as an object in itself than as a version of an object that would accommodate and justify the various perspectives on an actual physical object. More the convergence of a series of narratives than an iteration of properties of an actual object, the transcendental *Ding an sich* does not postulate a metaphysical, as opposed to a physical, realm. Rather, the transcendental functions to register the existence of competing perspectives and to make those competing views count not as mere variety but as the basis for agreement. This is as much as to say that objects, in Kant's account, become multiple, that they are important not for demonstrating that one cannot know how an object "really" is because there are many competing and equally persuasive perspectives on it. Instead, objects become new loci for the argument about individuals and collective wholes, because they are always one, always self-unified, until multiple human agencies introduce multiplicity into them. If objects cannot unite individual humans because humans introduce multiplicity into those objects by seeing them as portions of varying units, Kant's account of transcendentalism can. Transcendentalism, that is, does not concern itself with the flight from the social and political (as McGann suggests) but rather with establishing the possibility of the social and political.

It has seemed to me worthwhile to rehearse not just the old debate between Lovejoy and Wellek but also some of the main features of Kant's aesthetics to clarify the issues that have been at stake in recent criticism of the Romantics. For in establishing aesthetic formalism, Kant made it increasingly difficult to think of the relationship between individuals and objects and individuals and groups. As Steven Knapp has forcefully argued, the aesthetic object that a New Critical theoretician like W. K. Wimsatt could describe as a "concrete universal" was an aesthetic object by virtue of including all the meanings associated with it. It became a strangely overstuffed unified entity, a way of containing multitudes. And the tendency to make aesthetic objects increasingly capacious, to see them as concrete embodiments of multiple sets of correspondences and coherences, found its internal correlate in the New Critical emphasis on irony and ambiguity, the discovery of competitive versions of meaning within poems as well as "outside" them, in the versions that their interpreters provided. Texts, that is, were never merely texts for the New Criticism, however frequently that claim is put forward by way of rebuke. Texts were, instead, continually expanding, through an understanding of reception that incorporated it into the text itself, and a very expansive version of context was thus always being made identical to text. A poem was not just what a reader thought it to be; it was what all readers thought it to be.[3]

The New Critical account of the literary object as a concrete universal thus justified interpretations of literary works in a way that extended Kant's basic account of natural objects. According to Kant, the pleasure that we take in natural objects is not merely free but even gratuitous, beside every point we can think of, since we are not interested in discerning someone else's mental states through them and our pleasure does not involve knowing them for what they are. In the hands of the New Criticism, the interpretation of literary works could proceed along similar grounds. Pleasure in literary works, always appearing gratuitous in relation to an understanding of other persons or objects, proceeded by making literary interpretation a multiplying double of the literary work, the multiple other self to its physical unity.

To this extent, the New Criticism itself represented a direct continuation of the tradition of Romantic aesthetics. Yet another aspect of New Critical practice constituted a direct contradiction to this gesture. As the New Criticism emphasized the lyric—especially the Romantic nature lyric—as the paradigmatic literary form, it laid particular stress on the notion of "voice." Thus, against the interest in aesthetic objects that had emerged from the fact that they were not seen as indices to other persons and their intentions, the New Criticism set the model of the individual lyric speaker. According to this reasoning, the drama of the lyric could be distinguished from eighteenth-century accounts of theatrical representation (and deception between persons) primarily on the grounds that the lyric isolated an individual speaker with an unspecified imaginary interlocutor (usually seen as a surrogate for the reader) and occasionally, as in the model of the conversation poems, provided an interlocutor hovering around the margins of the poem. That is, the New Critical vein of Romantic criticism embraced a fundamental contradiction. On the one hand, the Romantic commitment to lyrics addressed to natural objects, objects without consciousness, objects without psychology, provided an essential step in the New Critical justification of interpretation as an act of treating an aesthetic object as if it were not already occupied by an originary intention. On the other hand, this very emphasis on defining literary works as if they were fundamentally distinct from all the marks of humanness, and certainly of individual psychology, combined with the view that this statement about intentionless objects must always occur as if it were a formal equivalent of an extreme impersonation of voice, tone, mood. The distinction between poet and poetic speaker, so frequently invoked and relied on, thus amounted to a doctrinal position that ran into headlong conflict with the equally cherished indifference to authorial intention. The New Criticism treated lyric tone as a way of evoking the impersonation of an explicitly impersonal—or, better, apersonal—state. Instead of speaking of an intention to make poetry about the pleasures of intentionless objects, it spoke, rather, of an intentionless object that seemed to ape the tone of the individual human voice. Thus, having made literary works seem interpretable because they could be compared with the intentionless objects of nature, the New Criticism made intentionlessness appear in specifically human—and intentional—form. A poem could *be* rather than *mean* because, like a flower—or a rock, stone, or tree—it appeared rather than expressed. Yet this poem as nature continually appeared as a curious natural ventriloquism of human speech, as if nightingales, for instance, could talk and we could understand them. The New Criticism had understood two crucial elements of Kant's argument about aesthetic experience—that we cannot explain aesthetic pleasure in an object that carries no intentions in it except through an argument in favor of formalism, and that pleasure in formalism is absolutely dependent on the object's not turning out to be an intentional object in our absence. Kant's central example of this latter point is that anyone hearing the song of a nightingale and taking pleasure in it finds his or her pleasure interrupted by learning that the song has been produced not by a nightingale but by a young boy replicating the bird's song. From Kant's perspective, the pleasure in the sounds is absolutely destroyed by the recognition that there was someone else attached to their production and that they therefore came with a meaning (*Critique* 145). What the New Criticism had not understood was the strangeness of presenting this formalist justification of aesthetic pleasure in essentially dramatic form (albeit with the dramatic circle intensely restricted to a lyric speaker and selected natural objects). For the process of lyric dramatization undid the argument through which a poem could seem to be like a rock by making it sound as though one had to imagine a rock standing just so and using just such a word or tone, as if assuming the angle at which Corporal Trim stands in *Tristram Shandy*. Having divested the poem of psychology on one level (to argue for a reception-based account of interpretation), it reinserted it on another.

In a sense, Harold Bloom's criticism reverses this pattern. Where the New Critics had lent individual, dramatic tone to formal objects, Bloom made individual psychology look like the most formal object of all.[4] His account of poetic influence projected a resolution of the split between psychology and formalism by treating psychology as ultimately formal rather than experiential and individual. It was formal, moreover, not because it had a predictable course or regular structures but because it lacked such structures. That is, psychology became formal in the moment in which Bloom could claim the priority of "misreading" over "reading," and stress the analogy between our misreading of texts and our misreading of persons. The crucial formalist event in his thinking is therefore the yoking of the claim that "the meaning of a poem can only be another poem" with the claim that "Poetry (Romance) is Family Romance. Poetry is the enchantment of incest, disciplined by resistance to that enchantment" (*Anxiety* 94, 95). Imagining a text as a representative of a person with thoughts, feelings, an individual or even a collective psychology is, for Bloom, an unavailable option. For he takes the message of the Freudian family romance to entail the inevitability that individual psychology is as articulate as the natural sublime. The New Criticism had relegated biographical criticism to insignificance, thus dispatching authorial psychology, and had then reintroduced an impersonation of psychology in the formal emphasis on the lyric speaker. Bloom, by contrast, insists that individual psychology is, already, formal, just as legible, and just as illegible, as any individual poem. Like Lacan with his more global formalization of psychology in language, Bloom sees the formalization of psychology in poetry. His psychology of influence then achieves nothing less than an accommodation of the notion of psychology to the model of interpretation derived from Kant's account of the natural sublime, so that psychology appears less the story of the ego and its development (as in American ego psychology) than the narrative of the impossibility of that story's being heard. Psychology is no longer in competition with formalism, and individuality is so irrelevant as no longer to need to be smuggled into a poem's delivery system as "voice" or "tone." It has become the formal itself.

Yet the question of how many poems there are becomes a particularly pressing one as Bloom elaborates his literary history. On the one hand, no poem can mean anything independently in this system. As with other formalist accounts, the meaning of a poem must be another poem, because the relationship or contrast between one poem and another is the only thing that enables one to have a poem that is not merely a version of the most extreme subjectivism on the part of the reader. On the other hand, Bloom can justly describe this as a "story of intra-poetic relationships" (5) and can say that individual poems are all part of the one great poem that is continuously being written, because an individual poem can come into being only by means of the existence of another individual poem. Like a poetic version of the children's game the Farmer in the Dell, in which the individuals are brought into existence as direct by-products of their relationships to other individuals, the unity of all poetry is essential for there to be either individual poems or multiple poems.

This much seems coherent and explicable in Bloom's system of literary history. It founds literary history on the strictly ahistorical grounds of formalism (in psychology, in poetry) and can thus assert without the slightest degree of embarrassment or confusion that a poem can reflect the influence of a poem that the writer had never read. Experience is, on this level, not an issue. Yet the question of anxiety in Bloom's account of influence introduces its own equivalent to the incongruously dramatic lyric speaker of the New Criticism. For anxiety comes to be the engine for the formalist machine, lending a motive to explain how the system of poem on poem came to produce itself as its own effect. Without anxiety, that is, it becomes impossible to say how the first poem in a sequence came to be a first poem; for anxiety is the force not of the earlier poem at all but of the later poem whose "strong reading" makes the earlier poet, as well as himself or herself, come into existence. (The farmer, that is, was not a farmer until he was taken by a wife.) The vocation of the poet becomes necessarily anxious, because it relies so thoroughly on someone else, the action of reception that one can never take into one's own hands.

Moreover, Bloom does not rely merely on the impossibility of one's knowing a poem or a person for what it, he, or she "really" is. The trajectory of his narrative also insists on the radical inequality of the various parties to the confrontation. One cannot, Bloom suggests, adequately engage the dead. Derrida has argued that a connection between writing and violence is inevitable rather than incidental. Writing, in his analysis of Jean-Jacques Rousseau's "Essai sur l'origine des langues," does not merely enable an individual human to speak in his or her own absence; it insists on the absence of the speaker, and in doing so, brings that absence about, wreaking its own violence on the persons whom it could be thought to represent. Bloom's argument about the "belatedness" of poets is something like the reverse of this. Whereas for Derrida self-expression is impossible in language because language constitutes itself as an assault on the notion of selfhood that might stand to be expressed, for Bloom self-expression is both inevitable and unsatisfactory. The poem of self-expression ceases to function as self-expression because its violence cannot count as an act of violence against one's poetic progenitor. If the Freudian treatment of family romance imagines that the fundamental inequality between fathers and sons, parents and children, may ultimately eventuate in a recognition of the mortality even of the father, then Bloom's narrative clings to the absoluteness of the inequality between living poet and dead poetic progenitor, the figure whom one could never possibly engage on equal terms. The history of poetry must then be the history of decline, because the individual poet comes into being as a poet through a process that involves his enacting a form of self-mutilation.[5] To be a poet, then, is to take on a fight that is, by definition, not to be won. For it is to contend with poetic ancestors whose invulnerability lies in their being dead. Derrida's speakers continually produce language in excess of intention, so that language comes to make intentional states both insufficient and superfluous. Bloom's poetic speakers, however, take formalism's problematic miracle, the ability to read the dead language of a poem (or any other document), as its own predicament. Poems, like persons, are for Bloom themselves examples of *nature morte* (understood not as still life but as dead and speechless nature). One could not, in this view, explain one's reading of a poem by recourse to the intentions of the person who wrote it, because the formalist psychological gesture is to insist that those intentions are certainly unknowable within the enlarged space of family romance. If this magnifies the place of poet-readers, the later interpreters who get to have their way with earlier poems, then Bloom's argument is that the self-generating aspect of poetry writing as poetry reading becomes the later poets' acts of violence on themselves rather than on their precursor poet. Like Joseph Lancaster's ingenious plans for making the students in his schools the instruments of their own punishment, Bloom's account of poetic violence converts the comparative harmlessness of textual indeterminacy into a poet's self-punishment. To be a poet is continually to get agency wrong. If understanding a precursor poet inevitably involves misprision, in a misreading that has only its "strength" to justify it, writing poetry is an action that is fatally suspended between a commitment to individual experience with intentions and effects and an acquiescence in a systematic literary history that renders such individual effects inconsequential. For the very pattern of writing a poem that is another poem, being a poet by virtue of being another poet, makes identity itself a tragic notion. Whether or not literary history tells a tale of the decline of poetry, poetry testifies to a feeling of decline that derives from one poet's inability to coincide with himself or herself.

While for Bloom the moral of Kant's reconfiguration of aesthetics is the primacy of individual psychology (which becomes generative because of its inability to found individuality), for Geoffrey Hartman it is a phenomenological encounter between nature and the human imagination. Here the notion of developmental psychology, of a growth of consciousness, reformulates what counts as an object. For the Freudian interpretation of psychology, of developing consciousness, with which Hartman works is less concerned to derive individual identity from objects, to make epistemology depend on ontology, than to epistemologize ontology, to make the identity of objects and persons involve an interpenetration between the ways in which one knows and the objects that one can know. His important *Wordsworth's Poetry: 1787–1814* essentially traces the development of Wordsworth's career—through 1814—as a charting of maturation, so that the poetry is everywhere seen as the story of "the growth of the poet's mind." "In some sense *emergence* itself, our unsteady growth into self-consciousness, became the subject" (xvi).

Hartman's project, thus characterized, might sound like an account of

Romantic solipsism or individual psychobiography. Yet his phenomenological reading makes "consciousness of consciousness" the story of the marriage of Wordsworth's mind to nature, the blending of consciousness and objects, so that the appearances of things no longer seem to be surfaces to be penetrated but are instead the object of the quest. This means that individuality is itself a peculiar oxymoron, because the relational aspects of perception become more important than a subject-object dichotomy would suggest. As Hartman puts it, "Things may be lost in each other but they are not lost to each other" (xvi). Identity is continually fluid, participating in the various objects that have become objects through what once would have counted as subjective perception.

The argument proceeds, then, by superimposing a series of narratives on one another. Ontogeny recapitulates phylogeny, as individual poetic development rehearses literary history. Thus, when Hartman recalls that he had "said somewhat dramatically" that "two powers . . . fought for [Wordsworth's] soul—Nature and Milton" (xiv), Milton becomes the name of an imagination of the separability of perception (imagination) and nature. Both individual poems and Wordsworth's individual poetic history become the more and less miniature examples of the progress of poetry, as they represent in smaller and larger units the modulation away from the visionariness that would have separated the terms. An acceptance of nature, as opposed to its repudiation in sublime visionariness, comes to represent for Hartman "Wordsworth's great counter-myth to Milton: that Nature itself led him beyond nature and to the borders of vision" (xv).

Romantic nature poetry is for Hartman, then, not the site of simplicity, of the naturalness of nature, but of phenomenological contest, in which nature becomes an antagonist to individual consciousness: "Nature, time, memory, and poetry itself, can only fitfully bind an imagination which is radically in excess of nature as of every socializing principle" (211). In this description, "imagination" moves into synonymy with "disequilibrium" or "untranslatability." It is all that will not compute or find an adequate substitute or correlative. It is individual consciousness without an object, as Hartman indicates very clearly when he continues:

> If the word "imagination," because associated with "image," seems inappropriate to describe the special consciousness that brings a man home to himself, another term should be coined. Yet in one sense the term is quite appropriate, for what is popularly understood by imagination is the first, strong, "imaginal" reaction to this pointed and mortalizing state of mind. The images we associate with imagination are an antidote to self-consciousness drawn in part from consciousness itself. It is certainly true that wherever you find self-consciousness raised to a certain pitch there you will find imagination: cause and effect are so close, that they are, by metonymy, interchangeable.     (211)

Self-consciousness, in other words, can intensify to such a point that it can become its own opposite, anti–self-consciousness, by virtue of becoming imagination, with imagination being understood as something like fixation on images. Whereas imagination functions as a principle of transcendence in the moments in which it seems to tend toward casting out nature, imagination here functions in the opposite way, as a principle of immanence.

The conflict between imagination and nature, that is, does not merely get resolved; it becomes its own cure. For if nature and the imagination had seemed continually to present themselves as two, as fundamentally irreconcilable as things and persons, imagination becomes the human faculty of identifying with things. Imagination, by absorbing all of the elements of division into itself, becomes the means of establishing unity for all the terms outside itself. In other words, imagination, as soon as it can represent both consciousness and anti–self-consciousness, has rendered all other kinds of doubleness irrelevant or resolvable.

Hartman's recurrent and favored example of the operations of the imagination is that of the place. He, on the one hand, provides a literary historical genealogy for the idea of place as he identifies it in Wordsworth's poetry, in the form of the classical genius loci, the spirit of the place. He, on the other hand, makes this genealogy superfluous with the account he gives of imagination as attachment to times and places. And in his extension of Wordsworth's "spots of time" passages, from book 12 of *The Prelude*, to his identification of a more generalized "spot syndrome" in Wordsworth's poetry, he makes the phenomenological view of the imagination more important than the visionary, as the recurrent narrative is one in which places—in time and in space—function to reconcile the human and the natural that would compete in a visionary scheme. The "spots" materialize as interruptions of the Hegelian progressive narrative that Hartman sees Wordsworth's account of consciousness constructing. The pattern that he observes in the "spot" he locates in "The Vale of Esthwaite" recurs throughout his commentary: "What that spot signifies, what memory or deed it hides, is impossible to determine" (85). While the illegibility of the spot makes it unavailable for the purposes of knowledge, of maturation conceived as progressive understanding, the spot can nevertheless become a mediator between the human and the natural by operating as a force field that exerts its hold on them both. However incommensurable they may be from the standpoint of epistemology, they become equivalent as objects of the *idea* of a spot, a moving force without motive.

Hartman provides, then, a phenomenology of equivalence. What you can't know becomes what you can resemble by becoming subject to the same set of conditions. Yet when Paul de Man, in "Wordsworth and the Victorians," attacks Arnold's influential Wordsworth criticism, his line of argument suggests the ways in which this pattern of phenomenology is, from his standpoint, less distant from the visionary model that Hartman had substituted it for than might have been immediately apparent. For Hartman's reading has been willing to yield on the score of epistemology; phenomenology, in his handling of it, has identified itself with the renunciation of claims to knowledge. Yet in his depiction of the "spot syndrome," natural objects and human consciousness (by virtue of becoming the object of the force of the spot) become analogous, as Romantic self-consciousness has been reinterpreted to be anti–self-consciousness. Consciousness seems most itself when it becomes all that one thought of as its opposite—an object seen as the absence of thought.

This narrative of the oscillation between consciousness and anti–self-consciousness makes Romantic literature a depiction of the ways in which human consciousness can imitate an object, in an impersonation of thingness. And if such a concern figures prominently in much of de Man's work, his later efforts to describe a difference between phenomenality and materiality mark a change from this approach. What de Man identifies as the "prosaic materiality of the letter" builds the question of epistemological uncertainty—otherwise known as indeterminacy—into the ontological status of language itself. Jean-Paul Sartre, following Husserl, identified what he called the "hyletic ambivalence" of aesthetic objects as the ability of "one and the same impressional matter" to appear as a "thing-object or as an image-object" (*Imagination* 141). Similarly, de Man, following but also adapting Derrida, can be seen to use rhetoric and reference, process and phenomenon, as composite names for the "hyletic ambivalence" of written language itself. Another way of putting this point is to say that rhetorical tropes are not deviations from names or descriptions of objects but they become themselves objects; moreover, words and phonemes are, similarly, objects in themselves as well as parts of signs. And the deconstructive insight is that language does not simply fail to refer to objects, or fail to refer to them "adequately." Language does not fail to produce communication. Instead, it creates a communication that is always inadequate because the language that would be its mere medium has its own ontological status. By being an object, that is, language always makes the medium of knowledge operate as its own static, the ontological that continually exceeds any epistemological claims that might seem to be at issue. If deconstruction opposes itself to the view that objects are constructed to carry consciousness and intentions in them, the mark of that opposition occurs in its insistence on language as an ongoing proliferation of understandings, explanations, and references that does not merely fail to saturate a context but makes the context in principle unfillable. For it is expanding that context, producing more things in the form of words, even as it is filling it with accounts of objects and expressions of consciousness.

The deconstructive position lays stress on the tension between epistemology and ontology, not merely to emphasize the impossibility of arriving at *a* (much less, *the*) correct interpretation of anything but also to suggest that the intentional self loses control of meaning in the moment that intentions have to be entrusted to objects that are always, themselves, multiple. This position is frequently seen to lead to political quietism, to an undermining of the notion of agency that involves what de Man (rather melodramatically) sees as language's innocently lacking sense (*Allegories* 293).

Against the New Critical incorporation of all possible meanings into a textual object, de Man sets the opacity of such objects to any and all interpreters. In his reading of Rousseau's descriptions of his theft of a ribbon and his false naming of Marion, de Man traces out the narrative of the movement from phenomenality to materiality that will be the subject of his "Phenomenality and Materiality in Kant." In "Excuses" the gesture of describing the progression from one interpretation to another yields to the identification of "Marion" as neither a name that refers to a person nor the name for Rousseau's psychological projection; it is simply "noise." Similarly, in "Phenomenality and Materiality in Kant" he sets out from Kant's use of examples of sublimity—the heavens as a vault, the ocean seen as poets see it—to get at "what the eye reveals" rather than at the sensory appearance of the idea (*Ideenschein* for Hegel). This line of argument makes it possible for him to challenge Kant's heuristic description of the aesthetic as "guaranteeing the architectonic unity of the system" by bridging the gap between the pure reason and the practical reason, the domains of the human perception of the external world and of the freedom of moral self-determination. For de Man's claim is that the examples of flatness, of what appears to the eye, mark the aesthetic as materiality per se and thus indicate that Kant is, in providing an account of aesthetics as materiality, undoing "the very project" of producing a system based on "transcendental and ideological (metaphysical) principles" (143).

The example of "Marion," the examples of the flatness of the starry heavens or the ocean, and the related account that de Man gives in "Pascal's Allegory of Persuasion" all conduce to the same end: they convert a process of accumulating interpretations or elements of a series of analogous things (such as numbers) into a process of discarding those elements, as if merely by following the elements of a serial progression, one would arrive at something entirely different. To make this move is to imagine that materiality might come to be an available notion, that one might, as de Man seemed to be suggesting in his depiction of a "linguistic moment," find a way of cordoning off the ontology of language from epistemology. And while it would be correct for de Man to claim that the successive explications he gives of the name "Marion" are all equally available, the basic point to be made is that they all rely on their availability because of the materiality of the "noise" "Marion." There is, in other words, no sequential development that enables one to progress from a straightforwardly referential account, to a psychologically complex referential account, to a metaphorical or substitutive account, to the purely material account of "Marion" as "noise." The "noise," far from being the punch line of the narrative, never conceals or reveals itself any more or any less at any given point in narrative time. It only testifies to the ways in which the materiality of language involves language in an endless doubleness, a hyletic ambivalence that can make individual words look like their own quotations, as the material version of a name (its being "noise") faces off against the nominal or referential version of matter (its being a "name"). The deconstructive emphasis on the simultaneously material and formal aspects of language enables de Man to argue that the fact of something's having been said is no proof of anything other than the existence of the linguistic material. The "noise" makes multiple interpretations possible by rendering it impossible to tell from the material at hand what difference any intention or reference might make.

Whereas the New Criticism had emphasized the inevitable multiplication of meanings as a result of the ambiguity of literary meaning, de Man compounds ambiguity with the ambivalence of the linguistic sign itself. Even the smallest, most self-identical unit (the name, the phoneme) fails to be identical with itself, because the linguistic sign is part matter (the signifier), part intention or performance (the signified). But in making it look as though this ambivalence could ever be reduced to a narrative in which the "meanings" of language could lead to the "materiality" of language (as if matter were one meaning among others), de Man vitiates the force of his own argument, which is, properly speaking, a version of Heidegger's adaptation of the Kantian transcendental *Ding an sich* for materialism.

It is in the understanding of materialism that de Man's position provokes "a certain unexpected convergence," as Terry Eagleton happily puts it, with Marxist accounts of materialism. For although many have seen Marxist materialism as precisely a form of the determinism that de Man repudiates in repudiating formalism, Eagleton finds himself "in entire agreement" with de Man's view that "aesthetic ideology involves a phenomenalist reduction of the linguistic to the sensuously empirical, a confusing of mind and world, sign and thing, cognition and percept, which is consecrated in the Hegelian symbol and resisted by Kant's rigorous demarcation of aesthetic judgment from the cognitive, ethical and political realms." The formal move, for both, is the ideological move. It is ideological, moreover, because it is, in Eagleton's words, "in danger of converting the accidents of meaning to organic natural process in the characteristic manner of ideological thought" (*Ideology of the Aesthetic* 10).

Materialism thus comes to be the name of indeterminacy, which can look political because it reads formalism as a process of imagining that sequences are themselves versions of mastery and servitude. As a totalitarian government is to the innocent individual, formalism is to the innocent word or phoneme. Thus Eagleton can proclaim that the aesthetic "represents on the one hand a liberatory concern with concrete particularity, and on the other hand a specious form of universalism" (9), and de Man can argue that the crowning achievement of Kant's *Critique of Judgment* occurs when Kant, "that most inconspicuous of stylists," turns out to be untranslatable and one notices "how decisively determining the play of the letter and of the syllable, the way of saying (*Art des Sagens*) as opposed to what is being said (*das Gesagte*)" is ("Phenomenality" 144).

As for Lovejoy and McGann, so for Eagleton and de Man. The particularity of materiality becomes a model for the political in the moment in which formalism, as opposed to materialism, seems like an inappropriate conversion of the accidental and contingent into the model of internal unity and internal self-regulation that had seemed so central to Romantic accounts of the natural organism. Materialism, that is, seems to avoid misreading accidents as design and thus seems to avoid the violent, totalizing gesture that even the making of sense out of sense has come, from this perspective, to entail (thus the bodies and the mutilations of bodies that de Man establishes as analogues to the material of language and the rhetorical formalization of them).

The irony of this view of materialism, however, is that it repeats the argument for organic unity—not a letter or a syllable could be different—as if it were a refutation of that argument. For the classic formulations of the notion of organic unity in Goethe, in Schelling, in Coleridge—all resolve themselves into the same claim—which is less that the whole governs the individual parts than that the individual and particular parts cannot be changed. In other words, everything that can be seen as an element—every letter or syllable—comes to look like a vital organ. De Man's progressive restriction of the range of his analysis—the individual word ("Marion"), the syllable, the letter—may change the scale on which the organic argument works, but it alters nothing fundamental about its contours or its force.

Although some Marxist critics have, as Eagleton says, dismissed de Man's position as merely a version of formalism, the point of convergence between a political account and a linguistic account is that both make the claim that what we call nature is actually culture, a culture enabled, legitimated, and freed to oppress by virtue of its looking like nature. What we count as natural, the argument goes, we take as a causal principle, as a law of nature. And reversing that collapse of the natural into the human therefore seems to count as a demystification of illegitimate political might. If we apply such an interpretation to any natural-rights theory of government, or to any conjectural history of the origins of society from the state of nature, we can convincingly make the case that de Man and Derrida make—that nature turns out to resemble civil society "as we know it," that it, in its invariable misapplication, becomes evidence of the self-evidence of society in its current configuration.

If society's territorial imperative in relation to nature is the disease, then materialism, whether Marxist or deconstructive, would restore nature to us. In the light of deconstruction's insight into the similarities between returns to nature and returns to culture, this claim may sound hopelessly counterintuitive. The "unexpected convergence" between de Man and Eagleton emerges, however, in a curious logic of objects. Through a series of gliding emphases, the claim that the interpretation of any linguistic object does not yield a single or univocal meaning becomes, in de Man's hands, the rationale for seeing language as if it were nature. Language may have appeared to distinguish humans from animals; language may look as though it were getting made by humans every time they open their mouths. Yet the veritable frenzy of all this linguistic activity suggests, for de Man, its inefficacy. The multiplicity of human meanings becomes evidence for deconstructive materialism of meaning's inability to "take," to become part of an object. Marxism, in the mode of McGann or Eagleton, would challenge the legitimacy of the constructs that naturalize our cultured world; deconstructive materialism, in the mode of de Man, would demonstrate the collapse of those constructs even in the moment of their apparent application (as when there may be differences of opinion about the idea or the interpretation of a word, but what remains unaltered is the persistence of the matter, the "noise").

Kant's account of aesthetics had made the sublime in general and the beautiful in part an occasion for examining what one perceives in objects without intentions. The deconstructive materialist understanding of this insight has been to see it as presenting a false analogy between subjects and objects, an analogy that ultimately converts objects into pseudosubjectivities; the Marxist materialist understanding emphasizes the ways in which the notion of aesthetic autonomy enables aesthetic objects to establish themselves as exemplars of a "specious universalism" (Eagleton, *Ideology of the Aesthetic* 9). In both cases, the repudiation of consciousness in materialism goes beyond a claim about the impossibility of making subjects and objects equivalent. In both cases, the truth of consciousness is not objectivity (in the sense of grounding itself on objects) but becoming object-like (in the sense of likening itself to objects). And the progressive reduction in scale—de Man's concern with the phoneme, Eagleton's interest in particularity—demonstrates a common project: to produce more objects. Deconstruction thus discovers objects in objects (in a reinterpretation of "properties" of things as things themselves), while Marxist materialism discovers individuals in universals. Individuals have been likened to objects in a way that converts what once seemed like the privacy of the individual—mental reservation—into the physical reservation of the object. For both versions of materialism, the possibility of that reserve calls out for ceaseless iteration, the particularization of particularity, the production of more objects out of partial objects.

De Man is right to suggest that context does not determine meaning;

Eagleton is doubtless right to point to the difficulties involved in the Marxist analysis of base and superstructure. They are right, however, in their answers to misformulated questions. For these descriptions conceive context, base, superstructure, and ideas as objects, when the relationship between one object and another is every bit as indeterminate as materialism suggests. In a thoroughly material world, things fail to determine other things, and by virtue of that failure they also fail to become things. Trying to have objects without intentions turns out to be having no objects at all. While objects can exist even for an aesthetic experience that does not postulate original constructive intention, Kantian aesthetics (as Derrida suggests in his *Truth in Painting*, esp. 119–47) indicates how deeply some notion of intentionality counts toward establishing a thing as a thing.

The "unexpected convergence" between a Marxist materialism and a deconstructive materialism occurs, ultimately, in a claim about how many natures there are. What I have been arguing is that the Romantic "discovery" of nature that Kantian aesthetics epitomizes is every bit as important as everyone has said. What I have also been arguing is that this "discovery" does not involve empirical reality, an acceptance of nature as a universal ground for human experience. Human pleasure in nature did not come to represent realism or empirical reality, what we must face up to, but became the enabling example for an argument on behalf of formal idealism. Yet far from being escapist or unreal, Romantic formal idealism remains as real as it gets. Our pleasure in nature and our scientific knowledge of it are alike important for identifying not reality but reality production as an inescapable process of supplying intentional states to the very matter that we identify as incapable of having intentional states. If deconstructive materialism and Marxist materialism combine to depict materialism as a commitment to the material conditions of production (the noise or inscription that is the matter of speech or writing), they do so by imagining the intentional states that are the necessary conditions of phenomenological experience as themselves the problem. What the legacy of Romantic thought demonstrates is how far the nonmaterial extends. The mere act of seeing the world of matter as nature makes ideology less a cultural construction than an assertion of the constructedness of seeing a world of things.

### Notes

[1]I should state, quite baldly, that I use *formalism* and *formal idealism* as descriptive rather than evaluative terms. Insofar as they are value words in my account, they are positive rather than pejorative.

[2]I find de Man's "Intentional Structure of the Romantic Nature Image" a partic-

ularly powerful essay in large measure for having understood the force of aesthetic intention by way of Husserlian phenomenology. See H. Bloom, *Romanticism* 65–77.

[3]Obviously, this account of the New Criticism sees the affective fallacy as an inadequate retreat from the implications that had been set in motion by the intentional fallacy, particularly in the discussion of an interpreter's ability to appeal to a verbal meaning that was, on the basis of all lexicographical evidence available, nonexistent to a given author. See Wimsatt and Beardsley's discussion in "The Intentional Fallacy" of the significance of the word *vegetable* in Marvell's "To His Coy Mistress."

[4]Bloom's interest in formal taxonomies—the various types of influence that he elaborates—from this vantage looks like an effort to formulate the psychological so that it will involve neither the diagnostic terms of psychoanalysis nor the rhetorical terms of literary analysis.

[5]Gilbert and Gubar have noted the maleness of Bloom's line of poetic influence and have provided their own account of a female line in *The Madwoman in the Attic*.

## Selected Bibliography

Aers, David, Jonathan Cook, and David Punter. *Romanticism and Ideology: Studies in English Writing, 1765–1830*. London: Routledge, 1981.
Discussing writers from Blake to Hazlitt, the three authors provide accounts of the social relations of Romantic writing.

Averill, James. *Wordsworth and the Poetry of Human Suffering*. Ithaca: Cornell UP, 1980.
This study provides both a context for and an analysis of the place of sentiment in Wordsworth's poetry.

Bewell, Alan. *Wordsworth and the Enlightenment: Nature, Man, and Society in the Experimental Poetry*. New Haven: Yale UP, 1989.
Drawing on social as well as literary history, Bewell situates Wordsworth's early poetry in context and makes literary periodization itself epitomize the difficulty of identifying context.

Bialostosky, Don. *Making Tales: The Poetics of Wordsworth's Narrative Experiments*. Chicago: U of Chicago P, 1984.
Bialostosky emphasizes the dialogic relationship between Wordsworth and Coleridge in the production of *Lyrical Ballads*.

Bloom, Harold, Paul de Man, Jacques Derrida, Geoffrey Hartman, and J. Hillis Miller. *Deconstruction and Criticism*. New York: Seabury, 1979.
The essays in this volume combine commentary on Romantic texts with assessment of the place of deconstructive criticism.

Brisman, Leslie. *Milton's Poetry of Choice and Its Romantic Heirs*. Ithaca: Cornell UP, 1973.
Brisman uses the competing claims of active choice and passive influence

to discuss literary transmission in the case of the Romantics' relationship to Milton.

———. *Romantic Origins*. Ithaca: Cornell UP, 1978.

Linking Romantic imagination with the dream of autogenesis, Brisman argues for the primacy of poets' myths of the past over biographical and historical facts.

Butler, Marilyn. *Romantics, Rebels, and Reactionaries: English Literature and Its Background, 1760–1830*. New York: Oxford UP, 1982.

Butler distinguishes between the revolutionary context of Romantic writing and that writing itself to challenge simplistic identifications of political and poetic revolutions.

Chandler, James. *Wordsworth's Second Nature: A Study of the Poetry and Politics*. Chicago: U of Chicago P, 1984.

Chandler offers a detailed political argument that Edmund Burke and his intense pleadings on behalf of custom inform much of Wordsworth's major poetry.

Chase, Cynthia. *Decomposing Figures: Rhetorical Readings in the Romantic Tradition*. Baltimore: Johns Hopkins UP, 1986.

In chapters on Wordsworth and Keats, Chase provides interpretations that exemplify an emphasis on the rhetoricity of literary texts.

Christensen, Jerome. *Coleridge's Blessed Machine of Language*. Ithaca: Cornell UP, 1981.

Emphasizing Coleridge's critique of David Hartley's philosophy of association, Christensen illuminates the significance of Coleridge's fragmentary discourse.

Curran, Stuart. *Poetic Form and British Romanticism*. New York: Oxford UP, 1986.

Curran challenges psychologically and historically based interpretations in this sustained argument that Romantic poets did not so much abandon the traditional genres as intensify and revive them.

Eaves, Morris, and Michael Fischer, eds. *Romanticism and Contemporary Criticism*. Ithaca: Cornell UP, 1986.

The essays in this collection explore the impact of both recent critical modes and Romanticism.

Ellison, Julie. *Delicate Subjects: Romanticism, Gender, and the Ethics of Understanding*. Ithaca: Cornell UP, 1990.

Ellison treats Schleiermacher, Coleridge, and Fuller in the course of framing an argument "that gender is the site of self-consciousness about understanding, that theories of understanding are the site for reflection on interpretive ethics, and that ethical discourse is the site of gender awareness" (iii).

Ferguson, Frances. *Wordsworth: Language as Counter-spirit*. New Haven: Yale UP, 1977.

Ferguson emphasizes Wordsworth's views as they suggest the ways in which the self is produced by the alternate consciousness and automatism of language.

Fry, Paul H. *The Poet's Calling in the English Ode*. New Haven: Yale UP, 1980.

Fry treats the ode as epitomizing the transmission of claims of poetic vocation and influence.

Galperin, William. *Revision and Authority in Wordsworth: The Interpretation of a Career*. Philadelphia: U of Pennsylvania P, 1989.

Galperin challenges the common judgment that Wordsworth's career involved one great decade (1797–1807) and a long anticlimax, in arguing for the poet's commitment to revision.

Hertz, Neil. *The End of the Line: Essays on Psychoanalysis and the Sublime*. New York: Columbia UP, 1985.

In readings primarily informed by both psychoanalysis and a deconstructive, rhetorical approach, Hertz identifies the sublime in terms of an avoidance of closure.

Hogle, Jerrold E. *Shelley's Process: Radical Transference and the Development of His Major Works*. New York: Oxford UP, 1988.

Hogle sees Shelley's evanescent style not as obscuring some determinate meaning but as indicating a poetics of sublimation and self-veiling.

Jacobus, Mary. *Romanticism, Writing, and Sexual Difference: Essays on* The Prelude. Oxford: Clarendon–Oxford UP, 1990.

Jacobus's book combines both historical and theoretical concerns to discuss Romantic politics (sexual and otherwise).

———. *Tradition and Experiment in Wordsworth's* Lyrical Ballads (*1798*). Oxford: Clarendon–Oxford UP, 1966.

This examination of Wordsworth's early poetry both assesses its major influences and charts its departures from earlier models.

Johnston, Kenneth R. *Wordsworth and "The Recluse."* New Haven: Yale UP, 1984.

Johnston argues that "The Recluse" forms the rationale for Wordsworth's other poetry and demonstrates the poet's increasing commitment to a poetry of "human life."

Johnston, Kenneth R., and Gene Ruoff. *The Age of William Wordsworth: Critical Essays on the Romantic Tradition*. New Brunswick: Rutgers UP, 1987.

This collection includes essays on the Romantic era, its forms, and its legacy.

Johnston, Kenneth R., et al. *Romantic Revolutions: Criticism and Theory.* Bloomington: Indiana UP, 1990.
The essays chart the impact of political and theoretical readings of Romanticism.

Keach, William. *Shelley's Style.* New York: Routledge, 1985.
Keach ranges from Englightenment linguistic theory to versification in his account of the significance of language in Shelley's poetry.

Kelley, Theresa M. *Wordsworth's Revisionary Aesthetics.* New York: Cambridge UP, 1988.
Kelley explores Wordsworth's conflict between the poles of the sublime, self-transcendence, and the beautiful, or escape from the sublime's potential egotism.

Klancher, Jon P. *The Making of English Reading Audiences, 1790–1832.* Madison: U of Wisconsin P, 1987.
Drawing on a wide range of materials, Klancher identifies the place of Romantic literature in relation to newly emergent readerships.

Knapp, Steven. *Personification and the Sublime: Milton to Coleridge.* Cambridge: Harvard UP, 1985.
Knapp discusses the importance of the Romantic interest in personification in identifying the place of literature, its claims, and its hazards.

Levinson, Marjorie. *Keats's Life of Allegory: The Origins of a Style.* Oxford: Blackwell, 1988.
The author emphasizes the outraged reviews of Keats's poems to discuss, in particular, the production of middle-class literariness.

———. *The Romantic Fragment Poem.* Chapel Hill: U of North Carolina P, 1986.
Levinson argues that the formal features of the Romantic fragment poem are comprehensible in the light of historical projections.

———. *Wordsworth's Great Period Poems.* Cambridge: Cambridge UP, 1986.
Reading "Tintern Abbey," "Michael," the Intimations Ode, and "Peele Castle," Levinson sees Wordsworth's poetry as embodying a substitution of poetry for politics.

Liu, Alan. *Wordsworth: The Sense of History.* Stanford: Stanford UP, 1989.
Liu stresses, in his account of Wordsworth's changes in genre (from a narrative, historical mode to a more lyric and ahistorical mode), the poet's denial of contemporary culture.

Lockridge, Laurence S. *The Ethics of Romanticism.* Cambridge: Cambridge UP, 1989.
Lockridge, challenging the critical dismissal of ethics in Romanticism, argues for the centrality of ethical concerns.

Manning, Peter J. *Reading Romantics: Texts and Contexts*. New York: Oxford UP, 1990.
The essays fuse psychoanalytic, textual, and historical scholarship in discussions of Wordsworth and Byron.

McFarland, Thomas. *Romanticism and the Forms of Ruin: Wordsworth, Coleridge, and Modalities of Fragmentation*. Princeton: Princeton UP, 1981.
This study explores the concern with unitariness and fragmentariness in an uncovering of Romantic phenomenology.

McGann, Jerome J., ed. *Historical Studies and Literary Criticism*. Madison: U of Wisconsin P, 1985.
Various writers support both textual historical scholarship and an understanding of the political circumstance of literature.

Mellor, Anne K., ed. *Romanticism and Feminism*. Bloomington: Indiana UP, 1988.
These essays use both current feminist approaches and historical investigation of Romantic feminism.

Mitchell, W. J. T. *Blake's Composite Art: A Study of the Illuminated Poetry*. Princeton: Princeton UP, 1978.
Mitchell, analyzing the verbal and visual elements of Blake's art, argues that the visual does not so much illustrate the verbal as establish an opposing dialogue with it.

Modiano, Raimonda. *Coleridge and the Concept of Nature*. Tallahassee: Florida State UP, 1985.
Modiano traces the Romantic concept of nature with particular reference to the picturesque, the sublime, and the symbolic.

Parker, Reeve. *Coleridge's Meditative Art*. Ithaca: Cornell UP, 1975.
Parker examines Coleridge's meditative poems less as an expression of dejection than as a victory over morbid desolation.

Rajan, Tillotama. *Dark Interpreter: The Discourse of Romanticism*. Ithaca: Cornell UP, 1980.
Rajan charts the shift of the Romantic conception of artistic creation from a naive to a consciously ambivalent one that establishes a constant tension between illusion and its destruction.

———. *The Supplement of Reading: Figures of Understanding in Romantic Theory and Practice*. Ithaca: Cornell UP, 1990.
The writer discusses the relationship between hermeneutics, deconstruction, and cultural criticism in "structurally unsettled" literary texts.

Reed, Arden, ed. *Romanticism and Language*. Ithaca: Cornell UP, 1984.
The essays stress rhetorically oriented readings.

Robinson, Jeffrey. *The Walk: Notes on a Romantic Image*. Norman: U of Oklahoma P, 1989.
    Robinson presents a phenomenologically inflected reading of the importance of the walk as a social and literary key term for Romanticism.
Roe, Nicholas. *Wordsworth and Coleridge: The Radical Years*. Oxford: Clarendon–Oxford UP, 1988.
    Roe situates Wordsworth and Coleridge in the context of the revolutionary debate in England.
Ross, Marlon B. *The Contours of Masculine Desire: Romanticism and the Rise of Women's Poetry*. New York: Oxford UP, 1989.
    Ross analyzes the evolution of women's poetry in terms of the intersections between the Romantic ideology and masculinist assumptions.
Scrivener, Michael Henry. *Radical Shelley: The Philosophical Anarchism and Utopian Thought of Percy Bysshe Shelley*. Princeton: Princeton UP, 1982.
    Committed to disputing the view of Shelley as a recondite poet, this study emphasizes the political character of even the seemingly apolitical poetry.
Shaffer, E. S. *"Kubla Khan" and* The Fall of Jerusalem: *The Mythological School in Biblical Criticism and Secular Literature, 1770–1880*. Cambridge: Cambridge UP, 1975.
    Shaffer both describes the evolution of the mythological school of European biblical criticism and demonstrates its impact on the work of Coleridge and other nineteenth-century writers.
Simpson, David. *Irony and Authority in Romantic Poetry*. London: Macmillan, 1979.
    In readings of Blake, Wordsworth, Coleridge, Shelley, and Keats, Simpson links ironic language and the instability of the autonomous ego.
——. *Wordsworth and the Figurings of the Real*. Atlantic Highlands: Humanities, 1982.
    The work traces the problem of the figurativeness, or unreliability, of perception in Wordsworth's poetry.
——. *Wordsworth's Historical Imagination: The Poetry of Displacement*. New York: Methuen, 1987.
    Simpson looks to Romantic debates on issues such as the poor laws and property to argue that even the possibility of privacy is socially circumstanced.
Siskin, Clifford. *The Historicity of Romantic Discourse*. New York: Oxford UP, 1988.
    As an analysis of the "discursive power of English Romanticism," Siskin's book is committed to understanding the "imaginative mind" as "a culture-specific product."

Sperry, Stuart M. *Shelley's Major Verse: The Narrative and Dramatic Poetry.* Cambridge: Harvard UP, 1988.
In a new reading of the major poetry, Sperry emphasizes Shelley's extreme idealism.

Tannenbaum, Leslie. *Biblical Tradition in Blake's Early Prophecies: The Great Code of Art.* Princeton: Princeton UP, 1982.
Tannenbaum considers how biblical texts, refracted through the critical and exegetical traditions surrounding them, shaped Blake's early prophetic works.

Vendler, Helen. *The Odes of John Keats.* Cambridge: Harvard UP, 1983.
Vendler offers readings that take the individual poems as microcosms of the artistic potentialities of the language.

Weiskel, Thomas. *The Romantic Sublime: Studies in the Structure and Psychology of Transcendence.* Baltimore: Johns Hopkins UP, 1976.
Examining a variety of Romantic texts in terms of questions posed by psychoanalysis and structural linguistics, Weiskel focuses on the importance of the sublime in the Romantic period.

Wolfson, Susan. *The Questioning Presence: Wordsworth, Keats, and the Interrogative Mode in Romantic Poetry.* Ithaca: Cornell UP, 1986.
Rather than emphasize particular rhetorical figures, Wolfson examines a mode, the interrogative, and its significance for Romantic poetry.

# $\mathcal{V}$ictorian Studies

## GEORGE LEVINE

One of the great ironies of the extraordinary increase in interest in things Victorian within the academy during the last twenty-five years is that, although it has emerged most effectively from the left, it is contemporary with a similar growth of interest in Victorianism in politics and commerce and culture, of Margaret Thatcher and Laura Ashley and the National Trust, where it is clearly a reaction against the left. A preoccupation with Victorian objects can reflect an ideological emphasis on the ordinary, of daily life, of "unimportant" people in the life of a culture, or it can be a symptom of a new monied elitism, an acquisitive rather than a democratic or socialist thrust. That strange combination emerged in the work of Walter Scott 175 years ago, as he provoked a new concern for the texture of ordinary life and romanticized the past into a set of objects for purchase by ambitious writers and rich readers. The figure of William Morris, that brilliant and enormously talented first major English Marxist, might stand as a further emblem of the irony of this story, its unresolved tensions. Morris wallpapers and ties are now expensively worn and displayed and recognized as in good taste; his politics don't enter the marketplace of Liberty prints.

This unresolved tension in contemporary attitudes corresponds to a tension recognizable among many of the canonical Victorians themselves—in Ruskin and Morris in particular, but in Dickens and George Eliot as well. Victorian studies are often, even against their own most deliberate intentions, very Victorian indeed—political and formalist at once, subversive and reactionary, historicist and idealist. Within the academy, the emergence of Victorian literature as a serious object of study—as serious as the Renaissance, say, or Romanticism—was generated by critics like Raymond Williams, sustained even by such politically hostile inheritors as Terry Eagleton and students of popular culture like Richard Hoggart, and it flourishes among such ideologically engaged feminist critics as Mary Poovey, Nancy Armstrong, and Nina Auerbach. Victorian fiction is central to the radical theoretical positioning of Fredric Jameson and Edward Said; Bakhtin needed Dickens as a central case for his dialogic theory. And, more conservatively, within a tradition of Victorian scholarship that culminated with Cook and Wedderburn's prodigious and expensive edition of Ruskin, fascination with the Victorians has led to the production of astonishing scholarly monuments like, for example, editions of the letters of Thackeray, George Eliot, Newman, Darwin, and Carlyle (still in progress). Definitive editions have been in the works, at last, for Dickens, Eliot, and Tennyson (Ricks), for example; and Christina Rossetti was ushered into the canon by way of an important new edition of her poetry. Such an explosion of Victorian activity, even in its most "objective" forms, is full of political implications and reflective, most distinctly, of the explosion of the profession of English studies itself.

Too much has happened both in the profession and in Victorian studies in the last twenty-five years to make the telling of its story so straightforward a matter as this opening narrative may have implied. This volume as a whole testifies to the difficulties and arbitrariness of redrawing the boundaries of literary study and must question the very nature of "boundaries" in the act of affirming them. Yet it assumes, as I assume, that the activity is worth it. Telling the story of boundaries is as important as the boundaries to be established—especially since it is too late to imagine that they can be anything other than provisional—of this time, this place. And to discuss developments in the study of Victorian literature over the last quarter century or so, it will be necessary to tell one or several stories, recognizing each as peculiarly situated in a perspective, a moment, a historical and a distinctively professional place.

There is no single voice—certainly not mine—that can speak the plurality of Victorianisms; nor, given the implication of any narrative in the structures of contemporary discourse, is there a way to write a reconstruction of the constructions of Victorianism that will be outside those constructions. Moreover, although the critical wars among Victorianists have been relatively muted—compared at least with the battles fought in other areas—the enormous changes in Victorian scholarship have not come naturally. That scholarship would seem to have reflected its subject in emphasizing realism and referentiality, "character" and moral intention, and interpretative conclusiveness; and while this may be an oversimplification, the rejection of all these tendencies by modern criticism in almost any of its theoretical variations has entailed some significant contestation. My own relation to these positions and my understanding of what is entailed in rejecting or modifying them leads me to write now with a bias built from a career that began, as it were, somewhat to the left of Carnegie Hall, with the rejection of formalism for historicism and proceeded through a moment when historicism became infected by textualism. Not so surprisingly, then, I will produce a notion of a field that finds its new strengths in just that historicism and that infection. My skepticism about my own perspective has not reduced my confidence that, in whatever complicated way, Victorianism has remained a working and workable concept: its literature still needs to be thought of within the terms of a traditional description I will be offering, but that description must be reconfigured within a cluster of alternatives to which it is related and must be subject to fundamental linguistic and historical skepticism.

There has always been the problem, to begin with, of the "make-believe of a beginning," but there is the further problem of continuity and causality. Much recent criticism of Victorian fiction aims at exposing the discontinuities disguised by the strategies of coherence by which novelists make sense of their "stories." Yet I will attempt to construct continuities and coherence, suggest causalities, and mediate between discourse and an extratextual history even while recognizing that history is a discourse.

And then, of course, there is the old problem of "Victorian" literature—one that has been exacerbated by the dominant critical movements of the last quarter century. In what ways can it make sense to identify a literary period, Victorian or otherwise, to impose arbitrary dates on it, to imply some kind of coherence if not unity about the cultural artifacts of the time, and to distinguish them from those created in other periods? And there is the other obvious question: What use is there in deciding on that particular focus of attention?

The convenience of the term *Victorian* needs emphasizing. Unlike the Romantic period, Victorian literature is cut off by extrinsic facts: Queen Victoria's ascension to the throne, in 1837, and her death, in 1901. Of course, the facts themselves emphasize the arbitrariness of the construction (it is impossible, for example, to teach Victorian literature without reference to *Sartor Resartus* [1833]), and the plurality of Victorian cultures and literatures even within that frame make discussion of something as specifically "Victorian" awkwardly reductive. The inadequacy of any conception of the Victorian has, however, done nothing to diminish my sense of the necessity of thinking about literature within such a defined historical frame. In the case of the Victorians, the history of our contemporary professional and disciplinary development comfortably meshes with their texts.

Victorian literature had, when I began teaching it, a roughly agreed-on set of characteristics, problems, preoccupations. These characteristics were codified in the indispensable background works to literary study, most significantly Basil Willey's *Nineteenth Century Studies* and *More Nineteenth Century Studies*, Jerome Hamilton Buckley's *Victorian Temper* and Walter Houghton's *Victorian Frame of Mind*, books that offered a view of the Victorian as abundant, complicated, and at least intellectually contestatory but also as relatively unproblematic and coherent. From the perspective of the present, these still useful ventures in definition seem guilty of a naive critical humanism in their emphasis on an "intentional" and predominantly intellectual milieu; on individual creative artists and thinkers who defined through their work the problems and solutions in Victorian culture; on historical cause and effect; and on an essential Victorianism characterized by the ravages of doubt, by resistance to its dominant social conditions and to the capitalism that shaped it, and by a wary commitment to the secular and progressive.

On this accounting, Victorian literature, which seemed in the hierarchy of periods to be least satisfying formally at a moment of emphatic critical formalism, was located romantically somewhere around the death of the exuberance of Romanticism itself, in the enormous expansions of empire, though darkened by the industrial revolution and urbanization. Intellectually and morally, it was riven and defined by the debate laid out in Mill's essays on Coleridge and Bentham (the two "seminal minds" of the nineteenth century)— as F. R. Leavis codified them; it was solemnized by the growth of a Podsnapian middle class; further darkened by the loss of God (which became, subtly, his disappearance in J. Hillis Miller's book of 1963); marred by a false, Tennysonian optimism and a vulgar Dickensian sentimentality, with a fiction that seemed loose and baggy and a poetry that seemed watered-down Romantic; awkwardly moralized and set in the abundance of household bric-a-brac, where Romanticism struggled with morality, high seriousness with domestic banality; and finally it died symbolically with Victoria but in reality with post-Darwinian decadence and degeneration, Paterian and Wildean aestheticism, Lord Kelvin's announcement of entropy and the heat death, as scientific optimism fell to the bleak news science brought. In such a Victorian vision, larger than any of its multiplot, nineteen-part novels, or its vast narrative poems, like the *Idylls of the King* or *The Ring and the Book*, was God's (or no-God's) plenty for criticism and scholarship.

All of these tendencies are still recognizably Victorian, of course, but from here the formulations appear to have been radically simplified and ideologically selected: ideas seem too abruptly disconnected from the material conditions that produced them; *Victorianism* was too sharply defined by a radical split between a formalism shaped by modernist conservatism and a historicism that either leaned too heavily toward a mere intellectual accounting or insisted too insularly on an empiricism only vaguely connected to literary and cultural artifacts. Issues of gender complicate all the categories; notions of ideology make the science-religion battle seem like a diversion from issues of class, professionalization, and economics. The story is that students in the 1920s and 1930s would emerge from Emery Neff's classes at Columbia "thick with the dust of the industrial revolution"; such historicism, however, seems to have emphasized extraliterary context without quite getting around the terms the Victorians themselves used to describe that context. In the course of the past twenty-five years, the Victorian critique of Victorianism, by both its great voices and its modern critics, has been reread so as to emphasize the way criticism of middle-class individualism and laissez-faire economics could also, paradoxically, participate in them. This kind of revisionism, characteristic in particular of the work of new-historicist critics (and dependent, as I will be suggesting, on an emphasis on the medium rather than the meaning, on representation rather than the represented), implies that the great critical and historical works on Victorian literature and culture tended to disguise how fully scholarly imagination of the culture was itself culturally enclosed: how much it defined itself in the language the Victorians invented to shape and give meaning to the crises through which they lived.

The work of the last twenty-five years begins to mark a fundamental generational break, for whereas the fact of the Victorians' proximity was part of the excitement of such study, our power to see ourselves in the Victorians has become its greatest limitation. The sages' revulsion from the conditions of Victorian culture provided the terms of criticism (for example, Ruskin's remarkable lecture on traffic was routinely read as a satisfying and heroic exposure of capitalism bravely performed before the industrialist enemy); so modernism, even in its rejection of certain aspects of Victorianism, borrowed many of its high (moral) culture terms of critique from the Victorians themselves. The crucial break with this way of thinking came with a preoccupation with the textuality of history itself, the spuriousness of the idea of untheorized data, apart from the verbal medium in which they are recorded.

There are, it seems to me, two pronounced aspects to recent revisions of Victorianism: the textual and the ideological. They are intimately, although sometimes antagonistically, related. Perhaps not so oddly, these aspects correspond to the conventions of Victorian study that they implicitly criticize. The traditional emphasis in most literary studies was on philosophy, epistemology, "thought"—on such issues as the Victorian crisis of faith. This emphasis has been resisted and rejected by minority and gender studies, discourse theory, later Marxism, the new historicism, as they have sought to bring ideas, via the medium of representation, together with the dust-of-the-industrial-revolution studies through a preoccupation with ideology and with a culture's power to absorb individual resistance into its hegemony. There was also a strong postwar New Critical textualism, a literary formalism, which has been displaced by poststructuralist formalism and textualism—a pervasive preoccupation with language outside of which there is nothing. This textualism has at the same time made itself central to the ideological critique while forcing itself into that other primary tradition of Victorian studies—its preoccupation with history.

Thus the idea of the Victorian points not only backward to those years between 1837 and 1901 but forward to our own professional situation. The period is defined as much by how we choose professionally to imagine our fields as by its intrinsic qualities. That we choose differently now than we would have in the early 1960s has almost everything to do with the demographics of our profession, which in turn has everything to do with the social transformations of America through those years. The revisions in literary studies, and in the study of Victorian literature, correspond crucially to the fact that in the mid-1950s the country and academia were economically expansive. A new generation of faculty members from a much broader base of class and ethnic background moved uneasily into the high modernist formalism that, through Brooks and Warren, and an alliance of Yale and the Southern agrarians, like Allen Tate and John Crowe Ransom, had been determining the shape of literary education in the post–World War II years. For them, Victorian literature was something of a mistake; there weren't many Victorian poems in Brooks and Warren's *Understanding Poetry*, and the loose, baggy monsters of Victorian fiction simply couldn't be measured against Jamesian criteria. Rebelling against the rebellions of modernism, the new and increasingly large cohort of Victorian PhDs justified their professional interest in a field to which justice clearly had not been done by tending to move in one of two directions. Either they sought to locate the aesthetic in places T. S. Eliot, F. R. Leavis, and others had not been able to find it and create a new kind of formalism, or they insisted on a reemphasis on history and an interdisciplinary approach to texts hitherto hermetically treated. Curiously, the politics of interdisciplinarity seemed to gibe with the politics of late-1960s social movements, and the humanist left of the postwar PhDs blurred into the new left and produced the generation of scholars who now dominate literary theory, against the grain of the country but very much in the grain of their professional discipline. Modernism had made itself comfortably at home in the academy, which had assimilated its reverence for high culture and the political conservatism of its rejection of capitalism and the modern industrial society, of kitsch, and the merely popular; but in entering the academy, it underwent a sea change. From a high moral and aesthetic crusade, it turned into professional revisionism.

The Victorians' wedge into respectability was the novel. Even to this day, there has been relatively little done with Victorian poetry. Books on the novels proliferate, but there have been no substantive histories of Victorian poetry over the last twenty-five years; as Isobel Armstrong has put it to me, "The response to Victorian poetry has been sluggish since Eliot, backed up by Leavis, would have nothing to do with it." In the writing of this story, I find that the Victorian novel stands in formidably for Victorian literature as a whole. Many years ago, before I had any right to do it, I wrote that "all Victorian art aspires to the condition of fiction" (*Boundaries* 78). In more complicated ways, I believe that now, and see that the Victorian proclivity to fiction has conditioned my way of reading and understanding.

So I will proceed to tell a story I believe, the sense of its provisionality having for me largely theoretical weight; greater weight derives from the model of the Victorians themselves, who thought that telling stories is a way to knowledge. As Alexander Welsh has asserted, "invented fictions contribute to our understanding of history" (29). That there are other ways to tell the story

is self-evident, as the Victorians helped to teach later generations of storytellers, the more so because, before I set out to write my own, I asked a number
of Victorian scholars to tell me theirs. Theirs of course were significantly different, but helpful as well, and I am grateful to them all.[1] Nevertheless, contemporary awareness of the fictional sources of all narrative—historical,
autobiographical, or fictional—has done nothing and, I would argue, can do
nothing to end the need to make a story out of history, to impose continuities
even on the Victorians themselves. Stories make sense of things. And the
stories we tell about the Victorians have everything to do with how we position
ourselves within our discipline and against the society that sustains our work.

After so long a prologue, my story begins by moving back arbitrarily
from the arbitrary twenty-five years ago to the founding of *Victorian Studies*, in
1957, which was almost exactly contemporary with the publication of Raymond
William's *Culture and Society*, one of the most influential books of the last
half century. This moment reasonably focuses the two tendencies of the new
generation of Victorian critics to which I have alluded. *Victorian Studies* and
*Culture and Society* reasserted the great tradition of Victorian study that
emphasized historical depth. Key classroom texts like Carlyle's *Past and Present* or Ruskin's *Unto This Last* or Arnold's *Culture and Anarchy*, notorious
documents like the anonymous *Essays and Reviews*, Darwin's *Origin of Species*,
even, say, Newman's *Apologia* had always seemed inadequately available without some history, some intellectual or social context. While formalist studies
of even these sorts of books were increasing, the emergence of a politically
concerned historicism at a time when formalism dominated the academy represented not only a return to a traditional way of looking at Victorian texts but
a new social awareness, academic and otherwise—the new Victorian studies
and the 1960s not so coincidentally happened together, and some of the ideological ground for the academic convulsions of that decade was certainly laid by
those antiformalist professors who had been trained so successfully in formalism. Williams's Leavisian preoccupation with culture was opening onto a politically engaged criticism and the revivification and sophistication of Marxist
criticism.

The early modernist oedipal revulsion from Victorian literature was
obviously in part a revulsion—already an aspect of Victorian literature itself,
as in the career of Oscar Wilde—against social realism and its attendant
moralism. It was also, as Linda Dowling has shown, an aspect of a crisis of
language and of the assumption that underlay the very idea of high culture.
These formal aspects of the literature implied a surrender to merely popular
taste, a vulgarity and populism that threatened the class status of high culture
(as it had recently been defined by Matthew Arnold). The aestheticism that
marked the late Victorians' revulsion from the preceding generations was

clearly an ancestor of the formalism of the 1950s. In perhaps a characteristic Victorian way, students of the literature in those years were divided—not always self-consciously—by a commitment to the aesthetic and by a sense that the merely aesthetic was not only a denial of the fullness of moral and social commitment characteristic of mid-Victorian literature but a contemporary refusal to engage through literature with major political and social problems. Study of Victorian literature has almost always leaned toward social realism itself, and Neff's still interesting studies *Carlyle and Mill* and *Carlyle* formidably contextualize those writers' works within the social and economic changes of the first third of the nineteenth century. One strategy to deal with the divided consciousness was to reimagine formalist criteria and offer the Victorian writers as sophisticated alternatives to a sophisticated modernism. Another, not necessarily opposed strategy was to show that the Victorians were modernists after all—a project that has continued through the quarter century, modified in its later days by demonstrations that the Victorians were also postmodernist after all. The enterprise of criticism of Victorian literature throughout, however, was an attempt somehow to reconcile modernist sensibilities with Victorian engagement, even when it was not identified as Victorian.

It was with this sort of commitment that the young editors of *Victorian Studies*, led by Michael Wolff, self-consciously set about developing an interdisciplinary context for the study of literature and, indeed, blurring the boundaries between literature and other forms of discourse (although *discourse* was not at that time in their vocabulary with its current resonances). Victorian studies were precisely not analytic considerations of individual canonical texts; Williams's notion of culture came to pervade the work of many Victorianists at the time. A sense of the particular historical location of the idea of culture and the peculiarities of the culture of the Victorians—who, in a way, deceptively naturalized and universalized the idea—became important aspects of Victorian studies. Works like J. W. Burrow's *Evolution and Society* and George Stocking's essay "Matthew Arnold, E. B. Tylor, and the Uses of Invention," though obviously not by *literary* critics, were directly to the point of the renewed historical and social sense of literary study. And E. P. Thompson's *Making of the English Working Class*, along with some of the writing of Eric Hobsbawm, was of enormous importance in shifting attention of literary scholars from the most obvious canonical works to the activities of writers concerned with the working class and, indeed, to working-class and political writers. Social history, which has become such a contested field in recent professional debates within the American Historical Association, was closely linked with the new interdisciplinary Victorianism. As in the Victorian novel itself, attention was beginning to shift from large-scale political events to the history of everyday things, and works like G. Kitson Clark's *Making of Victorian England*—with its emphasis on social and cultural life—and Asa Briggs's *Victorian People* and *Victo-*

*rian Cities* (recently supplemented by *Victorian Things*) were crucial for Victorianists.[2]

But despite the commitment to context and interdisciplinarity, scholars of the 1950s and 1960s for the most part did not imagine the sort of denial of generic and categorical difference that has become commonplace in modern criticism, particularly with the notion that *all* forms of knowledge are discourse, science and literature and history together. Thus the tendency was, as Gerhard Joseph has put it to me, toward a "rather old-fashioned notion of the 'disciplines' . . . related to each other isomorphically, so that, say, political history, literary history, art history, etc., are seen to fit together in a more or less continuous fashion." The connections were rather unself-consciously understood as "seamless," for all these disciplines were governed by notions, as Joseph describes them, "of cause and effect, genre, organic form, the mimetic fit of discourse and social 'reality,' the centrality of the human subject." The radical transformation of the idea of "culture" and interdisciplinarity that came with the importation of Foucault, in particular, was only anticipated.

But while historical and interdisciplinary study (partly on analogy with the discipline of American studies, which was often invoked as precedent) gathered respectability and energy in the 1960s, the primary literary strategy of critics of Victorian literature at the time was an attempt to demonstrate that it could sustain formal and modernist analysis as successfully as, say, seventeenth-century poetry. In George Eliot studies, for example, Leavis's formalist moralism, in *The Great Tradition*, had already had important effects, but Barbara Hardy's *Novels of George Eliot* decisively provided formalist justifications that complemented and, to a certain extent, displaced the Jamesian criteria then dominant. Hardy's *Appropriate Form* extended that new post-Jamesian formalism to a much wider range of Victorian fiction. Dickens's reputation was more complicated, having received strong modernist sanction with Edmund Wilson's psychoanalytically oriented "Two Scrooges." But throughout the 1950s there was a kind of crisis of Dickens criticism, everyone deferring to his genius but few finding the formal grounds that seemed essential for canonization. (A noteworthy if perhaps extreme late formulation of this crisis comes in Robert Garis's *Dickens Theatre*, which gives overt expression to the governing assumptions of a kind of criticism that has in recent years been pretty thoroughly discredited. In order to save Dickens, Garis had to insist that he is not interesting symbolically or in his prophetic mode, nor capable of "organic coherence" or verisimilitude. He is a great novelist because he is a great entertainer, brilliant in spots, a performer who is always evoking applause. Garis defended Dickens by absolving him from responsibility for literary—that is, Jamesian—seriousness.)

Not accidentally, I believe, it was through Dickens, in Hillis Miller's *Charles Dickens: The World of His Novels*, that the first scent of postmodern

Continental philosophy wafted into Victorian criticism. Dedicated to George Poulet, the book became a text of phenomenological criticism and the first of Miller's still active efforts to bring to bear on traditional texts the insights of Continental—particularly French—thought. (A book of even greater influence by Miller, just before he turned to his deconstructive phase, is *The Form of Victorian Fiction*, which continues to read Victorian novels within the phenomenological framework that emphasizes consciousness—with his characteristic attention to the details of the texts—and in terms of their efforts at intersubjectivity: "An exploitation of the fact that one can in language imagine oneself as having direct access to another mind makes Victorian fiction possible" [3].) Before Miller, however, even the best of Victorian criticism went untheorized—took as a given the existence of aesthetic and ahistorical norms and focused intensely on individual genius. The peculiarly oppositional nature of our most recent criticism is not evident in this earlier work—not even in Miller's—despite its frequent resistance to dominant critical modes.

The social and historical emphasis represented by *Victorian Studies* was, for a while, less influential than the new formalism of poststructuralist thought. Foucault, indeed, became and remains a crucial figure for providing the means to reconcile formalist impulses of modernism with historicism, for it is through Foucault particularly that the "infection" of historicism with textualism most potently spread. The most interesting developments in Victorian studies during the 1960s and 1970s generally reflect those dual tendencies already well established in Victorian study—that is, the commitment to aesthetic criteria that had been encouraged by Jamesian and New Critical methods and value assumptions, and the historical and contextual energies manifest in Williams's influential work. The formalist-aesthetic tendencies moved toward deconstruction, and the best historical-contextual work issued from feminism and the social concerns that tended to cluster around it.

Yet the relation of Victorianism to the remarkable proliferation of new theoretical positions during the last twenty-five years is, from some perspectives, rather less exciting than, say, that of Romanticism. For Romanticism seems to have generated Northrop Frye's mythic criticism and to have attracted immediately theorist-critics like Paul de Man, Harold Bloom, and Geoffrey Hartman, while the Victorians turned out to be writers of the sort of literature that needed to be contested by the new textualism. Isobel Armstrong's comments to me on the relation of this phenomenon to Victorian poetry are worth quoting in full, not only because they focus attention on the gap in criticism of Victorian poetry but because they place Victorian literature accurately in relation to contemporary literary theory:

> [T]o "reinstate" Victorian poetry even quite brilliant people have resorted to pre-existing theories and formulas and "applied" them to a lumpen body peri-

odised as "Victorian poetry"—e.g., Herbert Tucker with deconstruction, Alan Sinfield with Marxism, Eve Sedgwick with her homosocial-male-bonding-bargain-over-the-body theory. They have not used this poetry to think with, as deconstruction did with Romantic poetry or as the new historicists did with renaissance literature or as daring and innovative narrative theorists and historians of ideas did with the nineteenth-century novel.

Narrative theorists did, indeed, think with and through Victorian narrative, but the predominant view in the early years of poststructuralist criticism was that most Victorian literature was merely conventional; ironically, this attitude eventually worked in its favor by making it an especially important ground for testing theories out, and this testing has led critics to see the Victorians as proto-poststructuralists. Part of the major revision in readings of Victorians over the past twenty-five years or so has come from the discovery within their texts of exactly the sorts of instability, discontinuity, and skepticism that they seemed literally to have denied. It has struck many critics that the Victorians were contemporaries of Nietzsche and often contended with the same kinds of problems as he.

But perhaps the most important critical development out of Victorianism was feminism. Obviously, Victorian study was not the *source* of literary feminism, but obviously, too, it was closely associated with first-wave feminism, particularly through Elaine Showalter's *Literature of Their Own* and then Sandra Gilbert and Susan Gubar's *Madwoman in the Attic* and Nina Auerbach's *Communities of Women* and *Woman and the Demon*. Such criticism not only reread canonical texts and shifted focus onto others that had long been ignored, but it led to the revaluation of writers like Elizabeth Barrett, Christina Rossetti, and Elizabeth Gaskell and to a reconfiguration of the canon. Its sustained emphasis on context, its archival efforts to exhume forgotten materials, its thickly textured historical interpretations were all, in fact, compatible with the historicist traditions of Victorian study that were getting lost under the textualism of New Critical analyses and then of deconstruction. (The stream of feminist criticism has broadened enormously since Showalter's crucial book, and the range—paralleling curiously its Victorian subjects—might perhaps be represented in its most recent shape by the remarkable three-volume compendium *Woman Question: Society and Literature in Britain and America*, edited by Helsinger, Sheets, and Veeder. These volumes stay close to the grain of the subject and are distinguished by extensive quotation, a wide interdisciplinary range of topics, and thoroughly informed commentary. Clearly an inheritor from the first-generation feminists, it breaks beyond its conventions by complexly denying any single, monolithic Victorianism, any single feminist vision.)

Feminist criticism was not only coherent with the traditional Victorianist preoccupation with social history, but by virtue of speaking from a position outside the dominant texts and language of what had been known as "Victorian literature," it implicitly and then explicitly began to call into question the assumptions, suggested in the previous paragraph, that governed most Victorian criticism hitherto. Feminists had to become aware that the medium of Victorian prose was not translucent but opaque, that it bore within it, systemically, elements that seemed to exclude the voice and vision of women; as a consequence, conventions of literary "genius" and ahistorical aesthetic standards had to be challenged before any important new work could get done. Historicism and textualism almost inevitably joined in the feminist enterprise(s), and feminism became in a way both the most significant critical activity among Victorian scholars and beautifully representative of the whole activity of recent Victorian criticism—textualist *and* historicist, preoccupied with social history, alert to the material base of aesthetic criteria, alert to the extraindividual pressures of ideological forces, and politically motivated. The new textualism was becoming "cultural studies" so that not only were canons changing and interpretations reversing, but the interest in particular texts was being displaced by an interest in cultural forms and political change.

The lines of this development can be traced in the journal *Victorian Studies*, which had represented originally a strong liberal humanist position in the growth of interdisciplinary study but moved, with editorial change, toward an explicit feminist agenda. The political impinged deeply on the aesthetic. Under the editorship of Martha Vicinus, the journal intensified its original preoccupation with social history and made explicit some of its political goals, generating at least two volumes that articulated the concern with feminist matters. *Suffer and Be Still: Woman in the Victorian Age* gathered a wide range of essays from scholars in many disciplines, some of whom went on to write significant monographs in such areas as medicine, sexual behavior, literature, the fine arts. The book sought to document the stereotypes against which modern feminism had to struggle, and in doing so became an excellent place to locate the assumptions out of which first-wave feminist criticism developed. The early 1970s were marked by a great explosion of such publications, what must be seen as a necessary laying of the ground for an emerging feminist criticism. Its orientation was not like that of the textually influenced feminist criticism of a few years later, but less theoretically complex, more empirical in its historicism. Vicinus also edited a follow-up volume, *A Widening Sphere*, working from the Victorian stereotype of "separate spheres" to study ways in which women were both confined by that stereotype and found ways to move beyond it. Vicinus has been equally important in breaking from the canon in the direction of working-class literature, as witness her *Industrial Muse*.

At the same time, however, canonical Victorian literature, with its commitment to domestic realism, to narratives of redemption and redeeming and reforming selves and societies, became the red herring against which both modernist and poststructuralist positions could define themselves. The focus of these implicit rejections was Victorian fiction. Partly as a consequence of having to defend itself, Victorian fiction became a focal point for testing and developing poststructuralist narrative theory; perhaps not surprisingly, as I have already noted, critics have even found that Victorian fiction is often itself poststructuralist, after all. (Here, Hillis Miller's two strong essays on *Middlemarch* ["Narrative," "Optic"], like Cynthia Chase's remarkable piece on *Daniel Deronda*, are much to the point.)

One influential example is Peter K. Garrett's *Victorian Multiplot Novel*, which uses (if a bit loosely) Bakhtin's notion of dialogism to define the peculiar qualities of the great Victorian novels whose looseness and bagginess have long been a trial to formalists. The traditional solution to the looseness was a criticism that identifies a unified project, an organicist coherence, in the ostensible multiplicity of novels like, for example, *Bleak House* or *Vanity Fair*. What distinguishes Garrett's reading as a product of this particular moment in critical history is his comfort (and originality) in locating an irreducible tension in the novels between opposing perspectives, a tension built into their language and form. As John Kucich has noted, the Bakhtinian dialogue in Garrett's formulation looks a lot like de Manian deconstruction. Kucich argues that however explicitly historicist such criticism may be, it misses the way in which the particular tensions of these fictions are embedded in particular social and historical situations (662).

The willingness and determination to find irreducible tensions in ostensibly unified novels, a mark of most postmodern textualist approaches, is evident, for another example, in D. A. Miller's *Narrative and Its Discontents*, a more explicitly deconstructionist argument. Miller produces remarkable and important readings of several novelists (the only Victorian being George Eliot), all of which demonstrate a tension taken as intrinsic to traditional narrative form—between the "narratable" and closure. Novels turn out to be interested (and interesting) only in insufficiency, incompleteness, dissatisfaction, instability, and deferral, for these are the conditions that make narrative possible at all. The very qualities of completion and satisfaction to which narratives aspire ensure the death of narrative itself. So in the great Victorian novels that seem to aspire to stability and completed meaning, the ends are at odds with the condition of the quests—that is, of the "narratable."

I pause over these two examples to emphasize the way the Victorians get themselves incorporated into the postmodernist condition—willy-nilly, they become part of that condition. Thus the very literature that postmodernism first defined itself against turns out on such readings to be either proto-postmodernist or the authentic thing! Much criticism went on from there to obliterate the wall between modernism and Victorianism that modernists had constructed, and the move to make the Victorians postmodernist too was inevitable. From different angles of approach the case for Victorianism and modernism has been made by Carol Christ, in her discussion of poetry *Victorian and Modern Poetics*; by me, for the novel, in *The Realistic Imagination*; and most recently and impressively by Peter Allan Dale, whose *In Pursuit of a Scientific Culture* demonstrates how even the discourse of positivism anticipates and leads to modernist positions.

Obviously, there is no simple sequence to be traced in these odd critical swerves, but the textualism of Foucault and deconstruction and the political animus of feminist study did at various times conflict and converge. Some of the consequences of this convergence have been among the most interesting and innovative work in the field. It becomes difficult now to allow such binary categories as textualism, historicism, contextualism, formalism. The influence of French feminism, for example, conflating somehow the approaches of deconstruction and of politically and historically engaged criticism, has been felt in the important work of, among others, Margaret Homans and, in another way, Mary Poovey. Homans's *Bearing the Word*, concerned with "what it meant for a woman to write in the nineteenth century" (xi), is in a sense "formalist," since it explores with analytic persistence the language available to women writers and the ways in which the dominant language resisted the representation of women's experience. But the project is an attempt to open the way to a representational language that can be used by women and recuperated for feminist projects. Formalism—including its sustained treatment of individual texts—moves here toward general theories of the linguistic possibilities of nineteenth-century art and toward a political engagement that puts aside aesthetic questions entirely.

That putting aside in favor of energetic engagements with social issues from a politically defined (not always, alas, self-consciously theorized) perspective is, as I have suggested in my earlier remarks about feminism, one of the marks of the criticism of the Victorians that have come to dominate at the moment of this writing. Through the blending of textualism and historicism that has come to be known, often loosely, as the new historicism, defined political projects have begun to dominate a great deal of Victorian criticism; and again, ironically, the activity looks—though in a new professional language—rather like the high-serious criticism of the Victorians themselves (who often take their lumps for being on the wrong side politically and effacing the marks of their political agenda through the language of universals). Carlyle, Ruskin, Arnold never in fact pretended that their criticism was not in the interests of a moral and political position. Even Arnold's celebrated "disinterest" is explicitly in the interest of thoroughly specified moral and social conditions, although Arnold writes as though the special interest must be deferred until we know the object as in itself it really is. The often brilliant newer textualist-historicist

critics of Victorian literature and culture carry the same sorts of high seriousness into the same sorts of multidisciplinary critical ventures with the
object of exposing ideological fraud and affirming another ideology. The new
textualism has become, in their hands, precisely *not* formalism.

An important combination of feminism, ideology, textualism, and historicism, Poovey's *Uneven Developments* might stand here as an example of
the way these strands of criticism, woven together from traditions of Victorian
study, feminism, Foucault, the new historicism, and deconstruction, have become central to the study of Victorian literature today. To be more precise, it
is not strictly Victorian literature but Victorian culture that is under examination, and from the perspective and in the interests of a contemporary political
position. Victorian literature engages now because it is a battlefield in which
a new conception of text, self, and social order is to be forged. The object is not
the literature but the strategies of culture itself. And to be fair, this essay
needs to be redefined in terms not of literary but of cultural studies. Part of the
point of much of this kind of criticism is to eliminate the category "literature"
entirely, or to make it cover all discourse—which would produce the same
effect.

So while she talks in detail about *David Copperfield* and *Jane Eyre*,
Poovey is equally at home in discussions of how women were treated medically,
of the Caroline Norton matrimonial case, of Florence Nightingale. And her
project is not to read texts but to use the reading of texts to show that gender
is not a natural development of natural instincts but a construction of representation itself and, as such, complexly unstable. Unlike some critics who work
this vein, Poovey allows the possibility of oppositional voices breaking through
the ideological system that governs language and representation. She recognizes that any representation is unstably constructed out of ideological forces
related not only to gender but to class and race as well.

The cluster "class, race, and gender" has come to the center of much
of the dominant criticism of Victorian literature in recent years. Feminism
blends into gender studies, and Poovey's book has its parallel, to take just
one other example, in Ludmilla Jordanova's *Sexual Visions*. The fact that
Jordanova's work, deconstructing from the perspective of a historian of science
the polarities of male-female, reason-emotion, parallels so closely the project
of *Uneven Developments* is itself a sign of the way literary studies have become
cultural studies. The new establishment of cultural criticism, emerging from
the disciplinary web of history (social, art, science), literature, philosophy,
tends to take as its object a reconception of the nineteenth century in terms of
its textual and material structuring of conflicts about race, class, and gender.
History is itself a script to be reread, and the point of the rereading is to
"denaturalize" categories we can see to have been constructed in the particular
conditions of Victorian culture, with a view to changing them in our own. While

English departments are still for the most part structured on the principles of professional literary history of twenty-five years ago, cultural studies has established itself among the most active of the younger generation of critics. Resistances to this new left of literary criticism is as likely now to come from the old left as from the few (not greatly respected) faculty members who forthrightly practice the modes of scholarship and criticism dominant in the postwar years.

Poovey's insistence on writing across generic boundaries is representative of new-historicist approaches. Although, in the still important work of John Holloway in *The Victorian Sage*, rhetorical analysis led to a recognition that the projects of Victorian fiction and nonfiction were remarkably similar, it was largely in the late 1960s and early 1970s that literary study of the Victorians began most seriously to call the dominant generic categories into question. My own *Boundaries of Fiction*, like *The Art of Victorian Prose*, co-edited with William Madden, sought—without the theoretical sophistication that might have been available through the French theorists whose work ultimately transformed the field—to break through the generic boundaries that had tended to control professional discourse. In the last fifteen years, by way of Foucault, through the work of Hayden White and the many important critics who have found the idea of discourse important, the boundaries between nonfiction and fiction have been all but obliterated. Criticism itself, as Hartman has urged, becomes an art. In the late 1960s and early 1970s, the notion of the fictionality of nonfiction began to justify the traditional practice of Victorian scholars and teachers of considering the work of, say, Carlyle, Newman, and Arnold in formalist terms, without more than minimal reference to their historical referents. (It is of some interest to the field of Victorian literature that for the most part this direction did not in fact lead to much significant development in the study of nonfiction prose. *The Art of Victorian Prose*, making its case by arguing for an aesthetic or poetics of prose nonfiction, was both influential and ineffective; but the best writing about nonfiction prose developed in a context of intertextuality with other literary modes.)

The attempt to break the boundaries between the genres required an entirely new sense of what the subject of study was, and this critics like Poovey have provided. It was one thing to show that great nonfictional works could be read as fictions, were governed by fictional tropes; it was quite another to realize that a real change in critical method required not a study of particular fictional or nonfictional works but a recognition that all artifacts of a culture might be governed by the same ideological forces, the same rhetorical habits. And this kind of insight has governed Poovey's work, and that of Catherine Gallagher, among others—work that takes as its subject not particular canonical (or noncanonical) writers but specific problems, cultural knots, social deformations. Gallagher's *Industrial Reformation of English Fiction* seems to foreground the question of fiction but in fact is concerned almost as much with nonfiction prose like Mill's *On Representative Government,* or *Culture and Anarchy,* and the whole early Victorian discourse over industrialism. The generic separation of nonfiction and fiction, which seemed twenty-five years ago an important aesthetic problem, seems now, in the light of work like Gallagher's, largely beside the point.

Preoccupation with representation has led to important work in many directions other than the overtly ideological and political. My own *Realistic Imagination,* obviously impelled in part by the way recent critical theory has turned all texts into "discourse" and all language into "fiction," emphasizes both the constructed nature of reality in Victorian fictions and the epistemological and moral struggle to get beyond construction to some grounded truth. On this reading, realism is both trapped in representation, and virtuous or successful only insofar as it accounts for its own strategies of creation and breaks through to "reality." The contradiction in Victorian novels is part of their distinguishing character and places them in a limbo somewhere in the direction of modernism. Robert Caserio's *Plot, Story, and the Novel: From Dickens and Poe to the Modern Period* attempts, with remarkable theoretical sophistication, to show how "story" for the Victorians became a means to meaning and to life itself. He contests the dominant form of the modern emphasis on representation at the expense of life and reference in order to affirm both the Victorian commitment to story and a critical practice that continues to make significant referential gestures through language and form.

In another mode, Linda Dowling takes the question of representation seriously enough to detect in late-nineteenth-century "decadence" a crisis of language itself. That is to say, she emphasizes the importance of language in any question of literary and cultural activity, as postmodernist theory would seem to require, and then investigates, in a brilliant archaeological process, the way language, from Locke to the late nineteenth century, came to bear the burden of the crisis. Language theory, she shows, disentangled language from its Adamic sources and based it in material conditions; language, then, became a medium not of high civilization and of the transcendent values of a superior (English) culture, but a literally "demoralized" medium. Dowling's important argument needs to be attended to not because of its very interesting conclusions about late-nineteenth-century decadence but because it recognizes that if representation, and thus language, is to be taken so seriously in critical discourse, it is the responsibility of the critic to understand as much as possible about how language itself is imagined, how its history was written, how, then, it was understood by its most sophisticated users.

Many of the most interesting and important works written in this quarter century do not seem directly influenced by the transformations in the field that I have been tracing (or inventing). Yet in almost all of them one finds that peculiar attention to the medium, to the language of representation, and to the way fictional and nonfictional discourses play into and out of each other, that is characteristic of the new theoretical approaches. And they are all beautifully written. I think, for example, of David DeLaura's splendid *Hebrew and Hellene in Victorian England*, a work that, with meticulous scholarship, traces what would probably now be called webs of intertextuality among Newman, Arnold, and Pater. DeLaura defines a literary, cultural tradition in a way that has transformed our thinking about these writers. Other significant books (and my choice here will be arbitrary) belong clearly to recent critical movements while being built in utter independence of them. Welsh's *George Eliot and Blackmail* is one of the most impressive pieces of interdisciplinary scholarship Victorian study has produced. While ostensibly about Eliot, it ramifies out into the study of all Victorian fiction and of some of the culture's major social and intellectual changes. In connecting Eliot's art to the information explosion at the start of the century and to Freudian theory of the end, it fulfills, more than theoretically energetic works usually do, contemporary criticism's commitment to cultural studies. And in the course of doing so, Welsh manifests the kind of respect for literature and for great literary texts that contemporary theory self-consciously eschews. Or again, Rosemary Jann's *Art and Science of Victorian History* sees history as implicated in traditions of artistic imagination and as wrestling with questions of truth in ways parallel to that of the fiction writers themselves. Without much theoretical apparatus she explores how history embodies the complex attitudes of the Victorians toward art and science, imagination and truth. Perhaps the most impressive and innovative book of recent years has been Gillian Beer's *Darwin's Plots*, which comfortably reads Darwin as literature and allows for an interplay (by means of interplay of discourse) between science and imaginative literature. Other books that have usefully developed this area of discursive interplay within disciplines are Sally Shuttleworth, *George Eliot and Nineteenth-Century Science* and, I would hope, my own *Darwin and the Novelists*. Finally, I would point out how the recognition of the discursive relations among ostensibly unrelated disciplines becomes the meat and potatoes of Victorian study, as in the kinds of essay collections that have made a difference during these years. Two representative ones are *Nature and the Victorian Imagination*, edited by U. C. Knoepflmacher and G. B. Tennyson, which is also impressively preoccupied with the imagination-science dualism, and *Victorian Science and Victorian Values*, edited by James Paradis and Thomas Postlewait.

The Knoepflmacher-Tennyson collection does take up almost as much poetry as fiction, but here, too, concern for intersecting Victorian discourses insufficiently emphasizes poetry. Oddly, language itself gets inadequate attention, and it is, perhaps, the failure to consider how central to the Victorian literary and cultural experience language theory was that helps account for the relative thinness of criticism of poetry and to treat it with quite the seriousness that the novel has attracted. Why is it, as Daniel Harris has put it to me, that there "has been no substantive history of Victorian poetry in the period to hand," or that poetry "has continued to prove resistant to the kinds of social studies more obviously undertaken in the novel," or that, as Isobel Armstrong reminds me, postmodern theory has had so little effect on its study? Outside of Herbert Tucker's work (see, in particular, *Tennyson and the Doom of Romanticism* and *Browning's Beginnings*), virtually no valuable theoretical works on the poets have emerged. To be sure, Hillis Miller's *Linguistic Moment* deals with some Victorian poets' explicit concern with language, but this deconstructive argument has by now a kind of inevitability that does not lead to the sort of revitalizing emphasis Victorian poetry needs. From the perspective of Daniel Harris, the major exception to the rule that poststructuralist criticism has not been adequately or seriously applied to Victorian poetry is Loy Martin's *Browning's Dramatic Monologues and the Post-Romantic Subject*, a Marxist interpretation that builds in part on familiarity with Bakhtin, V. N. Volosinov, and Gregory Bateson and arrives at a rich understanding of what Harris calls "the oral/written relation between speaker and writer." But Harris complains about Martin, as Kucich does about the theorists he discusses, that the theory is supported by no real demonstration of a "material base." One should add, of course, the work of Jerome McGann, both on Swinburne and the Rossettis. McGann writes with a fierce originality and a commitment to poetry and to thorough bibliographical and historical scholarship that has, indeed, made a difference.

As with the novel, there have been canonical changes, and Christina Rossetti (thanks in part to McGann), Elizabeth Barrett Browning, and Emily Brontë now receive far more respectful attention than they probably ever had. But these shifts have not touched Victorian poetry in a way either to integrate it with the massive movements bringing together historicism and textualism or to locate its own awareness of the crisis of representation that has preoccupied critics of the novel. In the blurring of generic boundaries characteristic of twenty-five years of Victorian criticism, the poetry infrequently participates. Dowling's work, which studies linguistic theory, philology, and mythography among the Victorians, would be indispensable to a rich and theoretically informed study of the poetry. (A recent collection, *The Sun Is God*, edited by J. B. Bullen, contains much promising material in that direction and includes essays on Swinburne, Tennyson, and Romantic poetry.) Nobody has yet shown what Isobel Armstrong argues, that "the work of Victorian poetry was very much more radical and challenging politically, epistemologically and linguistically than the novel was."

Questions of representation have moved complexly from strict literary analysis into what had traditionally been imagined as background study. Those questions have, as in other areas of literary study, effaced the difference between text and context, focusing on the constructed nature of all discourse, implying the fictionality of nonfiction. The contest over textualism within Victorian studies has been in part a dispute over the nature of the subject itself. Victorian *literature* as a category has been put to the question, and certainly generic differences have broken down. The subject has imperceptibly shifted from the great writers to the complicity of all texts in the hegemonic discourse of a Victorian culture dominated by a capitalist economy and a patriarchal structure; and the problem here, admirable as the effort is and impressive as are some of its results, is the tendency to imagine that in fact there was such a monolithic structure as the "patriarchal," the "capitalist." The tendencies to reductivism in the hands of critics who unreflectingly (and without reading Gramsci) inherit the idea of a "hegemonic discourse" are very powerful indeed and mar much otherwise fresh work. It is refreshing, therefore, to find Nancy Armstrong's *Desire and Domestic Fiction*, which concerns itself with these problems but finds that the very discourse that by other constructions excluded women also empowered them; that in fact the discourse of Victorian fiction invented (rather than repressed) the idea of the monstrous woman. However debatable the thesis, the argument is enormously valuable in complicating the idea of hegemonic discourse.

If one were to locate a quality that characterizes the wide range of approaches developed during the last twenty years, it would be "writing against the grain." One of the greatest of the various ironies that seem to me to have governed the development of Victorian criticism is that the approaches that gather the most potent institutional endorsement are the ones most explicitly contestatory—that reject (allegedly) dominant views or read against the apparently explicit "intentions" of texts. This is true across a broad spectrum of theories, but only for a brief moment in the history of these contestations has it been convincing that the new position is a minority position, that it runs counter to established institutional positions. Deconstructive readings, for example, did indeed invert dominant traditional readings of texts. Hillis Miller's rereading of *Middlemarch*, for example, turned an organicist, meliorist, aspiringly moral and unifying novelist into an aporetic one, a writer subversively interrogating the history she ostensibly affirmed. But such readings quickly became canonical themselves. And Cynthia Chase's de Manian analysis of *Daniel Deronda* was one of the first essays accepted by *PMLA* under its new procedures of anonymous submissions: it clearly got professional sanction not because of the importance of the critic, as might have been the case with Miller, but because the argument was recognizable and convincing. Garrett's Bakhtinian interpretation of Victorian fiction was quickly assimilated. Feminist readings that made the mad woman in the attic central rather than marginal quickly transformed our understanding of key texts like *Jane Eyre*.

Oppositional views are institutionally and professionally necessary, not in fact opposed by departments that hire and committees that tenure.

One of the most striking instances of this development can be traced in D. A. Miller's second book, *The Novel and the Police*. In his first book, Miller wrote against the grain in the sense of resisting traditional humanist readings of classic texts by positing an *intrinsic* self-division in narrative. Having thus established a strong position in the profession by virtue of a brilliant deployment of deconstructive techniques, in *The Novel and the Police* he writes against the grain in the sense of denying the ostensible commitments of the works he studies, demonstrating in a Foucauldian manner that novels literally affirm the powers of independent action and will have inscribed in the very language of their culture the "surveillance" that controls freedom and asserts the dominance of social forms over individual acts and intentions. Politically, Miller argues, oppositional writers turn out to be complicit with the ruling ideology. Such criticism, influenced of course by Foucault and by aspects of Jameson's arguments, among others, insists on the power of the systemic; it obliterates humanist, individualist, voluntarist positions in an effort to show that no author can write other than what the culture requires. That is, Miller writes oppositionally in order to show that nobody, especially not the Victorian novelists, can.

It is in this sense, reading against the author, that Miller's work seems to epitomize the dominant tendencies of a quarter century criticism. Criticism becomes interesting at the point when a force larger than an individual writer can be detected shaping and reversing literal assertion. Gaps and cracks and fissures are discovered. Ideological power is revealed. The effaced technology of representation, which allows the illusion of realistic depiction, is foregrounded, shown to be an effect of systematic and inhuman forces of language or ideology; the fictional reality is shown, then, to be complicit with the technologies it effaces.

The foregrounding of representation thus turns out to be the central move of almost every major critical practice—feminist, Marxist, deconstructive, new-historicist and Foucauldian, Lacanian—and it leads invariably to reading against the grain, and almost as invariably to professional advancement. I state this irony in a tone of what must seem like deep skepticism not to bemoan it but, first, to represent the dominant condition of recent criticism of the Victorians and, second, to suggest that the rhetoric of these practices needs to be altered to take into account its own professional dominance and the potential incoherence of its own positioning.

It is true that outside the world of literary theorizing, the position is by no means dominant; in that respect, its importance cannot be underestimated and its sense of being a minority position justified. Nor should it be ignored that while at almost every major academic institution in the country reading against the grain is valued, and reading with it regarded as rather old-fashioned and unrewarding, in the nonacademic institutions, like the NEH, such practice is looked on with suspicion and distrust. At the same time, given the importance to such criticism of self-conscious confrontation with one's own position, it needs to comprehend its own efforts to *be* oppositional (and perhaps to see that it gains its position of privilege in a culture where privilege is now peculiarly valued by its very act of opposition). I would want to argue that it should also allow the possibility of opposition in its subjects, that the Victorians are interesting not only because they are complicit with the ideological systems they often thought themselves resisting, but because they often tried to be oppositional and were remarkably alert to the constraints that language and convention imposed on them. I would argue, too, that the theoretical insistence on the "always already" argument, on the systemic control by ideological forces, on the power of *langue* over *parole*, language systems over individual voices, needs to be in constant play against alternative possibilities in particular situations.

The demand for full historicist reading has the virtue of requiring constant alertness to universalizing tendencies, the wrenching of particular situations and strategic moves from contexts. As Kucich has put it, "much recent Victorian narrative criticism appears unexamined, often verging toward a textualist formalism disguised as history. Though it would be intellectual cowardice to urge some sort of general return to 'factual' historical research, practical criticism of the last few years has demonstrated a real need for strategies with which to materialize its theoretical structures" (659). That demand seems to me to be crucial to the future of Victorian criticism that has otherwise profited so immensely from the great development in theoretical sophistication of the last quarter century. The possibility that Hans-Georg Gadamer is right, and that language has infinite possibilities of meaning and newness, ought at least to be considered.

What we have witnessed in the last twenty-five years, however, amounts to an almost total transformation of the landscape. The invasion of textualism and questions of representation, often from Continental sources, has led to inversions of standard readings of Victorian texts; a preoccupation with the medium of language itself, historically, epistemologically, even morally; a shift of focus from the generic separations to the way in which the culture's discourse cuts across disciplinary lines; longstanding revisions of the canon, the addition of particular writers and of particular books. George Gissing's *Odd Women*, for example, has joined Elizabeth Barrett Browning's *Aurora Leigh* and Elizabeth Gaskell's *Cousin Phillis*; Darwin has moved from background to foreground, as has Florence Nightingale. The revisions have been startling and healthy, for the most part, and the field as a whole is defining itself as oppositional. The critical establishment does not mind. The Victorians have long been used to such treatment. The boundaries have been redrawn, although in disappearing ink; they remain essential to both our literary and our political projects.

### Notes

[1] I want to thank in particular Isobel Armstrong, Pat Brantlinger, Daniel Harris, Gerhard Joseph, John Kucich, and Michael Wolff, for troubling to write fairly extensive "stories" for my use. During the last phases of the writing of this paper, Linda Dowling offered a few useful suggestions as well. One of the characteristics of Victorian studies that has kept me in the field all these years is that the discipline is full of intellectually generous people like these. Thanks, too, to Garrett White, who did important bibliographical work for me.

[2] Of course, lying behind all these is G. M. Young's masterful *Victorian England: Portrait of an Age*, which was on every graduate student's reading list. I would argue that Young's work, precursor of much later Victorian social history, ultimately derives from the work of another Victorian—Thomas Babington Macaulay—whose insistence on what we would now call a synchronic vision of the whole of English society in 1685 anticipated the reorientation of modern histories to a consideration of everyday life as part of history. Macaulay, of course, has fallen from favor among historians and even among those most dedicated to social history. But his relation to current activities in Victorian study is another of the ironies in which Victorian attitudes reemerge in the work of Victorianism's most hostile critics.

## Selected Bibliography

Any selection of books as focal points for reading about Victorian literature must be quite arbitrary. The arbitrariness will, indeed, militate against its usefulness. In the list below, I have surrendered any idea of locating *the* essential texts and simply note work of some importance in the development of our modern view of the Victorians and ones that have impressed me at one time or other. I make no claim that these are the best or even that I continue to like them. Rather, I offer this selection as a piece of my intellectual autobiography in the hope that the works may serve to engage readers in the excitement of the study of Victorian literature.

Beer, Gillian. *Darwin's Plots: Evolutionary Narrative in Darwin, George Eliot, and Nineteenth-Century Fiction.* London: Routledge, 1983.
A remarkable study of Darwin's language and its relation to Victorian narrative, illuminating central assumptions about language and storytelling in post-Darwinian literature.

Dale, Peter Allan. *In Pursuit of a Scientific Culture: Science, Art, and Society in the Victorian Age*. Madison: U of Wisconsin P, 1989.
A study of one of the major intellectual developments of Victorian culture, scientific positivism, that crosses the genres and makes crucial connections among them and with the development of modernism.

Gallagher, Catherine. *The Industrial Reformation of English Fiction, 1832–1867*. Chicago: U of Chicago P, 1985.
A work that takes industrialism as an important intellectual development and traces its impact on major philosophical and social issues of the period and, through them, on Victorian narrative. The implications extend well beyond the industrial novels.

Garrett, Peter K. *The Victorian Multiplot Novel: Studies in Dialogic Form*. New Haven: Yale UP, 1980.
One of the first uses of Bakhtinian "dialogism" in the reading of Victorian fiction. This book serves as a valuable introduction to the problems of narrative raised by Victorian large, loose, baggy monsters.

Miller, D. A. *The Novel and the Police*. Berkeley: U of California P, 1988.
A brilliantly irritating, unsatisfying, but important and original application of Foucauldian theory to Victorian fiction.

Miller, J. Hillis. *The Form of Victorian Fiction*. Notre Dame: U of Notre Dame P, 1968.
A crucial text in the development of poststructuralist readings of Victorian novels. Miller here begins his move from phenomenology to deconstruction.

Poovey, Mary. *Uneven Developments: The Ideological Work of Gender in Mid-Victorian England*. Chicago: U of Chicago P, 1988.
An examination of how gender is constructed in Victorian culture and how the instabilities in the ideology that construct it open the way for contestation.

Showalter, Elaine. *A Literature of Their Own: British Women Novelists from Brontë to Lessing*. Princeton: Princeton UP, 1977.
Perhaps the founding work of feminist study of the Victorians. Showalter's work opens the canon and begins the definition of a women's tradition in a way that still requires attention, criticism, and respect.

Welsh, Alexander. *George Eliot and Blackmail*. Cambridge: Harvard UP, 1985.
A book that, although ostensibly about a single writer, wonderfully explores a major phenomenon of the nineteenth century—the information revolution—as it impinges on narrative, psychology, and social theory.

Williams, Raymond. *Culture and Society, 1780–1950*. Garden City: Doubleday, 1958.
A genuine classic that remains indispensable in its exploration of the way ideas of culture in relation to social change are created and shape Victorian art and society.

controversy and misunder-
. Not even *postmodernism*,
nt, has been subjected to as
many opposing interpretations. Once the site of all that was radical, exciting, and above all *new* (the medieval Latin *modernus*, an adjective and noun, was coined from the adverb *modo*, meaning "recently, just now"), by the early 1970s modernism found itself under attack as a retrograde, elitist movement—at best, the final phase of the great Romantic revolution and, at worst, the aestheticist reaction formation to an alienated social life that had close links to fascism. Thus Fredric Jameson called his 1979 study of Wyndham Lewis *Fables of Aggression: Wyndham Lewis, the Modernist as Fascist*. By 1990, the pendulum had swung again: today modernism has become less a derogatory term than a neutral one, referring to the earlier twentieth century. Cary Nelson's study *Repression and Recovery: Modern American Poetry and the Politics of Cultural Memory 1910–1945*, for example, accepts the "modern" as a time period and then proceeds to argue that the accepted modernist poetic canon (Robert Frost, T. S. Eliot, Ezra Pound, Wallace Stevens, William Carlos Williams) is unsatisfactory because it serves to repress those other modernist poets— women, blacks, proletarian writers—whose work made a discernible cultural difference.

So forceful is the current drive toward revisionist history that we sometimes forget how radical the now-canonized modernists actually were. From Rimbaud's insistence, in 1873, that "Il faut être absolument moderne" (241), to Pound's 1918 declaration that "no good poetry is ever written in a manner twenty years old" (11), to D. H. Lawrence's demand, in a 1923 manifesto by that name, for "Surgery for the Novel—or a Bomb," to Virginia Woolf's observation, in "Mr. Bennett and Mrs. Brown" (1924), "On or about December 1910 human character changed" (194), modernism perceived its own mission as a call for rupture. As Yeats put it in his introduction to *The Oxford Book of Modern Verse 1892–1935*:

> The revolt against Victorianism meant to the young poet a revolt against irrelevant descriptions of nature, the scientific and moral discursiveness of *In*

*Memoriam* . . . the political eloquence of Swinburne, the psychological curiosity
of Browning, and the poetical diction of everybody.                          (xi)

Nor, as is often assumed today, was the modernist "revolt" merely or even
primarily aesthetic. In 1915, for example, Lawrence wrote to Bertrand Russell:

> But we shall smash the frame. The land, the industries, the means of communi-
> cation and the public amusements shall all be nationalised. Every man shall
> have his wage till the day of his death, whether he work or not, so long as he
> works when he is fit. . . .
>             Then, and then only, shall we be able to *begin* living.        (2: 289)

Within less than a year after this letter was written, Lawrence's *Rainbow* was
banned under the 1857 Obscene Publications Act, thus setting the stage for
Lawrence's lifelong battle against censorship. Joyce's *Ulysses* (1922) could not
be published in the United States until the landmark decision of Judge Woolsey
in December 1933 cleared the novel of obscenity charges. Poetry was less likely
to be judged obscene than the fiction of the period, but, again, it helps to
remember that a lyric like "The Love Song of J. Alfred Prufrock," now a "set
text" at Oxford and Cambridge, was dismissed, in the pages of the *Times
Literary Supplement*, as the senseless rambling of a confused mind, even as
William Carlos Williams's *Spring and All* (1923), published in an edition of
three hundred copies in Dijon, France, was almost entirely overlooked ("Nobody," Williams later recalled, "ever saw it—it had no circulation at all" [*Imaginations* 85]). And Gertrude Stein's works, following *Three Lives*, were shrugged
off as so much "automatic writing"—which is to say, pure nonsense.
        Given this situation, it is not surprising that, in its earliest phases,
modernist scholarship and criticism were conceived as a defense of the "new
writing" on the part of fellow writers and advocates. F. R. Leavis called his
favorable account of the early poetry of Pound and Eliot *New Bearings in
English Poetry*, and in the introduction to his groundbreaking *Axel's Castle: A
Study in the Imaginative Literature of 1870–1930*, Edmund Wilson declared
that "it is not usually recognized that writers such as W. B. Yeats, James Joyce,
T. S. Eliot, Gertrude Stein, Marcel Proust, and Paul Valéry represent the
culmination of a self-conscious and very important literary movement" (1).
        Throughout the 1930s and 1940s—indeed, well into the 1950s—the
most important studies of modernist works were produced by critics who,
whether or not they held university posts, were themselves aspiring poets or
fiction writers. Wilson was of course a novelist; the New Critics—John Crowe
Ransom, Cleanth Brooks, Robert Penn Warren, Allen Tate, R. P. Blackmur—
were primarily poets who took Eliot (and to a lesser extent Yeats or Hardy,
Frost or Auden) as their master. But what is less well understood is that

the writers on the left—Malcolm Cowley, Kenneth Burke, Philip Rahv, F. O. Matthiessen—had similar predilections and made similar literary assumptions: indeed, the modernist situation was one in which the conservative Eliot published *East Coker* in *The Partisan Review* even as the Marxist Delmore Schwartz was taken up with enthusiasm by Brooks and Warren in their anthologies *Understanding Poetry* and *Understanding Fiction*. Such crossovers occurred as a matter of course, given that, what we might call first-stage modernist studies, whether undertaken by a New York Jewish social critic like Lionel Trilling or by a High Church Episcopal southern agrarian like Cleanth Brooks, were committed to the doctrine, put forward by Eliot himself, that form and content were inseparable and hence a poem or novel or play was never primarily what we now call a social text, whose political unconscious might reveal much about the ideology and culture of the early twentieth century but first and foremost a unique work of art. As such, any literary text inevitably raised the issue of *value*, the unavoidable question being not "What are the ideological underpinnings of $X$?" or even "What does $X$ mean?" but "Is $X$ a good poem?"

Compare, for example, Matthiessen's *Achievement of T. S. Eliot* with Brooks's famous essay "The Waste Land: Critique of the Myth," in *Modern Poetry and the Tradition* (1939). "My double aim," wrote Matthiessen in the preface to the first edition (1935), "is to evaluate Eliot's method and achievement as an artist," and he proceeded to descry as "fatal" the attempt to "isolate [a poem's] ideas from their context," citing Mallarmé's aphorism that "poetry is not written with ideas, it is written with words" (vii). By 1947, Eliot's opinions had begun to make Matthiessen, a convinced Marxist, uncomfortable: in the preface to the second edition, he admitted that "my growing divergence from [Eliot's] view of life is that I believe that it is possible to accept the 'radical imperfection' of man, and yet to be a political radical as well" (ix). Yet his focus continued to be on the *poetic* quality of Eliot's oeuvre, especially on the relation of the lyric to the critical prose, by means of which he shed light on Eliot's use of the metaphysical conceit, the objective correlative, the "clear, visual images" derived from Dante, and the "auditory imagination" that animated the poet's intricate verse forms. Matthiessen's discussion was never narrowly formalist: he viewed Eliot's style as an index to his sensibility, especially to his residual Puritanism, whose characteristics are described in a brilliant short passage (9–10). In Matthiessen's view, Eliot's poetry has "integrity" and "authenticity" because it so justly embodies the tensions and difficulties of living in the fragmented and alien world of the twentieth century and refuses to minimize human suffering in the urban landscape of the present.

Brooks's reading of *The Waste Land* was more explicatory, less concerned with the "auditory imagination" and formal features, but it came to curiously similar conclusions, although now with a Christian twist. *The Waste Land* is coherent, Brooks argued, because it embodies a central paradox, the "contrast between two kinds of life and two kinds of death." "Life devoid of meaning is death; sacrifice, even the sacrificial death, may be life-giving, an awakening to life" (137). In an extremely close reading, Brooks went on to illustrate this point, concluding that the "basic method" of the poem is "the application of the principle of complexity. The poet works in terms of surface parallelisms which in reality make ironical contrasts, and in terms of surface contrasts which in reality constitute parallelisms" (167). Madame Sosostris, for example, may be a vulgar charlatan, but in a deeper sense she does "tell" the narrator's fortune quite accurately. And so on.

For all the Eliot criticism produced in the fifty years since Brooks published his essay, it is doubtful that his analysis of the basic motifs and thematic threads has ever been bettered. Like Matthiessen, Brooks took for granted that a "good" poem, however seemingly diffuse like *The Waste Land*, would exhibit unity, integrity, wholeness. So ubiquitous was this view that generations of students were trained to find what Reuben Brower called, in his important New Critical textbook, "the key design" of a given work. In Andrew Hoover's modern novel course at Oberlin College in the 1950s, we were trained to look for precisely such key designs: the search of father for son and vice versa in *Ulysses*, the interlocking triangles formed by the Mother-Paul-Miriam and Miriam-Paul-Clara relationships in *Sons and Lovers*, the tension, present in the minutest details of setting and plot, between innocence and experience in *Daisy Miller*. The very opening sentence of a "successful" modern novel— say, "Mrs. Dalloway said she would buy the flowers herself"—would point obliquely but surely to the novel's central theme and structure. *Reading*, under these circumstances, became a riveting experience, culminating in what we had learned to call an epiphany: the underlying *form* of the work became radiant.

By the mid-1960s, however, epiphany had predictably begun to give way to familiarity: the codification of modernism was now under way. Richard Ellmann and Charles Feidelson's well-known case book of primary sources, *The Modern Tradition: Backgrounds of Modern Literature*, exemplifies this codifying and canonizing process at work. The title is itself revelatory: modernism—the *frisson nouveau* that excited Leavis and Wilson, Matthiessen and Brooks—was now a "tradition" requiring explanatory "backgrounds," grouped, by Ellmann and Feidelson, in nine categories: symbolism, realism, nature, cultural history, the unconscious, myth, self-consciousness, existence, and faith. This last section, focusing on the renewed Christianity of writers from Kierkegaard to Karl Barth and Paul Tillich, is, not surprisingly, the shortest, even as the first, "symbolism," is much the longest. Indeed, for Ellmann and

Feidelson, as I shall show in a moment, modernism and symbolism are nearly synonymous.

*The Modern Tradition* was based on the premise that

> "modern" amounts to more than a chronological description. The term desig-
> nates a distinctive kind of imagination. . . . One characteristic of works we call
> modern is that they positively insist on a general frame of reference within and
> beyond themselves. They claim modernity; they profess modernism.    (v)

Here is a claim that immediately points to the difficulty of relating modernist studies to Victorian or Elizabethan or eighteenth-century studies. One didn't claim to be eighteenth-century or Victorian, one either was or wasn't. But modernism was here asserted to be *more than* (and hence implicitly *better than*) the merely contemporary; it was, so the authors imply, an advanced doctrine, an elite state of mind, a kind of secular religion. Given this premise, Kant and Goethe, Darwin and Schopenhauer, Blake and Baudelaire were in-cluded in the anthology as, so to speak, protomoderns.

Modernism, in any case, now took on the characteristics that have defined it ever since in the popular imagination: (1) the replacement of repre-sentation of the external world by the imaginative construction of the poet's inner world via the mysterious symbol; (2) the superiority of art to nature; (3) the concept of the artist as hero; (4) the autonomy of art and its divorce from truth or morality; (5) the depersonalization and "objectivity" of art; (6) alogical structure, or what Joseph Frank called "spatial form"; (7) the concrete as opposed to the abstract, the particular as opposed to the general, the perceptual as opposed to the conceptual; (8) verbal ambiguity and complexity: "good" writing as inherently arcane; (9) the fluidity of consciousness: Woolf's "Life is not a series of gig lamps symmetrically arranged; but a luminous halo, a semi-transparent envelope surrounding us from the beginning of consciousness to the end" ("Modern Fiction" 287–88); (10) the increasing importance attached to the Freudian unconscious and to the dream work; (11) the use of myth as organizing structure, the calling up of the Jungian collective unconscious and of archetypes; (12) the emphasis on the divided self, on mask versus inner self (Yeats), conduct versus consciousness; (13) the malaise of the individual in the "lonely crowd," the alienated self in the urban world, the "Unreal City" of *The Waste Land* or *Ulysses*; and, finally, (14) the *internationalism* of modernism, with its free flow of artistic currents between Moscow and Rome, London and Berlin, Dublin and New York, all roads leading to Paris, quite literally the hub of the cultural wheel, as in Sonia Delaunay's illustration for Blaise Cendrars's *La prose du Transsibérien*, and the French language being the vehicle that brought together Mayakovksy and Marinetti, Picasso and Tatlin, Pound and Remy de Gourmont, Rilke and Proust.

Here, in a nutshell, is the version of modernism still propounded in most studies of the period. From Irving Howe's *Idea of the Modern in Literature and the Arts* to Helen Vendler's *Part of Nature, Part of Us: Modern American Poets* and Malcolm Bradbury's *Modern World: The Great Writers*, the familiar topoi just cited appear with reassuring regularity. At the same time, the very consensus on the modernist traits, as Ellmann and Feidelson presented them, set the stage for the inevitable reaction, when the more or less monolithic character of the modernist tradition would be called into question. For one thing, as the Ellmann-Feidelson model had already made clear, many of the poets and philosophers of the earlier nineteenth century had laid the groundwork for the modernist aesthetic. The next step, therefore, was to establish those links to Romanticism that the modernist writers themselves had denied so vigorously.

Three books, all of them published in 1957, made the case that modernist poetry was still squarely in the Romantic tradition. In *The Romantic Survival*, John Bayley argued that the poetry of Yeats, Auden, and Dylan Thomas carries on the Romantic polarity between subject and object, the "isolated creating self" and the "hostile" universe (10), that indeed these poets were more Wordsworthian than, as Eliot would have it, "classical." Robert Langbaum's *Poetry of Experience* made a similar case, tracing the derivation of the modern dramatic monologue, the poem of singular perspective eliciting a mixture of sympathy and judgment from the reader, to the early Romantic meditative lyric, what M. H. Abrams called "the greater Romantic lyric," with its empiricist placement of the speaker in a particular landscape at a particular moment in time, the course of meditation leading to psychological change and renewed insight. And in his classic study *Romantic Image*, Frank Kermode argued that imagist poetics, far from Making It New, were the logical culmination of Romantic and fin-de-siècle *symbolisme*, the main difference being the increasing reduction of the discursive field in which the symbol was embedded.

Such studies of Romantic-modernist continuities—studies that treat the last two centuries as a coherent post-Christian, post-Enlightenment period, in which the acute problem becomes the relationship of the I to the other in a world stripped of, but still longing for, transcendence—have obviously been more congenial to students of poetry than of fiction or drama or the newer genres. Theater critics, for example, are hardly likely to link the modernist drama of Strindberg or Shaw to the closet drama of Shelley. But in the case of lyric poetry, the Romantic era (in both England and America) was such an obvious golden age that the modernist poet, not to mention the modernist critic, could hardly escape its spell. Indeed, one of the best recent studies of modernist poetry, Albert Gelpi's *Coherent Splendor*, makes a strong case for the "continuity between the two supposedly opposing ideologies [Romanticism and modernism] which is deeper and more interesting than the initial points of contrast. . . .

Emerson and Stevens, Whitman and Pound—or Emerson and Pound, Whitman and Stevens—are Janus-faces that turn around and face each other" (2, 5).

But the most radical case for the Romanticism of the literature called modernist has been that of Harold Bloom. In 1970 Bloom, whose early works like *The Visionary Company* dealt with the English Romantic poets, published a revisionist study of Yeats that marks a turning point in modernist scholarship. "Yeats," Bloom declared in the first sentence of the preface, "was a poet very much in the line of vision; his ancestors in English poetic tradition were primarily Blake and Shelley." Further, "Yeats, Hardy, and Wallace Stevens seem to me the poets writing in English in our century whose work most merits sustained comparison with the major poets of the nineteenth century." As for Eliot and Pound, "the Cowley and Cleveland of this age," Bloom's prediction was that they would, quite simply, "vanish" (v).

Such extreme statements were, of course, intentionally outrageous. Ellmann's Yeats (and Ellmann was Bloom's colleague at Yale) was primarily the poet of complex symbolism, dramatic irony, and the "right mastery of natural things." Bloom dismissed this Yeats (especially the ironist of *The Green Helmet* and *Responsibilities*) as writing "against the grain" (163), the "real" Yeats being no rhetorician or Public Man but a Shelleyan "antithetical quester" of visionary power. This assessment paved the way for a whole series of "antithetical" studies, beginning with *The Anxiety of Influence* and *A Map of Misreading* and culminating in *Wallace Stevens: The Poems of Our Climate*. As a group, these "misreadings" stood modernism on its head.

What were the assumptions behind Bloom's argument that "[m]odernism in literature has not passed; rather, it has been exposed as never having been there" (*Map* 28)? Simply put, that the purpose of poetry is to teach us, in Stevens's words, "How to Live. What to Do," by providing us with a coherent visionary universe, indeed a kind of humanist religion. Bloom took as his starting point Emerson's famous dictum that "it is not meters, but a meter-making argument that makes a poem,—a thought so passionate and alive that like the spirit of a plant or an animal it has an architecture of its own. . . . The thought and the form are equal in the order of time, but in the order of genesis the thought is prior to the form" (20). Given this emphasis on poetry as the genesis of visionary content rather than of form, it is not surprising that Bloom came to regard modernism as no more than a belated Romanticism, even as Romanticism is itself a belated version of Miltonic poetics. The best a twentieth-century poet could hope for, in this scheme of things, is the "diminished but authentic Romanticism" exemplified by Stevens, "the Freudian wisdom that accepts limitation without prematurely setting limits" (*Yeats* 215). Pound's "phalanx of particulars," Eliot's orthodoxy—these evidently represent a gray zone where the high calling of the poet degenerates into mere verse.

Bloom's theory of the "anxiety of influence," the notion that "poetic strength" can come only "from a triumphant wrestling with the greatest of the dead, and from an even more triumphant solipsism" (*Map* 9), that the poet must always "*misinterpret* the father by the crucial act of misprision, which is the rewriting of the father" (19), and that hence the meaning of a poem can only be *another* poem, need not detain us here, nor do I want to discuss, yet again, the Kabbalist "revisionary ratios" and "theory of crossings" that provide Bloom with his methodology (see Perloff, *Dance* 1–23, 174–76). Rather, I want to consider the larger implications of the Bloomian stance and its repercussions in the academy.

"Why," asks Bloom, "do we read one poet rather than another? We believe the lies we want to believe because they help us to survive. Similarly, we read (reread) the poems that keep our discourse with ourselves going. Strong poems strengthen us by teaching us *how to talk to ourselves*, rather than how to talk to others" (*Wallace Stevens* 387). In placing such a high value on the power of poetry to change life, to produce "discourse" that can sustain us, Bloom's version of modernism is best regarded as a kind of humanist holding operation against the barbarism at the gates—the barbarism of those poets for whom Milton and Wordsworth are no longer *the* precursors with whom they must wrestle and who, indeed, are no longer wrestling primarily with the "displaced Protestantism" that is, for Bloom, at the heart of *the* Anglo-American poetic tradition. In a now notorious essay called "The Sorrows of American-Jewish Poetry," Bloom declared that not a "single American-Jewish poet of undoubted major status has established himself in a century now more than two-thirds gone" (247). His attitude to feminist poetics and to the various ethnic and minority poetries has been even more dismissive.

In retrospect, it seems startling that so authoritarian and narrowly drawn a modernist canon as Bloom's did not come under fire sooner. Throughout the 1970s, Bloom functioned as guru, his disciples spreading the gospel in any number of books with titles like *Keats and the Sublime* (Ende) or *The Limits of Imagination: Wordsworth, Yeats, and Stevens* (Reguero). Even a "strong" feminist book like Sandra M. Gilbert and Susan Gubar's *Madwoman in the Attic* was based largely on Bloom's theory of the anxiety of influence.

Then suddenly the bubble seems to have burst. By the mid-1980s, younger poets were no longer lining up to receive the Bloomian accolade, and graduate students seemed barely to know who Bloom was, even though books kept coming off the presses and the Chelsea House volumes of essays on the major writers were appearing under his editorship. The rapidity of the shift from Bloom's Romantic and Freudian humanism to the more politicized ethos of the 1980s came home to me when a doctoral dissertation written under my direction, David Fite's *Harold Bloom: The Rhetoric of Romantic Vision*, was published by the University of Massachusetts Press. At the time the manuscript was accepted (1983–84), Bloom was still the subject of intense debate. By 1986, when the reviews of Fite's book began to appear, debate had moved elsewhere, and so the reviews were as pleasant and polite as they were unengaged.

What is it that had happened? Had Bloom become the victim of the fashionable new jargons? Or of the hegemony first of deconstruction and then of Marxist and feminist theory? Fite, who called his concluding chapter "Humanism in the Extreme: The Predicament of Romantic Redemption," followed Paul de Man in suggesting that Bloom's conception of the Romantic imagination as "autonomous, nonreferential, acting according to the sublime guidance of its own 'internalized' laws" precluded the possibility that there might be a "conceptual language adequate to it" (166). One might add that the Bloomian dilemma was the desire to have it both ways: to move, somehow, "beyond" the "mere" *explication de texte* attributed to formalist critics and yet to remain entirely within a *literary* universe. True, the anxiety of influence presupposes a temporality that previous "close readers" may have minimized: Ashbery had to wrestle with his precursor Stevens, who, in turn, wrestled with Whitman and Emerson. But temporality as Bloom conceived of it was a closed poetic system, as self-referential as Northrop Frye's mythic one and more self-referential, ironically enough, than the empirically grounded New Criticism and related movements of the 1950s and 1960s. The map of misreading—Bloom's form of geography—was undone by the very history it had been trying to suppress.

Indeed, if history has proved to be more of a problem for Bloom than for his Yale deconstructionist colleagues—Paul de Man, J. Hillis Miller, and Geoffrey Hartman—it is probably because deconstruction tended to deny the very possibility of period concepts and regarded terms like *modernism* with suspicion. "Modernity," wrote de Man, "exists in the form of a desire to wipe out whatever came earlier, in the hope of reaching at last a point that could be called a true present, a point of origin that marks a new departure" ("Literary History" 148). Since such a "point of origin" is obviously illusory, "modernity cannot assert itself without being at once swallowed up and reintegrated into a regressive historical process." Hence, "modernity and history seem condemned to being linked together in a self-destroying union that threatens the survival of both" (151).

This self-destroying union clears the air for the study of poetic language and rhetoric, examined theoretically rather than historically. One major branch of modernist studies has moved in this direction, producing, as in the case of Hillis Miller, superbly subtle (sometimes supersubtle) readings of "major" modernist poems like Yeats's "Nineteen Hundred and Nineteen" or Stevens's "Rock" (see *Linguistic Moment*) or of novels like *Mrs. Dalloway* and *Between the Acts* (*Fiction and Repetition*). But since Miller's were conceived as exemplary readings of difficult texts, rather than as commentary on modernism as such, they will not concern me here. Rather, I want to look now at the cultural—and primarily Marxist—critique of modernist ideology that came into prominence in the 1980s and has, until quite recently, dominated the academy.

One of the first important discussions of the link between modernism and authoritarian politics appeared in Kermode's *Sense of an Ending*. In the apocalyptic fictions of Pound and Yeats, Eliot and Wyndham Lewis, Kermode detected a dangerous turn toward explanatory myth and system building. Yeats, for example, all but looked forward to the universal bloodshed that would hasten the end of his own "broken-down, odious epoch and the start of another, aristocratic, courtly, eugenic" (107). In turning his back on the reality of everyday life for a "system of aesthetics" that might control history (*A Vision*), "Yeats is our first example of that correlation between early modernist literature and authoritarian politics which is more often noticed than explained: totalitarian theories of form matched or reflected by totalitarian politics" (108).

Pound and Lewis represent, of course, even more extreme cases of such "paradigmatic rigidity" (110). "It appears, in fact," Kermode concluded,

> that modernist radicalism in art—the breaking down of pseudo-traditions, the making new on a true understanding of the nature of the elements of art—this radicalism involves the creation of fictions which may be dangerous in the dispositions they breed toward the world. . . . there is to be order as the modernist artist understands it: rigid, out of flux, the spatial order of the modern critic, or the closed authoritarian society.                                               (111)

Considered in this light, Eliot's celebrated cult of "tradition" could be seen as a longing for "the continuity of imperial deposits," a "persistent nostalgia for closed, immobile hierarchical societies" (112).

I cite Kermode's commentary at some length because it set the stage for a much more critical assessment of modernism than that of the earlier decades. Kermode himself, it is only fair to say, did not claim that modernism was necessarily authoritarian or proto-Fascist; indeed, he cited Joyce's *Ulysses* as a counterexample to Eliot and Yeats, a work that "asserts the resistance of fact to fiction, human freedom and predictability against plot" (113). But Marxist criticism, from Georg Lukács on down, has questioned such theories of exception and has argued that, on the contrary, modernism, in the words of Russell A. Berman, "objectively corresponded to fascist tendencies regardless of the subjectively expressed political allegiances of the author" (95). Thus, whereas the more conventional discussions of a writer's politics—say, John A. Harrison's *Reactionaries* (on Yeats, Eliot, Pound, Lewis, and Lawrence) or

Robert Casillo's *Genealogy of Demons* (on Pound's anti-Semitism)—treat the writer's ideology as individual and volitional, the more sophisticated body of Marxist studies reads the modernist text as inevitably marked by what Jameson has called a definable "political unconscious."

Take the issue of symbolism. For Ellmann and Feidelson, as I noted above, *symbolisme*, as derived from Baudelaire and Mallarmé, was the cornerstone of modernist aesthetic. In his brilliant *Théories du symbole*, Tzvetan Todorov traced the "Romantic crisis" whereby the symbol came to embody the process of knowing itself, its indirection and mystery: "[the symbol] achieves the fusion of contraries; it is and it signifies at the same time; its content eludes reason: it expresses the inexpressible. . . . the symbol is produced unconsciously, and it provokes an unending task of interpretation" (206). And further: "in the symbol, it is the signified itself that has become a signifier; the two faces of the sign have merged" (213).

But why could consciousness no longer make contact with the external world except through the mediation of symbols? What was the political dimension of the cult of ineffability, mystery, plurisignification? Todorov, whose aim was primarily descriptive rather than evaluative, did not raise this question, but for a Marxist like Lukács, it was *the* question. The modernist drive toward symbolism rather than the realism of the great nineteenth-century novels (which Lukács takes to be the normative mode) was for Lukacs an indirect admission of failure. "Having recourse [to symbolism]," as Jameson explained it, "the writer implies that some original, objective meaning in objects is henceforth inaccessible to him, that he must invent a new and fictive one to conceal this basic absence, this silence of things" (*Marxism and Form* 197). The original "meaningfulness" of objects, in other words, a meaningfulness that "becomes visible only when their link with human labor and production is unconcealed," is lost in modern industrial civilization when objects are reified: thus Joyce's newspaper office in *Ulysses* is perceived as a cave of winds, and the furniture in James's *Spoils of Poynton* is more "alive" than the people who fight over its possession.

For Lukács this situation signified the artistic decline of modernist literature, its inability to portray life without erecting a wall of verbal mediation. For Jameson, however, such modernist "repression," as Theodor Adorno had shown with regard to music, could function as a sign of genuine engagement on the writer's part. Indeed, for Jameson the most "interesting" modernist works are those most revelatory of "the great collective and class discourses of which a text is little more than an individual *parole* or utterance." *Explication de texte*, in this context, becomes the search for the *ideologeme*, "the smallest intelligible unit of the essentially antagonistic collective discourses of social class" (*Political Unconscious* 76).

Consider Jameson's trenchant analysis of Wyndham Lewis's novels in

*Fables of Aggression*. Lewis, Jameson argued, has suffered neglect because his "expressionist" fiction doesn't fit the more "impressionist" model of "canonical modernism," with its "strategies of inwardness, which set out to reappropriate an alienated universe by transforming it into personal styles and private languages" (2). For Lewis, far from seeming to protest the "fragmentation of modern social life" as did his more famous contemporaries, aggressively affirms "the most extreme restatements of grotesque traditional sexist myths and attitudes"—for example, "the obsessive phobia against homosexuals" and a "polemic hostility to feminism" (4). But the very gap between style and narrative in Lewis's work, between the *molecular* and the *molar*—as Gilles Deleuze and Félix Guattari referred to micro- and macrostructure, the individual speech event and the larger narrative, in their *Anti-Oedipus*—creates a force field that can be interpreted as containing the most deep-seated aporias of capitalism.

Following Louis Althusser's definition of the ideological as a narrative representation of "the Imaginary relationship of individuals to their real conditions of existence" (*Lenin* 162), Jameson read Lewis's novels as displaying in their very diction and sentence structure "the return of the repressed." Modernism, by this argument, is not overtly "revolutionary," the "repudiation of the values of a business society and of its characteristic representational categories" (13), but the very adoption, in its language and narrative structure, of those ideologemes that reveal the contradictions of capitalist economic structures.

This argument and its later elaboration in *The Political Unconscious* has proved to be extremely appealing to academic critics. Methodologically, it meant that one could still do subtle interpretation, using psychoanalytic theory and Derridean interpretive modes, not in the interest, now, of explicating a given author's meaning but in order to "unpack" or "unmask" the *episteme*, as Foucault called it, of a whole age. Then, too, the choice of an overtly proto-Fascist writer like Lewis (or, as became increasingly common, of Pound and Celine) generated a certain excitement—a *frisson nouveau*—in the scholarly community: one was "permitted," indeed required, to grapple with writers who were overtly anti-Semitic, racist, sexist, and possibly Nazi, because their work revealed, in purer form than the more mixed writing of a Joyce or a Faulkner, the "truth" about the degraded life lived under capitalism.

Jameson's readings of Gissing and Conrad in *The Political Unconscious*, his revisionist studies of, say, the *nouveau roman* in essays like "Modernism and Its Repressed: Or, Robbe-Grillet as Anti-colonialist" have the genuine excitement of discovery: *Nostromo*, we learn, "is not really a novel about political upheaval" but "a virtual textbook working-out of the structuralist dictum that all narrative enacts a passage from Nature to Culture" (*Political Unconscious* 272). And so on. The difficulty in accepting Jameson's readings, however, is that we must, by his own account, accept his basic premise, which is that history has "a single vast unfinished plot," defined in Marx and Engels's *Communist Manifesto*, to wit:

> The history of all hitherto existing society is the history of class struggles: freeman and slave, patrician and plebeian, lord and serf, guild-master and journeyman—in a word, oppressor and oppressed—stood in constant opposition to one another, carried on an uninterrupted, now hidden, now open fight, a fight that each time ended, either in a revolutionary reconstitution of society at large or in the common ruin of the contending classes.    (20)

But suppose we don't believe in this particular dogma? Suppose we doubt the existence of this "single vast unfinished plot," this dialectical model of class struggle as an adequate description of the world as we find it, that indeed the literature of modernism does not provide us with dialectical models of oppressor and oppressed but a much more complicated and ambiguous universe? In that case, we may conclude that the "unpacking" of the "political unconscious" of this or that work is not the most fruitful avenue of criticism. Then, too, in the hands of Jameson's followers, the "ideologemes" to be uncovered are always more or less the same, so that a certain monotony sets in. Hidden power relations, the hidden inequities of a colonialism and an imperialism, masked as benevolence and hence waiting to be correctly interpreted— these are now reported on, in the case of modernist writers like Conrad and Forster, Joyce and Kafka, with the tedious regularity that used to be associated with topics like "Paradox in W. H. Auden's *Sea and the Mirror*" or "Organic Unity in *Gerontion*."

Still, the issues of power and inequity have also forced us to redraw the map of modernism in ways that have been extremely fruitful. This has especially been the case with feminist and minority remappings of the modernist field. From Malcolm Cowley and Edmund Wilson down to Harold Bloom (and Marxist criticism has hardly been exempt from the charge), modernism, as the earlier part of this essay makes amply clear, was the work almost exclusively *of* men *for* men—both the authors and their critics were safely male. And further: modernism pertained to *white* men, indeed white Christian men. Among women writers, Virginia Woolf (usually referred to as Mrs. Woolf) was the great exception (Edith Wharton, Willa Cather, Marianne Moore were among the others), but her work was generally construed as primarily a variant on Proustian impressionism and Joycean plot construction. Thus when I first read *Mrs. Dalloway* as an undergraduate, the consensus was that the novel's structure of simultaneity (e.g., Clarissa, Peter, and Septimus presented in scenes occurring at the same time, the transitions signaled by the striking of Big Ben) was to be understood as a somewhat simplified version of Joyce's elaborately patterned twenty-four time scheme in *Ulysses*.

We now have, thanks to the studies of Phyllis Rose, Jane Marcus, Alex Zwerdling, Maria diBattista, and many others, a different Virginia Woolf, a novelist, not of delicate "feminine" sensibility, concerned, as it used to be assumed, primarily with the delicate nuances of personal relationships, but a tough-minded writer, involved with the politics, the society, the family and gender relationships of her day. Such studies as Gilbert and Gubar's *No Man's Land: The Place of the Woman Writer in the Twentieth Century* (vol. 1, *The War of the Words*, came out in 1988; vol. 2, *Sexchanges*, in 1989; and there is one more volume to come) and Shari Benstock's *Women of the Left Bank: Paris, 1900–1940* (1986) have shown conclusively that Anglo-American modernism becomes a very different phenomenon when the writing of women, hitherto suppressed, is reinscribed into its narrative. The Gilbert and Gubar project raises larger theoretical issues; I want, however, to say something about *Women of the Left Bank*.

"The impetus for this study of expatriate women," writes Benstock, "was the desire to replace them in the Paris context from which they had been removed by the standard literary histories of Modernism" (ix). The women of the Left Bank include Edith Wharton, Gertrude Stein, Djuna Barnes, HD, Mina Loy, and Jean Rhys—surely a powerful group of writers that can no longer be ignored or relegated to the margins. Take the case of HD, for decades considered a relatively minor *imagiste*, affiliated with Ezra Pound, but now understood—thanks to the work of critics like Albert Gelpi, Susan Stanford Friedman, Rachel Blau DuPlessis, and Benstock herself—as a very different sort of modernist, whose imagination, especially in her autobiographical fictions like *Hermione* and her "palimpsestic" poems like *Helen in Egypt*, foreground a dialect between male and female, heterosexual and homosexual, violence and peace, science and beauty (Benstock 335–36) that really has no direct counterpart in the poetry of Pound or the fiction of Joyce.

The case of Stein is even more dramatic: regarded for years as a great "character," the doyenne of the leading literary and artistic salon of *entre deux guerres* and the amusing raconteuse of *The Autobiography of Alice B. Toklas*, Stein was regularly referred to as having exerted an important influence on male writers like Hemingway and Sherwood Anderson, with the proviso that, thank goodness, Hemingway, for one, transformed what Wyndham Lewis called "Miss Stein's baby talk" into something much more interesting, much less "boring." Again, it has only been in the past decade or so that Stein's *difference*—her genuinely radical modernism—has begun to be explored. At the same time, Stein's writing is so elusive, so difficult to categorize as "feminist" or "lesbian," "Jewish" or "expatriate," "deconstructionist" or "postmodernist," that the spate of recent books about her has not, to my mind, yet rectified the misunderstandings of early modernist studies.

Benstock's *Women of the Left Bank* is excellent as social history, less good at the critical reading of texts. Indeed, the sections on Stein and on Proust have a secondhand air, as if Benstock herself had not really *read* her way through *Tender Buttons* and *The Making of Americans*, much less *A la recherche du tempts perdu*. Then, too, a separatist history like this one is in danger of being as one-sided as the history it wishes to replace: in the case of HD and Barnes, especially, one wants to understand how the literary formations themselves are and are not like those produced by the male writers of their circle.

What is known as canon revision is perhaps more properly understood as canon reversal: a case of getting rid of *A* and putting *B* in its place. An example of such canon reversal is to be found in Nelson's *Repression and Recovery*, whose aim is "to revise our notion of the social function of poetry, an effort grounded in a series of rereadings of marginalized or forgotten poets— particularly women, blacks, and writers on the left—and in a theoretical discussion of poetry's cultural status as a discourse among others" (xi). In this variant of Marxist criticism, the effort is to "recover" those poets that the dominant histories have consistently "repressed," not primarily for the sake of their aesthetic value—the *aesthetic* being, for a critic like Nelson, a suspect (and itself politically motivated) category—but for their cultural and historical role.

Nelson has unearthed some fascinating and little-known material, both verbal and visual—pamphlet anthologies like *The Rebel Poets* (1917), IWW song sheets and broadsides, Communist journals like *Contempo* (1931–34)—and he usefully discusses the poets of the Harlem Renaissance (e.g., Claude McKay, James Weldon Johnson, Sterling A. Brown), not just as a separate group but in relation to the other poets of the 1920s and 1930s: proletarian poets, women poets, and, for that matter, a number of black women poets not part of the "Renaissance," like Angelina Weld Grimke and Gwendolyn Bennett. Nelson's account of proletarian poetry, which was published in profusion throughout the 1930s in collections like S. A. De Witt's *Rhapsodies in Red* and in short-lived pamphlets like *Fire!* and *When the Sirens Blow*, recaptures an important chapter in American cultural history and reminds us that from Joe Hill's *Little Red Song Book* of the 1900s to the *New Masses* of the 1930s there was a proletarian lyric that was accessible, popular, and inspiring.

As someone who remembers singing the Joe Hill songs, especially "Pie in the Sky," when I was a teenager at work camp, I find this material extremely interesting even as I cannot accept the theory of modernism that Nelson builds around it. He admits that "literary history is never an innocent process of recovery," that "we recover what we are culturally and psychologically prepared to recover" (11), but since his own canon is primarily designed to *include* that which has been formerly *excluded*, he places, side by side with his black and proletarian poets, Dada poets like Lola Ridge, Mina Loy, and Charles Henri

Ford, expatriate women poets like Laura Riding and Stein, and objectivists like Louis Zukofsky and Charles Reznikoff, the latter because of their Marxist connection. The difficulty is that most of these, so to speak, neglected others, diametrically opposed the straightforward and popular proletarian lyric to be found in, say, the *New Masses*: the Stein of *Tender Buttons*, for example, would have had no use for Lucia Brent, whose 1929 "Black Men" evokes a lynching in the lines, "Tonight the earth is leper-pale and still; / The moon lies like a tombstone in the sky. / Three black men sway upon a lonely hill" (Nelson 119). In making exclusion or marginalization the sine qua non of inclusion in the "new" canon, Nelson thus skews the picture, especially since the exclusions that concern Nelson are always ideologically defined—Communists, women, blacks—whereas it might be useful to explore why certain once-popular white male poets of the period 1910–45—Madison Cawein, say, the so-called great Western poet whose work appeared side by side with Ezra Pound's in *The Egoist* and *Little Review*—have been so wholly "repressed" by a later generation. Most modernist writers, or should I say most writers, have, after all, been forgotten.

"From the Modernism that you want," the poet David Antin once quipped, "you get the postmodernism you deserve." Perhaps the greatest difficulty, for contemporary criticism of modernism, is to assume that there must be one metanarrative that will "explain" the term or movement once and for all. If, from his Marxist perspective, Nelson wishes to argue that proletarian poetry of the American 1930s deserves a central place in a revised canon, well and good, but what is not clear is why Nelson's version of modernism is not just as guilty of "systemic distortions" as is the "single master narrative" (7) it claims to replace. Indeed, the real question is why we continue to be haunted by the desire to set up anything so totalizing as a modernist model in the first place. In *The Dismemberment of Orpheus*, Ihab Hassan drew up a chart, admittedly schematic, of the differences between modernism and postmodernism. Here, with a few omissions, is Hassan's schema:

| *Modernism* | *Postmodernism* |
|---|---|
| Romanticism/Symbolism | Pataphysics/Dadaism |
| Form (conjunctive, closed) | Antiform (disjunctive, open) |
| Purpose | Play |
| Design | Chance |
| Hierarchy | Anarchy |
| Mastery/Logos | Exhaustion/Silence |
| Art Object/Finished Work | Process/Performance/Happening |
| Distance | Participation |
| Synthesis | Antithesis |

| Modernism | Postmodernism |
|---|---|
| Presence | Absence |
| Centering | Dispersal |
| Genre / Boundary | Text / Intertext |
| Paradigm | Syntagm |
| Hypotaxis | Parataxis |
| Metaphor | Metonym |
| Lisible [readerly] | Scriptible [writerly] |
| Master Code | Idiolect |
| Origin / Cause | Différance / Trace |
| God the Father | The Holy Ghost |
| Metaphysics | Irony |
| Determinacy | Indeterminacy |
| Transcendence | Immanence |

Interestingly, many of Hassan's modernist attributes are the same as Ellmann and Feidelson's—for example, "symbolism," "design," "art object," "centering"—only now they take on a negative aura vis-à-vis their postmodern counterparts (e.g., "chance" rather than "design," "play" rather than "purpose," "open" rather than "closed" form, "dispersal" rather than "centering," and so on). One of Hassan's purposes surely—both here and in other versions of this chart (see *Postmodern Turn*)—was to justify the seeming peculiarities of postmodern literature to an audience still accustomed to the structures of modernism; he wanted to show and, to my mind, succeeded in showing, that the "new" literature was characterized by indeterminacy and *difference*, by "dispersal" and "absence," by "open" and "disjunctive" form.

The difficulty—and here we find a repetition of the romanticism-modernism conundrum—is that so many of these postmodern qualities were already present in the work of the early century—work that, indeed, cannot be accommodated to Hassan's left-hand column. Closure in the *Cantos*? Kafka's *Trial* or Kurt Schwitters's *Merzbau* as "finished works"? The "master code" of Stein's *Stanzas in Meditation* or of Tristan Tzara's *Approximate Man*? "Centering" in Williams's *Spring and All*? "Distance" in Lawrence's *Birds, Beasts and Flowers*? Hierarchy in Stevens's *Auroras of Autumn*? Duchamp's *Fountain* as "synthesis"? Conrad's *Nostromo* as "readerly" rather than "writerly" text?

As we come to the end of the century, it is the variety of modernisms that strikes us; indeed, the "totalization" often attributed to modernism belongs much less to the literature of modernism than to its theorists. Hence the measure of dissatisfaction one feels reading even such excellent books as Sanford Schwartz's *Matrix of Modernism* or Michael Levenson's *Genealogy of Modernism*. The aim of the former is "to explore the affiliations between Modernist poetics and contemporaneous developments in philosophy," specifically Henri Bergson, William James, F. C. Bradley, Nietzsche, and Husserl. Earlier critics,

Schwartz contends, have taken an "atomistic approach" to "the Modernist movement," treating literature independently of philosophy, whereas his own method is to "construct a matrix that brings together a significant number of philosophers and poets, and articulates the relationships among them" (4).

The difficulty with this approach is that philosophical writing becomes "context," literature "text," a dichotomy poststructuralist criticism has taught us is dubious. Further, despite the many striking links Schwartz is able to set up—between, say, Nietzsche's concept of metaphor and Eliot's, or between William James's and Pound's suspicion of abstraction—the equation of modernist literature with Anglo-American literature even as its philosophical "matrix" is almost exclusively Continental, and the further assumption that Eliot and Pound "stand for" modernism, limits the value of Schwartz's generalizations.

Levenson's *Genealogy of Modernism* covers much of the same ground but treats its material historically rather than generically and hence makes more modest, and more convincing, claims than Schwartz's book. He begins with the early modernist tension—most notable in Conrad—between the "rhetorical call for the sensory apprehension of life's surfaces" and the opposing demand for "inwardness and depth" (1), a tension later taken up by T. E. Hulme, who set up the image—visual, concrete, intuitive, expressive—over against the "seductions of metaphysics" (*Genealogy* 47). Here, Levenson argues, is the "distinctive early Modernist doctrine," circa 1910, a doctrine that, in the course of the transformation of impressionism and symbolism into imagism and finally vorticism, hardened into the aggressive call for an autonomous, spatialized, dehumanized art. By the time of *The Waste Land*, the dark side of modernism had come to the fore—its "suspicion of progress," its "hostility toward individualism and modern democracy," its "insistence on hierarchy and order" and the "need for an outer authority to restrain inner caprice" (210). Here, indeed, is "modernism" as it appears on the left side of Hassan's chart.

As an account of Eliot's and Pound's move away from the openness and genuine radicalism of pre–World War I "modernist" aesthetic, Levenson's book (modestly subtitled, for that matter, *A Study of English Literary Doctrine 1908–22*) is excellent. Again, however, it is important to remember that Eliot was only one kind of modernist and hardly the most typical kind, that the map of modernism would look rather different if it centered on Joyce or on Stein instead. Or if we forget about centering modernism to begin with. Many of the best modernist studies, after all, are studies of individual authors, like Ian Watt's *Conrad in the Nineteenth Century* or John Bishop's astonishing *Joyce's Book of the Dark*: Finnegans Wake. Space considerations make it impossible to consider all such studies here, but I want to say something about a branch of modernist criticism now producing vigorous debate: namely, the relationship of the international avant-gardes of the early century (e.g., futurism, Dada, surrealism, expressionism, constructivism) to the work of the more mainstream modernists (e.g., Yeats, Eliot, Joyce, Faulkner, Woolf, Shaw). Here the starting point remains Renato Poggioli's *Theory of the Avant-Garde*, whose title Peter Bürger intentionally adopted when, in the 1970s, he challenged what he took to be Poggioli's excessively optimistic case for the conjunction, in the pre–World War I period, of the political and the aesthetic avant-garde, arguing, contra Poggioli, that the avant-garde (Bürger's example is primarily Dada) contained the seeds of its cooption by the dominant bourgeois culture and was hence doomed to failure. In his *Five Faces of Modernity*, Matei Calinescu details the nineteenth-century background, both historical and ideological, for this debate and provides a fascinating account of the evolving meanings of those slippery terms *avant-garde, decadence*, and *kitsch* and their role in the transformation of modernism into postmodernism. And in a highly original oppositional study, *The Theory Death of the Avant-Garde*, Paul Mann takes up the question To what extent does the current discourse about the fabled death of the avant-garde itself create that death?

These books provide the theoretical underpinning of such more specific works as Dickran Tashjian's *Skyscraper Primitives: Dada and the American Avant-Garde 1910–25*, Cecelia Tichi's *Shifting Gears: Technology, Literature, Culture in Modernist America*, Laurence Goldstein's *Flying Machine and Modern Literature*, Andreas Huyssen's *After the Great Divide: Modernism, Mass Culture, Postmodernism*, and my own *Futurist Moment: Avant-Garde, Avant-Guerre, and the Language of Rupture*, which focuses on the utopian phase of modernism in its futurist formation (in France, Russia, and Italy as well as in Anglo-America), immediately before the First World War. In connection with my own research, I want further to mention a monumental work on this early stage of modernism: L. Brion-Guerry's three-volume compilation *L'année 1913*. Brion-Guerry includes essays on every facet of her chosen year; more important, she also includes source material (manifestos, critical programs, essays, letters) that nicely complement the material in Ellmann-Feidelson; and she provides, in her final volume, elaborate charts of what was happening, in every field of artistic endeavor, in politics and social life all over the world in 1913.

To scan these charts alone is to understand that modernism can never be dismissed as the era of closure, spatialization, order, centering, proto-Fascism, and so on. Indeed, it is almost impossible to think that so many varied art works, novels, plays, poems, ballets, works of architecture, and so on could be produced in the single year 1913. *L'année 1913* also forces us to reconsider the time frame of modernism; as I learned when I studied the futurist moment, the war marked a watershed in artistic production from which we have never recovered, putting an end to first-phase modernism with its utopian, radical, largely optimistic momentum. It can be and has been argued that what we now think of as the great modernist innovations, from stream of consciousness, to simultaneity, to collage-montage, and the mixing of genres, were all in place by 1914 and that the work of the next three decades served largely as refinement and dissemination. For others, the key date comes later: 1922, say, the year of *The Waste Land*, the publication of *Ulysses*, and the ferment in Paris described in *Women of the Left Bank*; or again, a case can be made for the modernism of the 1930s—the ethnographic surrealism of the Bataille-Leiris circle, the poetics of *négritude* in Aimé Césaire and Léopold Senghor, and, in Anglo-America, the politically radical phase of the Auden group, the objectivists, the Harlem Renaissance, and the proletarian writers discussed by Nelson.

Whatever the decade that strikes us as quintessentially "modern," one of the features of our period—and I alluded to this phenomenon at the beginning of this discussion—is the continuing relationship between "creative writer" and "critic." Not only were the early defenders of modernism themselves poets or fiction writers, but from Beckett's *Proust* to Walter Benjamin's essay on Proust in *Illuminations*, from Lawrence's *Study of Thomas Hardy* to Auden's essay on Lawrence's *Birds, Beasts, and Flowers*, from Donald Davie's two books on Pound to Charles Tomlinson's appraisal of Williams and the objectivists in *Some Americans*, from Djuna Barnes's 1917 interview with Valentine de Saint-Point to Lyn Hejinian's recent essays on Stein in *Temblor* and Charles Bernstein's essays on Laura Riding and Charles Olson in *Content's Dream*—it is the poets and novelists themselves who continue to tell us what modernism was.

It is in this context that I conclude with a note on a modernist critic I have not yet mentioned—Hugh Kenner. When I was preparing this essay, I realized that Kenner's is a name one never comes across in the many textbooks on new theoretical directions, textbooks like Hazard Adams and Leroy Searle's *Critical Theory since 1965*, for the simple reason that Kenner doesn't fit into any school. Neither a New Critic nor a Russian formalist, an old or a new historicist, a phenomenologist or a structuralist, a Heideggerian or a Marxist or a feminist, Kenner is not the subject of critical monographs as is Harold Bloom, say, or Stanley Fish. Yet the more modernist literature one reads, the more one realizes that no other critic of modernism has made as much difference as has Kenner.

How do we characterize the methodology of *The Pound Era*; of *Dublin's Joyce, Joyce's Voices*, and *Ulysses*; of the two books on Samuel Beckett; of *Stoic Comedians, A Homemade World*, and *A Sinking Island*? From the time that he wrote—in six weeks, as he tells us in the preface to the new edition—*The Poetry of Ezra Pound*, Kenner's has been an advocacy-criticism, his aim being to elucidate how particular texts *work* and why, in his view, they work well.

To carry out this mission, Kenner absorbs the atmosphere of his subject: in writing on Beckett, he writes like Beckett; in writing on Pound, he writes like Pound. At the same time, his criticism is by no means impressionistic or even, strictly speaking, text-based, for it shifts without warning from the work to the life, from the work to the culture that produced it, from a word used in a poem or short story to that word's etymology, and so on. Another way of putting it would be to say that Kenner is himself writing as a poet-scholar.

Thus *The Pound Era*, as many of its original reviewers remarked in exasperation, is itself a collage with the "And then . . ." structure of the *Cantos*. It begins with a narrative about Pound's introduction to Henry James on a Chelsea street and skips about, in only loosely chronological order, covering topics like the troubadours, "Knot and Vortex," "The Invention of China," and "The Sacred Places." For Kenner, the modernist revolution is, above all, a question of reforming the language in the light of late nineteenth-century deadness and middlebrow cliché; in his concern for language, both in its ability to refer (Kenner is brilliant at tracking down allusions, say, to a particular fresco or medieval text) and to create its own resonances, Kenner slights many things: plot, character (indeed, he has little sense of the novel as representation), ideology. His politics (at best, he has played the aesthetic card, ignoring the "political unconscious" of his chosen writers as well as the ideological implications of his own position; at worst he has seemed to condone Pound's fascism and Eliot's anti-Semitism), his residual sexism and perhaps unconscious homophobia (*The Pound Era* does slight two women writers who certainly belong to its narrative, Stein and HD; and *A Sinking Island* is unnecessarily dismissive of Woolf and the Bloomsbury and Auden groups)— these qualities have earned Kenner the hatred of many academics today, even as others have objected to the mannerism and occasional coyness of his style.

In response, it could be argued that Kenner has never pretended that his criticism is objective or disinterested. Rather, his is a scholarly *inside* view of modernism, or a certain branch of modernism, by one who is himself a "belated" modernist. But Kenner's modernism is by no means Cleanth Brooks's or Lionel Trilling's. A Flaubertian with an obsessive concern for le mot juste (and Kenner has written very well on Flaubert), Kenner, like Pound, goes in fear of abstractions. Whereas the New Critics had little taste for the later Pound or for Williams, and certainly not for Louis Zukofsky and George Oppen, Kenner has championed these writers as the true modernists; along with Conrad, Joyce, Wyndham Lewis, Marianne Moore, and, to a somewhat lesser degree, Yeats and Eliot, these constitute his canon, and Beckett is, to his mind, their great successor in the next generation. Kenner is thus the vorticist, antisymbolist, literalist side of modernism, the side of precision, technique, and what we might call a doggedly secular vision rather than a yearning for transcendence. Williams's dictum "A poem is a small (or large) machine made out of words" might also be Kenner's. The world, he implies again and again, is what it is, so let's forget about all the theorizing and get on with it. Good literature, in this view, is a source of intense pleasure.

It may be that Kenner's particular mix of aesthetic, historical, and scholarly criticism is an anachronism in the contemporary academy. But as we move toward the millennium, it may also be that, to cite one of the poets (Stevens) Kenner most seriously underestimates: "It Must Give Pleasure." In the future, modernist studies will, I predict, return to the *eros* of its wonderfully various texts and away from the *thanatos* that so often accompanies their critical dissection and exposure. For how could the extraordinary body of work that we call modernist—the work that literally extends from A to Z (Apollinaire to Zukofsky, Hugo Ball and Djuna Barnes to Yeats, Conrad and Césaire to Woolf and Williams)—remain for any length of time in the suspect ideological corner that critics of the 1960s and 1970s, perhaps still too close to their modernist parents (just as the modernists insisted on trashing their Victorian ancestry), wanted to put it? It has been my experience that undergraduates, almost all of them coming to *Ulysses* or *Tender Buttons* for the first time, are completely captivated. "Modernism," after all, now has the charm of history on its side even as it remains, at the end of the twentieth century, our Primal Scene.

## Selected Bibliography

The following items are arranged chronologically; they date from 1965 to 1990.

Miller, J. Hillis. *Poets of Reality: Six Twentieth-Century Writers*. 1965. New York: Atheneum, 1969.
The six "poets" are Conrad, Yeats, Eliot, Dylan Thomas, Stevens, and Williams. Written during Miller's phenomenological phase, before the advent of deconstruction, this is a brilliant and profound treatment of modernist imagery and rhetoric in the face of the increasing doubt as to existence of a world outside the text.

Kermode, Frank. *The Sense of an Ending: Studies in the Theory of Fiction*. New York: Oxford UP, 1967.
This is one of the first critical works to take up the question of the authoritarian politics of Anglo-American modernism, the reliance of its fictions on explanatory myth and system building.

Benjamin, Walter. *Illuminations*. Ed. Hannah Arendt. Trans. Harry Zohn. New York: Schocken, 1969.
The essays collected in this book date from the 1920s and 1930s, but their

impact on Anglo-American studies was not felt until they were translated into English. Benjamin doesn't set out to define modernism, but his essays on Proust, Baudelaire, Brecht, and Kafka, and the famous "Work of Art in an Age of Mechanical Reproduction," are central to the understanding of a modernist sensibility.

Bloom, Harold. *Yeats*. New York: Oxford UP, 1970.

Together with Bloom's more theoretical books, especially *The Anxiety of Influence* and *A Map of Misreading*, this work argues that modernism is no more than a belated version of Romanticism, that Yeats's poetic mode is a revisionist version of his precursors Blake and Shelley, the poet being at his weakest when he tries self-consciously to be a modernist. Eliot and Pound are dismissed as "the Cowley and Cleveland of this age."

Kenner, Hugh. *The Pound Era*. Berkeley: U of California P, 1971.

In conjunction with other Kenner studies, like *A Homemade World: The American Modernist Writers* and *Joyce's Voices*, this work captures the uniqueness and greatness of modernist aesthetic. It is a brilliant "inside" re-creation of the period written by a critic who espouses modernist aesthetic rather than denigrates its ideology. In its historical sweep and the acuity of its analyses of individual texts, *The Pound Era* is unique.

Jameson, Fredric. *Fables of Aggression: Wyndham Lewis, the Modernist as Fascist*. Berkeley: U of California P, 1979.

Jameson presents a powerful version of the radical position that the seeds of Fascism were contained in modernist aesthetic, that indeed the ideologies of modernism and those of Fascism went hand in hand. Jameson's political readings are closely text-based.

Levenson, Michael H. *A Genealogy of Modernism: A Study of English Literary Doctrine, 1908–1922*. Cambridge: Cambridge UP, 1984.

The author traces the historical evolution of English modernism from the individualism and inwardness of such early twentieth-century writers as Conrad and Ford Madox Ford to the increasingly dehumanized and spatialized art of the 1920s and 1930s. The transformation of Eliot's and Pound's aesthetic is central to Levenson's narrative.

Chefdor, Monique, Ricardo Quinones, and Albert Wachtel, eds. *Modernism: Challenges and Perspectives*. Urbana: U of Illinois P, 1986.

This collection, the outgrowth of the Claremont Conference on Modernism in 1985, is notable for its range and variety. Clement Greenberg's "Beginnings of Modernism," an essay on Manet as "first modernist," represents what is still perhaps the standard position on the question; but others, like Robert Wohl's "Generation of 1914 and Modernism," Russell A. Berman's "Modernism, Fascism, and the Institution of Literature," and Jo-Anna

Isaak's "Revolution of a Poetics," take very different stances toward modernist innovation.

Perloff, Marjorie. *The Futurist Moment: Avant-Garde, Avant-Guerre, and the Language of Rupture*. Chicago: U of Chicago P, 1986.

Both Perloff's earlier *Poetics of Indeterminacy: Rimbaud to Cage* and *The Futurist Moment* argue for an alternate antisymbolist modernism found in Italian and Russian futurism, in the French avant-garde of Apollinaire and Cendrars, and in its American incarnations in Stein, Pound, and Williams. The focus is on the "heroic" phase of modernism on the eve of the Great War.

Gelpi, Albert. *A Coherent Splendor: The American Poetic Renaissance, 1910–1950*. Cambridge: Cambridge UP, 1987.

This study complements Harold Bloom's critique of modernism (see above). Like Bloom, Gelpi takes modernism to be a carrying out of the Romantic quest for imaginative transcendence, but, for Gelpi, the result is a poetic renaissance of great force and brilliance. Although the emphasis is on the canonical modernist poets Eliot, Pound, Williams, Stevens, Frost, and Crane, Gelpi includes long chapters on HD as well.

Calinescu, Matei. *Five Faces of Modernity: Modernism, Avant-Garde, Decadence, Kitsch, Postmodernism*. Durham: Duke UP, 1987. (Rev. ed. of *Avant-Garde, Decadence, and Kitsch*. Bloomington: Indiana UP, 1977.)

In tracing the shifting meanings of the five terms in question, Calinescu demonstrates just how varied modernist paradigms have been. The writer is primarily concerned with Continental literature and theory.

Nelson, Cary. *Repression and Recovery: Modern American Poetry and the Politics of Cultural Memory, 1910–1945*. Madison: U of Wisconsin P, 1989.

This revisionist redrawing of the map of American modernist poetry makes a forceful, if somewhat extreme, case for the replacement of the canonical poets by hitherto neglected groups: minority and women poets and especially the left proletarian poets of the 1930s. Nelson's work is an interesting exemplar of the new cultural studies.

Williams, Raymond. *The Politics of Modernism: Against the New Conformists*. Ed. Tony Pinkney. London: Verso, 1989.

This important book was in draft form at the time of Williams's death in 1988 and was not yet available at the time this essay was written. Williams is especially interested in the relation of modernist literature to the condition of travel, cultural dispersal, exile, and estrangement that characterizes the early twentieth century. "In remaining anti-bourgeois," he writes, modernism's "representatives either choose the formerly aristocratic valuation of art as a sacred realm above money and commerce, or the revolutionary doctrines, promulgated since 1848, of art as the liberating vanguard of popular consciousness" (34).

Scott, Bonnie Kime, ed. *The Gender of Modernism: A Critical Anthology.* Bloomington: Indiana UP, 1990.

This collection came out after this essay was completed; it purports to "challenge the old definitions and the critical canon of modernism." Among the writers whose work is reprinted and discussed are Djuna Barnes, Willa Cather, Nancy Cunard, HD, Zora Neale Hurston, Mina Loy, Marianne Moore, Jean Rhys, Dorothy Richardson, Gertrude Stein, and Rebecca West. *The Gender of Modernism* is one of the fullest treatments of an alternate feminist tradition that, so its proponents say, should replace the old-style modernist canon. But in foregrounding gender issues it may neglect those of race and class (see Nelson above).

Eysteinsson, Astradur. *The Concept of Modernism.* Ithaca: Cornell UP, 1990.

This excellent study, which appeared after I had completed my own essay, is an invaluable survey of evolving and conflicting views of modernism. But it is by no means just a survey: Eysteinsson takes "the most important task facing modernist studies" to be the "need to ask ourselves how the concept of autonomy, so crucial to many theories of modernism, can possibly coexist with the equally prominent view of modernism as a historically explosive paradigm" (16). Eysteinsson is especially good at exposing the problems inherent in Lukácsian reflection theory, on the one hand, and Theodor Adorno's separation of art from bourgeois culture, on the other.

# $\mathcal{P}$ostmodernist Studies

## JOHN CARLOS ROWE

Today, the coherence of the postmodern literary avant-garde is a part of history, and our confusion regarding the meaning of the term *postmodern* is no longer the effect of a deliberate strategy to disorient us. In our present context, the ambiguity of the postmodern is a consequence of the different ways the term has been used to characterize a wide range of social, aesthetic, economic, and political phenomena. It would be nice to believe that the literary postmoderns succeeded in invading other areas of contemporary life and that the transgressive function of postmodernity worked over the past twenty-five years to produce a useful conversation among these areas of everyday life.

Had this been the case, then my task would be vastly simplified. Were the term *postmodern* still clearly identifiable as a literary or aesthetic function in contemporary culture, then I could summarize and analyze the most influential scholarly studies of this postmodernism. I am afraid that the actual history of postmodernity tells a very different story, in which the vanguard role of aesthetic postmodernity turns out to be primarily the effect of larger socioeconomic forces. In what might be characterized as a counternarrative, the postindustrial social and economic factors still reshaping national and global politics constituted a postmodernity in which traditional disciplinary distinctions were fundamentally challenged. The crisis of the academic disciplines was matched by a comparable conflict between nonacademic and scholarly fields, such as "literature" and its "critical interpretation." Keeping in mind other efforts to define with some scholarly precision the meaning of *postmodernism* (see selected bibliography), I want to reconstruct the key elements that went into the composition of what we now *live* as the postmodern condition. This may seem an odd strategy in a volume of this kind, but it is a necessary one in view of the conflictual qualities of the term. To identify the study of postmodernism with some of the historical-critical texts that have sought to represent it, instead of with, as I shall try to describe, some of the thinking that went into defining the term, would be to betray the spirit of postmodernism itself. In short, any effort to distinguish clearly and simply the study of postmodernism from its practice or experience would be a quixotic effort to comprehend postmodernism with the tools of an enlightenment rationality that postmodernism claims to have left far behind.

I must make one further qualification of a method that already departs considerably from the format of other contributions to this volume. However we understand postmodernism, we must acknowledge it as a global phenomenon. Just how the postmodern has appeared and achieved definition in the United States, Japan, France, Brazil, Panama, Israel, or South Africa, for example, would require careful study of the specific cultural and political histories of these societies, as well as the general issue of the modern nation itself, in both its First World and Third World definitions. Of course, since it would be impossible to deal with the global significance of postmodernism in any detail in an essay of this length, my focus is the impact of the postmodern on the professional study of literature and culture in the United States. The extent to which I address other cultures is determined largely by the influence of such cultures on that professional study in the United States. In this context, the emphasis on European and United States intellectual relations is both understandable and problematic. What is sometimes termed "Euramerican" intellectual hegemony is a modern phenomenon that cultural critics of various sorts have called into question. Yet insofar as a certain kind of postmodernity has come to dominate the United States academy, it is one shaped more by European thinkers than by any other source. In this regard, my emphasis on Euramerican influences merely describes what has been the dominant pattern in the United States in the past twenty-five years. As my essay suggests, such Western provincialism I, along with other cultural critics, consider a serious limitation, with its own ideological consequences, to the influence of postmodernism on educational institutions and practices in the United States.

I address three different kinds of postmodernism in this essay: the literary experimentation that came to dominate fiction in the United States between 1965 and 1975; poststructuralist and deconstructive scholarly approaches between 1975 and 1985; the general outlines of a "postindustrial society," increasingly dominated by service and information-related industries, that begins to change social and personal behavior from the 1960s to the present. There is considerable arbitrariness in any such dating, and my particular breakdown tends to emphasize the discreteness of literary, critical, and socioeconomic postmodernisms. Let me write at the outset, then, that my periodization of these versions of postmodernism is designed ultimately to construct a working relation among them without succumbing to the usual dodge that postmodernism is, by the very terms of its own radical ambiguity or strategic undecidability, an indefinable concept.

Postmodern writers in the late 1960s and early 1970s, accepting the charge that the novel was dead, bid it good riddance. The most notable and vocal postmoderns worked primarily in prose fiction, and they generally preferred the term *fiction* to *novel*. Ronald Sukenick's *Death of the Novel and Other Stories* (1969) implies in its title an abandonment of the traditional concerns of the novel to represent social reality, the complex relation between psychological and social experience, and the essential terms governing our "lived" realities. *Reality* and *realism* were attacked by the postmoderns as mystified terms. The moderns had attempted to criticize the conventions of everyday life, proper behavior, and thus the consensually established terms for reality; the postmoderns claimed to go beyond their modernist ancestors by abandoning reality altogether. "Reality is a nice place to visit," John Barth said in an interview in 1964, "but you wouldn't like to live there" (Enck 11). *Antirealism, counterrealism* (Barth), *fabulation* (Robert Scholes), *the fantastic* (Tzvetan Todorov), *surfiction* (Raymond Federman) were only some of the terms used to describe the postmodernists' rebellion against literary realism and social reality.

Literature itself had been "exhausted," as Barth argued in his famous 1967 essay "The Literature of Exhaustion" (*Friday Book* 72). The great plots had been used again and again; centuries of stylistic innovation and formal experimentation had left contemporary writers with nothing new to say or do. That "nothing," of course, was the starting point for the postmoderns, itself the key to the treasure of a new literature, what Barth would subsequently call "the literature of replenishment" (*Friday Book* 193). Postmodern literature took the very terms used to criticize literature and transformed them into the slogans for its revolution. Literature is nothing, and that nothing can save us from a world too insistently material; the existential abyss was turned into a virtual geography of the literary imagination. Sukenick's *Out* (1973) was composed of self-obliterating characters, and the narrative moved literally to the blank space, the virginal white page of Mallarmé's pure poetry. In *V.* (1960), Thomas Pynchon focused on the quest for an elusive feminine figure narratively transformed into a machine dismantled toward the end of the text. Barth's *Lost in the Funhouse* begins with a "frame-tale" that consists solely of "Once upon a time there" printed vertically on the first page and "was a story that began," also printed vertically, on the next page. The corners of this literary Moebius strip were lettered, and "Frame-Tale" consisted of the convenient directions: "Cut on dotted line. Twist end once and fasten *AB* to *ab, CD* to *cd*" (1–2). The rest of the collection of Barth's "fiction for print, tape, live voice" was virtually wrapped in the endless Moebius loop of storytelling.

"Man would sooner have the void for his purpose than be void of purpose," Nietzsche wrote at the end of *The Genealogy of Morals* (299), and it is as good a slogan as any for the postmoderns' obsessive fixation on nothingness, absence, triviality, exhaustion, entropy, and blankness. The social and historical alienation of the individual that had been a central theme for the moderns became a formal building block, a fictional donnée, for the postmoderns. The moderns, who had examined the social disintegration of industrial societies, used the literary themes of fragmentation, alienation, decadence to represent the failure of social reality and everyday life; the residual commitment to literary "realism" remained in their works. Postmodern writers sought to turn the oppressive conditions of urban life into possibilities for literary creation and an ultimate transvaluation of those circumstances. They seemed intent on "negating negation," or so dwelling on the insignificance of literature and the marginalization of the artist as to turn these negative qualities into positive virtues. The result was an intensely self-conscious style carried to the virtual limits of language. The hallmark of postmodern literature was its obsessive concern with its own possibility of production. The questions writ large at the entrance to every postmodern fiction were: Why write? and Why read?

Postmodern literature did have answers to those questions, and they seemed exhilaratingly revolutionary at the time. We write because we are defined by our use of language; humankind, *homo faber*, is nothing other than the individual's representation of himself or herself. Self-conscious use of language is a liberation from the bonds of convention, from habitual and unreflective speech. How we express ourselves defines us, for better or for worse, and thus literary technique is not simply a minor category of literary study but a key to human knowledge. *How* we know is finally more important than *what* we know; or, in another version, *what* we know is nothing but a function of *how* we know. Because literature, unlike other modes of production, begins with the raw materials of existing language, the literary author must be more attentive to the ways in which everyday language works, as well as to the more specific literary uses of language prompting any avant-garde aesthetic movement. In effect, the literary author is a specialist in linguistics, but of a kind fundamentally different from the academic linguist intent on analyzing the basic rules by which a language—or all languages—functions. The literary author *knows* language only by *using* it and knows the conventions of language only by violating them with unconventional styles and avant-garde forms.

Like their predecessors, postmodern writers insisted on the special qualities of literary language to defamiliarize the ordinary, thus offering an opportunity to combat the automatization of individual existences in the urban mass. It is no surprise that the protagonist of modern and postmodern narratives is generally an artist or at least a poetically sensitive figure. But postmodern writers were often more ambivalent than the moderns about literature effecting large-scale social transformations. The utopian dimensions of modernism are commensurate with the ambitions of its major works. Pound's *Cantos*, William Carlos Williams's *Paterson*, Eliot's *Four Quartets*, and Faulkner's Yoknapatawpha narratives, for example, argue variously for major social changes initiated by literary works that address economic, political, scientific, religious, psychological, and philosophical issues. Much as they differ from traditional epics, then, many modern narratives in both verse and prose share the epic's utopian vision of a redeemed or ideal social order.

Postmodern writers were more modest, in part because they had witnessed the dramatic failure of the modernists' social ambitions. The Frankfurt school writer Theodor Adorno said shortly after World War II that "to write poetry after Auschwitz is barbaric" (*Prisms* 34). Moderns like Yeats, Mann, and Eliot obliquely predicted a reign of terror and destruction in the aftermath of the First World War, but none anticipated the mass murder of the Holocaust. In their literary efforts to save Western societies from their own destructive potential, Pound and Wyndham Lewis found a certain appeal in fascism. Postmodern writers in the United States, on the contrary, trivialized the political functions and contents of literature, even though their most provocative works appeared in a period—roughly 1965 to 1975—when "not to be part of the solution is to be part of the problem," as Huey Newton had insisted. The great issues of that period—civil rights, women's rights, and the Vietnam War— helped produce a powerful New Left political coalition. Yet postmodern experimentalists marginalized these questions in their works. John Barth, John Hawkes, William Gass, William Gaddis, J. P. Donleavy, Ronald Sukenick, to mention only some of the familiar names, had little to say, at the time, about the war, women's and minority rights, the battles waged at home against African Americans ("race riots") and antiwar activists. The few exceptions were writers like Norman Mailer and Philip Roth, who had established their careers in the 1950s, when "existential realism," despite its bourgeois obsession with the absurd and the alienated individual, retained some of the commitment to represent social and political realities that had characterized its European models, notably the works of Sartre and Camus.

Even these exceptions to the apolitical rule used the techniques of the postmoderns to render concrete political issues in oblique, often equivocal, ways. Mailer's *Armies of the Night* (1968) took the major antiwar march on Washington of the year before as its subject; in his *Why Are We in Vietnam?* (1967) the war was at least a titular topic. In both works, however, Mailer argued that it was our failure to comprehend the entanglement of our deepest psychic drives with our most visible cultural myths that had led us to war in Southeast Asia and at home. In his insistence that such understanding could be achieved first by literary means, through the metaphoric connections possible only through poetic logics, Mailer adapted postmodern techniques to modernist literary ambitions and utopianism. By the same token, Mailer mocked and parodied liberal reformers and intellectuals, including one of his several alter egos, for their superficial grasp of much deeper and more complicated issues. In this regard, he resembled many of his postmodern contemporaries, who viewed direct political activism with skepticism while preserving literature as a means of patiently investigating the nearly hopeless social and political conditions of our lives.

One reason for this caution was that postmodern experimentalists were often hard-pressed to compete with the growing influence of the mass media. Television and film declared themselves players in, not just observers of, the Vietnam War and the antiwar movement. Antiwar demonstrators unfurled the North Vietnamese flag during protests, and news photographs of Jane Fonda in Hanoi, the chief of police of Saigon executing a Viet Cong suspect, and a naked Vietnamese girl burned by napalm assumed much more than merely reportorial significance. Both the demonstrators and those covering news events employed, often in very contrary ways, mass media to capture and express economically the historical moment and specific political issues; such use of the mass media in itself constituted a mode of *symbolic action* often claimed by literary artists. One of the consequences was that the *literary* response to contemporary political and social issues was frequently to insist on more complex genealogies for current events. Robert Coover's *Public Burning* (1976) and Pynchon's *Gravity's Rainbow* (1973) are familiar examples of the literary effort to "explain" the Vietnam War. It is not enough to argue simply that these highly political and arguably leftist works arrived too late to make a difference in the New Left political coalition. *Gravity's Rainbow* may be the great work about "why we are [still] in Vietnam," but the political and historical issues are represented as so complex, so intertwined with our psychic lives, that resistance, or the "counter-force," in Pynchon's final section heading, seems at best elusive and at worst conventionally literary. In a similar sense, Coover uses *The Public Burning* to relate Richard Nixon's rise to political power to the virulent anti-Communism of the McCarthy era. The witch-hunt that culminates in the electrocution of Julius and Ethel Rosenberg as spies anticipates our special brand of imperialism in Southeast Asia. In both Pynchon and Coover, however, the specific events of the Vietnam era are barely mentioned, as if the consequences of the historical motives analyzed in these novels—the Vietnam War, racism, sexism, and the increasingly rigid class distinctions of the 1970s—go virtually without saying.

Wary of the moderns' unrealized ambitions for literature's transvaluation of the age, the postmoderns claimed instead to provide a more detailed critical understanding of our social situation. In a certain sense, they became academic, insofar as they made special claims on a growing number of intellectual disciplines and often their specialized languages. The multidisciplinary interest of much contemporary work in the humanities has at least one recent origin in literary experimentation. The postmoderns' claims to understand how language functions by means of the strategic deformation of verbal conventiohs implied that any significant social change would depend on our knowledge of language and its determination of thought and values. By the same token, this knowledge led to a familiar intellectual skepticism with regard to the bases for specific social and political praxes. The rhetorical complement of such skepticism was irony, which is the distinctive stylistic characteristic of postmodern literary experimentation.

The moderns had attempted to redefine, even redeem, the individualism destroyed by urban and industrial life. However protean, contradictory, or pluralistic, the modern artist precariously clung to the special integrity of personal consciousness or style. The postmoderns no longer had such confidence in the redemptive powers of individualism, although their responses to and diagnoses of the "death of the subject" are extremely various. In philosophical terms, the postmodern subject is a verbal or semiotic fiction, constructed in part by the language acquired through normal development and acculturation and in part by the specific employment of language in concrete situations— speech acts. "Self-expression" thus offers only limited freedom and paradoxical identity. Characters in Donald Barthelme's stories speak in clichés, the "dreck" of contemporary society, and thus are defined ontologically as "waste products." In Pynchon's fictions, characters are named for idioms, like the protagonist's ex-husband in *The Crying of Lot 49* (1967), Mucho Maas, or for consumer commodities, like Stanley Kotecks. The names of characters in Barth's *Chimera*—Scheherezade, Perseus, Bellerophon—suggest how dependent identity is on the mythic narratives that tell *us*. Barth himself appears as the genie of *1001 Nights*, in keeping with the assumption that the "author" is nothing but another character in the narrative of history. For the postmoderns, the subject is merely a literary character in that ultimate novel, history. Figures like Malcolm in James Purdy's *Malcolm* (1959) or Chance, the gardener in Jerszy Kosinki's *Being There* (1971), are simply blanks or radical innocents, determined entirely by the historical fictions they encounter.

The negative consequence of such *historicism* was a trivialization of history, in part because postmodern aesthetics seemed to comprehend abstractly the entire historical process. The details were uninteresting. Nevertheless, such an approach motivated a scholastic-like commitment to represent historical "stories" accurately, even in the midst of the most playful literary experiments. Scholars are still finding historically precise materials incorporated into *Gravity's Rainbow*, and these are often among the most "fantastic" of Pynchon's stories in that work. Barth's fictional variations on the *1001 Nights* and Greek myths in *Chimera* are by no means purely fanciful but rely on legitimate versions of these narratives. Ishmael Reed's *Mumbo Jumbo* (1972) uses footnotes, photographs, and bibliography to argue that his fictional history of jazz, the Harlem Renaissance, the United States occupation of Haiti, and the persecution and eventual deportation of Marcus Garvey by the federal government, for example, constitutes a way for the repressed history of African Americans to become readable.

Reed's suggestion that the postmodern author function can reveal an otherwise repressed history is shared by other experimentalists. The novel, of course, has always claimed a special historical function, generally to represent those aspects of history ignored by professional historians. The historiographical assumption of postmodernist aesthetics, however, was that the *textual* characteristics of history made it malleable and thus available for literary revision and adaptation. Not only did this view exaggerate considerably the historical authority of creative writers between 1965 and 1975; it also prompted investigations of the literary *infrastructure* of history in the place of more concrete, politically relevant reinterpretations of modern events. Like so many avant-garde movements, postmodernism seemed intent on demonstrating the universality of its own aesthetic tenets. Barth argued in "The Literature of Exhaustion" that the noted self-consciousness of postmodern literature is characteristic of all literature and myth and thus the "origin" of all storytelling. Postmoderns became adept at recycling familiar myths, often in order to recall us to the mythopoetic sources of all human experience. With certain exceptions, like Reed's account of how and why modern African American history has been repressed by a white ruling class (Reed's "Atonists"), most postmoderns stressed the mythic dimensions of history for the sake of two finally banal conclusions: our daily lives are governed by fictions we accept as real and true; we can play with those stories to find some limited self-expression in an otherwise deterministic history. The distinction between "good" and "bad" myths was based on a clear, albeit questionable, ethical claim: good myths announce their human and thus fictional origins; bad myths disguise such origins and insist on their truth and reality. Good myths invite further elaborations and "versions," thus remaining adaptable to historical and human changes; bad myths discourage revision and insist on universality. At root, this was postmodern literature's defense against the charge that its own aesthetic principles made it difficult to distinguish between literature and propaganda. "Propaganda," the postmoderns argued, "is bad literature."

The claim to historical authority is not the only basis for the noted multigeneric and multidisciplinary characteristics of postmodern fiction. Avant-garde literary movements generally reject traditional genres and canons, claiming to overcome their limitations. The moderns in particular had deliberately transgressed conventional generic boundaries. Pound called Flaubert his "true Penelope," and Wallace Stevens insisted on the "elemental prose" of poetry. Williams chose "antipoetic" subjects for his poetry, while Eliot's *Waste Land* parodied the footnotes and commentary of scholarship, such as Jesse Weston's *From Ritual to Romance*. The postmoderns also mixed and transgressed genres, but prose fiction was given special privilege. Whereas the Anglo-American New Critics often claimed the lyric as the fundamental literary form, on which other poetic and even prose genres built, later experimentalists considered the lyric's celebration of an individual voice to be both a literary and a philosophical anachronism. Among contemporary poets identified as postmodern, such as John Ashbery and A. R. Ammons, the lyric became a poetry of loss and mourning, most often for poetic voice itself. The primary mode of postmodern writing would have to be characterized as *pastiche*, in which the limitations of previously dominant genres such as lyric, epic, and the realistic novel were identified (see Jameson, "Postmodernism").

The postmodern interests in philosophy and linguistics—or "theories of language"—were far more central, shaping in many instances the historical subjects and themes of many of its literary works. Writers produced a wide range of nonfictional works in these academic disciplines; William Gass's *On Being Blue: A Philosophical Inquiry* (1976) and Walker Percy's *Message in the Bottle* (1975) are typical. Of course, literary authors in many different periods have also written criticism and nonfictional prose, and avant-garde literary movements are noted for aesthetic manifestos, anthologies of new writing, critical readings of previous literary movements, and assessments of contemporaries. The moderns produced a great volume of such work, much of which helped establish twentieth-century academic practices and institutions of literary criticism. Their successors, however, claimed a special coordination of their theoretical and practical work, often constructing fictional pieces around theoretical problems and issues. Barth's *Chimera* is an extended reflection on the relations among myth, literary narratives, and ordinary language use. Coover's *Universal Baseball Association, J. Henry Waugh, Proprietor* (1968) can be read as a contribution to sociological game theory, especially as such theories have developed in the wake of Wittgenstein's efforts to establish human knowledge on the basis of the language game. Pynchon's fiction reexamines the possible intersections of thermodynamic entropy, informational entropy, and figurative or literary language. Much of Hawkes's and Percy's fiction reassesses the authority of such crucial Freudian concepts as oedipal triangulation, the symbiotic relation of eros and thanatos, and sublimation.

In this context, the cliché that postmodern writing tends to be "academic" makes considerably more sense. Despite their literary criticism and nonfictional prose, the moderns were suspicious of academic writing they associated with what Williams would call "the Traditionalists of Plagiarism" in *Spring and All* (94). The postmoderns showed special respect for scholarly and critical modes of writing, even when they satirized and parodied the seriousness or narrowness of academic writing. The fact that many writers lived and worked in academic communities during the period of literary experimentation contributed to both the specialized and the often multidisciplinary qualities of their writing. Such a material explanation, though, must be complemented by other factors. In particular, the postmoderns were attracted to academic issues as a defense against their reluctance to write more politically specific work. Russell Jacoby's argument about the transformation of the American intellectual from social activist to academic specialist may be flawed by his nostalgia for the 1930s' left, but there is a measure of truth to the argument that the United States university has more often been the means of *containing* and *controlling* dissent than its breeding ground.

There is, however, a more positive way to understand the closer working relations between postmodern writers and the academy. At about the time of the emergence of postmodern literature as a coherent movement—that is, 1965–75—the humanistic disciplines in this country were undergoing profound changes attributable primarily to the influences of structuralist and poststructuralist theories developed in Europe. The customary date for the introduction of structuralism and poststructuralism to the United States is the October 1966 conference held at Johns Hopkins University, The Languages of Criticism and the Sciences of Man: The Structuralist Controversy. Although the conference focused on the work of structuralists in the several disciplines constituting the "sciences of man," the "controversy" of its title centered on two poststructuralist papers, one by Eugenio Donato, "The Two Languages of Criticism," and the other by Jacques Derrida, "Structure, Sign, and Play in the Discourse of the Human Sciences."

By the middle of the 1980s, the poststructuralist methods we identify with Derrida's deconstruction were referred to generally as "postmodern writing," but in 1966 there was no direct relation between the postmodern literary avant-garde and poststructuralist theory. There are, however, several indirect connections worth considering. The postmodern experimentalists followed their predecessors' special regard for a comparative approach to literary history that stressed cosmopolitan over national traditions. For the postmoderns, the influential works rarely fit the prevailing definitions of the United States literary canon. Barth's pastiche of the eighteenth-century picaresque narrative, *The Sot-Weed Factor* (1960), is based on the writings of Ebenezer Cooke, a minor poet in colonial Maryland, but the novel quite self-consciously draws on Cervantes, Smollett, Swift, and Fielding to develop a distinctly American plot that is curiously European in its telling. In a similar fashion, Hawkes relies on influences as diverse as Flannery O'Connor, Quevedo y Villegas, Joris-Karl Huysmans, and Louis-Ferdinand Céline. In *Gravity's Rainbow*, Pynchon's influences range from Jacobean drama to Henry Adams and German films of the Weimar period. Nevertheless, the literary influences and thus alternative canon of the postmoderns tended to be predominantly European, and it often focused on just those works and movements that had comparable significance for the poststructuralists: the symbolistes, decadents, and high moderns. To be sure, the writers of the Latin American "boom" also had a strong influence on postmodern experimentalists in the United States, but often because they shared aesthetic ideas and styles derived from European models.

Poststructuralism helped move the humanities, especially the study of literature, closer to the practices of literature itself, confusing hopelessly for some the traditional boundaries between literary production (e.g., creativity) and literary reception and understanding (reading and interpretation, professional or casual). Like the postmodern experimentalists, the poststructuralists insisted on the fundamentally linguistic construction of social and psychic reality. Jacques Lacan's famous declaration "The unconscious is structured as a language" was effectively revised to read: "The unconscious *is* a language," a claim for which there was much evidence not only in Lacan but also in Freud's own works.[1] For poststructuralists, language determines and shapes thought; both truth and reality are comprehensible only in terms of the signifying practices that make their conceptualization possible. The building block of structural linguistics had been Ferdinand de Saussure's thesis that language functions by means of signs and that each sign is composed of an acoustic image, or material means of transmission—the signifier—and a conceptual image or intellectual referent—the signified. The relation of signifier and signified was revised by Derrida to the irreducible *différance* of signifiers, so that the conceptual or intellectual reference of any speech act was understandable only as the repression or condensation of a potentially endless chain of signifiers. Thus "ideas" and "concepts" had to be reinterpreted as "compositions" of signifiers, and the analytical procedures established by philosophers (especially in the Anglo-American tradition) for understanding complex ideas were transformed at a stroke into rhetorical strategies.

Because of the strong and still current criticism that poststructuralism and, more specifically, *deconstruction* revolve around an ahistorical paradigm of language, we must remember that poststructuralism attacked structuralism on the very grounds that it ignored the complexities of historical language use. Theoretically, Derrida's translation of the structuralist "sign" into what he termed the *trace* or *différance* was motivated by a fundamentally *historical* understanding of language. In effect, poststructuralism argued that thought, truth, reality, and meaning itself could never be comprehended properly outside their sociohistorical conditions of production. And this assertion applied as well to the act of comprehension or analysis. Every aspect of human experience became a "text"—that is, a signifying system, including the acts of reading and interpretation by which we receive such texts. "Understanding" is actually an act of interpretation, and "analysis" always produces supplementary meaning.

Often accused of being ethically relativist or radically skeptical, as was the postmodern literary avant-garde, poststructuralism actually gave academic credibility to the moral conviction that the more self-conscious we are about the ways we use language, the more likely we are to improve our social and human relations. Poststructuralism thus seemed to offer a moral justification compatible with the ethics of literary postmoderns, but there is a significant difference between the two movements in this regard. By insisting on the inevitability of repression in any act of communication, deconstructive theorists exposed the naïveté of the literary distinction between "good" and "bad" myths. No writer can control effectively the reception and uses of his or her work; every text, however radical, remains indebted to the very language (and thus social order) that has motivated its rebellion. Even with such knowledge, the canniest deconstructive writer still clings to the "intention" of his or her message, and "self-deconstruction" becomes a logical impossibility. At a stroke, deconstructionists rejected postmodernism's neat distinction between literature and propaganda and challenged the validity of its moral insistence on rigorous "self-consciousness." Not only did they call into the question the very possibility of "self-consciousness"; they treated "self-consciousness" as yet another mystification with a specific sociohistorical locus—modern bourgeois culture.

To be sure, the most influential poststructuralists—Derrida, Lacan, Foucault—wrote in profoundly *literary* styles, even though their subjects were philosophy, psychoanalysis, and intellectual history. Their forms also challenged radically the traditions of scholarly writing in their nominal disciplines. Derrida's *Glas*, printed in double columns, the left-hand side consisting of a commentary on Hegel and the right-hand on Genet, is often read as an example of postmodern literature. The title, *Glas*, "knell" in French, suggests the death knell of Western modernity, tolling as it does the historical passage from Hegel to Genet. More than just a book printed in double columns, *Glas* is an effort to deconstruct the customary linearity of writing and reading in Western languages; it accomplishes this task in a number of related ways. Quotations and footnotes are inserted into the columns and printed in smaller type; comments are printed as postils in larger type between the columns. Gaps, ellipses, and other verbal and formal suspensions further accentuate the nonlinearity of a text that is multiple, *intertextual*. *Glas* is perhaps the most sustained instance in the 1970s of what we now call the computer hypertext, on which music, imagery, and writing can be composed by means of laser disk technology.[2] Lacan substitutes the analytical categories of Freudian psychoanalysis with successive, displacing metaphors that cannot be read in the customary cumulative fashion of scholarly arguments, while Foucault combines texts from literature, the visual arts, medicine, the sciences, anthropology, linguistics, politics, and psychoanalytical case studies, commonly interpreting their rhetorical subtexts and secret affinities with each other. By the end of the 1970s and early 1980s, books like Elizabeth Bruss's *Beautiful Theories: The Spectacle of Discourse in Contemporary Criticism* were written on the poetic and literary values of what began to be called postmodern theory.

Poststructuralism's insistence on the textuality of human reality and thus its fundamental historicality was actually a profound challenge to literary study as an academic discipline. Literature exists as a special discourse precisely because we choose to ignore the highly stylized characteristics of all language use.

For literature to exist as a discipline, we must make distinctions between instrumental and figurative languages, as well as discriminate between "denotative" and "connotative" meanings, "literal" and "figurative," "nonfiction" and "fiction," "creative" or "expressive" and "scholarly" or "expository" writing. If literature is simply a function of all language use, relatively foregrounded or backgrounded in any given speech act, then the existing institutions of literature and its study must be deconstructed to reveal the ways they have served to legitimize the false distinctions and dangerous hierarchies of "high art" over popular culture and folk art; enduring classics over journalism, protest and didactic writing; the original and avant-garde over the conventional.

In theory, poststructuralism criticized dominant literary canons, which governed twentieth-century curricula, and their exclusion or trivialization of popular and mass culture. By asserting the inevitably political motives for and consequences of any act of communication, poststructuralism supported abstractly the claims of minorities, women, and other marginalized groups for voices, writings, and literatures of their own. If deconstruction helped expose repression in and through the normative discourse of a society, then those repressed and excluded would speak in ways theoretically compatible with the larger sociopolitical aims of deconstruction. There is still a poststructuralist logic to such desirable coalitions with marginal social and political groups that strikes me as too tidy and academic. If deconstruction makes the "otherness" of the text speak, then the speech of the other seems to be a logical consequence of deconstruction. Deconstruction itself teaches that no such "logical necessity" (a category, after all, of analytical philosophy) can be the basis for political coalitions among different groups in real historical circumstances. The slippage from the "otherness" of what is repressed in ordinary acts of communication to the "other" obscures the specificity of actual social "others." The very generality of the "other" suggests a totalizing system likely to disregard differences of race, gender, class, culture, and history.

Between 1966 and 1975, feminists, African American scholars, and scholars of popular culture and mass media shared this suspicion of deconstruction and poststructuralism in general. American feminists were particularly wary of poststructuralist theory because it claimed as predecessors yet another venerable tradition of masculine theorists, from Hegel and Nietzsche through Freud and de Saussure to Lacan and Heidegger. By this, I do not mean that feminists criticized simply the fact that the major predecessors of deconstruction happened to be men, although this case was sometimes made. They argued instead that the assumptions of these thinkers were shaped by their European cultures and reflected inevitably the patriarchal values of those societies. Lacan's revisionary interpretations of Freud still relied on the centrality of the phallus (the oedipal paradigm) in the process of social acculturation. Derrida's productive deconstructions of Hegel and de Saussure paid little attention to

questions of gender, even though Hegel offered repeated justifications for bourgeois gender hierarchies and de Saussure treated highly gendered languages,
such as French, as if "masculine" and "feminine" were simply convenient grammatical tags.

By the same token, African American scholars asserted that poststructuralist considerations of "repression" and "exclusion" were largely esoteric, often excessively psycholinguistic, issues, rather than concepts designed
to address explicitly the continuing effects of racism. Like feminists, these
scholars noted that the intellectual genealogy of poststructuralism consisted
primarily of white European thinkers, often writing in the midst of Europe's
colonial expansion. The Eurocentrism of Hegel, the bourgeois orientation of
Freudian analysis, and the inevitable ethnocentrism of structural linguistics
were not sufficiently deconstructed by poststructuralists to give voice in any
genuine way to the thoughts and writings of peoples of color.

The dominant academic applications of deconstruction between
roughly 1975 and 1985 did not do much to challenge these suspicions of feminists and scholars of minority and non-European cultures. Especially as it was
practiced in literary studies in this country, deconstruction did not abandon
the established canons and authors but instead embarked on revisionary readings of these figures, together with complementary interpretations of minor
works and authors. Acknowledging the power of such canons and thus the
impossibility of simply dismissing their values and works, poststructuralist
theorists argued that they would have to be deconstructed to reveal their
ideological assumptions. Just who "they" were was often at issue, since many
deconstructive readings of authors as canonical as Emerson and Melville, Shelley and Trollope, Shakespeare and Henry James implicitly "saved" these authors from critical and scholarly traditions that had conventionalized their
works. Often enough, these writers were liberated from such traditional constraints insofar as they could be read as "modern" or "postmodern" in their
interests.

"Literary deconstruction," or the "aestheticization of deconstruction,"
is commonly associated with the Yale school, which flourished between 1975
and 1985, so-called because of the prominence at that university of such critics
as Geoffrey Hartman, J. Hillis Miller, Paul de Man, and Harold Bloom. Derrida
became a regular visitor at Yale in 1975, and the Yale school declared itself in
a manifesto of sorts, *Deconstruction and Criticism* (Bloom et al.), published in
1979. Yet the identification of deconstruction in America with the Yale school
and the critical tendency to treat even those five theorists as virtually equivalent have too often been means of containing and controlling poststructuralist
theories.[3]

After 1979, if I may use the publication of *Deconstruction and Criticism* as a heuristic turning point, deconstruction divided into literary and

political versions. In the second decade of deconstruction's influence on scholarship in the humanities in this country, literary deconstruction achieved the greater popularity, even though its political counterpart, especially in its feminist versions, was having greater effect on the traditional study of literature. In its aestheticized version, deconstruction was relatively easy to understand and to practice, and in this form served specific purposes in the micropolitics of American universities. Any literary text calls attention to its figurative dimensions, its explicit *style*, and in so doing often challenges the referential functions of ordinary language. The literary author characteristically resists critical paraphrase and insists on a literary "excess" as his or her genius. In this regard, literature has always read critically, if not precisely deconstructively, the language of the marketplace.

During this period, the adaptability of deconstruction to customary literary values was also motivated by the socioeconomic condition of professional literary studies. Aestheticized deconstruction helped relegitimate literary study—departments, faculties, curricula—at the very moment that most formal disciplines in the humanities were faced with declining undergraduate enrollments and majors and their customary complements: a decrease in graduate students, fewer academic jobs, and reduced funding for all activities.

It is quite clear that deconstruction revitalized literary texts and authors that by the middle of the 1970s had in many ways been exhausted by previous historical and formal methods of study. This renewed interest often resembled that claimed by the postmodern literary avant-garde. For both postmodern writers and deconstructors, there was cultural evidence all around them that literature was vanishing as a central social discourse. Just as postmodern experimentalists had accepted "the literature of exhaustion" as the paradoxical basis for a new literature, so literary deconstruction argued that the "exhaustion" of canonical texts called for drastically revisionary approaches. Deconstructive critics generally attributed such depletion to the narrowness of critical approaches and offered to revitalize traditional texts with an *intertextuality* that engaged literature, philosophy, history, and linguistics in a much wider conversation.

These scholars did not treat the specific historical situation of literature in the West very seriously; reports of the novel's demise were often considered exaggerated by literary defenders prepared with statistics documenting sharp rises in the sales of popular and serious fiction, as well as studies of growing literacy and comparative demographic figures that seemed to demonstrate steady increases in the reading population since the nineteenth century. In fact, few deconstructive critics had much interest in statistical studies of declines or increases either in enrollments or in the reading population. For them, the only fact that mattered much was that human beings used signs to function in the world and were always likely to do so. Thus how we read and interpret those signs, whether they come to us in the form of literary texts or bank statements, determines our modes of knowing and being. Versions of literature have changed and will change, but the essentially *literary* reflection on the nature and function of language will remain and explain.

But the argument that literature—that is, as a mode of representation concerned centrally with representation itself—was dying had little to do with the statistics and much to do with how such literature was received and used. One of the consequences of the Vietnam War, often termed the "living-room war," was the transformation of television into the principal medium of social debate. Not only news but melodramas, situation comedies, and police shows engaged major social and political issues in the "new realism" on television in the late 1960s and early 1970s; around the same time, film had also assumed growing authority to address such issues. Technological advances, such as the portable Minicam, developed during the Vietnam War, helped expand news coverage of world events. And television and film documentaries and docudramas became increasingly popular.[4]

Literacy figures would have to be measured against the number of hours readers and nonreaders alike watched television or attended films. Above all, such statistics fail to measure what *influence* literary works have on the lives and behaviors of those who read them. For the gloomiest cultural prophets, the decline of literary influence was reflected in the deterioration of literacy skills. As Neal Postman argues in *Amusing Ourselves to Death: Public Discourse in the Age of Show Business*, television and film as media are not conducive to complex rhetoric and profound discussion. Despite a new age of television interpretations of everything from presidential addresses to significant sports events, Postman and others insisted that our capacities for knowledge are conditioned by television's demand for condensed statement rather than extended debate.

For both traditional scholars, like Postman, and literary deconstruction, reading and interpretation require intellectual effort—hard work—implicitly discouraged by the forms of television and popular film. In a similar manner, Postman and many deconstructors argued that such diligent labor would be rewarded with a certain empowerment of the reader that ultimately meant greater political power. Postman's notion of such empowerment is rather modest and conventional: the educated citizen is a good citizen, one who can make intelligent decisions. Literary deconstruction often offered a more ambitious, albeit elusive, political reward: to understand how a culture represents itself gives one access to culture's secret authority, transforming one into Shelley's fantasy of the poet as unacknowledged legislator of the world.

Between 1965 and 1985, however, neither postmodern literature nor postmodern theory realized such bids for political empowerment when measured against the influence of the mass media. On the contrary, the mass media increasingly encroached on established intellectual and academic territories. By the mid-1970s, the talk show, originally designed to promote new films, books, and television programs—that is, with primarily an advertising function—had become yet another forum for the public discussion of social issues. Admittedly, this new format evolved into culturally hysterical modes, like the *Geraldo* show, which focuses on social pathologies of all sorts, and the confrontational "town hall" approach of Morton Downey, Jr. But more modest programs, ranging from *Merv Griffin* to *Donahue* and *Oprah Winfrey*, effected an interesting transition in which the combination of show-business promotion and social debate helped lend even greater credibility to Hollywood's authority on matters of national concern. As a consequence, the viewing public looked increasingly to film and television for the discussion of those topics traditionally addressed by serious fiction and professional historians and political scientists.

Even in its narrowly literary mode, deconstruction resulted in micropolitical changes in the teaching and study of literature in the university, not all of which should be treated cynically as defenses against the embattled situation of literature and humanistic study. Often criticized for intensifying academic specialization by insisting on the essentially infinite signifying potential of any given text and thus demanding intricate, sometimes baroque, interpretations of even the briefest works, deconstruction was actually less favorable to the sorts of subspecializations that had accompanied the twentieth-century professionalization of literary study. Postmodern theory relied on a limited number of theoretical texts that generally challenged their respective disciplines. By a "limited number," I do not mean to endorse the common criticism of deconstruction that it builds primarily on the writings of Hegel, Nietzsche, Freud, de Saussure, Husserl, and Heidegger: that is, the tradition of modern and masculine philosophy, adjusted to include the challenges of psychoanalysis and linguistics. Any list of the major figures for deconstruction would be long indeed and by no means governed by these six moderns, but despite many variations there was a reading list of sorts that cut across disciplinary and historical specializations.

Although subspecialization in literary studies continues to this day, deconstruction helped encourage debates across historical and generic lines and to frame literary topics in ways that often had significance for a wide range of professionals. One negative consequence of the reading list in critical theory was the often mechanical application of these theoretical texts to specific literary works without much consideration for the historical differences between theory and literary practice. Derridean and Lacanian readings of Chaucer, Shakespeare, and Milton are by now as common as those of Joyce, Beckett, and Pynchon. And in defending themselves against frequent criticism that such readings ignored historical differences, literary deconstructors tended to universalize the claims of their theoretical models, often on the apparent warrant of the chief poststructuralist theorists.

But even the common language of critical theory, riven as it was by internal debates and vigorous attacks from more traditional scholars threatened by its ostensible challenges to their customary practices and values, hardly echoed outside the academy. And because, between 1965 and 1985, the real battle for academics, especially in the humanities, involved the challenge posed by mass media, the internal upheavals in the American university, insofar as they concerned educational and research issues, resulted in only modest adjustments to the division between intellectual and public debate, between education as professional training and education as equipment for living.

I have written thus far primarily in the past tense to suggest that both postmodern literature and poststructuralism, particularly in its literary versions, are part of our recent history. I shift now consciously to the present, in which other feminist and minority studies, especially as they are generally described as postmodern, suggest more significant changes in the traditional practices and study of literature. I have mentioned already the suspicion of poststructuralist theories shared by feminists and African American scholars in the 1970s.[5] This distrust was compounded, I think, by the treatment of gender and race in postmodern experimental literature between 1965 and 1975. Not only were experimentalists in that period primarily white men, but their works were profoundly patriarchal and often racist. Gass's *Willie Master's Lonesome Wife* (1971) is a startling example, difficult to find today except in research libraries, because it metaphorizes the narrative itself as Willie Master's wife, inviting the reader to "play" with her *body*, which at one point constitutes the centerfold of the text. In a similar manner, Barth's *Chimera* appears to address positively the demands of feminists by casting Scheherezade and her sister, Dunyazade, in roles as brilliant storytellers and by causing the heroic Perseus to learn the meaning of his life from the stories woven by his savior, the Egyptian priestess Calyxa, who tells the majority of *Perseid*. In fact, these feminine characters are little more than the modernists' feminized muse, alter egos for the masculine imaginary. In the novels of Hawkes, liberated sexuality generally has fearful consequences, and women are represented quite conventionally as helpless victims or demoniac seducers.

African Americans are treated in similarly problematic ways in postmodern literature. Pynchon's version of the systematic extinction of the Herero tribe under German colonialism in Southwest Africa acknowledges how integral genocide was to colonial ideology, but then transforms the Hereros in both *V.* and *Gravity's Rainbow* into virtual embodiments of Western cultural entropy. Their blackness becomes a sign of their nihilistic "choice" to refuse to propagate and thus die out in Pyrrhic defiance of their European colonizers. *Chimera* more liberally argues for the shared, albeit repressed, origins of Egyptian, Greco-Roman, Muslim, and Christian myths, but Barth's comparative mythology effectively legitimates a white, middle-class, and very American synthesis of cultural heritages. Like Willie Master's "lonesome wife," the *cultural body* of the Muslim may be "played with" in Barth's version of the *1001 Nights, Dunyazadiade*, which is itself a comic version of the bourgeois sentimental romance.

The ends of deconstruction have often been declared to be the beginnings of cultural criticism, but once again we must avoid repeating the mistakes of a liberal evolutionary model for historical change. Contemporary cultural criticism in the United States has strong roots in the New Left political coalition of the 1960s and in the political work of feminist and black activists. As I have argued, the New Left acknowledged the postmodern critique of representation as fundamental to its methods and aims, but such a critique subordinated critical writing to political action. For all its idealism and naïveté, the New Left recognized that the struggle for power over the means of representation was not an internal academic debate but a public conflict among the mass media, governmental institutions, and various political interests.

The New Left acknowledged the subtle and pervasive power of popular mythologies, and it produced its own postmodern literature in the form of works intended to foster political activism. *The Autobiography of Malcolm X* (1965), Eldridge Cleaver's *Soul on Ice* (1968), Frances FitzGerald's *Fire in the Lake* (1973), and Kate Millett's *Sexual Politics* (1971) are only a few examples of this other postmodernism. Each work addresses in its own way the "construction" either of race, gender, or cultural identity in and through a wide range of texts that are doing the work of cultural mythology. The ideological artistry of the texts explored by these writers—ranging from casual habits of speech to foreign policy reports and including established literary classics—is what requires a critique of representation. Political empowerment for the antiwar movement, the Black Muslims and Black Panthers, and feminists is complemented by efforts to read critically the ways we internalize and personalize—*domesticate*—racism, sexism, and nationalism. By the same token, the very terms *postmodern* and *poststructuralist*, especially as scholars have tended to interchange them, may exclude certain works and authors crucial to New Left politics.

Many works of the black arts movement of the late 1960s and 1970s are by no means formally postmodern. As I have noted, many African American artists understood the white, bourgeois, masculine assumptions of postmodern fiction. Reed may engage the issues of that fictional experimentalism, but *Mumbo Jumbo* is a sustained critique of the aesthetic ideals of modernism surviving in postmodern fiction. The political and historical commitments of black women writers in the 1970s are obvious; the writings of Alice Walker, Toni Morrison, and Paule Marshall explicitly address the racist assumption that "black" means "black male." As innovative as their writings are, however, they too do not fit the category of postmodern experimentalism, but they belong to what I would describe as "postmodern politics"—that is, a politics that conceives of resistance and social reform as dependent on a critique of representation. Morrison's *Sula* and Walker's *Color Purple*, to mention only two familiar examples, revolve around quests for emancipation that rely on an analysis of the dominant discourse and the empowerment of black feminist speech.

It is worth recalling that the term *cultural critic* was used frequently in the 1960s and early 1970s to designate the writer as activist, especially as he or she departed from the proprieties of scholarship and the narcissism of the literary avant-garde. In his introduction to *Soul on Ice*, Maxwell Geismar wrote: "Cleaver is simply one of the best cultural critics now writing, and I include in this statement both the formal sociologists and those contemporary fictionists who have mainly abandoned this province of literature for the cultivation of the cult of sensibility" (xii). Residual elements of the New Left's postmodern politics still play a significant role in contemporary cultural criticism. It is fair to say, however, that the writings of the New Left and the black arts movement, radical as they were in terms both of politics and of literary form, have received far less scholarly attention than postmodern experimentalism and poststructuralism. One of the reasons for such relative neglect must be the ongoing literary prejudice against political forms and contents. The New Critical assumption that literature distinguishes itself from overt political action continues to have a powerful influence, even in those theories and literary practices that are the most overtly hostile to the aesthetic values of the New Criticism. Another reason is, of course, the ethno- and androcentrism of literary study in the United States. Much as poststructuralism challenged the hierarchies of class, race, nation, and gender, it inadvertently reinforced these "centered structures" by relying on works and authors still compatible with the general aims of Western civilization.

Yet in the past decade this limitation has been addressed in part by the appropriation of poststructuralist theories by feminist and African American scholars, among others. Admittedly, much pioneering work in feminism and cultural criticism has ignored poststructuralism or vigorously condemned its ethnocentrism and abstraction. But in other instances there has been a productive, albeit uneasy, crossing of postmodern politics and postmodern theory. I think that the most successful efforts to relate postmodern politics and poststructuralism can be traced to the influence of Continental feminism. In particular, the writings of Luce Irigaray, Julia Kristeva, and Hélène Cixous have used the conventional criticism of poststructuralist theory for its neglect of gender and race to *revise* the basic assumptions of poststructuralism to include gender and race as central issues.

The Continental feminist challenge to poststructuralism depends on an elaboration of one of deconstruction's principal claims: that the apparently undeniable materiality of experience is in fact constructed of verbal materia. The body itself, its biology, and nature are always already representational effects, so that issues of *gender*, rather than *sexuality*, would have to be reinterpreted in terms of their specific historical and cultural conditions of production. The often oblique and playful equation of verbal production with more material modes of production had an important political consequence for poststructuralist feminists. If all human *production* is to be understood in terms of *representation*—that is, as already shaped and informed by certain hermeneutic assumptions and values—then the economy of so-called natural production and reproduction would have to be considered central not only to any simple economic system but also to the more sophisticated economy of cultural production. Political, economic, psychological, and legal rights of a woman to the productivity of her own body were inextricably related to a woman's rights to the representation of that body. Production, reproduction, and representation occupied the same "body," at once a physically discrete and textual body.

Insofar as the construction of feminine gender in patriarchal societies relies on a complex intertextuality of economics, biology, the law, psychology, sociology, and the various arts, it appears to be an appropriate site for comprehending yet other practices of social marginalization according to race, religion, and class. And because postmodern feminism insists on both the exploitative power of language and its emancipatory potential, it proposes to build a coalition politics for marginal social groups on the basis of their access to and employment of cultural representation. In this regard, the abstract logical necessity of deconstruction to find in the discourse of the other a common cause against the formalized, referential, centered discourse of the real works itself out in more politically specific ways. Constituted by various forms of social and psychological repression, women and minorities must "speak" the otherness that so threatens the patriarchal, Eurocentric voice and consciousness.

The marginalization of women from the national interests and cultural traditions of Western society has encouraged a certain strategic antinationalism and identification with other peoples oppressed by various forms of colonial domination. A woman's body has often enough been treated as a territory to be "conquered" or a fearful "dark continent" in need of enlightenment.[6] Here the materiality of metaphor, itself a key concept in deconstruction, becomes understandable, since the metaphorization of a woman's body has had undeniably material consequences. It would be historically naive, of course, to claim that postmodern feminism is unique for its identification with other marginalized groups. Nineteenth-century women's rights activists worked vigorously for the abolition of slavery, and turn-of-the-century suffragists forged coalitions with working-class activists and the underclass in general. The legacy of feminist activism is one of the advantages that feminism has over less explicitly political versions of poststructuralism. Too often, the tradition (or counter-tradition) in which deconstruction claimed to work remained a version of *Geist-esgeschicte*, even though deconstruction strove to reveal the ideology of the histories of ideas. Yet even such a critical reading of the political implications of idealist history tended to stress deconstruction's historically privileged position as an avant-garde movement.

Like postmodern feminism, recent approaches to African American culture have the advantage of a heritage of political critique and activism that may well enable them to effect significant changes in our study of literature. The postmodern dimension of African American scholarship and theory has openly acknowledged its development out of the New Left, as well as a long tradition of activism and cultural self-definition. In the past half decade, African American theorists have added to the work of feminists in developing a diverse, yet coherent, theory and politics of cultural difference. In 1984, Henry Louis Gates, Jr., edited *Black Literature and Literary Theory*, whose essays explicitly relate structuralist and poststructuralist theory to the study of African and African American literatures and cultures. The January 1990 special issue of *PMLA*, a project coordinated by Gates, focuses on the topic of African and African American literature. In both collections, the study of internal colonialism—slavery and socioeconomic racism in the United States, Eurocolonialism in Africa, and postcolonial political constructions of the Third World by the United States and Europe—are coordinated issues. One of the crucial theoretical links in such work is the critical reading of anthropology as a Western discipline, whose professional practices have helped legitimate various modes of colonial and postcolonial domination. Critical anthropology, which draws on the work of postmodern researchers like Paul Rabinow, George Marcus, and Clifford Geertz, is one of the justifications for speaking of postmodern African American theories.[7] The African American appropriation of postmodern literary and anthropological theories has found deconstruction a useful method for exposing the racial unconscious of liberal societies and their more profound complicities with Eurocolonialism. This new critique attempts to interpret the ways in which explicit political forms of domination are internalized and "lived"—that is, *psychologized*. Because literature, the arts, and academic disciplines often play crucial roles in such a process, the analysis of ideology depends on a deconstruction of the boundaries separating the various disciplines through which racism perpetuates itself.

Much as the critical theory of colonial discourse draws on deconstruction's critique of aesthetic ideology, it aligns itself with traditional modes of

African American scholarship and political activism in ways that give it special authority. The new theorists work in the scholarly traditions of African American cultural definition. This is evident not only in the collaborative work of theoretical statements like *Black Literature and Literary Theory* but in such scholarship as Gates's thirty-volume series, the Schomburg Library of Nineteenth-Century Black Women's Writers, which makes available the rich heritage of black women's writings.

Even in its examination of the philosophical subject and the more specific bourgeois myth of the literary "author," deconstruction tended to reinforce the practice of criticism as a tour de force performance, even when the performer might be described as a textual composition. In and of itself, deconstruction produced primarily the collaborations of an avant-garde movement: manifestos, common issues, a reading list that encouraged discussion across disciplines and subspecializations. Yet it did not fully escape the models of belletristic authorship and critical argument that belong to the limited history of liberal bourgeois culture. Insofar as teaching and pedagogy are shaped by our research habits (or, at least, ought to be), the structure of the curriculum in literature and the hierarchies of the college classroom were not fundamentally changed by deconstruction.[8] Postmodern feminism and cultural criticism have challenged the subject position of the scholarly author and the classroom teacher by producing collaborative scholarship and encouraging team-taught, multidisciplinary curricula. And by acknowledging specific intellectual and political antecedents, these approaches have been able to balance the attractions of the avant-garde with the authority of tradition, especially when such traditions have meant the countertradition of resistance and critique.

The consequences of the new coalition of feminism, African American theory, and the critical study of colonial discourse remain to be seen, but it is likely that it will have profound influences not only on *what* is taught and written about but also on the very departmental structure of most American universities. There has been considerable professional discussion of the restructuring of the humanistic disciplines and their institutional forms, in part because postmodern critical theory in its many versions has challenged repeatedly these discrete epistemic specializations and in part because overspecialization in higher education has provoked fierce public debate regarding the desirability of scholars conducting research in narrowly defined fields. Thus far the official warnings about abandoning departmental structures have been dire: economic disaster, vulnerability to administrative manipulation, irrational tenure decisions, the destruction of affirmative action programs and of programs dedicated to women's and minority studies.[9] While we must keep such warnings in mind, we must also listen to what postmodern feminism and cultural criticism are trying to tell us about our outdated divisions of the human sciences.

With or without our professional decisions, however, the existing disciplines of the humanities are likely to change formally in significant, even drastic, ways in the next two decades. The reason I make such a confident prediction brings me to my final category of the postmodern, one that has haunted the more specific postmodernisms from the literary experimentalists of 1965–75 to the contemporary work of feminists and African Americanists. The essentially *textual* character of all social reality and the enormous power of signifying systems—that is, of representation—is not some literary discovery or humanistic insight but stems from the nature of the postindustrial societies of the West. The postmoderns of the early 1970s celebrated and even fetishized the irreducibly figurative qualities of what we now call the information age. Information must now be comprehended in terms utterly different from those of industrial societies, in which the instrumentality of language to refer either to natural or to manufactured objects seemed unquestionable. In the service- and information-oriented economy of the United States of the post–World War II era, few commodities are understandable outside the rhetoric of both their production and their consumption. I do not mean simply to say that advertising has become such big business that we can no longer see the true object behind the hype, the practical utility through the aura of fashion and status. Important as advertising has become not only to our economy but to our conception of the arts, it is only a secondary effect, a sort of inevitable by-product, of a far more profound mode of production.

Today, the value of what is produced either in words or from material substances is measured by the extent of its circulation, rather than its consumption. The "infinitely productive text" dreamt as a sort of ideal by postmoderns and poststructuralists alike, is now the utopian image of capitalism revived, healthy as never before and likely to achieve the sort of geopolitical dominance once nightmarishly projected into our ultimate paranoia, the Red threat of the cold war. All that the early postmoderns offered as forms of resistance to a bourgeois world of automated reflexes and dehumanization is now available in the shopping mall. Television presents us not with stereotypes, not with the "idealized" bourgeoisie of *Donna Reed* and *Leave It to Beaver*, but with the polymorphous diversity of the new family shows, in which virtually every combination is spun off the empty concept of the vanishing family. Upper-middle-class black families (*The Cosby Show*), white Yuppies (*Thirtysomething*), gender-role-reversed families (*Who's the Boss?*), decidedly *un*-nuclear families (*My Two Dads* and *Full House*) are jostled by their parodies and send-ups, *Roseanne* and *Married . . . with Children*. Big-box-office art-films about the Vietnam War, such as *Apocalypse Now, Coming Home*, and *Deer Hunter*, provoke their challenges in Stallone's aggressive Rambo, who in turn is "answered" by the more liberal, yet still militaristic and patriarchal, *Platoon*, which can produce its own anti-Vietnam response, by the same director, Oliver

Stone, *Born on the Fourth of July*. Television and film are, of course, established disciplines of study in most major universities, but the effect of such scholarship on literature—its genres and canons—is surprisingly small in the light of the dramatic impact these media have had on the popular conception of what constitutes figurative or literary representation. Literary genre theory, for example, is hopelessly narrow in its disregard of television and film. And to speak of the "literary canon" without considering the influences of popular literature, the Western on film and television, *I Love Lucy*, and *Perry Mason*, is to reduce the canon to a purely academic topic.

The endless conversation and debate often cited by postmodern liberals as the ultimate morality of the textualist position has been achieved in the mass media, both on the Business Channel and the talk show. The crudity of Downey's aggressive staging of the most confrontational groups is toned down as the media represent every position and permit any discussion. Herbert Marcuse called this liberal entertainment of any adversarial position, without substantially changing the system, the "repressive tolerance" of late capitalism. For better or for worse, we *are* this ceaseless conversation, debate, and rebuttal, from the commentaries on the evening news and Sunday's *Firing Line* to the next wave of television sit-coms or popular films taking stands on political issues.

If the literary postmoderns paid little attention to mass media, then they paid even less attention to the banal details of postmodern economics. The conversation among different positions that seems to simulate the polyglot dialogue still held as a utopia by many of today's cultural critics is made possible only according to certain basic economic facts. With few exceptions, the dizzying figurality of our postindustrial society admits only those with the capital, only those with the financial power to play. The African American activists and their confronters the neo-Nazi fanatics on Downey or Geraldo Rivera are finally just bit players, whose debates are nothing but theater and whose views are tamed by the larger drama: the production of semiotic power represented in the new authors of our age. Neither "Downey" nor "Geraldo" is the name that matters here; the actual authors are the invisible, anonymous "producers," who are today our best and most dangerous cultural critics. Analyzing, as they must, market shares and segments, they can lay claim to the concrete evidence of their accuracy in assessing cultural trends: the ratings.

How, then, did literature and its study change under the influence of the postmodern? In more traditional and scholarly terms, I have tried to explain the impact of a restricted postmodernism on the formal discipline of literature and its curriculum. Insofar as postmodernism fails to take account of the economy, it misses the ways in which contemporary society has turned the world into *theater*, transformed *life* into *art*, all for the sake of the usual passions of the artist: power and control of the audience. In order for analysis to proceed within the American university, scholars of literature will have to take seriously the influence and complexity of mass media and elaborate the existing logics of poststructuralism to deal more concretely with the aesthetic ideology of postmodern societies. Literature as it was can't be saved; knowing what we do now about its own contributions to ideology, we may not even want to save it. If we are to comprehend even this death of literature, then we will have to assess more accurately and less academically just who sets the stage for our public debates, however various and technologically accessible they appear to have become over the past two decades. The degree to which postmodern *writers* (a word that is itself designedly archaic) can come to terms with mass media and their audiences will help determine whether writing—as either literature or its interpretation—will be erased or transformed by what are today the predominantly electronic cultures of a new global postmodernity.

### Notes

[1] Lacan himself offered the revision on numerous occasions, despite the popularity of the slogan and its simile. In "Agency of the Letter in the Unconscious," Lacan argues: "The unconscious is neither primordial nor instinctual; what it knows about the elementary is no more than the elements of the signifier" (170).

[2] The advertising copy that Derrida wrote for Editions Galilée to promote *Glas* describes the text in this manner: "In the first place: two columns. Truncated above and below, cuts also in their sides: incisions, tattoos, incrustations. At first reading, it seems as if two texts are set up, one against the other or one without the other, without communication between them. And in a certain deliberate fashion, that is true, as far as pretext, object, language, style, rhythm, and law are concerned. A dialectic of one side, a galactic [motion] of the other, heterogeneous and indiscernibly dependent on their effects, sometimes nearly hallucinatory. Between the two, the bell clapper of another text, speaking another 'logic': in proper names of obsequy, penetration, restriction, taboo . . . of death" (my translation).

[3] For an excellent critical reading of the Yale school, see the essays collected in *The Yale Critics*, ed. Arac, Godzich, and Martin.

[4] The most familiar examples of the "new realism" on television in this period are *All in the Family*, which explored the working-class family's complicity in the perpetuation of racism and sexism, and *Maud*, which examined the impact of feminism on the bourgeois family. For the recent influence of documentary on the development of docudrama, see Rowe, "From Documentary to Docudrama."

[5] In "The Race for Theory," Barbara Christian argues that the elitism of critical theory, especially in its poststructuralist versions, is integral to its arguments and methods and that the noted "difficulty" and "sophistication" of deconstruction are means of preserving critical theory as a white, ethnocentric discipline. Christian criticizes both the "new philosophers" (Lacan, Foucault, Derrida, et al.) and Continental feminists, the latter for imitating the styles and arguments of those writers even while condemning

their blindness to issues of gender. Christian's argument is, perhaps designedly, undialectical. By stressing the inherent racism of poststructuralist theory, rather than the failure of poststructuralism to elaborate the implications of its own theories for a critique of race and gender, Christian invalidates the useful work of many contemporary feminists and African American scholars that has been significantly influenced by poststructuralist theory. Further, Christian's call for a return to the *literary* work and the self-evident values of expressive writing is based on a misunderstanding of the political aims of the postmodern critique of literature as a discrete mode of representation.

[6]Kolodny, in *The Lay of the Land* and *The Land before Her*, has examined critically the various ways writers in the United States have "feminized" nature, thus combining the aims of patriarchal and territorial domination, gender hierarchies, and the ideology of imperialism.

[7]Clifford and Marcus edited the most influential volume of essays concerned with postmodern or poststructuralist anthropology, *Writing Culture*.

[8]Deconstruction *has* had direct influences on pedagogy. The application of poststructuralist theories of language to basic instruction in English composition, for example, has by now achieved general recognition, on evidence of essays published in such journals as *College English* and at such annual conferences as the CCCC. The pedagogical and curricular possibilities of deconstruction are developed with considerable sophistication by Ulmer in *Applied Grammatology*.

[9]The MLA and other professional organizations have sponsored several national conferences in recent years to discuss the future of traditional departments of English, comparative literature, and the foreign languages. The reports of these conferences generally conclude that abandonment of the traditional departmental structures will place faculty members and their students at considerable risk with administrations, primarily with regard to adequate funding for teaching and research. By the same token, several foreign language departments around the country have decided to redefine themselves as concerned chiefly with culture rather than language or language and literature. See *The English Coalition Conference* (Lloyd-Jones and Lunsford).

## Selected Bibliography

Bhabha, Homi, ed. *Nation and Narration.* New York: Routledge, 1991.
    A collection of essays that demonstrates how postmodern theories have influenced cultural criticism concerned with relations between First World and Third World cultures. The work provides good representation of the different approaches of cultural criticism understood by the terms *critical study of colonial discourse* and *postcolonial studies*.

Collins, Jim. *Uncommon Cultures: Popular Culture and Post-modernism.* New York: Routledge, 1989.
    A good example of how poststructuralist theory has been transformed into postmodern cultural theory. In Collins's theorization of postmodern popular cultures as fundamentally decentered and intertextual, concepts of deconstruction have been translated from strictly literary into cultural terms.

Connor, Steven. *Postmodernist Culture: An Introduction to Theories of the Contemporary*. Oxford: Blackwell, 1989.
An exploration of how various poststructuralist and post-Marxian theories (Lyotard, Jameson, Baudrillard) inform recent developments in architecture and the visual arts, literature, performance, TV, video, and film, music, and fashion. Connor moves cautiously toward a cultural politics based on the promise of postmodern avant-gardes.

Foster, Hal, ed. *The Anti-aesthetic: Essays on Postmodern Culture*. Port Townsend: Bay, 1983.
An interesting historical marker, in which the transformation of the postmodern from an aesthetic avant-garde to a sociopolitical and sometimes economic condition is recorded. This explicitly leftist collection includes ideological criticism of the arts by Jameson, Habermas, and Said and, like Huyssen, attempts to reconcile it with the more aesthetic impulses of deconstruction.

Gates, Henry Louis, Jr., ed. *"Race," Writing, and Difference*. Chicago: U of Chicago P, 1986.
A collection that represents the influence of postmodern and poststructuralist theories on the study of minority discourse, colonial and postcolonial discourse, and the relation between them.

Giroux, Henry A., ed. *Postmodernism, Feminism, and Cultural Politics: Redrawing Educational Boundaries*. Albany: State U of New York P, 1991.
A fine collection of essays on the relation between theories of postmodernism and feminism and a good introduction to Giroux, who addresses cogently the practical applications of feminism, minority discourse, multiculturalism, and other versions of cultural criticism in the classroom.

Hassan, Ihab. *The Postmodern Turn: Essays in Postmodern Theory and Culture*. Columbus: Ohio State UP, 1987.
A good historical account of Hassan's career, including essays from 1967 to 1987. Hassan's fundamentally *literary* definition of postmodernism is what subsequent theorists like Huyssen, Collins, Connor, and Andrew Ross challenge.

Hutcheon, Linda. *A Poetics of Postmodernism: History, Theory, and Fiction*. New York: Routledge, 1988.
———. *A Politics of Postmodernism*. New York: Routledge, 1989.
Two books that indicate how the concept of a postmodern socioeconomic condition has recently changed postmodern aesthetics and theories. Planned virtually as two voices in a dialogue, Hutcheon's *Poetics* and *Politics* suggest that postmodernism must be transformed from a mere literary and cultural discussion into a social, political, and economic praxis.

Huyssen, Andreas. *After the Great Divide: Modernism, Mass Culture, Postmodernism.* Bloomington: Indiana UP, 1986.

An extraordinarily wide-ranging and theoretically sophisticated effort to reconcile the Marxian utopianism of the Frankfurt school and the postmodern condition. Huyssen's effort to interpret the "divide" between modernity and postmodernity in terms of changing attitudes toward "mass culture" reconfigures the humanities as "cultural studies."

Jameson, Fredric. *Postmodernism; or, The Cultural Logic of Late Capitalism.* Durham: Duke UP, 1991.

A qualification of Jameson's insistence that postmodernism is the inevitable cultural product of late capitalist excess. Hints are provided of some alternative and thus emancipatory potential that Jameson recognizes in the popular modes of expression made possible by capitalism's decentered and often schizophrenic status.

Lyotard, Jean-François. *The Postmodern Condition: A Report on Knowledge.* Trans. Geoff Bennington and Brian Massumi. Minneapolis: U of Minnesota P, 1984.

At once an interpretation and an enactment of the postmodern. It is one of the best examples of postmodern theory, insofar as it refuses to employ the customary analytical methods of enlightenment rationality to explain such a complex and antirational phenomenon. And yet it is a study commissioned by the Conseil des Universités of the government of Quebec nominally to explain how educators and intellectuals can meet the requirements of the postmodern.

Newman, Charles. *The Post-modern Aura: The Act of Fiction in an Age of Inflation.* Evanston: Northwestern UP, 1985.

A work originally received as a conservative attack on the excesses of postmodern literary experimentalism. Newman calls attention to the ways that postmodern socioeconomic forces shaped cultural phenomena, including literature and the visual arts.

Nicholson, Linda, ed. *Feminism/Postmodernism.* New York: Routledge, 1989.

A representative selection of feminist approaches to postmodern culture, in both its emancipatory and postfeminist possibilities. Feminist cultural criticism has challenged the patriarchal order; feminist politics has helped shape a postmodern utopia consisting of diverse social, sexual, and psychological models for social behavior and its interpretation.

Poster, Mark. *The Mode of Information: Poststructuralism and Social Context.* Chicago: U of Chicago P, 1990.

A study demonstrating how the technologies developed in the television, film, and computer industries are anticipated in the conceptual shifts articulated by poststructuralist theorists like Baudrillard, Foucault, Derrida, and

Lyotard. Poster's work explores the influence of poststructuralist theories on scholarship in social history.

Ross, Andrew. *No Respect: Intellectuals and Popular Culture.* New York: Routledge, 1989.

An attempt to translate postmodern academic theories dealing primarily with literature and philosophy into useful approaches to popular culture. Ross represents well the adaptation of poststructuralist theories to the study of postmodern culture from the perspective of cultural criticism.

Ulmer, Gregory L. *Applied Grammatology: Post(e)-Pedagogy from Jacques Derrida to Joseph Beuys.* Baltimore: Johns Hopkins UP, 1984.

A demonstration of the relevance of deconstruction to education. For Ulmer, the postmodern avant-garde of deconstruction remains self-evidently emancipatory and eccentric to the main currents of Western societies.

Wilden, Anthony. *System and Structure: Essays in Communication and Exchange.* London: Tavistock, 1972.

An important historical marker that shows how European structuralism confronted the communications media and artificial intelligence at the very moment, in the early 1970s, when the structural linguistic model was being transformed by poststructuralist theorists like Derrida.

Williams, Raymond. *Television: Technology and Cultural Form.* London: Fontana, 1974.

An extraordinarily clairvoyant book that examines how Marxism and British cultural materialism of the 1970s addressed television as a defining, if not central, medium in the formation of social experience and cultural values.

Woodward, Kathleen, ed. *The Myths of Information: Technology and Postindustrial Culture.* Madison: Coda, 1980.

A collection of essays describing the efforts of critical theorists in the late 1970s to connect literary postmodernism with postindustrial technology. Contributors like Baudrillard, Huyssen, and Wilden reflect the struggle of academics to address the transformation of purely theoretical issues into social and cultural realities.

# American Literary Studies to the Civil War

## CECELIA TICHI

For some twenty-five years, from the close of World War II through the 1960s, American Literary Studies to the Civil War seemed to be a clear, straightforward rubric. It performed—as it continues to perform—taxonomic service in classroom texts and in college and university catalogs. Within the rubric a certain evolutionary literary coherence, even progress, was presumed to be demonstrable, as instructors and critics located in prose and poetry the growing expressions of democratic consciousness and of such values as individualism and self-reliance. Certain topics and themes were shown to undergo development—for instance, in the *from-to* model based on the notion of aesthetic or thematic incipience leading to fulfillment (e.g., from nature in Jonathan Edwards's *Personal Narrative* to Emerson's *Nature*). Thus it was in no way considered disruptive for teaching or scholarship to subdivide American literature to the Civil War into such areas as colonial, revolutionary, early national, transcendental, American Renaissance.

And if few scholars assented to the simplicity of the homogeneous melting pot, the acceptance of such formulations as the American Adam (Lewis) or the American Renaissance (Matthiessen) reinforced the importance of certain patterns of texts considered to be major because they demonstrated salient parts of the American identity and its aesthetic expression. "American" in those years seemed synonymous with "United States," and teachers and students were in the main untroubled by conceptual problems implied in a body of literature representing a developing nation-state but claiming the whole of two continents as its purview.

This postwar epoch in American literary study, however, began to undergo major revaluation in the 1970s, when scholars pointed out that the canonical texts thought to constitute American literature excluded the cultural record of indigenous peoples, ethnic and minority groups, women, and non-Anglo colonial powers. A post-1960s generation of scholars and editors, moreover, invoked the terms of this rubric with growing awareness of myriad complexities embedded in virtually every word. The term *American* began to seem hegemonic and inaccurately univocal, while the largely Marxist challenge to the belletristic tradition made *literary studies* itself a problematic category. If *Civil War* has often been read as a contradiction in terms, newer scholarship additionally would point out that, given Michel Foucault's arguments on social discipline, the phrase is a tautology. Suffice it to say that for the past twenty-five years, every term in the title of this essay and every ramifying subcategory has undergone dynamic, radical change.

"Always historicize!" begins Fredric Jameson's *Political Unconscious*. And that is one crucial heuristic enterprise of contemporary critics of American literature from the colonial era through the mid-nineteenth century. The other is a change of subject positions. The two are of course related. Historicizing, as Jameson comments, can follow two paths, of the object and of the subject (9). Critical theory, particularly deconstruction, has let critics do both. The critical byword has become "the social construction of—," the prepositional object of that phrase including not only texts but temporal periods, authorial careers, and scholars' own argumentative positions. No category of literary text, period, approach is considered to be a natural one, from Puritan New England to the reputation of Nathaniel Hawthorne to the mid-nineteenth-century American Renaissance; and the inquiry into the process of naturalization necessarily results in the vigorous decentering of all literary categories.

The classroom anthologies show this new decentering, from the once-standard *American Tradition in Literature* (Bradley, Beatty, and Long), which as recently as 1974 opened with a section called "The Puritan Culture," down to *The Harper American Literature* (McQuade et al., 1986), which repositioned the literary origins with the Renaissance discovery narratives, and now *The Heath Anthology of American Literature* (Lauter et al., 1990), which, committed to a multiethnic, multiracial, and doubly gendered canon, opens with a section entitled "Native American Traditions" and boasts the work of "time-honored favorite authors placed alongside the writings of women and minority authors whose importance is only now being recognized" (iii). And just as the anthologies measure the shift in the canon, the literary history compendiums reveal the changed census of those considered qualified to form it and comment on it. Of the contributors to *Literary History of the United States*, edited by Robert Spiller et al. (1946; rev. ed. 1953), all fifty-five were white men, while *The Columbia Literary History of the United States*, edited by Emory Elliot (1986), lists seventy-four contributors, sixteen of whom are women and at least four of whom are specialists in ethnic or minority American texts.

The simple rubric American Literature to the Civil War is thus deceptively constant in its continuing use in classroom texts, in course titles, and even in journal titles (*American Literature, Early American Literature, Studies in American Fiction, American Literary History*). A post-1960s generation of scholars and editors by no means invokes the term without awareness of its ideological complexities.

For the colonial period, New England Puritanism continues to be a scholarly force field. And though the issue of New England's exceptionalism will concern us momentarily, suffice it to say here that books beget books, and arguably the sheer quantity of studies of seventeenth-century New England (by one estimate, a book or article for every one hundred persons alive in New England in 1650) engenders vigorous continuing scholarship (Wood 26). A 1986 investigation, for instance, of John Cotton's rhetoric and the ways in which the spoken word was aural sculpture for the New England Puritans is indebted to Larzer Ziff's 1962 biography of John Cotton (Kibbey), while a 1990 study of identity formation in colonial New England acknowledges its paternity in Perry Miller's *New England Mind*: "My primary scholarly inspiration came from that prime inspirer of American Puritan studies, Perry Miller" (Canup vii).

Miller's position as founder of contemporary colonial studies continues secure (Wood). His two-volume *New England Mind* (*The Seventeenth Century*, 1939; *From Colony to Province*, 1953) had located in colonial Puritanism what he termed "the meaning of America," a heroic and individualistic mission. From a congeries of Puritan texts, Miller configured a paradigmatic univocal construct, the Puritan mind. His Puritans struggled with anxieties and fears and with their human scale as motes in the cosmos, but they were intellectual heroes in the New World wilderness, tough-minded, courageous, bold, robust, and central to Western civilization: "Puritanism was one of the major expressions of the Western intellect [and] achieved an organized synthesis of concepts which are fundamental to our culture." Committed to the idea of a Puritan "single intelligence," Miller was a self-identified cartographer and anatomist, "map[ping] the intellectual terrain of the seventeenth century" and "the anatomy of the Puritan mind" (*New England* 1: viii, vii).

Miller's drive, as he put it, to expound "the innermost propulsion of the nation" (*Errand* viii) rhetorically suited midcentury industrial America, and his insistence on a purely intellectual formulation for the founding psyche doubtless served the position of the United States as the democratically triumphant nation of World War II. The nation that twice used the atomic bomb needed vindication as democratic *and* rational, impervious to raging passions. According to Miller, the New England mind, struggling to exploit the triad of reason-will-understanding, the best of the postlapsarian mental components, strove not only to apprehend God's will but also to contain the unruly and wayward passions: "Reason, free and independent, is the king and ruler of the faculties, and its consort, the will, is queen and mistress. . . . [L]ogic was a corrective of sinful passions." Miller offered a heroically cerebral American paternity that put passion into the service of the intellect, where it was contained. Puritan "regeneration would take the form of a reinvigoration of rational discourse" (*New England* 1: 247, 263). There is no nuclear-age demonic Dr. Strangelove among Miller's rational, national founders.

Puritan passions, however, have been the unabated focus of subsequent scholarship, beginning in the early 1970s with the inversion of Miller's interpretation of the Puritan "errand into the wilderness," the phrase from a sermon by John Danforth and one centered on the lamentations of the Old Testament prophet Jeremiah. Miller considered the sermon to be testimony to the crisis of diminished piety and zeal on the part of the second-generation Puritans. Subsequent critics began to see eschatological affirmation where Miller read Puritan self-admission of decline. The newer scholarship, in a tradition initiated by Ernest Lee Tuveson, Aletha Joy Bourne Gilsdorf, and others but developed most fully by Sacvan Bercovitch, redirected colonial studies away from the previously dominant exegesis on the Puritan intellect. In a move that upended the heuristic subject position, it argued that the Puritan glass, or perhaps tankard, was not half empty but half full. Exegesis of Puritan millennialism enabled the formulation of the American self and its Christic mission in the New World (Bercovitch, *Puritan Origins*). This approach also located in Puritan lamentation a covert imperative for national renewal that, in literature, took the form of a recurrently inscribed sense of national mission extending from the seventeenth century into the presidential rhetoric of the television age (Bercovitch, *American Jeremiad* and "Horologicals"). "The New World ministers, already committed to a scheme which would not admit of failure, compensated for their thwarted errand by constructing a legendary past and prophetic future for the country. . . . The popular aspect of the legacy [of the Jeremiad] consists in the exuberant national eschatology embodied in the American Dream" ("Horologicals" 43, 75).

Identified as a middle-class culture, America in this configuration embodies a myth leading the country into the millennium prophesied in the New Testament book of Revelation. From the early 1970s into the later 1980s, colonial American literary study flourished via scholarly exegesis on eschatology, especially on the ways in which the Puritan American self and the United States are susceptible to recurrent renewable commitment to the national destiny. During those years, most of us working in the area of Puritan studies exploited the schema in our own scholarship, whether it focused on, say, biography or the American landscape (Middlekauff; Tichi, *New World*).

As presentism is invariably a part of scholarly findings, it is the case that just as the idea of the Puritan mind should find favor in a particular postwar climate, so should the millennialist arguments be enabled by the cultural moment of the 1960s (roughly 1965–75), the Vietnam War era, in which many in literary studies perceived the United States not as a global democratic benefactor but as a militaristic empire. Responding in the late 1970s to a question from the audience after a talk at the Boston Public Library, Bercovitch spoke for scholarly cohorts when he asserted that it is precisely the critic's situation in contemporary history that promotes scholarly insights, customarily by turning presumed truth into exposed myth. Because ideology discloses itself as a result of historical processes, he remarked, the eschatological literary discourses had become particularly accessible as the United States began to decline as a global imperial power.

The continuing diminution of United States imperial authority, together with its economic decline, is plausibly the historical basis for yet another change in colonialists' critical subject positions. Continuing the investigation of the literary history of the seventeenth-century emigrants' emotional lives, recent scholarship now concerns itself not with messianic passions but with those of anguish, grief, and mourning. Thus Anne Bradstreet, the Puritan poet who admitted that the sight of the New World made her nauseous, comes to the fore as a poet of feminist sensibilities at odds with patriarchal Puritanism (W. Martin 15–76). The discourses, moreover, of intellectual heroism and of imperial millennialism, other scholars argue, occlude another kind of discourse, that of the anguished Puritan as immigrant. Recent work emphasizes the dreadful ordeal of the errand, the psychological deracination of a people caught in a double bind, their native land in chaos, their alternative the upheaval of dislocation in the New World (Delbanco).

This newer position calls into question the kinds of Puritan colonial texts accorded privileged status over the past quarter-century. The premise of a paradigmatic masculine mind permits the scholar to construct a composite *Ur*-text from fragments of many kinds of writings, including sermons, diaries, and tracts. (Deconstructive theory, in fact, has come relatively late to colonial American literary studies, probably because one element necessary to its operation—the antecedent New Critical presumption of textual integrity—has always been a tenuous proposition in a field of study so dependent on the pastiche, or composite text.) Yet even the intact text, such as the Danforth sermon "Errand into the Wilderness," has been positioned as inclusively corporate, representative of a group of visible saints (as the Puritan church members were called). And the spiritual biography, such as Cotton Mather's "Nehemiah" on Governor John Winthrop (in the *Magnalia Christi Americana* [1702]), has been presented as representative of the univocal middle-class "American self" (Bercovitch, *Puritan Origins*). In all of these, the literary text is exclusively self-referential to one presumably homogeneous group, the Puritans, and is emphatically masculine even as it subsumes two genders. Reference to all others, whether Satanic Indians, heretics, or those outside the circle of church membership, essentially reinforces both Puritan centrality and the otherness—the alien status—of non-Puritans.

The poststructuralist moment, however, in colonial studies currently reveals itself in scholarly claims for a different kind of representative text. Such a text extends beyond the patriarchal male realm to bring into juxtaposition the newer categories of critical inquiry, gender and race and, implicitly, class.

Gender was a salient issue in the 1637–38 antinomian controversy in which the Puritan wife and mother Anne Hutchinson, in her lay preaching, contested the spiritual authority of Puritan patriarchy and became a "disturber in Israel" with her female narrative of dissent (Lang, *Prophetic Woman*). Hutchinson left no written text (her voice recorded only in the transcript of her trial on charges of heresy), although her story, obsessively retold by others, was to ramify into, and to problematize, nineteenth-century American fiction and the essay (Lang).

Seventeenth-century studies have now identified the work that lends itself to considerations not only of gender but of the heuristics of race and class, resisting the totalizing tendencies indicated in such a term as *American self*. It is Mary White Rowlandson's *True History of the Captivity and Restoration of Mrs. Mary White Rowlandson* (see Lang, "Introduction"). The narrative describes the months during which Rowlandson, a mother and a Puritan minister's wife, was held captive by the Algonquians during King Philip's War (mid-1670s), as the colonists called it, when a confederation of Indian tribes led by their chief, Metacom ("King Philip"), fought the colonists because they feared loss of lands and tribal annihilation. Rowlandson's account began what has been called the first American literary genre, the captivity narrative. For the past three decades it has been, in excerpts, a staple of the classroom anthologies, in which interpretive headnotes customarily emphasized its importance in depicting Puritan trials and doctrinal orthodoxy on the colonial frontier.

Yet in the 1990s Rowlandson's text is being reread as an ethnographic juxtapositioning of two cultures, colonial whites and the indigenous Americans, and involving two genders, even as it presumes that the central experience of New England Puritanism is that of mourning (Breitwieser; Lang, "Introduction"). The title of a 1990 critical study devolving from Rowlandson's narrative is indicative: *American Puritanism and the Defence of Mourning: Religion, Grief, and Ethnology in Mary White Rowlandson's Captivity Narrative* (Breitwieser). It argues that the fundamental Puritan experience is loss at every level (social, economic, personal) and that the most profound psychological impulse, accordingly, is grief and mourning. The mandate of the clerical leadership becomes, essentially, a valediction forbidding mourning, a channeling of thought and feeling away from grief into a spiritual utilitarianism. Loss is identified as the central ethos of Puritanism, though it is suppressed and repressed everywhere in the official culture. Loss becomes overwhelmingly present in its absence, and the Puritans become one ethnic group over and against another, the Algonquians. In this configuration, Rowlandson's text is dissonant, not only because its author was a woman whose intrinsic aggression was to write but because it is about mourning and because, as a captivity narrative of cross-cultural encounter, it becomes as well an ethnographic text of a kind dangerous to establishment Puritanism. Cultural relativity inadvertently comes into play: "If what seems white can turn out to be red ... it is also the case that what has been thought red can turn out to be analogous to white. . . . Thus reversibility . . . reappears as a property of relative cultures" (Breitwieser 170–71). An understanding of what constitutes a rhetoric of dissonance in Puritan texts becomes the scholarly imperative. And the opening of ethnological rhetoric to discussion enables scholars to exploit ethnographers' and ethnographic historians' findings.

One critic asks, "What explains this remarkable scholarly attention [to New England Puritanism]?" and answers that it is "what" Puritanism seems to say about contemporary America, that there is "something" in it that still resonates in the late twentieth century, that in "some way or another" Puritanism has been, as Miller called it, an "ideal laboratory" for the study of America. The ineffable "what" and "something" both work ineffably, "some way or another" (Wood 26). Even though the Puritans themselves promulgated the myth of their exceptionalism (Gura 215–34), it may be surprising to find late-twentieth-century scholarly assent to the notion even by those historicizing the construction of New England Puritan studies: "the originating, generative power of the Puritan imagination continues to shape the way we tell the American literary story, indeed the way we explain the development of American culture" (D. Weber 101).

As some scholars recognize, the presumption of New England Puritan literary exceptionalism is, strictly speaking, neither a colonialist concern nor an antiquarian one, ramifying as it does directly into the nineteenth-century "classic" American literature, the canonical texts of Emerson and Thoreau, Hawthorne and Melville. The notion of a sui generis originating power is under challenge as research discloses the social construction of literary New England long represented *as if* it were a natural phenomenon (Baker, "Figurations" 148–49; Baym, "Early Histories," *Novels*, and *Women's Fiction*; Buell 193–250; Tompkins 3–39). Historically, one study finds, a kind of New England academic interlocking directorate "made literary works and authors display the virtues and achievements of an Anglo-Saxon United States founded by New England Puritans." That New England's exceptionalism emerges in such research shows the extent to which the literature of the South was systematically excluded from schoolbooks on American literature, just as New England was systematically privileged as *the* literature of this nation. "When in the second decade of the twentieth century, academics defined . . . 'American literature,' they did so by appropriating and sophisticating a narrative already constructed in the plethora of American literary history textbooks" that "encouraged respect, veneration, and gratitude toward these men who had achieved American literature on behalf of the rest of us" (Baym, "Early Histories" 459–60).

The argument that New England is a regional literature (Buell) with a literary history of intraregional responses (Bell), and that its putative national scope is the result of its social construction by academic-publishing elites rooted in Boston (Baym, "Early Histories," *Novels*, and *Women's Fiction*; Tompkins) may renew scholarly efforts to historicize and to develop theoretical positions toward the literature of other regions. The South, despite prodigious scholarship (e.g., R. B. Davis's three-volume intellectual history of the colonial South), to date has not commanded such attention. Yet the articulation of the idea of the South as an Eden from which the inhabitants are dispossessed because of the inherently corruptive institution of slavery establishes the theoretical basis on which Southern colonial studies might proceed (see L. P. Simpson). Lewis Simpson's work points up the need for a multivalent theoretics of regional Americas. The recent conception, moreover, of four distinct sets of English folkways disseminated in North America (see Fischer) and persisting in the subcultures of the United States may renew interest in a moribund regional American literary studies.

As of now, the paradoxical centrality of the marginal text has become a fruitful approach to earlier American literature and marks a distinct change in scholarly direction. For the revolutionary and postrevolutionary–early national periods, for instance, traditional scholarship has focused on the texts that explicitly expound the problematics and potential of republican political principles—texts such as the Declaration of Independence, the *Federalist* papers, or the verse of the Connecticut Wits, Timothy Dwight, Joel Barlow, David Humphreys, Jonathan Trumball (e.g., L. Howard). Recently, however, critical theory has concentrated on other categories of texts, heretofore considered at most obliquely concerned with issues central to the formation of the Republic. These reveal their "cultural work . . . redefining the social order" (Tompkins xi). Early American fiction is one such textual category: "because the novel as a form was marginalized by social authorities [including clergy, educators, political figures], because novelists could neither support themselves by their trade nor claim a respectable position within society because of it, the early American novel . . . was ideally suited to evaluate American society and to provide a critique of what was sorely missing in the exuberant postrevolutionary rhetoric of republicanism" (Davidson 218).

The Gothic novel, in this scheme, is particularly important as a social critique. Charles Brockden Brown's *Wieland*, for instance, in which an idyllic Philadelphia country-house life is disrupted by the arrival of a ventriloquist whose multiple voices are the catalyst for murder and mayhem—this text becomes engaging not for the solution of formal and thematic problems thought to be intrinsic to a "primitive" American fictional form nor for its psychoanalytical probings, but instead for the ways in which it pleads for the restoration of civic authority in a tumultuous postrevolutionary movement (Tompkins 40–61). Gothic novels can be seen, additionally, as criticisms of a hierarchical traditional society and of "the excesses of individualism" (Davidson 212–53).

Marxist and feminist approaches have also led to reconfigurations and revaluations of revolutionary and postrevolutionary–early national canonical and noncanonical texts—for instance, in work asserting the apposition between the narrative and the legal brief (R. A. Ferguson) and thus breaking the generic barrier between the belles lettres and documentary texts by insisting on the conceptual, structural, and argumentative enmeshment of letters and legal texts. And feminism has forced into unprecedented focus the patriarchal premises and presumptions of the canonical texts of the era, from Franklin's *Autobiography* to Jefferson's *Notes on the State of Virginia* (C. Jordan; Kerber). Feminist heuristics have so rigorously exposed patriarchy in the literature of this period and so thoroughly critiqued its arrogation of the power of social control by white males that the recent scholarly apologia for the revolutionary writers finds itself repudiating or redefining the nature and contingent status of patriarchy itself (Fliegelman).

Studies of the mid-nineteenth-century American Renaissance are also decentering the literary canon both by the reinterpretation of "major" texts and by the inclusion of those texts long thought to be marginal. Though the term was coined in 1829 by Samuel Knapp (see Gunn, "Kingdoms" 222), the rubric, as all Americanists know, was forcefully renewed by F. O. Matthiessen's *American Renaissance: Art and Expression in the Age of Emerson and Whitman*, itself a monumental act of canon formation, one that displaced the genteel "fireside" writers (Henry Wadsworth Longfellow, James Russell Lowell, John Greenleaf Whittier, Oliver Wendell Holmes) and instated a new constellation of major literary figures, among them Emerson, Thoreau, Hawthorne, Melville, and (as Emerson's designated poet-literatus) Whitman. In Matthiessen, the New England literary hegemony would remain intact, revivified—and also vivifying, as a vigorous post–World War II American literary criticism took flight from his scholarship (see Gunn, *Matthiessen*; Cain; Arac). As Charles Feidelson, Jr., remarked at the outset of his own influential *Symbolism and American Literature*, "The first large-scale attempt to define the literary quality of American writing at its best was Matthiessen's *American Renaissance*" (3).

The central postwar critical texts—Henry Nash Smith's *Virgin Land: The American West as Symbol and Myth*, Feidelson's *Symbolism and American Literature*, R. W. B. Lewis's *American Adam*, Richard Chase's *American Novel and Its Tradition*, Daniel Hoffman's *Form and Fable in American Fiction*, Leo Marx's *Machine in the Garden*, and, towering above these, Matthiessen's *American Renaissance*—all emphasized the United States as a country of democratic values encoded in a "classic" mid-nineteenth-century literature centered in New England, itself implicitly a synecdoche of the nation. This generation of theorists, moreover, was the first to incorporate New Criticism in approaches to American literature. They brought the social dimensions of New Criticism into organicist readings of individual texts. "The theorists of American literature conceived the social structure of the literary work as a microcosm of collective psychology or myth and thus made New Criticism into a method of cultural analysis" (Graff, *Promise* 217). It is no coincidence that the myth-symbol school of American studies flourished at this time (H. N. Smith; L. Marx), based on the premise that patterns of symbol embedded in the literary text manifest the ethos of the nation. By precept and example, the work of these scholars has continued to influence the terms and the design of scholarship; for instance, one study presumes that "the problems of American politics and the problems of American literary genius may be said to belong to the same family of problems" (Marr 39; see also Porte).

The newer scholarly subject positions, however, reject as invalid any claims to the organicism implied in the term *family of problems*. Accordingly, they have approached antebellum American literature very differently. It may well be that the nickname *cold war criticism* will become the term by which post–World War II studies are known in retrospect. The "cold war consensus" (Pease, *Visionary Contacts*) is being defined as ideological in its very contention that the major American literary texts (those of indigenous "genius") transcend ideology. Recent scholarship finds that cold war consensus to be earmarked by its argument and its presumption that the "classic" texts enact democratic freedom in their structural openness and thus oppose (and repudiate) the closed systems denoting totalitarianism (Pease, *Visionary Contacts*; Bercovitch and Jehlen).

Such retrospect is possible, in fact inevitable, when critical subject positions change to the extent that both culture and text are seen as a field in which power is contested and in which the text inscribes the contention of competing and combative forces. From Roland Barthes's essay "The Death of the Author" and Michel Foucault's "What Is an Author?" the very conception of authorship has undergone the process of historicization that discloses how problematic is the term, how coordinate through the centuries with the unprecedented rise of individualization and private property. The *author* cannot now be presumed to stand outside a situated world of roiling forces—political, economic, ideological, cultural. The premise of transcendent democratic truths embodied in texts of aesthetic genius is thus reassessed as ideologically self-serving to certain groups, especially to white male elites, and enactive of its own historical moment, such as the cold war.

In new-historicist terms, then, the criticism of the 1940s through 1960s becomes cold war criticism, an ideological construct, "a holistic master story of large-scale structural elements directing a whole society," when in actuality "selves and texts are defined by their relation to hostile others," such as "despised and feared Indians, Jews, Blacks" (Veeser xiii), and to disciplinary power represented in figures of institutional authority, such as Hawthorne's judge, Jaffrey Pyncheon, in *The House of the Seven Gables* or Melville's Captain Ahab. Previous criticism is seen to be flawed because of its evasion of these matters. Thus Matthiessen's treatment of mid-nineteenth-century American texts is condemned for its "most extravagant idealization: the diminishment of the Civil War. . . . rather than facing up to divisions within the renaissance, Matthiessen divided the renaissance from the war. . . . His wish for wholeness led to disconnection" (Arac 97–98).

While American Renaissance has served for decades as a course title in countless colleges and universities, current scholarship is reconfiguring the terms of the rubric. Studies of antebellum American literature bring texts previously excluded or marginalized onto the field; they reread the "renaissance" texts in light of the proposition that the written text, the author, and his or her culture coexist in a dynamic interplay of contending forces—a point demonstrable in work on Hawthorne.

For decades, scholars demonstrated Hawthorne's indebtedness to *The Faerie Queene* as a source for the character Pearl in *The Scarlet Letter*, citing as one instance Hawthorne's naming his daughter, Una, after Spenser's allegorical character. Currently, however, Hawthorne, Una, and *The Scarlet Letter* are positioned as "interactive, contingent and interdependent participants in a collective process" (Herbert 287). *The Scarlet Letter* does not, in these terms, become the transmuted form of autobiographical or sociocultural and literary influences on Hawthorne, much less the work of art transcendent of these forces. Indeed, the presumption of such transcendence is discredited, downgraded into mere reification. "Instead of reifying Hawthorne's entangled brooding on Una's character into transcendent aesthetic terms, *The Scarlet Letter* extends that brooding and complicates the entanglement" (287).

Melville, to cite another canonical example, is similarly recontextualized, approached as a participant in a network of dynamic associations—familial, political, cultural, economic—in all of which he becomes a figure of historical contingency. The conception of Melville as author, recent critics assert, has been reified in scholarly emphasis on his separateness from his sociocultural contexts. To call Melville a genius or great author is emphatically to remove him from his cultural milieu. To enshrine him (or, for that matter, Emerson or Thoreau or Poe) in a fraternal pantheon of singular cohorts is to stress his separateness, his distinctness from the society he inhabited, which inscribes itself in his texts. Selfhood becomes not an index of singularity but a term referring to the historical process of which any individual, including the writer, is necessarily a part. The text, accordingly, is not seen to be an entity transcendent of its time but one inscriptive of it. In this sense, author, text, and context merge. And to approach Melville or any other canonical author in this way is not to be iconoclastic but to reclaim that figure and the texts from reification—and to rescue scholars from their roles as monument makers, agents of reification. Thus Melville is viewed as being involved in nineteenth-century American imperialism even in his family relationships, those of "subversive genealogy," and *Moby-Dick* is revealed to enact the politics of imperialism, with Ahab exploiting Third World labor to plunder the globe's natural resources (Rogin; Dimock).

The "renaissance," not surprisingly, becomes a historical moment in which unexamined literary-cultural associations, in particular the economic, are investigated, as scholars draw from the work of Marx, Georg Lukács, and Raymond Williams to explore the ways in which the commodification of labor and the permeation of social relations by a market economy manifest themselves in literary texts previously thought impervious to such matters. The study of industrial capitalism in the United States reveals its development to be considerably earlier than once was thought, not a post–Civil War phenomenon but one occurring in the antebellum decades (Gilmore; Porter, *Seeing* and "Reification"; Shulman). According to the premises of new historicism, the "classic" American writers are no longer simply oppositional critics of marketplace values but inevitably, if inadvertently, complicitous with them.

Their response to an insurgent corporate capitalism is shown to be formal, not only discursively resistent to the market system for its exploitation of workers' wage slavery but participating in—in fact, enacting—the presumptions of the new economic order. Although Melville's "Tartarus of Maids" has long seemed a trenchant critique of the evolving industrialism—testimony to his opposition to systematic murder by wage slavery—his acquiescence in the new order has lately come to light. For instance, the cetology chapters in *Moby-Dick*, in which Melville's sources on whales and whaling are printed verbatim, are read as the writer's raw materials that, when processed through the imagination, emerge as a finished product, a literary symbol, to be marketed as fiction for profit (Gilmore). The novel thus takes on the character of a factory. And the domestic novel, in which the sacrosanct home is customarily thought to be exempt from commercial values, instead reveals the infiltration of the market at its worst: *Uncle Tom's Cabin* "show[s] the involvement of the home and its keeper in the practice of slavery . . . slavery as itself a domestic institution [with] an intrusion of the marketplace into the home" (Lang, *Prophetic Woman* 197–98).

Even the most visionary of nineteenth-century literary symbols, Emerson's "transcendent eyeball," when examined in the context of industrial capitalism becomes the signifier of a society that alienates individuals from themselves and their work and insinuates itself within the social consciousness. Such a society "generates people who assume a passive and 'contemplative' stance in the face of objectified and rationalized reality—people who seem to themselves to stand outside that reality because their own participation in producing it is mystified" (Porter, "Reification" 189). Emerson and Thoreau, from this viewpoint, become figures whose contemplative stance and visionary attributes are products of nineteenth-century economic history. In fact, the visionary is redefined as the inevitable outcome of capitalist alienation, and transcendentalism thus takes its place as a phenomenon grounded in economic history.

With increasing aggressiveness, critics have repudiated the once-eulogized American individualism, its major exponent being the Emerson of "Self-Reliance." Of course, the postwar critics had drawn careful distinctions among writers with claims to individualism, especially juxtaposing Captain Ahab against the Thoreau of *Walden*. The two are individualist antitheses, with Ahab portrayed as the nemesis of the ideal, the very "embodiment of his author's most profound response to the problem of the individual free will *in extremis*. . . . he can see nothing but his own burning thoughts since he no longer shares in any normal fellow-feelings [and] refuses to be deflected from his pursuit by the stirring of any sympathy for others" (Matthiessen, *American Renaissance* 447–51). Ahab thus became a "fearful example of the self-enclosed individualism that . . . brings disaster both upon itself and upon the group of which it is a part" (459). In postwar critical terms, he is "a false culture-hero, pursuing a private grievance (rather than a divine behest) at the expense of the mankind in his crew . . . a Satan, a sorcerer, an Antichrist" (Hoffman 234). Investigators who take this approach read *Moby-Dick* as "a book about the alienation from life that results from an excessive or neurotic self-dependence," one in which Ahab is "guilty of or victimized by a distorted 'self-reliance' " (Lewis 105). The critic who celebrates *Moby-Dick* for embodying the "great cultural heritage" of the United States warns nonetheless that Melville must not be seen to approve Ahab's "intensity, power, and defiant spirit" because he represents the deformation of individualism and self-reliance (L. Howard, *Literature* 176–77). And if the cold war version of Captain Ahab echoes the horrors of Hitler and totalitarianism (and, retrospectively, in U.S. history, indicts the unchecked predations of the robber barons, as Matthiessen remarked), he also stands interpretively as an alienated anti-individualist.

Thoreau, on the contrary, was presented in the postwar era as the exemplar of the democratic common person, recommitting himself to American traditions of hard work and artisanship, his *Walden* also making a claim for "communal security and permanence," for "order and balance" (Matthiessen, *American Renaissance* 172–73). He was a "visionary hero" who "demonstrates his freedom in the liberation of others," thus working on behalf of other human beings to further the greatest cause of freedom (Lewis 21). Thoreau's "aggressiveness," though regrettably "excessive" for his time, is vindicated when his democratic "symbol of the hermitage" is exported to India for Mahatma Gandhi's successful struggle for independence (L. Howard, *Literature* 158–60). Thoreau, then, becomes the democratic heroic individualist precisely because he represents the dutiful and responsible postwar American working person committed to communal security and stability, and also to social order. In postwar criticism, then, the individualist must either be brought within the democratic fold, as was Thoreau, or, failing that, be consigned to un-American realms beyond—that is, to the alienationist domains of insanity, abnormality, deformity.

Beginning in the 1970s, however, a challenge to the ideal of American individualism as hostile to human interests and pernicious in its effects was undertaken. Narratives on American environmentalism were shown to endorse violence against the self and others; representations of life on the frontier were felt to be tributes not to personal and national independence and courage but to deracinative isolation and alienation. Regenerative energies were seen to be aroused precisely in violent, aggressive action (Kolodny, *Lay of the Land*; Slotkin).

Critics have continued to challenge individualist ideals. Studies of eighteenth-century commodity capitalism and the concomitant picaresque novel, both in England and America, reveal the imperative of incessant social upheaval that defines individualism as "change, difference, possibility, mobility, restlessness, flux," qualities that thwart stable cultural relationships and, when convergent, represent "the excesses of individualism" (Davidson 167, 219). And one recent study of individualism in the United States, *Habits of the Heart*, acknowledges in brief that "sometimes the flight from society is simply mad and ends in general disaster," offering Ahab as the consummate example of "asocial individualism" unredeemed by the postwar critics' solace of a democratically pervasive and enduring Ishmael (Bellah et al. 144–45). In this sense, Thoreau becomes not the exemplar of visionary democracy but the isolate in whom the potential to be an "inspiring friend replaces the need for any actual friendship" and who "etherealizes friendship to the point of mutual evanescence" (Pease, *Visionary Compacts* 263). "Thoreau did not want a friend of his own. . . . what he wanted in a friend was a confirmation of the self" (J. W. Warren 59). The masculine ethos of individualism in Thoreau, as well as in Cooper, Emerson, and Melville, is reidentified as egocentric narcissism: "The American myth of the individual has encouraged the development of narcissism, not only in the psychological sense of an individual's unsuccessful resolution of an early failure in identity but in a cultural sense. . . . The male individualist . . . sees himself as all-powerful and all-encompassing, and he sees only himself" (J. W. Warren 13).

If marketplace capitalism is one heuristic by which to critique the development of individualist ideology and its literary consequences, another is the inverted subject position focused on the founding of the New World. According to a line of argument that bypasses the colonial New England tradition, the dominant nineteenth-century canonical texts devolved from the European Enlightenment's projection of a mythic, pristine New World, the crucial concept being that of the *discovery* of America. This is not the nation understood to have developed through historical processes but instead perceived to be a world come upon intact, existing essentially outside of history. And the kinds of literary production emerging from that position were predetermined by it: the discovered, pristine America, existing primarily in a state of perfection, by its very definition admits of no change; literary representations of social or personal change in a fluid context were thus precluded. The literary opportunity is one of entitlement—and of tremendous constraint. It is chiefly one of ratification and celebration of the quotidian world whose representative American incarnates the continent itself (thus the scholarly title *American Incarnation*, with its pun on *nation*). "The American, and therefore the American artist, is identical with America and sufficient unto all of it. He incarnates America and encompasses its entire consciousness" (Jehlen, *American Incarnation* 132). Thus the novel—the genre central to historical process—is excluded because it is precluded, since nineteenth-century American genre and ideology must be inextricably connected in the dominant literary forms. What remains is nonfiction and the romance: the Emersonian or Thorovian essay and the likes of *The Scarlet Letter*. Literary efforts at the novel as a historical narrative (e.g., Hawthorne's *The Marble Faun* or Melville's *Pierre*) are doomed to fracture because they attempt the intervention of history into an America that is conceptually ahistorical.

Other reassessments of antebellum American literature resist the notion of dominant literary forms and inject the traditional rubrics—the Age of Emerson and Whitman, the American Renaissance—with irony as they redefine the period by widening its scope to include texts previously marginalized or excluded altogether, especially those categorized as belonging to popular culture or to sentimental (i.e., women's) fiction. While Matthiessen traced a trajectory "from Coleridge to Emerson" (*American Renaissance* 133), writers such as David S. Reynolds now argue that popular culture, particularly vernacular religious rhetoric, was at least as important a source for Emerson and his major-figure cohorts. Colloquial revivalism is now asserted to be an integral part of the formation of Emerson's discourse (as well as that of Whitman and Poe), and the "renaissance" shown to be so riddled with "subversive" works that "the major texts [become] artistic renderings of irrational or erotic themes predominant in a large body of overlooked sensational writings of the day" (169).

The sensational, mass-market press filled with ghoulish crimes, sex scandals, felonies, celebrity criminals, and the like becomes permeable with the previously sacralized literary productions of the canonical figures, and scholarly rubrics indicate this newer high culture–low culture inclusivity: Poe and Popular Irrationalism, Hawthorne and Crime Literature, *The Scarlet Letter* and Popular Sensationalism (Reynolds). Robert S. Levine argues that a pervasive cultural paranoia, much of it anti-Catholic and extending from the colonial era through the nineteenth century, recurrently engendered texts centered in anxiety about conspiratorial subversion. In this sense literary studies become cultural studies, diminishing the possibility of sensationalist, even prurient exposés of canonical figures. "Beneath" the American Renaissance, in Reynolds's phrase, may be an unfortunate and misleading preposition when criticism shows the more accurate term to be "within."

Locating divers kinds of texts *within* the period, moreover, investigators looking at the sentimental tradition most closely identified with women writers and readers have taken a prominent position over the past decade. The *feminine*, a word disparaged in Hawthorne's dismissal of the "damned mob of scribbling women" (meaning his commercially successful women-author rivals), and sustained in the title of Fred Lewis Pattee's historical examination *The Feminine Fifties* (1940), had continued to be a term of opprobrium even in the scholarship that, in the 1970s, initiated the revaluation of the sentimental (see Ann Douglas, *Feminization*).

The long-forgotten body of popular texts written by and for nineteenth-century women has now come to the fore in analysis that earns the title "sentimental power" (Tompkins 122–201). Such examinations, begun originally as bibliographic study to determine authors, titles, sales figures, and audiences for nineteenth-century sentimental fiction (Baym), utilize that data to formulate arguments on the sociocultural power of these texts, whose authors include Susan Warner, E. D. E. N. Southworth, Elizabeth Stuart Phelps, Louisa May Alcott, and especially Harriet Beecher Stowe. If a positivist, materialist, and scientific-technological bent dominated later nineteenth- and twentieth-century American history, feminist criticism argues, that direction nonetheless must not conceal a mid-nineteenth-century ethos of evangelistic piety—much less prevent the study of it. The terms of the mid-nineteenth-century moral universe now demand exegesis, and the texts that represent that universe should be included in any configuration of American antebellum literature. No longer can these texts be dismissed as naive or ingenuous, such dismissal itself understood as having served a particular critical-political agenda in postwar literary criticism (Baker, *Figurations*; Tompkins).

Nor is sentimental, domestic American fiction divided along gender lines exclusively. The sentimental tradition is currently understood to include both the women writers and the canonical Hawthorne. Jane Tompkins (11) points out that Hawthorne was most valued in the mid-nineteenth century not for the ironic dark fiction the era of T. S. Eliot came to value but rather for the tales that moralize on domestic topics ("Sunday at Home," "A Rill from the Town Pump," "Little Annie's Ramble"). In interdisciplinary cultural studies, still best known as American studies, the study of sentimental fiction has been extended into cognate forms, especially into nineteenth-century American sculpture; for example, such objects as Hiram Powers's *Greek Slave* are only ostensibly classically derivative and, like the sentimental tradition itself, have been too long dismissed as vapid. Instead, as Joy S. Kasson shows, such sculpture enacts the tensions and political divisions of its antebellum era, including slavery, feminism, class divisions, the developing capitalist and marketplace economics.

The sentimental, moreover, is not solely a category for the scrutiny of domesticity and evangelistic piety. For instance, scholarship involving the "hard facts" of American literary culture, including the rhetoric of extirpation of the Indians in James Fenimore Cooper's fiction, includes an extended discussion of Stowe's *Uncle Tom's Cabin* under the heading "The Sentimental Novel and Slavery" (P. Fisher 87–127). And the legacy of Hutchinson, the "prophetic woman," is shown to be the narrative paradigm splaying into the texts of Emerson, Hawthorne, and Stowe (Lang). Beyond the issue of the social construction of gender and text lies the related but separate matter of sexuality and its construction over time. The seemingly "exaggeratedly male" Walt Whitman proclaiming his virility and phallic power becomes, in recent analysis of his poetic persona, a figure who is alternately female and transsexual, just as Poe is reread as a writer whose heroes are androgynous, embodied pleas for the human wholeness that must encompass the male and the female (Gilbert; C. Jordan 133–51). American literary studies, long dominated by an overarching presumption of masculinity in its primary and critical texts, may well continue to elicit kindred studies of sexuality and gender like that on Whitman (and like those currently appearing on Hemingway).

Another recent direction in American literary study involves the role(s) of the reader in the formulation of the text. The process of interpretation in which readers are thought to construct a text has also come in for particular attention as reader-response theory is applied to American literary study that asks, What are the cultural or political shapings of reading and what a priori literary conventions affect interpretation and assessment? Answers to such inquiry reveal that the reception of texts differentiates according to national-cultural patterns. *Moby-Dick*, for instance, was received differently in England and the United States. The British, preoccupied with literary conventions, evaluated the novel according to prescriptive rules for fiction and found it wanting because it defied taxonomic convention; American reviewers, less constrained by normative rules, were less exasperated by Melville's mix of genres (Mailloux 169–78). And the reader-response theorist now takes us through a Hawthorne story like "Rappaccini's Daughter" to disclose the process of the time flow of reading, its constraints and liberations, while the scholar of African American literature finds this methodology to be particularly useful for texts in which "the distinctions between telling and writing on the one hand, and hearing and reading on the other, are far more profound than they usually are determined to be in those interpretive groupings constituted by other types of fictive narrative" (Mailloux 80–92; Stepto, "Distrust" 306).

Those students of American literature conversant largely (or solely) with the traditions of Western civilization, moreover, are increasingly impaired, as scholars of ethnic and racial literary traditions explore the intratextual functioning of cultural-rhetorical patterns indigenous to non-Western groups. As one states, "It is well worth it to interpret America not narrowly as immigration but more broadly as ethnic diversity and include the pre-Columbian inhabitants of the continent, the kidnapped Africans and their descendents, and the Chicanos of the Southwest" (Sollors, *Beyond Ethnicity* 8). (It would be interesting to hear the postwar critics reevaluate their major studies in this light, as Henry Nash Smith did, acknowledging that *Virgin Land* ignored the populations of indigenous groups on the North American continent, whose very existence gives an ironic dimension to the term *Virgin* [see "Symbol and Idea"].)

The civil rights movement of the 1960s gave impetus to the study of African American literature, beginning with the examination of figures and images of the black in the literature and culture of the United States (Yellin; Boskin) and proceeding with an analysis of the ways in which American literary history excluded African American texts from "traditional, orthodox patterns of a spiritually evolving American literature" (Baker, "Figurations" 149). Studies of canonical texts have disclosed their criticism of racism—for instance, Melville's *Benito Cereno*, the story of the suppression of a slave mutiny, has been the focus of scholarship revealing Melville's scathing critique of the paternalistic white male, a type prominant in antebellum political life of the North and South, and his prescience in blasting the plantation myth as politically and psychologically repressive (Sundquist; Rogin 210–15).

More recently, African American literature has been subjected to theoretical analysis of its rhetorical structures (Gates, *Signifying Monkey*). Generations of Western writers have exploited their literary innovations to surpass or to destroy the work of their predecessors, this argument says, but the African American tradition operates very differently and needs to be understood in its development from the sophisticated folk cultures of Africa. (According to one scholar, the marginalization of those traditions in the hegemonic development of the West via classical Greece and the Hebrews had profoundest impact in nineteenth-century concepts of race and therefore has special bearing on the period under discussion here; see Appiah, "Race.") "Black people," then, have embraced "a system of rhetorical strategies peculiar to their own vernacular tradition," in which "the Signifyin(g) Monkey is the figure of a black rhetoric in the Afro-American speech community," existing to "embody the figures of speech in the black vernacular," and as the principle of self-consciousness in that vernacular, becoming "the meta-figure itself" (Gates 53). The African American text, moreover, is not fixed in a determinate sense but works by indeterminacy and uncertainty, so that simultaneous plurality of meanings is possible: "The ironic reversal of a received racist image of the black as simi-anlike, the Signifying Monkey, [is] he who dwells at the margins of discourse, ever punning, ever troping, ever embodying the ambiguities of language." In African American texts he becomes the "trope for repetition and revision, in-deed [the] trope of chiasmus, repeating and reversing simultaneously as he does in one deft discursive act" (52). (The opening of ethnically and racially diverse traditions continued and was accelerated by the Columbian quincen-tennial year, 1992, in which academic conferences and scholarly publications focused on earlier Caribbean American literature and the literature of New World cross-cultural encounter. This work departs from the perspectives of the Mexican historian Edmundo O'Gorman, who emphasizes the "invention" of America, as well as from Tzvetan Todorov's argument on the Western Euro-pean "conquest" of Mexico.)

The kinds of scholarship discussed in this essay have not come to the fore without a degree of resistence and hostility on the part of a generation of Americanists educated in the New Criticism, well trained in bibliographic and research methods and plying these skills to excellent results in the college classroom, in journal articles, and in books. One can point, moreover, to the continuation of exemplary scholarship of a traditional design in this poststruc-turalist moment—for instance, in studies of national character in Hawthorne and Melville, of democratic ideals pursued in the praxis of rhetoric, of Cooper's politics or of Thoreau's classical influences, or of the relation of popular histori-cal romance to Hawthorne's fiction (McWilliams, *Political Justice*; Dauber; Richardson; Bell).

The controversy over the newer methodologies, however, is essentially one of epistemology and of its political orientation as a struggle for the control of meaning. Professional, collegial, and scholarly endeavor are all seen at this point as overtly political. Editorial succession—for instance, for the journal *American Literature*—becomes a matter not only of the maintenance of schol-arly scrupulousness but of ideological positioning, as groups of researchers perceive their interests to be potentially furthered or frustrated by a likely appointee. Disagreement about the openness of the long-established "flagship" journal to newer viewpoints has had the market-economy effect of the forma-tion of a new, competing periodical, *American Literary History*, which is explic-itly hospitable to articles on "theoretical problems" (perhaps implying lack of receptivity to such work in other, established journals).

At this juncture, as groups of Americanist scholars contend for inter-pretive legitimation and critical assent, those cognizant of both the postwar and post-1960s scholarship can point out certain as-yet unresolved (and even unacknowledged) problems in criticism. This is to say that the practitioners of the newer critical approaches can find themselves unwittingly in a vexed rela-tion to the scholarship of their predecessors, the very scholarship they are challenging. Suppose one were to read Leo Marx's *Machine in the Garden*, for instance, as a cold war fable on a pastoral America threatened with the nuclear invasion figured in the machine and therefore to historicize that text as a critical act of the nuclear age mentality. To do so would require the elucidation of the American literary pastoralism so closely defined in *The Machine in the Garden*. Thus one historicizes the very texts whose data and argumentative shape are necessary for the foundations of one's own argument. The risk is one of simultaneous exploitation and reification, the latter an act that contemporary scholarship deplores.

The community most receptive to the new historicism, moreover, awaits the cogent theoretics who would justify and guide its assimilative practices. If the new historicist faults the New Critic predecessor for explaining away the irreconcilable and the contradictory in the sacralizing name of paradox and irony, for example, then the new historicist must bring to visibility—and account for—those lines of cultural and literary contention that pose challenge to—even threaten to subvert the plausibility of—the new historicist's own disclosures. As it is, new historicism implies a territorial comprehensiveness that functions to exclude realms fraught with oppositional possibility.

Those trained in traditional methods, at the same time, must be aware that literary study cannot be unaffected by historical process, that every literary critic belongs to an incessantly changing intellectual-cultural world, that no position, argument, stance can be impervious to change, as those scholars currently historicizing the discipline of literary studies have so well revealed. New Criticism was certain to have a limited shelf life, but so will any other "ism," though it remains to be seen whether poststructuralists will be any more prepared for what succeeds them—perhaps some neocanonicalism marshaled in arguments as yet unforeseen as the category of the aesthetic begins to reinsinuate itself in literary study. Any examination of changing patterns in American literary study ought to take notice of scholarship reflecting on the history of the profession, including Giles Gunn's *Culture of Criticism and the Criticism of Culture*, Jonathan Culler's "Literary Criticism and the American University," and Gerald Graff's *Professing Literature: An Institutional History*.

Those who may feel that the insurgence of newer approaches represents certain professional betrayal might, in fact, find it useful to survey the social construction of an anthropological text considered especially congenial to literary study. Clifford Geertz's "Deep Play: Notes on the Balinese Cockfight" has been taken up virtually as a fable for critics, appearing as it did at the point in the history of New Criticism at which every possible interpretation of any given canonical text seemed already to have been published, ultimately with diminishing returns, and few could conceive of the usefulness of yet another interpretive refinement of a Hawthorne tale or Thorovian essay—in sum, when younger scholars could but feel themselves relegated to roles of acolytes to the preceding generations, producing secondhand versions of the arguments of their own scholarly parents.

At that point, enter Bali, in Geertz's term "the well-studied place" whose mythology, art, ritual, social organization, law, and child-rearing practices had all been "microscopically" examined by the authoritative master scholars (Gregory Bateson and Margaret Mead) but that now could suddenly yield itself anew as a text. Long overlooked as mere cultural minutiae, the Balinese cockfight, the heretofore marginal text, discloses previously unnoticed dimensions of intrapsychic struggle, social status, hierarchy, morality. The authorities had somehow missed these important dimensions, just as the master scholars of American and other literatures had undertaken massive studies but somehow overlooked crucial heuristics that would reopen the texts especially to the researchers of the succeeding generation. Though Geertz has recently been attacked for splitting language from reality (Bercovitch and Jehlen 12–13), the motives for literary scholars' affinity with his work are self-evident. The lesson of the cockfight is that the imprint of august scholars need not deter one, that "exhaustive" or "microscopic" examinations are only spuriously so, that the seemingly marginal text can yield insights of central importance, that the canonical text holds surprises if only one knows how to look for them. The lesson is cyclical and applicable to American literary study.

## Selected Bibliography

Baym, Nina. "Early Histories of American Literature: A Chapter in the Institution of New England." *American Literary History* 1 (1989): 459–88.

——. *Novels, Readers, and Reviewers: Responses to Fiction in Antebellum America*. Ithaca: Cornell UP, 1984.
Two titles that survey the range of antebellum fiction, its market and audiences, and historicize the literary hegemony of New England.

Bercovitch, Sacvan. *The American Jeremiad*. Madison: U of Wisconsin P, 1978.
A literary theory of nationalism rooted in Puritan eschatology.

——, ed. *Reconstructing American Literary History*. Cambridge: Harvard UP, 1986.
Revaluative essays on the early republican era through the mid-nineteenth century and beyond.

Bercovitch, Sacvan, and Myra Jehlen, eds. *Ideology and Classic American Literature*. New York: Columbia UP, 1986.
Language and politics of mid-nineteenth-century texts examined by diverse groups of scholars.

Breitwieser, Mitchell. *American Puritanism and the Defence of Mourning: Reli-*

*gion, Grief, and Ethnology in Mary White Rowlandson's Captivity Narrative*. Madison: U of Wisconsin P, 1990.
A new theory of New England Puritanism based on a heuristics of race, gender, and, implicitly, class.

Buell, Lawrence. *New England Literary Culture: From Revolution through Renaissance*. New York: Cambridge UP, 1986.
A reconceptualization of New England literature.

Davidson, Cathy N. *Revolution and the Word: The Rise of the Novel in America*. New York: Oxford UP, 1986.
A study of the rise of the novel and its relation to political life of the early Republic.

Dimock, Wai-chee. *Empire for Liberty: Melville and the Poetics of Individualism*. Princeton: Princeton UP, 1989.
A new-historicist consideration of the Melville oeuvre.

Gates, Henry Louis, Jr. *The Signifying Monkey: A Theory of African-American Literary Criticism*. New York: Oxford UP, 1988.
A theory of language and signification in African American literature.

Gilmore, Michael T. *American Romanticism and the Marketplace*. Chicago: U of Chicago P, 1985.
An analysis of the insurgence of industrial capitalism in mid-nineteenth-century America and the response of Emerson, Hawthorne, and Thoreau.

Jehlen, Myra. *American Incarnation: The Individual, the Nation, and the Continent*. Cambridge: Harvard UP, 1986.
On the European projection of an America extrinsic to historical processes and the literary result of that conception of a nation whose citizens are its incarnation.

Jordan, Cynthia. *Second Stories: The Politics of Language, Form, and Gender in Early American Fictions*. Chapel Hill: U of North Carolina P, 1989.
Two generations of patriarchal texts and the permutations of language of gender.

Kasson, Joy S. *Marble Queens and Captives: Women in Nineteenth-Century American Sculpture*. New Haven: Yale UP, 1990.
Cultural study of sculpture, contemporary medicine, feminism, and social practices in the arts.

Lang, Amy Schrager. *Prophetic Woman: Anne Hutchinson and the Problem of Dissent in the Literature of New England*. Berkeley: U of California P, 1987.
The culturally obsessive narrative of the seventeenth-century Puritan woman as it reemerges in Emerson, Hawthorne, Stowe.

Mailloux, Steven. *Interpretive Conventions: The Reader in the Study of American Fiction*. Ithaca: Cornell UP, 1982.
Reader-response theory in the interrogation of American texts.

Michaels, Walter Benn, and Donald E. Pease, eds. *The American Renaissance Reconsidered: Selected Papers from the English Institute, 1982–83*. Baltimore: Johns Hopkins UP, 1985.
Revaluation of canonical texts and arguments for the inclusion of popular, sentimental, and ethnic texts.

Reynolds, David S. *Beneath the American Renaissance: The Subversive Imagination in the Age of Emerson and Melville*. New York: Knopf, 1988.
The permeability of popular and canonical texts in antebellum America.

Rogin, Michael Paul. *Subversive Genealogy: The Politics and Art of Herman Melville*. Berkeley: U of California P, 1979.
A new-historicist and psychoanalytical study of Melville and his culture.

Shulman, Robert. *Social Criticism and Nineteenth-Century American Fictions*. Columbia: U of Missouri P, 1987.
A discussion of the impact of capitalism on canonical texts of the American Renaissance.

Tompkins, Jane. *Sensational Designs: The Cultural Work of American Fiction, 1790–1860*. New York: Oxford UP, 1985.
Examines the social power of the sentimental and the social construction of literary careers, principally that of Hawthorne.

Warren, Joyce W. *The American Narcissus: Individualism and Women in Nineteenth-Century American Fiction*. 1984. New Brunswick: Rutgers UP, 1989.
Argues that male narcissism in the guise of individualism precluded the participation of women in canonical texts.

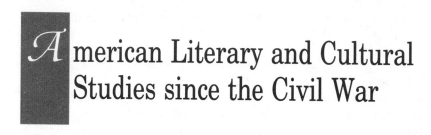

# American Literary and Cultural Studies since the Civil War

PHILIP FISHER

## From Myth to Rhetorics

The essential books of the last fifteen years in the literary and cultural study of American life represent the work of a new generation within American studies, and they represent, at the same time, a new idea of what it might mean to do American studies and how one would go about doing it. In combination they also represent the rich diversity of explanations and materials in the study of American culture. Films and photographs, Supreme Court decisions and industrial manuals, educational and domestic theory, the popular culture of Horatio Alger and the standard genres of domestic fiction: a culture in its full institutional and individual variety has been brought into play.

One way to characterize this newness would be to say that, in this generation of American studies, interest has passed from myth to rhetorics. *Myth* in this perhaps too simple formula is always singular, *rhetorics* always plural. Myth is a fixed, satisfying, and stable story that is used again and again to normalize our account of social life. By means of myth, novelty is tamed by being seen as the repetition or, at most, the variation of a known and valued pattern. Even where actual historical situations are found to fall short of myth or to lie in its aftermath, the myth tames the variety of historical experience, giving it familiarity while using it to reaffirm the culture's long-standing interpretation of itself.

Rhetoric, in contrast, is a tactic within the open questions of culture. It reveals interests and exclusions. To look at rhetorics is to look at the action potential of language and images, not just their power or contrivance to move an audience but the location of words, formulas, images, and units of meaning within politics. Rhetoric is the place where language is engaged in cultural work, and such work can be done on, with, or in spite of one or another group within society. Rhetorics are plural because they are part of what is uncertain or potential within culture. They are the servants of one or another politics of experience. Where there is nothing openly contested, no cultural work to be done, we do not find the simplification into one and only one rhetoric. Instead we find the absence of the particular inflammation and repetition that rhetoric always marks. We find no rhetoric at all, only the ceremonial contentment of myth. Rhetorics are also distinct from ideology. Within the term *ideology* we are right to hear a combination of calculation, cynicism about social truth, a schoolteacher's relation to the pupils, indoctrination, and propaganda. Whether as reality or hope, ideology implies that one part of the legitimacy of authority is a monopoly on representation, and this is exactly the condition in which rhetorics become irrelevant.

To understand what a move from myth to rhetorics might involve, it is useful to look at two things: first, how the claim of a unitary myth worked and was used during the period that we might call the transfer of literature to the American university; second, the counterelement to central myths within American studies—the force of regionalism.

## *Myths and the University*

The new field of American studies came to maturity in the years just before and after the Second World War. Its description of American experience had as its audience both Americans themselves and, even more important, a wider world in which American culture had begun to work as a kind of world culture. Both Europeans and Americans were asked to consider in mythic terms a prior state of American experience, one whose essence and importance lay in the fact that it no longer existed but had generated the cultural heart of American experience. But to this prior culture of Puritan mission, frontier, wilderness, garden, and innocence, contemporary Americans were just as much outsiders as Europeans and Asians were.

In this charged pre- and postwar atmosphere of cultural victory and cultural defeat, Americanists undertook the search for a central myth of America. Such key works as Henry Nash Smith's *Virgin Land*, Leo Marx's *Machine in the Garden*, R. W. B. Lewis's *American Adam*, and Richard Slotkin's *Regeneration through Violence* encouraged a study of literature, everyday culture, and history around a shared mythic content that captured American uniqueness and national identity. American studies as an academic field in its first generation took this myth of America to be its central topic and its method for linking the classics of American poetry, fiction, and painting to the culture of images, newspapers, sermons, political rhetoric, and, especially, popular fiction and verse. Here the western and the sermon met.

The first of these all-encompassing myths of America had, in fact, been defined half a century earlier. This was the frontier myth of Frederic Jackson Turner, a hypothesis as Turner called it, but ultimately a story rather than a scientific speculation, and a story whose appeal lay in the curious fact that it described just those social features that had been lost forever in the formal, official closing of the American frontier noted in the census of 1890. Although Turner's great myth appeared before what we might call the capture of American culture by the universities, an event that took place in the 1930s and 1940s, his strategy of discovering one fundamental fact or myth that explained the identity of America as a nation set the stage for the mythic cast of the first generation of the academic study of American culture. After the frontier myth, the most important global explanation lay in the myth of the Puritans, their mission, the unique significance of intellectuals and ideology within the Puritan experience, the primacy of New England's religious forms for American political experience, and the residue of Puritan energy, now changed to commerce and self-cultivation, that remained as a permanent trace within the national character. If the frontier myth was a myth of the West, the Puritan myth was a myth of New England culture, asserting its right to a permanent steering function in national life. Where the western myth was democratic, based on the experience of immigration and self-reliance, the New England myth was ultimately a myth of the importance of intellectuals and, with them, of the crucial role played by writing and those who provide ideology, self-description, and history—the importance, finally, of preachers and their later descendants, the intellectuals of the nineteenth century and the university professors of the twentieth.

In spite of the built-in resistance of our literature and its awkward wildness, no cultural fact is more decisive over the past fifty years than the wholesale movement of every component of our literary life, past, present, and future, into the universities. American studies and American literature have everywhere arrived at legitimacy. American poets have been signed up as writers-in-residence. Our men and women of letters, following Philip Rahv and Irving Howe, have become professors, trading in their general audience of educated adults for a classroom full of students eighteen to twenty-five years old, and a secondary audience of their professional colleagues who have now become the main readers of their opinions. Our little magazines are now subsidized by colleges, where they too are now in residence, and they find their primary guaranteed sales to the periodical rooms of university libraries. The paperback revolution of the 1950s and 1960s that promised at first to democratize our culture by making inexpensive editions widely available, has ended up filling our bookstores with texts instead of books, texts designed for adoption as required reading in courses.

The high-level professional work on the new subject of American literature has been shaped to a remarkable degree by the residence of culture within the academic world. The university and the professor think, as they must, in terms of courses—that is, in terms of a coherent set of books or themes that fit into the fifteen-week semester. Such distinguished critical studies as

F. O. Matthiessen's *American Renaissance*, Marx's *Machine in the Garden*, or Smith's *Virgin Land* represent our past as a set of model courses. The great interest in myths of the frontier, the machine, the Puritan errand into the wilderness (see P. Miller, *Errand*), American violence, or American individualism served to give shape to the academic year in an ordered, consecutive, thematic way with developments and oppositions. The problem of the American romance, as opposed to the novel, or the description of so arbitrary a period of our history as what is known as the Gilded Age, redesigned the past to fit the intellectual needs and temporal rhythms of the newly professionalized study of the past.

The most common thread of the first generation of the study of America has been what could be called the disappointment of myth by fact, the failure of reality to live up to the ways in which it has been imagined. America is first mythologized as the second Eden, its purpose linked to the Puritan mission, or pictured as a frontier or free space for the unbounded individual, but then, in each case, the myth is betrayed by fact. The promise is unkept. As the purity of what was imagined grew stained over time, American reality, by means of the apparatus of myth, took on the look of a fallen state. The frontier had been closed. The high moral purpose of the Puritans had given way to commerce and commercial purpose. The innocence had blood on its hands. What was there had the look of heavily discounted possibility; what might have been had been disappointed in the act of making. Significantly, one of the master texts of a whole generation of American study was Henry James's *The Ambassadors*, perhaps from an academic point of view the most perfect book ever written by an American. James's hero Strether creates a myth of Paris, a myth of his charge, Chad, a myth of Chad's relation to Mme. de Vionnet. Each myth is betrayed by fact, stained by the complexity of the real world. An entire academic generation saw its own love of criticism, observation, nuance, disappointment, myth, and defeat in James's novel.

As the great academic popularity of James's novel made clear, if there has been one history lovingly traced by intellectuals over the past fifty years, it has been the history of intellectuals themselves. From the work of Perry Miller in the late 1930s, the explanation of America as a long history of Puritan hope and decline resulted from the fact that, looking into the past to find not necessarily its chief actors but precisely those congenial figures whose analytic and critical stance most resembled their own, the academic intellectuals discovered in Puritan writing what was for them the most intelligible feature of the past, the one mirror most filled with familiar features. The Puritans too were intellectuals, engaged in holding up a mirror of admonition or exhortation to their society. In theocratic New England they embodied one of the most secret self-images of all intellectual cultures, a world in which the critics and intellectuals of society were not marginal but actually in power.

The Puritan intellectuals had their successors in the radical critics of society from the mid-nineteenth century to the 1950s and 1960s. Utopian intellectuals of the left in the 1930s found in the radical Puritans of three hundred years earlier their own model for the role and hoped-for importance of the intellectual within politics and society. However marginal intellectuals have been actually within American culture, the study of America has reclaimed them.

Useful as the history of intellectuals as written by their own aspiring descendants might be, it amounts only to a rather timid look into the most friendly and probably most unrepresentative district of the American past. The actors in exploration and settlement, in enterprise and invention, in the making of cities and the long history of money and speculation in America, in the tangled history of black and white, Native American and settler, political and personal rebellion, have been the primary characters of the American story, even if, unlike the intellectuals, they have seldom been their own best historians.

Myth creates a fault line between what ought to have taken place and what did. It permits ideas and facts to criticize each other. Like the rebellion of an individual or like the more collective movements of reform, myths embody what Henry Adams in his *Education* called the "spirit of resistance." The search for central myths—myths that were already closed off, as the frontier was at the moment of its first description as the most vital experience for the foundation of an American identity—was inseparable from the study of resistance within culture, whether in the Gothic style of *Pierre* or in the reflective emigré style of *The Ambassadors* or the self-ironic Adams of *Education*. The appetite for resistance led Lionel Trilling to propose that all culture in the modern period was basically adversarial, at war with the commonplace or everyday social energies and beliefs. In European society of the nineteenth century, this adversarial position reflected the failure of self-belief in the emerging middle classes that had at last arrived at political and cultural power equivalent to their economic importance. But in the United States the source was quite different. It lay in a utopian or even moral radicalism combined with or concealing the resentment of artists and intellectuals at their rather small voice in a national life dominated by business and politics.

The belief in spiritual radicalism led to a focus on those writers, like Melville, who said their "No! In thunder." Such oppositional figures as the hero of Melville's *Pierre* or of "Bartleby the Scrivener" or, in real life, Thoreau defiant of Concord and moving two miles away to Walden Pond or spending a night in jail, Henry James withdrawn to England because American reality was not thick enough, the protagonist of *The Scarlet Letter* stubborn and free: these defiant, adversarial figures, along with the challenging distance they created in standing out by standing against their world, are what the study of the tension between fact and all that resisted fact brought to the center. Within

American studies the study of America had become the study of dissent. The rebels and dissidents came to the front as the leading patriots. It was the era of Thoreau, Henry Adams, and Bartleby, not of Emerson and Whitman.

By an accident of timing, American literature arrived in the university at a highly politicized moment. Its arrival coincided with the polarization between right and left or, in European terms, between fascism and communism in the period between the two world wars. The study of resistance was attractive, in part, because both the conservative right and the liberal left had rejected one key feature of what had been a synthesis in the most vital parts of nineteenth-century American culture. The right was hostile to democracy; the left to capitalism. They shared a distrust of the optimism, energy, confidence, and what might be called the surprisingly guiltless relation that figures like Emerson, Whitman, James Fenimore Cooper, or Francis Parkman had had to their own past. The lack of apology or contrition, the robust feeling of the right to be where and as they were in spite of slavery, Indian massacres, the failures of national politics to be dignified or even honest, the violence of the West, the polyglot hustle of the new cities—such guiltless self-regard seemed shallow to a left and to a right equally convinced, from different sides, of the nightmare of history. A whole new meaning of the term *innocence* had to be invented to make it seem that only some youthful unawareness of evil could explain the pride or health of Twain, Whitman, William James, or Emerson. That the greatest figures of our literature were not oppositional figures seemed almost beyond belief. But it was a fact. There is no margin of frictional energy that accounts for Emily Dickinson or Theodore Dreiser or William Faulkner. Whitman and Emerson continue to embarrass by their failure to have seen through democracy and capitalism or, rather, by their having imagined themselves to have seen into the philosophic and temperamental depths of those two systems and to have found them both profound and humane, exhilarating and enduring.

One key to the new ground claimed by critical work of the last few years has been the implicit rejection of this heroism of oppositional dissent and its replacement by collaborative and implicational relations between writer or speaker and culture. Emerson, Harriet Beecher Stowe, Twain, and William James are the masters of this new relation, not Melville and Thoreau. Richard Poirier's books on the tactics of Robert Frost within language (*Robert Frost: The Work of Knowing*) and the cultural meaning of Emerson (*The Renewal of Literature*) set out important accounts of the rich entanglement of writer and culture. In Poirier's account, the work always lives off and lives through the spaces open within the language and especially within the plural languages of culture.

The pressures of cultural life are plural and not a single hegemonic ideology that must be resisted, subverted, or surrendered to. Cultural life, in this formulation, is open to the activity of rebalancing and reconstruction that the literary work makes possible. Poirier's is an aesthetics of survival that represents at the same time a confident aesthetics of pleasure within the forces of culture and the possibility of mastery over them, what we might call the outwitting of the up-to-then apparently dead ends of language and feeling, the traps of rhetoric and commitment. In this respect, his work is remarkably similar to the claims of the major book within African American theory, *The Signifying Monkey*, by Henry Louis Gates, Jr. For Gates, signifying is a way of taking over cultural formulas, living off and living within whatever is given, because whatever is given can always be topped, reformulated, bent to build in whatever it was designed to place or to place out. In his theory of culture, the trickster once again displaces the victim as the essential subjectivity and actor within the cultural script. One major weakness of the theory of ideology and myth has always been its specification of subjectivity as either that of power, victim, or coopted dupe. What Gates celebrates in the trickster, Poirier had earlier called the "performing self," and the great model of this performance might be sketched out by combining the moves of Huck Finn and Whitman with those of Emerson and Frost. These tactics of freedom in the face of the givenness of reality are normative for Emersonian artists in the face of an already given set of forms, for adolescents discovering and differentiating themselves within a world of parents and parental society, and for African American culture and its practices within and yet above the surrounding culture into which they have been thrown.

A simple catalog of moves within collaboration would include boasts, lies, tricks, exaggeration, the mastery of language, even an entrepreneurial relation to language, the play with masks and roles, the caginess of Frost and Emerson, the folksy and the elusive. All are wrapped together as elements of a heightened self-consciousness and strategic style of thinking. They define the cultural location where the signifying monkey meets the performing self, where the ambiguity of Hawthorne and the glib half-serious language of Twain meet the canniness of Frost and the daring extravagance of Emerson's and Whitman's verbal bravado. Gates and Poirier have returned the study of moves within culture—the moves of the trickster—to their real importance over against the "No! In thunder" of opposition and the sentimental pathos of the many narratives of victims crushed by all-pervading scripts of power.

Sacvan Bercovitch's study of Hawthorne and what Bercovitch calls the "a-morality of compromise" interrogates and deflates the rhetoric of oppositional purity in favor of a remarkable and nuanced idea of politics, a term of extraordinary importance as an alternative to the purity of cultural dissent and protest. Politics and, along with it, the pragmatics of action and compromise within a given temporal horizon and in the face of specific counterforces that cannot be defeated but must be enlisted in a joint project define the essence of a stance beyond the merely gestural "No! In thunder" but equally beyond the various forms of radical purity—the expatriation of Henry James, the internal expatriation of Thoreau at Walden, the aloof aristocratic unemployment of Henry Adams, the utopian posture of Thoreau or the history of intellectual socialism and communism in the hundred years between the fall of the Paris commune in 1870 and the collapse of that utopia in the face of the crisis in real-existing socialism at the end of the 1980s.

Like the texts by Poirier, Gates, and Bercovitch, but from an entirely different direction, Walter Benn Michaels's book on naturalism and the 1890s—*The Gold Standard and the Logic of Naturalism*—has demolished the oppositional simplicity in what had seemed the easiest period to locate the author automatically outside and over against the culture of capitalism. In my own book *Hard Facts*, the nineteenth-century models of cultural work are deliberately taken to be different from and more varied than the work of protest and negation or its opposite, pious complicity and conscious or unconscious propagation of a single leading ideology. In its literature a culture practices and memorizes its own self-relation, only one part of which involves its relation to what it takes to be its past, to what circumference of action and choice it holds itself accountable for in the present, and what future it takes to be its promise to itself, as opposed to the merely abstract or utopian bad infinity of possibilities. Cultural work is pragmatic, not Hegelian. Its plural objects are local, open matters, necessary cases, hard facts. One measure of cultural work is not realism but a certain decay within realism that announces that some local fact of culture has been altered or restabilized so that the work now done has made the earlier representation obsolete—that is, no longer realistic. For later periods the effectiveness of that work can be felt in what now seems like excess or exaggerated emphasis—what we sweep to the side as genre. What feels sentimental, in the bad meaning of the term, in Stowe or Wordsworth, Dickens or Dostoevsky, is exactly the marker of suffering now casually within the field of vision that once had to be forced into representation. What is now noticed as shrill in Whitman—once the work of Whitman to center the sexual and democratic self has succeeded—becomes obsolete, part of the genre or category of the egotistical sublime, the excess of Romanticism, the emotional fraud of mid-nineteenth-century boosterism, whether for land schemes, political candidates, or, in Whitman's case, self-description and construction of the role and stance of the democratic poet.

Cultural work is one concept of a cultural pragmatism, a concern with the effective strategies of culture that includes, at the level of individual psychology, such strategies as performing and signifying. Poirier's Emerson, in *The Renewal of Literature*, is a model of the tough-minded intellectual within American culture. One part of his model is that bravery of fools that Emerson shared with Whitman and Twain. Bercovitch's Hawthorne, with the notion of politics and the intriguing morality of compromise, is a second, equally important cultural model. Both are elements of the major recuperation of American philosophical pragmatism that has been a significant project of the new collaboration between American philosophy and American literary studies in the 1970s and 1980s.

The worldliness and local field of vision of pragmatism has always existed as the rough alternative both to dissent and to the spiritual purity of transcendentalism, utopianism, and puritanism—those three overlapping, radical energies within our culture. In the books of Stanley Cavell and Richard Rorty, the philosophical and literary tradition of American pragmatism has been returned to central interest in our cultural life. The easy combination of the literary and the philosophical is only one of the novelties of this recent examination of pragmatism. The contingency, irony, and solidarity that Rorty has brought together as key terms in one of his titles define a posture of liberal generosity and a dismissal of the vehemence and refusal of solidarity with one's own culture that are the classic tonal pitch of self-appointed radicalism. That Emerson and William James stand also for a genuinely popular and culturally central relation of the intellectual to society is no small part of their value and interest. They are, we might say, anti-Nietzschean models of the intellectual.

Cavell, Rorty, and Poirier have laid the basis in recent books for a profound and profoundly impure—that is, contingent and political—tradition of American intellectual culture. At the same time it is notable that Cavell and Poirier have created analyses of culture that broke the barrier between high culture and the innovative commercial and popular culture of our own time. Cavell has brought both philosophy and Hollywood into the register of literary vision. His work on film, especially on the Hollywood comedies of marriage and remarriage—*Pursuits of Happiness*—has set a new configuration in place of the older-style American studies negotiation between "major authors" and the "wider culture." Poirier's *The Performing Self* did similar decisive work in building analytic paths into the complex languages of popular music, political writing, and such authors as Frost and Norman Mailer. Gates's *The Signifying Monkey* is the key recent revision of our description of the text culture in its links to the strategies and range of everyday oral and written performance. An encyclopedic summary of what used to be called "our classic authors" in terms of this wider culture of possibilities was achieved by David Reynolds in his book *Beneath the American Renaissance*.

## *Regionalism and Central Culture*

Alongside the search for grand unifying myths, with their inevitable narrative of a fall into imperfection and disappointment, a second element shared the stage within American studies between the 1930s and the 1970s—

the claim of pluralism within American culture. This diversity, which resists the single shelter of myth or ideology, has again and again risen to dominance in what we might call the episodes of regionalism in American cultural history.

Cultural life in American swings like a pendulum between a diversity of sectional voices and an ever-new project of unity, between the representation of the nation as made up of weakly joined districts and the depiction of a central national order. A hundred and fifty years ago our then strongly sectional culture was split along geographical lines: the New England mind, the southern way of life, the West of the pioneers, with their energy and violence. Each section had its own voices and themes, its own philosophies and religions, its unique spirit and humor. A common identity was rebuilt out of these regionalisms by the Civil War, by the mythic figure of Lincoln, by the railroads and telegraph, which conquered a geography grown too large for the earlier Federalist unity of Washington and Jefferson, and by the elaboration of an American way of life made up of Singer sewing machines, Coca-Cola, Remington rifles, and Ford Model T's—a way of life created around democratically available mass-produced goods rather than by the right to vote or to own property.

Each swing to regionalism has split the country along different fault lines, and each rewon unity involves not a return to a lost identity but a new plane of association. In early twentieth-century America a regionalism that was not geographic but ethnic appeared as a result of the massive immigration that had taken place between 1870 and 1914. The local color was not that of climates and regions but of what are called, metaphorically, hyphenated Americans: Jewish Americans, Italian Americans, Irish Americans, Wasps and Chinese Americans, Poles, Swedes, and Russians. It was a regionalism of languages, folk customs, humor, music, and beliefs set over against the pull of what came to be called Americanization.

In the case of ethnic regionalism it was not the railroads and the everyday objects of a thriving economy that created the unifying force, as they had done earlier. To this regionalism was opposed the core culture of public education and the pull of economic advancement, always purchased at the price of a surrendered culture, most obviously by the requirement within the schools and business world of the English language. A third unifying force was mobility itself. Only if immigrants remained in a ghetto, the ghetto of arrival, could the coherence of language, way of life, religion, and, most important, marriage within the ethnic group be preserved. To move even once was to enter the general American condition. And the two world wars and the democratic experience of the army worked, as the Civil War and the Revolutionary War had earlier, to fuse an identity that superseded the ethnic diversity of the late nineteenth and early twentieth centuries. Thus the pots in which the melting actually occurred were the schoolroom, the offices of the business world, the new suburbs out beyond the territorial inner city, and, finally, the fields of battle. Unity within American culture has always been a postwar unity, whether Federalist, after the Revolution, capitalist, after the Civil War, or contemporary American, after, and resulting from, the two world wars.

In recent years a further episode of regionalism, neither geographical nor ethnic, has begun. The regionalism of our own times, which comes on the heels of the generation that elaborated the myth of America within the shadow and aftermath of World War II, is one of gender and race. The civil rights movement after 1954 had, as its cultural side, the debate over black identity in America. The women's movement that followed, just as the nineteenth-century suffrage movement had followed and drawn its vocabulary from the abolitionist movement against slavery, set the model for the denial of what came to be called *essentialism*, the claim to an overriding common human identity. Later gay and lesbian movements, as well as ethnic identities that were now conceived not along the model of the earlier hyphenated identities but along the more radical model of black or female identity, reopened the full spectrum of regionalized culture. Native American, Chicano, gay, black, lesbian, female: once again, an episode of regionalism set out its claims against, in this case, a central technological culture made up of the new media—television and film—but also against the older forces of education and mass representation. The model that black or female identity set in place for regionalism was refractory in a novel way because these regional—as opposed to universal—models for identity were the first within American experience that neither mobility nor the succession of generations would alter. Earlier geographic or ethnic identities had been episodic in that the mechanisms of the culture itself would erase them over time. California, with its new "identity," was obviously composed of people who had shed—by means of the simple act of driving across the country and choosing to settle there—their prior New England, midwestern, southern, or western identities. Jewish Americans who moved to the suburbs of New York City and watched their children marry Italian Americans, German Americans, or Wasps may have seen the fading and erasure of these regionalisms in the lives of the grandchildren who went off to school in Chicago or Los Angeles. Earlier American regionalisms had been temporary and easily bargained away once the alternatives were attractive enough. The weak hold of geography could be seen in the all-purpose category "Sun Belt," which encompassed not only the states from Florida through Texas to Southern California but also, in the case of Florida, the new security of retirement and the simple desire for a warm and convenient climate that would lead Americans to desert and shed their regional identities, homes, and friends even late in life for a carefully calculated new start. By contrast, to be black or female was an unnegotiable identity, one that could not be dissolved by those American master plots: education, intermarriage, mobility. Insofar as other groups, including ethnic groups, took over the black model, they chose to see their own regional identity as final and began to argue for their own language, education, and culture.

In American universities the departments of American studies, established in the 1930s, 1940s, and 1950s, found themselves in the 1960s and 1970s quickly regionalized into departments of black or African American studies, Jewish studies, women's studies, Native American studies, Chicano and Asian American studies, and, in some cases, gay studies. One consequence of these new identity claims was what the proponents viewed as an aggressive unmasking of the myths of the previous generation, among other things a series of overwhelmingly white male myths of America. The pastoral, the western, the Puritan mission, the frontier experience of individualism, self-reliance, and democratic values: all had, at their center, white male actors with various supporting casts. The self-appointed task of unmasking hegemony, essentialism, and the many disguised operations of power within the culture has defined what could be called the *fundamentalism* of this third and most recent swing of regionalism. We have lived for twenty years within a scholarship that could be more and more clearly identified as, in effect, the unnegotiable regional essentialism of gender, race, and ethnicity. This new regionalism demanded and made claims for a wider membership within the university on behalf of women, blacks, and others while supplying the new members with an automatic subject matter: themselves, their own history and rights within the national array of culture.

The new American studies has grown up alongside but also as an alternative or aftermath to this regionalism, which tore apart the previous unifying and singular myths of America. The key limitation to this new phase, as well as to all earlier regionalisms, was its need to define itself and thrive only within a highly politicized atmosphere. Regionalism is always, in America, part of a struggle within representation. It is seldom or never a matter of tolerance, the blooming of a thousand, or even of three, flowers. In the regionalism of the last two decades, identity is formed by opposition: black-white, female-male, Native American–settler, gay-heterosexual. Because of this opposition, identity is located above all in the sphere of politics—that is, in the sphere of felt opposition, of movement, laws, demands, negotiations over representation, and, in the university, in struggle over curriculum and requirements. The new American studies has stood outside this regionalism by locating a set of underlying but permanently open national facts around which all identities are shaped. It is with these permanently open cultural questions that the many rhetorics of our culture are engaged. Among these permanently open, that is, never won or lost, national facts are democratic culture and its demands; the culture of freedom that permits conditions of dominance, whether economic, sexual, or cultural, and has permitted even permutations of slavery as one aspect of the nature of freedom itself; the creation of a national life that is economic rather than religious or, in the anthropological sense, cultural. This troubled utopian core of enterprise, freedom, and democratic culture, baffled by preexisting social facts while never surrendering to them, is central to much of the best recent work in American studies.

## The Civil War within Representation

One consequence of the new American studies has been to replace the traditional concept of the American Renaissance with the new category of a literature located within the Civil War and driven by the particular concepts of freedom and independence, politics and compromise that the war period, with its preparation and aftermath, froze into place. Recent European historical work, particularly Reinhart Koselleck's essays on the concept of revolution in his book *Future's Past*, has brought to the center of attention the part played by civil wars in the grounding and contesting of national identity in the three hundred years between the Thirty Years' War and the English Civil War of the seventeenth century and the end of the general European civil war of 1914–45. Like the American Civil War, or the French and Russian revolutions with their phases of civil war, all such conflicts put at risk the very existence of the society itself in the name of uncompromisable values. Periods of civil war are periods without ideology, because two or more rhetorics of self-representation, national purpose, and historical genealogy are in wide enough circulation to elicit complete support, even to the point of making people willing to die for them. Civil war is the alternative condition to what we call, following Foucault's relentless analysis, the power of the centralized state, the structured, all-pervading system for stabilizing and describing a fixed social reality.

In contrast to the condition of two or more contesting powers that we can, in a shorthand way, express by the notion of civil war, the very idea of a cultural period like that of Romanticism or the American Renaissance leads us to look for a unified set of ideas and aesthetic practices. We then come to think of such concepts as the ideology of the American Renaissance or some other period. Writers can be viewed as expressing or dissenting from that ideology. Ideology, dissent, a sense of identity and of an authoritative discourse within each period are all interdependent notions. Once the idea of civil war as a normative situation within representation replaces that of ideology, the entire array of concepts falls away together.

In literary studies of the last ten years what has been called the new historicism has, as a result of the strong influence of Foucault and modern experience of totalitarianism and its analysis by, among others, Hannah Arendt, Max Horkheimer and Theodor Adorno, focused on the fate of representation within absolutist states or societies. The English Renaissance, taken as a glorious period of monarchy, along with its secondary pressures and exceptions, became the natural topic for new-historicist demonstrations.

The condition of civil war can be taken to be the fundamental alternative to that of monarchical power, self-display, uniform discourse, ideology, and controlled representation. American new historicism has its basis in the representational situation not of monarchy but of civil war. To see the central American historical episode as the civil war is to bring to the front the power of rhetorics, incomplete dominance of representation, and the borrowing or fusing of successful formulas of representation. The actual war of the 1860s stands in for the pervasive, continuously unsettled, open struggle within American culture. All cultural history in the United States is the history of civil wars.

The civil wars between contemporaries are only a local version of what, to use an Emersonian formulation, should be seen as the fundamental, permanent conflict in any society that is, as the United States is, an economy rather than a culture. That underlying civil war, as Emerson described it in his essay on Napoléon, is between the young and the old, between power that represents work done in the past and the effort of the young, who will displace all that is being defended in order to make room for themselves in the world. Railroads overthrew canals and water-based transportation, and no sooner had they succeeded than the automobile and long-distance truck overthrew the railroad. No sooner did Western Union have a monopoly on long-distance communication than the telephone industry emerged to make that monopoly worthless.

The representational topic of monarchy is the inheritance, diffusion, and protection of already-held power. The subject of civil war is the unstable contest for short-term control that is uninheritable and, in the end, undefendable. Power is not the topic of this historicism but its weak long-term expectations in a culture in which economic dominance is not located in land— that one genuinely scarce, readily transferable, and not easily variable basis of hegemony.

## Print Culture without the State

The ordinary culture within which our classic authors and painters have worked has to be called a print culture, but now understood in a wider sense than the Gutenburg culture of the book. A photograph is also called a "print," as is the copy of a film. Newspapers and journals, advertisements and billboards are also, in this sense, prints, offprints, and reprints. In his book on the profession of the author in America, Michael Warner sets out the model of the printer Benjamin Franklin, with his new-made career within print culture, a culture replacing the oral culture of sermon, oratory, and statements linked to the personal presence of the speaker and the audience's identification with the spoken words. After Franklin all American authors, photographers, and filmmakers are printers.

In his important book on American photography, Alan Trachtenberg has defined the photographic print as a cultural text within the Civil War, the reform movements of the 1890s and 1930s, and the modernist aesthetic of the early twentieth century. In the photographic images of the war itself, Trachtenberg reads the rhetoric of representation as it appeared within the camera—which, like the machine gun, was one of the new instruments of this conflict. The very existence of photographs during wartime for the first time, alongside or combined with day-by-day newspaper reporting from the battle-field, set up a contest for the control and definition of this new visual genre. The photograph and newspaper did not define an ideology of the war experience and certainly not a myth. Instead, they embodied the rapidly shifting competitive rhetorics within the as-yet-unstabilized representation that would only later, with victory and time, become what we know as the "Civil" War.

Unlike myths that take on all possible historical circumstances as illustrations and by this means become universal explanations, rhetorical analysis is never universal. One important reason for the local nature of the analysis of rhetorics found in recent work is the lack of what might be called, in the European sense, the state in American experience and therefore an absence of any monopoly of either power or of violence on the part of the state. Centralization of power on the European model, and with it the centralization of the power of representation and self-conception as it has been described by Foucault, was never present in America. Unlike French schools, American education has always been local, variable, responsive, for good and ill, to local pressures and the demands of the moment. When, in the twentieth century, state control over, and funding of, culture became fundamental and deeply ideological in Europe and throughout much of the world, politicized between the radical cultural projects of the right and the left, American culture developed an almost singularly market- and consumer-based formula of funding, selection, and survival. American newspapers, music, film, radio, publishing, and television were all competitive, decentralized, and in the hands of ever-new players. Only the highly paradoxical analysis of European intellectuals, like those of the Frankfurt school, with their horror of popular or commercial culture, could have invented the claim that this unsponsored and competitive culture itself expressed an even more rigid and tricky ideology than the more obvious overt ideologies of twentieth-century European experience, the so-called ideology of capitalism (see Jay). But by 1945 no European intellectual could any longer imagine what it might mean to live in a society without a state that owned, sponsored, and used for its own purposes all the media of cultural life.

Even outside the arena of cultural conflict, or civil war per se, American culture provided the richest possible resources for escape, invisibility, and defiance. The right to "move on" or "head out west" was only one of the possibilities that limited the creation of a state. More important was the economic commitment to a rapidly changing culture of invention, with its dizzy cycles of the amassing, loss, and transfer of wealth and power. The economic commitment was far more decisive than the purely individual right to escape or move on, but even the apparently individual mobility was historically profound because it was the means of renewing the act of immigration—leaving behind and moving on—that was each individual's first drop of American identity. In fact, such an economic pressure—what has been called the "creative destruction" of the market economy—is a form of willed, collective instability, because it accepts the future as an already bankable asset that can be borrowed against to speed up the overthrow of the past. In a speculative culture, for instance, the profits of the railroads fall into an investment pool, where, since they are expected to yield the highest returns, they no longer are invested back into the railroad system itself but into the automobile industry, whose only purpose is to overthrow the railroads as the fundamental transportation system. By means of the speculative system, the past becomes the silent partner of a future that will abolish its own hold. A culture of speculation is opposite in its action to those of preservation, inheritance, and self-reproduction, which we tend to take anthropologically as the human norm. Pierre Bourdieu's *Outline of a Theory of Practice*—precisely because it is concerned with societies whose primary goal is reproduction in the widest sense of self-replication and continuation, as is, over time—can never describe an Emersonian or speculative society whose commitment to self-destruction in the name of its own next possibility is far more important than its interest in the transfer of the forms of the past to a future generation.

For these reasons analysis within American studies will always be of sectors of a diverse culture characterized by the absence of a monopoly of power. These studies will always be historical and not anthropological, because of the commitment of the culture itself to a rapid building up, wearing out, and replacement of systems of all kinds by new arrays of persons and forces. The updraft is strong, the door of immigration both to and within the country is open, the exhaustion of control is always imminent and control itself is porous. Because America had no experience of monarchy, it has a permanent democratic core working against not only the centralization of power but, more important, its inheritance or preservation over time.

In the absence of a state, we find ourselves freed of the intellectual component of the systematic state: ideology. We have rhetorics because we have no ideology, and we have no ideology because we lack the apparatus of ideology: a national religion, a unitary system of education under the control of the state, a cultural life and media monopolized by the state by means either of ownership or of subsidy. Ideology is a cultural mechanism of stabilization and transmission, neither of which is a primary topic of a culture of speculation. The study of rhetorics is our necessary alternative to the study of ideology. Rhetorics are the sign of the play of forces within cultural life, and at the same time of the power of invention and obsolescence within culture. Rhetoric is the mark of temporary location and justification. The nuances of provisional justification and defense, the opening up of newness within culture without escaping the grip of the master problems and resources of the culture: this is what is at issue within the newest writing on American literature and culture.[1]

### Note

[1]This essay has been adapted from the author's introduction to his volume *The New American Studies* (Berkeley: U of California P, 1991).

## Selected Bibliography

Bercovitch, Sacvan, ed. *Reconstructing American Literary History*. Harvard English Studies 13. Cambridge: Harvard UP, 1986.
A particularly thoughtful group of essays, on literary issues and texts from the eighteenth century to the present, that reflect what the editor refers to as "the self-reflexiveness that characterizes this period of critical interregnum."

Cavell, Stanley. *In Quest of the Ordinary*. Chicago: U of Chicago P, 1988.
One of Cavell's recent collections of essays that display his efforts to recuperate the writings of Emerson and Thoreau for serious philosophical reflection and show how their pragmatist absorption with the ordinary and the familiar constitutes a profound response to the modern problem of skepticism.

Fisher, Philip. *Hard Facts: Setting and Form in the American Novel*. New York: Oxford UP, 1987.
A study of the way cultural forms like novels transform certain of the disagreeable facts at the center of social experience—in nineteenth-century America, the removal and destruction of Native American peoples, the enslavement of African Americans, and the later commercial objectification of all Americans—into something not only palatable but naturalized.

Gates, Henry Louis, Jr. *The Signifying Monkey: A Theory of African-American Literary Criticism*. New York: Oxford UP, 1988.
An important work that focuses on the trickster in African American literary experience, a figure whose talents for signifying, for redescription, constitute

a subjectivity that can elude the structures of rhetorical and ideological closure associated with the dominant society.

Gunn, Giles. *Thinking across the American Grain: Ideology, Intellect, and the New Pragmatism.* Chicago: U of Chicago P, 1992.

A study of the renaissance of pragmatism in contemporary American intellectual culture and its application to a variety of literary and critical contexts.

Lewis, R. W. B. *The American Adam: Innocence, Tragedy, and Tradition in the Nineteenth Century.* Chicago: U of Chicago P, 1955.

A definitive study of the myth of the American Adam in the nineteenth century and of some of the tragic collisions to which its moral and spiritual pretensions were exposed in the literature of the last two centuries.

Marx, Leo. *The Machine in the Garden: Technology and the Pastoral Ideal in America.* New York: Oxford UP, 1964.

An examination of the development of nineteenth-century American literary pastoralism as a response to the social, political, and emotional threat of the rise of industrialization.

Matthiessen, F. O. *American Renaissance: Art and Expression in the Age of Emerson and Whitman.* New York: Oxford UP, 1941.

A classic study of the American literature of the mid-nineteenth century that displaced the Fireside Poets as the preeminent authors of the period with a new canon that included Emerson, Thoreau, Whitman, Hawthorne, and Melville.

Michaels, Walter Benn. *The Gold Standard and the Logic of Naturalism.* Berkeley: U of California P, 1987.

An exploration of the way literary and other cultural forms helped create value in the emergent environment of corporate capitalism at the end of the nineteenth century, as the literary romance mitigated the experience of alienation, trompe l'oeil painting served as a critique of money, and the contract became a device that eroticized slavery.

Miller, Perry. *Errand into the Wilderness.* Cambridge: Harvard UP, 1956.

A work that summarizes some of the themes that circulated in Miller's numerous and often majesterial studies of the Puritan mind, from the role of the jeremiad in American culture to the place and function of millenarianism in the American psyche.

Poirier, Richard. *The Renewal of Literature: Emersonian Reflections.* New York: Random, 1987.

A recuperation of a pragmatist tradition of American writing that runs from Emerson and the elder Henry James through William James, Gertrude Stein, Robert Frost, and Wallace Stevens to John Ashbery and, furthermore, shows how this body of writing, in addition to providing a countertradition to the high modernism of Ezra Pound and T. S. Eliot, may suggest a cultural alternative to postmodernism.

Reynolds, David. *Beneath the American Renaissance: The Subversive Imagination in the Age of Emerson and Melville*. New York: Knopf, 1988.
A path-breaking study that rereads the work of what are here held to be the seven major writers of the middle years of the nineteenth century (in addition to Emerson, Thoreau, Hawthorne, Melville, and Whitman—Edgar Allan Poe and Emily Dickinson) against the background of a rich but little-known world of sensational and popular literature on which they drew for many of their themes, characters, settings, and even idioms.

Rorty, Richard. *Contingency, Irony, and Solidarity*. Cambridge: Cambridge UP, 1989.
A more effective demonstration than any of his other books that Rorty has breathed new life into pragmatist motifs and concerns and resituated them at the center of contemporary cultural existence.

Ruland, Richard, and Malcolm Bradbury. *From Puritanism to Postmodernism*. London: Routledge, 1991.
A literary history from the colonial era to the present that reflects the shift from ideological explorations of essential American myths to a pragmatic concern with the conversation between different American rhetorics and styles.

Trachtenberg, Alan. *Reading American Photographs: Images as History, Mathew Brady to Walker Evans*. New York: Hill, 1989.
An analysis of the translation of the history of American photographs into a social text. The approach not only affords a new way of reading that history but turns it into a theory of how American culture has itself been read.

# $\mathcal{F}$eminist Criticism

## CATHARINE R. STIMPSON

In 1970, Kate Millett published *Sexual Politics*. It rocketed her to international fame. *Sexual Politics* symbolized the beginning of feminist criticism, for it was "the first major book of feminist criticism" in the United States (Showalter, *New Feminist Criticism* 5). This movement has now created and re-created critical maps in five ways: (1) by charting the course of women as writers, who they are, how and why they write, their reception and reputations—a job that Elaine Showalter has named "gynocritics"; (2) by charting the cultural representations of gender, patterns of masculinity and femininity, a complementary task that Alice A. Jardine calls "gynesis"; (3) by showing the complex relations among these representations and patterns of masculine dominance and then asking for the erasure of such patterns (feminist critics are like cartographers of the vanishing rain forest who say both *see* and *stop* the damage); (4) by establishing the unreliability of other maps because they overlook or misconstrue women and the issue of gender; (5) by so doing, stimulating vigilance about the processes of map making themselves.

Like air and language, women and representations of women and gender are everywhere. Necessarily, then, feminist criticism finds all of culture and literature interesting: single authors, periods, or genres; other critical methods; high, folk, mass, and popular culture. Given such scope, feminist criticism is less a single map of culture than a portfolio of maps, their common and unifying features the five activities I have noted. Feminist criticism has also self-consciously traced its own evolving intellectual and institutional nature.[1] My addition to this record begins with a comment about *Sexual Politics*, which, although autobiographical, reflects some of the cultural ferment in which feminist criticism developed. I then describe relationships among women, education, literary studies, and feminism and end by outlining three rubrics of feminist criticism: the defiance of sexual difference, the celebration of sexual difference, and the recognition of differences, a movement into pluralism. Although feminist criticism is an international activity that cuts across the arts, academic disciplines, and the media, I restrict myself to feminist literary criticism, especially in the United States.

*I*

Kate Millett and I are old friends. I first heard her voice over the telephone in New York in the mid-1960s. I was living over an Irish bar in an unfashionable section of the East Side, going to graduate school at Columbia University and serving as a part-time lecturer at Barnard College, its affiliated women's college. Kate was living on the Bowery, hoping to enter Columbia and teach at Barnard. She had a first from Oxford, but Columbia, she said, was insisting that she take an exam if she wished to be exempted from its master's degree requirement. She had heard that I had a degree from Cambridge and had done the exam. What was it like?

We met, then, because we were academics who were young and making our way. Feminist criticism had had its honorable antecedents. In 1949, Simone de Beauvoir had published *The Second Sex*, her narrative of women's existential otherness. A mark of otherness is one's inability to shape one's psychological, social, and cultural identity; Beauvoir analyzes men's depictions of women in biology, psychoanalysis, history, and literature. In 1957, Carolyn G. Heilbrun had reread *Hamlet* and Shakespearean criticism to find a new Gertrude, a queen both lustful and "intelligent, penetrating . . . gifted" (17). A decade later, Katharine Rogers had traced the representation of misogyny from Genesis and the classical Greeks to Faulkner. Tillie Olsen, Ellen Moers, Elizabeth Hardwick, and Diana Trilling had written about women and culture. Nevertheless, in the 1960s, most feminist critics were young and making their way. They were graduate students, nontenured faculty members, journalists, writers, editors. Kate and I wanted to be accepted in the academy that we treasured, to have our degrees and lecterns. We also wanted to be different. Ambition, not the desire to marry the boy next door, had taken Kate out of Saint Paul, Minnesota, and me out of Bellingham, Washington. Within a few weeks, we were sharing an office at Barnard. She looked more conservative than I, in her long skirts, pumps, and hair drawn back in, yes, a bun. I jumped around the corridors in miniskirts, tights, and unruly, unkeyed, naturally curly locks. The discrepancy between a woman's decorous appearance and flaring subjectivity—in a Jane Eyre, for example—was to become a theme for feminist criticism. I might have looked the more radical, but I was, intellectually, the more conservative, prudent, and buttoned-up.

One evening, in 1966, we went to a meeting in a church basement because Kate had seen a mimeographed flyer and said we should check out this civil rights organization for women. It was the New York chapter of the National Organization for Women. We joined and became activists as well as graduate students and part-time faculty members. Although a mote in the environment of New York, our demonstrations had some dear panache and flair. Despite their rages, flurries, and insecurities, these years were oddly beyond happiness or unhappiness. Of course, we were happy or unhappy, euphoric or sodden. We were, however, out there, self-consciously avant-garde, swinging on the edge of culture and shouting into the voids below and beyond us. We were aware that we had a history. When we demonstrated on Park Avenue against the consumer products of Lever Brothers, Marcel Duchamp inspired our iconography and Susan B. Anthony our message. Yet our naïveté was so ebullient that we felt as if we were new, speaking a natural language without stodgy nouns.

Using a language with nouns, we were writing our dissertations as well. Mine, done in a spirit of scurry and grim duty, is safely filed away, accessible in the archival coziness of *Dissertation Abstracts*. I would read Kate's chapters at Barnard, on the Bowery, on summer weekends with Kate and Fumio, her husband. Her dissertation was to become *Sexual Politics*, a fusion of an explosive historical moment and her brilliance, passions, and training, the discipline of studying with Allen Tate at the University of Minnesota, of doing Anglo-Saxon and Middle English at Oxford, of having the stern correctives to her Victoriana and grammar of Steven Marcus at Columbia. She knew "the tradition," which gave her critique of the tradition its bite. Constructing her theory of sexual politics, she was both applying feminist ideas to and deriving them from culture. To oversimplify, she was arguing that the relations between men and women are power relations: that men tend to have the power and that sexuality enforces their power. She was to use the techniques of close reading to explore the discourse of such gender relations. Her first chapter on Henry Miller, Norman Mailer, and Jean Genet was to demonstrate how destructively men wrote about women and their sexuality but how brilliantly Genet, the male homosexual, had critiqued gender roles. "Kate," I twitted and yelped in alarm, when I first read her sections on D. H. Lawrence, "you can't say these things about Lawrence. He's a great writer."

My twittings anticipated Sandra Gilbert and Susan Gubar's response to Millett a few years later. Their sophisticated matrilineage of feminist criticism places Beauvoir as the "mother of all modern feminists" and Millett as a "slightly disreputable but always interesting older sister, whose energetic reevaluations of literature in *Sexual Politics* were enormously ambitious and influential, if somewhat flawed" ("Review Essay" 158). My yelps also foreshadowed the polemical charge that feminist criticism lacks literary sense and values and that it spurns great literature, especially that of dead white men. I would now say that Lawrence is a central figure in twentieth-century literature in English; that serious readers and historians of modern culture must know him; that he is, literally, a "dead white man" but that this phrase is, at best, a flippant bit of shorthand for dominant figures in Western culture; that we must all be very clear about the meaning and criteria of "greatness"; that these criteria have shifted over time; and, finally, that Kate was correct in writing a devastating exposure of his theories of sex and gender.

For my yelps and twittings, I am thanked in the preface to *Sexual Politics* (xv). For her genuine originality, Kate lost her job. Before *Sexual Politics* was published, the English Department at Barnard refused to renew her contract. When *Sexual Politics* did appear, when *Time* magazine put Kate on a cover, she was marginal to the academy whose thought and curricula her book was to change.

## II

The combination of being intellectually talented but institutionally marginal is one characteristic of the history of women, education, and literary studies.[2] Indeed, a women's movement, whatever its specific name and historical context, arises when enough women and men find this combination unbearable. Of course, like men, women have always been educated in the general language, roles, and customs of their culture. My female ancestors, in the damp peasant cottages and wet fields of Wales and the English Midlands, learned how to speak, stitch, plant, cook, give birth, and pray. However, the institutions that have dominated literary and rhetorical studies (churches, universities, schools) have also historically shunned women as participants in these studies. If women were to become critics, let alone feminist critics, such practices would have to change.

To be sure, in the West, during the Middle Ages and the Renaissance, some convents were centers of learning for women. During the Renaissance, a handful of women struggled successfully for a formal education. The first woman to earn a doctorate of philosophy, Elena Lucrezia Cornaro Piscopia, a Venetian noblewoman, did so in 1678 at the University of Padua. However, the processes of modernization were necessary for the manufacturing of a sturdy framework of ideas about women that broadly legitimated the notion of women as thinking beings. These ideas postulated that women were capable of self-definition and of the life of the mind. Indeed, the cultivation of the life of the mind is indispensable to self-definition. Think of the hot-tempered Englishwoman Sarah Fyge Field Egerton. Born in the late seventeenth century, she was one of six daughters of an apothecary and sometime poet. Her rebelliousness and creativity enraged her father. Expelled from home, she married—first a lawyer and then a clergyman. Neither alliance seems to have been a tribute to wedded bliss. More happily, we hope, she wrote. In an early eighteenth-century poem, "The Emulation," she declares:

And shall we Women now sit tamely by,
Make no excursions in Philosophy,
Or grace our Thoughts in tuneful Poetry?
We will our Rights in Learning's World maintain,
Wits empire, now, shall know a Female Reign. . . .

According to the logic of the modern, if women could think, they should participate in the institutions that organize scholarship and culture. To exclude women harms them as individuals. It is also morally unjust and socially stupid. As Heilbrun writes, "Where the university must change is in allowing the energy of women to be exercised fully and to its own ends. Nothing is perhaps so wasted in our culture as the energies of women" ("Politics" 240). Women and men—of all classes, races, and nationalities—were willing to translate these modern beliefs into actions. Inevitably, the claims for the thinking woman bred resistance and created a great theme for women writers and critics: the tension between their desire to think and write and the prohibitions and inhibitions against acting on this desire. A pervasive trope is the woman's ultimate decision to substitute the pen that symbolizes writing for the needle that symbolizes her more traditional labor. Fortunately for feminist criticism, modernity persisted. When major institutions of higher education continued to exclude women, women's colleges came into being. By the end of the nineteenth century, the family of higher education had three siblings: the all-male institutions, the big brother; the all-female institutions, the spunky sister; and the coeducational institutions, the androgyne, who tolerated sister but preferred the company of older brother.

In coeducational and women's institutions, some women sought to reform research and the curriculum to reflect experiences of women. In the United States, in the last part of the nineteenth century and first part of the twentieth, women explicitly studied sex and gender. The prophets of women's studies, they "launched the modern study of sex differences" (Rosenberg xiii). They offered courses about women, sex, and gender at such diverse places as the University of Chicago, Wellesley College, Goucher College, and the University of Washington (Solomon 87). Their most famous intellectual daughter was Margaret Mead.

Sadly, these curricular experiments were largely ignored or abandoned until women's studies rediscovered them in the late 1960s and 1970s. Their fate is one sign of the uneven development of modern societies, an asymmetry that has deeply affected women scholars and critics. For modern societies have been prepared to educate men and women to some degree, and to educate some of them to a high degree. Women have been especially welcome in the arts and humanities. However, modern societies have not been ready to abolish gender roles, even if they constrict the lives of many women. To be sure, in the

United States, women could get a literary education; they could be literary scholars and critics. Yet until now, they could not occupy the same cultural space as men. They could spurn Cinderella's glass slipper but not evade the glass ceiling. In the 1970s, two feminist critics surveyed twenty-four widely used anthologies of literary criticism. Of a total of 653 essays, only 16 (2.4%) were by women (Lanser and Beck 79).

In the 1960s, the struggle by and for the thinking woman reemerged. A number of reasons account for its appearance: a push for general educational reform; a demand for social justice and racial equality that generated a renewed commitment to gender equity; some worry about the dissipation of the talents of educated women; the entrance of women of all races and classes into the public labor force, which provoked fresh questions about their education; and new technologies of reproduction, such as birth control, which helped to redefine women's sexuality. These same forces reinvigorated feminism. Contemporary feminism structures itself as a broadly gauged educational reform movement. At once transgressive and redemptive, it would tear up old maps and draw more trustworthy new ones. Linking transgression and renewal, Barbara K. Smith, the black feminist critic, introduces her anthology: "I sincerely hope that *Home Girls* is upsetting, because being upset is often the first step toward change" (liii).

More specifically, feminism would

- improve child-rearing and socialization practices so that young children would not be forced to conform to stereotypes;
- organize small consciousness-raising groups in which women would learn from each other about themselves in order to change their lives if they chose to do so. Here and elsewhere, women would express themselves—no matter how enraged, outrageous, crazy, or lustful they might be;
- attack the cultural studios that produce the often trumped-up representations of women;
- create and rediscover cultural alternatives, different systems of representation and expression, another art, literature and literary criticism, film, music, journalism, religion. Feminism would even produce its own languages and dictionaries.[3] It was, Annette Kolodny wrote in "Dancing through the Minefield," an influential essay about pluralism in feminist criticism, "the catalyzing force of an ideology that . . . helped to bridge the gap between the world as we found it and the world as we wanted it to be" (144);
- transform, or at least alter, the sites of formal education from child care to research centers. Nothing—no institutional practice, no intellectual practice, no infrastructure, no character structure—could go unexamined. For they were as tied together as fuel and motor or the cords in the Gordian knot.

This explicit alliance among feminism, education, and culture has had its triumphs, so many that some now conclude that feminism has given way to postfeminism. An English professor writes, "feminists are beset by the fear that academe will declare premature victory for women in higher education. . . . the students themselves may believe that the crisis has passed" (Burgan 74). Mariam K. Chamberlain notes that five major changes in higher education have occurred since the late 1960s. First, most overt discrimination, which official policies and practices formalized, has disappeared. Certainly, in the modern languages and literatures, the hiring, promoting, and paying of women has improved in twenty years (Huber). Second, educators are aware of sex discrimination as an issue. Third, women have organized themselves to end this discrimination. Fourth, women's issues have become a part of institutional infrastructures; for example, in 1968 the MLA formed its Commission on the Status of Women. And fifth, the study of women exists and has entered the curriculum (Chamberlain 16–17).

Quantitatively, the growth in research and teaching about women, within interdisciplinary women's studies programs and within specific disciplines, is impressive. In 1969, in the United States, there were sixteen or so courses devoted to the subject of women and gender; there are now over thirty thousand on the undergraduate level alone. A significant proportion of literature departments have added courses about women writers or writing about women. In fall 1989, the Schlesinger Library at Radcliffe College had forty-eight items on its list of current periodicals, from *Affilia: Journal of Women and Social Work*, through four journals with *gender* in their title; through *Sage: A Scholarly Journal on Black Women*, edited at Spelman College since 1984; to *Women's Studies Quarterly* (*Schlesinger*). Of special help to feminist criticism have been *Feminist Studies*, founded in 1969, its first issue appearing in 1972; *Women's Studies*, founded in 1972; *Signs*, in 1975; and the *Women's Review of Books*, in 1983. Established after 1970, publishers such as the Feminist Press in the United States, Virago in Great Britain, and Editions des Femmes in France issued the writing by women, old and new, on which feminist criticism fed. University and mainstream publishers also recognized a new women's market. A 1987 list of the best-selling works of university press fiction in the last twenty-five years had "The Yellow Wallpaper," by Charlotte Perkins Gilman, in seventh place, with 145,000 copies; *Their Eyes Were Watching God*, by Zora Neale Hurston, in fourth place, with 240,000 copies (Lanser 437).

Not surprisingly, feminist criticism has provoked opposition. In part, the resistance swells up from a general fear, which men and women share, of any new map—be it of heaven or of earth. In part, the opposition arises because of the linking of "feminism" and "criticism." This antagonism, far sharper than to a more neutrally named Study of Women and Literature, takes three forms. The first is intellectual, a serious and informed disagreement from within and without of aspects of feminist criticism. Posing two good, cautionary questions, the critic Eugene Goodheart asks if feminist criticism does not reverse the hierarchy of values it exposes and substitute a superior, "female" truth for a "male" truth. Moreover, does feminist criticism not aggrandize women's historically inferior status, leading to undue claims and privileges because "of victimization or oppression" (185)?

The second form is psychological, a fear of the loss of traditional cultural authority. In 1979, Heilbrun detected a malaise in literary studies. Critics, she said, were either repeating themselves or losing themselves in abstract theory. Only feminist criticism was alive. Yet men were mocking it (several of the initial reviews of *Sexual Politics* do convey a hard, ridiculing tone). "Men's fears are palpable. Men have long been members of a profession whose masculinity can, particularly in our society, be questioned. I suspect that the macho attitudes of most English professors, their notable male bonding, can be directly attributed to the fear of female dominance" ("Bringing the Spirit" 24).

Finally, the third form of opposition is political—that is, a clash of worldviews and ideologies. For this camp, feminist criticism is nothing but feminism, which itself is not a changing mixture of ideas and social action but an ideological grid to impose over education and culture or, to put the matter more colloquially, the grim agenda of a bunch of man-hating women's libbers. In November 1989, a visitor to a class in feminist criticism returned to tell of alarming scandals, "intellectual fare" that was "so esoteric and yet so vulgar, so free-wheeling and yet so dogmatic, so full of political energy and yet ultimately so futile" (D'Souza 210). The more reductive feminist critics give up supportive evidence for this charge. In "American Feminist Literary Criticism," Cheri Register, a more careful scholar than I now make her seem, called for a "prescriptive criticism," a set of five moral, social, and psychological standards by which to evaluate a literary work: (1) Does it serve as a forum for women? (2) Does it help to achieve cultural androgyny? (3) Does it provide role models? (4) Does it promote sisterhood? (5) Does it augment consciousness-raising? ("American" 18–19).

The "politics" of feminist criticism needs plain speaking. For admirable reasons, which the narrative of education in repressive societies underscores, the American academy has endorsed two principles: that intellectual inquiry should struggle to be neutral and "value-free" and that the academy is properly the site of such inquiry. The equivalent of these principles in literary criticism is vulgarly captured in the word *Arnoldian*. That is, criticism is the disinterested search for aesthetic and literary value. Feminist critics have at least two major responses to such positions. The first is to agree with them but to point to the academy's treatment of women and women's writing as an overwhelmingly demonstrable example of the academy's violation of its own standards. What, then, does it say about the standards if they are so easily stirred and so friable? How can feminism inspire and pressure the academy to stand by its own standards?

The second response is to question the epistemological viability of the principles themselves, an act compatible with modern critiques of rationality and objectivity. All institutions and individuals act ideologically and, broadly speaking, politically. That is, we all act on a set of values, beliefs, and interests. Membership in a race or a gender roughly carries such a set with it that influences our intellectual and critical judgments—to one degree or another. As a result, an academic's self-identification as "value-free" and "apolitical" is itself an ideological act. The question is not "Am I political or nonpolitical?" but rather "What are my political protocols? How do I defend them? Am I willing to belong to a free, pluralistic, interpretative community?" Moreover, the second response continues, all of us think *perspectively*, from a *standpoint*. Feminist theory and criticism is a self-conscious perspective, a standpoint, or, to change the metaphor from sight to sound, a voice to join a polyvocal, equitable discourse. This conversation will not uncover values lying out there—as if they were precious ores. There are no values "out there" that human beings have not created. Values are not like minerals. Rather, our conversation will examine our cultural, intellectual, and literary traditions in order to ground and then reground the values—moral, political, cultural, literary—by which we choose to live.

## *III*

As feminist criticism has grown during the past decades, it has not gone through stages neatly and consecutively—as if it were a Piagetian child or a fashionable creature putting on one set of clothes for breakfast in 1970, another for lunch in 1980, another for dinner in 1990. Rather, three activities have supplemented, corrected, and overlapped with each other.

1. *The defiance of difference.* Like Millett in *Sexual Politics*, feminist critics believe that sexual difference often means sexual discrimination and repression. To see this is to see and feel the world anew. The writer must find a language for these freshly experienced realities. The title of a famous Adrienne Rich essay, a deliberate adaption of Ibsen, is "When We Dead Awaken: Writing as Re-vision." Angry because of the past, joyous because of the possibility of ripping away from this past, feminist critics take on two interdependent projects.

The more important is to create fairer cultural and educational institutions, to rewrite literary history, and to redesign the curriculum. However, before this is possible, feminist critics must document the reasons for their revolt. In part, this task is historical and sociological, proving that social structures discriminate against the woman who would write, study, and teach. In

"Women Who Are Writers in Our Century: One Out of Twelve," Olsen states that the standard records of literary achievement—reviews, textbooks—show eleven male writers for every one woman. Her explanation pervades feminist criticism and annoys some of its opponents. The fault is not in women's biology but in society's treatment of women: the cultural and religious devaluation, the lack of female literacy and education, the conflict between work and family life.[4]

In part, the task of documentation is critical, showing how "male structures of power are inscribed (or encoded) within our literary inheritance and the consequences of that encoding for women—as characters, as readers, and as writers . . ." (Kolodny, "Dancing" 162). What happens, for example, to our theories of genre if we include women and gender? Celeste Schenck proposes that we traditionally think of Western genre theory as "prescriptive, legislative . . . its . . . preoccupations . . . the establishment of limits, the drawing of exclusionary lines" (285). When feminist critics look at genre theory, they see women being "edged into marginalized, noncanonical genres as a result of their exclusion from central cultural concerns." For example, women turn to the ballad tradition, the mystery, or, in the eighteenth century, the novel. Moreover, the stress on genre as form, as norm, has bred a diagnosis of the writing of women, who exist on the cultural margins, as itself formless, normless, "shapeless and indeterminate" (286). We also see how the various genres seem to organize themselves around the psychosexual development of each gender—the epic, for example, around men's martial conflict.

Finally, the task of documentation is pedagogical, to analyze the curriculum as the Praetorian Guard of this inheritance. Why should *Portrait of the Artist as a Young Man*, in which the artist is very much a young man, be taught as a narrative of universal human experience? The fact that Stephen Dedalus is male is no mere contingency but a crucial element of his identity—his relations to literature, country, and church; his relationships to others. A portrait of the artist as a young Catholic woman in late nineteenth-century Ireland might have a family likeness to Joyce's work, but at most only a family likeness.[5] What, for example, would her dreams of priesthood be? Delirious fantasies?

Not surprisingly, as feminist criticism has matured, it has reevaluated the question of men in feminism. Can men, the class whose powers feminism anatomizes so severely, help feminism? Neither the exploration of misogyny in literature and history nor a suspicion that men might yet again appropriate women's work is over. Nevertheless, three activities have potential: the study of women's representations of men, the inverse of the study of men's representation of women; the understanding of masculinity as a social and literary construct, the counterpart and counterpoint to femininity; men's work as credible feminist critics, which Jonathan Culler, in *On Deconstruction*, helped to start with his deconstructive, destabilizing interrogation of the meaning of "reading as a woman."[6] The situation of "men in feminism" offers feminists a chance to practice an ethics of criticism. Both Robert Scholes and Wayne C. Booth have used feminist criticism approvingly in their ethics of reading, Scholes in *Protocols of Reading* and his argument with deconstruction, Booth in *The Company We Keep* and his definitions of a "bad book." Now feminist critics can go beyond gender as a litmus test of the good reader and ask about the generosity and intelligence with which the good reader sees gender at work and play.

2. *The celebration of difference.* In *A Room of One's Own*, Virginia Woolf created the figure of Judith Shakespeare, William's imaginary and suicidally frustrated sister. Judith Shakespeare became a primary symbol of women's cultural deprivation. Yet revisionary acts of attention discovered more than the grave of Judith Shakespeare—a rich landscape of women's writing waiting to be recovered and nurtured. Despite enmity and indifference, despite the anxiety enmity and indifference engender, women had written and spoken extensively—in formal and informal, respected and despised genres. After listening to Audre Lorde read, Naomi Schor confessed, "Somehow . . . my topic had changed from the anxiety to the joy of difference" ("For a Restricted Thematic" 189). Revealing these accomplishments, feminist criticism returns to and transvalues the metaphor of the needle, of sewing and weaving. It now serves as a figure for women's artistic work, the stitching and piecing together of textual quilts and tapestries.

On one level, the celebration of women's difference has produced a number of critical studies, biographies, and anthologies that cohere around a single figure (for example, Woolf), a tradition (British women novelists), a genre (life stories or science fiction), a theme (mother-daughter relations), or a group (Mary Helen Washington's anthologies of black women's writings). The discovery and recovery of writing by women, together with these studies, have irrevocably altered our literary history. The past looks different now. On another level, the celebration of women's difference poses a hard but obvious theoretical question: What *are* the differences between men and women? What are their sources? A critic's answer to this depends inevitably on her or his larger theory of human nature. Some of the appeal of various schools of psychoanalysis to the feminist critics who adhere to them is that they seem to explain why men and women develop different gender identities and how such identities shape language. The question about gender difference leads to a second, equally hard, equally obvious literary puzzle: How do women differ from men as writing and reading subjects?

In brief, how much does gender matter to literature? Is there a difference between "female" and "male" writing that emerges from two classes that are each united by biology? If so, is women's writing (*écriture féminine*) stylistically marked by fragmentation, lyricism, alogicality? Is women's writing thematically marked by a special treatment of war or marriage? Or is the difference between "feminine" and "masculine" writing one that emerges from two classes, each united by a psychosocial position? If this is so, then biological men might write from a feminine position, biological women from a masculine position. Moreover, if *this* is so, then a woman's signature could mark the writing of either a man or a woman. Or is the difference between "feminist" writing and "nonfeminist" writing, two classes each united by ideas? Or as many argue, are these limited, self-limiting questions? Does the act of writing not burn away all biological and social distinctions in the crucible of the imagination? Does writing not transmute language into literature, a world in which men and women might dwell as unequal characters but is nevertheless a self-regulating world in which men and women dwell equitably as readers? Or, as I believe, is it not feasible to consider all of these possibilities at once? Why must one cancel and stamp out the others?

Several feminist critics have been skeptical about the search for a "woman's difference." In 1981, Myra Jehlen admonished some feminist critics for glamorizing the sentimental novels and women's studies for focusing only on women and thereby creating "an alternative context, a sort of female enclave apart from the universe of masculinist assumptions" ("Archimedes" 576). She legitimately calls for a radical comparativism between men's and women's writings and a connection of them both to the larger world. Nevertheless, some of the most adventurous, intelligent feminist critics gather evidence of stylistic, thematic, or generic differences: Barbara Christian, Hélène Cixous, Rachel Blau DuPlessis, Susan Stanford Friedman, Sandra Gilbert and Susan Gubar, Margaret Homans, Julia Kristeva, Nancy K. Miller, Elaine Showalter, Patricia M. Spacks. The internal logic of feminist criticism demands such an investigation. For there is no reason to study women unless "women" represent something else again. Interestingly, the more historically specific the evidence of difference is, the more persuasive it is. Women's traditions do exist. However, a "woman's difference" from a man emerges most plausibly in a precise time and place. The "woman's difference" in the Greek oral tradition differs from the "woman's difference" in the modernist novel and poem. The more we multiply the number of "women's differences," the more we fragment the category of woman and the less universal "a woman's voice" becomes. The more particular a "woman's voice" becomes, the more numerous the differences become—not only between men and women but among women.

3. *The recognition of differences.* The study of the differences among women is no more monolithic than the subject of women itself.[7] Given the thorny, lovely, idiosyncratic creativity of individual talents, feminist critics have asked about the careers of single authors. A persistent theme has been

the ways in which these authors—a Zora Neale Hurston, a Willa Cather—have resisted cultural instructions against their writing or against their writing with flamboyant candor. Acting on feminism's hope of claiming the virtues of autonomy for women, feminist critics have also studied the genres that are narratives of the self—the diary, biography, autobiography, or, to use Domna Stanton's term, *autogynography*. Stanton points out that virtually no criticism of women's autobiography existed until feminist criticism in the 1970s, another erasure of women as writers (7).

Feminist critics have also questioned the meaning of a woman author's membership in a social group or groups. So doing, they have revitalized the sociology and study of the materiality of literature. These groups might be sexual, economic, racial, ethnic, regional, colonial or postcolonial, national, religious. Whatever the community, belonging to it is a vital element of identity that a writer, reader, or critic must at the very least acknowledge. Such elements form a variety of compounds with each other and with gender. A Protestant African American woman writer born in Mississippi will differ from a Protestant Anglo woman writer born in Arizona. Because some groups have more power and prestige than others, their women will have more power and prestige than others. Nellie Y. McKay writes, "We, women and men of our time, have come out of a history which has separated us for hundreds of years, in the many different situations of our lives, and has left us with the difficult task of attempting to locate our common center amidst confusions of hierarchies and multiple oppressions" (161). Significantly, in 1970, the year of *Sexual Politics*, Toni Morrison published *The Bluest Eye*, her first novel, which opens with a bitter parody of a school reader's idealization of the brightly white family of Mother, Father, Dick, Jane, kitten, and dog.

In the 1970s, feminist critics divided into several different critical communities. The term *critical community* has two meanings. One refers to a cluster that unites the principles of feminism and feminist criticism with participation in a particular social group, primarily one that claims minority or marginal status. A priori, this status ensures some misrepresentation in the culture at large. For such critics as Biddy Martin or Bonnie Zimmerman, being a lesbian defines a group; for such critics as Paula Gunn Allen or Rayna Green, being an American Indian does so. Painfully, an allegiance to women and the allegiance to a social community often conflict with each other, a dilemma for the critic that her literature might also dramatize. "Chicano women are underrepresented in professional sectors where Anglo women have made important advances," states the author of the first book-length study of Chicana poets. "Inequalities based on ethnicity and gender help explain why the identities of Chicano scholar and Chicana feminist continue to seem ambiguous and contradictory" (Sánchez ix). The community then provides a common subject position. To a degree, but only to a degree, it also provides subject matter. A black feminist critic may write primarily about black writers, but, clearly, she need not and often does not.

The virtues of a passionate engagement with and care for one's subject matter are obvious. So are the dangers of parochialism and special pleading. However, the development of each group has entailed an internal critique that lessens the threat of parochialism and special pleading. An example: in 1977, Barbara K. Smith asked for a book that would make her life visible, an act of black feminist criticism that would include lesbians and draw sustenance from a black feminist movement. In 1980, Deborah E. McDowell, in "New Directions for Black Feminist Criticism," agreed with the call for the study of black women's literature but found Smith insufficiently precise. A few years later, Hazel V. Carby, regarding Hortense Spillers and Barbara Christian as well, found black feminist criticism "a problem, not a solution . . . a sign that should be interrogated, a locus of contradictions" (15).

The second meaning of critical community is that of theoretical affinity. By the mid-1970s, feminist criticism was an international movement with a wide, conflicting range of theoretical concerns. Indeed, the potential partners for a feminist critic are a narrative of contemporary critical methods and the quarrels among them. To each partner, the feminist critic brings her questions about women and gender. She can choose, inter alia, liberal humanism and its belief in authenticity and autonomy of character; neo-Marxist theories of ideology; cultural studies and its explorations of culture and social relations; deconstruction, a strategy of reading with its emphasis on the differences within language; revisionary psychoanalysis and its various pictures of the body and the psychosexual development of the gendered subject; semiotics and its exploration of sign systems; reader-response theory and its investigation of the dramas between text and reader; structuralism and its analysis of the laws and elements of literature; or the stunning complexities of poststructuralism and its radical skepticism about psychological autonomy, master narratives, and the possibilities of representation, truth, and "real experience." Here, the study of literature often broadens into a study of textuality. Here, too, the "self," for many a psychological good that women are to seek, metamorphoses into "the subject," a linguistic identity, "a relational position demarcated by language" (Gallop and Burke 106). One reason for the importance of the work of Nancy K. Miller and Teresa de Lauretis is its effort to reconcile the strands of feminist criticism, to conceptualize women as both a self, "a real historical being," and a subject, a "fictional construct" (Alcoff 431). Inevitably, the movement into theory jump-started a countermovement against theory, a feminist parallel to a reaction elsewhere in literary criticism.[8] For theory seemed, to many, a self-involved, arcane enterprise that threatened pluralism and literature's double promise, first, of humanistic, mimetic insights into life and, next, of a stimulus to social change. Theory might be stripping the feminism from feminist criticism.

In 1985, *Sexual/Textual Politics* publicized some of the disagreements within feminist criticism. The author, Toril Moi, takes her title from Millett and swipes at various other feminist critics. Moi's book has its weaknesses, for it inaccurately describes feminist criticism as if it consisted of but two competing camps: an empirical "Anglo-American" and a theoretical "French." So doing, it glibly dismisses those feminist critical communities (black, lesbian, black-lesbian, Third World) who locate themselves in a sociocultural space from which they do their criticism. Moreover, unlike Patricia Yaeger in *Honey-Mad Women*, Moi refuses to confront systematically the question of what to do in the classroom or the world at large if one believes in both intellectual freedom and in certain moral and political principles.

Yet Moi's reading of *Sexual Politics* is an interesting guide to larger aspects of feminist criticism. Rightly, she praises Millett for speaking both to the academy and to a much larger audience beyond its borders. Like Elizabeth Janeway, Adrienne Rich, or Alice Walker, Millett showed that feminist criticism appealed to a wide spectrum of readers. As a voice, Millett is "neither submissive nor lady-like." Her style itself challenges cultural authority. Moi, however, condemns Millett, seeing gaps that later feminist criticism had to fill. For Millett does not acknowledge what female intellectual precursors she had, especially Beauvoir.[9] This lack is one aspect of Millett's refusal to write about women. Neither thinking nor reading back through her mothers, she has no sense of women's textual resistance to power. Finally, Moi charges, Millett is a misreader, ignorant of form, messy with facts. In particular, Millett misreads psychoanalysis and confuses the "phallus" with the "penis," a linguistic construction with a biological event. Here Moi is unfair to Millett, but Millett does reflect an ambivalence about psychoanalysis that haunts feminist criticism.

Given Moi's sharpness, it is surprising that she ignores other weaknesses in Millett that render Millett an incomplete prophet of feminist criticism: the use in her preface of the generic *he*, which masculinizes the reader of her book; the ahistorical use of the term *patriarchy*; the almost total erasure of lesbianism, especially ironic since Millett's autobiographies were later to write the lesbian and women's sexual pleasure into contemporary literature; the lack of attention to the mass media and the visual text as powerful signifying forces. Although Millett does not subscribe to the theory that literature flatly imitates life, a blow of reductionism that has weakened much feminist criticism, she assumes that life is there, a priori to language. No poststructuralist, she wants literature to interpret the interpretable. Moving, as most feminist critics do, between dissent and hope, she also endorses a master utopian narrative about history in which we can be nonviolent revolutionaries who will regain an Eden of a common humanity. The last words of *Sexual Politics* are, "It may be that we shall even be able to retire sex from the harsh realities of politics, but not until we have created a world we can bear out of the desert we inhabit" (507).

Yet I wish to praise this book. My gesture is more than nostalgia, friendship, and old-girl cronyism. I doubt if any fair-minded critic is unhappy that *Sexual Politics* was written. Many honest critics would probably admit that they wish they had written it and could take some credit for the cartographers of culture it inspired. My essay has accented the contests among these cartographers, their variety and multiplicity, a variety and multiplicity that are conditions of the late twentieth century itself. My essay, however, has also outlined their unity. This mingling of heterogeneity and unity is manifest in the relations between feminist criticism and the question of the canon. A literary canon doubly announces the presence of cultural power. First, a canon is meant to embody the authoritative values of a culture. Second, the forces that draw up and transmit a canon (in criticism and education) have the strength to do so. I could run up and down Broadway in New York City, waving a copy of *Sexual Politics* and clamoring for one and all to read and teach it, but if no one had any compelling reason to listen to me, I would be just another crazy urban jogger.

Feminist critics unite in their belief that canons in the United States have excluded the literature of women and minorities, no matter how meritorious this literature might be. The canon, then, should "open up" to include the work of women and minorities. In addition, accepting the work of Annette Kolodny, Paul Lauter, Barbara Herrnstein Smith, or Jane Tompkins, many feminist critics agree that a canon constructs value as much as it reflects value; that the canon is contingent not universal; that the canon is a fiction about aesthetic and intellectual supremacy.

So believing, feminist critics have been reluctant to canonize their own texts or, more generally, those of women writers.[10] Gilbert and Gubar, in their *Norton Anthology of Literature by Women: The Tradition in English*, distinguished their map of literary history, which shows "exuberant variety yet strong continuity" (xxvii), from a rule book of literary value. Despite their pains, Gilbert and Gubar took some lumps from divers hands—accusations of extracting only feminist sentiments from women's writings, of ignoring experimental and anglophonic writers, of accepting the standard periodization of literary history, and of replicating the rules of the existing canon, substituting women for men as they did so (Heinzelman).

However, every critical school must structure the culture it studies. This activity makes a critical school a school. Feminist criticism has looked long and hard at other ordering performances and queried the values of many of them. It still rejects strict hierarchies of literary value. Despite its fascination with women's traditions, feminist criticism also continues to suspect linear notions of literary history. A woman's text has neither one mother, nor one father, nor even two parents. It is now time to devise more coherent theories of literary value, maps of the good that are neither cut in stone nor scuffed in sand. It is also time to expand on the work of a Millett or a Gilbert and Gubar and publish major cultural histories that include the findings and concepts of feminist criticism. Yet, in this labor, theory and history will do well to think of writing and reading, not as fixtures but as incessant activities, exchanges, a multiplicity of tongues and discourses that "argue and interrogate the status claimed for each by their practitioners . . . a reading of the internal difference by which the letter refuses any univocal meaning." Feminist reading, like all reading, is a "movement," a "getting together and . . . getting across . . . its itinerary incomplete and its destination deferred" (Jacobus, *Reading Women* 292). Perhaps such perpetual mobility is a source of electric mourning. It is also a source of glory.[11]

### Notes

[1]Nelson suggests that being part of a movement has motivated these self-descriptions. "Feminism has a much stronger sense of being a collaborative enterprise and thus has more impetus to continue updating and rearticulating its collective identity and common ground" ("Feminism" 117). In a succession of review essays and an anthology, Showalter has written a valuable history: "Review Essay," 1975; "Toward a Feminist Poetics," 1979; "Feminist Criticism in the Wilderness," 1981; *The New Feminist Criticism*, 1985; "Women's Time, Women's Space: Writing the History of Feminist Criticism," 1987; "A Criticism of Our Own," 1989. In the last, a comparison of African American and feminist criticism, she outlines four stages: in the 1960s, a feminist critique of male culture and a female aesthetic that celebrated women's culture; in the 1970s, gynocritics, her term, adapted from the French, for the study of women's writing; in the late 1970s, poststructuralist, or "gynesic," criticism; and in the late 1980s, gender theory, the comparative study of sexual difference. Other helpful surveys are Kolodny, "Review Essay," 1976; S. J. Kaplan, "Review Essay," 1979; Register, "Review Essay," 1980; Greene and Kahn, a collection of review essays, *Making a Difference*, 1985; Neely, "Feminist Criticism in Motion," 1985; Messer-Davidow, "The Philosophical Bases of Feminist Literary Criticisms," 1987; June Howard, "Feminist Differings," 1988; Gilbert and Gubar, "The Mirror and the Vamp," 1989; Stimpson, "Woolf's Room, Our Project," 1989, a graph of the immense influence on feminist criticism of Virginia Woolf's *Room of One's Own*; Draine, "Refusing the Wisdom of Solomon," 1989.

[2]I adapt this section from my paper "Knowing Women." Lanser and Beck provide a brief history of modern women as critics.

[3]See Wittig and Zeig, a dictionary from a lesbian perspective; Kramarae and

Treichler, from a general feminist perspective; and Daly, from a radical and cultural feminist perspective.

[4]L. Robinson, *Sex, Class, and Culture* is an influential merger of radical and feminist criticism.

[5]Three publications are excellent guides to the writers, ideas, and discoveries of this stage: Gornick and Moran, *Woman in Sexist Society* (1971); *College English* 32.8 (May 1971), largely based on a 1970 Modern Language Association annual convention program that the MLA Commission on the Status of Women had organized; and *College English* 34.1 (October 1972), guest ed. Elaine Hedges, the results of the 1971 MLA Annual Convention. In addition to Olsen and Rich, the contributors to these programs and issues became significant feminist critics: Florence Howe, Annis Pratt, Lillian Robinson, Elaine Showalter.

[6]*Misogyny, Misandry, and Misanthropy*, a special issue of *Representations*, allies the study of cultural misogyny with new-historicist methods. Jane Miller deepens investigation of women's equivocal representation of men. Jardine and Smith, Boone and Cadden, Claridge and Langland are anthologies that rethink the "men's question."

[7]The literature about differences is vast. Some especially useful texts include D. Fisher, *The Third Woman*, an anthology of American Indian, Asian American, black, and Chicana writing; Eisenstein and Jardine, *The Future of Difference*, the papers from an exceptionally important 1979 conference about our multiplicity of differences; *Feminist Readings*, a special edition of *Yale French Studies*, with a collective editorship; it includes Spivak's skeptical reading from a postcolonial perspective of French feminist theory, "French Feminism in an International Frame"; Johnson, *A World of Difference*, a mediation among deconstruction, feminism, texts by men and women and by African American and white women; *Feminist Studies* 14.1 (1988), about differences and deconstruction, in a journal known for its attention to history and material culture; and Fuss, *Essentially Speaking*, an analysis of the relations between the doctrine of essentialism and difference.

[8]Pungent critiques of theory include Baym, "Madwoman," and Christian, "Race," with a response by Awkward.

[9]In conversation, Millett told me she now regrets not rereading Beauvoir more closely. Moi also rightly places M. Ellmann, *Thinking about Women* as a precursor of feminist criticism.

[10]One exception is Moers, *Literary Women*, a quick-witted, erudite, often dazzling book that is nevertheless deliberately limited to "major" figures, the "writers we read and shall always read" (xi).

[11]My essay gives Millett, *Sexual Politics*, its place. I regret the many crucial texts I could not list in the selected bibliography. My criteria for those I did are influence, intellectual power, and the inclusiveness of their references to other critics.

## Selected Bibliography

Abel, Elizabeth, ed. *Writing and Sexual Difference.* Chicago: U of Chicago P, 1982.
  A major collection that was among the first to examine the relations of writing to the concepts of "gender" and "difference."

Beauvoir, Simone de. *The Second Sex.* Trans. and ed. H. M. Parshley. New York: Knopf, 1953.
  The single greatest influence on feminist theory and criticism, which has also pointed out Beauvoir's great errors.

Carby, Hazel V. *Reconstructing Womanhood: The Emergence of the Afro-American Woman Novelist.* New York: Oxford UP, 1987.
  A synthesis of black women's history and black feminist criticism that offers "a materialist account of the cultural production of black women intellectuals" (17).

Christian, Barbara. *Black Women Novelists: The Development of a Tradition, 1892–1976.* New York: Greenwood, 1980.
  An early, systematic history of fiction written by African American women.

de Lauretis, Teresa, ed. *Feminist Studies/Critical Studies.* Bloomington: Indiana UP, 1986.
  An interdisciplinary collection that links feminist politics to critical studies, associations central to later criticism.

Flynn, Elizabeth A., and Patrocinio Schweickart, eds. *Gender and Reading: Essays on Readers, Texts, and Contexts.* Baltimore: Johns Hopkins UP, 1986.
  A collection that brings together historical, psychological, and critical investigations of the difference between women and men as readers.

Gallop, Jane. *The Daughter's Seduction: Feminism and Psychoanalysis.* Ithaca: Cornell UP, 1982.
  A study of the relations between contemporary feminist thought and French schools of psychoanalysis, especially Jacques Lacan.

Gilbert, Sandra M., and Susan Gubar. *The Madwoman in the Attic: The Woman Writer and the Nineteenth-Century Literary Imagination.* New Haven: Yale UP, 1979.
  A map of women writers in the nineteenth century, their anxieties and resistances.

Heilbrun, Carolyn G. *Toward a Recognition of Androgyny:* New York: Knopf, 1973.
  An exploration in myth and literature of the figure of the androgyne that transcends sexual difference.

Jardine, Alice A. *Gynesis: Configurations of Woman and Modernity*. Ithaca: Cornell UP, 1985.
    A reading of the feminine, or *gynesis* (*gyn* = *woman; sis* = *process*), in writing, especially texts that question traditional humanism.
Jehlen, Myra. "Archimedes and the Paradox of Feminist Criticism." *Signs* 6 (1981): 575–601.
    A guide in the shift from the study of women writers to the study of gender, literature, and ideology.
Marks, Elaine, and Isabelle de Courtivron, eds. *New French Feminisms: An Anthology*. New York: Schocken, 1981.
    The anthology that introduced French feminist writing to the United States.
Miller, Nancy K. *Subject to Change: Reading Feminist Writing*. New York: Columbia UP, 1988.
    A collection about the meaning of "the female signature."
Rich, Adrienne. *On Lies, Secrets, and Silence: Selected Prose, 1966–1978*. New York: Norton, 1979.
    A selection from the writer second only to Beauvoir in influence on feminist thinking about literature and culture.
Showalter, Elaine. *A Literature of Their Own: British Women Novelists from Brontë to Lessing*. Princeton: Princeton UP, 1977.
    Another map of women's literary history, this showing "feminine," "feminist," and "female" stages.
Spivak, Gayatri Chakravorty. *In Other Worlds: Essays in Cultural Politics*. New York: Methuen, 1987.
    The essays of the scholar who first brought together deconstructive, feminist, neo-Marxist, and postcolonial criticism.

# 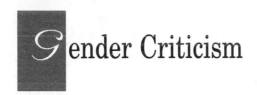ender Criticism

## EVE KOSOFSKY SEDGWICK

"Gender criticism" sounds like a euphemism for something. In practice it is a euphemism for several things and more than that. One of its subtexts is gay and lesbian criticism. There can be no mystery about why that highly stigmatic label, though increasingly common, should be self-applied with care—however proudly—by those of us who do this scholarship. For instance, I almost never put "gay and lesbian" in the title of undergraduate gay and lesbian studies courses, though I always use the words in the catalog copy. To ask students to mark their transcripts permanently with so much as the name of this subject of study could have unpredictably disabling consequences for them in the future: The military, most churches, the CIA, and much of the psychoanalytic establishment, to mention only a few plausible professions, are still unblinking about wanting to exclude suspected lesbians and gay men, while in only a handful of places in the United States does anyone have even nominal legal protection against the routine denial of employment, housing, insurance, custody, or other rights on the basis of her or his perceived or supposed sexual orientation. Within and around academic institutions, as well, there can be similarly persuasive reasons for soft-selling the challenge to an oppression whose legal, institutional, and extrajudicial sanctions extend, uniquely, quite uninterruptedly up to the present.

Besides code-naming a range of gay- and lesbian-centered theoretical inquiries, "gender studies" also stands in a usably unmarked relation to another rubric, "feminist studies." Feminist studies might be defined as the study of the dynamics of gender definition, inequality, oppression, and change in human societies. To the extent that gender is thus at the definitional center of feminist studies, "gender studies" can sometimes be used as an alternative name for feminist studies, euphemistic only in not specifying, as the "feminist" label more than implicitly does, how far inequality, oppression, and struggle between genders may be seen as differentially constituting gender itself. *Women's* studies today is commonly defined, at least in practice, by the gender of its object of study (at my university, for instance, the women's studies program will not cross-list courses unless a majority of the texts read are by women). In contrast to women's studies, feminist studies, whose name specifies the angle of an inquiry rather than the sex of either its subject or its object, can make (and indeed has needed to make) the claim of having as privileged a view of male as of female cultural production.

What, then, can or does distinguish the project of gender studies from that of feminist studies? Sometimes, as I have suggested, "gender studies" is another, equally appropriate way of designating "feminist studies"—the reasons for offering the emollient name no more than tactical. In other instances, however, "gender studies" can mean "feminist studies" *minus* feminism or, in another version of the same deadening equation, "women's studies" (in the most positivist meaning of the term) *plus* some compensatory entity called "men's studies." Although they offer an illusion of enhanced inclusiveness, these are the arithmetics that can give "gender studies" a sinister sound to the very scholars most involved in active gender critique. The assumptions behind these usages are intellectually as well as politically stultifying. To assume that the study of gender can be definitionally detached from the analysis and critique of gender inequality, oppression, and struggle (that is, from some form of feminism) ignores, among other things, the telling fact that gender analysis per se became possible only under the pressure of the most pointed and political feminist demand. It ignores, that is to say, the degree to which the otherwise available analytic tools of Western culture had already been structured by precisely the need to naturalize or to deny, and hence to allow the continuance of, a gender inequality already assumed. To figure gender studies as a mere sum of women's studies plus something called "men's studies," meanwhile, reduces both women's studies and the supposedly symmetrical men's studies to static denominations of subject matter and reduces any understanding of relations between genders to something equally static and additive. That genders are constituted as such, not only in dialectical relation to each other but in relation to the oppression historically exercised by one over the other, is a knowledge repressed by this impulse toward the separate but equal. Things get even worse when the rationale for an additive gender studies agenda involves not a nominally depoliticized and positivist study of women as women and men as men but rather the conscious promotion of masculist viewpoints (under the men's studies rubric) as a remedial "balance" against feminist ones. One can only summon up the foundational feminist assertion that colleges don't need something called "men's studies" because so much of the rest of the curriculum already fulfills that function: the function, that is, not only of studying the cultural production of men but of furthering the interest many of them have in rationalizing, maintaining, or increasing their gender privilege over women.

It seems, then, that insofar as "gender studies" actually is the study of gender, its most substantive and intellectually respectable meanings make it coextensive with "feminist studies," and gender criticism coextensive with feminist criticism. Where, then, to look for the distinctive projects of gender criticism beyond its overlap with feminist criticism? In the context of this volume, where feminist criticism has its own topical assignment, distinct from this chapter, it seems particularly possible to insist on the question. And where, for that matter, to look for the already fecund connection of gender criticism with the agendas of gay- and lesbian-centered critique to which I began by alluding? *Homosexual* is not, after all, today understood as the name of a gender, though it alludes to and is defined by reference to gender. Nor has the feminist analysis of mutually constitutive relations and oppressions *between* genders proved to have an adequate purchase on how relations, identities, and oppressions are constituted, as in the exemplary gay instance, *within* genders. Yet so far the greatest success—institutionally as well as intellectually—of gender criticism per se has been specifically in gay and lesbian criticism.

For gender criticism not coextensive with feminist criticism, the most distinctive task may be not to do gender analysis but to explore what resists it: to ask, with respect to certain categories that can't be a priori disentangled from gender, nonetheless, *What isn't gender?* "Gender criticism" might here be taken to mean, then, not criticism *through* the categories of gender analysis but criticism *of* them, the mapping of the fractal borderlines between gender and its others. And if gay and lesbian criticism is so far the typifying site of such interrogations of gender analysis, then the first other of gender would seem to be, in this defining instance, sexuality.

## Sex and Gender

Sex, gender, sexuality: three terms whose usage relations and analytical relations are almost irremediably slippery. The charting of a space between something called "sex" and something called "gender" has been one of the most influential and successful undertakings of feminist thought. For the purposes of that undertaking, *sex* has had the meaning of a certain group of irreducible, biological differentiations between members of the species *Homo sapiens* who have XX chromosomes and those who have XY chromosomes. These include (or are ordinarily thought to include) more or less marked dimorphisms of genital formation, hair growth (in populations that have body hair), fat distribution, hormonal function, and reproductive capacity. Sex in this sense—what I'll demarcate as "chromosomal sex"—is seen as the relatively minimal raw material on which is based the social construction of gender. Gender, then, is the far more elaborated, more fully and rigidly dichotomized social production and reproduction of male and female identities and behaviors—of male and female *persons*—in a cultural system for which "male-female" functions as a primary and perhaps model binarism affecting the structure and meaning of many other binarisms whose apparent connection to chromosomal sex may often be exiguous or nonexistent. Compared with chromosomal sex, which is seen (by these definitions) as tending to be immutable, immanent in the individual, and biologically based, gender is seen as culturally mutable and variable, highly relational (in the sense that each of the binarized genders is defined primarily by its relation to the other), and inextricable from a history of power differentials between genders. This feminist charting of what Gayle Rubin refers to as a "sex/gender system" ("Traffic" 159), the system by which chromosomal sex is turned into, and processed as, cultural gender, has tended to minimize the attribution of a person's various behaviors and identities to chromosomal sex and to maximize their attribution to socialized gender constructs. The purpose of that strategy has been to gain analytic and critical leverage on the female-disadvantaging social arrangements that prevail at a given time in a given society, by throwing into question their legitimative ideological grounding in biologically based narratives of the "natural."

*Sex* is, however, a term that extends indefinitely beyond chromosomal sex. That its history of usage often overlaps with what might now more properly be called "gender" is only one problem. ("I can only love someone of my own sex." Should *sex* be *gender* in such a sentence? "M. saw that the person who approached was of the opposite sex." Genders—insofar as there are two and they are defined in contradistinction to each other—may be said to be opposite; but in what sense is XX the opposite of XY?) Beyond chromosomes, however, the association of *sex*, precisely through the physical body, with reproduction and with genital activity and sensation keeps offering new challenges to the conceptual clarity or even possibility of sex-gender differentiation. A powerful argument can be made that a primary (or *the* primary) issue in gender differentiation and gender struggle is the question of who is to have control of women's (biologically) distinctive reproductive capability. Indeed, the intimacy of the association between several of the most signal forms of gender oppression and the "facts" of women's bodies and women's reproductive activity has led some radical feminists to question, more or less explicitly, the usefulness of insisting on a sex-gender distinction (see, e.g., MacKinnon, "Agenda"). For these reasons, even usages involving the sex-gender system within feminist theory are able to use *sex-gender* only to delineate a problematical space, rather than a crisp distinction. My loose usage here will be to denominate that problematized space of the sex-gender system, the whole package of physical and cultural distinctions between women and men, more simply under the rubric "gender." I adopt this terminology to reduce the likelihood of confusion between *sex* in the sense of the space of differences between male and female (what I'll group under *gender*) and *sex* in the sense of sexuality.

For meanwhile the whole realm of what modern culture refers to as "sexuality" and *also* calls "sex"—the array of acts, expectations, narratives, pleasures, identity formations, and knowledges, in both women and men, that tends to cluster most densely around certain genital sensations but is not adequately defined by them—is virtually impossible to situate on a map de-limited by the feminist-defined sex-gender distinction. To the degree that *sexu-ality* has a center or starting point in certain physical sites, acts, and rhythms associated (however contingently) with procreation or the potential for it, the term in this sense may seem to be of a piece with *chromosomal sex*: a biological necessity for species survival, tending toward the individually immanent, the socially immutable, the given. But to the extent that, as Freud argued and Michel Foucault assumed, the distinctively sexual nature of human sexuality has to do precisely with its excess over or potential difference from the bare choreographies of procreation, sexuality might be the very opposite of what we originally referred to as chromosomal sex: it could occupy, instead, even more than gender the polar position of the relational, the social-symbolic, the con-structed, the variable, the representational.

In "Thinking Sex," an influential essay published in 1984, Rubin hy-pothesizes that although the question of gender and the question of sexuality are inextricable in that each can be expressed only in the terms of the other, they are nonetheless not the same question. In twentieth-century Western culture, Rubin argues, gender and sexuality represent two analytic axes that one may productively imagine as being as distinct from each other as are, say, gender and class or class and race. Distinct, that is, no more than minimally but nonetheless usefully.

Under this hypothesis, just as one has learned to assume that no issue of racial meaning fails to be embodied through the specificity of a particular class position—and no issue of class, for instance, through the specificity of a particular gender position—so no issue of gender would fail to be embodied through the specificity of a particular sexuality, and vice versa; but nonethe-less, there could be use in keeping the analytic axes distinct.

An objection to this analogy might be that gender is *definitionally* built into determinations of sexuality, in a way that neither gender nor sexuality is definitionally intertwined with, for instance, determinations of class or race. Without a concept of gender there could be, quite simply, no concept of homo- or heterosexuality. But many other dimensions of sexual choice (auto- or allo-erotic; within or between generations, species, etc.) have no such distinctive, explicit definitional connection with gender; indeed some dimensions of sexual-ity might be tied not to gender but *instead* to differences or similarities of race or class. The definitional narrowing in this century of sexuality as a whole to a binarized calculus of homo- or heterosexuality is a weighty but an entirely historical fact. To use that fait accompli as a reason for analytically conflating sexuality per se with gender obscures the degree to which the fact itself requires explanation. It also, I think, risks obscuring yet again the extreme intimacy with which all these available analytic axes do after all mutually constitute one another: to assume the distinctiveness of the intimacy between sexuality

and gender might well risk assuming too much about the definitional separability of either of them from determinations of, say, class or race.

It may also be, as Judith Butler argues in *Gender Trouble*, that a
damaging bias toward heterosocial or heterosexist assumptions inheres un-
avoidably in the very concept of gender. This bias would be built into any
gender-based analytic perspective to the extent that gender definition and
gender identity are necessarily relational between genders—to the extent, that
is, that in any gender system, female identity or definition is constructed by
analogy, supplementarity, or contrast to male, or vice versa. Although many
gender-based forms of analysis do involve accounts, sometimes fairly rich ones,
of intragender behaviors and relations, the ultimate definitional appeal in any
gender-based analysis must necessarily be to the diacritical frontier between
different genders. This necessity gives heterosocial and heterosexual relations
a conceptual privilege of incalculable consequence. Undeniably, residues,
markers, tracks, signs referring to that diacritical frontier between genders
are everywhere, as well, internal to and determinative of the experience of
each gender and its intragender relations; gender-based analysis can never be
dispensed with in even the most purely intragender context. Nevertheless, it
seems predictable that the analytic bite of a purely gender-based account will
grow less incisive and direct as the distance of its subject from a social interface
between different genders increases. It is unrealistic to expect a close, textured
analysis of same-sex relations through an optic calibrated in the first place
to the coarser stigmata of gender difference (see King; de Lauretis, "Sexual
Indifference"). The development of an alternative analytic axis—call it sexuality—must be, therefore, if anything a peculiarly central project to gay-lesbian
and antihomophobic inquiry.

The gravity of gender division and gender oppression does have, however, the consequence that one can never take for granted how much women's
same-sex relations will have analytically or experientially in common with
men's; the sense of talking about "gay-lesbian" critique at all is itself always,
and with good reason, contested. Still, it does seem that the interpretive frameworks within which lesbian writers, readers, and interlocutors are likely to
process male-centered reflections on homo- and heterosexual issues, and vice
versa, are currently in a phase of destabilizing flux and promise.

Until recently the lesbian interpretive framework most readily available to critics and theorists was the separatist-feminist one that emerged
from the 1970s. According to that framework, there were essentially no valid
grounds of commonality between gay-male and lesbian experience and identity;
on the contrary, women-loving women and men-loving men were thought to be
at precisely opposite ends of the gender spectrum. The assumptions at work
here were indeed radical ones: most important among them was the stunningly
efficacious re-visioning, in female terms, of same-sex desire as being at the

very definitional center of each gender, rather than as occupying a cross-gender or liminal position between genders. Thus, women who loved women were seen as more female, and men who loved men as quite possibly more male, than those whose desire crossed boundaries of gender; the self-identification of the virilized woman gave way, at least for many, to that of the "woman-identified woman." The axis of sexuality, in this view, was not only exactly coextensive with the axis of gender but expressive of its most heightened essence: Feminism is the theory, lesbianism is the practice. By analogy, male homosexuality could be, and often was, seen as the practice for which male supremacy was the theory (see, e.g., M. Frye 128–51; Irigaray 170–91). A particular reading of modern gender history was, of course, implicit in and then propelled by this gender-separatist framework. In accord with, for instance, Adrienne Rich's understanding of many aspects of women's bonds as constituting a "lesbian continuum" ("Compulsory Heterosexuality" 79), this history, found in its purest form in the work of Lilian Faderman, de-emphasized the definitional disconti-nuities and perturbations between more and less sexualized, more and less prohibited, and more and less gender-identity-bound forms of female same-sex bonding. Insofar as lesbian object choice was viewed as epitomizing a specificity of female experience and resistance, insofar as a symmetrically opposite under-standing of gay male object choice also obtained, and insofar also as feminism necessarily posited male and female experiences and interests as different and opposed, the implication was that an understanding of male homo- or heterosexual definition could offer little or no affordance or interest for any lesbian theoretical project. Indeed, the powerful impetus of a gender-polarized feminist ethical schema made it possible for a profoundly antihomophobic reading of lesbian desire (as a quintessence of the female) to fuel a correspond-ingly homophobic reading of gay male desire (as a quintessence of the male).

Since the late 1970s, however, there have been a variety of challenges to this understanding of how lesbian and gay male desires and identities might be mapped against each other. Each development has led many theorists to a refreshed sense that lesbians and gay men may share important though con-tested aspects of their histories, cultures, identities, politics, and destinies. These new perspectives have emerged from the "sex wars" within feminism over pornography and sadomasochism, which seemed to many pro-sex femi-nists to expose a devastating continuity between a certain, theretofore privi-leged feminist understanding of a resistant female identity, on the one hand, and, on the other, repressive nineteenth-century bourgeois constructions of a sphere of pure femininity. Such challenges arose as well from the reclamation and relegitimation of a courageous history of lesbian transgender role-playing and identification (see E. Newton; Nestle; Hollibaugh and Moraga; Case; de Lauretis, "Sexual Indifference"). Along with this new historical making-visible of self-defined mannish lesbians came a new salience of the many ways in which male and female homosexual identities had in fact been constructed through and in relation to each other over the last century—by the variously homophobic discourses of professional expertise but also and just as actively by many lesbians and gay men (see Grahn). The irrepressible, relatively class-nonspecific popular culture in which James Dean has been as numinous an icon for lesbians as Garbo or Dietrich has been for gay men seems resistant to a purely feminist theorization (see Golding; Dyer). It is in these contexts that calls for a theorized axis of sexuality as distinct from gender have developed. And after the antisadomasochism, antipornography liberal-feminist move toward labeling and stigmatizing particular sexualities joined its energies with those of the much longer established conservative sanctions against all forms of sexual "deviance," it remained only for the terrible accident of the HIV epidemic, and the terrifying societal threats constructed around it, to reconstruct a category of the pervert capacious enough to admit homosexuals of any gender. The newly virulent homophobia of the past decade, directed alike against women and men even though logically its medical pretext ought, if anything, to give a relative exemptive privilege to lesbians,[1] reminds ungently that it is more to our friends than to our enemies that sexually nonconforming women and men are perceptible as distinct groups. At the same time, however, the internal perspective of the gay movements shows women and men increasingly, though far from uncontestingly and far from equally, working together on mutually antihomophobic agendas (see, e.g., Winnow). The contributions brought by lesbians to current gay and AIDS activism are weighty, not despite but because of the intervening lessons of feminism. Feminist perspectives on medicine and health-care issues, on civil disobedience, and on the politics of class and race as well as of sexuality, for instance, have been centrally enabling for the recent waves of AIDS activism, while the extensive repertoire of intellectual strategies amassed and tested by feminism has been of incalculable benefit to emergent gay and lesbian theory. What these developments return to the lesbians involved in them may include a more richly pluralized range of imaginings of lines of gender and sexual identification.

## *Historicizing Sexuality*

It is indicative of the disjunctive positioning of sexuality in gender criticism that the book that made *sexuality* a usable critical term—the book whose 1978 English publication thus probably offers the best date for the inception of gender criticism in the present sense—should have been itself virtually uninterested in gender, so that the task of fitting analyses of gender and of sexuality to each other has remained a conceptually intractable, hence a vibrant, one. That book, Foucault's *History of Sexuality: An Introduction*, enabled a newly productive discourse of sexuality by clarifying the extent to which modern sexuality is already produced through and indeed as discourse. Foucault first shows that prior understandings of sexuality (including the psychoanalytic and Marxist) have depended heavily on what he calls the "repressive hypothesis," the understanding of sexuality as a quantitative absolute of a distinctive kind of energy, immanent in the individual, whose silencing and regulation is the supposed task of political and cultural power.[2] Although Foucault is far from claiming "that sex has not been prohibited or barred or masked or misapprehended since the classical age" (12), he finds the proliferation of modern discourses of sexuality more striking than their suppression. Or rather, he perceives that there may be no "rupture" at all between "repression and the critical analysis of repression" (10). Responding to the paradox of a society that "speaks verbosely of its own silence, [and] takes great pains to relate in detail the things it does not say" (8), he sees the modern period as defined instead by "the multiplication of discourses concerning sex in the field of exercise of power itself: an institutional incitement to speak about it, and to do so more and more; a determination on the part of agencies of power to hear it spoken about, and to cause *it* to speak through explicit articulation and endlessly accumulated detail" (18). Thus, the would-be-liberatory repressive hypothesis itself comes to be seen as a kind of ruse for mandating ever more of the verbal proliferation that had also gone on before and around it.

Instead of envisioning "power" as something exercised prohibitively from the top of society downward, against a sexuality envisioned as forcing its way upward from the level of the individual, Foucault thus describes both sexuality and power as relations that are incessantly and locally produced and productive at every level of modern culture, through "the task of passing everything having to do with sex through the endless mill of speech" (21). He locates the imperative to utterance in the premodern institutional discourses of law and especially religion (both founded on protocols of confession) but most symptomatically in the newly prestigious ones of psychiatry, psychoanalysis, demography, medicine, and education.

By refusing to distinguish between sexuality "itself" and the discourses that structure, delimit, and (he argues) produce and reproduce it, Foucault undoes the positivist assumption that to write historically about sexuality involves increasingly direct, immediate knowledge or "understanding" of some unchanging sexual essence. On the contrary, he argues that modern sexuality is so intimately entangled with the historically distinctive contexts and structures now called "knowledge" that such knowledge can scarcely be a transparent window onto a separate realm of sexuality: rather, it constitutes that sexuality.

Indeed, he goes beyond this. His ultimate argument is that sexuality per se came into existence, not with the first sexual acts or even sexual prohibitions, but during the long process, culminating in the nineteenth century, by which, as sex learned an infinity of new paths into discourse, the value of truth itself—in particular the truth of individual identity—came to be lodged in the uncovery or expression of the truth of sexuality.[3] That is, what distinguishes modern sexuality from premodern sex is the extreme, indeed unlimited, epistemological pressure everywhere placed on it, and the epistemological centrality in turn accorded it in the wider field of all knowledges and institutions.

No doubt it will be clear why the analysis offered in Foucault's book has proved problematic in relation to other forms of politically oriented analysis. As in most of Foucault's writing, the accounts of agency, or for that matter of causality or change, are elusive at best. His dissolutive insistence on the most local or molecular vantage makes class identity, interest, or struggle—or gender identity, interest, or struggle—extraordinarily difficult to keep in focus. His renunciation of any economic metaphor based on scarcity or deprivation would seem to silence most forms of materialism. His refusal to distinguish between the realms of power and of eroticism is only one example of the resistance his work mounts to moralistic—indeed, to any ethicizing—appropriation; and while fugitive utopian or elegiac moments certainly animate his writing, what is more solidly founded there is an analysis of the utopian impulse as yet another alibi of the repressive hypothesis (6–8).

No doubt it will also be clear, however, why Foucault's volume was to prove so catalytic for literary study. Coarsely put, the work justifies a view of writing as a form of sex, indeed as its most direct form; at the same time, it justifies a view of sexuality as the central repository of the truth-values of modernity. How could these assertions not be deeply energizing for writers and scholars—at least if Foucault is right in his estimate of the prestige, the promise of epistemological force, the "sex appeal" of sexuality in our century? This is also to say, of course, that, far from offering resistance to the modern "scheme for transforming sex into discourse" (20) and "interplay of truth and sex" (57)—processes that Foucault treats as historically unidirectional and inescapable—his book has instead accelerated that trajectory and loaded it with ever greater explanatory force. Rather than attempt vainly to impede it, he has, if successful, merely displaced and repropelled it unpredictably by making less tenable the repressive hypothesis by which its subjects have concealed its itineraries from themselves. "Merely" displaced and repropelled: but that is a more direct path of rhetorical efficacy—of historical intervention, which is to say, in Foucault, of seduction—than most critical works admit to undertaking. Thus, again excitingly for any writer, this work has seemed to offer new accesses to the performative force of writing. In the unmentioned, only slightly displaced continuity between what the book *says* and what it seems to *make happen*, readers can register the gap of unrationalized rhetorical force that the author has already thematized in the distance between what the repressive hypothesis says (sex is forbidden) and the almost hilarious proliferation of sexualized discourse that it in fact effects.

## Specifying Sexuality

So far we have discussed a fairly unified, though vast, field of phenomena around "sexuality" that Foucault's volume at once describes and enacts. But the fact is that the work has not issued in a new movement of "sexuality criticism." Rather, its strongest effects have been radically partial—partial enough, perhaps, even to call into question the mapping of that neatly unified "sexual" field. That is to say, the discursive progeny of *The History of Sexuality* has been, not the mythic "sexuality criticism," but a renewed, ambitious, assertive, splendidly explicit, and unprecedentedly institutionalized movement of gay and lesbian criticism. The metonym for *sexuality* that *The History of Sexuality* effectually installs is *homosexuality*.

Yet the least clear thing about this book is the sense in which it can be said to be a gay book. The author is not explicit about his own sexuality between its covers, and the few, brief discussions of the history of homosexuality per se (the index lists three references) are embedded in discussions of other sexualities or of sexuality more broadly. Take, for instance, the book's most famous and agenda-setting formulation about the history of homosexuality, under the heading "*incorporation of perversions* and a new *specification of individuals*":

> As defined by the ancient civil or canonical codes, sodomy was a category of forbidden acts; their perpetrator was nothing more than the juridical subject of them. The nineteenth-century homosexual became a personage, a past, a case history, and a childhood. . . . [His sexuality] was everywhere present in him: at the root of all his actions because it was their insidious and indefinitely active principle; written immodestly on his face and body because it was a secret that always gave itself away. . . . [T]he psychological, psychiatric, medical category of homosexuality was constituted from the moment it was characterized—Westphal's famous article of 1870 on "contrary sexual sensations" can stand as its date of birth—less by a type of sexual relations than by a certain quality of sexual sensibility. . . . The sodomite had been a temporary aberration; the homosexual was now a species.          (42–43)

Foucault's discussion here of the invention of "the homosexual" is presented as an exemplifying instance of a process of specification, of the emergence of *identities* where previously there had been *acts*, that also included "all those minor perverts whom nineteenth-century psychiatrists entomologized by giving them strange baptismal names: there were Krafft-Ebing's zoophiles and zooerasts, Rohleder's auto-monosexualists; and later, mixoscopophiles, gynecomasts, presbyophiles, sexoesthetic inverts, and dyspareunist women" (43); and those other "figures" and "privileged objects of knowledge," the hysterical woman and the masturbating child (105). The newly reified homosexuality, in short, is but one representative example of "these thousand aberrant sexualities" that came, in their plurality, to define sexuality itself (44).

Yet the discursive context in which Foucault's book does its performative work is not, as it happens, one that prominently features the classification of "these thousand aberrant sexualities." The rhetorical strategy of the book is to allow a reader to imagine, as it were by default, that the nineteenth-century social formations that emerge from its narrative are in essence those of the present day: "We 'Other Victorians,' " the first chapter is entitled. But in the late-twentieth-century scene of the book's actual address, after the lapse of the century elided in "We 'Other Victorians,' " to specify someone's sexuality is not to locate her or him on a map teeming with zoophiles, gynecomasts, sexoesthetic inverts, and so forth. Hysterical women are no longer taxonomized, and to imagine, as nineteenth-century psychiatry did, "the masturbator" as a particular *kind of person* distinct from other kinds of people would seem laughable.[4] This change does not reflect any lightening of the burden of meaning placed on issues of sexual definition since the period described by Foucault. Rather, it reflects an astonishing simplification of the fraught identity categories through which sexuality is conceived. In the late twentieth century, if I ask you what your sexual orientation or sexual preference is, you will understand me to be asking precisely one thing: whether you are homosexual or heterosexual. And whether or not you find these terms inadequate or even irrelevant to your particular desires and velleities, you will be confident in interpreting "sexual orientation" as a reference to that differential and only that.

This startlingly coarse dichotomy effect operates, unremarked, in and on the reading gestalt of Foucault's study. It operates all the more decisively for its silence, however, and in ways that inevitably drive wedges in at the joints between the book's constative and its performative projects. The first dichotomy effect of the book is to install homosexuality in a more than just metonymically representational relation to sexuality as a whole. That the other "species" identities attached to nonconforming sexual desires in the nineteenth century have only lost taxonomic power since then, while homosexual identity has so decisively gained it, implicitly installs homosexual-heterosexual definition as *the* (unasked) question of Foucauldian sexuality; but beyond that, as we must discuss further, Foucault seems to exclude even the hetero side of any homo-hetero dichotomy from the purlieus of sexuality, insofar as sexuality itself is composed of "a world of perversion" (40).

In Foucault, dynamics and meanings attributed to "sexuality" repeatedly act and mean differently when they are read in the light of the homosexual metonym. Foucault's generalizations about sexuality often seem acutely truer when applied to homosexuality—but truer because different and, again, different because truer. He says, for instance, "What is peculiar to modern societies . . . is not that they consigned sex to a shadow existence, but that they dedicated themselves to speaking of it *ad infinitum*, while exploiting it as *the* secret" (35). But what could be less secret than the, as it were, surplus *the*-ness of one particular secret within the open secret of sex, the one named by Christianity and multiple reinscriptions of Western law as the unspeakable itself, *nefandam libidinem*, "that sin which should be neither named nor committed" (qtd. in Boswell 349, 380), the crime "of so black a hue, of so abominable a nature, that we cannot pretend to give any report of it," "so detestable and repugnant to the common feeling of our nature that by no word can it be described without committing an outrage against decency" (qtd. in E. Cohen 200)[5]—videlicet, "the love that dare not speak its name" (Alfred Douglas 28). The particular case of homosexuality here marks an intensification of, but by the same token a certain discontinuity from, the knowing reification "sex."

Similarly, if the regime of sexuality in general is seen by Foucault as instituting knowledge relations that are ultimately productive of that obscure object of desire, the unconscious, how much the truer must this be of the particular knowledge relations around the secret, relentlessly spectacularized, and therefore utterly social space of tacit homosexual-heterosexual definition: the closet? The complex communities of blackmail, complicity, condescension, glamorization, and every sort of cognitive leveraging that are incessantly generated around any closet or the mere space of the possibility of one, enabled in the past century by the newly reduced homo-hetero meaning of "sexual preference," render potent and priceless on many different markets the commodity of ignorance, especially self-ignorance. Foucault writes:

> Thus sex gradually became an object of great suspicion . . . the fragment of darkness that we each carry within us: a general signification, a universal secret, an omnipresent cause, a fear that never ends. . . . We tell it its truth by deciphering what it tells us about that truth; it tells us our own by delivering up that part of it that escaped us. From this interplay there has evolved, over several centuries, a knowledge of the subject; a knowledge not so much of his form, but of that which divides him, determines him perhaps, but above all causes him to be ignorant of himself. . . . Causality in the subject, the unconscious of the subject, the truth of the subject in the other who knows, the knowledge he holds unbeknown to him, all this found an opportunity to deploy itself in the discourse of sex. (69–70)

Here again, however, in narrating what appears to be the demystifyingly historicized story of sexuality per se and its centrality to a Western common sense described in the tropes of Lacanian psychoanalysis, Foucault chooses not to make explicit the privileged referent of his "universal" noun phrases in the locus of a particular homosexual-heterosexual question. His refusal constitutes the closet of homosexual-heterosexual definition *as* "the unconscious" of this text: not in the sense that a certain homo- or heterosexual specificity is cognitively unavailable to the author but in the sense that the text's refusal to verbalize it forces its articulation or denial rather on the reader, whom the text thus interpellates as "the other who knows . . . the knowledge [the text] hold unbeknown to [itself]"; Foucault founds the reader as the knowing Other of "that which divides [the text], determines [it] perhaps, but above all causes [it] to be ignorant of [it]self."

Foucault's analysis of the confessional tradition makes clear, if nothing else did, both how strongly and how resistantly this book is marked by its positioning at the end of the century that stretched between Karl-Heinrich Ulrichs (arguably the first European man to come out as a homosexual) and the gay liberation movement of the late 1960s. Even given the French context of its writing, more urbane and less hygienically dichotomized than the American context of its reading whose effects I here describe, Foucault's account of the confessional owes as much to the sacralized new ritual of coming out as to the psychoanalytic ritual that appears to be its first referent:

> a ritual of discourse in which the speaking subject is also the subject of the statement; . . . a ritual that unfolds within a power relationship . . . ; a ritual in which the truth is corroborated by the obstacles and resistances it has had to surmount in order to be formulated; and finally, a ritual in which the expression alone, independently of its external consequences, produces intrinsic modifications in the person who articulates it.          (61–62)

For Foucault to posit a historical continuity between religious confession and coming out is also, however, to unfold the reasons for his skepticism about the latter act.

> From the Christian penance to the present day, sex was a privileged theme of confession. A thing that was hidden, we are told. But what if, on the contrary, it was what, in a quite particular way, one confessed? Suppose the obligation to conceal it was but another aspect of the duty to admit to it (concealing it all the more and with greater care as the confession of it was more important, requiring a stricter ritual and promising more decisive effects)?          (61)

Characteristically, Foucault dislocates a conventional understanding of the individual will involved in political action. The conditions that make sense of the speech act of coming out, he suggests, actually constitute it as a nominal defiance that marks the place of a more disabling acquiescence: acquiescence in the lie of the repressive hypothesis, that speech and silence are, in the discourses of sexuality, each other's polar opposites.[6] The dignified and, in his terms, more profoundly resistant strategy of this book is to refuse either to conceal or to reveal the "sexuality" (i.e., either the homo- or the heterosexuality) of its speaker and concomitantly to articulate the reader, rather than the text itself, as the agent of the implied *dis*articulation of the supposedly unified field of "sexuality."

## *Performing Foucault*

Post-Foucauldian work in gender theory has both profited and suffered from the ruptures of this founding text. In *Forget Foucault*, Jean Baudrillard remarks that Foucault's followers have tended to ignore how actively his discourse, "a mirror of the powers it describes," proffers disillusion about "the effect of truth it produces"; historians, Baudrillard notes, have instead used it to refine and perpetuate a positivist order of "the truth, nothing but the truth" (10–11). In its own terms, this historical work has been extremely valuable, taking up Foucault's challenge to denaturalize by putting into narrative form present understandings of what sexuality is and entails. Yet every morning's newspaper brings proof of the violently contradictory and volatile energies surrounding the issues of homo- and heterosexual definition and shows over and over again how preposterous must be anybody's urbane pretense at having a clear, simple story to tell about the outlines and meanings of what and who is homosexual and heterosexual. Jeffrey Weeks points out the thoroughgoing, coercive incoherence of the homophobic etiological models that prevail in our culture, according to which homosexuality is classified at the same time as "sin" *and* as "disease," something "you can be born with . . . , seduced into . . . and catch . . . all at the same time" (45). Antihomophobic analysis shares this divided conceptual heritage: the most current theoretical form in which this conflict appears is in the debate in gay and lesbian studies between "social constructionist" and "essentialist" understandings of homo- and heterosexual identities. The conflict, within both homophobic and antihomophobic ideologies, has a long history; it is the most recent link in a more enduring chain of conceptual impasses, a deadlock between what might be called more generally *universalizing* and *minoritizing* accounts of the relation of homosexual desires or persons to the wider field of all desires or persons. Universalizing discourses are those that suggest that every person has the potential for same-sex, as for other-sex, desire or activity; minoritizing ones are those that attribute each of these desires to a fixed, unchangeable segment of the population. Each kind of account can underpin both virulently homophobic and supportively antihomophobic ideological formations. As we have seen, post-Foucauldian historical narratives have seemed to show universalizing paradigms, such as the terribly influential Judaeo-Christian proscription of particular *acts* called "sodomy" (acts that might be performed by anybody), as being displaced after the late nineteenth century by the definition of particular kinds of *persons*, specifically "homosexuals." A classically based but enduring honorific subtradition of durable and significant pedagogic-pederastic *bonds* between men of different ages was also seen as having been displaced by the new, minoritizing view of homosexual identity. It may, however, as we have seen in reading Foucault, be more descriptive to say that since the late nineteenth century the different understandings, contradictory though they are, have coexisted, creating in the space of their contradiction enormous potentials of discursive power.[7]

Other, more theoretically or rhetorically adventurous work "after" Foucault has opened new disciplinary territory by embodying or enacting its contradictions less numbly. This development has been especially necessary, and especially powerful, in the critical analysis of what Foucault made it possible to think of as the "discourse of AIDS." His conceptual centrality to activist understandings of the disease that silenced him is only one of the nightmarish overdeterminations typical of AIDS. Of those overdeterminations, the sickening rhyme between the disease's patterns of depredation and the lines of proscription already drawn by a homophobic and racist culture is the obvious and almost overwhelming one. To dismantle the murderous monolith that AIDS has kept threatening to forge out of the accidents of a virus; out of the established homophobic moralisms of state and church; out of the insatiable modern momentum toward increased surveillance; out of a centuries-old intertextual narrative linkage between fatality and male-male desire; out of the institutional consolidations of advanced medical research and its ideology-drenched forms of figuration; out of an invidious capitalist health-care delivery system; out of the incoherences of modern discourses of addiction and the "foreign substance"; out of imperialist needs to constitute the Third World as at once the incubator of Western illness and the laboratory of Western medicine; out of the vengeful iconographic traditions of both expert technical imaging and popular media—that pressing need has consolidated, under an academic banner of "cultural studies" but by no means confined to academia, a new axis of inquiry involving literary and communications theorists, film theorists, art historians, historians of medicine, artists, film and video makers, feminist community and cultural activists, and AIDS activist groups like ACT UP.

The generative energy that Foucauldian analysis has made available for this form of intellectual-political activism is still, however, intimately inscribed with the contradictory imperatives (of truth, of performance; of proliferation, of specification) transmitted by his work. For example, like thousands of other gay men lost to AIDS, Foucault acquired a sexuality visible to a broad public only when journalism (belatedly) specified his cause of death. It was AIDS that engraved the impoverishing homo-hetero dichotomy most indelibly on the retrospect of his work; slowly but unrelentingly, the obituary process revoked his potent refusal of (what he had figured as) confession. The epistemological stress that Foucault showed to be lodged in modern sexuality has not been dislodged by the crisis of AIDS; rather, it has been yoked violently to an epistemological stress now also attached to death. In the age of AIDS, the hidden sex of the obituary has been framed as a question of authority. In *New York Times* usage throughout the first decade of the epidemic, for example, cause of death was customarily given as an unattributed fact—that is to say, as one transparently known to the *Times*. In obituaries of unmarried, nonclergy men under sixty who didn't die in accidents, however, a "hospital spokesman" or a sibling or partner of the dead person was always specified as the source of information, whether or not AIDS-related illness was given as the cause of death and presumably whether or not it actually was.[8] Precisely by proffering a named authority—by making the authority process, atypically, visible—the *Times* in these cases solicits and tendentiously points the skepticism of obituary readers: a skepticism normal obituary practice repels. It has been characteristic of the discourse around AIDS to be so tied to a truth imperative whose form is intransitive but whose angle is killingly partial. Last year a friend of mine, being treated for a skin rash, came under pressure from his doctors to agree to an HIV-antibody test he had decided he did not want to take. The male doctor sent the female doctor out of the room, the better to set the stage for man-to-man epistemological heroics: "Don't you," the doctor, scalpel-eyed, at last bore down, "want *to know*?" "No, I don't," my friend bravely replied. "I think you're the one who wants *to know*."

Activist analysis can do everything but except itself from these dynamics, a truth dramatized in a pivotal text, *AIDS: Cultural Analysis, Cultural Activism*, edited by Douglas Crimp. This exemplary presentation of AIDS-related cultural radicalism deconstructs and critiques the scientific and media iconography of the disease and suggests strategies of ideological and cultural resistance; authors of the essays include women and men, lawyers, gay theorists, a sex worker-activist, named and unnamed people living with AIDS within and outside of academia, and scholars and artists in the cultural studies fields. The strategic enablements of Foucault's constructivist archaeology are everywhere visible in the volume, beginning with Crimp's introductory manifesto, "AIDS does not exist apart from the practices that conceptualize it, represent it, and respond to it" (3).[9] The anti-idealist motive of Foucault's historicizing work is immensely productive in the book, for example, in Simon Watney's useful formulation:

> AIDS is increasingly being used to underwrite a widespread public ambition
> to erase the distinction between "the public" and "the private," and to establish
> in their place a monolithic and legally binding category—"the family"—under-
> stood as the central term through which the world and the self are henceforth
> to be rendered intelligible.                                                    (86)

And the volume seems to mobilize, by some relatively unproblematized mechanism, a confident sense of political agency (Crimp writes, "We don't need to
transcend the epidemic; we need to end it" [7]); an assertive ideology of rights
(titles include "A Patient's Bill of Rights" and "Further Violations of Our
Rights"); and a protean and utopian sex affirmativeness (the work ends with
Crimp's words "we are now reclaiming our subjectivities, our communities, our
culture . . . and our promiscuous love of sex" [270]).

The dissonant note in the volume, but also its most ambitious theoretical moment and in many ways its effectual centerpiece, is an essay by Leo
Bersani with the characteristically confrontational title "Is the Rectum a
Grave?" Bersani's essay performs skeptical operations on what the volume
otherwise presents as uninterrupted continuities between analysis and politics.
Bersani deprecates as "pastoral" any gay-affirmative polemics, implicitly including virtually all the others in the volume, that are based on an ideology of
sexual "pluralism":

> [T]he rhetoric of sexual liberation in the '60s and '70s . . . received its most
> prestigious intellectual justification from Foucault's call—especially in the first
> volume of his *History of Sexuality*—for a reinventing of the body as a surface
> of multiple sources of pleasure. Such calls, for all their redemptive appeal,
> are, however, unnecessarily and even dangerously tame. The argument for
> diversity has the strategic advantage of making gays seem like passionate
> defenders of one of the primary values of mainstream liberal culture, but to
> make that argument is, it seems to me, to be disingenuous about the relation
> between homosexual behavior and the revulsion it inspires. The revulsion, it
> turns out, is all a big mistake: what we're really up to is pluralism and diversity,
> and getting buggered is just one moment in the practice of those laudable
> humanistic virtues. Foucault could be especially perverse about all this: chal-
> lenging, provoking, and yet, in spite of his radical intentions, somewhat appeas-
> ing in his emphases.                                                          (219)

Bersani, on the contrary, is impatient with any assumption that sex in general
"has anything to do with community or love" (215) or that the desires or habits
of gay men are likely to be especially infused with political or protopolitical
subversions of a status quo. A politically redemptive pluralism has, in his view,
nothing to do with the real force of sex. Stubbornly locating both the cause of
homophobic revulsion and the recalcitrant, invaluably resistant center of male

homosexual desire in a single practice, a single organ, a single role, the receptive position of one man in anal intercourse with another, "a self-shattering solipsistic *jouissance* that drives them apart" (222), Bersani celebrates "the inestimable value of sex as—at least in certain of its ineradicable aspects—*anti*communal, *anti*egalitarian, *anti*nurturing, *anti*loving" (215; emphasis added). "If, as Weeks puts it, gay men 'gnaw at the roots of a male heterosexual identity,' it is not because of the parodistic distance that they take from that identity, but rather because, from within their nearly mad identification with it, *they never cease to feel the appeal of its being violated*" (209).

Bersani frames his essay as an anti-Foucauldian intervention, by way of Freud, on a scene where Foucault's own analyses are viewed—by Bersani, by the other authors—as seamlessly continuous with an ideological praxis also identified with Foucault: the supposed "call for" a redemptive rediscovery of the pluralized body. Some features of Bersani's account, notably its refusal of diachronic historical narrative, do distinguish it sharply from any Foucauldian project. But I am much more impressed by the ways his essay performs, in relation to the volume as a whole, the propulsive rhetorical work of political refusal or blockage whose terms were also set by the same text of Foucault's.

In Bersani's treatment of sexual pluralism, as in Foucault's treatment of the repressive hypothesis, the exposure of a culture-wide lie supposed to inhere in liberal sexual politics is the most relished trope: "In short," as Bersani says at one climactic moment, "to put the matter polemically and even rather brutally, we have been telling a few lies" (206). But these emphatic gestures of disabuse must also entail, by reaction, an equally marked truth effect; and for each theorist, the very strength of the truth effect constitutes an argumentative obliquity. Bersani, after all, is asking readers to imagine a sexuality whose (redemptive) essence ("our primary hygienic practice of nonviolence" [222]) is that, given the irreducible opacity of its relation to the unconscious, it cannot be recuperated for redemptive projects. Meanwhile Foucault suggests a sexuality whose (true) essence is that it has no noncontingent connection to Truth. And Bersani's relation to the repressive hypothesis is in turn as double as Foucault's. His essay begins with the announcement, "There is a big secret about sex: most people don't like it" (197). Like Foucault, he disavows any connection between, on the one hand, the secret *he* has to reveal about sex and, on the other, the conventional exposure of how repressed and repressive are many people's relation to the "smoldering volcanoes" of sexual desire (198). Noting that the aversion to sex he wants to discuss, the one that is not the same as repression, has "both benign and malignant forms" (198), Bersani first specifies that its malignant forms include the homophobic and AIDS-phobic manifestations also documented and decried elsewhere in the volume. The essay then moves to its withering appraisal of the redemptive gay-liberationist rhetoric of sexual pluralism and from there to its own proposal of the "arduous representational discipline" (209) by which gay male desire, at least the specific one in which Bersani is interested, can be accorded its proper value on the basis of its dangerous truth "as a mode of ascesis" (222).

Interestingly, however, Bersani never explicitly identifies the "benign" form of the aversion to sex. Is that more properly represented by the gay liberationist position he sees as a pious, perhaps necessary, lie or by Bersani's own position, which celebrates sex precisely and exclusively for the way it creates, in its participants, aversion—the passionate turning away, the "anti-communal" and "antiloving," the *jouissance* that "drives" men "apart"? The introductory gesture of the essay seems to join speaker and reader in an enunciatory compact of people who "like" sex against some distinguishable majority of those who "don't." But what's "like" got to do with it? And what reader, on Bersani's rebarbative showing, could fully identify with her assigned, confidently sex-affirmative place in this schema? It seems as though, to the degree that the essay is structured by the revelation of the "secret" that sex is commonly aversive, it makes a polemical point (the rather vulgar one that the repressive hypothesis so regularly enables: one's opponents can't say the truth because they are not truly sexual) and at the same time a theoretical point that quite undoes the presumptive community of its address. It positions a reader, if compellingly, incoherently. By the same token, although Bersani insists that the meaning of a particular sexual act is of far more consequence than gay life-style or identity, concepts with which he is especially impatient, the rhetoric by which he sets out to unmask that normalizing minority identity depends, as it happens, on constant appeals to a conventional, identity-based semiotic presumed to be internal to each of his readers.[10] Note, for instance, his use of the second person (flattering? threatening?—full, in any event, of unspoken identity presumption) in describing "the classic put-down: the butch number swaggering into a bar in a leather get-up opens his mouth and sounds like a pansy, takes you home, where the first thing you notice is the complete works of Jane Austen, gets you into bed, and—well, you know the rest" (208).

"And this," Bersani continues, "brings us back to the question not of the reflection or expression of politics in sex, but rather of the extremely obscure process by which sexual pleasure *generates* politics" (208). To trace these multidirectional dynamics discredits Bersani's essay no more than it does Foucault's book. On the contrary, what would most discredit the argument of either would be the very possibility of a self-transparent, performatively inert relation among the politics of sexuality, the truth-claiming language in which sexual epistemologies may be explored, and the experiential material that gets called sexuality itself. What, rather, I hope the terms I have assembled account for is a more unexpected effect: that, far from discrediting either its own argument or (more predictably) the impugned politics of the rest of the collection in which it appears, Bersani's essay, bursting as it is with transverse aggressions, seems to have served for many demanding readers to *legitimate* the project of gay-liberation-based AIDS cultural criticism represented by this important volume. If that is so, it is not, I think, because the essay offers the generalized spectacle of what Anthony Trollope would call "moderate schism" (169–70; see also D. A. Miller, *Novel* 114–39). The validation that Bersani offers is far more substantial than a mere staging of internal controversy to confirm the elasticity and differentiability of a fairly new political movement. He makes one assertion to whose truth the very frustrations of the felt pressure toward programmatic clarity all minister: each eclipse, collapse, or collision of authorial or readerly positionings makes more serious and present to the reader that extreme obscurity, noted by Bersani, in the "process by which sexual pleasure *generates* politics." "While it is indisputably true that sexuality is always being politicized, the ways in which *having sex* politicizes are highly problematical" (206). It seems that to thematize, and at the same time but unrationalizably to dramatize, the deep epistemological fractures that necessarily gape under the pressure of a new political need and possibility may actually render that possibility more intimately recognizable. It may do so especially to an audience whose present need for both sexual theory and sexual activism is tied so closely to our repeated, publicly specularized, politically motivating, shared but at some level immiscibly private and implacably privative experiences of loss, mourning, and dread.

## *Denaturalizing Heterosexuality*

In volume 1 of *The History of Sexuality*, Foucault performs the emergence of homo-hetero as *the* defining axis of modern sexuality silently. But he does explain there how asymmetrical the speech relations around the two poles of that axis have become and must presumably remain, in his description of "a centrifugal movement," in the eighteenth and nineteenth centuries, "with respect to heterosexual monogamy":

> Of course, the array of practices and pleasures continued to be referred to it as their internal standard; but it was spoken of less and less, or in any case with a growing moderation. Efforts to find out its secrets were abandoned; nothing further was demanded of it than to define itself from day to day. The legitimate couple, with its regular sexuality, had a right to more discretion. It tended to function as a norm, one that was stricter, perhaps, but quieter. . . .
>
> Although not without delay and equivocation, the natural laws of matrimony and the immanent rules of sexuality began to be recorded on two separate registers. (38–40)

Thus, since Foucault defines modern sexuality as the most intensive site of the demand for, and detection or discursive production of, truth, it seems as though this silent, normative, uninterrogated "regular" heterosexuality may not function as sexuality at all. Think of how a central concept like public/private is organized so as to preserve for heterosexuality the unproblematicalness, the apparent naturalness, of its discretionary choice between display and concealment: "Public" means the space where cross-sex couples *may*, whenever they feel like it, display affection freely, while same-sex couples *must* always conceal it. "Privacy," to the degree that it is a right codified in United States law, is differentially centered on the married, cross-sex couple's protection from scrutiny, a scrutiny to which (since *Bowers v. Hardwick*) same-sex relations by contrast are unbendingly subject. Thus heterosexuality is consolidated as the *opposite* of the "sex" whose secret, Foucault says, "the obligation to conceal ... was but another aspect of the duty to admit to" (61). To the degree that heterosexuality does not function as a sexuality, however, there are stubborn barriers to making it accountable, to making it so much as visible, in the framework of Foucauldian projects of historicizing and hence denaturalizing sexuality. Especially since Jonathan Ned Katz's notation of the relative novelty of the word *heterosexuality* in its current sense—his notation, in particular, that the term postdates the coinage *homosexuality*—it has been widely felt that a history of heterosexuality was a necessary and possible project (147–50, 232n; for a thorough overview of the vexed chronology of the two terms, see Halperin 155n1, 2, 158–59n17). My impression is, however, that it has proved a theoretically recalcitrant one and that it will continue to do so. Yet the work of undoing the exemptive discretionary privilege of heterosexuality is no less pressing than other tasks of gay and lesbian critique.

Foucault says that, after the turn of the century, "if regular sexuality happened to be questioned ... it was through a reflux movement, originating in ... peripheral sexualities" (39); the same is true for future interrogations of normative heterosexuality, interrogations that can and (I would even say) must begin from, and perhaps return to, the definitional centers of the achieved and loved "perversion." It must also begin from gay and lesbian studies. My own instinct is that, in the discursive ecology of which we may take *The History of Sexuality* as a model—an ecology structured on the one hand by a plurality of perverse histories and local possibilities, on the other by an abyssally reductive homosexual-heterosexual divide that it seems impossible to stop performing— it will be productive for this purpose to go back and look further at the matrix of perversions that have *not* become distinct modern identities. We might ask, at the same time, why they have not and how they do function within and around the identities, and in particular the heterosexuality, violently carved out from among them. I make this suggestion not in order to resuscitate a "utopian" past of undifferentiated sexual plurality, which never existed and whose evocation on this scene tends most often to be a repressive evasion of the modern gay or lesbian subject, nor in order to invest heterosexuality with a speciously perverse glamor, designed to recruit impressionable youth into that sad, lonely, degrading, and ultimately dangerous life-style. Rather, I am interested in adding to the specificity and accountability of our understanding both of cross-sex possibility and of the heterosexist imposition.

As I have said, I don't think any denaturalizing project concerning heterosexuality can be conceptually simple, nor are any of its possible motivations likely to be perspicuous. Psychoanalysis—which, as Jean Laplanche explains, shows "perversion" to be already internal to the origin of any sexual desire—offers to teach us many useful techniques for this project (23–25); but to the degree that it is non- or even antihistorical, its denaturalizing work tends to perpetuate an atmosphere of chronic scandal or pathos instead of suggesting any possibility of change. At the same time, making heterosexuality historically visible is difficult because, under its institutional pseudonyms such as Inheritance, Marriage, Dynasty, Domesticity, and Population, heterosexuality has been permitted to masquerade so fully as History itself—when it has not been busy impersonating Romance. And these holding-company names accrue legitimacy by remaining in undefined and shifting relation to anything one might call heterosexuality-as-sexuality.

At present "the family" and "the homosexual" are functioning as each other's principal defining Others, obviously in an intimate relation to the desperate and murderous denials and enforcements around AIDS in this culture. The relation of domesticity to gender is also, as it has long been, one replete with constitutive contradictions, perhaps best epitomized in Catharine MacKinnon's trenchant dictum: "Privacy is everything women as women have never been allowed to be or have; at the same time the private is everything women have been equated with and defined in terms of *men's* ability to have" ("Feminist Jurisprudence" 656–67). But the ecology of this, too, is subject to change. If we ask, for instance, why the issue of gay and lesbian marriage should be surfacing so strongly just now, in the early 1990s, as a potentially feasible, and to some a desirable, program of our politics, the answer will have much to do with the effects of AIDS, certainly, but also perhaps increasingly to do with the untheorized, politically still unarticulated but steady and growing pressure being brought to bear on all urban lives by homelessness (see Stoddard's and Ettelbrick's discussions of the current salience of the gay-marriage issue). It seems telling that the movement for recognition of domestic partners, long oriented toward and progressing slowly around struggles over health benefits and bereavement leave, should have scored major court victories rather on the issue of rent control and eviction. If, as it is hard to help fearing, "the homosexual" is being replaced by "the homeless" as the definitional other of domesticity, as the abyssal specter against which the name of the family and the name of marriage are to be brandished, then this may be a moment in which the tacit, exclusive identification of "the domestic" with "the heterosexual" may be effectively challenged. But such a challenge might depend on exacerbating other splits also internal to the community of those identified by sexual dissidence: on excluding the poor, the racially marked, or those of us whose "primary attachments" may be plural in number, experimental in form, or highly permeable. As it happens, the most formally innovative writing now being done in gender and sexuality theory—I mean, for example, the work of Cherríe Moraga and Audre Lorde—is stimulated by just the multiplicity of these definitional fractures. To calibrate the costs and consequences of such a challenge is one of several urgent projects that require new terms for analyzing class and race, along with sexuality, as—in the fertile sense that "gender studies" makes possible—what isn't gender.

## *Professional Boundaries, Political Connections, Erogenous Zones*

The difficult politics and erotics of representation, as all of us know, hardly stop short inside the threshold of the text. Although the present account of gender criticism has not focused, as it might have, on direct applications to readings of literary texts, I have meant it to suggest several distinctive ways in which gay-lesbian inquiry has raised specifically representational issues that traverse, exceed, and alter the definitional boundaries of our discipline. I turn now, in conclusion, to the representational issues raised by its presence, along with that of other explicitly political projects, within the university.

It is very hard to come up with useful images for the synecdochic relation of academic institutions to the larger world of productive institutions in our culture. One important thing about academia is how drastically it tends to condense. The very name *university* conveys its ambition to represent something huge in a disproportionately tiny space: a space that thereby tends to be rendered, of course, unreal or hyperreal, so that the desublimation of its untransformed relations across the local "real"—for instance, its infrastructural labor relations, its health-care provisions, its effects on real estate values and municipal tax bases, its symbiosis with various industries and communities—requires repeated wrenching acts of re-recognition. Moreover, the condensation that the university effects on its universe is not only uneven but tendentious, partial, and intermittent in its coverage: increasingly important segments of the society can seem to escape its purview entirely.

Beyond being condensed, and thus tending toward the unreal or the hyperreal, in its synecdochic relation to the universe it claims to represent, the university is also in an anachronistic relation to it. People may choose an academic vocation, not in the first place because of their cognitive talents or because they have particular political values or identifications, but because academic labor, at least at its most privileged and visible levels, is still in many ways so amazingly unrationalized. Compared with industrial or with other service labor—even compared with the other professions—our fealty to the stop clock and to time discipline, to the bottom line of profitable or even of quantifiable results, to the public and private stresses of office or factory inter- action, to the suppression or denial of affective charge, and in particular to the forcible alienation of our labor in the service of projects conceived by and for someone else is still, for some, almost miraculously attenuated. Projects conceived in relation to identity politics, such as feminist or gay-lesbian inquiry, are continually testing and redefining the limits of such a professional exemp- tion. Delusive as some of these freedoms may be, the space of work for at least some in this industry can seem strikingly close to an idealized preindustrial workspace of task orientation, work continuity, and the relatively meaningful choice of tasks based on perceptible need and aptitude.

The complex temporality of our representational space has a variety of consequences. First, and most obviously, it means that academia and aca- demics are always almost definitionally in danger of embodying various simply nostalgic or reactionary politics. Second, it means that the many, very distinctly rationalized and alienating aspects of academic labor, which form all or most of the conditions of work for many academics, always risk being occluded or mystified by this more elegiac ideal. Third, it of course marks the vulnerability of this space to the scouring triumphalism of capitalist rationalization; while the relatively decentered structure and the diffuse status economy of United States higher education pose some resistance to our instant, wholesale Thatch- erization, this state's hypersensitivity to interventions into the discourses of gender and of homo- and heterosexuality, in particular, may represent the threshold of an extreme risk. Fourth, and more encouragingly, our anomalous temporality is one of the things that allows academia to function as a kind of cognitive gene pool of precisely anachronistic ideas, impulses, or information that, unusable under one set of political circumstances, might be preserved in this relatively unrationalized space to emerge with a potentially priceless relevance under changed circumstances. And fifth, I think many of us are very responsive to the utopian potential of this vision of relatively unalienated, sometimes collaborative labor. No less dangerously grounded in the retrospect than any other utopian formation, it can nevertheless afford energies and leverages for change both within and around the institution.[11]

In an influential recent essay, "Theory, Pragmatisms, and Politics," Cornel West has written that "to be an engaged progressive intellectual is to be a critical organic catalyst whose vocation is to fuse the best of the life of the mind from within the academy with the best of the organized forces for greater democracy and freedom from outside the academy" (34–35). An image that keeps recurring to me, as a way of recording both the extreme condensation and the extreme temporal discontinuities by which our profession represents the world around it, is that of the progressive academy as one of several erogenous zones for our culture.[12] This image seems thematically available to me, no doubt, as it might not to some "otherwise engaged" intellectuals, because the path of my own engagement travels so much through the politics of gender and sexuality. Even for other political projects, however, the erogenous-zone metaphor may usefully record some of the representational circumferences across which we struggle to orient ourselves. For example, Naomi Schor has identified the clitoris as the appropriate figure, in rhetorical theory, for the trope of synecdoche itself, a trope that she argues may be retrieved from the gender-binarized structuralist and poststructuralist conflation of all figures into (an often phallically figured) metaphor and (an often vaginally figured) metonymy ("Female Paranoia" 219). The clitoris also makes literal, as for that matter may mouth, anus, and some other zones chargeable as erotic, the space of an irreducible difference from procreation that homosexuality may be in the best position to represent, as well, for other sexualities—perhaps even, if it can stand for a displacing resistance to the untransformed reproduction of labor, for other institutions.[13]

Emily Dickinson, in her underquoted poem 1377, writes:

> Forbidden Fruit a flavor has
> That lawful Orchards mocks—
> How luscious lies within the Pod
> The Pea that Duty locks—
>                             (592)

In this reading,[14] of course, the P that Duty locks would have to stand, in the first place, for the Profession or its Professional—the highly innervated node that might be hot enough to, as West puts it, "fuse" an individual history with a collective future, and the mind of the academy with (implicitly) the body of the political. The P could also stand for the locked potentials of pleasure whose release in the form of unalienated labor would signify a decisive rupture in the arid economy of our current surround.

I value the erogenous image, however, also because it records, in addition to desire and pleasure, the equally strong pressure of the nondiscretionary or even the compelled in any of our relations to political life. The local, intense, irrepressible throb that marks a site of "sexuality" seems in a way to militate against West's judicial, almost connoisseurial program of fusing "the *best* of the life of the mind from within the academy with the *best* of the organized forces for greater democracy and freedom from outside the academy." His formulation seems to suggest an Apollonian—one might say Arnoldian—

political privilege of distinction that must, after all, be thought to inhere in the life of the mind. I would be surprised, and indeed disturbed, to learn that most of us use such methods to arrive at the politics that really motivate us or, for that matter, at our truly productive critical projects and insights. If each of us held an open competition of politics and ideas in the privacy of our mind, choosing *the best* and following it both within and outside the academy, then we would be as likely as not to find an Edward Said in the vanguard of feminist theory, an Elaine Showalter in the private councils of the PLO. Or, for that matter, some new movement of an even more right-thinking and ideologically sound description could sweep into view tomorrow—indeed, a new one could sweep into view every year—and each of us would perforce enroll in its train. Of course, the degree to which some such labile economy *does* obtain marks at the same time a commoditized faddishness, a valuable sinuosity, and a very considerable level of underlying privilege and entitlement that do characterize a certain set of critical milieus. But the truth is, we forge our politics out of the impacted, anachronistic residuum of who we are and what we need, even as we do understand who we are and refine the art of our necessities under the pressure of our politics and theory.

This is hardly to say that our theory or politics can be read in any transparent way from anything so static or given as to be called *identity*. If gay and lesbian theory demonstrates any one thing, it demonstrates—more radically even than can the theory of gender or race—how difficult, distortive, and incoherent, though at the same time how profoundly consequential, are such processes as the self-assignment or allo-assignment of a definitional identity within a hierarchized system of specification. I would be the last critic to argue that the rigid notation of gender, class, race, sexuality could map the important data for anyone's locus of creativity and struggle. Yet the fact remains that each person, like each institution, *has* such loci of maximum potential and has them characteristically. Our paths to them are very particular paths, and often—perhaps always—oblique; if cognitive work can expand or transform them, the process is a slow one that goes finger's breadth by finger's breadth. It is a rare figure (one thinks, perhaps, of Lorde) who has managed to feel and think a way through to an experiential understanding that makes more than one politics, one's own politics. The process cannot be an a priori one for the approach to any new or other politics.

One consequence of this condensation and embeddedness is the extreme difficulty, not at all to say impossibility, of doing or thinking coalition politics at more than a superficial level. A second consequence, one that has been severely underestimated by the current academy, is simply the recalcitrance of the barrier that a relative privilege in our mode of labor is inevitably going to oppose to most of our investment of real creativity, courage, and steadfastness in a class-based political analysis. Another consequence, however, is the very possibility of any political commitment that can be responsive to a strong theoretical moment but whose energies, needs, and desires (and for this we are very fortunate) can also, in altered forms, outlast it.[15]

### Notes

[1]I do not, of course, intend to suggest that lesbians are less likely than persons of any other sexuality to contract HIV infection when they engage in the (quite common) acts that can transmit the virus with a person (and there are many, including lesbians) who already carries it. In this particular paradigm clash between a discourse of sexual identity and a discourse of sexual acts, the former alternative is uniquely damaging. No one should wish to reinforce the myth that the epidemiology of AIDS is a matter of discrete "risk groups" rather than of particular acts that can call for particular forms of prophylaxis. That myth is dangerous to self-identified or publicly identified gay men and drug users because it scapegoats them, and it is dangerous to everyone else because it discourages those outside the "risk groups" from protecting themselves and their partners. But for a variety of reasons, the incidence of AIDS among lesbians has indeed been lower than that among many other groups.

[2]According to the repressive hypothesis, the history of sexuality could only be that of the "negative relation" between power and sex, the "insistence of the rule," the "cycle of prohibition," the "logic of censorship," and the "uniformity of the apparatus" of scarcity and prohibition: "Whether one attributes it to the form of the prince who formulates rights, of the father who forbids, of the censor who enforces silence, or of the master who states the law, in any case one schematizes power in a juridical form, and one defines its effects as obedience" (Foucault, *History* 82–85).

[3]About early psychiatric investigations, for instance, Foucault writes: "The important thing is that they constructed around and apropos of sex an immense apparatus for producing truth, even if this truth was to be masked at the last moment. The essential point is that sex was not only a matter of sensation and pleasure, of law and taboo, but also of truth and falsehood, that the truth of sex became something fundamental, useful, or dangerous, precious or formidable: in short, that sex was constituted as a problem of truth. What needs to be situated, therefore, is not the threshold of a new rationality whose discovery was marked by Freud—or someone else—but the progressive formation (and also the transformations) of that 'interplay of truth and sex' which was bequeathed to us by the nineteenth century, and which we may have modified, but . . . have not rid ourselves of" (*History* 56–57).

[4]In "Jane Austen and the Masturbating Girl," I discuss further the relation between the history of masturbation and that of homosexual and heterosexual identities.

[5]Boswell quotes a legal document dated 533 and a 1227 letter from Pope Honorius III. Cohen quotes press characterizations of the accusations in the 1810 Vere Street scandal, given in Trumbach's *Sodomy Trials*.

[6]Foucault comments: "Silence itself—the things one declines to say, or is forbidden to name, the discretion that is required between different speakers—is less the absolute limit of discourse, the other side from which it is separated by a strict boundary,

than an element that functions alongside the things said, with them and in relation to them within over-all strategies. There is no binary division to be made between what one says and what one does not say; we must try to determine the different ways of not saying such things, how those who can and those who cannot speak of them are distributed, which type of discourse is authorized, or which form of discretion is required in either case. There is not one but many silences, and they are an integral part of the strategies that underlie and permeate discourses" (*History* 27).

[7] I make this argument much more fully in *Epistemology of the Closet*. We have recently witnessed a perfect example of this potent incoherence in an anomalous legal situation of gay people and acts in this country: The Supreme Court in *Bowers v. Hardwick* has notoriously left the individual states free to prohibit any *acts* that they wish to define as "sodomy," by whomsoever performed, with no fear at all of impinging on any rights safeguarded by the Constitution. At the same time, a panel of the Ninth Circuit Court of Appeals ruled in 1988 (in *Sergeant Perry J. Watkins v. United States Army*) that homosexual *persons*, as a particular kind of person, are entitled to Constitutional protections under the equal protection clause.

[8] For instance, on a day chosen at random, a married male law professor of 61 "died of a heart attack"; a twice-married 91-year-old female art collector, like an 85-year-old male ex–Cambodian Premier, simply "died"; a married male author of 74 "died of heart failure"; a married 86-year-old male executive "died of congestive heart failure"; an 86-year-old male dentist with a son and three grandchildren "died of a heart attack," as did a 70-year-old married male probation officer; a 91-year-old married male surgeon "died after a long illness" and so did another man, a 51-year-old Zairian band leader with 17 children; an unmarried but 90-year-old male jazz drummer "died of kidney failure"; and a Polish political leader who was only 47, but who had a wife and son, "died of bladder cancer." But in the obituary of a 30-year-old actor, survived by his mother, grandmother, and two brothers, "a spokeswoman for the New York Shakespeare Festival, Barbara Carroll, said he died of a heart attack" (*New York Times*, 18 Oct. 1989:11). Interestingly, this invidiously differential practice seems to have changed literally overnight (on Sunday, 10 June 1990): since Monday, 11 June 1990, it has evidently been *Times* practice for all obituaries to specify the source of information about the cause of death. On 14 June 1990, for example, reports of non-HIV-related deaths were attributed to a "mortuary spokeswoman" or to the "family" or (in two cases) to the "wife" of the deceased; the epistemological status of these reported deaths is no longer different from that of an advertising executive who "died of complications from AIDS, a company spokesman said" (B13). The net result seems to be that AIDS has installed an evidentiary skepticism in the media's views of any report of death.

[9] Crimp continues: "This assertion does not contest the existence of viruses, antibodies, infections, or transmission routes. Least of all does it contest the reality of illness, suffering, and death. What it *does* contest is the notion that there is an underlying reality of AIDS, upon which are constructed the representations, or the culture, or the politics of AIDS" (3).

[10] "What," Bersani retorts against a comment quoted from Foucault, "is '*the* gay life-style'? . . . More importantly, can a nonrepresentable form of relationship really be more threatening than the representation of a particular sexual act . . . ?" (220). As

evidence for one of his assertions, however—one that contradicts the theory he has just been quoting from several other gay men—he offers the phrase "All gay men know this" (208).

[11] Clearly, however, the very force of this utopian investment can sometimes work against what many would ordinarily think of as its guiding political principles. On hiring and graduate-admissions committees, for instance, I see in myself as well as in my colleagues how much this utopian investment in a potential for unalienated intellectual-affective labor and collaboration leads us to think in individualistic terms about choosing potential soul mates for ourselves or finding companions for our deepest projects, where in any other context of economically consequential personnel decisions we would view very skeptically choices that did not have the firmest demographic or statistical support. It is this mechanism and our institutional defenses of it, of course, that have made academia much slower than many other industries to show significant numerical effects under equal-opportunity laws. The possibility that mechanistic and number-based change may precede and even be a prerequisite for deeply rooted imaginative change can be difficult for us to conceive; it becomes even more difficult as we become more involved with the sense of our profession as a space that could be at once representative, exceptional, and transformational.

[12] This image was suggested to me by Karen Swann's discussion (in a personal communication) of feminist criticism as an erogenous zone for the larger project of literary criticism.

[13] I might make explicit, too, that I find I can only hear West's evocative phrase "critical organic catalyst" as a weirdly elongated way of pronouncing "clitoris."

[14] It was Paula Bennett who, in an important article, first called attention to the clitoral salience of this poem.

[15] Some portions of this chapter are adapted, with the permission of the University of California Press, from the introduction to my *Epistemology of the Closet* (1990).

## Selected Bibliography

Bartlett, Neil. *Who Was That Man? A Present for Mr. Oscar Wilde*. London: Serpent's Tail, 1988.
  An openly performative experiment in first-person critical writing that offers, at the same time, the best archaeology now available of late-Victorian male homosexual experience.

Bray, Alan. *Homosexuality in Renaissance England*. London: Gay Men's, 1982.
  The most theoretically interesting and productive attempt so far to apply Foucauldian paradigms to pre-eighteenth-century European male sexuality.

Butler, Judith. *Gender Trouble: Feminism and the Subversion of Identity*. New York: Routledge, 1989.
  A formidable demonstration of how densely the concept of gender itself (in both philosophical and psychoanalytic traditions) is imbricated with heterosexist presumptions and histories.

Crimp, Douglas, ed. *AIDS: Cultural Analysis, Cultural Activism*. Cambridge: MIT P, 1988.
The most ambitious collection of cultural criticism on AIDS.
de Lauretis, Teresa. "Sexual Indifference and Lesbian Representation." *Theatre Journal* 40 (1988): 155–77.
A sophisticated attempt to develop lesbian theory that has antiracist emphases at its center. Leans heavily on Irigaray for basic premises.
Foucault, Michel. *The History of Sexuality: An Introduction*. Trans. Robert Hurley. New York: Pantheon, 1978. Vol. 1 of *The History of Sexuality*. 3 vols. 1978–86.
The most influential of the texts at the origin of constructivist views of sexuality.
Halley, Janet E. "The Politics of the Closet: Towards Equal Protection for Gay, Lesbian, and Bisexual Identity." *UCLA Law Review* 36.5 (1989) 915–76.
A particularly powerful synthesis of theoretical and legal issues involving representation and self-representation of sexualities.
Irigaray, Luce. *This Sex Which Is Not One*. Trans. Catherine Porter, with Carolyn Burke. Ithaca: Cornell UP, 1985.
The locus classicus of a descriptively powerful but dehistoricizing and perhaps more than potentially homophobic understanding of Western culture as a male "hom(m)o-sexual monopoly." Essays offer resources for necessary feminist critiques of psychoanalytic and deconstructive understandings of women's sexuality and pleasure.
Lorde, Audre. *Sister Outsider: Essays and Speeches*. Trumansburg: Crossing, 1984.
A collection by the poet, activist, and writer of discursive prose who most persuasively presents the promise of a critical understanding of the intersection of plural axes of oppression including gender, sexuality, and race.
Moraga, Cherríe. *Loving in the War Years: Lo que nunca paso por sus labios*. Boston: South End, 1983.
Vibrantly complex and formally daring meditations (essays and poetry, in English and Spanish) on intersections of lesbian with Chicana identity.
Rich, Adrienne. "Compulsory Heterosexuality and Lesbian Existence." *Women, Sex, and Sexuality*. Ed. Catharine R. Stimpson and Ethel Spector Person. Chicago: U of Chicago P, 1980. 62–91.
The germinal and controversial essay in which a "lesbian continuum" of all bonds among women is posited.
Rubin, Gayle. "Thinking Sex: Notes for a Radical Theory of the Politics of Sexuality." Vance 267–319.
Written in response to the "sex wars." Begins to lay some theoretical foundations for an analysis of sexuality hypothetically distinct from that of gender

(though its rights-based manifesto may be at cross-purposes with its nominally Foucauldian analytic framework).

—. "The Traffic in Women: Notes on the 'Political Economy' of Sex." *Toward an Anthropology of Women*. Ed. Rayna R. Reiter. New York: Monthly Review, 1975. 157–210.
Synthesizes work of Lévi-Strauss, Freud, Lacan, and Engels to posit a transhistorical paradigm of the male traffic in women. Originated the concept of the "sex/gender system."

Sedgwick, Eve Kosofsky. *Between Men: English Literature and Male Homosocial Desire*. New York: Columbia UP, 1985.
Attempts, beginning with the paradigm of Rubin's "Traffic in Women," to historicize questions of male homo/heterosexual definition and homophobia and to place antihomophobic analysis at the center of feminist theoretical agendas.

—. *Epistemology of the Closet*. Berkeley: U of California P, 1990.
Presents the hypothesis that virtually every important epistemological crux in twentieth-century Western thought has been marked by the centrality and the intractable conceptual incoherence of issues of modern male homo/heterosexual definition.

Vance, Carole S., ed. *Pleasure and Danger: Exploring Female Sexuality*. Boston: Routledge, 1984.
Proceedings of the famous Barnard Conference, whose disruption was a climactic event in the struggles between sex-radical feminists and antipornography, antisadomasochism feminists in the early 1980s. An influential collection in putting sexuality and pleasure at the center of certain, highly contested feminist agendas.

Yingling, Thomas E. *Hart Crane and the Homosexual Text: New Thresholds, New Anatomies*. Chicago: U of Chicago P, 1990.
Offers new, widely generalizable models for undoing the suppression of gay stylistics and thematics in opaque modernist literary texts.

# African American Criticism

## HENRY LOUIS GATES, JR.

### I

For those of us who were students or professors of African American literature in the late 1960s or through the 1970s, it is a thing of wonder to behold the various ways in which our field and the works we explicate have moved, if not exactly from the margins to the center of the profession, at least from defensive postures to a generally accepted validity. Few, if any, scholars of African American literature encounter today the sort of hostility, skepticism, and suspicion the field elicited a quarter-century ago. Accordingly, the status of black literature within the academy has also changed dramatically. Courses and programs in the field are now commonplace: African American literature has never been more widely taught or analyzed. We have come a long way since the early 1920s, when Charles Eaton Burch (1891–1941), as chair of the department of English at Howard University, introduced into the curriculum a course entitled Poetry and Prose of Negro Life, and a long way, too, from the middle 1930s, when James Weldon Johnson (1871–1938), then the Adam K. Spence Professor of Creative Literature and Writing at Fisk University, became the first scholar to teach black literature at a white institution, New York University, where he delivered an annual lecture series on "Negro literature."

What has happened within the profession of literature to elevate the status of African American and other "minority" texts? It is difficult to be certain about the reasons for the heightened popularity of any area of study. Nevertheless, we can isolate several factors that, in retrospect, seem to bear directly both on the growth of student interest in these fields and on the vast increase in the number of teachers attempting to satisfy student demand.

One factor would seem to be the women's movement within African American literature. Since 1970, when Toni Morrison's *The Bluest Eye*, Alice Walker's *Third Life of George Copeland*, and Toni Cade Bambara's anthology *The Black Woman* were published, black women writers have produced a remarkable number of novels and books of poetry. Walker, Morrison, Gloria Naylor, and, in poetry, Rita Dove have won Pulitzer prizes and National and American Book awards; before 1970, Ralph Ellison and Gwendolyn Brooks were the only black writers who had been accorded these honors. The works by black women novelists, especially Walker and Morrison, have sold in record numbers, in part because of an expanded market that includes white and black feminists as well as the general black studies readership. What has happened, clearly, is that the feminist movement, in the form of women's studies on campus and the abandonment of quotas for the admission of women to heretofore elite male institutions, has had a direct impact on what we might think of as black women's studies. Indeed, black studies and women's studies have met on the common terrain of black women's studies, ensuring a larger audience for black women authors than ever before.

Scholars of women's studies have accepted the work and lives of black women as their subject matter in a manner unprecedented in the American academy. Perhaps only the Anglo-American abolitionist movement was as cosmopolitan as the women's movement has been in its concern for the literature of blacks. Certainly, Richard Wright, Ralph Ellison, and James Baldwin did not become the subjects of essays, reviews, books, and dissertations as quickly as Morrison and Walker have. Zora Neale Hurston, of course, attracted her largest following only after 1975, precisely when other black women authors rose to prominence. The women's studies movement in the academy has given new life to African American studies, broadly conceived.

Forecasts of the death of African American studies abounded in 1975. Although the field had benefited from a great outburst of interest in the late 1960s, when student protests on its behalf were at their noisiest, it had begun to stagnate by the mid-1970s, as many ill-conceived, politically overt programs collapsed or were relegated to an even more marginal status than they had had before. American publishers, ever sensitive to their own predictions about market size, became reluctant to issue works in this field. Morrison, however, herself an editor at Random House, continued to publish texts by black women and men, from Africa and the Caribbean as well as from the United States. The burgeoning sales of books by black women, for many of whom Morrison served as editor, began to reverse the trends that by 1975 had jeopardized the survival of black studies. Morrison's own novels, especially *Tar Baby* (1981), which led to a cover story in *Newsweek*, were pivotal in redefining the market for books in black studies. The popularity of—and the controversy surrounding—Michele Wallace's *Black Macho and the Myth of the Superwoman* (1978) and Ntozake Shange's *For Colored Girls Who Have Considered Suicide* (1977) also generated a great amount of interest in the writings of black women.

Simultaneously, within the academy, scholars of black literature were undertaking important projects that would bear directly on the notion of their field. Whereas in the late 1960s, when black studies formally entered the curriculum, history had been the predominant subject, a decade later, literary studies had become the "glamour" area of black studies. While the black arts movement of the mid-1960s had declared literature, and especially poetry, to be the cultural wing of the black power revolution, it had little effect on the curricula offered by traditional departments of English. This intervention would be dependent on the studies produced by a group of younger scholars— Donald Gibson, June Jordan, Houston A. Baker, Jr., Arnold Rampersad, Geneva Smitherman, Mary Helen Washington, Carolyn Fowler, R. Baxter Miller, and others—many of whom had been trained by an older generation of African Americanists. That generation included such literary critics as Charles Davis, Michael G. Cooke, Darwin Turner, and J. Saunders Redding, some of whom had been recruited to previously segregated schools in response to student demands for the creation of black studies.

For a variety of reasons, and in a remarkable variety of ways, these scholars began to theorize about the nature and function of black literature and its criticism and, simultaneously, to train an even younger generation of students. While it is difficult, precisely, to characterize their interests, it seems safe to say that they shared a concern with the literariness of African American works, as they wrestled to make these texts a proper object of analysis within traditional departments of English. Whereas black literature had generally been taught and analyzed through an interdisciplinary methodology, in which sociology and history had virtually blocked out the literariness of the black text, these scholars, after 1975, began to argue for the explication of the formal properties of writing. If the "blackness" of a text was to be found anywhere, they argued, it would be in the practical uses of language. So at a time when theorists of European and English-language literature were offering critiques of Anglo-American formalism, scholars of black literature, responding to the history of their own discipline, found it radical to teach formal methods of reading.

Of the several gestures that were of great importance to this movement, I can mention only three here. In chronological order, these are Dexter Fisher's *Minority Language and Literature: Retrospective and Perspective*, Dexter Fisher and Robert Stepto's *Afro-American Literature: The Reconstruction of Instruction*, and Leslie Fiedler and Houston A. Baker, Jr.'s *Opening Up the Canon: Selected Papers from the English Institute, 1979*. Conveniently, for my argument here, each of these anthologies, the published results of seminal conferences, expresses a different aspect of a larger movement.

The first two collections grew out of conferences sponsored by the MLA, while the third was sponsored by the English Institute. "In an effort to address the critical, philosophical, pedagogical, and curricular issues surrounding the teaching of minority literature," Fisher explains in her introduction to the book, the MLA in 1972 formed the Commission on Minority Groups and the Study of Language and Literature. (Until the early 1970s, black scholars did not find the MLA a welcoming institution; they formed instead the predominantly black College Language Association, which thrives today. The commission's establishment was an attempt, in part, to redefine the MLA sufficiently to "open up" its membership to black and other minority professors.) Beginning in 1974, the commission sponsored various colloquiums, funded by the NEH, "to stimulate greater awareness and to encourage more equitable representations of minority literature in the mainstream of literary studies" (8). Fisher's book stemmed directly from a conference held in 1976, at which forty-four scholars, publishers, and foundation program officers came together to consider "the relationship of minority literature to the mainstream of American literary tradition." Fisher writes in her preface:

> The question of the "place" of minority literature in American literature raises a deeper, and perhaps more controversial, question: "In what ways does minority literature share the values and assumptions of the dominant culture, and in what ways does it express divergent perspectives?" This question has implications not only for curriculum development and critical theory, but also, and even more important, for the role of the humanities in bringing about a truly plural system of education. (9)

The conference's participants, including J. Lee Greene, Mary Helen Washington, Michael G. Cooke, Michael Harper, Geneva Smitherman, and Houston A. Baker, Jr., each a specialist in African American literature, explored the relations between "principles of criticism" and social contexts. As Fisher nicely puts it:

> The emergence of the Black Aesthetics Movement in the 1960s focused attention on the dilemma faced by minority writers trying to reconcile cultural dualism. Willingly or otherwise, minority writers inherit certain tenets of Western civilization through American society, though they often live alienated from that society. At the same time, they may write out of a cultural and linguistic tradition that sharply departs from the mainstream. Not only does this present constant social, political, and literary choices to minority writers, but it also challenges certain aesthetic principles of evaluation for the critic. When the cultural gap between writer and critic is too great, new critical approaches are needed. (13)

Above all else, the conference was concerned with "revising the canon of American literature," a matter that Fiedler and Baker would explore in even broader terms three years later at the English Institute.

In the same year that Fisher's volume appeared, she and Stepto, a professor of English, American, and African American studies at Yale, convened, again with NEH funding, a two-week seminar at Yale entitled Afro-American Literature: From Critical Approach to Course Design. The five seminar leaders—Fisher, Stepto, Robert O'Meally, Sherley Anne Williams, and

Henry Louis Gates, Jr.—defined their purpose as "the reconstruction of instruction": "in this case," as Fisher and Stepto put it, "to design courses in, and to refine critical approaches to, Afro-American literature yielding a 'literary' understanding of the literature" (vii). The "literary," Stepto explains, is contrasted with the "sociological," the "ideological, etc." Noting that "many schools still do not teach Afro-American literature, while other institutions offering courses in the field seem to be caught in a lockstep of stale critical and pedagogical ideas, many of which are tattered hand-me-downs from disciplines other than literature" (1), Stepto and his colleagues, with all the zeal of reformers, sought to redefine African American literary study by introducing into its explication formalist and structuralist methods of reading and by providing a critique of the essentialism of black aesthetic criticism that had grown out of the black arts movement. These scholars were intent on defining a canon of both African American literature and its attendant formal critical practices.

As bold and as controversial as the Fisher-Stepto volume was within African American literary studies, the volume edited by Fiedler and Baker was perhaps even more daring, since it sought to explode the notion that English was, somehow, or could ever be, somehow, a neutral container for "world literature." Indeed, the institute's theme in 1979 was English as a World Language for Literature. The volume, featuring papers by Dennis Brutus and Edward Kamau Brathwaite on South African and Caribbean literature, respectively, carries a succint yet seminal introduction by Baker that suggests something of the polemics generated by the notion that English might be anything but the most fertile and flexible language available to any writer for the fullest expression of literary sensibility. Baker's laconic remarks suggest the heated responses of the institute's audience to the participants' critique of the "neocolonialism" of traditional English studies and to Baker's observations that "the conception of English as a 'world language' is rooted in Western economic history" and that we must juxtapose "the economic ascendancy of English and the historical correlation between this academy and the processes of modern thought." English literature, Baker concludes, is not what it appears to be:

> The fact that a Sotho writer claims that he has chosen English because it guarantees a wide audience and ensures access to the literary reproduction systems of a world market may be less important as a literary consideration than what the writer has actually made of the English language as a literary agency. One might want to ask, for example, what summits of experience inaccessible to occupants of the heartland have been incorporated into the world of English literature? What literary strategies have been employed by the Sotho writer to preserve and communicate culturally-specific meanings? What codes of analysis and evaluation must be articulated in order to render accurate explanations for a Sotho or a Tew or a Yoruba literary work in English? (xiii)

These foundational volumes proved to be, each in its own way, enabling gestures for the growth of sophisticated theories and critical practices in African American as well as African and Caribbean literatures. In the past decade, scores of books and hundreds of essays—reflecting structuralist, poststructuralist, gay, lesbian, Marxist, and feminist theories and practices—have been devoted to the study of black literature. Even the essentialism of race itself, long a sacrosanct concept of African American studies, has been extensively reanalyzed in terms of social construction.

What, then, is the current state of the field? To begin, virtually no scholar today would contend that the texts written by black authors cohere into a tradition because the authors share certain innate characteristics. Opposing the essentialism of European "universality" with a black essentialism—an approach that in various ways characterized a large component of black literary criticism since the black arts movement—has given way to more subtle questions. What follows the critique of the essentialist notions that cloaked the text in a mantle of "blackness," replete with the accretions of all sorts of sociological clichés, is a "postformal" resituation of texts, accounting for the social dynamism of subjection, incorporation, and marginalization.

Black literature, recent critics seem to be saying, can no longer simply name "the margin." Close readings are increasingly naming the specificity of black texts, revealing the depth and range of cultural details far beyond the economic exploitation of blacks by whites. This heightened focus on specificity of text has enabled us to begin to chart the patterns of repetition and revision among texts by black authors. In *Notes of a Native Son*, Baldwin described his own obsession with "race" in his fiction: "I have not written about being a Negro at such length because I expect that to be my only subject, but only because it was the gate I had to unlock before I could hope to write about anything else" (8). Accordingly, many black authors read and revise one another, address similar themes, and repeat the cultural and linguistic codes of a common symbolic geography. For these reasons, we can think of them as forming literary traditions.

Wright once argued, polemically, that if white racism did not exist, then black literature would not exist, and he predicted the demise of the latter with the cessation of the former. It is difficult to deny that certain elements of African American culture are the products of cross-cultural encounters with white racism. But black culture is radically underdetermined by such encounters and can never be reduced to them. While it is important to criticize nativistic essentialism, in doing so we can lose sight of the larger social dynamic, the factors that make people come together into groups in the first place. Developments in African American studies have helped to reveal the factitious nature of an "American" identity; that which had been systematically excluded has not been revoiced as a mainstream concern.

\*   \*   \*

We might think of the development of African American criticism over the past three decades in a number of distinct stages, beginning with the black arts movement of the mid- and late-1960s. The black arts movement, whose leading theoreticians were Amiri Baraka and Larry Neal, was a reaction against the New Criticism's variety of formalism. The readings these critics advanced were broadly cultural and richly contextualized; they aimed to be "holistic" and based formal literature firmly on black urban vernacular, expressive culture. Art was a fundamental part of "the people"; art for art's sake was seen to be a concept alien to a pan-African sensibility, a sensibility that was whole, organic, and, of course, quite ahistorical. What was identified as European or Western essentialism—masked under the rubric of "universality"—was attacked by asserting an oppositional black or "neo-African" essentialism. In place of formalist notions about art, these critics promoted a poetics rooted in a social realism, indeed, in a sort of mimeticism; the relation between black art and black life was a direct one.

In response to what we might think of as the social organicism of the black arts movement, a formalist organicism emerged in the mid-1970s. This movement was concerned with redirecting the critic's attention toward the literariness of the black texts as autotelic artifacts, to their status as "acts of language" first and foremost. The use of formalist and structuralist theories and modes of reading characterized the criticism of this period. The formalists saw their work as a corrective to the social realism of the black arts critics.

In the third stage, critics of black literature began to retheorize social—and textual—boundaries. Drawing on poststructuralist theory as well as deriving theories from black expressive, vernacular culture, these critics were able to escape both the social organicism of the black arts movement and the formalist organicism of the "reconstructionists." Their work might be characterized as a new black aesthetic movement, though it problematizes the categories of both the "black" and the "aesthetic." An initial phase of theorizing has given way to the generation of close readings that attend to the "social text" as well. These critics use close readings to reveal cultural contradictions and the social aspects of literature, the larger dynamics of subjection and incorporation through which the subject is produced.

This aspect of contemporary African American literary studies is related directly to recent changes in critical approaches to American studies generally. Black studies has functioned as a strategic site for autocritique within American studies itself. No longer, for example, are the concepts of black and white thought to be preconstituted; rather, they are mutually constitutive and socially produced. The theoretical work of feminist critics of African American literature, moreover, has turned away from a naively additive notion of sexism and racism. Especially in this work, we have come to understand that critiques of essentialism are inadequate to explain the complex social dynamism of marginalized cultures. Implicit in both kinds of reflection has been a rethinking of the trope of marginality itself, and particularly the relation between marginality and centrality. In the remainder of the essay, I wish to submit this trope to the sort of pressure to which it has become increasingly exposed in recent theorizing in African American literary studies, by both feminist and nonfeminist critics.

## II

With the growing attention to "minority discourse," we have all come to recognize many of its master tropes and terms and seen how its politics has fixed on a spatial vocabulary of margin and center. What is recently new, however, is the convergence of different constituencies on a shared list of concerns. They have come to focus not just on the heterogeneous forms of marginalization (territorial, temporal, biological, cultural) but on the ways in which these categories subtend each other, and the relation of the more "naturalized" subject positions (e.g., race and gender) to the broader categories of social normality and deviance.

At the same time, many critics remain trapped within old problematics; we fail to be adequately self-conscious about the larger institutional and disciplinary contexts in which our work as "marginal" critics takes shape as well as about the historical forces that have constructed the margin as an object of study. Since the formation of the margin has moved to the center of literary history and theory, it is important now to rethink this cartography.

What follows is a catalog of the sometimes obliquely interrelated issues that arise under the general rubric of marginalization; among other things, I hope this inventory will suggest the practical and theoretical enrichment that can result from bringing together diverse perspectives. Our task, in recasting familiar arguments in minority discourse, is to disrupt some of the comforting concepts that seem to foreclose any truly critical inquiry; to encompass the essential continuities among disparate phenomena of marginalization, of center-periphery power relations; and yet to remain responsive to the essential differences within (that other totalizing category) "difference."

### Canon Formation and the Construction of Cultural Identity

The twin problematic of canon formation and nation formation is background to much debate at the boundaries of literary studies, and it sponsors the ideology of tradition that has long been in the service of minority legitima-tion. As Kwame Anthony Appiah observes, recent debates have left us "attuned to the ways in which the factitious 'excavation' of the literary canon can serve to hypostatize a particular cultural identity" ("Out of Africa" 161).[1] Self-inven-tion is then depicted as discovery. Emmanuel Wallerstein's observation is to the point:

> Any ethnic group exists only to the extent that it is asserted to exist at any given point in time by the group itself and by the larger social network of which it is a part. Such groups are constantly created and recreated; they also constantly "cease to exist"; they are thus constantly redefined and change their forms at amazingly fast rates. Yet through the physical maelstrom some "names" maintain a long historical continuity because at frequent intervals it has been in the interest of the conscious elements bearing that name to reas-sert, revalorize the mythical links and socialize members into the historical memory.                                                                      (qtd. in Higham 199)

Clearly, the endless reconstruction of a "national literature," however subtle and differentiated, remains the hidden object of much of our literary criticism. It would be easy to demonstrate its operation through the ideology of "tradition," whose tyranny remains little abated even today. And, for better or worse, the margin has borrowed this instrumentality. As the German critic Robert Weimann argues, however:

> [W]hen "tradition," or *Erbe*, is defined historically not only by what is preserved but also by what is repressed, not only as liberating but, in the words of Marx, also as burdensome, then the notion of "order" or even the formulation of a canon will, as an act of historicity, appear more deeply heterogeneous and contradictory.                                                                      (272)

If minority discourses in America seem to embrace the ideology of tradition, it is because they remain at a stage where the anxiety of identity formation is paramount.

Such concern shows up, for example, in African American literary criticism and theory as the privileging of the "vernacular," which is frequently exalted as its *fons et origo*. "Folkish ideology" emerges in a variety of contexts; in the case of black nationalism, Adolph Reed, Jr., observes, this folkish essence has been

> hypostatized to the level of a vague "black culture"—a romantic retrieval of a vanishing black particularity. This vision of black culture, of course, was grounded in residual features of black rural life prior to migrations to the

North. . . . As that world disintegrated before urbanization and mass culture, black nationalism sought to reconstitute it.

The limitations of the "nationalist elaboration" is displayed "both in that it was not sufficiently self-conscious and that it mistook artifacts and idiosyncrasies of culture for its totality and froze them into an ahistorical rhetoric of authenticity" (73–74).

If a nationality comes into its own through the production of literature, the apparatus of recognition—the "selection of classics" to which E. R. Curtius refers—remains integral to its realization. Inevitably, the process of constructing a group identity, at the margins as at the very center, involves active exclusion and repudiation; self-identity requires the homogeneity of the self-identical. Ironically, then, the cultural mechanism of minority self-construction must replicate the mechanism responsible for rendering it marginal in the first place. To recur again to Weimann: "the process of making certain things one's own becomes inseparable from making other things (and persons) alien" (qtd. in Krieger).

## Representation versus Articulation

In *Modernism and the Harlem Renaissance* Baker writes that "modernist 'anxiety' in Afro-American culture does not stem from a fear of replicating outmoded forms or of giving way to bourgeois formalisms. Instead, the anxiety of modernist influence is produced in the first instance by the black spokesperson's necessary task of employing audible extant forms in ways that move clear *up*, masterfully and re-soundingly away from slavery" (101). Of course, what is really at stake here is the black spokesperson's identity *as* black spokesperson. The constitution of social groups is politically conceived here as a *representation of interests*; yet as Ernesto Laclau and Chantal Mouffe's analysis suggests, the field of politics can no longer be so understood, "given that the so-called 'representation' modifies the nature of what is represented," so that "the very notion of representation as transparency becomes untenable" (58). Laclau-Mouffe's intervention becomes of great significance in the discourses of marginality, where we move between the problematic of literary representation to one of representation of interests (the "black spokesperson" paradigm). Some minority intellectuals who would otherwise repudiate the discursive episteme of literary representation as mimesis do not question the model of the transparency of political representation. What Laclau-Mouffe offer as an alternative perspective accepts "the structural diversity of the relations in which social agents are immersed, and replaces the principle of representation with that of *articulation*. Unity between these agents is then not the expression of a common underlying essence but the result of political construction and struggle" (65).

As I argued earlier, if a peripheral ethnicity is to come into its own through the production of literature, the mechanisms of recognition—the "selection of classics"—remains integral to the attainment. But this too is bound up in the issue of the spokesperson, the dynamism of representation, the site of which is the community of representatives. In fact, at the level of high theory, this whole social struggle is taking place by proxy, with the intellectual community providing the mediation necessary to a "central" reception. Bruce Robbins writes, "As soon as a text is chosen not from the West but from 'the rest,' in fact, attention to its positionality becomes a *sine qua non*: without an act of historical location, it may not 'mean' at all" (156).

## *The Economy of Authorization*

Intellectual formation occurs today in an international arena. In short, we misrepresent the intellectuals, literary critics, academics of formerly colonized spaces if we ignore that they occupy "First World" institutions and roles and inherit the colonizer's architecture of knowledge and its intellectual structures. The Third World intellectual thus engages willy-nilly in the play of spokesperson, or *porte-parole*, the economy of discursive authority that Pierre Bourdieu has explicated so incisively through his idea of "l'économie des échanges linguistiques." Since authority comes to language from outside, Bourdieu argues, "the authorized *porte-parole* can act by words on other agents, and thereby on things themselves, only because his speech concentrates the symbolic capital accumulated by the group which has mandated him and which provides the *basis of power*" (*Ce que parler* 73; cf. J. B. Thompson 48).

Hence a progressive dialectic of authorization between center and periphery. The empowerment of the periphery, then, logically proceeds from the center, but from there on the colonial relation can easily be reversed.[2]

## *Subjection and Agency*

It is easy to understand the disgruntlement of many marginal critics toward those imperial modalities of thought known to them as "theory": in which the subject is called into question; in which reflectionist notions of artistic production are dismissed as naive; or, most generally, in which the category of the experiential is demystified as a purely textual artifice.[3]

When Wlad Godzich writes of the reasons for "the sense of loss of historical agency that accompany the fragmentation of the self characteristic of social abstraction" (Foreword xx), he touches on an important issue. For the dimension of agency is of crucial importance to the marginal spokesperson: after all, the social construction of group identity is also, in an extended sense, the construction of agency.[4] But it will be clear why hostility of nationalists toward the social antiessentialism of discourse theory is misguided. It is one thing to understand social agents as constructed, the result of articulatory practices, rather than as arriving already constituted on the stage of history. It is another thing to oppose such agential construction, even if you think that (as Appiah has suggested) the demands of agency may entail a misrecognition of its genesis (see Gates, "Critical Remarks"; Appiah, "Conservation"). Such a theoretical vantage is neutral with respect to any particular pragmatic program.

Practices of ideological subjection are typically opposed by what Foucault terms "reverse-discourse," which are still contained by such practices. The pragmatic double bind of the marginal critic is implicit here: to go beyond reverse discourse would require us to dismantle the identities to which—and by which—we are subjected, the instrument of our subordination. But actively to dismantle this identity may also be to jeopardize our collective agency. (At the same time, one can no longer ignore the argument that the dispersion of agency tends only to stabilize the existing order and thus proves pragmatically self-defeating; see M. Mann; Giddens, *Class Structure*; J. B. Thompson 61–64; Jameson, *Political Unconscious* 54n; Appiah, "Conservation".)

## Production of Agonism

Theorists often imply that the margin, or the other, is inevitably the endangered target of annihilation or assimilation. Godzich, for example, contends that "Western thought has always thematized the other as a threat to be reduced, as a potential same-to-be, a yet-not-same." Its paradigm, he argues, is that of the Arthurian quest, in which the "alien domain is brought within the hegemonic sway of the Arthurian world: the other has been reduced to (more of) the same." Indeed, "it is ideologically inconceivable that there should exist an otherness of the same ontological status as the same, without there being immediately mounted an effort at its appropriation" (Foreword xiii).

Yet this argument does not acknowledge that the margin is *produced* by the center, the other, by the self or same and proceeds as if the two did not define a mutually constitutive system. Our characteristic stance on these matters—as champion of the politically disenfranchised—constantly blinds us to the ways in which the margin (that is, its positionality) is an effect of the cultural dominant rather than an autonomous agency of subversion, the dissolution or cooptation of which is the dominant's dearest wish.[5] Since (as Michel Pêcheux argues) the very meaning of discourses subsists on such conflictual relations, the periphery is, as it were, never someplace else.[6] A less blinkered view is offered by Sneja Gunew, who argues:

> The textual production of marginal minorities exists to confirm hegemonic textualities. And these minority writings have been in general homogenised as the area of plurality, disruption, non-closure, deferred meaning and process; in other words, as affirming the dynamism of the centre and its ability to accommodate change—change which is safely contained.     (142–43)[7]

The threat to the margin comes not from assimilation or dissolution—from any attempt to denude it of its defiant alterity—but, on the contrary, from the center's attempts to *preserve* that alterity, which result in the homogenization of the other as, simply, other. The margin's resistance to such homogenization, in turn, takes the form of breeding new margins within margins, circles within circles, an ever-renewed process of differentiation, even fragmentation, so that, for example, black women's writing asserts its distinctness from women's writing, which it depicts as white and middle class and so discredits it by *centralizing* it. For the center has, at least in certain spheres, conferred special authority on the marginal voice. These are the antinomies of center and periphery: where the center constructs the margin as a privileged locale, you assume authority by representing yourself as marginal, and, conversely, you discredit others by representing them as central—a tidy peripeteia best exemplified in the establishment of what the Brazilian scholar J. G. Merquior calls the "official marginality."

But if we are trading on the margin, whose currency are we using? It is useless to pretend that the discussion takes place in some neutral matrix, that our terms of argument are innocent. When, for example, Harold Bloom writes that "the popular myth of the alienated artist or intellectual is largely based on the late, decadent phase of Romanticism but it is soundly based there" (*Ringers* 345), we are reminded that the articulation of marginality has functional significance within modern culture (see Rieff). Obviously, the divide between dominant and adversial culture is basic to our conception of the intellectual. But the ideology that would thematize the artist or intellectual as adversarial (however reassuring to artists and intellectuals themselves) is, of course, not itself adversarial—far from it. At the same time, the stereotype cannot help but inform our response to the elevation of marginality as not just the stakes or subject but the privileged *site* of cultural critique.[8]

## *Margins on the March*

But as we saw earlier, the periphery is never someplace else. Where, finally, does this lead? To begin with, we have to examine the strategic function of the conceptual divide between "minority" (internal) and "Third World" or "post-colonial" (external) discourses, which is to deflect the broader implications of what is called internal colonization. Keeping inside and outside distinct is a means of keeping the other elsewhere. But othering, we might say, starts in the home. The grammarian's term *barbarism* encapsulates the social and linguistic freight of our condition: internal transgression is figured as the savagery beyond our borders; and, projectively, vice versa. As John Guillory argues,

> The question of reading and writing belongs to the whole problematic of social reproduction, because what one learns to read is always another language. The internal differentiation of language produced by the classical educational system as the distinction between a credentialed and non-credentialed speech reproduces social stratification on the model of the distinction between the tribe or nation and its sociolinguistic other, the "barbarian."
>
> ("Canonical" 501)

Nevertheless, much theorizing about Europe and its others depicts the production of cultural alterity as an act of self-reflection that requires the complete evacuation of that other's specificity. The other is figured as a form or space merely; a "dingy mirror," as Wright described Africa.[9]

Such a view typically takes little interest in the actual effects of such projections on its hapless screens. This view is harder to maintain when we shift to the model of internal colonization, the others—sexual, racial, ethnic others—within our cultural borders. At the same time, and conversely, there has been little attention to the ways in which these tendencies to textualize otherness within certain fixed parameters may operate even in the process of the margin's (self-)articulation and construction. The double vision we need here would take in the relation between, on the one hand, the way the subjects are constructed or represented to themselves and, on the other, the way they are represented within the putatively dominant culture.

### *Notes*

[1]Appiah's essay provides an elaboration and a case study of the intersection of literary history and identity politics.

[2]This underwrites the contrapuntalism between authentication and authorial control in Stepto's study of African American narrative, *From behind the Veil*, since

their meeting ground is, of course, *authorization*. But the basic operation has long been understood. Langston Hughes's character Jesse B. Simple observes one instance of this dynamic: "Harlem won't accept a writer unless he is already famous."

[3]The shift from the "discursive episteme of representation" and the disruption of the subject compromises the experiential basis of minority-critical authority. "What is most important about the black woman writer is her special and unique vision of the black woman," Washington avers, in a characteristic move. "That these writers have firsthand knowledge of their subjects ought to be enough to command attention and respect" (x). But one should not be too quick to dismiss the claims for the authority of experience. Poirier has asked whether Howells, who "read his life as the history of his times," was so different from "critics who now celebrate the fact, as did Zola in his novels about the various industries and occupations, that a new book has at last 'made available' some aspect of reality hitherto sequestered? The novel has been called many things, but is it at last only a procurer?" (*"Politics"* 345).

[4]Two concerns—identity and agency—come together in the central Althusserian thesis, "ideology interpellates individuals as subjects" (*Essays on Ideology*), since "subject" here has a double import: the individual is both conceived as an autonomous agent (person who makes history) and subjected to—defined in terms of—an imaginary identity. "The Negro," Fanon writes, "is never so much a Negro as since he has been dominated by whites" (*Wretched* 212). And, of course, as Macdonell argues, "given the principle that, while ideologies take shape antagonistically (under the dominance of ruling ideology), ruling ideology can operate divisively, granting mastery and imposing submission, it should be possible to analyse the historical, including the current, relations between ideologies that come from positions of race or gender as well as from class positions" (36).

[5]Since "postmodernism," as cultural dominant, is associated with commodication of the margin—what Guillory terms the "cachet of the non-canonical"—the situation grows ever more complex in contemporary Western culture. And, of course, the cooptative powers of "multiculturalism"—another cozy mainstream value—hardly needs remarking.

[6]Thus, for example, the demonization of sexual deviancy is an integral part of the social regulation of sexuality *simpliciter*. Freud "problematises the category of normal sexuality by showing how its other, homosexuality, isn't at all over there, alien and removed (foreign), but at the very heart of heterosexuality itself" (Dollimore, "Homophobia" 8).

[7]Compare Spivak's discussion of "how Europe consolidated itself as a sovereign subject by defining its colonies as 'Others,' even as it constituted them, for purposes of administration and the expansion of markets, into programmed near-images of that very sovereign itself" (F. Barker et al. 1: 128).

[8]Compare Seidel's observation, in the context of territorial dislocation, that "experiences native to the life of the exile seem almost activated in the life of the artist: separation as desire, perspective as witness, alienation as new being" (x).

[9]Thus Slemon finds that "the system of knowledge that constitutes Others as subjects has little to do with practices or values intrinsic to them, with the political, religious, and social codes by which Others live. Rather, it is an exercise in self-reference, a projection outward of one's own systemic codes so that they come to inscribe on to the

territory of the Other—necessarily read as discursively vacant, 'uninscribed earth'—a set of values and meanings that can be recuperated by reference to one's own inherited markers of cultural recognition" (103).

## Selected Bibliography

Baker, Houston A., Jr. *Blues, Ideology, and Afro-American Literature: A Vernacular Theory*. Chicago: U of Chicago P, 1984.
A pioneering study of black literature and culture that, bridging Marxian and poststructuralist concerns, inaugurated postformalist African American criticism.

Baraka, Imamu Amiri, and Larry Neal, eds. *Black Fire*. New York: Morrow, 1968.
A classic compilation of the black arts movement, for whom art and act were one.

Carby, Hazel V. *Reconstructing Womanhood: The Emergence of the Afro-American Woman Novelist*. New York: Oxford UP, 1987.
A major work of literary and social scholarship that showcases the insights of cultural studies applied to African American literary history.

Christian, Barbara. *Black Women Novelists: The Development of a Tradition, 1892–1976*. New York: Greenwood, 1980.
A trailblazing study of the subject, motivated by the concerns not of a theorist but of an engaged reader.

Fiedler, Leslie, and Houston A. Baker, Jr., eds. *Opening Up the Canon: Selected Papers from the English Institute, 1979*. Baltimore: Johns Hopkins UP, 1981.
Includes essays by Dennis Brutus and Edward Kamau Braithwaite on literature and the diaspora.

Fisher, Dexter, and Robert B. Stepto, eds. *Afro-American Literature: The Reconstruction of Instruction*. New York: MLA, 1979.
A showcase of the formalist backlash.

Gates, Henry Louis, Jr., ed. *Reading Black, Reading Feminist: A Critical Anthology*. New York: NAL, 1990.
Features influential critical essays by Mary Helen Washington, Mae Henderson, Hortense Spillers, Michele Wallace, Deborah McDowell, Hazel Carby, and many others feminist critics and theorists.

Gayle, Addison, ed. *The Black Aesthetic*. Garden City: Doubleday, 1971.
A collection of representative texts of the eponymous tradition.

Hull, Gloria T., Patricia Bell, and Barbara Smith. *All the Women Are White, All the Blacks Are Men, But Some of Us Are Brave: Black Women's Studies*. Old Westbury: Feminist, 1982.

Widely influential collection of black feminist essays.

Rampersad, Arnold. *The Life of Langston Hughes*. New York: Oxford UP, 1986.
The outstanding literary biography of an African American figure. This
study of black America's unlikely "representative man" spurred renewed
interest in biography as a branch of literary study.

Sollors, Werner. *Amiri Baraka/Leroi Jones: The Quest for a "Populist Modernism."* New York: Columbia UP, 1978.
A model single-author study of a figure who embodies the contradictions of
modern black literary culture.

Spillers, Hortense, and Marjorie Pryse, eds. *Conjuring: Black Women, Black
Fiction, and Literary Tradition*. Bloomington: Indiana UP, 1985.
An important collection of essays by a wide variety of scholars.

Stepto, Robert. *From behind the Veil: A Study of Afro-American Narrative*.
Urbana: U of Illinois P, 1979.
A touchstone of modern African American criticism, pursuing a socially
capacious formalism.

Wall, Cheryl, ed. *Changing Our Own Words: Essays on Criticism, Theory, and
Writing by Black Women*. New Brunswick: Rutgers UP, 1989.
Addresses contemporary issues in feminism and African American criticism.

# Marxist Criticism

## WALTER COHEN

Karl Marx and Friedrich Engels (1840s–1890s) took as their central task the revolutionary surpassing of the historically and qualitatively new miseries produced by industrial society. Although no brief summary can do justice to their vast, complex, and hardly homogeneous work, a few major issues stand out. An insistence on the dialectic (loosely speaking, the contradictory relatedness) of objectivity and subjectivity or, in a more contemporary vocabulary, of structure and subject separates their position from both determinist and voluntarist views of society or history. Perhaps their two central categories, mode of production and class struggle, coexist—at times uneasily—in just such a relation of unity and tension. Although the precise meaning of these terms, like virtually all others in Marxist thought, remains problematic, *mode of production* generally refers to the way in which a society makes material goods. It includes, among other things, both physical objects and the social relations that people enter into in the process of production. In any postsubsistence society, the mode of production has a primarily inherent, contradictory dynamic that eventually issues in a crisis. It structurally establishes a conflict between lower and upper class, between the immediate producers and the appropriators of the surplus they produce. For Marx and Engels the resulting class struggle is the driving force of history. The working class, which emerges in significant numbers with the advent of industrial capitalism, is the first exploited class with both the desire and the ability to overthrow the exploiters and reorganize society in its own universal socialist interests. Marx and Engels interpreted events in their lifetime as significant steps toward that revolutionary outcome, while describing their own theories as the reflex of proletarian struggle in the world of ideas.

Explanatory primacy clearly rests in their writings with the mode of production and class struggle rather than, for instance, with literature, which unsurprisingly does not receive systematic attention. In constructing a Marxist theory of literature, one therefore has the option of synthesizing Marx's and Engels's numerous scattered comments on art and literature or of working out somewhat more independently the aesthetic implications of their central theories. Marx had an extensive knowledge of the canonical texts of European literature in the original languages and a corresponding appreciation of the relative autonomy of form, combined with an antipathy to tendentious literature. Coming from a different background, Engels began by favoring overtly committed art but subsequently came to recognize the power of Marx's position. Both looked for the social grounding of a literary work and valued its fidelity to history without, however, insisting on a normative form of representation. Engels reintroduced tendentiousness in some late remarks but insisted that a work's political position correspond to the actual rather than the wished-for movement of history and that it emerge from the form rather than from direct statement by the author or authorial mouthpiece. Thus a realist aesthetic is one, though hardly the only, plausible inference to be drawn from the literary criticism of Marx and Engels.

As twentieth-century work has demonstrated, their major social theories have an even wider range of possible implications for the understanding of art. The creation of literature can be viewed as a productive activity on the model of economic production. The dialectical relation between form and content provides a model not only for the inner logic of the literary work or for the connection between that work and society but also for the movement of history itself. The notion of consumption points suggestively toward reception aesthetics. The theory of commodity fetishism, which both explains and challenges the objective social necessity of the misperception of relations between people as relations between things, offers a method of connecting surface and deep structures in a literary text. Yet another influential position depends on the claim that social being determines consciousness. And in what may still remain the central formulation, economic and social forces together constitute the base (or infrastructure or substructure) on which is erected the superstructure—the state, politics, law, culture, ideology, religion, values, philosophy, and the arts. Since the relation between base and superstructure is dialectical, determination flows in both directions. But the main line of force runs from the base to the superstructure rather than the other way around.

The two subsequent generations of Marxists contributed more systematic studies of literature than had Marx and Engels but without introducing many major theoretical inflections or breakthroughs. The leading intellectuals of the decades immediately prior to World War I continued the project that had occupied Engels in the years between Marx's death in 1883 and his own in 1895—the consolidation of Marxist thought in the first era of an international working-class movement. In Germany, which had the largest proletarian party, Franz Mehring concerned himself with the legacy of bourgeois culture—with the synthesis of Kantian aesthetics and Marxist theories of ideology and with the working class's appropriation of European and especially German literary classics. In Russia, Georgi Plekhanov provided a systematic social theory of art that, in its emphasis on genetic rather than dialectical relations, contributed to the strong deterministic currents in the Marxism of the era. The younger generation, which was formed by the far more volatile world of the first two decades of this century, commented on literature in the context of revolutionary upheaval and hence in an occasional fashion. Following the 1905 revolution, Lenin wrote a series of essays on Tolstoy that advance a political theory of reception. During the period of relative cultural openness after the Bolshevik consolidation of power, Trotsky meditated on the relation between literature and revolution, defending bourgeois art at the expense of its proletarian rival.

The real boom in Marxist aesthetics occurred in the interwar years with the construction of a range of often competing systems. The condition of possibility of this creative development was a break with the past that should be seen as a crisis or, rather, a catastrophe. The Russian Revolution of 1917 gave rise to visions of the rapid international march of socialism, but defeats in Poland, Hungary, and Germany in the next few years revealed instead the reconsolidation of capitalism. The triumph of fascism in Italy in 1922 was followed by the advent of the Stalinist era in the Soviet Union at the end of the decade and the ascendancy of nazism in Germany in 1933. The close of the revolutionary era was thus succeeded by the violent suppression of the working class on an international scale. Marxist intellectuals found themselves cut off from the social movements that were their raison d'être, even at times if they remained members of the Communist party. Their writings correspondingly reveal a shift from their predecessors' concerns with economic, social, and political issues to the less immediately urgent matters of philosophy and aesthetics. Advance onto a new terrain depended on retreat from the original ground of Marxist thought. It is from this period that one can date the emergence of a distinctively Western Marxism, a tradition that lasted at least into the 1960s and that shapes much of contemporary American Marxist criticism.

The significance of the new departure was obscured from view for more than a generation by the international prominence of the Communist, and indeed specifically Stalinist, norm of socialist realism that came to be known as Zhdanovism after A. A. Zhdanov, Stalin's minister of culture in the early post–World War II years. In the writings of Christopher Caudwell, the most important British Marxist critic before the 1950s, a crude functionalism coexists in unresolved tension with utopian Romantic idealism. Caudwell's studies are noteworthy for their scope and ambition if not for their success. They range from a theory of the origins of poetry in primitive agriculture through a history of the alienated literature of England from the Renaissance to the present—in which changes in artistic form are correlated with social and technological evolution according to an undialectical application of the base-superstructure model—to a contradictory call for a proletarian poetry that would galvanize the masses and ultimately result in the socialist reunification of art and production.

Elsewhere during the interwar period, however, a number of basic

Marxist literary-theoretical categories were first worked out—reification, realism, production, hegemony, dialogism. The Hungarian Georg Lukács's *History and Class Consciousness*, published in German and partly marked by immediate postrevolutionary optimism, radically extends Marx's brief account of the fetishism of commodities by stressing its Hegelian interplay between subject and object. The notion of reification (that is, "thingification"), which Lukács generally substitutes for fetishism, locates in the dominance of commodity production the explanation for the necessarily fragmented, abstract, formalistic appearance of reality. Only the proletariat, through the process of revolutionizing itself and the world, can pierce this reified surface and gain access to the contradictory, concrete totality that is society. The aesthetic implications of this argument are not self-evident, and indeed the 1930s saw the elaboration of at least three competing paradigms in various ways dependent on the reification model. Eventually, for Lukács, naturalism, which he labels abstract objectivity, and modernism, which he calls abstract subjectivity, both reproduce reification—albeit while protesting the phenomenon—without understanding its causes and nature. Only realism, a literary procedure closely associated with mimesis, reflection, contemplative reception, and the base-superstructure model, is capable of revealing the content beneath the form, the underlying movement of history. It seems to share this cognitive capacity only with Marxism. Insofar as realism is normatively identified with the nineteenth-century novel, this theory aims at the appropriation of the best of the bourgeois past by the socialist present, at political rapprochement between liberal capitalism and the Stalinist Soviet Union (against fascism), and at an ahistorical and reactionary attack on experimental art, much of it produced by the left. But if the formal features of the theory are specified at a higher level of abstraction— as the concrete, totality, and narration—the result, though still problematic, is far more formidable.

Beginning in the 1930s, the Frankfurt school (Max Horkheimer, Theodor Adorno, Herbert Marcuse, and, later, Jürgen Habermas) takes a very different path, modifying the original theory of reification in at least two ways that fundamentally undermine its revolutionary implications. First, under the pressure of both nazism and Stalinism, these writers, though accepting Lukács's diagnosis of modernity, reject the belief that the working class will overcome reification. Second, they trace back the process of rationalization that shapes various contemporary societies to the ancient origins and very nature of reason. The Enlightenment critique of reason is thus turned against itself in a Nietzschean fashion, the traditional instrument of critique now transformed into the object of critique. These pessimistic, indeed quietistic conclusions lead to a scathing attack on emergent mass culture (termed "the culture industry" by Horkheimer and Adorno), to a suspicion of left-wing committed art, and, by contrast, to an anti-Lukácsian valorization of high modernism, which through its very negativity is alone able to resist reification and thereby keep faith with a potentially revolutionary future.

Like Lukács's attack on modernism, the critique of commitment is partly directed against the combination of tendentiousness and anti-illusionistic estrangement effects characteristic of Bertolt Brecht's epic theater. Although Brecht offered telling (but at the time unpublished) critiques of Lukács's own position, the leading theoretical defense of Brecht's dramaturgy came from Walter Benjamin. In a sense, Benjamin may be located between Adorno and Brecht, but his aphoristic, essayistic, wildly heterogeneous writings, though apparently intended as parts of a single project, defy easy categorization. In his hands commodity fetishism is interpreted through an abiding concern with allegory. Just as allegory posits an arbitrary relation between meaning and the consequently devalued world of objects, so the commodity is defined by an arbitrary relation between its use value and exchange value, between its material specificity and its meaning, or price. Once a commodity's physicality is thereby stripped of intrinsic significance, it attracts the wishes, the dreams, the anxieties of the consumer. Here as elsewhere in Benjamin, the subjectivist twist coexists with a fascinated attention to the material objectivity of commodities, which are in turn connected on the one hand to various aesthetic forms and on the other to the technological innovations of industrial society. The resulting productivist aesthetic deliberately downplays the individual work of art in favor of technique, understood not as style but as the means of production, as technology, as institution. In the tendency either to overlook the importance of social relations or to presuppose that such relations have already been transformed by socialism, Benjamin's and Brecht's assessment of modern technology's liberating potential for artistic production is unduly optimistic. Yet it opens the way both for the analysis of cultural institutions and for something other than a blank rejection of the advanced technologies that mark those institutions.

Two other figures of the 1920s and 1930s, Antonio Gramsci and Mikhail M. Bakhtin, stand apart from this German tradition in different ways. Undertaken in a fascist prison, Gramsci's most important work concerns not philosophy or aesthetics but political theory. His central category of hegemony (loosely, domination by consent) is designed to explain and ultimately overcome the greater resistance of western Europe than of Russia to revolutionary insurgency. This perspective also produces original contributions on ideology, cultural institutions, the functions of intellectuals (a term meant to encompass professionals and managers, as well as intellectuals in the ordinary sense), and the relation between high and popular culture or between dominant and subordinate cultures. More generally, Gramsci assigns a crucial role to culture in the long-term, shifting struggle between capital and labor for the allegiance of the majority of the population. The resulting model is open to question not only because of its possible overvaluation of culture and undervaluation of democracy but also because of the ambiguities and inconsistencies inevitable in a lengthy, fragmentary undertaking like the *Prison Notebooks*. It nonetheless remains perhaps the most compelling account of twentieth-century capitalist democracy produced in the Marxist tradition.

Gramsci is an eccentric figure within Western Marxism because of his political preoccupations; Bakhtin and his circle (P. N. Medvedev, V. N. Vološinov) fall outside the category on geographical grounds. Yet they are the exceptions who prove the rule. Indebted like Brecht to the Russian formalists, Bakhtin stresses the dialogic principle, the multiple social voices—often divided along popular-elite lines—that constitute discourse and particularly novelistic discourse. The formalist, even stylistic, criticism that results may be understood as a protest against the univocal official Marxist discourse imposed in the Soviet Union under Stalin. Although the works signed exclusively by Bakhtin lack the explicitly Marxist framing of the volumes published partly or wholly under Medvedev's and Vološinov's names, they have proved the most suggestive for subsequent Marxist literary and cultural criticism.

The center of European Marxist thought migrated from Germany to the east in the generations after Marx's and Engels's deaths and then returned to Germany following World War I. The westward march resumed after World War II—with Italy and especially France coming to prominence—and in a sense continues to this day. Between 1890 and 1970, a significant Marxist intelligentsia emerged only in countries with a prominent Communist party. But another institutional affiliation ultimately carried equal, if not greater, weight: in the decades immediately following World War II, nearly all leading Marxist intellectuals entered academic life. The central international figure of the period is undoubtedly Jean-Paul Sartre, whose existential, humanist, subjectivist, praxis-oriented Marxism, with its methodological emphasis on mediation (on the nonimmediate relations among the various elements of social life), directly challenges Stalinist norms. This position has fared better politically than philosophically, given its inability to reply effectively to the emergent structuralist critique of a human-centered, and usually male-centered, perspective. As a result, Sartre's major later works have perhaps not had the influence they deserve. Prominent during the same period as Sartre, Lucien Goldmann is more centrally located in the Hegelian Marxist tradition. His genetic-structuralist approach to literature has little in common with structuralism despite the terminological similarity. Directly derived from the early Lukács, it establishes homologies among social class, worldview, and literary form. The salutary demonstration of coherence is thus purchased at the expense of obscuring the process of mediation.

These positions were in a sense overtaken in the 1960s by Louis

Althusser's writings, in which the formal innovation is to downplay historical narrative and to reinterpret Marxism as a synchronic structure, especially through a substantially modified base-superstructure model. The insistence on the scientificity of Marxism, the theoretical rejection of human-centered historical agency, and the emphasis on the relative autonomy of the superstructures are designed to distinguish a refurbished Leninism from two potent antagonists. On the one hand, Althusser openly opposes the humanist, often Hegelian tradition in Marxism (early Marx, early Lukács, the contemporary French Communist party, Sartre). On the other hand, and more obliquely, he challenges a reductively determinist notion of the influence of the base on the superstructure, in particular the Stalinist (and French Communist party) assumption that, with the overthrow of capitalism in Russia, political and cultural life was progressively transformed as well.

Perhaps because of the linguistic roots of this model, its obvious problems—the ungrounded assertion of scientificity, the radical expansion and consequent depoliticization of the category of ideology, the almost total denial of human agency—have not proved disabling for literary-theoretical analysis by Althusser, Pierre Macherey, Etienne Balibar, Terry Eagleton, and others. The distinction between science and ideology and the location of art in a vexed relation to ideology offer the possibility of a sympathetic criticism that does not require the weighty cognitive claims for literature fundamental to Lukács's theory of realism. The implicit pessimism of structuralist social theory, though reminiscent of Horkheimer and Adorno's position, results instead in a privileging of Brechtian disruption of the apparently complete coherence of capitalist structures. Similarly, the method of symptomatic reading is particularly attendant to contradiction; hence, in a manner somewhat akin to deconstruction, it can either demystify orthodox texts or recover their heterodox elements. Finally, the theory of ideological state apparatuses, adapted from Gramsci, provides a useful point of entry for the study of literary and critical institutions.

Certain parallels to this problematic can be found in postwar Italy. Galvano Della Volpe shares with Althusser an anti-Hegelian, anti-Lukácsian commitment to a scientific Marxism, as well as a consequent need to distinguish science from art. Although the contrast between univocal science and polysemic art is far less sharp than Althusser's oppositions are, it too leads to a rejection of the ideal of aesthetic wholeness and an accompanying valorization of modernism. Even more than Althusser's later work, Della Volpe's broad appreciation of art runs the danger of undermining ideological analysis. For reasons that probably have little to do with intellectual quality, however, recent Italian Marxist thought—the writings of Lucio Colletti and Sebastiano Timpanaro and even the explicitly literary-theoretical work of Della Volpe—has had little if any effect on American criticism. The same is probably true of work during the past quarter century in the former Communist countries, which continues to remain terra incognita in the United States. The publications of the contemporary semiotician Yury Lotman and his colleagues, from the former Soviet Union, may be a partial exception. The situation of Robert Weimann, from what was until recently the German Democratic Republic (East Germany), is a little different: his studies of Shakespeare, which resemble Bakhtin's reading of Rabelais, have influenced American (and British) criticism more than his theory of reception has. One might also point to the aesthetic theory of Stefan Morawski in Poland and to the writings of Agnes Heller and other Hungarian Lukácsians. Until very recently, theorists from Czechoslovakia and the former Yugoslavia had an international significance for Marxist philosophy rather than for Marxist aesthetics; the current interest in the work of the Slovenian cultural critic Slavoj Žižek is either an exception or the beginning of a new trend.

Two contemporary figures, both perhaps reformist socialists, have been particularly important. In the former West Germany, Habermas has broadened the work of the Frankfurt school during the last thirty years by returning it to institutional analysis and, more recently, by focusing on language and communication. His far-reaching revision of Marxism locates the destructiveness of capitalism in the progressive colonization and reification of the "life world"—the realm of culture, intersubjectivity, norms, and social integration—by autonomous systems like bureaucracy or the economy, which operate along the axes of power or money according to the logic of instrumental reason. Against this tendency, Habermas calls for the revitalization of the life world in terms of communicative rationality. During the past decade, he has belatedly received considerable attention from literary and cultural critics in this country for his often polemical engagement with contemporary French thought, which he accuses of celebrating a postmodernity that facilely dismisses modernity's enduring commitment to the Enlightenment project of liberation. He has been criticized for positing a hopelessly utopian notion of rational consensus; for clinging to the anachronistic ideal of a general theory of history and society; for asserting an oppressive standard of truth and objectivity that effaces differences of gender, race, and even class; for operating within a self-evidently limited Eurocentric framework; and hence for unduly scaling down both the possibility and the necessity of social change. But Habermas's partial vulnerability to these charges is to a considerable extent a consequence of the extraordinary depth and breadth of his enterprise, for which there may be no real analogue in contemporary Western thought.

In England, Raymond Williams's cultural materialism utilizes criticism of literary texts and other cultural forms to promote a general socialist vision of British society. After 1970, Williams frequently refers to the Continental Marxist tradition and insists on retroactively inserting his entire corpus into that tradition. This apparently new departure indicates less a shift of perspective than a selective appropriation in which the foreign thinker enriches the text by ultimately speaking in the same voice as Williams does. That voice, with its interest in the relations between social being and consciousness and its consistent emphasis on the creative, practical consciousness of ordinary people, seems to grow out of the author's own working-class background, the significant presence of working-class culture in England, and the importance of the Labour party. The strength of this stance is its emphasis on the potentially transformative role of culture, literary and otherwise. Its weakness is a tendency to minimize or at least not to specify adequately the forces that resist change. Nonetheless, Williams's work occupies the central position in the emerging field of cultural studies in both England and, to a considerable extent, the United States.

A different relation to the Marxist heritage characterizes Eagleton's criticism. Eagleton came to international prominence in the late 1970s on the strength of his powerful adaptation of Althusserian thought to literary theory in the English-language world. Yet an overview of his career reveals a systematicity not in the advocacy of a particular version of Marxism but in the dissemination of as many versions of Marxism (and not of Marxism alone) as possible. His procedure ranges from theoretical critique to a practical application that tests out the analytical power of the model. Although Eagleton's work lacks the broad cultural perspective of Williams's, it is marked by a far greater sensitivity to the specifically formal features of literature. Again, the very limitations of its deliberate eclecticism have also widened the range and deepened the sophistication of Marxist and, more generally, radical criticism, while encouraging the development of a genuine pluralism in a discourse once plagued by its dogmatic certitude.

Finally, Ernesto Laclau and Chantal Mouffe's *Hegemony and Socialist Strategy* offers a self-conscious post-Marxism that emerges from a poststructuralist reading of Gramsci. Marxism is found guilty of foundationalism and essentialism. It spuriously appeals to an ultimate material grounding in its central category, mode of production, and assumes the virtually ontological unity of the working class as a collective subject fundamentally committed to the fight for socialism. The struggle for hegemony, Laclau and Mouffe believe, means that these Marxist claims cannot be taken for granted, that the identity and interests of individuals and groups are neither pregiven nor immutable, that socialism must be reduced from *the* goal of the left to an important moment in the central enterprise of a radical democratic politics, and that, accordingly, the new social movements of the postwar period—ecology, antiracism, feminism, gay rights, and so on—are not necessarily less important, and indeed may be more important, than the venerable socialist project. These claims are developed in the first three chapters of *Hegemony and Socialist Strategy* at a high level of abstraction.

But in the immediately following and concluding chapter, a relatively empirical account of trends since 1945, traditional Marxist categories immediately reassert their primacy. The authors argue that the switch from extensive to intensive capitalist accumulation leads to the spread of capitalist relations of production and the commodification of social life, stimulates the development of an increasingly intrusive bureaucratized welfare state, and makes possible the expansion of the mass media. From these unprecedented developments a whole range of new conflicts and movements arise. Hegemonic practice has the task of organizing these disparate movements into a relatively unified, distinctive force for radical democracy. Although this impressive line of reasoning is compatible with the preceding theoretical model, it does not follow from that model. The model offers no hint of what the central features or important struggles of an epoch are likely to be. The resulting gaps between theory and practice and between structure and subject unwittingly reveal an enduring dilemma of an entire tradition. *Hegemony and Socialist Strategy* produces not a post-Marxist break but a sharpened, still problematic, and scaled-down Marxist political theory.

Laclau and Mouffe represent an opening out of Western Marxism in a fashion related to their substantive position. Their integration of philosophy and politics, like Habermas's integration of philosophy and sociology, marks the mutually beneficial reconciliation of this predominantly cultural heritage with classical Marxist concerns. The two authors are biographically anomalous as well: Mouffe is the only woman treated so far, while Laclau, who is Argentine, is the only non-European. Their ability to inflect Marxist theory in the direction of the new social movements may partly result from this distinctiveness. By contrast, among the overwhelmingly white, male, middle-class, European thinkers considered here, issues of race and gender have rarely arisen. The position of race is occupied by the problem of anti-Semitism and the question of nationalities. The oppression of women, which had received sustained attention from Marxists in the late nineteenth century, is either ignored or subsumed under economic and class categories. The partial exception to this rule, the feminist writings of Alexandra Kollontai in the heady days following the Bolshevik Revolution, were rejected in the Soviet Union and had no influence elsewhere. The absence of women from the roster of Marxist cultural critics, as opposed to the absence of women's issues from the writings of Marxist cultural critics, slightly misrepresents the Marxist intellectual tradition as a whole, however. The important work of Rosa Luxemburg—perhaps the central example—focuses on economic and political theory.

The exclusive attention to Europe by the Marxist cultural thinkers considered here may be understood along similar lines. Marxist social thought from Asia, Africa, the Middle East, and Latin America has had a considerable effect in the West. But only in the past few years has Marxist cultural theory from outside Europe begun to influence American criticism, either because the distinctive conditions that made Western Marxism possible have not been duplicated elsewhere in the world or because the relatively linguistic orientation of much philosophy and aesthetics renders international transmission unusually problematic. This shift is a response both to the new prominence of what is usually designated either Third World or postcolonial literature and to modest demographic and more significant ideological changes in college literature departments in this country. A decade from now an international overview of Marxist cultural theory may look rather different.

But the preceding survey offers a selective account even of European Marxism, in ways that cannot be reduced to judgments of prestige or stature. It downplays social thought while giving equal attention to cultural theory and literary criticism, and it passes over even important cultural theorists—Karl Korsch, Ernst Bloch, Henri Lefebvre, and Maurice Merleau-Ponty, along with several other writers mentioned briefly above—unless they have proved influential in the United States. The figures treated at greater length can arguably be grouped into two main categories. The reification tradition, which stresses the autonomous logic of the commodity, extends with varying degrees of plausibility from Lukács through Benjamin, Horkheimer and Adorno, Sartre, Goldmann, and Habermas. A more tenuous hegemony line, with its emphasis on social institutions and practices, connects Gramsci to such otherwise disparate writers as Williams and Althusser, as well as to Laclau and Mouffe. Certain affinities and influences would also link Althusser to the postwar Italian Marxists, Eagleton, and even Brecht and Bakhtin. Yet too much should not be made of this pattern, which obscures both similarities between the two groups and differences—often polemically expressed—within each group. And if one is committed to dualities, it might be more useful to locate the unity of all these writers in the necessary confrontation with the constitutive, overlapping tensions of Marxism—between subject and object, agency and structure, theory and practice, science and ideology. Equally important, the relative emphasis here on the heterogeneous, open, and creative character of Marxist thought, to the neglect of its theoretical coherence or even of its sharply defined, polarized debates, depends on a series of underlying philosophical and political judgments. Discussion of those judgments is best deferred, however, until after a review of the American Marxist tradition.

That tradition does not come easily into focus, in part because of its immigrant communities and evident discontinuities. The discontinuities result in part from self-destructive political behavior but even more from political repression, especially after each of the world wars. A crucial question is the relation between the present moment and the Marxist cultural and literary criticism that emerged during the 1930s in response to and as part of a mass, though by no means predominantly socialist, working-class movement. That criticism is usually associated with a polemical advocacy of the norms of Stalinist socialist realism by Mike Gold and to a lesser extent Granville Hicks in the Communist journal *New Masses*. Yet it is important to recall the diversity and vitality of Marxist culture in this period and indeed as late as the 1950s, to recognize that its relative lack of interest in aesthetic questions perhaps indicates strength as much as weakness. Moreover, Marxism significantly influenced Philip Rahv, Edmund Wilson, Kenneth Burke, Malcolm Cowley, F. O. Mathiessen, Dwight MacDonald, Irving Howe, and C. L. R. James, among many others. In the late 1930s, intellectuals began defecting from Marxism for a variety of reasons. More decisive, however, was the repression of the left, which also predates World War II but which turned into a systematic purge only after 1945 and then continued for two decades before a new upsurge of radicalism seriously undermined its efficacy. Marxist literary critics and theorists were driven from colleges and universities, from the mass media, and from major publishing houses. At the theoretical level, New Criticism rose to prominence in part by successfully challenging a crude and reductive caricature of the domestic Marxist heritage.

The names listed in the previous paragraph reveal, however, that this heritage was not completely expunged from the record. But insofar as these critics continued to write in a radical vein, the absence of a broad leftist intellectual community meant that their work would be appropriated as idiosyncratic, isolated, individual achievements rather than as contributions to a larger socialist enterprise. The limited exception is James, the Trinidadian peripatetic revolutionary Marxist activist and philosopher; theorist of Pan-African, Caribbean, and African American liberation; and historian, cultural critic, and artist. Resident and politically active in the United States for fifteen years until his deportation in 1953, unshakably convinced that ordinary people can carry through a revolutionary transformation of the world in their own interests, James seems effortlessly to bridge the major gaps of Western Marxism—between theory and practice, elite culture and popular culture, Leninism and democracy, Europe and the Third World, class and race. Because of space limitations, he will have to stand in for the many, largely ignored Marxists who rejected both of Western Marxism's basic options—either Communist party membership or distance from political involvement. The unjust neglect of James's own work until very recently renders premature any confident assessment of the adequacy of the alternative posed by his cosmopolitan synthesis. But it obviously has considerable appeal today, and beginning in 1968, when James was allowed to visit America again, it had a marginal influence on the New Left and perhaps a rather more substantial effect on young black workers and intellectuals.

In general, however, when major activist movements reemerged in the 1960s, they were almost entirely cut off from their predecessors and not least from the indigenous tradition of Marxist cultural criticism. The considerably more impressive body of European Marxist theory was equally inaccessible. In 1960 little was available beyond a substantial amount of Marx and Engels (unstudied and untaught) and bits and pieces of the Frankfurt school and Sartre (removed from a political context). It took more than a decade to change the situation significantly, and much work remains to this day. The enormous price that the New Left in particular paid for this loss of the past—in knowledge, experience, constituency, and organizing skills—is still not adequately appreciated. Yet enforced discontinuity has its advantages, albeit lesser ones—in this instance, a powerful responsiveness to the heterogeneity of emergent progressive social movements that finds its delayed disciplinary echo in the diverse political approaches currently prominent in American academic literary study.

The Marxist criticism that came out of the New Left was part of a general rise of radical and often explicitly Marxist scholarship in most areas of the humanities and social sciences. In literature departments the relation between its two main forms reproduces the hierarchical structure of American higher education. On the one hand, a group of activist critics, including Louis Kampf, Paul Lauter, and Richard Ohmann, adopted an institutional and pedagogical focus whose central ongoing vehicles of expression are the Radical Caucus of the Modern Language Association and the journal the *Radical Teacher*. Rooted in the English departments of four-year and community colleges rather than in research universities, their work addresses the structure of the academic workplace and especially the teaching of undergraduates. It extends to educational efforts outside colleges and indeed outside the formal school system entirely. Their writings reveal relatively little concern with theoretical problems but a deep sensitivity to matters of gender and race in addition to class. Here Marxism is one major component of a broad, radical enterprise. Such work clearly has the potential to speak to the situation of the vast majority of college teachers of language and literature in the United States.

On the other hand, a different kind of Marxism simultaneously emerged, this one devoted to the construction of theory on the Continental European model. Not surprisingly, then, it was initially located in foreign language departments and especially in German, where a small number of job-seeking émigrés from West Germany brought their powerful native Marxist tradition along with them. This work had virtually no effect outside German studies in the United States until the founding of the journal *New German Critique* in the mid-1970s, and most of it remains untranslated. Only in the past decade have English and to a lesser extent comparative literature departments assumed a central position in American Marxist literary theory. Regardless of its departmental affiliations, however, this theoretical orientation has been a phenomenon of research universities rather than of colleges. It sometimes seems narrowly professional in its focus on conferences, publication—its central journal is appropriately called *Social Text*—and the training of graduate students. Perhaps analogously, emphasis on the classical categories of Marxism may leave little room for serious attention to a variety of other forms of oppression, although this absence is much less evident in recent work. Like its Continental predecessors, American Marxist theory inevitably has an elitist feel. Given the structure of higher education in this country, it also is accorded far greater prestige than the more activist pedagogical Marxism described above.

A defense of the project of Marxist theory, though not necessarily of that project's priority, would undoubtedly emphasize the importance of developing an American Marxist intelligentsia across generational lines and of entering into international Marxist discussions. But if such considerations explain the necessity of a scholarly, publication-centered undertaking, they do not adequately account for the prominence of theory, especially in the light of the relatively empirical American Marxism that has developed over the last fifteen years in the social sciences. Several other forces converged to produce this result. For Marxist criticism to regain entry to the academy, it had to overcome its reputation for reductiveness by providing evidence of methodological sophistication. Partly in response to the political upheavals of the time, the paradigm—though not the practice—of New Criticism collapsed by the end of the 1960s at the latest, leaving a conceptual vacuum in literary study. Thus an opening appeared for a new theoretical justification of the discipline that would in addition be able to speak to the critical atmosphere of the time. Marxism was only one and hardly the most successful of the options offered. Finally, the downturn in political activity by the early 1970s implicitly validated the appropriateness of a relatively detached project. Yet necessary conditions are not sufficient ones. To understand how Marxist literary theory became established in the United States, one might recall that some of the members of the Frankfurt school who fled the advance of fascism in the late 1930s and came to this country remained here after the war. In the 1960s one of them, Marcuse, emerged as the intellectual mentor of the radical movement in the United States and parts of Western Europe. And he is among the twentieth-century German cultural theorists who are considered in conjunction with Sartre in Fredric Jameson's 1971 study, *Marxism and Form*.

Situated against a narrowly native tradition of Marxist criticism, Jameson's book, with its unusual erudition, sophistication, and complexity, seemed to come from nowhere. In practice it established what has proved to be the main line of contemporary American Marxist criticism. Of course, the long-term significance of *Marxism and Form* was unclear twenty years ago, and it is often obscured today as well, when Jameson's subsequent writings and a variety of other developments are felt—incorrectly—to have reduced the volume to a historical document. The first half of the book treats the German tradition, including Adorno, Benjamin, Marcuse, Bloch, and Lukács; the remainder is evenly divided between long chapters on Sartre and on dialectical criticism. In focusing on other theorists and critics, then, Jameson is not so much critical as metacritical—a stance that bears a certain resemblance to Paul de Man's in *Blindness and Insight*, published the same year. That stance should not be seen merely as the ordinary consequence of producing a commentary on criticism and theory, however. Rather, in at least two ways it designates the necessary methodological procedure of any serious intellectual enterprise. First, metacriticism acknowledges the importance of self-consciousness, of reckoning the interpreter into the interpretation. A Hegelian dialectic links the subjective critic to the object of criticism as part of the process by which a synthetic, totalizing perspective is achieved. More specifically, this second-order orientation acquires a contemporary urgency from the opacity, the reification of modern life and art, a crisis that requires the act of metacommentary in order to reconnect the fragments into a totality, to penetrate beneath surface abstraction to underlying concreteness. Finally, for Jameson, because other disciplines are symptoms rather than diagnoses of the crisis, literary criticism bears a special responsibility for carrying out this reconstituting task. Although American literary study of the last two decades has rejected the totalizing enterprise called for here, it has strikingly taken on the more general obligation that Jameson stresses—the development of a theoretically innovative critical analysis of contemporary culture and society.

Since most of these themes and procedures remain central to Jameson's subsequent work, they receive consideration below. Here it is worth dwelling instead on the critic's and the work's significance during the 1970s. Simply put, *Marxism and Form* made Marxist criticism stick in the United States. After its appearance, dismissive remarks about that criticism's inevitably dogmatic, reductive predictability, though still frequent, could no longer be seriously sustained. During the remainder of the decade, Jameson attracted increasing interest with the publication of two more books and a number of articles. Several talented students, many of whom have since established themselves as thoughtful critics, came to study with him at San Diego. Working primarily with those students, Jameson was instrumental in starting the Marxist Literary Group, which organizes sessions at national and regional MLA conventions, publishes a newsletter, and runs an annual summer institute. At the end of the decade, he cofounded the journal *Social Text*, which, as the title suggests, is designed to bring recent advances in literary theory to bear on broad cultural and social problems. More generally, Jameson provided a model for younger critics drawn to Marxism but in search of a method. An entire generation remains indebted to him: without his example their work would be unimaginable.

*The Political Unconscious*, which appeared a decade after *Marxism and Form*, marks a shift from the earlier work both in nature and in influence. In 1972 Jameson had published *The Prison-House of Language: A Critical Account of Structuralism and Russian Formalism*. *The Political Unconscious* synthesizes the predominantly German tradition of *Marxism and Form* and the predominantly French tradition of *The Prison-House of Language*—if one understands these national rubrics more as methodological than as national categories. The work combines a continuing allegiance to Sartre and especially to Lukács with an appropriation of Vladimir Propp, Jacques Lacan, Claude Lévi-Strauss, A. J. Greimas, Gilles Deleuze and Félix Guattari, and especially Althusser. Furthermore, although the first half of the volume pursues a meta-theoretical tack reminiscent of the two earlier works, the emphasis falls more clearly on the construction of Jameson's own theoretical perspective. And the second half moves to practical criticism, albeit of a distinctive type, presenting readings of Honoré de Balzac, George Gissing, and especially Joseph Conrad.

Opinion remains divided on both the character and the success of the synthesis between diachronic dialectics and synchronic structuralism. Yet the very notion of synthesis itself, as well as the prominence of metacommentary and especially of totalizing claims for Marxism, suggests that *The Political Unconscious* effects the subordinate incorporation of structuralism into an encompassing Hegelian Marxist project. Thus Jameson "conceives of the political perspective . . . not as an optional auxiliary to other interpretive methods . . . but rather as the absolute horizon of all reading and interpretation" (17). This perspective consists of three concentric frameworks. In the first or political phase, the text remains coincident with the individual literary work but functions as a symbolic act designed to provide formal solutions to unresolvable social problems. In the larger second or social framework, the text enters the field of class struggle as an antagonistic, dialogical, collective discourse organized into minimal units of intelligibility called ideologemes and involved in conflicts over legitimation, hegemony, popular culture, and subversion. The third and ultimate semantic horizon is history, understood by Jameson as the contradictory, simultaneous coexistence of several modes of production. The text is here rewritten as part of a permanent cultural revolution, which is apprehended through attention to the ideology of form. The later chapters on the novelists repeat this procedure at the level of extended example, moving from the symbolic act in Balzac through the ideologeme in Gissing to the ideology of form in Conrad. In other words, Jameson's solution to the dilemma posed by the aestheticizing tendency of Western Marxism is to reinscribe literary theory in the classical categories of Marxism and thereby to see literature as an agent in the fundamental struggles of human beings. The result is grandly synthetic in a fashion unknown in North American criticism at least since Northrop Frye's *Anatomy of Criticism* (1957).

The efficacy of the synthesis is another matter. The argument oscillates uncomfortably between a traditional Marxist appeal to history as ground
and a more poststructuralist or Althusserian notion of history as absent cause.
Jameson insists:

> The human adventure is one; . . . long-dead issues . . . can recover their original
> urgency for us only if they are retold within the unity of a single great collective
> story; only if . . . they are seen as sharing a single fundamental theme . . . ;
> only if they are grasped as vital episodes in a single vast unfinished plot.
>
> (19–20)

The critic, he continues, is engaged "in detecting the traces of that uninterrupted narrative, in restoring to the surface of the text the repressed and buried
reality of this fundamental history." But only a few pages later, it turns out

> that history is *not* a text, not a narrative, master or otherwise, but that, as an
> absent cause, it is inaccessible to us except in textual form, and that our
> approach to it and to the Real itself necessarily passes through its prior textu-
> alization, its narrativization in the political unconscious.    (35)

A similar difficulty troubles the chapter on Balzac, which has recourse to Lacan
for a critique of the centered subject and for the categories of the imaginary,
the symbolic, and the real. The assertion without any substantive argument
that Lacan's work, which concerns "the individual biological subject, is not
incompatible with a broader historical framework" (153) leads to the vulnerable
conclusion that the novelist's "heterogeneous narrative registers [depend], as
their condition of possibility, upon a psychic situation in which the centered
subject has not yet emerged" (179).

The chapter on Conrad integrates the use of metacommentary, deployed in order to discover some coherence in the bewildering variety of interpretations of the novelist, with the notion of reification, utilized as a mediatory
code to connect style with narrative and both with society. Though the terms
work well together, separately each poses problems. The practice of metacommentary rests on the assumption that proper interpretation concerns not interpretation itself but the impossibility of interpretation. This method opens up
a process of infinite regress that undermines not only its own privileged position
but also any larger totalizing claims. An emphasis on reification limits the
surface of the text to symptoms while finding meaningfulness only in the
depths. To sustain this approach, Jameson must ignore a considerable amount
of overt social material in the novels, ending up instead with a vague intellectual history in which Conrad is compared with a range of writers extending
chronologically from Balzac to Sartre. More generally, the broadly narrative,

totalizing framework of Jameson's writing sometimes obscures important specificities and differences, whether these are formal concerns such as the nature of lyric or social ones such as racial or sexual oppression.

There are possible replies to such objections and to many others that have appeared in print. Yet despite the criticisms leveled against it, *The Political Unconscious* inaugurated a second moment in contemporary American Marxist criticism in which that criticism played a considerably expanded role in the discipline of literary studies. The leading Marxist critic in the United States and a respected theorist in the 1970s, Jameson became in the 1980s one of the central figures in American and, increasingly, international literary study. *The Political Unconscious* received book-length commentary as well as the attention of several special issues of journals. And Jameson's recent writing has significantly influenced such emergent fields as Third World studies, film criticism, cultural studies, and especially the theory of postmodernism. His most ambitious text to date, *Postmodernism; or, The Cultural Logic of Late Capitalism* (1991), marks a third stage in his career, in which literary theory is replaced at the center of his work by the broadly cultural concerns that have formed part of his subject for more than two decades. In retrospect, this eleventh volume by Jameson—there are also well over one hundred articles—seems like the logical culmination of the project for literary study outlined twenty years earlier at the end of *Marxism and Form*. Yet in the introduction, Jameson calls *Postmodernism* merely "the third and last section of the penultimate subdivision of a larger project entitled *The Poetics of Social Forms*" (xxii).

The title of the book accurately, though ambiguously, conveys its strong and distinctive thesis. Jameson argues not only that postmodernism is related to the current—late or multinational—stage of capitalism, nor even only that it is the dominant or hegemonic form of culture of this stage, but that late capitalism is defined by its cultural logic, by postmodernism. He seeks not just to explain what the cultural logic of late capitalism is but to argue that the logic of late capitalism is cultural. He does not simply answer the question, What kind of *cultural* logic is specific to late capitalism? He asks what kind of *logic* is specific to late capitalism, to which the answer is a *cultural* logic and specifically postmodernism. Postmodernism refers to a stage in the capitalist mode of production that accords cultural production a distinct function. It occurs when the process of modernization is complete, when the commodity has penetrated and colonized previously impervious arenas of life, including both culture and the psyche, so that there no longer is any outside. This central claim registers the effect of the mass media and more generally of the information revolution, and it suggests why the United States is the home of postmodernism, whose crystallization Jameson dates to 1973.

The thesis also governs a series of secondary hypotheses, many of which turn on a powerfully developed contrast with modernism. A shift in perception from time to space results in the preeminence of a depthlessness evident in a new culture of the image and in a concomitant decline of temporality, historicity, and totalizing thought. In a similar process at the private level, the schizophrenic subject emerges from the waning of affect and the fragmentation of the psyche. New emotional intensities—both exhilaration and paranoia—develop in response to the unrepresentability of contemporary high-tech machinery. The previously constitutive distinction between high culture and mass culture collapses; critical distance in the arts disappears with the replacement of parody by pastiche; and television supplants film as the dominant cultural form. But Jameson also attends to ostensible countertendencies—to survivals of the modern, to utopianism, and to the return of the historical repressed. And he considers and correlates an enormous range of issues and materials—experimental video, nostalgia films, art and architecture, the novel, recent American literary theory and the problem of interpretation, the new social movements and the question of agency, the resurgence of religious fundamentalism, decadence and difference, the ideologies of postmodernism and of the market, the significance of demography, and, as a response to the spatial character of postmodernism, what he calls cognitive mapping.

Many of these "texts" are analyzed in a series of detailed close readings that immerse the reader in the feel of the postmodern and make up more than half the book. Though the other parts of the volume—the introduction, opening two chapters, and very lengthy conclusion—also offer specific analyses, they carry the burden of the larger generalizing claims. The possible tension between these two parts self-consciously defines the project. *Postmodernism* attempts to think historically about a world that has lost that capacity, to totalize a phenomenon defined by differentiation. More striking still, it is as much an instance of postmodern theorizing as a theory of postmodernism; it both analyzes and exemplifies its object of inquiry; it both *is* and is *about* postmodernism. At the stylistic level, Jameson's complex dialectical sentences, in which everything connects to everything else, attempt to register at least the phenomenon, the appearance, of nonrelatedness. At the structural level, the individual close readings strive simultaneously for the exemplary and the eccentric. Thus the chapter on experimental video fails to make a serious argument for the applicability of the provocative theses to the central medium of commercial television; the essay on architecture begins by suggesting the possible irrelevance of the analyzed building to postmodernism in general and even to postmodern architecture; and the discussion of the novel is anachronistically limited to the *nouveau roman*. This is the point of the enterprise, however— to reconstruct the system from the experience of dispersal and heterogeneity.

The almost inevitable objections to such a highly controversial project have already emerged in response to the titular essay (first published in 1984), which has provoked widespread commentary, including a collection of critical appraisals. The fundamental charge is that Jameson cannot have it both ways. From certain postmodernist perspectives, the totalizing, periodizing, and politicizing thrust of the argument seems misguided and futile at best. From certain Marxist perspectives, the acceptance of fragmentation seems self-defeating despite Jameson's insistence that there is no alternative, that one cannot in any simple way take sides for or against the phenomenon, that a serious radicalism must work through—rather than around—postmodernism. At a lower level of generality, the identification of postmodernism and late capitalism may appear arbitrary, overstated, or at least premature: even otherwise sympathetic readers may resist the claims for the hegemonic status of postmodernism and for the specifically *cultural* logic of late capitalism. Though many other criticisms are also possible and though discussion of Jameson's arguments has only begun, this study is bound to transform the debate about the nature of postmodernism and perhaps more generally of the advanced capitalist world as well.

A movement similar to Jameson's, from literary to cultural studies, has marked both American Marxist criticism more generally and American literary criticism as a whole in the last several years. It may thus be useful to speak of *Postmodernism* as a crucial text of a third moment in contemporary American Marxist criticism. But whatever the appropriate demarcations, the last decade has witnessed a remarkable increase in the quantity and almost certainly the quality of that criticism. Most of the publications are articles and first books by relatively young scholars. Like the other forms of political criticism currently prominent in the United States, the Marxist work is a sign that the generation of the 1960s has come of academic age. As suggested above, that generation had much earlier unwittingly opened professional doors for itself by challenging with some success the ideological structures of higher education. The liberal academic backlash against the policies of the Reagan administration, though recently replaced by a conservative counteroffensive, for a time allowed room for more radical criticism. The example of the work of Jameson and now others as well has continued to provide both a defense and a model for younger Marxists and other politically oriented critics—in other words, a method of pursuing an academic career while, on an optimistic interpretation, keeping some faith with social activism. Thus although Jameson's writings remain preeminent, the very success of his effort to invent and disseminate a powerful American Marxist criticism may be contributing to a paradoxical but desirable outcome—the continuing increase in his stature combined with the relative decline in his importance due to an end to his isolation and to the growing acceptance, duplication, and extension of his project.

Current Marxist literary scholarship takes a number of forms. One is the further elaboration and contestation of theoretical and methodological agendas. Within Marxism itself the often fierce polemics of the 1970s between

Hegelians and structuralists have died down into peaceful coexistence. Today one finds Lukácsians as well as Althusserians. More important, the vast majority of Marxist critics, like Jameson, draw readily not only on a spectrum of Marxist thinkers but also on a variety of other theoretical perspectives. As noted earlier, Marxist literary theory reentered the university as part of a general turn to Continental theory. And that theory, unlike New Criticism, retained some connection to Marxism. The loose but sometimes tense alliance between Marxist and poststructuralist critics, which rests on institutional, generational, ideological, and philosophical affinities, has gradually resulted in significant mutual influence. Yet few theorists have attempted to imitate Jameson's totalizing strategy, in part, perhaps, because the problems he seems to come up against look less like subjective failings than objective limits, at least at the present. In any case, the rise of eclecticism, which by now is nearly as pronounced in American Marxist criticism as it is in contemporary British Marxist literary study, represents a reaction against what is obviously felt to be an excessively abstract insistence on methodological and theoretical rigor. Recent political criticism, and not only in Marxism, often gains range and flexibility by sacrificing precision and consistency.

A balance sheet evaluating this shift cannot yet be drawn up with any confidence, but something of the feel of Marxist criticism at its best today may emerge from consideration of the work of Gayatri Chakravorty Spivak. Spivak is often associated with the effort to connect Marxism and deconstruction, and she has herself emphasized the centrality of deconstruction to her criticism. But Spivak is paradigmatic because her writing draws significantly not only on Marxism and deconstruction but also on psychoanalysis, feminism, and Third World studies, among many other approaches. Unlike Jameson she explicitly rejects any global, totalizing aspiration, a rejection at one with the shape of her oeuvre over the last fifteen years—no book-length project but a vast number of essays, some of which she has collected in a single volume, *In Other Worlds*. Although the individual articles intersect, the work makes no attempt to establish an overarching unity at the level of theory, substantive argument, or object of inquiry. Within a single piece, one regularly encounters references to theoretical roads not taken, a shifting and multilayered vocabulary, and quite often a sense of fragmentation.

The deliberately antiprogrammatic character of this strategy enacts the conviction that in literary discourse "the truth of a human situation *is* the itinerary of not being able to find it" (77). The potential disproportion between the enormously complicated methodological machinery and the actual conclusions reached is thus precisely the point. With genuine consistency she argues that "Marxism and feminism must become persistent interruptions of each other" (249). But the mode of interruption often takes a different form: "it is . . . the deconstructive view that keeps [her] resisting the essentialist freezing of the concepts of gender, race, and class" (84). From this perspective, deconstruction carries out a second-order critique of categories that, however problematic and untotalizable, remain primary. It does so by "its insistence that in disclosing complicities the critic-as-subject is herself complicit with the object of her critique" (180). This complicity is revealed by an allegorical approach to the literary text, which one "must wrench . . . out of its proper context and put . . . within alien arguments" (241). The "alien arguments" are those of high theory, which in an elegant reversal becomes the object of the literary text's critique: "If thus placed in the arguments from Western Marxist-Feminism, Western Liberal Feminism, and French high theory of the Female Body, [Mahasweta Devi's] 'Stanadayini' can show us some of their limits and limitations" (241).

Designed to produce politically useful readings, this complex procedure poses a number of problems. What persuasiveness does a radically decontextualizing interpretation possess? The reply that every appropriation decontextualizes may not adequately answer this question. But even if it does, the danger remains that the "literariness of literature," which invites "us to take a distance from the continuing project of reason" (249–50), has been asked to bear excessive allegorical weight, that relatively little follows from a single text's demonstration of the inadequacies of a theory. Spivak does not explain the practical, strategic, nonauthoritative basis for determining political utility. She is hardly alone: analogous dilemmas can be found in Michel Foucault and Eagleton, among many others. In the absence of a criterion of judgment, the rejection of foundationalism often leads to its covert return—here, most likely in the form of the primary categories noted above. Similarly, Spivak asserts but does not really show that her deconstructive operation avoids the risk of going to the opposite extreme, of revealing the metaphysical character of all discourse, and of undermining the distinctions between helpful and destructive positions. One may again wonder if race, class, and gender provide ultimate points of reference. But however these issues are evaluated, the systematic antisystematicity of this project, which recalls Laclau and Mouffe's work, sets it apart not only from Jameson's more Lukácsian endeavor but also from the eclectic Marxism it may seem to resemble. Although Spivak may be at her best in her relatively recent work on India, her practice of a consistently and immensely sophisticated, politically committed criticism that is sensitive to a range of forms of injustice and oppression has no real parallel in the United States today.

Spivak's work is also representative to the extent that it focuses as much on practical criticism as it does on theory. The partial shift away from theory is connected to the tendency toward eclecticism. Recent practical Marxist criticism addresses the literary canon in at least two ways. First, it has undertaken a reevaluation of the central texts, figures, movements, and historical problems of that canon as traditionally constituted. Research along these lines finds its most powerful theoretical rationale in Lukács's claims that canonical texts are in fact great, that they are great because they are realistic, and that therefore they resemble Marxism in revealing the true movement of history. Like some of his pre–World War I predecessors and Eastern European successors, Lukács argued for *Erbschaft*, for the inheritance—and appropriation—of the best of the bourgeois past in the socialist present. Despite its evident elitism, this position should not be lightly dismissed in the absence of a compelling alternative theory of the canon. Its practical consequences have an additional pragmatic justification in the United States today: Marxist critics cannot always choose the ground of contestation. The literary canon interpreted in certain ways continues to play a role in class formation and ideological legitimation. Marxists have no option but to attempt to gain some influence on the meanings produced by still powerful cultural artifacts. Yet there are reasons for doubting whether the traditional canon could ever play a central role in the fundamental task of creating a broad radical or socialist culture. The rereading of the canon should therefore be seen as a necessary defensive, delegitimizing, neutralizing, ground-clearing, modestly constructive, and primarily preparatory activity.

Second, Marxism challenges the racial, sexual, and class biases governing the inclusion and exclusion of texts in the received canon. But there is nothing distinctively Marxist about the recovery of writings by, for example, women or African Americans. Marxists have contributed to this important process but probably have been the dominant force only in the study of Third World literature, a position almost certainly related to the traditional centrality of Marxism in the critique of imperialism. More generally, much recent work combines class analysis with the elucidation of sexual and racial hierarchies in accounts of canonical texts, a project with the strengths and weaknesses noted above. The other major mechanism by which to expand the canon, the restoration of working-class literature to visibility, *is* a distinctively Marxist project. But it has far less promise and has enjoyed far less success in the United States than in England. Instead, North American Marxists have sometimes substituted an interest in preindustrial popular culture. In the absence of a convincing account of the relation of that culture to the subordinate cultures of today, however, the potential political value of this line of inquiry remains problematic.

A number of forces have thus converged to promote the study of culture and especially of mass culture, which, along with ethnic and Third World studies, are the fastest growing areas of American Marxist "literary" study. The turn to culture radicalizes the efforts to widen the literary canon by calling into question the centrality of the category of literature itself. It entails a refusal to identify culture with high culture and hence a self-conscious distancing from the elitism that is hard to avoid in discussions of literature. British Marxists, especially Williams and members of the Birmingham Center for Contemporary Cultural Studies, have done much more in this area than their American Marxist counterparts have. In the United States, attention has focused on mass culture and recently on the question of postmodernism in particular. This emphasis responds to the overwhelming power of the mass media in this country, a power that is increasingly global in its effect. But it may also implicitly register doubts about the viability of alternative approaches to culture—about, that is, the insurgent potential of the culture of the people, of workers, of women, or of ethnic minorities. The issue here is not the absence of critical cultural activity in these and other groups but the suspicion that such activity can have significant influence only by passing through the production, distribution, and consumption networks of mass culture and by finding a way to convert those networks to radical ends. On this view, there can be no path to a radical or socialist popular culture that simply evades these important multinational corporations. But Marxist cultural theorists have not yet developed anything like an adequate strategy for waging the struggle over democratic control of mass culture.

Finally, the institutional perspective toward which such studies tend can be self-reflexively focused back on the institutions of criticism and of higher education. A considerable amount of recent Marxist work has examined higher education. On the structure of the academic discipline of literature, however, the United States once again lags far behind England.

Readers already familiar with Marxist thought have probably recognized the Hegelian totalizing framework of the preceding discussion. How can this perspective be reconciled with the earlier insistence on the heterogeneity of the European Marxist tradition? For better or worse, the answer is that the potential contradiction between the two positions is deliberate. Emphasis on diversity means more than a recognition of obvious facts or even of the need for Marxism to break definitively with its dogmatic tendencies. Flexibility and responsiveness to changing conditions depend on an openness of outlook and a range of resources. By contrast, a totalizing imperative registers the value of relational thinking, the potentially unsurpassed persuasiveness of general explanations. One might project the structural tension between these two poles along a historical axis, imagining an oscillation over time between synthetic and analytic impulses, each of which would repeatedly engage in demystifying critiques of the other.

From this unstable standpoint, the goal of Marxist criticism is to contribute to the formation of a radical cultural practice that is an important part of a broad movement of social transformation. Its specific procedure, which might go under such labels as ideological analysis or cultural critique, has the responsibility of both demystification and reconstruction. To the field of literary study, Marxist thought brings an emphasis on complex, hierarchically structured forms of connectedness, which are defended on the grounds of explanatory power and moral urgency. Such an emphasis aims at transforming not merely critical practice but also the relationships of academic critics to their immediate institutions as well as to the society at large. From literary study, Marxism takes a methodological sophistication and focus on culture less common in more traditional areas of Marxist inquiry. This bidirectional relation to literary criticism (contributing generalizing theory, carrying away a concern with particularity) corresponds in some respects to the contradictory imperatives of totalization and dispersal evoked earlier. This dual perspective might prove more generally suggestive not only to artists who are concerned with the social resonance of their work but also to larger movements for change that are determined both to respect cultural specificity and to break with the long and enduring heritage of self-destructive fragmentation on the American left.

These movements may take on a specifically Marxist character; more likely they will not. But if they do not, if Marxism is felt to be insufficiently comprehensive, the solution will surely not be a combination of class and gender or even of class, gender, and race. Despite the fine current work establishing such linkages, two or three final instances—whether class, gender, and race or some other categories—add up to less than one. The attraction of traditional Marxism is its coherent explanatory and strategic stance. No synthesis of, for example, Marxism and feminism will achieve as much for the simple reason that the number of forms of hierarchy, injustice, and oppression is indefinitely large. A genuinely post-Marxist, rather than non-Marxist, position will have to be responsive to this reality, will have to appropriate important motifs from Marxism and many other theories of inequality without degenerating into a new pluralism.

Even such scaled-down claims attribute considerable validity to Marxism. Searching criticism of central Marxist propositions began over a century ago and continues today on economic, social, political, and historical grounds. In many areas, persuasive replies have not been forthcoming. But the absence of alternatives to Marxism is equally striking. Although the modern social sciences have assimilated a considerable portion of Marxist thought, the results have not proved consistently satisfying. This is especially true in these disciplines' tendency not to replicate the fundamental combination of the analytical and the insurgent that is one of Marxism's enduring sources of appeal. To the extent that Marxism has now become effectively identified with the oppressor rather than the oppressed, however, its long-term vitality is by no means assured. In literary and cultural studies, this issue has arisen in recent decades in the poststructuralist critique of Marxism's essentialist, totalizing models, models that in extreme formulations are said to lead directly to the gulag.

Most, perhaps all, of the thinkers of the past quarter century who are re-viewed in this essay attempt to address these problems, with the uncertain results described. Yet the gravitational pull of Marxism on even those theo-rists determined to break free of its orbit—Laclau and Mouffe or Foucault—testifies to its continuing centrality within the radical tradition, to the absence of any other comparably comprehensive oppositional and transformational perspective.

In this light what has American Marxist criticism accomplished? As suggested earlier, never before has there been so much or so much good Marxist criticism in the United States. It has been reasonably successful in theoretical and cultural studies, in Third World studies, in English and American litera-ture from the Renaissance on, and in German, Latin American, and perhaps French literature. Not surprisingly the situation is less impressive in Spanish literature, in classical and medieval studies, and in the literatures of present or former Communist countries. The absolute gains notwithstanding, Marxist work forms only a small proportion of the total amount of criticism published today. The same goes for the number of Marxist professors of literature, al-though here too one may suspect that actual effect exceeds percentage of repre-sentation. This is not to say, however, that Marxism compares in influence with feminism or even necessarily with other currently dynamic approaches such as deconstruction, new historicism, or psychoanalysis. If one's purview is limited to the classroom, New Criticism continues to outstrip all these schools, perhaps all of them combined. It is possible, however, that in the coming years the more recent theories and methods, perhaps including Marxism, will increase both relatively and absolutely in pedagogical significance as tradi-tional forms of criticism gradually decline.

An international perspective sheds further light on the American situ-ation. In England, Marxist criticism is considerably more prominent. This disparity results from the far greater weight of British left-wing, working-class culture and from the far greater resistance of British universities to Marxist initiatives—a resistance compounded of the ideological hostility shown by the literature profession and the Tory-induced financial crisis of higher education. American critics, whether or not they are Marxists, have begun to reap the benefits of British work. More generally, both England and the United States have witnessed a striking development of Marxist thought at almost the very moment when the tradition has suffered devastating reversals in much of western Europe, eastern Europe, the former Soviet Union, and, in a different way, the People's Republic of China. It is not clear whether Anglo-American intellectuals will also outgrow the foolish passions of youth or—in a paradoxical but perhaps more hopeful scenario—whether the consistently innovative and imperialistic character of American culture will render contemporary Marxist work here a useful model for critical activity in other countries.

Realization of the optimistic alternative depends in part on how one assesses the institutional and social position of Marxist academics. In allowing Marxists to enter the professoriate, the ruling class arguably coopted negativity or at least retrospectively found a way to keep potential troublemakers off the streets. This conclusion seems unduly pessimistic if not simply misguided. More likely, militant protest opened the university to Marxists and other radicals over the resistance of elite groups, who rightly thought they had something to lose. Although some Marxist intellectuals would undoubtedly have become full-time activists had academic careers not been available to them, others would have entirely lost contact with left-wing politics. Equally important, higher education plays a significant role in the social and ideological dimensions of class formation. Only in contrast to the far more immediately pressing demands of protest struggles do the gradual and less dramatic counterhegemonic agendas of radical academics seem nugatory. Marxist and other leftist critics have taken genuine if inadequate steps toward remaking their disciplines. But the restructuring of the field, which now seems possible, is not the same as the transformation of an institution. No such outcome can reasonably be envisaged in large or elite universities, with their inextricable ties to corporate and state power. Yet if it is not possible to democratize higher education, it *is* possible to convert it into a terrain of ideological contestation. The real but limited progress here will prove important, however, only when it issues in sustained campus activism.

Events in the academy are of course influenced by developments in the society and the world as a whole. The most dramatic of these in recent years, repeatedly alluded to above, have occurred in eastern Europe and the former Soviet Union, where mass movements have swept away Communist regimes. The consequences of the demise of Communism, which may become a global phenomenon, will not emerge with any clarity for some time. Revulsion against neo-Stalinism could carry Leninism, Marxism, socialism, social democracy, and even liberalism along into oblivion—without mitigating the destructive aspects of the very capitalist system that gave Marxism its cogency in the first place. But the removal of Communism from the political landscape could instead open the space for new radical popular movements to take up many of the traditional themes of Marxism, though no doubt in a different vocabulary. At least in the United States, the important point is that the outcome is not predetermined, that the choices made by oppositional intellectuals could make a difference.

It therefore seems fair to conclude that, however substantial the advances, Marxist critics have not adequately dealt with the basic difficulties: articulating a comprehensive theory that nonetheless respects important differences; developing a strategy for the radical reappropriation of mass culture and its complex technologies; establishing practical connections between academic work and efforts to construct alternative cultures and institutions; and, more generally, forming linkages between academic Marxism and working-class and other oppositional movements. These limitations are interrelated. Overcoming them requires an initial recognition that the dilemma of any academic radicals seeking to connect up with popular organizations is exacerbated for Marxist intellectuals by the absence of a radical working-class movement which might give direction and timeliness to their work; that the evolution of American capitalism and not of American capitalism alone will result in the ongoing relative diminution of the industrial working class and probably of its unionized component as well; and that although the working class in a broader sense will continue to make up the majority of the employed population, members of that class may prove increasingly unlikely to define themselves exclusively or even primarily in terms of class. It is from some such point of departure that solutions to the urgent problems confronting Marxist critics become, if hardly inevitable, then at least imaginable.

## Selected Bibliography

Althusser, Louis. *For Marx.* 1965. Trans. Ben Brewster. London: NLB, 1977. Althusser's first collection; see especially "Contradiction and Overdetermination," "The 'Piccolo Teatro': Bertolazzi and Brecht," and "Marxism and Humanism."

Bakhtin, Mikhail M. *The Dialogic Imagination: Four Essays.* 1975. Trans. Caryl Emerson and Michael Holquist. Austin: U of Texas P, 1981. Written between 1934 and 1941; see the discussion of Rabelais and "Discourse in the Novel."

Benjamin, Walter. *Illuminations.* Ed. Hannah Arendt. Trans. Harry Zohn. New York: Schocken, 1969. A wide-ranging compilation from the 1920s and 1930s; includes pieces on Brecht, Baudelaire, the mechanical reproduction of art, and the philosophy of history.

Eagleton, Terry. *The Ideology of the Aesthetic.* Oxford: Blackwell, 1990. Three hundred years of primarily German aesthetic theory; ends with postmodernism.

Gramsci, Antonio. *Selections from the Prison Notebooks.* 1948–51. Ed. and trans. Quintin Hoare and Geoffrey Nowell Smith. New York: International, 1971. Written between 1929 and 1935; for the concept of hegemony, see "State and Civil Society."

Habermas, Jürgen. *The Philosophical Discourse of Modernity: Twelve Lectures.* 1985. Trans. Frederick G. Lawrence. Cambridge: MIT P, 1987.

A defense of modernity against poststructuralism; notable chapters on Foucault and Habermas's own theory of communicative reason.

Horkheimer, Max, and Theodor W. Adorno. *Dialectic of Enlightenment*. 1944. Trans. John Cumming. New York: Herder, 1972.
Probably the central text of the Frankfurt school, written in American exile and noted for its critique of Western rationalism and of the emergent "culture industry."

Jameson, Fredric. *The Political Unconscious: Narrative as a Socially Symbolic Act*. Ithaca: Cornell UP, 1981.

———. *Postmodernism; or, The Cultural Logic of Late Capitalism*. Durham: Duke UP, 1991.

Laclau, Ernesto, and Chantal Mouffe. *Hegemony and Socialist Strategy: Towards a Radical Democratic Politics*. Trans. Winston Moore and Paul Cammack. London: Verso, 1985.

Lukács, Georg. *History and Class Consciousness: Studies in Marxist Dialectics*. 1923. Trans. Rodney Livingstone. Cambridge: MIT P, 1971.
Lukács's major work; includes a central, long essay on reification.

Marx, Karl, and Friedrich Engels. *The Marx-Engels Reader*. Ed. Robert C. Tucker. 2nd ed. New York: Norton, 1978.

Sartre, Jean-Paul. *Critique of Dialectical Reason: Theory of Practical Ensembles*. 1960. Trans. Alan Sheridan-Smith. Vol. 1. London: NLB, 1976.
Sartre's major Marxist philosophical work, concerned with praxis, collectivities, and totalization.

Spivak, Gayatri Chakravorty. *In Other Worlds: Essays in Cultural Politics*. New York: Methuen, 1987.

Williams, Raymond. *The Country and the City*. New York: Oxford UP, 1973.
Williams's major work; a social rewriting of the history of English literature since the Renaissance.

———. *Marxism and Literature*. Oxford: Oxford UP, 1977.
An introductory survey inflected toward Williams's characteristic concerns.

# $\mathcal{P}$ sychoanalytic Criticism

## MEREDITH SKURA

Freud's psychology . . . touches at the very heart of human
interest. For that reason, however, people resent and reject what
does not appeal to them in his psychology, and thus distort it.

—Walter Lippman (1915)

[Freud's discovery was that] the true center of the human being is
henceforth no longer what it has been considered to be. . . . To
install the ego in the center of the perspective, as is done in the
present [ego-psychology] orientation of analysis, is only one of
those returns to which any calling into question of man's position
finds itself exposed.

—Jacques Lacan (1955)

I have no patience with this post-Freudian psychology, which
usually consists of Freud's psychology with all the difficult parts
left out.

—J. C. Hill to Anna Freud (1977)

In 1981 and 1982, when the MLA last assessed literary study, the
results were published in two separate volumes: one describing literary study
itself (Gibaldi) and a second describing "interrelations" between literature and
other disciplines like psychology (Barricelli and Gibaldi). But this volume includes psychoanalysis within literary study itself—just as courses on Freud
are now taught by English rather than psychology departments and just as
literary criticism now deals with the "psychoanalytic" issues of subjectivity,
sexual difference, and power. With titles like "Is the Rectum a Grave?" (Bersani) and "Female Chatter: Meter, Masochism, and the *Lyrical Ballads*"
(Pinch), criticism sounds increasingly like psychoanalysis. If a discipline is
seen as a "field"—so much ground to be covered or fought over—this "blurring
of the borders" (D. Gunn 219nl) gives evidence for Shoshana Felman's claim
that "there are no *natural* boundaries between the academically defined disciplines of literature and psychoanalysis" (*Literature* 9).

Change was inevitable. Once criticism no longer needed to define itself as "new" by differentiating itself from other disciplines, it opened itself to changes of all kinds—a process made more attractive, perhaps, by boredom with the old dogmas and familiar texts and more necessary by the entry of new constituencies into the graduate schools and the openness to new philosophies from abroad. Whatever the cause, New Criticism has been challenged, as have the assumptions on which it was based: the nature of authors and readers, texts and language, and the presumed separation of an aesthetic realm from psychological and political pressures. Most important, we have become increasingly self-conscious both about what we as critics are doing and about the fact that we *are* doing something rather than discovering what is there. We speak less about interpretations and more about interventions. We pay attention not only to the boundaries but even more to those who draw—and redraw—them, for whatever reasons.

It is hardly surprising that psychology—or, rather, psychoanalysis—would be implicated in these changes. Along with Marxism, Freud's late-nineteenth-century discoveries helped initiate the radical questioning of consciousness and its representations—of subjectivity—that has now reached literary study, and his work shaped the terms in which we cast our self-scrutiny. In decentering the Cartesian consciousness ("I [am conscious of] think[ing]; therefore I am"), Freud showed that we are not who we think we are and that we do not always mean what we say. His hermeneutics of "suspicion," as Paul Ricoeur has called it (32–36), and Jacques Lacan's even more radical interrogations are implicit in literary critics' new questions. Yet even as you read this argument testifying to a radical questioning of everything previously staked out as "literary studies"—especially coming upon it in the context of this volume—you are aware that interrogation itself is something of an unquestioned necessity by now, and it might itself bear interrogation. What have we gained, and what have we lost, by redrawing the boundaries to include psychoanalysis?

## I

Criticism has long since left the clinic behind. But it is still useful to begin an examination of psychoanalytic literary criticism by clarifying what we mean by "psychoanalysis" itself, because criticism's roots remain in the clinical exchange where the issues are defined. The three quotations at the head of this essay, spanning more than half a century, may sound as if they are in agreement about psychoanalysis: all three lament the repression of Freud's most radical discoveries. But in fact each writer is accusing another of doing the repressing. Psychoanalysis has been divided into territories, though as one analyst has said, there are "porous boundaries" between them (Cooper 255); and the International Psychoanalytic Association recently devoted its annual meeting to the topic Psychoanalysis: The Common Ground (see Wallerstein). Literary critics have ignored many of these conflicts by associating psychoanalysis solely with Freud or, more recently, with Lacan, but no one figure constitutes analysis; nor is the conflict created by the difference between theorists. It is inherent in the nature of psychoanalytic investigation, and it began with Freud's first work as he tried to link mind and body, psychology and biology, an interpretive with a natural science.

Thus, despite the association of Freud with "sex," Freud's innovation was in large part a method of interpretation, and the book that remained most important to him was called not *Dreams* but *The Interpretation of Dreams*. That the unconscious may be repressed is the cornerstone of Freud's theory, but it is neither eradicated nor mute. It is a form of thinking always available if we listen with care; it has been called the "unspoken motive," the "whispered meaning," the "discourse of the other" (Kaplan and Kloss; Lesser; Lacan). Psychoanalysis is a "talking cure" rather than a medical treatment, and Freud came increasingly to focus on the talking as an end in itself when he found his patients not only describing past conflicts but acting them out again with the analyst. This "transference" of neurotic expectations to the current situation provoked a corresponding "countertransference" on the part of the analyst, and they both interfered with "objective" analysis of the unconscious. Instead, the transference itself became a primary object of analysis.

Much as he emphasized the interpretive process, however, Freud always linked it to the pressure of what he called *instincts*, a term referring broadly to a range of conflicting, not purely physical agencies that hover, rather, "on the frontier between the mental and the somatic" ("Instincts" 121–22). As Ricoeur has argued, it is Freud's dual concern with dreams and sex, mind and body, meaning and motive that constitutes his originality. Psychoanalysis may be a "talking cure" (Freud, "Lectures" 13, 21), but it never forgets that it analyzes, as John Forrester suggests, "language caught up in a sexed and mortal body" ("Psychoanalysis" 172). And, I would add, that body has a history. For Freud, "the ego is first and foremost a bodily ego" ("Ego" 26–27), and it still bears the traces of its earliest stages when soma and psyche were neither distinguished from each other nor differentiated from the mother-child unit. It is based not only on instinctual satisfactions like feeding and excreting but also on interaction with the mother—on tactile, rhythmic, imitative, proprioceptive aural and visual experiences that reinforce or qualify one another in various ways. Gradually these "inner" sensations are joined by identifications with beloved "outer" objects, and, with every new stimulus, the infant learns to integrate the two and to separate something marked "inside" from the rest. The nascent ego takes final form as it confronts and integrates social demands.

The Freudian ego is thus anchored in both instinctual id and cultural superego, and the Freudian subject is shaped by both material and social pressures, including embodiment and prolonged infantile dependence on other people, as well as discontent at having to fit into civilization.

Since the first third of the century, revisionist Freudians have continued to work on what Geoffrey H. Hartman has called the "Freudian boundary" between consciousness and the body (*Psychoanalysis* xix), and they share Freud's dual focus on interpretation and psyche, meaning and motive, linguistic and material conditions of existence. Thus they have continued to develop increasingly nuanced ways of understanding the act of interpretation and the dialogue between analyst and patient. The question that had begun early psychoanalytic inquiry was, What sexual wishes does this material fulfill for the patient? But by 1956 Paula Heimann was reminding analysts that they also had to ask, "Why is the patient now doing what to whom?" (307). It became increasingly clear that to answer these questions analysts had to begin by analyzing themselves. "Since a psychoanalytic investigation can only be carried out by a human mind," Hans Loewald writes, "we cannot conceive of one in which the analyst's [counter]transference and resistance are not the warp and woof of his activity" (56).

But along with this stress on interpretation and transference, the neo-Freudians also share Freud's assumption that transference is the manifestation of a self constituted by its material history in the body. They differ about which aspects of history are important, but they all anchor the psyche in a material world. Anna Freud and the ego psychologists focus on internal struggles between instincts and the ego, the reality-oriented aspect of the psyche that copes with instincts. Melanie Klein, one of the earliest object-relations analysts, includes aggression among the instincts, but she sees the presence of both sex and aggression as less important than the infant's fantasies about its loved "objects," especially the mother. W. R. D. Fairbairn moves even further from instinct theory than Klein does, describing an "object hunger" or object libido that is even more primary than sexual libido is. Whereas Freud says that the ego is a bodily ego, the object-relations analysts say it is a relational ego, defined by how it acts toward and feels about other people. The principal difference between Freud's and the neo-Freudians' interest in the history of the subject is that the neo-Freudians go further back. While Freud focuses on the oedipal conflict between a well-defined self and the world of the father and sees castration as the primary threat to integrity, the object-relations analysts study the origins of the self in relation to the mother and in the process of "hatching" from a preoedipal unity with her. "There is no such thing as an infant," D. W. Winnicott said, only a baby-and-mother (see "Theory"). The baby develops a sense of self as the mother "mirrors" the baby's actions through her response to them: the mother's delight, disapproval, or indifference contributes to the child's sense that he or she is capable, bad, or irrelevant. The danger, according to object-relations theory, is not castration but rather a failure of the self to cohere in the first place, a "basic fault" or "wound." Heinz Kohut's self-psychology and Otto Kernberg's narcissism theory both build on these object-relation assumptions about an original stage of narcissistic entitlement. The "self" evolves as the vicissitudes of this narcissistic self-image inevitably shatter it.

During the same period in France, however, Lacan was developing a psychoanalysis aimed at correcting what he saw as misreadings of Freud. With his provocative style and his flagrantly unacademic behavior, Lacan challenged not only the psychoanalytic establishment but also its values and its faith in rationality. Calling for a return to Freud's radical insights, Lacan conducted an unrelenting campaign against the "mirage of consciousness" and its complacencies, especially insofar as consciousness creates the illusion of a coherent, autonomous self existing prior to the language it uses. His essays not only proclaim but act out Freud's originating discovery of the otherness of the unconscious, its energy and inventiveness, its power both to compel and to disrupt any effort to make sense of it. Drawing on free association as well as argument, Lacan's prose forces the reader to acknowledge the complexities of language and subjectivity; it offers what Anthony Wilden calls a "curious mixture of penetration, poetry and willful obscurity" that most readers find either prophetic or contradictory ("Lacan" 311).

Given the rhetorical thrust of his work, Lacan "is not the sort of author who can be made obsolete by the detection of serious flaws in his thinking," as William Kerrigan has said ("Introduction" xxii). Nonetheless several themes do reappear throughout the essays and lectures with the force of standard, sometimes remarkably familiar arguments. Like object-relations theorists, Lacan de-emphasizes instinct and stresses dependence (or "prematuration"); he describes a process of mirroring that creates the sense of self; and he places the vicissitudes of the intersubjective "demand" for recognition (rather than the biological "need" for food) at the center of the infant's experience. Most of all, he focuses on what object-relations analysts call the narcissistic wound— the child's inevitable loss when emerging from the narcissistic fantasy of union with a totally devoted preoedipal mother—though Lacan assimilated this loss to oedipal castration. Like them he postulates a resulting lack, and thus a desire, that drives the subject—uselessly—to seek satisfaction in replacement after replacement for what has been lost. But instead of unifying these observations into either a self- or an object-relations psychology, Lacan tries to rescue Freud from reductive psychologizers. Speaking from a philosophical more than a medical tradition, he is less interested in finding cures than in questioning the very categories of "self" and "object" assumed by other analysts.

As a result, one major difference between Lacan's psychology and that of the object-relations theorists is Lacan's greater skepticism about the developmental process. For Lacan, the fact of intersubjectivity means there can be no coherent subject—and no satisfactory relations to objects. Object-relations analysts see the self emerging gradually into mutual relation with others. For Lacan, any protoself is annihilated by the other. In fact, at times Lacan argues that there is no self but only the false self of the ego, which, far from being autonomous, is created by "an alienating series of identifications" ("Freudian" 128). ("[The ego] is autonomous! That's a good one!" ["Freudian" 132].) The ego belongs to the realm of the imaginary, which is roughly equivalent to Freud's "fantasy," except that it is imposed by perception or identification instead of arising from "within." The prototype of the ego is the infant's identification with the image in the mirror at a time when "he" or "she" is nothing more than an incoherent, disunified mass of sensations. The image is true to nothing except the fact of the infant's tendency to deny the chaos by assuming false images. Lacan continually ridicules the prevailing—and, to him, naively optimistic—orthodoxy of the ego psychologists whose image of a "total personality" happily adjusting to reality and learning to be nice he terms a "white-nigger" notion tied to conformist views of mental health ("Freudian" 133). Desire, for Lacan, is never assuageable in reality. Lacan's call is to question what passes for reality, not to accept it, and certainly to question all authoritative versions of it. Freud's discovery, Lacan says, was precisely to put truth into question ("Freudian" 118).

Like Freud and the neo-Freudians, Lacan believes that the subject comes fully into being only by leaving the narcissistic fantasies of the imaginary order and entering the symbolic order, or the intersubjective structures of culture and language that Claude Lévi-Strauss describes. Here subjectivity is secondary to the social structure; what matters is the player's position in the exchange game, not his desire for the woman being exchanged. Lacan's theory focuses on the painful oedipal confrontation with the father, whom he took to be the original other—or rather with the name, or concept, of the father—who makes the restrictive laws that sustain any culture, like the incest prohibitions that sustain the kinship system. (Lacan puns on "le nom [name] du père," that which says "non" [no].) The subject becomes a subject only after recognizing the other *as* other, only by taking into account other points of view and other views of the self. Entry into the symbolic is thus repressive because the sheer fact of recognizing an other—and recognizing that you want to be recognized by the other—is a catastrophic affront to narcissism. But, however repressive, it is necessary.

So far Lacan, arguing that "one must assume one's castration" (Gallop, *Reading Lacan* 20, 59), sounds like the moralist Freud grimly resigned to the necessity of civilization. But a second major difference between Lacan and

Freud (and neo-Freudians) is that Lacan equates the symbolic not with inter-subjective relations in general but with language in particular. For Lacan, "castration" is not a physical lack, just as the phallus is not a penis. The subject is "castrated" because he—or she—must accept the arbitrary language of the father along with the paternal sexual prohibitions, a language whose meanings one can never fully control, whose prefabricated structures are inadequate to the expression of one's desire. One becomes a subject only by speaking the other's language and thus being subjected to the particular limitations and restraints that only language creates. First of all, the signifier "I" (as distinguished from the stable ego or self-image to which the "I" refers) has no more continuous content than the shifting pronoun "I" as used by one speaker and then by another. The subject is not a person but a position, an "I" defined relationally, by his or her difference from the "you" he or she addresses. Second, language can never fully express the subject or the subject's desire, because all signifiers are ambiguous: what *tree* means to me is not necessarily what it means to you. The very act of speaking creates a split-off aspect of the subject that cannot be communicated directly but only in the nonreferential play of the signifier—the puns, parapraxes, wordplay, and silences that the analyst listens for. For Lacan, the unconscious, instead of expressing itself in language or, in his famous dictum, merely being "structured like a language," thus comes into being only in language.

Lacan's revisionary claim that the subject is constituted by the symbolic, by the intersubjective system of language and culture into which that subject is born, promises to supplement Freud's largely individualist psychology and mitigate one of the most glaring lacks in classical analysis. The Freudian subject may be socially constructed insofar as "society" consists of the nuclear family, but otherwise Freudian analysis provides no way of taking cultural influences into account. To explore the role of cultural and linguistic systems in producing as well as manipulating the subject, most theorists have therefore drawn more on Lacan than on Freud. Many feminists have found useful Lacan's overt identification of culture with patriarchy, and gender with social or linguistic construction; others find his emphasis on the phallus just as restrictive as Freud's focus on the penis, and they argue that Lacan simply substitutes a male metaphysics for the male member. Like Freud, he leaves no space for the political, and he merely makes gender a universal, ahistorical effect of language instead of making it a universal effect of biology as Freud does. The resulting debate at the border between feminism and psychoanalysis has generated much of the most exciting work in psychoanalytic theory today and has expanded Freud's problematic view of gender. Marxists have also found the concept of a socially constructed "political unconscious" useful, and Louis Althusser's fusion of ideology and the unconscious is a Lacanian move.

The American psychoanalytic establishment has largely ignored Lacan, objecting to an imbalance it sees in his work that counters the one in ego
psychology. Taken literally, Lacan's arguments result in a theory detached
from the material details of clinical experience that grounds Freud's work and
in a model of the subject detached not only from biological determinism but
also from phenomenology and history. It is not just that Lacan's subject is the
one who speaks and takes positions in the symbolic order but has no substance.
(How far is it from Descartes's "I think; therefore I am" to Lacan's "I know that
I think that *you* think I am; therefore I am"?) The problem is the degree to
which even Lacan's imaginary realm is disembodied—and the degree to which
the realm of the real (or the material "given," which is shaped by the imaginary
and ordered by the symbolic) all but disappears. It is difficult to tell the imaginary from the symbolic, as Wilden notes ("Lacan" 174), because even the illusory ego, the false self mired in the imaginary (that realm of "shit and diaper
rash," as Lacan puts it ["Freudian" 120]), is itself disembodied, in that it
consists of nothing but a visual image. Lacan's model for ego formation is based
on the purely visual exchange of the mirror phase, where the infant who may
not yet be the one who "says" is still the one who "sees" rather than feels,
smells, tastes, or moves against the world. The mirroring depends on a distance
sense, vision, as if that were the only feedback the infant ever received from
experience—or as if the visual mirroring were a sufficient model for the rest.
Lacan's account of the mirror stage, as he says, is a "myth" or a theory, independent of the subject's actual history with mirrors or mothers. In privileging
language over the immediacy of all nonvisual as well as visual experience in
that history, Lacan comes close to losing the real baby in the imaginary bath-
water or at least to dissolving the traces of its past. In place of the past, he
emphasizes what Freud calls *Nachtraglichkeit*, the present revision or representation of a past event. Freud sees the subject in terms of an infantile past
that he now reworks, a reality that fantasies distort and memories "screen." For
Freud the present is infantalized by a real past, just as past "memories" of
infancy are only now constructed by the present act of interpretation in analysis. But Lacan stresses revision in one direction only, backwards, so that the
past is inseparable from recapturing the past, psyche inseparable from history.

So it is with the body as opposed to symbolic representations of it.
For Lacan, historically located experiences of sex and aggression—the motive
forces in Freud's concept of the unconscious—become "desire" and "death,"
forces emerging from and located wholly in the impersonal and universal constraints of language. Post-Lacanian feminists, as well as neo-Freudians,
counter Lacan's dismissal of the preverbal, bodily realm of "primary process"
thinking that can subvert the patriarchal symbolic order. Julia Kristeva describes an ungendered realm of bodily experience arising in infancy; instead

of being opposed to language (and culture), it has its own ongoing "semiotic" discourse of sound and rhythm. Hélène Cixous and Luce Irigaray gender a similar realm as feminine, stressing its origin in children's relations to their mothers' bodies and to their own and identifying its voice in an "écriture féminine" that draws on the female body (as in the meeting of two lips that Irigaray describes) rather than the male for its metaphors. Post-Lacanian materialists like Gilles Deleuze and Félix Guattari also focus on a realm of desire existing before oedipal repression and the symbolic. For them, both Lacan and Freud facilitate the capitalist move to identify desire as lack, thus fueling consumption.

Lacan's practice of psychoanalysis then does not just privilege the psychoanalytic dialogue; for Lacan, there is nothing apart from the psychoanalytic dialogue. Ernst Kris says, in effect, that psychoanalysis is nothing but the human being seen from the point of view of psychic conflict; Lacan might say that it is nothing but the subject's discourse seen from the point of view of verbal contradiction. Thus there is no repression for Lacan, only metaphor; no repressed unconscious, only another interpretation. For Lacan, the unconscious or the "discourse of the other" in one's own speech is no harder to understand than poetry is. In fact Lacan implies that resistance comes primarily from the analyst who tries to reify the past and the unconscious and to freeze the flow of analytic dialogue into an answer. The patient's problem, for Lacan, is precisely the assumption that the analyst does have such knowledge, that the analyst is the "subject [who is] presumed to know," that there is something else to know, apart from the dialogue with the analyst (*Fundamental Concepts* 232).

Lacan's emphasis on the psychoanalytic dialogue constitutes, he says, a return to Freud or, rather—with a surprising faith in historical progress toward truth—a return to what Freud would have said if he had only had access to the sophisticated linguistic theory we now have. Insofar as it counters positivist maps of the mind, it is a return. But Lacan counters the positivist Freud not by supplementing him but by obliterating him. Freud decenters "consciousness" but returns "the unconscious" to the center; Lacan replaces both with "discourse." Freud questions the obvious manifest meaning of his patients' narratives but always substitutes another meaning; Lacan suspects all meaning. Freud says the ego is not master in its own house; Lacan says there is no house—the very spatiality of that metaphor, with its assumptions about a substantial self that is "inside" while the world is outside, is itself a neurotic fiction, an imaginary creation that evades the more fluid truth of subjectivity. Instead, Lacan would substitute topologies of counterintuitive relations—the mind as Möbius strip, the subject as doughnut or Borromean knot.

## II

The split between Freud and Lacan is inscribed in the varieties of contemporary "psychoanalytic" criticism, a phrase that belies the rift already dividing Freud's portmanteau word. The "psyche" group—Freudians, Kleinians, object-relations theorists, Winnicottian interpreters—takes its readings to be evidence for somebody's mind; but the "analysis" group—Lacanians—directs attention away from any individual mind existing before or outside the act of analysis from which we deduce its existence. Lacanians direct attention away from the author's unconscious to the text in which we find it or even more to the intersubjective process through which we believe we find it.

The "psyche" group goes back to Freud. Much as Freud liked to claim that poets discovered the unconscious before he did, he still saw the text as someone's symptom to be analyzed. Even in the most high-minded discourse, Freud found other concerns expressing themselves in such remarkably subversive ways that he had to develop a new technique for interpreting them. No one has been able to read literature the same way since. Apart from his ear for primitive sexual and aggressive content, two simple changes in interpretive strategy made all the difference. First, Freud insisted on the truth of figurative language and rhetorical indirections. He showed that the apparently primary or "manifest meaning" was a function of every aspect of the text—symbols, allusions, gaps, puns, repetitions, and clang associations—even, or especially, those that seemed irrelevant. He made us aware of other dimensions of communication, so that, for example, a little girl who resents her mother's smothering attention will dream of being locked in a mummy case. Freud's is the one psychology, Lionel Trilling claimed, that makes "poetry indigenous to the very constitution of the mind" ("Freud" 49). Critics like William Empson listened to texts the way analysts listen to their patients' free associations; others, also like analysts, studied the strange logic of image patterns or mythic structures. Second, Freud postulated a reason for all this indirection by reinstating the "wish," thus asking his version of the contemporary query, Who benefits? Just at the time New Critics were severing the text from any human intention or effect, Freud linked it up again. There is always a hidden agenda as well as a hidden meaning in what we say; the text is not only a thing but also the end result of a process that performs work and serves a psychic function.

Freud's followers agreed, but they differed in identifying which function literature served. Freud always considered fantasy an escape, at best one that had been defensively concealed: "a (disguised) fulfillment of a (suppressed or repressed) wish," as he described the dream text (*Interpretation* 4: 160). Kleinians saw artistic fantasy instead as a way of making reparation for one's destructive wishes. Ego psychologists added that art not only defends against and counteracts wishes but also helps artists adapt by meshing their wishes and defenses into what Erik Erikson called the "peculiar time-space"—the artist's public, social "frame of reference" (qtd. in Swann 14)—what we might call the symbolic order in its widest sense. Object-relations analysts went furthest from the escape theory to describe art as the sole means of constituting the world as separate from the self in the first place. Like the child's "transitional object," as Winnicott has called it—Linus's blanket—the text is neither wholly part of the self nor wholly external, neither purely imagined nor confined to reality. It creates a "transitional space" where the author can work out otherwise irreconcilable conflict between fantasy and reality, self and other— whether the other is the resistant medium (hard marble, the limits of language) or the alien audience.[1] Whereas analysts examining the writer's "style" had originally looked for instinctual or defensive patterns, they also began to explore styles of "collaboration" with an audience (Rosen) and finally the writer's entire collection of habitual ways of interacting with both inner and outer "realities"—the writer's "identity theme" (Holland, *The I*).

In general, however, though neo-Freudian criticism has expanded its domain in this way to include interpsychic transactions, it still remains anchored, like Freud's psychology, in the experience of a body with a unique personal history stretching back to infancy. The best neo-Freudian psychoanalytic criticism stays in touch with the details both of the text and of its total authorial or readerly context, what Lacan might call the real and imaginary of the author and reader. It traces the surprising ways in which preoccupations recur, are transformed, and collide as they weave patterns linking text and context. In thereby emphasizing details that may be minor or irrelevant within the text but that serve as vital intertextual nodes, it also suggests alternative ways of reading the text itself. It constitutes a not-so-vulgar Freudianism that is still the basis for all psychoanalytic criticism. But though illuminating at its best, Freudian criticism too often treated fantasies as static thematic patterns, ignoring the ways in which they result from dynamic compromises among desires and points of view—particularly from current desires implicated in the reading process itself. The efforts of psychoanalytic critics became all too predictable, and Freud's exhilarating discoveries hardened into efforts to fit literature onto procrustean couches. Psychoanalysis slid toward what Norman Holland has called the "here a phallic symbol there a phallic symbol" school of interpretation; or to the search for *the* Oedipus complex that had already bored Stanley Edgar Hyman in 1949 (160); or to the "allegorizing of a particularly silly kind" that formerly psychoanalytic Frederick Crews went on to reject (166). Disappointed with the failure of psychoanalysis to expand on its own discoveries, Hartman spoke for many critics when he asked, "What does it matter that the drift of an interpretation is descendental rather than ascendental, that sex rather than lofty ideals proves to be the key?" (see "Richards"). And Hartman wasn't only complaining about phallic symbols; the idea of a "key" itself had by then become somewhat vulgar.

Meanwhile Lacan gave impetus to the "analysis" group when he published a provocative sally into literary criticism as the opening chapter in his first book of essays (*Ecrits*). It was devoted to an analysis of Edgar Allan Poe's story "The Purloined Letter," and it supplied no key, or so he thought. The story is worth exploring in some detail here since the analysis shows how Lacanian and Freudian interpretations differ. For one thing, Lacan's analysis is not only a message but also an openly dialectical move. It defines itself not only by what it says about the text but by what it is saying to previous Freudian interpreters, in particular to Marie Bonaparte. Bonaparte's reading (in *The Life and Works of Edgar Allan Poe*), along with Holland's recent neo-Freudian response to the debate, will thus be considered as part of the context for Lacan's.

Poe's tale about M. Dupin's miraculous analytic power is narrated by Dupin's admiring friend, who reports on two visits to Dupin: the first, in which he learns about the theft of the letter, and the second, a month later, in which he hears about the solution. In the first scene, the prefect of police, unable to recover the Queen's letter, comes to Dupin for advice. The problem, he says, began when Minister D_____ intruded on the king and queen just after the queen had received the embarrassing letter. The queen kept the letter from the king's attention by casually leaving it out in the open, but, although the king was fooled, Minister D_____ saw what was going on and took the letter, leaving another in its place. The queen of course could do nothing without arousing the king's suspicion about the letter, but immediately afterward she offered the prefect of police a reward to find the letter. The prefect searched every recess of D_____'s apartment, even probing the furniture with long needles, but he found nothing. Can Dupin help?

Dupin, however, says very little. In the second scene one month later, the prefect returns, even more anxious. After Dupin extracts a promise of part of the reward, he produces the missing letter, pockets the money, ushers out the prefect, and then tells his friend how he got the letter. Dupin realized that D_____, like the queen, must have left the letter unhidden; and so he arranged to steal it from D_____ in the same way that D_____ stole it from the queen, leaving one like it in its place. D_____ has not yet realized the theft, but when he reads the letter's unexpected message—an insult from Dupin—he will know all. Dupin's cleverness in finding the letter, as he tells the friend, finally, has not only earned him the reward but also allowed him to get back at D_____ for an old injustice.

Bonaparte assumes that Poe was a coherent though conflicted entity and that the tale bears evidence of his struggle to rework his own past experience. She looks for fantasies linking the tale to Poe's life, and her analysis is prefaced by a biography of Poe, though it bypasses the text's narrative structure and many of its details. Poe, she explains, was at the center of two, or perhaps three, oedipal triangles, focused first on his dying mother, Elizabeth, and then on his sickly adoptive mother. Elizabeth herself had been involved in an adulterous triangle, and her lover's letters were among the pitifully few possessions she bequeathed to the three-year-old Edgar when she died—though they were then appropriated by his unsympathetic adoptive father. Losing his parents so early, Poe had no opportunity to work through infantile fantasies about maternal betrayal and castration or about his hated father's intrusions. The fantasies haunted his life as he repeated his childhood by marrying a sickly child bride and remaining dependent on alcohol, and they haunted his tales. "The Purloined Letter" re-creates his childhood situation, though this time with a defensively happy ending. "The Queen of France," Bonaparte says, "like Elizabeth, is in possession of dangerous and secret letters, whose writer is unknown." The letter that is stolen from her by the minister and then stolen back by Dupin— like the real letters symbolizing Elizabeth's adulterous sexuality—is "the very symbol of the maternal penis" (483). The two thefts represent primitive versions of the oedipal struggle for possession of the maternal penis: First the minister/adoptive father steals it from the king/Poe's real father, and then the poet Dupin/Poe steals it from the evil minister/adoptive father. Dupin/Poe's current triumphant mental powers are a compensation and "revenge" for his being left out of the secrets when he was a child; and the narrator is Poe's alter ego, admiring his own creation.

Bonaparte's interest remains focused on the author, though she tacitly assumes that the text "contains" his fantasies and that any reader can retrieve them more or less intact. Holland's analysis of "The Purloined Letter" begins with the reader instead of the author (see "Re-covering"), but like Bonaparte he assumes the reader to be a coherent entity with a unique past history. In reading, Holland argues, as in every other activity, each reader tries to reenact his or her own "identity theme" or characteristic style of seeing and behaving. Each reader's transaction with the text is different, though it may be reworked later to achieve a consensus with other readers. Holland, a professional interpreter, sees his own identity theme "combin[ing] a passionate desire to know about the insides of things with an equally strong feeling that one is, finally, safer on the outside" (*Five Readers* 39). His analysis of Poe proceeds accordingly. He notices, for example, the story's attention to the potential hiding places in D_____'s apartment, and he links them to Poe's secrets from us: Poe does not tell us the names of D_____ or the prefect, and he doesn't even reveal the identity of "the royal personage" (the queen?) who first received the letter. He doesn't tell us how Dupin got the letter until after we learn that Dupin has it; and, of course, he never tells us what is in the letter. In fact, Poe never talks to us at all; only the narrator does. Dupin's power to find answers only emphasizes this hide-and-seek game in the tale. Poe's story, we might say, displaces attention from the queen's past (unrevealed) secret sexual activity (concealed in the letter) to the current intellectual activity necessitated by the theft of the letter. All sex and violence remain "hidden" outside the room—in the queen's past; in the "madman" planted out on the street; in the story of Thyestes and Atreus that Dupin quotes in his false letter; and most of all, in Dupin's prior rivalry with D_____, mentioned as if incidentally, only at the end.[2]

Moving from text to his own history, Holland notes that he read the tale when he was schoolboy himself—like Dupin's schoolboy, who could "read minds." He had his own private sexual secrets in those days: a thirteen year old's version of the queen's forbidden sexual activity. He finds something of his boyhood hidden activity in D_____, who, as Poe's prefect says, "is, perhaps, the most really energetic human being now alive—but that is only when nobody sees him"("Re-covering" 310). Holland identifies even more closely with Dupin, who discovers other people's secrets, like an interpreter of texts. Thus while Bonaparte looks for a specific sexual secret hidden behind the tale, Holland finds a conflict about secretiveness manifest in its telling: this is a story "about hiding which is also about not hiding" ("Re-covering" 309). But like the letter itself, these disturbing acts are hidden in plain sight. We may never learn what was in the letter, but we get the picture. The story allows Holland to both see and not see inside, a strategy, he says, that appeals to him.

Lacan's analysis of the story implicity challenges Bonaparte's. Bonaparte reduces Poe's characters, one by one, to parental figures in Poe's life and fantasies; but Lacan analyzes structures or relations between characters. Lacan points out that Poe's story consists of a single "scene" of three "glances" (where "glance" is a visual assessment of the object) repeated twice. Each time, there is one figure (in the queen's place) who possesses a "hidden" letter and sees that a second figure, a bystander, does not see the letter; the second figure (in the king's place), the by-stander, who sees nothing; and a third figure (in the minister's place) who not only sees the letter but also knows that the first doesn't see that he sees. The subjectivity of the characters is determined not by their psychology but by their position in this dynamic structure and, in particular, by their belief about what those in the other positions know. Any figure who changes position changes "personality." Minister D_____ displays a canny cleverness when he plays the thief in scene one, but when he assumes the queen's role in scene two, he takes on her feminine qualities; Dupin's success is a function not of his intelligence but only of his position in the second triangle. Like the characters, the letter is also determined by its position in the structure. Where Bonaparte says that the letter represents the maternal penis, Lacan says the letter doesn't *represent* anything—or not anything that can be decided. The letter is given meaning only by its *function* in the structure;

like the signifier of unconscious desire, its hidden content is indeterminable: "she has it and doesn't want him to see it; therefore I want it," no matter what "it" is. What matters is the signifier, not the signified.

The difference from Freudian theory is clear. Bonaparte traces one kind of repetition—between details in the text and details in Poe's life—and Holland traces another: between concerns in the text and concerns in his past life. But both are analyzing a relation between a text (given, for Bonaparte; for Holland, created by his attention to it) and a mind separate from it. Lacan by contrast analyzes the text, not anyone's mind. Where Bonaparte finds a meaning for the story, Lacan takes the story to be an allegory for the absence of meaning. Bonaparte undermines the story to expose Poe's fantasies, but Lacan undermines claims to know (Bonaparte's as well Poe's) what those fantasies are. Jacques Derrida has since suggested, however, that Lacan's interpretation is not that different from Bonaparte's after all. His identification of the letter with "signification in general," that is, with the maternal phallus, is not so different from her identification of the letter with the maternal penis. Derrida might also have noted that Lacan comes to an equally Bonapartean conclusion in his essay on *Hamlet*: if there is something rotten in Denmark, Lacan says there, it is "connected with the position of the subject with regard to the phallus. And the phallus is everywhere present . . ." ("Desire" 49). We veer from the Freudian Scylla of the "here a phallic symbol" school to the Lacanian Charybdis of "the phallus is everywhere present."

As Lacan's self-consciousness about interpretation implies, one of the greatest strengths of Lacanian criticism is not so much in practical criticism of specific texts but in theory. During the 1970s Lacan provoked a change in psychoanalytic literary theory as critics began to look away from the old Freudian answers about texts to Lacan's questions about all discourse. Hartman's complaint about Freud's "descendental key," quoted above, introduced a collection of essays entitled *Psychoanalysis and the Question of the Text*, and only a year earlier Felman had edited a collection of Lacanian essays called *Literature and Psychoanalysis: The Question of Reading: Otherwise*. Instead of new "keys" or readings of particular texts, Lacanian critics had begun to challenge the claims of psychoanalysis to explain a text in metalanguage superior to, more inclusive or more insightful than, the text itself. As Felman puts it, "[W]hile literature is considered as a body of *language*—to be interpreted—psychoanalysis is considered as a body of *knowledge*, whose competence is called upon to interpret" (*Literature* 5). The way to change this master-slave relation, she says, is not simply to reverse it but rather to initiate a dialogue between equals. If psychoanalysis finds the unconscious of literature, literature should look for the unconscious of psychoanalysis.

It's not clear whether Felman means that psychoanalytic theory is dependent on literature—the evidence she gives is Freud's dependence on literary myths for terms like "Oedipus complex"—or that psychoanalytic criticism is dependent on literature, or perhaps that psychoanalytic criticism is based on literary criticism. But such questions have ceased to matter as literary critics respond to her call, and others like it, with some remarkably diverse new kinds of commentary. Here, at the level of theory at least, psychoanalytic and literary discourse confront each other in new ways. Critics have compared psychoanalysis and postmodernism as theories (e.g., Flieger's *Purloined Punchline*). They have reversed the old paradigm of psychoanalyzing literature and instead have criticized, historicized, or psychoanalyzed psychoanalytic discourse, putting Freud's work in the position of patient. Derrida has deconstructed key texts in Freud's theoretical papers, as have Cynthia Chase ("Transference"; "Butcher's Wife") and Samuel Weber (*Return*); among Freud's clinical papers, his analysis of Dora has proved fertile in generating commentary on transference, gender issues, and the status of theory as narrative (see "Fragment"). The resulting confrontation suggests a new psychoanalytic poetics that attempts, as Felman says, "not to solve or *answer* the enigmatic question of the text, but to investigate its structure; not to name and make explicit the ambiguity of the text, but to understand the necessity and rhetorical functioning of the textual ambiguity" (*Literature* 119). There have also been new analogues for the text drawn from psychoanalysis; the text is not inferior to but just as sophisticated as the interpretive process (Skura), or even identical to it, as in Roland Barthes's *Lover's Discourse*.

Though theory has predominated, practical Lacanian criticism of particular texts has also emerged, building on Freudian techniques of close reading. Some of this criticism inevitably moves toward the kind of allegorizing found in older Freudian criticism, assimilating the narrative to what Gayatri C. Spivak calls "the unfolding of . . . a few classic psychoanalytic scenarios," albeit Lacanian rather than Freudian scenarios ("Letter" 222). Thus Lacan sees the fate of the signifier allegorized in Poe, or Herman Rapaport finds the fate of the Lacanian subject thematized in Theodor Fontane's *Effi Briest*. Given Lacan's Foucauldian foregrounding of the knowledge that is always inseparable from power, it is not surprising that some of the most successful Lacanian practical criticism has dealt with genres like the detective story, which turn specifically on the power of "knowing." Here the critic can analyze and deconstruct the claims of the fictional "subject [who is] presumed to know" (like Poe's prefect), who tries to rise above and understand the text. Freud was also interested in detective stories—nearly every story he analyzed, from *Oedipus* at the core of his dream book, to *Gradiva*, the *Sandman*, and *Macbeth*, was about people who solved riddles about themselves. But Freud was interested in the affective context of detection and in what he took to be the answers it produced. He played detective in *Oedipus* to give a new answer to Oedipus's question, Who am I? For Lacan, however, detection only raises questions.

Nothing is revealed; and nobody gets upset; no Oedipus tears his eyes out. As the Lacanian analyst Serge Leclaire says elsewhere, "Oedipus . . . plays the part of the sphinx" (113).

Most often and most fruitfully, Lacanian practical criticism has focused not on the text but on the exchange mediated by the text, not on the structures but on their production and reception in the narrative or reading process. Here, too, the difference from Freudian approaches is instructive. Freudian interpretation of the narrative or reading process implies a fully psychologized and embodied author or reader. In Lacanian analysis, the author, rather than being a person who happens to have written a story, is simply the writer of that story, existing solely in the exchange mediated by the text. The author can disappear entirely: Barthes, partly under the influence of Lacan, ostentatiously psychoanalyzed the writings of Jules Michelet without referring them to the author. Or the author becomes a product of reading the text: critics always treat poetry as an effect of the author, Felman says, but, she notes, "I would here like to reverse this approach, and to analyze a particular poet as a symptom of poetry" (*Lacan* 27). More often the author is simply a position, a point of view. Freud asks of a text, Why is the author saying this? but Lacan first asks, Where is the author? Freud talks about the unconscious as the *andere Schauplatz*, the other scene; but Lacan talks about another perspective, another camera angle. Lacanian criticism lends itself particularly well to narratology (R. C. Davis; Rimmon-Kenan) and to the "entanglings of a writer's thematic concern with issues of epistemology and rhetoric," as Neil Hertz puts it; it traces ways in which "the specularity of reading . . . devolves into narcissistic dramas of power" (220, 223). Art criticism has been influenced by this emphasis on the antagonisms and identifications between viewer and object (see, e.g., Fried's study of the "theatricalization" of the relation between painting and beholder, and his suggestion that Courbet tried to "undo his own [structurally male] identity as beholder of his pictures by transporting himself quasi-bodily into them in the act of painting" [43]). Finally, Lacanian emphasis on point of view, along with its interest in the imaginary or the visual, has made it particularly congenial to film criticism, as in Laura Mulvey's influential (and by now controversial) analysis of the gendered gaze.

The most frequent concern of Lacanian literary criticism has been the reader of the text, though this reader may be conflated with the author in a particularly "writerly" or problematic text. Freudians tend to put the reader in the place of the psychoanalyst, but for Lacanians the reader is always the patient; the master (analyst)–slave (patient) relation in psychoanalytic transference is thus re-created in reading. The reader sees the text, Felman says, as " 'a subject presumed to know'—as the very place where meaning and the *knowledge* of meaning reside" ("Open" 7). Would-be interpreters are therefore mastered by the text; they undergo what Lacanians call a "transference" to the text, though in keeping with Lacan's stress on knowledge and power, this is a more restricted phenomenon than Freudian transference, and it consists in the act of reading or interpretation only. While the Freudian Holland includes his past memories as part of his "transference" to Poe's "Purloined Letter," Elizabeth Wright by contrast is interested only in what she calls Holland's "Lacanian transference"—that is, his use of punning language like Lacan's when he now reads Poe (*Psychoanalytic* 67). Holland thinks he is mastering the text by explaining how it works, Wright says. But it's not what Holland says that is revealing—it's what he unwittingly does as he reenacts the very structures he seeks to explain.

Transference awe has been demonstrated spectacularly in Jane Gallop's *Reading Lacan*, Gallop's response to the author who really is seen as the subject presumed to know, though it is not clear that postmodern readers are mastered so easily by other texts. Even more important to the readers' "transference" than their slavish attitude toward the master text, however, is their involuntary "repetition" of something in it. As Felman describes it, the reading transfers a process from the text to the reader's analysis of it. Lacanians have demonstrated increasingly complex examples of the effort to master a text being undermined by "transference" to that text, as in Felman's now classic analysis of Henry James's *Turn of the Screw*—another mystery story ("Turning" 97). James's governess-narrator provides an interpretation of the mysterious ghosts who seem to haunt her charges, but we never learn whether or not she is correct—or whether there are even any ghosts at all. Felman argues that the story forestalls all possible answers—particularly Freudian ones—by deconstructing them. The reader

> can choose either to *believe* the governess, and thus to behave like Mrs. Grose [not an insightful person], or *not to believe the governess*, and thus to behave precisely *like the governess*. Since it is the governess who, within the text, plays the role of the suspicious reader, occupies the *place* of the interpreter, to *suspect* that place and that position is automatically *to take it.* . . . The text thus constitutes a reading of its two possible readings, both of which in the course of that reading, it deconstructs.                                    ("Turning" 190)

In Edmund Wilson's "Freudian" analysis of the governess, Felman argues, "it is precisely by proclaiming that the governess is mad that Wilson inadvertently *imitates* the very madness he denounces, unwittingly participates in it" (196).

Felman unsettles the reader and opens a space for a fresh understanding of the reading process in general. But her specifically anti-Freudian conclusion depends on her assuming precisely what she wants to prove, namely that there are only "two possible readings," which just happen to be the two possible readings that James deconstructs in the text. Both those readings fall into the category of old-fashioned Freudian character analysis like Wilson's; and even Felman says that Wilson is not representative of all Freudian analysis (187). What about the possibility of a neo-Freudian reading more attuned to narrative structure and its effect on the readers while still in touch with this past? Such a reading might suggest that James's mystery is "sexy" to us now in part because all sex was mysterious when we first discovered it and that the "secret" is secretiveness itself, not only as a symbolic phenomenon but as reminder of past secrets. When the adult governess spies on two children, she reverses the usual situation in which a child (like James's Maisie) spies on adults to find out what they do. Oedipal stories are often cast as mysteries (as in "The Purloined Letter" and, of course, *Oedipus* itself); the uncertainty of meaning is a repetition of the oedipal child's experience. Though not a final explication of the tale, this interpretation at least avoids Felman's trap.

Barbara Johnson contributed another landmark of revisionary criticism of psychoanalysis, which, while avoiding Felman's ad hominem argument, goes even farther than Felman in claiming that all readings inevitably reenact the text (see "Frame"). In a subtle and telling analysis, Johnson argues that if Lacan repeated Bonaparte, then Derrida, exposing Lacan's repetition, repeats what he criticized in Lacan; and Johnson herself, exposing Derrida, closes by acknowledging that in her analysis too the sender may again unwittingly receive "his own message backwards from the receiver" ("Frame" 505). Her reading demonstrates the special strength of Lacanian reading based not on Lacan's literary criticism but on his skeptical theory of discourse. The most obvious gain is that the new skepticism has led to the "closer" form of close reading that Hartman desired from psychoanalysis: Lacanian criticism builds on Freud's by looking for the unconscious in the text's performative aspects, in being suspicious of its rhetorical as well as representational strategies—as Freudians too often were not. It therefore emphasizes a new dimension of reading.

Such skepticism about the possibility of interpretation, however, derives not so much from Lacan as from Derrida. The appearance of Derrida as an influence on the new psychoanalytic critics returns us to this essay's opening questions about boundaries between psychoanalysis and literature and about what has been gained and lost by redrawing them to include Lacanian analysis. Felman argues that the difference between extraliterary Freudian criticism and the more properly literary Lacanian criticism is that Freudians search for a "master signifier" while Lacanians refuse to identify any latent meaning as the ultimate truth. But Freudian criticism has given up that particular form of reductionism. The real difference is not between reductionism and complexity but between optimism and pessimism—two different attitudes toward complexity. Freudians tend to see the complex latent meanings as integrated into a multiply functioning text, but for Felman "poetry is precisely the effect of a deadly struggle between consciousness and the unconscious" (*Lacan* 50). Where neo-Freudian Kris spoke of "regression in the service of the ego," post-Lacanian Wright instead sees the power of the unconscious to subvert the ego. As in Lacan's own writing, Lacanians expose what Malcolm Bowie has called "the forces of darkness and light in mighty combat" (148). It is this combat that has revitalized literary critics already primed by deconstruction to value "the warring forces of signification within the text" (Johnson, *Critical Difference* 5).

Yet despite postmodern ties, Lacan has finally bequeathed to his American followers an oddly New Critical sort of reading. In an effort to counter reductive analogizing either to a signified reality (the New Critics' "heresy of paraphrase") or to the psychology of a unified author or reader (the "intentional" or "affective" fallacies), Lacanian criticism is in danger of short-circuiting the particularity of this exchange. Where the New Critics fetishized the verbal icon, Lacanians have created a rhetorical icon, purposely isolated from any humanistic context. Where the New Critics studied textual patterns, Lacanians study impersonal rhetorical "style" detached from any authorial personality. Wright, for example, explores ironies that cannot be attributed either to character, author, or reader (see her "New Psychoanalysis"), and Gallop includes in "Lacan's" style a variety of printer's errors and typos (*Reading Lacan* 39). For Lacanians a text means everything it can mean, whether the author and reader could intend the meaning or not. Potential chains of signifiers stretch to the horizons of language—from *tree* to oak, pine, and Christmas; to Mr. Forrester; to family tree; to the repeated mention of symmetry; to another critic's reference to "not seeing the forest for the trees" in her commentary on this text; and so on, through the plenitude of linguistic signification.

In going this far, Lacanian criticism, by isolating the interpretive exchange from all reference to personal identity, erases the major difference between *psycho*analysis and literary criticism. It adapts the analysis but jettisons the psyche—and thus collapses the encounter between disciplines into the dyadic relation Lacan associates with the imaginary. It offers a reading of psychoanalysis that sees only sameness to literary criticism. Even where the criticism does seem to draw on psychoanalysis, it does not. The analysis of "transference," which suggests a promising use of the psychoanalytic encounter to understand the literary encounter, is not psychoanalytic. It takes only the notion of transference that it had already found in literary theory, in reader-based reception theory, and in text-based deconstruction. It is not surprising, then, that a psychoanalyst commenting on Felman's essay on "transference" in *The Turn of the Screw* concluded, "Not a psychoanalytic perspective but a literary one has clarified the text and the 'structure of the reading experience' " (Coen 7). John Knapp, speaking for the other side in an antipsychoanalytic critique of psychopoetics, concurs: "[S]upposedly interdisciplinary [psychoanalytic] thinking is really a branch of post-modernist literary thinking and cannot be separated from academic literary analysis [but] the vocabularies of the two are virtually indistinguishable" (259). The boundary between literature and psychoanalysis, in other words, has disappeared. Literature may sound like psychoanalysis, but in its Lacanian guise, psychoanalysis has become a form of literary criticism. No wonder it has been given a place in this volume.

The easy conflation between disciplines is puzzling because, until now, the fate of a psychoanalytic idea among literary critics has been determined by its incompatibility with "the literary" and its capacity to disturb or even to scandalize. While opponents resist this power, supporters celebrate it; and each new Freudianism establishes itself by maintaining its claim to call more into question, by trying to be unholier than thou. Thus when Freud was rejected by the American majority, he found acceptance in America among the young intellectuals who were rebelling against their parents' humanist values—intellectuals who were "humanists turned upside down," who "had an antithesis" for each humanist virtue (F. J. Hoffman 59, 60). Once Freud became too familiar to scandalize, his influence declined. It took Lacan to make a fresh impression on literary critics, once again through the same marginal channels. Lacan has been taken up in America not by the psychoanalytic establishment but by those who find that he offers a "radical critique" of "essentialist assumptions of human integrity" and "lays the groundwork for a provocative dismantling of the powerful assumptions surrounding 'human nature' with which we are saddled" (Frosh 138). Lacan, literally speaking from the position of outcast in his own society, was from the first associated with subversion, with the 1968 revolution in Paris, and with his own dramatic skirmishes against the hidebound French psychoanalytic establishment. Though Lacan speaks of the analyst's power deriving from his being taken for "the subject presumed to know," it also derives from his being taken for the subject who shows that *they* don't know, the subject who scandalizes.

But despite claims to return to Freud, Lacan re-created the scandal of Freudian analysis only by going beyond Freud, only by challenging still more fundamental aspects of humanism. Perhaps all intellectual history, like Poe's "Purloined Letter," consists of a repeated structure of interactions, with one position left open each time, a kind of temporary chair for the current succès de scandale; and, for the moment at least, Lacan is the visiting professor. (Wright has recently suggested, however, that the post-Lacanian antipsychiatry movement associated with Deleuze and Guattari may be a more productive mode of psychoanalytic criticism today because it "recovers some of the scandal" that Lacan, like Freud, has lost ["Another Look" 626].)

But it is appropriate to ask what the scandal is about and whether it is more a matter of Andy Warhol's "fifteen minutes of fame" than of truly revolutionary paradigm shifts. It is also revealing to ask who is being scandal-ized by whom and why. Each Freudian believes, "*They* repress what is most difficult, but *I* have the courage to face it." Yet facing what is currently identified as "difficult" is not always so difficult, and it even has satisfactions of its own. Lacan may have decentered human beings and replaced psychology by signification; this, he said, is what scandalizes ego psychologists and other Americans. But he has thereby placed the literary critic emphatically at the center of human activity. He rids us of one complacent assumption—that we can trust consciousness, that we can know who we are. But he replaces it with another—that we can always have access to subjectivity through analyzed language, that the unconscious is always available, at least to us, to the critics who know about language. Lacan himself has become the subject who is supposed to know, and he allows us to identify with him. Proposing his science of language as an interrogation of all discourse, Lacan shores up the hubristic claims of the 1982 MLA volume on the "interrelations of literature": "Literature, as the hub of the wheel of knowledge, provides the logical locus for the interrogation of knowledge" (Barricelli and Gibaldi iv). He shores up our confidence that, having been trained as readers, we are prepared to analyze all of culture.

If, ten years later, Lacanians are still reaffirming the literary critic's position at the hub, we critics do not yet need to begin worrying about being decentered. But we might take care lest our "interrogation" become an inquisition, and we close our borders to all except those who convert. Partly through psychoanalysis itself, we have become sensitized to the way in which claims that "*they* repress" or "*they* are vulgar" are integral to claims for our own integrity and sophistication. It might be appropriate to end by noting one last complementary blindness in both Freud's and Lacan's theories, as a final reminder of the need for caution in our own claims to knowledge. Neither of these two patriarchs took account of his dependence on the specific *female* patient he sought out—as mirror?—as the basis for a theory that not only ignored women (except as a male derivative) but also gave only a limited view of men. Freud's model of the psyche remained close to his descriptions of the female hysterics, his first patients, who, having repressed their sexual fantasies, were split within. For Freud the split in the ego was always internal: superego and id, mind and body, meaning and motive, psychology and biology. For him, even his own psychoanalysis was figured tellingly as an internal split, as a mind operating on its own body: "The task which was imposed on me in the dream of carrying out a dissection *of my own body*," he said in *The Interpretation of Dreams*, "was thus my *self analysis* which was linked up with my giving an account of my dreams" (5: 454). However ruthlessly Freud explored such internal conflicts, he tended to avoid external conflicts, with other researchers like Wilhelm Fliess and with previous theorists.

Lacan's model for the subject is also based on a female patient, the paranoid woman, who was his first case. Her split was projected outward, and her enemies were all external. The ego, Lacan said repeatedly, is a paranoid ego; and his own conflicts were all external as well. What Stanley Leavy calls Lacan's "conspiratorial view of psychoanalytic history" (38), along with the witty running attack on ego psychologists, is not a mere accident of style, any more than Lacan's obscurity is accidental. In part, perhaps, it is true that the ego psychologists are always out there and that Lacan's paranoia, even now, after the fact, is appropriate. But Lacan's relevance may instead derive from the fact that it is the "ego psychologist" within who is always most dangerous. Just as Freud omitted accounts of his battles with others, Lacan omitted any battles within the boundary of the self. Perhaps critics will find ways in the coming decade to integrate these complementary strategies of ignoring boundaries only to wind up ignoring either what is "inside" or what is "outside." Boundaries are necessary if the interpreter is to recognize the discourses they separate and to go between the two—to "translate" or "negotiate," as the root meaning of *interpretation* suggests.

### Notes

[1]For Rosen, for example, a psychoanalytic study of "style" not only accounts for the writer's typical way of accommodating fantasy to the givens of language and convention; it also accounts for the writer's typical way of using this accommodation to provoke a "collaborative response" from the audience (452).

[2]As if approving of Poe's defensive intellectualization in the story, Mabbott notes that "its great merit lies in fascination of the purely intellectual plot and in the absence of the sensational" (3). That is the goal: thought only; no sensations.

## Selected Bibliography

For psychoanalytic theory, especially for Lacan and for the object-relations analysts (e.g., Klein, Winnicott) who have been most influential for literary critics, see the fuller bibliographies where noted below. Since the new psychoanalytic literary criticism is characterized by variety and experimentation, it is often best represented not by individual authors but by the exploratory anthologies that began to appear in the late 1970s.

Adelman, Janet, " 'Anger's My Meat': Feeding and Dependency in *Coriolanus*." *Shakespeare: Pattern of Excelling Nature.* Ed. David Bevington and Jay L. Halio. Cranbury: Associated UP, 1978. 108–24.
One of the best examples of contemporary neo-Freudian criticism.
Bal, Mieke, ed. *Psychopoetics—Theory.* Spec. issue of *Poetics* 13 (1984): 301–420.

Issue on psychopoetic theory. See Bal's introduction for a rigorous categorization of possible relations between literature and psychoanalysis.

Cohen, Ralph, ed. *Psychology and Literature: Some Contemporary Dimensions.* Spec. issue of *New Literary History* 12 (1980): 1–218.

Davis, Robert Con, ed. *Lacan and Narration: The Psychoanalytic Difference in Narrative Theory.* Baltimore: Johns Hopkins UP, 1983.
Contains examples of a variety of approaches, as well as a good bibliography of works by, about, and influenced by Lacan.

Feldstein, Richard, and Henry Sussman, eds. *Psychoanalysis and* . . . . New York: Routledge, 1990.

Felman, Shoshana, ed. *Literature and Psychoanalysis: The Question of Reading: Otherwise.* Spec. issue of *Yale French Studies* 55–56 (1978): 3–508. Baltimore: Johns Hopkins UP, 1982.
The anthology most often associated with the beginning of the new psychoanalytic criticism. See especially Felman's introduction and essay and Johnson's essay.

Gallop, Jane. *Reading Lacan.* Ithaca: Cornell UP, 1985.
Good introduction to a (feminist) Lacanian style of reading that is both Gallic in its playfulness and Anglo-American in its willingness to unfold and explain its own wit.

Garner, Shirley Nelson, Claire Kahane, and Madelon Sprengnether, eds. *The (M)Other Tongue: Essays in Feminist Psychoanalytic Interpretation.* Ithaca: Cornell UP, 1985.
Excellent examples.

Hartman, Geoffrey H., ed. *Psychoanalysis and the Question of the Text.* Baltimore: Johns Hopkins UP, 1978.
Largely theoretical essays exploring the boundary between psychoanalysis and literature.

Hogan, Patrick Colm, and Lalita Pandit, eds. *Criticism and Lacan: Essays and Dialogue on Language, Structure, and the Unconscious.* Athens: U of Georgia P, 1990.
Useful essays on Lacan and his relation to feminism, narrative, and religion as well as "the work of art."

Holland, Norman. *The I.* New Haven: Yale UP, 1985.
A theory of the self that attempts to correlate Freudian and post-Freudian psychoanalysis with cognitive psychology. See also Holland's *Dynamics of Literary Response* for an excellent account—with many practical illustrations—of mainstream psychoanalytic literary criticism; see his *Five Readers Reading* for a psychoanalytic reader-response theory, again richly illustrated.

Kaplan, E. Ann, ed. *Psychoanalysis and Cinema*. New York: Routledge, 1990.

Kurtzweil, Edith, and William Philips, eds. *Literature and Psychoanalysis*. New York: Columbia UP, 1983.

Marks, Elaine, and Isabelle de Courtivron, eds. *New French Feminisms: An Anthology*. New York: Schocken, 1981.
Luce Irigaray on *écriture féminine*, in "The Laugh of the Medusa," and other important essays.

Meltzer, Françoise, ed. *The Trial(s) of Psychoanalysis*. Spec. issue of *Critical Inquiry* 13 (1987): 215–414.

Rimmon-Kenan, Shlomith, ed. *Discourse in Psychoanalysis and Literature*. London: Methuen, 1987.
Essays emphasizing the rhetorical structures and textual strategies of texts but restoring the human dimension to these linguistic, semiotic, or narratological structures.

Roland, Alan, ed. *Psychoanalysis, Creativity, and Literature: A French-American Inquiry*. New York: Columbia UP, 1978.
See especially the essays by Serge Dubrovsky and André Green.

Skura, Meredith. *The Literary Use of the Psychoanalytic Process*. New Haven: Yale UP, 1981.
Critical overview of the different interpretive models drawn from psychoanalysis.

Smith, Joseph H., and William Kerrigan, eds. *Interpreting Lacan*. Psychiatry and the Humanities 6. New Haven: Yale UP, 1983.
Though mostly not about literature per se, these essays focus on and clarify both Lacan's and Freud's interpretive assumptions and strategies.

Wright, Elizabeth. *Psychoanalytic Criticism: Theory in Practice*. London: Methuen, 1984.
Historical-critical account tracing relations among various schools; includes extensive bibliography.

# econstruction

## DEBORAH ESCH

### *Territorial Interests*

In April 1987, the *Washington Post* ran a front-page story disclosing that American officials had known since 1979 that the Soviet Union was planting listening devices in the United States embassy complex under construction in Moscow. According to then Assistant Secretary of State Robert E. Lamb, a special counterintelligence task force had been set up to find and "neutralize" the devices. "We knew the Soviets were going to bug us," Lamb testified before the House Subcommittee on International Operations. But counterintelligence had not anticipated that the Soviets would use "the structure itself as part of the bugging": the devices, as it turned out, were embedded in the precast concrete blocks and reinforcing bars used in the construction of the embassy walls and floors. Work on the edifice was halted only in August 1985, six years after construction had begun. Richard Dertadian, deputy assistant secretary of the State Department's Foreign Building Office, reported to the committee that the government was contemplating, as one of its options, the "deconstruction" of the top two or three floors of the embassy chancery. Asked what it might cost to "deconstruct" part of the building, Dertadian ventured that the cost would equal roughly what the United States had already spent to erect the chancery, with the total amounting to most of the sum appropriated for construction in the first place.[1]

A story of superpower intrigue reported prominently, if belatedly (befitting the *Post*)—history chronicled more or less as it unfolds—may also serve as an allegory of events taking place elsewhere, in the ostensibly rarefied and circumscribed sphere of literary studies. The reiteration, in quotation marks, of "deconstruction" and "deconstruct" in the reported exchange appears to be an instance of one institutional jargon citing (however unwittingly) another, translating what has become a more or less technical term in academic discourse into a usage of another order, which is cited in turn by the media.[2] But is it possible, in such a case, strictly to demarcate, or even denominate, the respective realms: academic, bureaucratic, journalistic? What is at stake in their articulation, especially when it confers priority of place on one over another? And what justifies reading this report of a cold war skirmish (whose geopolitics are already outdated, at least as of the "deconstruction" of that boundary of boundaries the Berlin Wall, the dissolution of the Soviet Union, and the profound transformations that have since taken place) as an allegory of whatever "deconstruction" may have to do with "redrawing the boundaries: the transformation of English and American literary studies"?

The seeking and acquiring of intelligence by means of acoustic surveillance is a predictable part of the give-and-take of international relations: the value of such knowledge lies, of course, in its translatability into the terms of power vis à vis the adversary. Not foreseen in this episode was the transformation, via a certain technology, of the very architecture of the institutional structure into a relay of information potentially damaging to the embassy and to the territorial (or, in the parlance of the planners, the "national security") interests it represents. "U.S. counterintelligence agents had first thought they could 'neutralize' and turn their knowledge of Soviet bugging efforts to the advantage of the United States, but then discovered the devices were planted inside the building materials" (Ottaway A1). Despite the "highly sophisticated countermeasures" brought to bear on the situation, officials were thus compelled to acknowledge—well after the fact—the vulnerability of the structure itself to wholesale "deconstruction."[3]

Language, knowledge, power, technology, institutions: these are among the persistent preoccupations of deconstruction as it has come to intervene in and transform literary studies, among other disciplines and practices. Moreover, the *Post*'s account employs "a figure of what some might be tempted to see as the dominant metaphorical register, indeed the allegorical bent of 'deconstruction,' a certain architectural rhetoric. One first locates, in an architectonics, in the art of the system, . . . that which, from the outset, threatens the coherence and the internal order of the construction. . . . It is required by the architecture which it nevertheless, in advance, deconstructs from within. It assures its cohesion while situating in advance . . . the site that lends itself to a deconstruction to come" (Derrida, *Memoires* 72). A temporal dimension thus complicates—before the fact—the spatial metaphorics of the architectural model (signaled in the temporal ironies of the embassy incident: the foreknowledge of the Soviet bugging operation, the failure to anticipate its use of precast materials, the post hoc disclosure):

> [T]he very condition of a deconstruction may be at work, in the work, *within* the system to be deconstructed; it may *already* be located there, already at work . . . participating in the construction of what it at the same time threatens to deconstruct. One might then be inclined to reach this conclusion: deconstruction is not an operation that supervenes *afterwards*, from the outside, one fine day; it is always already at work in the work. . . . Since the disruptive force of

> deconstruction is always already contained within the architecture of the work, all one would finally have to do to be able to deconstruct, given this *always already*, is to do memory work. (73)

Yet as Derrida will remind his readers time and again, the multiple logics and rhetorics of deconstruction do not depend on the figuration strongly suggested by the term's association with the architectonic, with a system of assembly or reassembly: for it is precisely "everything that can be reassembled under the rubric of logocentrism," including many of the foundational concepts of Western metaphysics, that deconstructive analysis subjects to scrutiny. Logocentrism comprises "the system of speech, consciousness, meaning, presence, truth, etc." that is itself an effect—an effect to be analyzed—of "a more and more powerful historical unfolding of a general writing," a multiple network of traces that cannot be subsumed under philosophy's traditional understanding of writing as a medium of communication at one remove from the plenitude and self-presence of speech, nor exhausted by "a hermeneutic deciphering," by "the decoding of meaning or truth." In the "very schematic" but still indispensable formulation of a general deconstructive strategy that concludes the essay "Signature Event Context," Derrida notes that "an opposition of metaphysical concepts (for example, speech/writing, presence/absence, etc.) is never the face-to-face of two terms, but a hierarchy and an order of subordination." And he goes on to assert what the *Post* allegory may be said to confirm, that "deconstruction cannot limit itself or proceed immediately to a neutralization" of such oppositions, nor can it be content to inhabit, however uneasily, the field they constitute; rather, "it must, by means of a double gesture, a double science, a double writing, practice an *overturning* of the classical opposition *and* a general *displacement* of the system. It is only on this condition that deconstruction will provide itself the means with which to *intervene* in the field of oppositions that it criticizes, which is also a field of nondiscursive forces" (*Margins* 329).

The double gesture of deconstructive intervention, then, is not restricted to or determined by architectural metaphors or the conceptual and nonconceptual orders they may be taken to figure. "It doesn't mean, for example, that we have to destroy something which is built—physically built or culturally built or theoretically built," for deconstruction puts in question the authority of precisely those rhetorical structures: "the metaphor of foundations, of superstructures, what Kant calls 'architectonic' etc., as well as the concept of the *arche* . . ." (Derrida, "In Discussion" 8). Yet the recent appropriation of deconstructive thought in architectural theory and practice is one indication that this "dominant metaphorical register," if not necessary or inevitable, is at any rate telling, not least (as the *Post* allegory once again attests) in the reminder it affords of the way in which deconstruction may be bound to and implicated in structures already in place, as well as liable to its own analysis:

"Operating necessarily from the inside, borrowing all the strategic and economic resources of subversion from the old structure, borrowing them structurally, that is to say without being able to isolate their elements and atoms, the enterprise of deconstruction always in a certain way falls prey to its own work" (Derrida, *Of Grammatology* 24).

Such considerations must figure in any attempt to assess the effects of deconstruction on literary scholarship, criticism, and pedagogy over the past two decades, and to redress misunderstandings and misrepresentations of those effects. The most recurrent of the latter have characterized deconstruction as "pure verbalism, as a denial of the reality principle in the name of absolute fictions" (de Man, *Resistance* 10), as a reduction to linguistic phenomena of nondiscursive forces, including those presumed to constitute the social and historical contexts of literary production and reception: characterizations that seem to forget or ignore deconstruction's beginnings as a critique of logocentrism. To some extent, this misunderstanding and its perpetuation (along with the concomitant charges of political quietism or conservatism) are themselves effects of certain features of deconstruction's initial intervention into the field or fields of literary study, particularly in North America. The keen interest in Saussurean linguistics, Lacanian psychoanalysis, and structuralist anthropology that marked the theoretical scene in France in the 1960s and 1970s was a determining consideration for deconstructive analysis, whose evolving concerns and strategies have been highly responsive to time and place. And given the specificity of its beginnings in a critical engagement with the tradition of Western philosophy (e.g., the critique of speculative dialectics—its determination of difference as contradiction and its resolution of classical binary oppositions through an idealizing, totalizing third term—by way of a Derridean "logic" of *différance*), deconstruction did not at the outset always concern itself explicitly with a thematics of politics and history. But a reflection on the political dimensions of deconstructive analysis and of the fields in which it intervenes was and is readable, for example, in Derrida's early and repeated insistence on the necessity, in reading philosophical as well as literary texts, of overturning and displacing the terms of their foundational structures:

> To do justice to this necessity is to recognize that in a classical philosophical opposition we are not dealing with the peaceful coexistence of a *vis à vis*, but rather with a violent hierarchy. One of the two terms governs the other (axiologically, logically, etc.), or has the upper hand. To deconstruct the opposition, first of all, is to overturn the hierarchy at a given moment. To overlook this phase of overturning is to forget the conflictual and subordinating structure of opposition. Therefore one might proceed too quickly to a *neutralization* that *in practice* would leave the previous field untouched, leaving one no hold on the previous opposition, thereby preventing any means of *intervening* in the field effectively. We know what always have been the *practical* (particularly *politi-*

*cal*) effects of *immediately* jumping *beyond* oppositions, and of protests in the
simple form of *neither* this *nor* that.                                        (*Positions* 41)

And if deconstruction did not, from the first, consistently foreground its own
potential as an instrument and a mode of institutional critique, the indissocia-
bility of deconstructive textual analysis from questions of disciplinarity and
the institution, of "an *institutionalized system of interpretation* in which precisely the question of the institution itself had come to be obliterated" (Weber,
Introduction ix), has become increasingly evident over the course of its elaborations. Deconstruction and its corresponding pedagogy, often in productive conjunction with feminism and psychoanalysis, have challenged and dislocated
disciplinary boundaries, including those associated with literature and philosophy as well as history, anthropology, theology, and law. More fundamentally
still, Derrida's investigations of the institutional and political conditions of
academic work include studies of the history of the university (and its founding
"principle of reason"), its roles and responsibilities with regard to the politics
of research and teaching in advanced technological societies. At stake in these
analyses is the implication, as well as the transformative potential, of what
appear to be the least "end-oriented" and programmable of disciplines (including literature) in a larger military-industrial, technoeconomic network.[4]
      Samuel Weber formulates succinctly the emerging emphasis on the
institutional and political in the trajectory of Derrida's work of reading and
writing:

> Whereas the earlier, more classically deconstructive writings of Derrida—up
> to *Dissemination*, which can be seen as a kind of pivot—sought to demonstrate
> the problematic status of certain major attempts, in the Western intellectual
> tradition, at systematic closure, i.e., at institutionalization, his subsequent
> writings have carried this demonstration further and, in a certain sense, in a
> different direction. Having established a certain structural instability in the
> most powerful attempts to provide modes of structuration, it was probably
> inevitable that Derrida should then begin to explore the other side of the coin,
> the fact that, *undecidability notwithstanding*, decisions are *in fact* taken, power
> *in fact* exercised, traces *in fact* instituted. It is the highly ambivalent *making*
> of such *facts* that has increasingly imposed itself upon and throughout the
> more recent writings of Derrida as well as upon the field of problems and
> practices associated with his work.                              (Introduction x)

Weber's own work, together with that of Wlad Godzich, Werner Hamacher,
Tom Keenan, Philippe Lacoue-Labarthe, Avital Ronell, Gayatri Spivak, and
others, attests to the multiple ways in which deconstructive analysis can be
brought effectively to bear on a range of institutional and political questions
as they inform literary and cultural studies.

Derrida himself has insisted on the necessity of engaging texts not simply or primarily on the basis of their discursive contents, "but always as institutional structures, and, as is commonly said, as being political-juridical-sociohistorical—none of these last words being reliable enough to be used easily" ("Some Statements" 86). In an interview whose express focus is deconstruction and architecture, he contests yet again the charges of verbalism and textualism, of an exclusive concern with the conceptual and discursive at the expense of more "practical" matters:

> Deconstruction is not simply a matter of discourse or a matter of displacing the semantic content of the discourse, its conceptual structure or whatever. Deconstruction goes *through* certain social and political structures, meeting with resistance and displacing institutions as it does so. . . . to deconstruct traditional sanctions—theoretical, philosophical, cultural—effectively, you have to displace . . . "solid" structures, not only in the sense of material structures, but "solid" in the sense of cultural, pedagogical, political, economic structures.                    ("In Discussion" 7–8)

When the traditional sanctions are those of literary studies in the North American academy, the structures in question are solid indeed. But, as Derrida observes in "The Laws of Reflection: Nelson Mandela, in Admiration," force (including the force of deconstruction) presupposes resistance (13).

## *The Invasion of the Corpus Snatchers*

That the deconstructive impulse and its attendant institutional displacements have met and continue to meet with resistance is not news—not even to those who know deconstruction primarily as a media event. The aggravated wartime scenario of our *Post* allegory stamps the same newspaper's earlier reporting on deconstruction's incursion into the field of "literary criticism" (fig. 1). This time, the symptomatic article appeared not above the fold on page 1 but in the Style section of the Sunday edition. The headline, "War of the Words," and the secondary head, "A New Brand of Literary Criticism Has Scholars Everywhere Up in Arms," reprise a hyperbolic rhetoric of armed struggle that has characterized mainstream journalistic representations of deconstruction from the first.[5] Given its publication in the American capital's newspaper of record, whose readership includes those who make determinations on federal funding for scholarly research in the humanities, the account is not simply one among others, and it warrants commentary on grounds of its own positioning as well as the positions it rehearses.

Accompanying the feature is a half-page cartoon illustration that an-

*Fig. 1.  Illustration by Dan Sherbo, from the* Washington Post *(6 Mar. 1983). Reproduced by permission of Dan Sherbo.*

nounces its generic affiliations: science fiction and horror. Flanked by sinister spaceships in the shape of graduation caps, the monstrous figure of a tweed-clad "alien being" wreaks destruction in a campus-turned-terrordome, zapping hapless students with an unforgiving X-ray vision, all under the lurid banner "Humanities vs. the Deconstructionists." The lead paragraphs gloss the comic-book graphics:

> It's the first horror movie about English teachers. It's called "The Beast From the Unfathomable" or, if you prefer, "Humanity vs. the Deconstructionists." It's in black-and-white and 2-D, but there are those who find it plenty scary just the same.
> The plot up to now:
> Alien spacecraft (rumored to bear the Air France emblem) have been sighted over college campuses from Yale to northern Alabama. Meanwhile, red-blooded young American scholars have begun speaking a strange language thick with words like "semiotics," "prosopopoeia," "apotropaic" and "diacritical." Attempts to treat the condition with bed rest and vitamin C have come to naught. (Lardner G1)

In the passage from the splashy banner to the fine print, "Humanities vs. the Deconstructionists," a formulation in which a disciplinary distinction is at stake, becomes "Humanity vs. the Deconstructionists," in which the future of the human race itself appears to be in jeopardy. (Thanks to the disparity in order of magnitude between the two terms opposed in the second case, the question of what Washington policymakers call a "level playing field" arises: but of course the outcome of this war game has been decided in advance. Just let the "deconstructionists" try to overturn *this* opposition, to intervene in *this* field of forces). The alarmist and xenophobic rhetoric first casts this threat to life as we know it as an invading force, which is readily metamorphosed into an infectious epidemic that defies conventional treatment (with overtones that are particularly sinister in the age of AIDS).

The scenario then "Dissolve[s] to Cambridge, Mass.," presumptive location of the symbolic Center for Disease Control and "headquarters of the national resistance to just about everything that has happened in the criticism and teaching of literature over the last 15 years, for a word from the resistance leader, Walter Jackson Bate, Kingsley Porter university professor at Harvard." The report goes on to cite Bate's manifesto "The Crisis in English Studies," an influential essay that deplores the academy's abandonment of the Renaissance concept of humane letters, as a consequence of the "new ersatz specialism" and the increasing interest in and pursuit of theory in the "flagship of the humanistic fleet," English studies (Bate 49, 46). What we are witnessing, in Bate's view, is "a wholesale reshuffling of values—a reshuffling downward, which is always easier than a reshuffling upward—down from the classical ideal of the central importance of literature to a self-imposed modesty and skepticism about its centrality" (49). According to the *Post*, "Bate's Paul Revere-like alarm, first sounded in Harvard Magazine, has been widely heard. 'I've never written anything that got so much in the way of correspondence,' says Bate, whose previous works include Pulitzer Prize-winning biographies of John Keats and Samuel Johnson." Bate's essay deploys to great effect a rhetoric of crisis likewise enlisted by such defenders of the traditional humanistic faith and upholders of cultural standards as René Wellek (in "Destroying Literary Studies," published in the *New Criterion*), Allan Bloom (in *The Closing of the American Mind*), and William Bennett (in his capacities as chair of the National Endowment for the Humanities and secretary of education in the Reagan administration)[6]: "The humanities are not merely entering, they are plunging into their worst state of crisis since the modern university was formed a century ago. . . . the humanities are not only in the weakest state they ever suffered but seem bent on a self-destructive course, through a combination of anger, fear, and purblind defensiveness; the strongest help from enlightened administration in universities is indispensable to prevent the suicide (or, at least, self-trivialization) that will result" (46).

That the dimensions of the "crisis" are "not merely," "not only" ideological but institutional and political emerges in a call to battle that is strategically sounded: "My appeal is to administrations of universities and colleges, and also to alumni and educated people generally. It is often said that war is too important to leave to the generals—the 'experts.' So with the whole cultural heritage . . . that we call literature; it belongs to all of us. I couch this appeal in general terms, yet terms that are fairly specific when the cards are down and a tenure appointment is to be made, as it must be, every week throughout major universities in this country" (52–53). Just as specific is the targeting of proponents and practitioners of "the strange stepchild of structuralism known as 'deconstructionism' "—as in the passages from "The Crisis in English Studies" selected for citation by the *Post*, in which Bate poses a version of the House subcommittee's question to the State Department official regarding the embassy incident: What price deconstruction?

> "At least a quarter of the profession acts as though it were intimidated," says Bate, by a "nihilistic view of literature, of human communication and of life itself" [the latter a virtual quotation from *Newsweek*'s early misreporting on deconstruction as "a decidedly nihilistic theory of life" (Woodward et al. 82)].
>
> He sees a trend that, unchecked, will "isolate literature still more into a self-sealed and autonomous entity, into which few students, few of the general public, indeed few—if any—writers of the past 2,000 years could be able to enter or could wish to enter."

> ... Bate and his allies indict deconstruction as nihilistic, whimsical, abstruse and incapable of distinguishing great literature from trash—and for spreading these maladies not only within the relatively small circle of avowed deconstructionists, but out among a far broader and more dangerous community of dupes and fellow-travelers. (Lardner G1, G10; Bate 52)

The *Post*'s characterization of deconstruction, an assemblage of quotations from Bate and other professors of the humanities, culminates in one whose morbid tonality belongs more properly to the obituary page than to the Style section: " 'The long, solemn imposture of what passes for "modern literary theory" may now be reaching its point of turn,' writes Cambridge University's George Watson. 'Its more recent pronouncements, certainly, have a pale, autumnal air' " (G10). The clear and present danger to "humanity" and the "humanities" would seem to be subsiding.

One reason for the uniformity and familiarity—indeed, the almost rote quality—of these pronouncements about deconstruction may be the dense intrication of the professional academic's vested interest in discrediting this latest challenge to established habits of thinking and teaching with a journalistic penchant for simplification and domestication, labeling, and sloganeering (signaled in the reduction of the heterogeneous processes and effects of "deconstruction" to the axiomatics of "deconstructionism" or "deconstructivism"—a distinction that, as Derrida notes, "doesn't have the reality of a border which some would cross and others wouldn't. It is always being crossed, erased and retraced, retraced by being erased" ["Some Statements" 75]). Andrzej Warminski, among others, has analyzed

> the self-generating, balanced, closed economy of exchange that constitutes talk about deconstruction in America: an economy in which academics tell reporters what deconstruction is and then quote these reporters to tell other academics (and themselves) what it is, in which academics report to and report reporters, in which reporters report themselves—a self-contained informational relay system of self-reporting and self-quotation.... A contentless, meaningless, formalistic, nihilistic system if ever there was one—but, like all systems, terroristically coercive in policing its territory and enforcing its law.... What does this system have to contain? ("Deconstruction" 45)

Such a system—deconstruction's normalizing reappropriation by academic critics and reporters alike—makes for a very "solid" set of structures: ideological, cultural, institutional. Within this framework, acoustic surveillance yields nothing new in the way of information (or intelligence)—only quotations of quotations of quotations, which have the currency, and about the force, of gossip. What do these formations tell us about the character and the effects of deconstruction's intervention into literary studies and about the modes of resistance it has encountered?

## *The Resistance to the Resistance to Theory*

Wherever they originate, the resistances in question may be most legible after the fact, and specifically as they are inscribed in their institutional effects. Deconstruction undertakes to counter such effects in kind, as well as to trace, in the institutionalization of literary theory in the North American academy, what may also be "the displaced symptoms of a resistance inherent in the theoretical enterprise itself" (de Man, *Resistance* 12).[7] The institutional determinations of the present volume—commissioned by the Modern Language Association's Committee on Research and Publication to outline the transformations in literary studies in English over the past quarter-century— suggest as one example of deconstruction's engagement with these resistances an essay commissioned for a comparable project roughly ten years ago. At that time, Paul de Man was asked by the MLA's Committee on Research Activities (before it was incorporated, in a renegotiation of administrative boundaries, into the Publications Committee) to contribute the chapter on literary theory to a volume entitled *Introduction to Scholarship in Modern Languages and Literatures*, edited by Joseph Gibaldi. By his own account, de Man's submission, "Literary Theory: Aims and Methods," had difficulty meeting the well-defined scholarly and pedagogical criteria of such a volume, whose chapters "are expected to follow a clearly determined program: they are supposed to provide the reader with a select but comprehensive list of the main trends and publications in the field, to synthesize and classify the main problematic areas and to lay out a critical and programmatic projection of the solutions which can be expected in the foreseeable future. All this with a keen awareness that, ten years later, someone will be asked to repeat the same exercise" (*Resistance* 3). The essay, declined by the committee for its obvious failure to conform to these expectations, eventually appeared under the title "The Resistance to Theory." In it, de Man elaborates two orders of resistance that bear not only on its own fate but more generally on deconstruction's impact on literary criticism and theory—on what we might, following Geoffrey Hartman, call "the fate of reading."

The institutional resistances to theory and especially to deconstruction amount in de Man's assessment to a "resistance to the introduction of linguistic terminology in aesthetic and historical discourse about literature" (12–13), a reaction motivated by ideological as well as professional investments in aestheticist and historicist approaches to texts. What de Man diagnoses, in response to Bate's "Crisis" essay, as a "return to philology" in contemporary theory coincides with his version of the deconstructive project, which he more often terms rhetorical reading or, simply, "reading." "Critical-linguistic analysis," closely allied to the descriptive sciences of philology and rhetoric, is in de Man's view a prerequisite for a genuine historical understanding of texts, as well as for an effective critique of ideology. That is to say, the responsible account of a work of literature (or any textual instance) takes as its initial object of inquiry "not the meaning or the value but the modalities of production and of reception of meaning and of value prior to their establishment—the implication being that this establishment is problematic enough to warrant an autonomous discipline of critical investigation to consider its possibility and its status. Literary history, even when considered at the furthest remove from the platitudes of positivist historicism, is still the history of an understanding of which the possibility is taken for granted" (7). In the North American context, deconstructive teaching thus takes place on ground prepared by the New Criticism, in encouraging students "to begin by reading texts closely as texts and not to move at once into the general context of human experience or history" (23) and training them to interrogate the way meaning is constructed and conveyed before they zero in on the meaning itself: to take account, for example, of specific complications in the relation between the meaning and the order of words, between semantics and syntax. At the same time, deconstruction distinguishes itself from the New Criticism (which understood the text as the stable, self-identical object of a stable, self-identical reading subject) in that it also "dislocates the borders, the framing of texts, everything which should preserve their immanence and make possible an internal reading or merely reading in the classical sense of the term" (Derrida, "Some Statements" 86). Instead of being taught first of all as a vehicle for the received ideas that are often equated with traditional humanistic knowledge, literature "should be taught as a rhetoric and a poetics prior to being taught as a hermeneutics and a history" (de Man, *Resistance* 25–26). The first order of priority is "the difficulty and importance of engaging as rigorously as possible with language as a medium and model [and] the products of this order of engagement should be carefully differentiated rather than casually deplored" (Findlay 395).

De Man argues, for example, that one can go a long way in reading and teaching texts on the basis of "the most familiar and general of all linguistic models, the classical *trivium*." He invokes the tradition of humane letters that he is accused of abandoning to show how this model, "which considers the sciences of language as consisting of grammar, rhetoric and logic (or dialectics), is in fact a set of unresolved tensions powerful enough to have generated an infinitely prolonged discourse of endless frustration of which contemporary literary theory . . . is one more chapter" (*Resistance* 13). De Man's recollection of the contestatory relations among the categories of the *trivium* thus furnishes an instance of the "memory work" performed by deconstruction, of the way in which "the disruptive force of deconstruction is always already contained within the architecture of the work" (Derrida, *Memoires* 73). A reconsideration of the *trivium*'s configuration of the several functions of language (and the disciplines to which they give rise) brings to light a hierarchical order whereby grammar has been assumed to be at the service of logic, which has in turn been posited as the link between the sciences of language and the sciences of the phenomenal world. The disruptive potential of rhetoric in this scenario is particularly at issue in the case of the literary text, which "foregrounds the rhetorical over the grammatical and the logical function" of language (de Man, *Resistance* 14). De Man would have the reader resist the tendency to preempt analysis by reducing the literary text to extralinguistic, extratextual conditions, a resistance effected pedagogically by teaching students how to read language as rhetoric and as writing.

In de Man's reinscription of the term, "reading"—as the pragmatic and hence unpredictable engagement with the specifics of language as an open-ended rhetorical and grammatological construct—is the locus of a second-order resistance: that of the reading (the deconstructive) operation itself to codification as method, to formalization as technique, to systematization as theory. "Mere reading, it turns out, prior to any theory, is able to transform critical discourse in a manner that would appear deeply subversive to those who think of the teaching of literature as a substitute for the teaching of theology, ethics, psychology, or intellectual history" (24). The radicality of reading as practiced and taught by de Man undoes language (especially but not only literary language) as a reliable epistemological ground:

> [R]eading disrupts the continuity between the theoretical and the phenomenal and thus forces a recognition of the incompatibility of language and intuition. Since the latter constitutes the foundational basis of cognition upon which perception, consciousness, experience and the logic and the understanding, not to mention the aesthetics that are attendant to them, are constructed, there results a wholesale shakeout in the organization and conceptualization of knowledge, from which language, conceived as a double system of tropes and persuasion, that is as a rhetorical entity, emerges as the unavoidable dimensionality of all cognition.
> (Godzich, "Tiger" x)

To the extent that it engages language as "a disruptive intertwining of trope and persuasion or—which is not quite the same thing—of cognitive and performative language" (de Man, *Allegories* ix), reading thus problematizes not only literature's aesthetic function (i.e., the presumed compatibility of linguistic structures with aesthetic values) but the very category of the aesthetic conceived, since Kant, as the articulation of pure with practical reason, of cognition with action. De Man's own readings of Kant's *Critique of Judgment* and Hegel's *Aesthetics* seek to question critically (rather than take for granted) the possibility of a passage from the epistemological to the ethical and political domains, by elaborating the ways in which, in the long wake of Schiller's domesticating interpretation,

> [a]esthetic judgment came to be replaced or overlaid by an ideological construct of values, now commonly taken to be the aesthetic, even though, de Man insists, the underlying judgment will not support such an overlay but will actively work to dismantle it. Only an activity such as reading can come in touch with this process and experience the resistance of the material to the ideological overlay.                                             (Godzich, "Tiger" xi)

It remains briefly to account for the way in which, in a further turn of the screw of interpretation and theory, the "return to philology" has come around, in turn, to a so-called return to history. Well before the self-denomination and self-institution of the "new historicism" (and its attendant "new politicism"), de Man sketched the conditions of its advent:

> We speak as if, with the problems of literary form resolved once and forever, and with the techniques of structural analysis refined to near perfection, we could now move "beyond formalism" towards the questions that really interest us and reap, at last, the fruits of the ascetic concentration on techniques that prepared us for this decisive step. With the internal law and order of literature well policed, we can now confidently devote ourselves to the foreign affairs, the external politics of literature.                               (*Allegories* 3)

Much recent work in literary and cultural theory would indeed seem to mark a turning away from "reading" (again, often misleadingly cast as aestheticism or textualism, as a "nostalgia for an unadulterated and uncontaminated Ur-text beyond the blemish of interpretation and history" [Gasché, Introduction xiv]) and a re-turn to questions, in Frank Lentricchia's phrase, of "criticism and social change," of literature's historical status and political effects—in some cases, as if this status and these effects could be determined apart from, in the absence of, the critical insights afforded by reading.

As a priority of the historicist turn has come the call, held by some to be long overdue, to historicize deconstruction itself, to contextualize and peri-odize a movement that has sought to question the viability of such an unprob-lematic return and recovery, particularly when it bypasses reading in favor of a more immediate invocation or thematization of "history." While the historical situating and self-situating of deconstruction are imperative, its "historicizing" has too often meant "playing the overall boring game which consists in applying the most worn-out schemes of the history of ideas to the specificity of what is happening now," a game whose moves include consolidating and closing off the heterogeneity of deconstructive operations into a totalizing theory, a set of theorems and theses: "deconstructionism" (Derrida, "Some Statements" 79). As Derrida notes, "the most recent and most interesting developments of Marxism and of what is called new historicism . . . institute themselves in reaction to a deconstructionist poststructuralism which is itself *either* nothing but a figure or a stabilizing reappropriation of deconstruction *or else* a caricatural myth projected by Marxists and new historicists out of self-interest or misunderstanding" (90). To the extent that an overly impatient "return to history" may overlook deconstruction's differences from deconstruction*ism*, its resistances to reappropriation in historicist terms—and to the extent that it forgets the irreducible textuality of history and histories—it risks positing nonreading in a systematic way. When the avoidance of reading becomes systematic, hegemonic, then reading in the sense posited by deconstruction, however circumscribed its apparent scope, becomes a counterhegemonic undertaking.[8] As we have seen, such an enterprise "operat[es] necessarily from the inside, borrowing all the strategic and economic resources of subversion from the old structure," and so is liable, always, to its own analysis. Yet it may prove crucial to any effective intervention in, and transformation of, the institutions in, for, and against which we work.

### Notes

[1]The transcript of the hearing before the House Subcommittee on International Operations reads:

> MR. MICA [Chair].    Mr. Dertadian, with regard to an option, we're going to introduce a new word that I learned in Moscow, to potentially deconstruct a portion of a building. Deconstruct the top two floors. How much does it cost to deconstruct a building, one or two floors?
>
> MR. DERTADIAN.    We're looking at various options, depending on what the option is decided on, and we are looking at options of deconstructing and demolishing, whatever the word is. It depends on how you are going to do this.
>
> MR. MICA.    Is it feasible that to deconstruct the top two or three floors of a building of the size that we're talking about it would cost—
>
> MR. DERTADIAN.    Yes.
>
> MR. MICA.    It is possible, but—
>
> MR. DERTADIAN.    It is possible.
>
> MR. MICA.    It is possible that it would cost almost as much to reconstruct from the beginning, or no? Is that out of the question? . . . I have been told that would be enormously expensive to do what this new term now envisions, possibly deconstructing a couple floors, maybe equal, and I may be wrong. That's all I'm asking you. You're the expert. What is the cost of rebuilding the entire building?
>
> MR. DERTADIAN.    . . . Based on some very preliminary work we've done in looking at options and what they would cost, it would probably cost about as much as we have already spent to deconstruct and rebuild.

MR. MICA.   So, in other words, we break even by starting over if we did the deconstruct route.

MR. DERTADIAN.   I don't think we break even, sir. . . . These are very rough figures.

("Security" 59–60)

I thank Tom Keenan for making available to me both the transcript of the hearings and the *Post* report.

[2]For Derrida's account of the way in which the word *deconstruction* initially "imposed itself," see "Deconstruction in America," "Letter to a Japanese Friend," and "Some Statements"; in the latter, Derrida calls for a vigilant use of quotation marks, "not as a formalist neutralization concerned with propriety but as the reminder of the necessary general contamination, of the transplants and irreducible parasitism which affect any theorem" (78). The term has been appropriated with varying degrees of care (with and without quotation marks) in a wide range of contexts, particularly in cultural reporting. Press coverage of the Rolling Stones' 1989 tour, for example, cited Mick Jagger's description of its "techno-baroque" stage set: "I tell people it's postmodernist-deconstructivist. But does anyone really know what deconstructivist means?" (P. L. Brown C12).

[3]Cf. de Man, writing in 1970 about the impact on literary studies of the new theoretical approaches: "Well-established rules and conventions that governed the discipline of criticism and made it a cornerstone of the intellectual establishment have been so badly tampered with that the entire edifice threatens to collapse" (*Blindness and Insight* 3).

[4]On these questions see in particular Derrida's "Conflict of Faculties" and "Principle of Reason."

[5]Warminski ("Deconstruction in America") has analyzed the pivotal role played by *Newsweek*'s "New Look at Lit Crit" (22 June 1981) in setting this tone. That article's first paragraph is symptomatic: "The study of literature has seldom been as genteel as its subject matter suggests. Teachers of literature are not only scholars but, inherently, critics as well, and they have always fought like intellectual infantry over the interpretations of literary texts. But in recent years the literary scene has dissolved into a state of all-out war" (Woodward et al. 80). The cover story in the same issue was, suitably enough, "A Dangerous Nuclear Game," on Israel's bombing of an Iraqi atomic reactor.

[6]In "Criticism and Crisis" de Man asks whether "there is not a recurrent epistemological structure that characterizes all statements made in the mood and the rhetoric of crisis" (*Blindness and Insight* 14). The uniform logic at work in these denunciations of the current state of the humanities suggests that the answer is yes.

[7]In a reading of "The Resistance to Theory," Kamuf observes that "because the institutionalization of literary theory in this country has tended to follow the way in which it can be made to serve an overarching pedagogical program and because literary theory, when it pursues its main theoretical interest, has to question the defining limits of any such program when applied to literary language, institutionalization can be made to appear in its effects—the marks it has left—on the movement of theoretical thought" (140).

[8]This line of argument is indebted to Warminski (*Readings in Interpretation* xxxv), who assesses the current critical scene in terms of the hegemony of nonreading

and the counterhegemonic, strategic force of reading. See also Godzich, "The Culture of Illiteracy" 34.

## Selected Bibliography

de Man, Paul. *Aesthetic Ideology*. Ed. Andrzej Warminski. Minneapolis: U of Minnesota P, forthcoming.
Essays on texts in the Romantic and idealist traditions that seek to recover the radicality of Kantian aesthetic judgment and to analyze the workings of ideology by way of a critical linguistic model.

———. *Allegories of Reading: Figural Language in Rousseau, Nietzsche, Rilke, and Proust*. New Haven: Yale UP, 1979.
Readings that, taken together, elaborate a rhetorical model of language as trope and persuasion (or performative), as well as a theory of allegory, including political allegory.

———. *Blindness and Insight: Essays in the Rhetoric of Contemporary Criticism*. New York: Oxford UP, 1971. 2nd ed. Minneapolis: U of Minnesota P, 1983.
An analysis of the operations of blindness and insight in the rhetoric of criticism and the ways in which reading problematizes received conceptions of literary history. The second edition includes "The Rhetoric of Temporality," on allegory and irony.

———. *The Resistance to Theory*. Minneapolis: U of Minnesota P, 1986.
Essays (including "The Resistance to Theory" and "The Return to Philology") and an interview that elaborate further the rhetorical model of language, analyze the relations of reading, theory, and pedagogy, and question the compatibility of linguistic structures with aesthetic values.

———. *The Rhetoric of Romanticism*. New York: Columbia UP, 1984.
Readings of Romantic and post-Romantic poetry that engage theoretical problems of rhetoric, temporality, and textuality as a provocation to literary history.

Derrida, Jacques. *Dissemination*. Trans. Barbara Johnson. Chicago: U of Chicago P, 1981 [*La Dissémination*. Paris: Seuil, 1972].
Three pivotal essays, on texts by Plato ("Plato's Pharmacy"), Mallarmé ("The Double Session"), and Sollers ("Dissemination"), that explore received notions of textuality, genre, and the status of the book.

———. *Glas*. Trans. John P. Leavey and Richard Rand. Lincoln: U of Nebraska P, 1986 [*Glas*. Paris: Galilée, 1974].
Readings of Hegel and Genet in juxtaposed columns of print that question the discursive and disciplinary borderlines delimiting philosophy, literature, psychoanalysis, and rhetoric.

————. *Margins of Philosophy*. Trans. Alan Bass. Chicago: U of Chicago P, 1982 [*Marges de la philosophie*. Paris: Minuit, 1972].
Key essays on the interarticulations of philosophy, literature, and linguistics, including "White Mythology," "*Différance*," and "Signature Event Context."

————. *Negotiations*. Ed. Deborah Esch and Thomas Keenan. Minneapolis: U of Minnesota P, forthcoming.
Essays and interviews from 1976 to 1991, including material on ethics and politics, nationalities and nationalisms, racism, and the law.

————. *Of Grammatology*. Trans. Gayatri C. Spivak. Baltimore: Johns Hopkins UP, 1976 [*De la grammatologie*. Paris: Minuit, 1967].
An analysis of the systematic repression of writing in Western philosophy, and an elaboration of a new "science" of grammatology; includes Spivak's detailed preface.

————. *The Post Card: From Socrates to Freud and Beyond*. Trans. Alan Bass. Chicago: U of Chicago P, 1987 [*La carte postale: De Socrate à Freud et au-delà*. Paris: Flammarion, 1980].
A far-reaching reflection, in (pseudo-)autobiographical and epistolary form, on the possible subversion of a fixed sequence, followed by critical essays on Freud and Lacan.

————. *Writing and Difference*. Trans. Alan Bass. Chicago: U of Chicago P, 1978 [*L'écriture et la différance*. Paris: Seuil, 1976].
Readings of Hegel, Lévi-Strauss, Freud, Artaud, Bataille, and Foucault analyze the problematics of writing in philosophy, psychoanalysis, anthropology, and literature.

Johnson, Barbara. *A World of Difference*. Baltimore: Johns Hopkins UP, 1987.
Readings that reinflect the analysis of "difference," bringing deconstructive strategies to bear on a range of literary texts and institutions.

Spivak, Gayatri Chakravorty. *In Other Worlds: Essays in Cultural Politics*. New York: Methuen, 1988.
Essays that engage a range of literary and cultural instances in their articulation and deployment of deconstructive with Marxist and feminist analyses.

Weber, Samuel. *Institution and Interpretation*. Minneapolis: U of Minnesota P, 1987.
Nine essays, on topics including deconstruction, hermeneutics, psychoanalysis, and professionalism, that interrogate the institutional organization of knowledge and the demarcation of the disciplines.

# New Historicisms

## LOUIS MONTROSE

### I

In the 1980s, literary studies in the American academy came to be centrally concerned with the historical, social, and political conditions and consequences of literary production and interpretation. From a multiplicity of sometimes convergent and sometimes incompatible perspectives, the writing and reading of texts, as well as the processes by which they are circulated and categorized, analyzed and taught, are now being construed as historically determined and determining modes of cultural work. What have often been taken to be self-contained aesthetic and academic issues are being reunderstood as inextricably linked to other social discourses, practices, and institutions; and such overdetermined and unstable linkages are apprehended as constitutive of the ideological field within which individual subjectivities and collective structures are mutually shaped.

In various combinations and with varying degrees of consistency and effectiveness, the intellectual forces identifiable as new historicism or cultural poetics, cultural materialism, feminism, and revisionist forms of Marxism have been engaged in redrawing the boundaries and restructuring the content of English and American literary studies during the past decade. My assigned task in this essay is to discuss "the new historicism." I place this term inside quotation marks to indicate my resistance to its now-conventional representation within critical discourse as a fixed and homogeneous body of doctrines and techniques. As such, the new historicism is the invention of its critics and commentators. The motives and methods of this invention are part of my present concern. But I also, and primarily, wish to discuss some of the heterogeneous and changing dimensions of the work frequently designated as new historicist and to situate it within the larger field configured by the mutually conditioning forces I have enumerated.

The critical forces I have conveniently if simplistically labeled as new historicism or cultural poetics, cultural materialism, feminism, and Marxism have in common a concern at once to affirm and to problematize the connections between literary and other discourses, the dialectic between the text and the world. In recent years, these forces have challenged, with considerable success, the dominant paradigms of New Critical rhetorical analysis and positivist historical scholarship in Anglo-American literary criticism. The enabling conditions of this challenge have been various in their origins and complex in their interactions (Boose; W. Cohen; Gallagher, "Marxism"; Wayne, "Power, Politics"). Here I shall merely suggest three factors that appear to be of widespread relevance. First, there has been taking place, for some time, an opening of the profession of English to scholars whose gender, ethnicity, religious or class origins, political allegiances, or sexual preferences (or some combination of these) complicate their participation in the cultural and ideological traditions enshrined in the canonical works they study and teach. Experiences of exclusion or otherness may, of course, provoke a compensatory embrace of the dominant culture, a desire for acceptance and assimilation; but they may also (and, perhaps, simultaneously) provoke attitudes of resistance or contestation. Such divided and dissonant positions may provide vantage points for the appropriation and critique of particular canonical texts—and, more important, for an appropriation and critique of the constitutive categories and normative procedures of literary studies. Second, the reorientation in the field under way since at least the beginning of the 1980s is largely the work of critics whose values were formed while they were students during the culturally experimental and politically turbulent 1960s. The burgeoning of the women's movement and of feminism during the 1970s, when most of them were seeking to establish their careers, had a profound social, institutional, and intellectual impact on this generation of critics—although, of course, the contours and consequences of that impact varied enormously, not only with the gender but also with the particular gender identities and attitudes of individuals and subgroups. In general, these critics responded to the radically altered sociopolitical climate of the 1980s—and, perhaps, for some of them, to the uneasy comfort they had now achieved within its academic establishment—with work that confronted ideologies and cultural politics of other times and places but resisted the articulation of its own assumptions and commitments. Third, the modes of criticism to which I have referred have variously reacted against and contributed to the intellectual ferment of the past two decades. Such ferment, summed up in the word *theory*, has challenged the assumptions and procedures of normative discourses in several academic disciplines. And in our own discipline, it has shaken if not undermined the aesthetic, moral, and ontological principles that prescribe the ideological dispositions of traditional literary studies. The theoretical field of poststructuralism is inhabited by a multiplicity of unstable, variously conjoined and conflicting discourses. Among the principles some of them share are a problematization of those processes by which meaning and value are produced and grounded; a shift from an essential or immanent to a historical, contextual, and conjunctural model of signification; and a general suspicion of closed systems, totalities, and universals.

In the United States, feminism and the women's movement have provided, in recent years, the most powerful infusions of intellectual and social energy into the practices of cultural critique, both written and lived. Across the disciplines, feminist theory and practice have called attention to the discursive construction of gender and sexuality and of social and domestic relations generally, and to the role of such constructs in the formation and regulation of exploitative social and cultural relations. In turn, this perspective has foregrounded the different subject positions from which readers interpret texts and from which they may negotiate or resist inscription into the positions constructed for them by the texts that they read. During the past decade, feminist analyses of discourses that construct and regulate hierarchies of gender and sexuality have increased in cultural and historical specificity; and, at the same time, they have analyzed with increasing subtlety the shifting articulations of gender and sexuality with each other and with the discourses of class and ethnicity. Such scholarship has explored the ways in which women's voices are marginalized, suppressed, ventriloquized, or appropriated in various literary and dramatic works—and in previous commentaries on those works; and it has spurred the recovery of marginalized or suppressed texts written by women. These projects have challenged liberal humanist claims that the literary and critical canons embody an essential and inclusive range of human experience and expression. By seeking openly and collectively to connect the spheres of critical practice, academic policy, and sociopolitical activity, feminist academics have demystified claims that scholarship and the academy stand apart from or above the interests, biases, and struggles of material existence; they have, as well, provided a model for the mutual articulation of intellectual, professional, and social concerns.

The recent revival of interest in historical, social, and political questions in literary and cultural studies is also, no doubt, a response to the acceleration in the forgetting of history that seems to characterize an increasingly technocratic and commodified American academy and society. A primary task for those who profess the humanities must be to disabuse students of the notion that history is what's over and done with; to bring them to a realization that they themselves live *in* history and that the form and pressure of history are made manifest in their subjective thoughts and actions, in their beliefs and desires. Of course, there is more than one way to implement a return to history. Disturbed by "the erosion of historical consciousness" in our society, the chair of the National Endowment for the Humanities has written that "by reaching into the past, we affirm our humanity. And we inevitably come to the essence of it. Because we cannot encompass the totality of other lives and times, we strip away the thousand details of existence and come to its heart" (Cheney, *American Memory* 7, 6). To resolve history into a simple antinomy of myriad expendable details and a single irreducible essence is precisely to refuse history—to refuse history by utterly effacing its *constitutive* differences, by effacing those complex historical formations in which not only the details but also the essences are produced, revised, challenged, and transformed. The emergent social-political-historical orientation in literary studies is characterized by an antireflectionist perspective on cultural work, by a shift in emphasis from the aesthetic analysis of verbal *artifacts* to the ideological analysis of discursive *practices*, and by an understanding of meaning as situationally and provisionally constructed. This orientation is pervasively concerned with writing, reading, and teaching as modes of *action*. And such academic concerns with the sociopolitical instrumentality of cultural and intellectual work are themselves forms of a sociopolitical praxis—although of highly variable and always conjunctural import and efficacy.

This general reorientation in literary and cultural studies is the unhappy subject of J. Hillis Miller's 1986 Presidential Address to the Modern Language Association. In his speech, Miller noted with some dismay—and with some hyperbole—that

> literary study in the past few years has undergone a sudden, almost universal turn away from theory in the sense of an orientation toward language as such and has made a corresponding turn toward history, culture, society, politics, institutions, class and gender conditions, the social context, the material base.
>
> ("Triumph" 283)

By such a formulation, Miller polarizes the discursive and the social domains. However, the prevailing tendency across cultural studies has been to emphasize their reciprocity and mutual constitution: on the one hand, the social is understood to be discursively constructed; and on the other, language use is understood to be necessarily dialogical, to be socially and materially determined. Thus Fredric Jameson can retheorize a Marxist concept of the social by appropriating a poststructuralist concept of the textual. He writes that history as material necessity "—Althusser's 'absent cause,' Lacan's 'Real'—is *not* a text, for it is fundamentally non-narrative and non-representational; what can be added, however, is the proviso that history is inaccessible to us except in textual form" (*Political Unconscious* 82). Miller identifies "theory" exclusively with domesticated varieties of deconstruction, conformable to formalist critical traditions in the United States. Theory so construed he privileges ethically and epistemologically in relation to what he scorns as "ideology"—an impassioned and delusional condition that "the critics and antagonists of deconstruction on the so-called left and so-called right" ("Triumph" 289) are said to share. Although his polemic indiscriminately (though hardly unintentionally) lumps them with the academy's intellectually and politically reactionary forces, the various modes of sociopolitical and historical criticism have not only been challenged and influenced by the theoretical developments of the past two decades but have been vitally engaged in their definition and direction. And one such direction is the understanding that "theory" does not reside serenely above "ideology" but rather is mired within it.

Miller's categorical opposition of "reading" to cultural critique, of "theory" to the discourses of "history, culture, society, politics, institutions, class and gender conditions," seems to me not only an oversimplification of both sets of terms but also a suppression of their points of contact and compatibility. The propositions and techniques of deconstruction are employed as powerful tools of ideological analysis when they are trained on the overdetermined and hierarchically structured binary oppositions that constitute the central tradition in Western thought. Derrida himself has suggested that "deconstructive readings and writings are concerned not only with . . . discourses, with conceptual and semantic contents. . . . Deconstructive practices are also and first of all political and institutional practices" ("But, beyond" 168). The notorious Derridean aphorism "*Il n'y a pas de hors-texte*" may be invoked to abet an escape from the necessities of history, to sanction a self-abandonment to the indeterminate pleasures and/or terrors of the text. However, the phrase may also be construed in terms of the Jamesonian "proviso that history is inaccessible to us except in textual form." That is to say, it may signify the pervasive ideological force of discourse in general and, in particular, the specific ideological force of those discourses that seek to reduce the work of discourse to the mere reflection of an ontologically prior, essential or empirical reality.

Traditionally, *ideology* has referred to the system of ideas, values, and beliefs common to any social group; in recent years, this vexed but indispensable term has come to be associated with the processes by which social subjects are formed, re-formed, and enabled to perform in an apparently meaningful world. In the well-known formulation of Althusser's essay "Ideology and Ideological State Apparatuses," "Ideology is a 'Representation' of the Imaginary Relationship of Individuals to their Real Conditions of Existence," a representation that "Interpellates Individuals as Subjects" (Althusser, *Lenin* 162, 170; Eagleton, *Ideology: An Introduction*). Representations of the world in written discourse participate in the construction of the world: they are engaged in shaping the modalities of social reality and in accommodating their writers, performers, readers, and audiences to multiple and shifting subject positions within the world that they themselves both constitute and inhabit. In such terms, our professional practice is, like our subject matter, a production of ideology. By this I mean that it bears traces of the professor's values, beliefs, and experiences—his or her socially constructed subjectivity—and also that it actively—if not always consciously, and rarely consistently—instantiates those values, beliefs and experiences. Like anyone else's, my readings of cultural texts cannot but be partial—by which I mean incapable of offering an exhaustive description, a complete explanation; but also incapable of offering any description or explanation that is disinterested, that is located at some Archimedean point outside the history I study, in some ideal space that transcends the coordinates of gender, ethnicity, class, age, and profession that plot my own shifting and potentially contradictory subject positions. In its pursuit of knowledge and virtue, the academic profession of literature is necessarily impure. From this perspective, any claim for what Miller calls an "orientation to language *as such*" (my emphasis) is itself—always already—an orientation to language that is being produced from a position *within* "history, culture, society, politics, institutions, class and gender conditions."

## II

In an essay published in 1986, I attempted briefly to articulate and scrutinize some of the theoretical, methodological, and political assumptions and implications of the kind of work produced since the late 1970s by those Renaissance specialists (including myself) who were then coming to be labeled as "new historicists" (Montrose, "Renaissance"). The focus of such work had been on a refiguration of the sociocultural field within which now-canonical Renaissance literary and dramatic works had been originally produced, on situating them in relation not only to various other genres and modes of writing from beyond the literary canon but also to other cultural domains, including the social practices and political institutions of early modern England (Goldberg, *James I*; Greenblatt; Montrose; Mullaney; Wayne; Whigham). The dominant mode of interpretation in English literary studies had long been to combine techniques of formal and rhetorical analysis with the elaboration of relatively self-contained histories of "ideas" or of literary genres and topoi—histories abstracted from their social matrices. In addition to such literary histories, we may note two other traditional practices of "history" in English literary studies. One comprises those commentaries on political commonplaces in which the dominant ideology—the unreliable machinery of sociopolitical legitimation—is celebrated by the historical critic as being the morally, intellectually, and aesthetically satisfying structure of understanding and belief, the stable and coherent world picture, that is shared by all members of the social body. The canonical literary works of the period in question are then discovered to reproduce, by synecdoche, the lucid organic form inhabited by the spirit of the age. The other historical practice is an erudite antiquarian scholarship that, by treating texts as elaborate ciphers, seeks to fix the meaning of fictional characters and actions in their reference to specific historical persons and events. Though sometimes reproducing the methodological shortcomings of such older idealist and empiricist modes of historical criticism, but often appropriating their prodigious scholarly labors to good effect, the newer historical criticism could claim to be new in refusing unexamined distinctions between "literature" and "history," between "text" and "context", in resisting a tendency to posit and privilege an autonomous individual—whether an author or a work—to be set against a social or literary background.

In his introduction to a 1982 essay collection, Stephen J. Greenblatt distinguished what he dubbed the "new historicism," both from an older, re-flectionist, and positivist literary historical scholarship and from New Critical formalism. He commented that "Renaissance literary works are no longer regarded either as a fixed set of texts that are set apart from all other forms of expression and that contain their own determinate meanings or as a stable set of reflections of historical facts that lie beyond them" (Introduction 6). Furthermore, he suggested that the contours of art and literature are socially and historically configured: distinctions "between artistic production and other kinds of social production . . . are not intrinsic to the texts; rather they are made up and constantly redrawn by artists, audiences, and readers." We might now add that the very identities, expectations, and practices associated with the positions termed artist, audience, and reader are themselves "made up and constantly redrawn" by the discursive processes in which they are engaged and that condition their own engagement with texts. Such a reciprocal fashioning is emphasized in Tony Bennett's concept of the "reading formation," described as

> an attempt to identify the determinations which, in operating on both texts and readers, mediate the relations between text and context, connecting the two and providing the mechanisms through which they productively interact in representing context not as a set of extra-discursive relations but as a set of intertextual and discursive relations which produce readers for texts and texts for readers. . . . Texts, readers and contexts . . . are variable functions within a discursively ordered set of relations. Different reading formations . . . produce their own texts, their own readers and their own contexts.    (74)

This concept implicates critics in historically and institutionally situated roles as privileged readers, whose specialized though hardly disinterested knowledge constitutes the past that they undertake to elucidate. From this perspective, a new historicism, or cultural poetics, must be positioned within our own reading formation.

The symbolic anthropology of Clifford Geertz conspicuously influenced work identifiable as new historicism, or cultural poetics, produced during the later 1970s and early 1980s (*Interpretation; Local Knowledge; Negara*). Geertz himself seems to have been engaged in a liberal humanist response to the quantifying scientism of American social science, on the one hand, and to the totalizing theoretical discourses of structuralism and Marxism, on the other. For Geertz,

> the term "culture" ... denotes an historically transmitted pattern of meanings embodied in symbols, a system of inherited conceptions expressed in symbolic forms by means of which men communicate, perpetuate, and develop their knowledge about and attitudes toward life.          (*Interpretation* 89)

In Geertzian symbolic anthropology, culture is the medium of semiosis, "a set of control mechanisms—plans, recipes, rules, instructions . . .—for the governing of behavior" (44); a system of codes regulates social life by "governing" the production of those ensembles of conventions, practices, and artifacts to which the word *culture* is often loosely applied. It is a version of what Marshall Sahlins has called "the symbolic or meaningful" concept of culture, in which "human action in the world is to be understood as mediated by the cultural design, which gives order at once to practical experience, customary practice, and the relationship between the two" (*Culture* viii, 55).

Geertz's work offered to literary critics and cultural historians not so much a powerful *theory* of culture as an exemplary and eminently literary *method* for narrating culture in action, culture as lived in the performances and narratives of individual and collective human actors. Geertz called his rhetorically self-conscious ethnographic practice "thick description" (*Interpretation* 3–30). "It is explication I am after," he avers, "construing social expressions on their surface enigmatical" (5). The ethnographer's enterprise is "like that of the literary critic" (9)—and, we might add, like that of a New Critic. Thus he describes his "concept of culture" in a metaphysical conceit:

> Believing ... that man is an animal suspended in webs of significance he himself has spun, I take culture to be those webs, and the analysis of it to be therefore not an experimental science in search of law but an interpretive one in search of meaning.          (5)

"Thick description" might be more accurately described as "interpretive narration": it seizes on an event, performance, or other practice and, through the interrogation of its minute particulars, seeks to reveal the ethos of an alien culture.

Unsurprisingly, Geertz's method and style have probably been more admired and imitated beyond the discipline of anthropology than within it. Anthropologists of various persuasions have been sharply critical of Geertz's tendency to sublimate the dynamics of material struggle into the forms of collective imagination; of what some see as his impressionistic descriptions of alien worldviews; and of the isolated or fragmentary "local knowledge" produced by thick description, its failure to relate " 'cultural texts' . . . to each other or to general processes of economic and social change" (Walters 551–52; see also Asad; Shankman; Crapanzano).

Geertz focuses on indigenous cultural meanings rather than on general social laws, on cultural cohesion rather than on social struggle. The latter interpretive bias—and its consequences for the work of social historians and literary critics influenced by Geertzian symbolic anthropology—has been the subject of considerable recent criticism, trenchantly summarized in Roger Keesing's remark that "cultures are webs of mystification as well as signification. We need to ask who *creates* and who *defines* cultural meanings, and to what ends" (161–62; see also LaCapra, *Soundings*; Pecora; Biersack). In other words, critique of the Geertzian mode of analysis concentrates on the ways in which a cultural poetics suppresses or subsumes a cultural politics.

## *III*

In a typical new-historicist essay or book chapter, the Geertzian model of thick description is evident in the initial deployment of an exemplary anecdote as a strategy of cultural and historical estrangement. In some examples of new-historicist work, such anecdotes may be elaborated into the interpretive units from which a sustained argument emerges; in others, the method may seem merely fashionable and formulaic, a vaguely associative accumulation of historical curiosities. Thus Walter Cohen characterizes new-historicist method (or, perhaps, antimethod) as "arbitrary connectedness": "The strategy is governed methodologically by the assumption that any one aspect of a society is related to any other. No organizing principle determines these relationships" (34). And in order to describe this phenomenon, Dominick LaCapra offers the generous choice of "facile associationism, juxtaposition, or pastiche . . . weak montage, or, if you prefer, cut-and-paste bricolage" (*Soundings* 193). New-historicist work has been particularly susceptible to such responses because it has frequently failed to theorize its method or its model of culture in any sustained way. Proceeding on the basis of tacit and perhaps inconsistent notions about cultural dynamics, new-historicist studies may sometimes seem to imply that the objects they analyze are connected merely by a principle of cultural contingency or by the wit of the critic ("arbitrary connectedness"); or, on the contrary, that they have a necessary connection that is grounded in a principle of cultural determinism ("containment").

Having first called his critical project a "cultural poetics" in *Renaissance Self-Fashioning* (4–5), Greenblatt returns to and develops the term in *Shakespearean Negotiations*. This enterprise is now defined as a "study of the collective making of distinct cultural practices and inquiry into the relations among these practices"; its relevant concerns are "how collective beliefs and experiences were shaped, moved from one medium to another, concentrated in manageable aesthetic form, offered for consumption [and] how the boundaries were marked between cultural practices understood to be art forms and other, contiguous, forms of expression" (5). Described, in conspicuously formalist and structuralist terms, as a study of distinctions among "*contiguous . . . forms of expression*" (my emphasis), cultural poetics tends to emphasize structural relations at the expense of sequential processes; in effect, it orients the axis of intertextuality synchronically, as the text of a cultural system, rather than diachronically, as the text of an autonomous literary history.

One of the implications of Greenblatt's formulation—an implication already present in the widespread early new-historicist reliance on Geertzian notions of culture—is that "art forms and other, contiguous, forms of expression" are expressive of some underlying causal principle or generative and restrictive cultural code, that they are thus organically related to one another, and that this genetic relationship among practices is manifested in their surface articulation as a tropological system. Thus Greenblatt writes in the essay "Fiction and Friction":

> The relation I wish to establish between medical and theatrical practice is not one of cause and effect or source and literary realization. We are dealing rather with a shared code, a set of interlocking tropes and similitudes that function not only as objects but as the conditions of representation.
>
> (*Shakespearean* 86)

The cultural model implicit in such new-historicist work seems to have its origins in a cross between Geertzian and Foucauldian conceptual schemes: specifically, between Geertz's integrative sense of culture, his construal of culture as a localized and collective system of symbols, and Foucault's early epistemic history, which elucidates similitudes and rejects causality "in order to establish those diverse converging, and sometimes divergent, but never autonomous series that enable us to circumscribe the 'locus' of an event, the limits to its fluidity and the conditions of its emergence" (Foucault, "Discourse" 230). Some elements of new-historicist critical practice that have puzzled or irritated its critics may be explicable (though not, therefore, always or easily defensible) as consequences of this implicit cultural model. Certain examples of new-historicist work imply that a culture is a shared system of symbols expressive of a cohesive and closed (a "restricted" or "sutured") ideology. The problematic or contested consequences of such a model tend to suggest its affinities with formalist modes of analysis. They include the methodological assumption of tropological rather than causal relations among new historicism's objects of study; the emphasis on culture as a text, on the discursivity of material life and of social and political relations; the critic's self-imposed limitation to the study of synchronic intracultural processes, exemplified in particular texts and textualized performances; and the apparent incompatibility of the cultural paradigm with the dynamics of ideological resistance, conflict, and change.

The terms in which the problematic of ideology and resistance came to be posed in new-historicist studies of the Renaissance—terms that have now become widely established in other fields of specialization—are those of a simplistic, reductive, and hypostatized opposition between "containment" and "subversion." These terms—which appear to be residues of a cold war ideology that had pernicious consequences in both international and domestic policy—prove once again to be wholly inadequate instruments of analysis and debate. Nevertheless, they are significant indicators of a shift of perspective within Anglo-American literary criticism and its ambient political culture. As the problem of ideology has become an acceptable and even a central topic of critical discourse in the American academy, so the emphases in sociocultural analysis have shifted from unity, reciprocity, and consent to difference, domination, and resistance. It is precisely this shift of emphasis from canonicity and consensus to diversity and contestation that, during the past decade, has been the focus of the national debate about the direction of the humanities—a debate that has been waged on the campuses and on the best-seller lists, in the public media and in the policy statements and funding priorities of government agencies. It is within the context of these cultural politics—and as their displacement—that the "new historicism" has been constituted as an academic site of ideological struggle between containment and subversion. This struggle may be reduced to the following scenario. Critics who emphasize the possibilities for the effective agency of individual or collective subjects against forms of domination, exclusion, and assimilation have energetically contested critics who stress the capacity of the early modern state, as personified in the monarch, to *contain* apparently subversive gestures, or even to *produce* them precisely in order to contain them. According to a now-notorious argument in Greenblatt's essay "Invisible Bullets," the ability of the dominant order to generate subversion so as to use it to its own ends marks "the very condition of power" (45). Thus a generalized argument for the "containment of subversion" is itself subversive of arguments for the agency of subjects, which it reduces to the illusory and delusive effects of a dominant order. The binary logic of subversion-containment produces a closed conceptual structure of reciprocally defining and dependent terms, terms that are complementary and mutually complicit.

One can readily see that the larger assumptions and implications of a "containment" position concerning the operations of ideology might be suspect or even alarming, not only to traditionalists who cherish liberal humanist ideals of individual self-determination but also to those cultural critics who have a stake in making their own discursive practice a direct intervention in the process of ideological reproduction. At its extreme, the "containment of subversion" position suggests a reading of Foucault that emphasizes the discontinuity of history and the inescapable subjection of subjects; it makes no theoretical space for change or for contestation. Such a position might be said to reinstate the Elizabethan world picture, but now transposed into the ironic mode. Recent commentators have, with increasing frequency, seized on the provocative argument of "Invisible Bullets," misleadingly ascribed to the essay the claims of a cultural law, and then inaccurately represented it as the central tenet of the new historicism—sometimes using it to characterize the work of those who have been explicitly engaged in contesting Greenblatt's thesis. Such assertions gain credibility and authority simply from their frequent repetition in print; nevertheless, subscription to the "containment hypothesis" in no way characterizes the work of all those writers identified as new historicists, any more than it characterizes all of Greenblatt's work—or, for that matter, all of Foucault's.

The putatively Foucauldian new-historicist argument for the dominant's production and containment of subversion is pungently characterized by Frank Lentricchia as "a prearranged theatre of struggle set upon the substratum of a monolithic agency which produces 'opposition' as one of its delusive political effects" ("Foucault's Legacy" 234). However, such a strict containment argument oversimplifies Foucault's subtle, flexible, and dynamic conception of power by suggesting that the volatile and contingent relations of power that saturate social space are actually determined by the crystallization of power in the state apparatus. Foucault emphasizes that

> [p]ower's condition of possibility . . . must not be sought in the primary existence of a central point, in a unique source of sovereignty from which secondary and descendent forms would emanate; it is the moving substrate of force relations which, by virtue of their inequality, constantly engender states of power, but the latter are always local and unstable. (*History* 1: 93)

For Foucault, power is never monolithic; and power relations always imply multiple sites not only of power but also of resistance. He writes that such sites of resistance are of variable configuration, intensity, and effectiveness:

> The strictly relational character of power relationships . . . depends on a multiplicity of points of resistance: these play the role of adversary, target, support, or handle in power relations. . . . Resistance . . . can only exist in the strategic field of power relations. But this does not mean that they are only a reaction or rebound, forming with respect to the basic domination an underside that is in the end always passive, doomed to perpetual defeat. . . . The points, knots,

or focuses of resistance are spread over time and space at varying densities. . . .
Are there no great radical ruptures, massive binary divisions, then? Occasionally, yes. But more often one is dealing with mobile and transitory points of
resistance, producing cleavages in a society that shift about, fracturing unities
and effecting regroupings, furrowing across individuals themselves. . . . It is
doubtless the strategic codification of these points of resistance that makes a
revolution possible, somewhat similar to the way in which the state relies on
the institutional integration of power relationships.               (1: 95–96)

Foucault's flexible conception of power relations may accommodate local instances of a subversion that is produced for containment, but it also acknowledges revolutionary social transformations and other possible modalities of
power and resistance. If, on the one hand, ideological dominance can never be
monolithic, total, and closed, then, on the other hand, revolutionary upheavals
occur relatively rarely; modes and instances of resistance—subversions, contestations, transgressions, appropriations—tend to be local and dispersed in
their occurrences, variable and limited in their consequences. Thus one need
look no further than Foucault's own work for confirmation of the hopeless
inadequacy of subversion-containment as an explanatory model for the dynamism and specificity of relations of power, and for the necessity to make more
subtle discriminations among the modalities of resistance and among their
various conditions of possibility.

    Within the context of the containment-subversion debate, my own
position has been that a closed and static, monolithic and homogeneous notion
of ideology must be replaced by one that is heterogeneous and unstable, permeable and processual. Raymond Williams's invaluable *Marxism and Literature*
theorizes ideology in just such dynamic and dialogic terms. By emphasizing
"interrelations between movements and tendencies both within and beyond a
specific and effective dominance" (121), Williams clarifies the existence, at any
point in time, of residual and emergent, oppositional and alternative values,
meanings, and practices. The shifting conjunctures of such "movements and
tendencies" may create conceptual sites within the ideological field from which
the dominant can be contested, and against which it must be continuously
redefined and redefended—and so, perforce, continuously transformed. An
ideological dominance is qualified by the specific conjunctures of ethnic, gender,
class, profession, age, and other social positions occupied by individual cultural
producers; by the heterogeneous positionality of the spectators, auditors, and
readers who consume, appropriate, and resist cultural productions; and by
the relative autonomy—the properties, possibilities, and limitations—of the
cultural medium being worked. In other words, allowance must be made for
the manifold mediations involved in the production, reproduction, and appropriation of an ideological dominance: for the collective, sectional, and individual

agency of the state's subjects, and for the resources, conventions, and modes of production and distribution of the representational forms that they employ. In its emphasis on a dynamic, agonistic, and temporal model of culture and ideology—a ceaseless contest among dominant and subordinate positions, a ceaseless interplay of continuity and change, of identity and difference—such a perspective opens cultural poetics to history.

Such binary terms as *containment* and *subversion, dominance* and *contestation* are always dialectical and relative; their configuration, content, and effect are produced in specific and changing conjunctures. During the 1940s and 1950s, literary-historical scholarship was much concerned to demonstrate the ideological orthodoxy of such canonical authors as Shakespeare. In the climate of recent cultural politics, however, it has become fashionable for critics to affirm their favorite canonical literary works to be "subversive" of their own canonicity. Frequently, such claims are based on analyses that are less historical and dialectical than formal and immanent, implying that "subversiveness" is an essence secreted in particular texts or classes of texts. However, as Jonathan Dollimore points out in his introduction to *Political Shakespeare*:

> Nothing can be intrinsically or essentially subversive in the sense that prior to the event subversiveness can be more than potential; in other words it cannot be guaranteed a priori, independent of articulation, context and reception. Likewise the mere thinking of a radical idea is not what makes it subversive: typically it is the context of its articulation: to whom, how many and in what circumstances; one might go further and suggest that not only does the idea have to be conveyed, it has also actually to be used to refuse authority *or* be seen by authority as capable and likely of being so used. It is, then, somewhat misleading to speak freely and only of "subversive thought"; what we are concerned with . . . is a social *process*. (13)

Crucial here is the concept of a "context of . . . articulation," which must include not only the social effectivity of a particular notion, formulation, or action but also the historical and social specificity of its subsequent representations; in other words, it must include the context of articulation—or, following Tony Bennett, what we might also call the reading formation—within which we retrospectively inscribe, identify, and interpret "subversion." Ideology can be said to exist only as it is instantiated in particular cultural forms and practices, including those traditionally categorized as literature and as criticism. All texts are ideologically marked, however multivalent or inconsistent that inscription may be. And if the ideological status of texts in the literary canon is necessarily overdetermined and unstable, it is so precisely as a condition and consequence of their canonicity. If, for example, I characterize *Hamlet* as a "complex" text,

I am not reverting to an aesthetics of immanence, unity, and closure; rather, I am describing the transformation of a *text* into an open, changing, and contradictory *discourse* that is cumulatively produced and appropriated within history and within a history of other productions and appropriations. In so historically and socially sedimented a textual space—an always-occupied space that signifies to a historically and ideologically sited reader—so many cultural codes converge and interact that ideological coherence and stability are scarcely possible.

## IV

In "Renaissance Literary Studies and the Subject of History," I did not characterize new historicism as a school, movement, or program but merely as an emergent historical *orientation* within our field of study. It seemed to me then that those identified with this orientation, by themselves or by others, were heterogeneous in their critical practices and, for the most part, reluctant to theorize those practices. The very lack of such explicit articulations was itself symptomatic of the residual elements of empiricism, formalism, and humanism that undermined attempts to distinguish any new critical paradigm from an older one. Furthermore—and in marked contrast to both their feminist and Marxist contemporaries in the United States and their cultural materialist colleagues in Britain—American male academics producing new-historicist work in Renaissance studies during the past decade tended to displace and contain the cultural politics of their own practice by at once foregrounding relations of power and confining them to the English past that was presently under study. In Britain—where class barriers remain more clearly articulated than in the United States; where, too, radical politics enjoy stronger traditions; and where the coercive pressure of the state on centralized educational institutions and practices has for some time been direct and intense—there has been a polemical emphasis by cultural materialist critics on the uses to which a historical *present* puts its versions of the national past (see Dollimore and Sinfield, "Culture" and *Political Shakespeare*). Such scholars have been concerned with the processes by which the canon of English Authors and Works incorporated into English culture and into the British educational system has helped to forge the ideology of the dominant social class and to perpetuate its hegemony. Cultural materialism derives its name, principles, and politics from the later, Gramsci-inspired work of Raymond Williams. In their brief, programmatic foreword to *Political Shakespeare*, Jonathan Dollimore and Alan Sinfield propound "a combination of historical context, theoretical method, political commitment and textual analysis" (vii) as the four principles of cultural materialism. Among these, explicit "political commitment" of the sort they suggest—

"socialist and feminist commitment [that] confronts the conservative categories in which most criticism has hitherto been conducted"—is conspicuously absent from the American new-historicist work with which they align their own. Analogous projects in the United States have been more feminist or Marxist than new historicist.

A complex amalgam of geographical, social, ethnic, institutional, and gender-specific factors were at work in producing, in the work of American new historicists, a domesticated Foucauldian emphasis on historical and cultural discontinuities, on the radical and fascinating otherness of the Renaissance. To the degree that it recuperated in practice the critical traditions and values that it (sometimes nostalgically) repudiated in principle, the emergent new historicism may have been perceived by some discomfited English professors as more palatable than the Marxist and feminist projects with which it was ambiguously linked. Such a response may partially explain the rapid installation of "The New Historicism" as the newest academic orthodoxy, its rapid assimilation and varying appropriations by the fractious "interpretive community" of Renaissance literary studies—and, too, the waves of opposition and attack following almost immediately on its canonization. Certainly, some who have been identified as exemplary new historicists now enjoy the material and symbolic tokens of academic success; and any number of clearly labeled new-historicist dissertations, conferences, and publications testify to an institutional authority and prestige. However, it remains unclear whether this "ism," with its appeal to our commodifying cult of the "new," will have been more than another passing intellectual fancy in what Jameson would call the academic marketplace under late capitalism. The new historicism has not yet faded from the academic scene, nor has it quietly taken its place in the assortment of critical approaches on the interpreter's shelf. But neither has it become any clearer that "the new historicism" designates any agreed-on intellectual and institutional program. There has been no coalescence of the various identifiably new-historicist practices into a systematic and authoritative interpretive paradigm, nor does the emergence of such a paradigm seem either likely or desirable. Instead, what we have been witnessing is the convergence of various special interests on an unstable signifier: *New historicism* has been constituted as a terminological site of intense debate, of multiple appropriations and contestations, not only within Renaissance studies but in other areas of literary criticism, in history and anthropology, and within the cross-disciplinary space of cultural studies.

During the past decade, as some historians and anthropologists have become increasingly concerned with the cognitive and ideological importance of narrative forms and rhetorical strategies, literary theory has come to exert an unprecedented extradisciplinary influence in the humanities and interpretive social sciences. For example, in a discussion of recent controversies in history, Lynn Hunt characterizes that discipline as "an ongoing tension between stories that have been told and stories that might be told. In this sense, it is more useful to think of history as an ethical and political practice than as an epistemology with a clear ontological status" ("History" 103). And, in anthropology, the ambiguous status of the ethnographer as participant-observer of the alien culture that is the object of study has been reproblematized by a focus on textual and ideological dimensions of ethnographic discourse (Clifford and Marcus; Marcus and Fischer; Wagner). It should be noted, however, that such trends have also met with considerable hostility from some historians and anthropologists, and that the opposition manifests a range of positions analogous to those critical of poststructuralist and new-historicist directions in literary studies. For example, some scholars in the tradition of empiricist Marxist historiography have produced their own version of the opposition between textuality and materiality; and having done so, they are compelled to insist on the logical and the political priority of the latter term (Fox-Genovese). At the other end of the political-intellectual spectrum, guardians of the Humanist tradition engage in an idealist and essentialist polemic against poststructuralist, textualist, and new-historicist modes of historiography (Himmelfarb).

Much of the most interesting work now being produced within our discipline is by younger scholars whose graduate studies have endowed them with a poststructuralist sensitivity to both the *instability* and the *instrumentality* of representation. In their dissertations and publications, these younger scholars are synthesizing elements of the engaged theoretical discourses of feminism, Marxism, postcolonialism, and gay and lesbian studies. Some of this work demonstrates that avowedly new-historicist perspectives are compatible with, and enabling of, such projects of cultural-political analysis and critique. It seems to me, however, that although it is sometimes construed as a cultural-political project unto itself, the merely academic phenomenon of new historicism is incommensurable with the worldwide social movements articulated by feminist, Marxist, postcolonial, and gay and lesbian discourses. A partial explanation of why *new historicism* has been at once so central and so contested a term may lie in the relative availability of new-historicist methods for deployment in projects of widely varying or obscure ideological direction.

Right-wing critics in the academy, the popular press, and the federal government have yoked new historicism with Marxism and feminism in an unholy trinity bent on sullying, with its political credo of race, class, and gender, the enduring and universal concerns of the great authors and works (D. Brooks; Cheney, *Humanities*; Pechter; Will). At the same time, some self-identified Marxist critics have been actively indicting new historicism for its reluctance to address processes of historical change, for its evasion of political commitments, for its tendency to confine its analyses to the texts of men working within the dominant discourse, and thus for its inadequate attention to the marginalized or suppressed voices of the colonized and the commons, as well as those of women (W. Cohen; Gallagher, "Marxism"; Holstun; Porter, "Are We Being Historical" and "History"). While some scholars, including both women and men, are fruitfully combining new-historicist and feminist perspectives in their research and teaching, others have represented these projects in terms of a gender-specific antagonism. This hostility seems to have its origins in a complex amalgam of gender politics, intellectual antipathies between new historicism and modes of psychoanalytic and essentialist feminism, and professional and institutional rivalries symptomatic of the academy at large. New-historicist work by men has been indicted for its effacements, objectifications, marginalizations, and appropriations of feminist discourses and/or of women (Boose; P. Erickson; Neely, "Constructing"; J. Newton; Waller). Whatever the critical practice of particular new historicists, there has never seemed to me to be any *necessary* problem of theoretical, methodological, or political incompatibility between new historicism and materialist and historicist modes of femininist criticism. And, indeed, work that is both feminist and new historicist is increasingly evident in many areas of literary and cultural studies. While some see new historicism as one of several modes of criticism engaged in constructing a theoretically informed, poststructuralist problematic of historical study, others see it as aligned with a neopragmatist and cynically professionalist reaction against all claims for the theorization of practice and all calls for an oppositional cultural politics. If some see new-historicist preoccupations with ideology and social context as threatening to traditional idealist and humanist values, others see a new-historicist delight in anecdote, narrative, and "thick description" as an imperialistic will to appropriate *all* of culture as the domain of literary criticism—to construe the world as an aesthetic macrotext to be cleverly interpreted by means of a formalist cultural poetics.

Inhabiting the discursive spaces currently traversed by the term *new historicism* are some of the most complex, persistent, and unsettling problems that professors of literature attempt to confront or to evade—among them, the conflict between essentialist and historically specific perspectives on the category of literature and its relations with other discourses; the possible relations between cultural practices and social, political, and economic institutions and processes; the consequences of poststructuralist theories of textuality for historical or materialist criticism; the means by which ideologies are produced, sustained, and contested; the operations that construct, maintain, destabilize, and alter subjectivity through the shifting conjunctures of multiple subject positions. My point is not that "the new historicism" as a definable project, or the work of individuals identified by themselves or by others as new historicists, can provide even provisional answers to each of these questions, but rather that "the new historicism" is currently being invoked in order to bring such problems into play, and to stake out, or to hunt down, specific positions on the ideological terrain mapped by them.

The poststructuralist orientation to history now emerging in literary studies I characterize chiastically, as a reciprocal concern with the historicity of texts and the textuality of histories. By the *historicity of texts*, I mean to suggest the historical specificity, the social and material embedding, of all modes of *writing*—including not only the texts that critics study but also the texts in which we study them; thus, I also mean to suggest the historical, social, and material embedding of all modes of *reading*. By the *textuality of histories*, I mean to suggest, in the first place, that we can have no access to a full and authentic past, to a material existence that is unmediated by the textual traces of the society in question; and, furthermore, that the survival of those traces rather than others cannot be assumed to be merely contingent but must rather be presumed to be at least partially consequent on subtle processes of selective preservation and effacement—processes like those that have produced the traditional humanities curriculum. In the second place, those victorious traces of material and ideological struggle are themselves subject to subsequent mediations when they are construed as the "documents" on which those who profess the humanities ground their own descriptive and interpretive texts. As Hayden White and others have forcefully reminded us, such textual histories and ethnographies necessarily although incompletely constitute, in their own narrative and rhetorical forms, the past or alien actions and meanings—the "history" or "culture"—to which they offer access.

In *After the New Criticism*, Lentricchia links "the antihistorical impulses of formalist theories of literary criticism" with monolithic and teleological theories of history (xiii–xiv)—visions of history that, in their unity, totality, and inexorability, can be grounded only on essentialist or metaphysical premises. I assume that among such visions of history belongs not only the great code of Christian figural and eschatological history but also the master narrative of classical Hegelian Marxism. The latter has been characterized by Jameson as "history now conceived in its vastest sense of the sequence of modes of production and the succession and destiny of the various human social formations"; this he projects as the "untranscendable horizon" of interpretive activity, subsuming "apparently antagonistic or incommensurable critical operations, assigning them an undoubted sectoral validity within itself, and thus at once cancelling and preserving them" (*Political Unconscious* 75, 10). (Perhaps we should now add, as a bathetic coda to the history of grand historical narratives, the recent pop theory that, with the collapse of totalitarian Communist regimes in eastern Europe, History as such has suddenly ended—the end having come somewhat short of the Marxian trajectory, in the supposed universal embrace of liberal democracy and consumer capitalism.) One of the most powerful theoretical challenges to the Marxian master narrative has come from within the Marxist tradition itself, in the post-Marxist analysis of Ernesto Laclau and Chantal Mouffe. In the polemical introduction to *Hegemony and Socialist Strategy*, they write that

> there is not *one* discourse and *one* system of categories through which the "real" might speak without mediations. In operating deconstructively within Marxist categories, we do not claim to be writing "universal history," to be inscribing our discourse as a moment of a single, linear process of knowledge. Just as the era of normative epistemologies has come to an end, so too has the era of universal discourses. (3)

Accordingly, "the rejection of privileged points of rupture and the confluence of struggles into a unified political space, and the acceptance, on the contrary, of the plurality and indeterminacy of the social, seem to us the two fundamental bases from which a new political imaginary can be constructed" (152). Similarly, against the monstrous marriage of unhistoricized formalisms and totalized history, Lentricchia opposes the multiplicity of "histories," characterized by "forces of heterogeneity, contradiction, fragmentation, and difference" (*New Criticism* xiv). It seems to me that the various modes of what could be called poststructuralist historical criticism—including new historicism or cultural poetics, as well as modes of revisionist, or post-, Marxism—can be characterized by such a shift from History to histories.

The conjunction of the terms *new historicism* and *cultural poetics* points to the characteristic mixture, in exemplary new-historicist work, of historicist and formalist, materialist and textualist or tropological, interests and analytical techniques (Liu, "Power"; Wayne, "New Historicism"). As I have suggested, this mixture is sometimes criticized as being—and may sometimes merely be—the symptom of a fundamentally antimaterialist, residual, or recuperative formalism. But it has also demonstrated the potential for development in the direction of a genuinely materialist and historicist formalism—a historical analysis of what Jameson calls "the ideology of form," which is inseparable from a historical analysis of the form of ideology. "The ideology of form and the form of ideology"; "the historicity of texts and the textuality of histories": if such chiastic formulations are in fashion today—when, in the wake of deconstruction, referentiality has become so vexed and tropology so conspicuous—it may be because they figure forth from within discourse itself the model of a reciprocally constitutive and transformative relation between the discursive and material domains. Rejecting "the distinction between discursive and nondiscursive practices," Laclau and Mouffe have asserted that "every object is constituted as an object of discourse, insofar as no object is given outside every discursive condition of emergence." They hasten to add that "the fact that every object is constituted as an object of discourse has *nothing to do* with whether there is a world external to thought, or with the realism/idealism opposition"; against the assumption that discourse is merely mental in character, they affirm "the *material* character of every discursive structure" (109, 110). One important implication for literary studies is the possibility of transcending the formalist-historicist opposition in a new mode of textualist-materialist critical practice:

> The main consequence of a break with the discursive/extra-discursive dichotomy is an abandonment of the thought/reality opposition, and hence a major enlargement of the field of those categories which can account for social relations. Synonymy, metonymy, metaphor are not forms of thought that add a second sense to a primary, constitutive literality of social relations; instead, they are part of the primary terrain itself in which the social is constituted.
>
> (110)

From a perspective that affirms *figuration* to be *materially* constitutive of society and history, the reorientation in literary studies of which Hillis Miller has complained—the turn from "language as such . . . toward history, culture, society, politics, institutions"—might be better construed as a widening and deepening of our central scholarly concern with language and reading. Literary criticism has for some time been making its traditional analytical strengths useful to new transdisciplinary projects of cultural analysis, and it has been doing so by studying the ways in which discursive forms and processes constitute "history, culture, society, politics, institutions."

## V

Recent invocations of *history* (which, like *power*, is a term now in constant danger of hypostatization) have often appeared to be responses to— or, in certain cases, nothing more than positivistic retrenchments against— various structuralist and poststructuralist formalisms that have seemed, to some, to question the very possibility of historical understanding and historical experience; that have threatened to dissolve history into what Perry Anderson has suggested is an antinomy of objectivist determinism and subjectivist free play, an antinomy that allows no possibility for historical agency on the part of individual or collective human subjects (*In the Tracks*). *Subject*, both a grammatical and a political term, has come into widespread use not merely as a fashionable synonym for *the individual* but precisely as a means of emphasizing that individuals and the very concept of the individual are historically constituted in language and society. Although it continues to thrive in the mass media, in political rhetoric, and in undergraduate essays, the freely self-creating and world-creating individual of so-called bourgeois humanism has, for quite some time, been defunct in the texts of academic theory. Against the beleaguered category of the historical agent, contending armies of theory have opposed the specters of structural determinism and poststructural contingency—the latter tartly characterized by Anderson as "subjectivism without a subject" (54). We now behold, on the one hand, the implacable code, and on the other, the slippery signifier—the contemporary equivalents of Predestination and Fortune.

Anderson remarks that the "one master-problem around which *all* contenders have revolved" on the battlefield of contemporary social theory is "the nature of the relationships between structure and subject in human history and society" (33). Variations on this problematic might juxtapose structure to history or to practice; might oppose system or totality, on the one hand, to strategy or agency, on the other. And, indeed, one such version has characterized the interplay of current historical-social-political orientations to English and American literary studies in the form of containment versus subversion. As I have already suggested, such formulations are no more adequate to our own situation than to that of Elizabethan England. I believe that we should resist the reductive tendency to formulate our conceptual terms in binary oppositions; rather, we should construe them as joined in a mutually constitutive, recursive, and transformative *process*.

I have in mind here such recent work in social theory as Anthony Giddens's concept of *structuration*:

> The structural properties of social systems are both the medium and the outcome of the practices that constitute those systems. . . .
> Rules and resources are drawn upon by actors in the production of interaction, but are thereby also reconstituted through such interaction.
> (*Central Problems* 69, 71)

Pierre Bourdieu's concept of *habitus*:

> Systems of durable, transposable *dispositions*, structured structures predisposed to function as structuring structures, that is, as principles of the generation and structuring of practices and representations. . . .    (*Outline* 72)

and Marshall Sahlins's concept of the *structure of the conjuncture*:

> History is culturally ordered, differently so in different societies, according to meaningful schemes of things. The converse is also true: cultural schemes are

historically ordered, since to a greater or lesser extent the meanings are revalued as they are practically enacted. . . .

By the "structure of the conjuncture" I mean the practical realization of the cultural categories in a specific historical context, as expressed in the interested action of the historical agents.          (*Islands* vii, xiv)

With such perspectives in mind, we might entertain the following propositions: that the processes of subjectification and structuration are both interdependent and ineluctably historical; that the apparent systematicity of society is produced, adjusted, and transformed by means of the interactive social practices of individuals and groups; and that there is no necessary relationship between the intentions of actors and the outcomes of their actions—in other words, that their effectivity is conjunctural or situational and, to varying degrees, contingent. The possibilities for action are always socially and historically situated, always limited and limiting. Nevertheless, collective structures may enable as well as constrain individual agency; and they may be potentially enabling precisely when they are experienced by the subject as multiple, heterogeneous, and even contradictory in their imperatives. Paul Smith articulates such a concept of agency:

> The symbolic realm, the *place* where we are in language and in social formations and which is also the *process* whereby we fit into them, *constructs* the ideological. . . . Resistance does take place, but it takes place only within a social context which has already construed subject-positions for the human agent. The place of that resistance has, then, to be glimpsed somewhere in the interstices of the subject-positions which are offered in any social formation. More precisely, resistance must be regarded as the by-product of contradictions in and among subject-positions. . . . Resistance is best understood as a specific twist in the dialectic between individuation and ideological interpellation.
>
> (25)

The possibility of social and political agency cannot be based on the illusion that consciousness is a condition somehow beyond ideology. However, the very process of subjectively *living* the contradictions *within* or *among* ideological formations may allow us to experience facets of our own subjection at shifting internal distances—to read, as in a refracted light, one fragment of our ideological inscription by means of another. A reflexive knowledge so partial and unstable may, nevertheless, provide subjects with a means of empowerment as agents. Thus my invocation of the term *subject* is meant to suggest an equivocal process of *subjectification*: on the one hand, it shapes individuals as loci of consciousness and initiators of action, endowing them with *subjectivity* and with the capacity for agency; and, on the other hand, it positions, motivates, and constrains them within—it *subjects them to*—social networks and cultural codes, forces of necessity and contingency, that ultimately exceed their comprehension or control.

The refiguring of the relation between the verbal and the social, between the text and the world, involves a rejection of some still-prevalent, alternative idealist, empiricist, and materialist conceptions of literature: as an autonomous aesthetic, moral, or intellectual order that transcends the shifting and conflicting pressures of material needs and interests; as a collection of inert discursive records of "real events"; as the superstructural reflection produced by a determining economic base. Recent theories of textuality have argued persuasively that the referent of a linguistic sign cannot be fixed, that the meaning of a text cannot be stabilized. However, writing and reading are always historically and socially situated events, performed *in* the world and *upon* the world by ideologically situated individual and collective human agents. In any situation of signification, the theoretical indeterminacy of the signifying process is delimited by the historical specificity of discursive practices, by the constraints and resources of the reading formation within which that signification takes place. The project of a new sociohistorical criticism in literary studies is, then, to analyze the interplay of culture-specific discursive practices, including those by which cultural canons are formed and reformed. By such discursive means, versions of the real, of history, are experienced, deployed, reproduced, and by such means they may also be appropriated, contested, transformed.

Any collective critical project must be mindful that it, too, is a social practice that participates in the very interplay of interests and perspectives that it seeks to analyze. All academic texts selectively constitute the objects of their literary-historical knowledge, and do so on frequently unexamined and inconsistent grounds. Integral to any genuinely new-historicist project, however, must be a realization and acknowledgment that our analyses necessarily proceed from our own historically, socially, and institutionally shaped vantage points and that the pasts we reconstruct are, at the same time, the textual constructs of critics who are, ourselves, historical subjects. Our comprehension and representation of the texts of the past proceed by a mixture of estrangement and appropriation, as a reciprocal conditioning by the discourses of the past and our discourses about the past (McCanles; LaCapra, "Rethinking"). Scholarship actively constructs and delimits its object of study, and the scholar is historically positioned vis-à-vis that object. Thus, a historical criticism that seeks to recover meanings that are in any final or absolute sense authentic, correct, and complete is pursuing an illusion. It also becomes necessary to historicize the present as well as the past, and to historicize the dialectic between them—those pressures by which the past has shaped the present and the present reshapes the past. Such a critical practice constitutes a dialogue between a *poetics* and a *politics* of culture.

Since the beginning of the 1980s—the period marked, according to Miller, by the lurch of literary studies "toward history, culture, society, politics, institutions, class and gender conditions, the social context, the material base"—segments of the American political establishment, the mass media, and the neoconservative intelligentsia have been attacking what they represent as the degradation of literature and the humanities within the academy, and of cultural production and performance in society at large, as a result of the leftist agendas of professors and artists. In the very process of mobilizing their attack, these forces have made manifest their own agendas for the policing of education and the arts. The campaign for curricular reform pursued by the National Endowment for the Humanities has played on a widespread anxiety about the perceived demise of "traditional values" since the permissive 1960s. Under the successive leadership of William Bennett and Lynne V. Cheney, the NEH has focused on the preservation of curricula reflecting the dominant culture and the maintenance of syllabi that emphasize the putative stability, cohesion, and inclusiveness of American values and beliefs. A succession of official NEH reports, which have been endorsed in numerous editorials and popular commentaries, have sought to discredit cultural analyses that stress alternative and oppositional perspectives in history, politics, class, race, gender, and sexuality.

Whatever other responses it may provoke, the hostile attention paid from beyond the groves of academe to developments in literary theory, curriculum, and pedagogy confirms that the academy is perceived as a site for the contestation as well as for the reproduction of ideological dominants; that there may be something important at stake in our reading, teaching, and revision of the literary canon; and that, if we suddenly discover ourselves to be culturally and institutionally empowered, we are now compelled to choose if, when, and how to employ that power. The politics of the academy extend beyond what we casually refer to as "academic politics": the study and teaching of cultural poetics are enmeshed in a larger cultural politics that is without disinterested parties, without objective positions. Nevertheless, the claim to just such disinterestedness, like the naive appeal beyond interpretation to "the text itself," is a means of legitimating the dominant interest. By our choices, not only of what to read but of how to read, we may bring to our students and to ourselves a heightened awareness that we are engaged in a politics of reading, a sharper sense of our own historicity, an apprehension of our own positions within a regime of power and knowledge that at once sustains us and constrains us. It is by reconstruing "literature" within an unstable and agonistic field of verbal and social practices—by redrawing the boundaries of literary study, and then by transgressing those boundaries—that we may articulate the humanities as a site of intellectually and socially significant work in the historical present.[1]

## Note

[1]Portions of this essay have appeared under the title "Professing the Renaissance: The Poetics and Politics of Culture" in the book *The New Historicism*, edited by H. Aram Veeser, published by Routledge in 1989.

## Selected Bibliography

This list of suggestions for further reading contains a number of studies exemplifying new-historicist and related modes of recent literary criticism. I have selected only books, emphasized collections and anthologies rather than single-author volumes, and included representative work in fields of literary study outside the English Renaissance.

Greenblatt, Stephen J. *Renaissance Self-Fashioning: From More to Shakespeare*. Chicago: U of Chicago P, 1980.
A seminal study in the cultural poetics of identity formation in Tudor and Jacobean England.

——, ed. *Representing the English Renaissance*. Berkeley: U of California P, 1988.
An anthology of essays on sixteenth- and seventeenth-century English culture and ideology, reprinted from the journal *Representations*. Many of the articles are characteristic of new-historicist methods and themes.

Hunt, Lynn, ed. *The New Cultural History*. Berkeley: U of California P, 1989.
A stimulating collection of original essays on current methods and topics in the practice of cultural history, by scholars from the United States, Britain, and France.

Levinson, Marjorie, Marilyn Butler, Jerome McGann, and Paul Hamilton. *Rethinking Historicism: Critical Readings in Romantic History*. Oxford: Blackwell, 1989.
A collection of revisionist studies of English Romanticism by British and American critics.

Michaels, Walter Benn, and Donald E. Pease, eds. *The American Renaissance Reconsidered: Selected Papers from the English Institute, 1982–83*. Baltimore: Johns Hopkins UP, 1985.
Revisionist studies of canonical and noncanonical American Renaissance writers in relation to nineteenth-century socioeconomic issues, and of the critical history of the American Renaissance in relation to twentieth-century ideologies.

Patterson, Lee, ed. *Literary Practice and Social Change in Britain, 1380–1530*.

The New Historicism: Studies in Cultural Poetics 8. Berkeley: U of California P, 1990.
Critical historicist essays on writing practices in late medieval England and on the discipline of medieval studies.

Veeser, H. Aram, ed. *The New Historicism*. New York: Routledge, 1989.
A lively collection of analytical and polemical essays from a variety of critical and disciplinary perspectives, on the genealogy, methods, and politics of the new historicism.

# *C*ultural Criticism

## GERALD GRAFF AND BRUCE ROBBINS

In an essay called "Distance," written during the Falklands/Malvinas war of 1982, Raymond Williams offers a critique of British television's coverage of the fighting. The reporting has had a dangerously sanitized abstractness, he suggests, because of the "culture of distance" that results from the management of society by professionals. Television, which comes "from the Greek for 'afar,'" is "professionally understood, managed and interpreted" in such a way as to distance the reality of war from the viewer (36–38). There is a sort of conspiracy: "The television professionals," who are "deeply integrated" with "military professionals," join with them to suggest that "war is a profession." In the "antiseptic presentation of the images of war" by this "professional culture of distance," a presentation that emerges from "models and . . . convictions without experience," the reality of violent death is disguised, distanced, alienated. "Throughout the crisis, across different opinions," Williams reports, "I have not heard any talk of that distant calculating kind from friends who had been in actual battles" (39–40).

Though the Falklands/Malvinas conflict has itself retreated into the distance for most of us, Williams's commentary has lost none of its bite. Here, as often, he is the exemplary cultural critic, attending with fervor and astuteness to the "popular" culture of television as well as the "high" culture of serious literature, to present urgencies as well as past monuments, and counteracting the abstraction of professional specialists by calling us back to the commonality of shared experience. Like George Orwell, about whom he writes so well, Williams speaks in a public, reasonable, jargon-free voice that aims to be both independent and representative. Together, these two adjectives define the heroic project of cultural criticism, which claims to be "critical" in opposing the social mainstream and yet "cultural" in speaking for that mainstream.

While admiring Williams's stand against the uncritical coverage of the war, we find problems in the understanding of cultural criticism that it exemplifies. A look at these problems should help explain why many critics today have sought a different model of cultural criticism, one less prone to place the theoretical reflection of the professional in opposition to the humane authenticity of culture. The new cultural criticism that has arisen under the auspices of academic theory, particularly poststructuralism, has questioned

the very distinction assumed by Williams between the personal and the professional. This fact helps explain why critics still working in the Williams tradition
tend not to recognize the newer forms of theory-oriented criticism as "cultural
criticism" at all, much less as a successor to that earlier tradition, and why for
many of these critics the advent of academic theory seems to spell the death
of the cultural critic and the public intellectual.

Consider Williams's equation of "culture" with "experience," which is
contrasted with abstract and theoretical representations of experience. Speaking in the name of "friends who had been in actual battles" (he himself fought in
Normandy in the Second World War), Williams obliquely invokes the familiar
formula of the one who speaks from experience: I know; I was there. The
formula gently strong-arms its reader into the proposition that, to understand,
all we need is to be there. But nothing could be less evident. Is physical
presence, in a battle of all things, really a sufficient guarantee of pertinent
knowledge? Is it even necessarily superior to a more distanced perspective?
For that matter, isn't individual experience itself shaped and inhabited by
those seemingly distant social and ideological structures?

Williams associates "the professional culture of distance" with new
weaponry capable of killing at distances that once seemed, and perhaps still
seem, inhuman, from "beyond the range of normal vision" (38). But could a
sailor stationed on a battleship struck by a tele-guided missile "know" anything
useful about the logic of battle or even about his "experience"? And, by extension, in a modern society determined by forces as distantly and invisibly deadly
as the Exocet missile, does "being there" really guarantee the authenticity of
social knowledge?

Williams contrasts "experience" with mass-mediated "models," implying that experience somehow contains its own understanding of itself, as if
experience, as Jacques Derrida might say, were self-identical and present to
itself, prior to explanatory categories. This appeal to the consensus-forming
power of primary "experience" is a compelling instance of what the concept of
"culture" itself has meant to the tradition of literary and social thought that
Williams assembles in his great work *Culture and Society* (1958), and it illustrates why that concept and that tradition are now regarded as controversial
in more recent culturally oriented theory and criticism.

For Williams, the first-hand experience of combat functions as a radical unifier, transcending the specialized abstractions and social divisions common in modern technological societies and restoring us to a sense of a single,
publicly intelligible whole. The voice of the Williams-like cultural critic seems
to say, "We're all in this together." Behind the hypothetical immediacy of
Williams's battlefield lies the model of the natural, rooted wholeness of an
"organic community," set over against the pseudocommunity of the culture of
professionalism. The organic community presumably affords the critic a central

point of view—Matthew Arnold, writing of Chaucer, called it a "central, a truly human point of view" ("Study of Poetry" 174)—from which to survey experience. Viewed from this central standpoint, experience ceases to seem dissociated, fragmented, and secondary and becomes innerly transparent, harmonious, and consensual. In Williams's own phrase in *Culture and Society*, culture is "the whole way of living of a people," with the adjective *whole* implying an internal coherence that relegates dissension, conflict, and incoherence to the exterior, the distance (83).

## *Culture and Its Ambiguities*

Williams favorably contrasts this anthropological meaning of culture, denoting the whole way of living of a people, with the normative meaning of Culture (with an idealized capital C), Arnold's "best that has been thought and known in the world" ("Sweetness and Light" 113). In the latter usage, Culture still claims to represent the organic voice of the people but actually has become a distant abstraction imposed on the people by a middle-class leadership that speaks only for a certain faction.

But this conflict between culture in the anthropological sense and Culture in the normative sense leads to a third way of using the term, one that refers neither to a people's organic way of life nor to the normative values preached by leading intellectuals but to a battleground of social conflicts and contradictions. It is owing partly to Williams's influence that the word *culture* is invoked today both to affirm the bourgeois idealism of Arnold and to challenge that idealism in the name of Marxist, feminist, and poststructuralist "cultural studies." In the one tradition, the cultural critic speaks for the social mainstream and defines its unifying concerns, while in the other the cultural critic sees such unifying concerns as a way of begging questions of power and inequality. The first meaning emphasizes organic unity and the dualism of the organic culture against technological false culture; the second emphasizes contradiction and the idea that the poles of any such dualism tend to inhabit each other.

The idea of culture as a people's "whole way of life" first arose in the late eighteenth century with the growth of Romantic literary nationalism and the concern with "national character" by writers such as Johann Herder, Friedrich Schlegel, and later Jules Michelet; the idea was subsequently developed into a methodology of modern literary history in the work of Hippolyte-Adolphe Taine and Charles-Augustin Sainte-Beuve. The central premise of this literary nationalism was that the measure of a civilization's value lay primarily in the respect accorded to its national literature, with ancient Greece being the most notable case in point.

The centrality of literature in the modern curriculum is a direct result of the prestige of this literary nationalism in the later nineteenth century, when the departments of modern languages and literatures were formed and defined on nationalistic lines. The preeminence accorded to literature reflected its promise as a political instrument for the socializing of otherwise heterodox groups into the mainstream of the national culture. When late-nineteenth-century educators urged that English literature replace the classical languages at the center of the school and college curriculum, they were animated by the belief that the literature of the native tongue (provided it was British, not American) was a superior means of acculturating the raw, uncultivated masses, many of them children of recent European immigrants, who were the subjects of the new compulsory schooling and the expansion of college education. The campaign to replace Greek and Latin with English literature would not have succeeded as rapidly as it did had not English and, later, American literature seemed the perfect instrument for socializing a threateningly heterogeneous ethnic population into the values of Anglo-Saxon culture.

The political aims and effects of this project were ambiguous in a way that has marked the politics of the word *culture* ever since. The teaching of literature expressed the desire to keep an expanding immigrant population under control, but it also expressed the desire to make meritocratic opportunities more widely available. Despite its traditional roots, literary study became identified with a democratic counterculture that challenged the social conservatism of the earlier classical curriculum. The present-day culture war over the humanities canon is the culmination of a century-long battle over the social function of the academic humanities and the extent to which their values should harmonize with or challenge the values of the larger society.

The emergence of the idea of culture as told by Williams in *Culture and Society* is the story of the making of a counterculture. Williams explains how the word *culture* appeared only as the organic way of life it denotes came to be threatened during the Industrial and French revolutions and how the word later came to serve, in the elaborations of the Romantics, Matthew Arnold, Walter Pater, T. S. Eliot, F. R. Leavis, D. H. Lawrence, George Orwell, and their successors, as "a court of human appeal" against the divisions and fragmentations of industrial society (xviii). "Culture," Williams writes, "was made into an entity, a positive body of achievements and habits, precisely to express a mode of living superior to that being brought about by the 'progress of civilization' " (254). This story, more or less as Williams tells it, has been for us the founding story of cultural criticism. At the story's center is a concept of culture that is presumed to be "critical," an antidote for a dissociated and disembodied social actuality.

This coupling of culture and the critical standpoint helps explain how the seemingly pedestrian study of literary texts could have taken on such grandiose and sweeping ambitions as a kind of self-appointed conscience of modern society. It is paradoxical, after all, that the rising pretensions of literary criticism took place during a period when literature itself was being relegated to an increasingly marginal role in the cultures of Europe and the United States. But it was precisely because literature was *not* socially central that it needed to proclaim its central position as society's conscience, representing a kind of counterdiscourse, "an abstraction and an absolute," in Williams's words, against which society would be judged (xviii).

Such a concept of culture in effect appoints cultural critics to the role Percy Shelley ascribed to poets when he called them the unacknowledged legislators of the world. When Arnold declared in his essay "The Study of Poetry" that, in an age of increasing skepticism, poetry would have to take the place of religion "to interpret life for us, to console us, to sustain us," he was clearly assigning poetry a role of social as well as quasi-religious leadership, with the critic serving as the intermediary who would interpret the new poetic religion of "culture" to the general public (161).

Contrary to the objections often heard today, recent academic Marxists and feminists were not the first to "politicize" literature and criticism: the cultural critics of the nineteenth century turned literary criticism into a kind of social and political action by other means. Culture, defined as universal values of "sweetness and light," was pressed into service to save society from engulfment by the "machinery" of private interest and opinion and the acrimonious contentions of democratic politics.

The story of how criticism became politicized has been most eloquently told by cultural critics of the postwar generation (who seem, however, as we shall see, to have forgotten their own statements in their dismay at the present generation's way of politicizing culture). Writing of nineteenth-century American literary criticism, Alfred Kazin observes in *On Native Grounds*:

> What had criticism in America usually been if not predominantly social, even political, in its thinking? From Emerson and Thoreau to Mencken and Brooks, criticism had been the great American lay philosophy, the intellectual conscience and intellectual carryall. It had been a study of literature inherently concerned with ideals of citizenship, and often less a study of literary texts than a search for some new and imperative moral order within which American writing could live and grow. (400–01)

In *A Margin of Hope: An Intellectual Autobiography* Irving Howe draws an even more explicit connection between the sense of social crisis and the tone of social exigency in modern criticism:

> In a secular age literary criticism carries a heavy burden of intention, becoming a surrogate mode of speech for people blocked in public life. Unable to fulfill

directly their visions of politics, morality, and religion, critics transfer these to the seemingly narrower channels of literary criticism. Precisely this spilling over of thought and passion has made criticism so interesting in our time—so perilous, too. The dominant formal claim of modern criticism has been an insistence upon treating literature as autonomous; the main actual circumstance for writing criticism has been a pressure for extraliterary connections. Ever since Arnold found that reflecting upon the place of poetry in an industrial society led him to worry about "a girl named Wragg," the most valuable critics have often doubled as cultural spokesmen, moral prophets, political insurgents.

(147)

As Kazin comments, criticism in America "had always been more a form of moral propaganda than a study in esthetic problems" (401).

But as Howe and Kazin have recognized, the moral propaganda of cultural criticism has always been contradictory. Clearly there was something contradictory in the very project of grounding an oppositional concept of culture in an organic and consensual ideal of society. How could the allegiances of culture be consensual and subversive of consensus at the same time? How was culture—and the teaching of culture—to be at once the essential expression of the national consensus and a profound critique of the national consensus? How could culture stand simultaneously for what the nation already was and what its progressive faction aspired to be?

## Culture versus Theory

*Theory* has proved to be as contested and ambivalent a term as *culture* in the history with which we have been concerned. On the one hand, the tradition of culture represented by critics like Williams, Leavis, Kazin, and Howe has seen no redeeming value in theoretical speculation. On the other hand, during the period when the postwar New Criticism in the United States and Britain contracted the scope of literary study to the autonomous work of literature itself, these same antitheoretical critics helped keep broadly cultural theorizing about literature and the arts alive.

E. P. Thompson's polemic against Louis Althusser, *The Poverty of Theory*, is perhaps the most explicit example of the quarrel of culture with theory, but the quarrel runs back through the whole *Culture and Society* tradition. In that tradition, immediate experience joins with culture to oppose theory, which is associated with professional elitism on the one hand and uncontrolled controversy and sectarianism on the other. Chris Baldick writes that, in this tradition, there is "a constant and deeply held distaste for theory among these critics, and an accompanying tendency which amounts to a cult of raw experience" (203). Again, whereas culture is taken to represent organic wholeness, theory epitomizes the alienation from personal and communal experience that Williams identifies with "the professional culture of distance." Theory becomes a preeminent case of the fragmented technocratic disciplinarity that combines with the other specialized machineries of modern industrialism to plunge society into the contention of ideologies.

The role of cultural criticism, then, comes to be identified with the need to shore up a supposedly once-intact social consensus threatened by the conflicts and hypertrophied self-consciousness of modern life. Hence stress is placed on the cultural critic's presumed transcendence of mere partisanship and "special interests." As Arnold writes, "The great art of criticism is to get oneself out of the way and to let humanity decide," to stand above "the turmoil of controversial reasonings," which can only lead to skepticism and cultural demoralization (qtd. in Baldick 32, 38). The Arnoldian cultural critic speaks for the voice of "humanity," against the liberal democratic individualist cult of "doing as one likes" (119–23). Like Arnold, Leavis also thinks of criticism as a missionary counterforce for consensus against "the dissolution of the traditions, social, religious, moral and intellectual, [that] has left us without that basis of things taken for granted which is necessary to a healthy culture" (qtd. in Baldick 193).

A "basis of things taken for granted": this phrase succinctly sums up the longing to be free of controversy, sectarianism, polemic, the clash of theories and countertheories that underlies the idea of the cultural critic still embraced by middlebrow critics today. And it is *theory*—a term with a diffuse range of associations, from multiculturalism and feminism to postmodern self-consciousness to the interpretive controversies of academic explicators—that is seen as the source of this unwanted and unnecessary plague of dissension. Theory, as Baldick writes, is seen as the symptom and the cause of "the modern disease of polemic and partisanship" (32).

Our very idea of the literary has come to be defined as a refuge from this disease of divisiveness that makes us think self-consciously about ourselves and our differences. As Terry Eagleton observes, from the nineteenth century onward, "the poetic is gradually redefined by English criticism as the organic, intuitive and stubbornly specific, inimical to conceptual analysis and global generality." Poetic discourse is defined as the antithesis of the discourse of "statement" and polemic and is associated, as Eagleton puts it, with "the priority of local affections and unarguable loyalties" ("Escape" 1291). The view propagated by the postwar New Critics that a poem is not a statement "about" something but a symbolic "embodiment" of attitudes had the effect of taking poetic discourse out of the realm of the arguable where disagreements can arise about it or where poems might engage in arguments with one another or with other writing. For the New Critics, argument and polemic were the instruments of a degraded "ordinary language," which meant that any text that argued or theorized could not be poetry, or not good poetry. And yet the view that poetry could not be argument or theory was unable to protect poetry from becoming the site of massive theoretical and interpretive disagreement.

This distaste for controversy, identified with the technocratic forces of antiliterature, comes across in attacks on literary theory today. In one such attack, Robert Alter, in *The Pleasures of Reading in an Ideological Age*, complains of "the new academic sectarianism" that results from "the division of the academic study of literature, especially in the United States, into competing sectarian groups, each with its own dogmas and its own arcane language" (14–15). In a similar fashion, Denis Donoghue, in a favorable review of Alter, speaks of the need to acknowledge a "trouble free zone of reading" that would protect literature from the menace of theoretical and political conflict (38). Like Arnold before them, Alter and Donoghue purport to speak from a central position above the mere sectarianisms of critical schools. Yet their polemics are themselves inevitably sectarian gestures, attempts to wrest back some of the influence that their critical school has lost.

The fear of theory and of overly conscious reflection, which are blamed for having destroyed a once-intact organic community, is a pervasive impulse in English literature itself: Geoffrey Hartman has labeled it the philosophy of "anti-self consciousness" ("Romanticism"). The philosophy can be traced from Coleridge and Carlyle through Arnold down to Lawrence's glorification of the predemocratic, preindustrial "living, organic, *believing* community" (*Studies* 6) and to similar communal visions in the work of Yeats and Eliot. Lawrence and T. E. Hulme located the moment of dissolution of the organic community at the Renaissance, while for Eliot it occurred at the end of the seventeenth century and for Leavis it came with the advent of industrialism and the rise of "technologico-Benthamite civilization" (*English Literature* 24). But whenever it is said to have first set in, the rise of modern theoretical reflection is lamented for its destruction of a cultural "basis of things taken for granted." Eliot finds this problem at the center of the poetry of Blake and Yeats, whom he takes to illustrate the price paid by poets who, unlike Dante, have not inherited a culturally shared belief system and are thus forced to use their poems as places to consciously work out their beliefs.

This doctrine has led Eliot's admirers and detractors alike to mistake him for an aesthete who argues that poets either need have or ought to have no beliefs at all. But Eliot's point is not that poets could or should have no beliefs but that they should not have to become aware of their beliefs as beliefs. In a rightly ordered society, according to Eliot, we would be able simply to live our beliefs without having to think and argue about them; the beliefs of poets and everyone else would already go without saying and thus not be noticed as beliefs. There would be no need for the kind of sectarian debate about beliefs that erodes our confidence in their authority and makes us think too much. That a community's beliefs have become recognizable as beliefs is a telltale sign that authentically organic culture has been replaced by the modern democratic chaos of ideological controversy. In the sociological idiom, culture has been replaced by association, *Gemeinschaft* by *Gesellschaft*.

The "problem of belief" that obsessively preoccupied the New Critical generation of Eliot and Leavis turned on the question of whether true art is compatible with a society in which beliefs are not simply given and taken for granted but continually negotiated and rationalized. In *The Use of Poetry and the Use of Criticism*, a searching reinterpretation of the cultural criticism tradition from the Romantics to I. A. Richards, Eliot saw clearly that the very emergence of criticism—we would now call it "theory"—presupposes a democratically disintegrated society, in which the beliefs embedded in art are no longer taken for granted and thus have to be elaborately analyzed and explained to the public by a cadre of critics and teachers. Eliot believed that a truly organic society would have no need for critics like himself, much less for the academic explicators whom he inspired and finally disparaged as "the Lemon-squeezer school of criticism" (*On Poetry* 113).

Eliot also recognized regretfully that writers who do not accept the state of culture as it is have no choice but to enter the arena of theoretical debate if they hope to change things, that resistance to theoretical reflection is the luxury of those who are content with the status quo. Thus Arnold was defeating his own missionary purposes when he refused to theorize about the nature of poetry and offered a set of "touchstones" instead. As Arnold observed:

> Critics give themselves great labor to draw out what in the abstract constitutes the character of a high quality of poetry. It is much better simply to have recourse to concrete examples; to take specimens of poetry of the high, the very highest quality, and to say: the characters of a high quality of poetry are what is expressed *there*. They are far better recognized by being felt in the verse of the master, than by being perused in the prose of the critic.
>
> ("Study of Poetry" 170–71)

Arnold encountered a double bind here: if his audience did not already appreciate the greatness of the touchstone passages he adduces—and why bother adducing them if they did?—then it is hard to see how they could have been helped by those passages. Arnold had to refuse to offer a theoretical argument about poetic greatness, lest he become caught up in the disease of partisanship and theoretical disagreement, but such a refusal made sense only on the assumption that his readers already knew what poetic greatness is. The very conditions that forced Arnold to appeal to the touchstones seem to guarantee the futility of this gesture, at least for any audience that did not already have the feel for poetry in its bones.

There is, in short, a performative contradiction in the attempt to argue for a "basis of things taken for granted." The efforts of Arnold, Eliot, and their whole tradition of cultural critics to protect from controversy the organic wholeness of beliefs only tended to foment more controversy. The complaint that the organic culture is being corroded by modern critical self-consciousness tends only to generate more of the critical self-consciousness being complained of. Bewailing the loss of the organic society—the preindustrial society of Carlyle and Coleridge, Eliot's Europe before the dissociation of sensibility, Leavis's England before the coming of "technologico-Benthamite civilization," Lawrence's "living, . . . *believing* community"—only generates a further surplus of that corrosive theoretical rationality on which the catastrophe is blamed.

But what distinguishes Eliot from Arnold before him and today's theory-bashing critics after him is his unsentimental if grudging recognition that the expansion of critical and theoretical reflection is an inevitable result of the dissolution of the kind of medieval consensus he admired. The theoretical impulse *is* profoundly threatening to any ideal of organic social consensus because it accepts the eruption of radical cultural contention and disagreement as a normal rather than a perverse condition. Theory, in our view, has become a name for the reflective or second-order discourse that breaks out when a community's previously unspoken assumptions are no longer taken for granted. These assumptions then become objects of explicit formulation and debate— very likely because the confines of the community are breached. Literary theory emerges when critics and teachers of literature no longer share agreements on the meaning of terms like *literature, meaning, text, author, criticism, reading, aesthetic value, history, teaching, discipline*, and *department*—and, of course, *culture*.

As Williams saw, the very appearance of cultural criticism's "keywords" (including *culture* itself) results from the breakdown of the consensus that had formerly made those words unnecessary. Examples today are the sudden prominence of the word *canon* and the expression "Western culture": a generation ago these terms were not as pervasive as they are now because what they stood for was not felt to be under challenge. When the canon was unproblematically what the humanities curriculum consisted of, there was little need for the word *canon*. When the only culture worthy of being taught seemed self-evidently Western, there was little need to designate it as such. The very prominence of a term like *canonical Western culture* implies that what the term denotes has lost its self-evident status and become a theoretical entity and a locus of conflict.

In this view, then, the theoretical impulse is both a result and a cause of what Sacvan Bercovitch has termed a condition of cultural "dissensus" ("Problem" 633). It exemplifies the situation that for Jean-François Lyotard and others has come to define the postmodern condition, in which the "metanarratives" or "master stories" that once structured the precritical common sense of the community now seem to be socially contested forms of ideology rather than foundational truths. Social communication according to this view thus dissolves into a plurality of "language games" whose rules are unstable and renegotiable from one conversation to the next.

It becomes easy to see why current feminists and postcolonials, who have always viewed as important the question of who speaks for whom, find something politically suspect in the Enlightenment idea of the cultural critic as a "universal intellectual," in Michel Foucault's disparaging term, one who claims to speak for humankind in general. The problem is dramatized again by Arnold, who invokes Chaucer's "central, . . . truly human point of view" and then illustrates his remark by adducing a passage from the Prioress's Tale that blames the Jewish people for the treacherous murder of a Christian child ("Study of Poetry" 174). The "central, . . . truly human point of view" turns out to be a blatantly anti-Semitic point of view.

## The Backlash

A powerful backlash against the trends we have described has set in, and many voices are calling for a return to the tradition of the Arnoldian cultural critic, which is said to have been replaced by soulless academic professionalism and a cult of political correctness. The backlash is immediately directed against the aggressively political thrust of the new trends, but its essential arguments long predate the coming of those trends. Both from the Left (as in Russell Jacoby's polemic, *The Last Intellectuals*) and from the Right (as in any recent issue of the *New Criterion*), we are told that the last several decades mark the decline and fall, if not the death, of the cultural critic. The age of theory, the age of methodology, the age of specialism—these are regarded as the plausible denominations for our period. It is felt that, with the "rise and fall of the man of letters" (John Gross's well-known book of the same title makes this argument), the critic who addressed the "common reader" of Samuel Johnson and Virginia Woolf in an idiom understandable to the general public has been replaced by the narrow academic specialist employing a jargon addressed only to other academic specialists.

The charge is that the academicization of criticism has spelled the triumph of impersonal methodology and theory over the personal intuition of the critic. Narrow professional interests have triumphed over the interests of the community. In this change, criticism is said to have suffered a loss at once of individual personality and of universal appeal. Instead of acting as a human being speaking to other human beings out of the resources of an individual sensibility, the critic becomes an anonymous technician whose mechanical "method" rather than any personal judgment dictates his or her interpretations, irrespective of the public interest, the needs of students, or the uniqueness of literary texts being interpreted.

Academic critics, the indictment continues, do not attempt to make difficult literary works accessible to a wider public but evolve a self-protective discourse of abstractions that comes between the literary work and the reader and makes literature even more inaccessible than it would be otherwise, while increasing the lay reader's dependency on the academic expert. These critics have thus allegedly been able to elevate themselves above both the public and the literary artist and to transform literary education from the teaching of great books to the teaching of research specialties—which today turn out to be tied increasingly to political agendas and insurrectionary theories.

This form of intellectual treason is one of the major charges of Allan Bloom's best-selling book, *The Closing of the American Mind*. Bloom argues that a liberal education ought to mean "reading certain generally recognized classic texts, just reading them, letting them dictate what the questions are and the method of approaching them—not forcing them into categories we make up. . . ." But today's professors, according to Bloom, turn their backs on the classic texts in order to engage in "endless debates about methods—among Freudian criticism, Marxist criticism, New Criticism, Structuralism and Deconstructionism, and many others, all of which have in common the premise that what Plato or Dante had to say about reality is unimportant" (334, 375).

These widespread dissatisfactions with academic criticism rest on a legitimate recognition of the unhealthy gulf that increasingly separates the concerns and discourses of academic critics and the constituencies that those critics still at least nominally claim to address. Yet the dissatisfactions also come, as we have been suggesting, from a refusal to acknowledge the possibility of legitimate disagreement over what counts as a great book, how texts should be read and taught, and what the aims and assumptions of humanitistic education should be. What has stimulated the proliferation of methodological "isms" that Bloom and others disparage in academic literary studies is not just the need of a professorial caste to elevate itself above the public and the artist. It is also the emergence of new conflicts over the meanings of cultural texts or the reemergence of older conflicts that can no longer be pushed out of sight. The attack on the academic "forcing" of texts "into categories we make up," in the name of a criticism that would "just" read the classics as they supposedly ask to be read, is in essence an attack on the existence of radical disagreement. It expresses the longing, which we referred to earlier, for a "trouble free zone of reading" (in Donoghue's phrase) that would somehow elevate culture above the realm of sectarian politics and debate.

The self-contradictory nature of the attack becomes clear when we note that its effect is not to draw us back to an uncontroversial, trouble-free reading of the classics but to provoke still more debate, a debate in which the traditional humanism of writers like Bloom and Donoghue becomes one more competing "ism," one more cultural and political agenda, among others. Thus when Bloom invokes the names of Plato and Dante in the passage just quoted, he does *not* let those authors "dictate what the questions are and the method of approaching them." In using Plato and Dante to denounce modern methodological tendencies of which those writers could have known nothing, Bloom "forces" them into categories made up by him, not them. To point out this problem is not to efface the distinction between legitimate and illegitimate readings of past writers, but it is to argue that our changing historical interests inevitably predetermine some of the questions we ask of past texts.

For this reason, the very effort to keep the conflict of methodologies and theories from interfering with the practice of "just" reading texts, without the intervention of theory and politics, only becomes one more methodology or theory of reading, one more polemical position in the conflict. Barring outright repression from the Right, the current trend toward increasing theoretical and methodological self-consciousness appears to be an inevitable result of the increasingly conflictual nature of the cultural and academic scene. This conflictual atmosphere can only be intensified by attempts to reinstate traditional cultural criticism under the banner of "the cultural heritage" or "our common culture" (see, e.g., W. J. Bennett, *Our Children*).

For us, then, the new theory-driven academic criticism represents not a symptom of terminal decline but the recovery of the aims of the older cultural criticism at a time when that older criticism is no longer adequate to express a dissensual cultural scene. If there has been a decline of criticism, in our view, it is seen in the stale middlebrow neoconservatism that continues to invoke a rhetoric of consensus that its own hysterical anger and resentment belie.

Nothing in the new academic cultural criticism draws more of this anger and resentment than its radical "politicization" of literature and literary study. Instead of upholding a "central, truly human point of view," gay and feminist studies, black studies and postcolonialism, neo-Marxism, the new historicism, poststructuralism, and post-Freudian psychoanalytic criticism fragment the culture of criticism and the criticism of culture into a myriad of special-interest groups, each with its peculiar grievances against the establishment. Rather than "We're all in this together," the motto of the new cultural criticism might well be "Whose common culture?"

Again, however, if our earlier point is correct, the contrast between old and new is less clear-cut than it at first appears. We have seen that the older cultural criticism, for which current middlebrow critics are nostalgic, was the first to "politicize" criticism, a fact conveniently forgotten today. Howe's statement, quoted above, that "the most valuable [literary] critics have often doubled as . . . political insurgents" acknowledges the politicization of literary criticism as a continuous and honorable motif. Yet recently Howe seems to have forgotten his own point (as well as the direction of his own career) when he objects that the preoccupation of today's literature teachers with "race, gender and class" is "better dealt with in courses in history and sociology" ("Teaching" 478). Granted, the politics of feminist, postcolonial, Marxist, and deconstructionist criticism cannot be conflated with the older forms of insurgent criticism to which Howe referred. Nevertheless, the recent politicization of criticism springs from the same "pressure for extraliterary connections" that Howe once recognized as a legitimate critical impulse.

In a typical specimen of the traditionalist argument in a recent *New York Times Book Review*, Cynthia Ozick bemoans the loss of the unitary culture of thirty years ago, when it was "patently not ... wrong to speak of literary culture as a single force or presence. That was what was meant," Ozick observes, "by the peaceable word 'humanities.'" Instead of peaceable words like *humanities* and *letters*, Ozick complains, we now have "a thousand enemy camps," specialized professional "fortresses" isolated by "crocodiled moats," and what used to be a literary culture "falls into a heap of adversarial splinters—into competing contemptuous clamorers for turf and mental dominance." Literary theorists, needless to say, emerge in Ozick's picture as the self-appointed police of the crocodile moats (3, 51).

Yet what Ozick depicts as the sad degeneration of a once-unified literary culture into a nest of "contemptuous clamorers for turf and mental dominance" could be less invidiously described as a simple result of democratization. What Ozick can see only as a fall into the crocodile pit will look to those formerly excluded as simply an opportunity, a situation in which those with Ozick's traditional view of literary culture no longer get to dictate the terms in which culture is discussed and studied. As for "the peaceable word 'humanities,'" this word has seemed "peaceable" only from inside a certain consensus that arbitrarily excluded the voices that might have injected more turbulence into it, groups that not long ago would have included Jews and women like Ozick herself. Ozick's figures of speech place her above the crocodiles in the theory pit, but one of the premises of a democratic culture is that those you describe as crocodiles will have the right to describe you that way in turn.

It has to be conceded that the attempt to reenliven the general discourse of culture through the agency of professional academic vocabularies is as yet a problematic and groping enterprise fraught with many difficulties and dangers. One can object that the attack on postmodern theory for retreating from public discourse into a superspecialized and rarefied vocabulary is a profound misrecognition, but the very pervasiveness of this misrecognition is evidence of the enormous gulf that still separates postmodern theoretical discourse from general public understanding. It is easy enough to argue in principle that postmodern theory is a struggle to constitute a new discourse of cultural generality that will transcend academic specialisms. But it is difficult in practice for that theory to make itself publicly intelligible and available. That difficulty, however, is what makes the teaching of theory and the attempt to prevent it such an important battleground in the larger conflict over who will define the term *culture* today. And the very fierceness of the battle suggests that the debate over theory and the politics of literature is far from being merely esoteric and trivial. If the lessons of the new theoretical cultural criticism were as merely esoteric and specialized as they are said to be, few of us would be getting so aroused over them.

## Cultural Studies

The idea of a criticism that is methodological and theoretical as well as broadly cultural may still seem a contradiction in terms. But this response reflects just those habits of categorization that the new theory-oriented cultural criticism attempts to change. In one sense, theory represents an attempt to "redraw the boundaries": it challenges the antithesis between literature and theory, literature and methodology, literature and politics, and the equation of democracy with immediate experience, organic community, and consensus. Theory argues that an authoritarianism behind the facade of democratically accessible intuition gives rhetorical power to the appeal to the unarguable loyalties of the common culture. From the theoretical perspective, we cannot assume a single, central culture that renders individual experience coherent and meaningful but rather inescapable cultural difference, division, and dissonance. As a ground of culture, theoretical controversy is inescapable, however repressed and unacknowledged it may be.

When culture is conceived as an organism, modern history tends to become a narrative of historical decline in which the advance of theory, rationalization, and professionalization can only be seen as a threat. The historian of anthropology James Clifford states the point well:

> Everywhere individuals and groups improvise local performances from (re)collected pasts, drawing on foreign media, symbols, and languages. This existence among fragments has often been portrayed as a process of ruin and cultural decay, perhaps most eloquently by Claude Lévi-Strauss in *Tristes tropiques* (1955). In Lévi-Strauss's global vision—one widely shared today—authentic human differences are disintegrating, disappearing in an expansive commodity culture to become, at best, collectible "art" or "folklore." The great narrative of entropy and loss in *Tristes tropiques* expresses an inescapable, sad truth. But

> it is too neat, and it assumes a questionable Eurocentric position at the "end" of a unified human history. . . . It is easier to register the loss of traditional orders of difference than to perceive the emergence of new ones.    (14–15)

In contrast to this view of lost cultural authenticity, Clifford has suggested that "cultures" be reconceived: not as static, bounded entities, on the model of villages to which the professional ethnographer travels in order to "experience" and study them first-hand, but as textual sites and processes, constitutively open to conflicting cultural currents and interpretations, and as themselves *including* travel, both "ethnographic" and other. In Clifford's sense, *culture* would no longer be opposed to *distance* but would presuppose it.

This argument liberates us from the necessity of opposing culture to the characteristically modern form of distance that Williams calls "professional." The traditional narrative of decline, not anything in the nature of either culture or professionalism, has opposed these concepts, seeing the rise of professionalism as a falling away from the wholeness of culture into a distance and division exemplified by academic methodology and theory. As long as the idea of a professional discipline of academic criticism is understood to be such a falling away, academic criticism remains dedicated to an end that by definition it can never achieve, for as a professional discipline it is conceived as a fragment rather than a whole.

Our point here is not to reject the concept of culture but to see it as a contested space. In this sense, the current conflict over the academic curriculum centers on which definitions and interpretations of the word *culture* will prevail. It is not that the academic humanities have become "no longer" consensual but that universities have attempted to cease excluding groups that formerly would have challenged the consensus of those traditionally in control. This point is conveniently forgotten by the many educators and critics who blame the crisis of the humanities on the dissolution of literary culture into special-interest groups.

The institutional name most often given today to the ensemble of new vocabularies and practices emerging on the site occupied by cultural criticism and theory is *cultural studies*. Though the content and direction of academic cultural studies are still very much open, its one uncontested principle has been respect for the lived experience of cultures in the plural, particular sense, which issues in a hospitable inclusiveness to "low" or uncanonical objects, activities, genres, and styles that Culture in the singular, universal sense had tended to neglect.

*Cultural studies* suggests that the aim of cultural criticism is something more than preserving, transmitting, and interpreting culture or cultures. Rather, the aim is to bring together, in a common democratic space of discussion, diversities that had remained unequal largely because they had remained apart. Cultural studies in this sense means a refusal of the universals of Arnoldian *Culture* with a capital C, but it means a refusal also to grant permanent immunity to the values, borders, and differences of plural, lowercase *cultures*. Contrary again to the popular charges, the multicultural trend of recent cultural studies has been not to exalt group "particularism" but to challenge it, to challenge the belief that blackness, femaleness, or Africanness are essential, unchanging qualities. Like texts, cultures are seen as indeterminate sites of conflict that cannot be pinned to a single totalized meaning.

We conclude, then, by adapting an argument from Ernesto Laclau and Chantal Mouffe's *Hegemony and Socialist Strategy*, a book well on its way to becoming the bible of oppositional cultural studies today. In our view, cultural studies can best find common ground with new social movements outside the university by creating a space of debate in which questions of cultural identity and political strategy are not defined in advance.

## Selected Bibliography

Baldick, Chris. *The Social Mission of English Criticism, 1848–1932*. Oxford: Clarendon–Oxford UP, 1983.
Analytic survey of early British cultural criticism.

Brantlinger, Patrick. *Crusoe's Footprints: Cultural Studies in Britain and America*. New York: Routledge, 1990.

Clifford, James. *The Predicament of Culture: Twentieth-Century Ethnography, Literature, and Art*. Cambridge: Harvard UP, 1988.
Central statement on the ambiguous intersection between anthropological and literary senses of culture.

Clifford, James, and George E. Marcus, eds. *Writing Culture: The Poetics and Politics of Ethnography*. Berkeley: U of California P, 1986.
Important collection of essays on the "literary turn" in ethnography.

Graff, Gerald. *Professing Literature: An Institutional History*. Chicago: U of Chicago P, 1987.
Institutional history of American criticism with perspective on current cultural conflicts.

Graff, Gerald, and Michael Warner, eds. *The Origins of Literary Studies in America: A Documentary Anthology*. New York: Routledge, 1989.

Grossberg, Lawrence, Cary Nelson, and Paula Treichler, eds. *Cultural Studies*. New York: Routledge, 1991.
An ambitious international collection on cultural studies.

Hall, Stuart, Dorothy Hobson, Andrew Lowe, and Paul Willis, eds. *Culture, Media, Language: Working Papers in Cultural Studies, 1972–79*. London: Unwin, 1980.
Good introduction to history and variety of work done at the Center for Contemporary Cultural Studies, University of Birmingham.

Mulhern, Frances. *The Moment of "Scrutiny."* London: NLB, 1979.
Definitive treatment of Leavis and his place in the development of British cultural criticism.

Nelson, Cary, and Lawrence Grossberg, eds. *Marxism and the Interpretation of Culture*. Urbana: U of Illinois P, 1988.
Epoch-making collection of the new cultural studies, highlighting the confrontation of Marxism with forms of poststructuralism.

Williams, Raymond. *Culture*. London: Fontana, 1981.
Along with the interviews of *Politics and Letters*, Williams's major rethinking of the problematic of *Culture and Society*.

# $\mathcal{P}$ ostcolonial Criticism

## HOMI K. BHABHA

> [F]or some of us the principle of indeterminism is what makes the
> conscious freedom of man fathomable. . . .
> —Jacques Derrida, "My Chances/*Mes Chances*"

## *The Survival of Culture*

Postcolonial criticism bears witness to the unequal and uneven forces of cultural representation involved in the contest for political and social authority within the modern world order. Postcolonial perspectives emerge from the colonial testimony of Third World countries and the discourses of "minorities" within the geopolitical divisions of east and west, north and south. They intervene in those ideological discourses of modernity that attempt to give a hegemonic "normality" to the uneven development and the differential, often disadvantaged, histories of nations, races, communities, peoples. They formulate their critical revisions around issues of cultural difference, social authority, and political discrimination in order to reveal the antagonistic and ambivalent moments within the "rationalizations" of modernity. To bend Jürgen Habermas to our purposes, we could also argue that the postcolonial project, at the most general theoretical level, seeks to explore those social pathologies—"loss of meaning, conditions of anomie"—that no longer simply "cluster around class antagonism, [but] break up into widely scattered historical contingencies" (*Discourse* 348).

These contingencies are often the grounds of historical necessity for elaborating empowering strategies of emancipation, staging other social antagonisms. For to reconstitute the discourse of cultural difference demands not simply a change of cultural contents and symbols; a replacement within the same time frame of representation is never adequate. It requires a radical revision of the social temporality in which emergent histories may be written, the rearticulation of the "sign" in which cultural identities may be inscribed. And contingency as the signifying time of counterhegemonic strategies is not a celebration of "lack" or "excess" or a self-perpetuating series of negative ontologies. Such "indeterminism" is the mark of the conflictual yet productive space in which the arbitrariness of the sign of cultural signification emerges within the regulated boundaries of social discourse.

In this salutary sense, a range of contemporary critical theories suggest that it is from those who have suffered the sentence of history—subjugation, domination, diaspora, displacement—that we learn our most enduring lessons for living and thinking. There is even a growing conviction that the affective experience of social marginality—as it emerges in noncanonical cultural forms—transforms our critical strategies. It forces us to confront the concept of culture outside objets d'art or beyond the canonization of the "idea" of aesthetics, to engage with culture as an uneven, incomplete production of meaning and value, often composed of incommensurable demands and practices, produced in the act of social survival. Culture reaches out to create a symbolic textuality, to give the alienating everyday an aura of selfhood, a promise of pleasure. The transmission of *cultures of survival* does not occur in the ordered *musée imaginaire* of national cultures with their claims to the continuity of an authentic "past" and a living "present"—whether this scale of value is preserved in the organicist "national" traditions of romanticism or within the more universal proportions of classicism.

Culture as a strategy of survival is both transnational and translational. It is transnational because contemporary postcolonial discourses are rooted in specific histories of cultural displacement, whether they are the "middle passage" of slavery and indenture, the "voyage out" of the civilizing mission, the fraught accommodation of Third World migration to the West after the Second World War, or the traffic of economic and political refugees within and outside the Third World. Culture is translational because such spatial histories of displacement—now accompanied by the territorial ambitions of "global" media technologies—make the question of how culture signifies, or what is signified by *culture*, a rather complex issue. It becomes crucial to distinguish between the semblance and similitude of the symbols across diverse cultural experiences—literature, art, music, ritual, life, death—and the social specificity of each of these productions of meaning as they circulate as signs within specific contextual locations and social systems of value. The transnational dimension of cultural transformation—migration, diaspora, displacement, relocation—makes the process of cultural translation a complex form of signification. The natural(ized), unifying discourse of "nation," "peoples," or authentic "folk" tradition, those embedded myths of culture's particularity, cannot be readily referenced. The great, though unsettling, advantage of this position is that it makes you increasingly aware of the construction of culture and the invention of tradition.

The postcolonial perspective—as it is being developed by cultural historians and literary theorists—departs from the traditions of the sociology of underdevelopment of "dependency" theory. As a mode of analysis, it attempts to revise those nationalist or "nativist" pedagogies that set up the relation of Third World and First World in a binary structure of opposition. The postcolonial perspective resists the attempt at holistic forms of social explanation. It forces a recognition of the more complex cultural and political boundaries that exist on the cusp of these often opposed political spheres.

It is from this hybrid location of cultural value—the transnational as the translational—that the postcolonial intellectual attempts to elaborate a historical and literary project. My growing conviction has been that the encounters and negotiations of differential meanings and values within "colonial" textuality, its governmental discourses and cultural practices, have enacted, *avant la lettre*, many of the problematics of signification and judgment that have become current in contemporary theory—aporia, ambivalence, indeterminacy, the question of discursive closure, the threat to agency, the status of intentionality, the challenge to "totalizing" concepts, to name but a few.

In general terms, there is a colonial contramodernity at work in the eighteenth- and nineteenth-century matrices of Western modernity that, if acknowledged, would question the historicism that analogically links, in a linear narrative, late capitalism and the fragmentary, simulacral, pastiche symptoms of postmodernity. This linking does not account for the historical traditions of cultural contingency and textual indeterminacy (as forces of social discourse) generated in the attempt to produce an "enlightened" colonial or postcolonial subject, and it transforms, in the process, our understanding of the narrative of modernity and the "values" of progress.

Postcolonial critical discourses require forms of dialectical thinking that do not disavow or sublate the otherness (alterity) that constitutes the symbolic domain of psychic and social identifications. The incommensurability of cultural values and priorities that the postcolonial critic represents cannot be accommodated within theories of cultural relativism or pluralism. The cultural potential of such differential histories has led Fredric Jameson to recognize the "internationalization of the national situations" in the postcolonial criticism of Roberto Retamar. This is not an absorption of the particular in the general, for the very act of articulating cultural differences "calls us into question fully as much as it acknowledges the Other . . . neither reduc[ing] the Third World to some homogeneous Other of the West, nor . . . vacuously celebrat[ing] the astonishing pluralism of human cultures" (Foreword xi–xii).

The historical grounds of such an intellectual tradition are to be found in the revisionary impulse that informs many postcolonial thinkers. C. L. R. James once remarked, in a public lecture, that the postcolonial prerogative consisted in reinterpreting and rewriting the forms and effects of an "older" colonial consciousness from the later experience of the cultural displacement that marks the more recent, postwar histories of the Western metropolis. A similar process of cultural translation, and transvaluation, is evident in Edward Said's assessment of the response from disparate postcolonial regions as a "tremendously energetic attempt to engage with the metropolitan world in a common effort at re-inscribing, re-interpreting and expanding the sites of intensity and the terrain contested with Europe" ("Third World" 49).

How does the deconstruction of the "sign," the emphasis on indeterminism in cultural and political judgment, transform our sense of the "subject" of culture and the historical agent of change? If we contest the "grand narratives," then what alternative temporalities do we create to articulate the differential (Jameson), contrapuntal (Said), interruptive (Spivak) historicities of race, gender, class, nation within a growing transnational culture? Do we need to rethink the terms in which we conceive of community, citizenship, nationality, and the ethics of social affiliation?

Jameson's justly famous reading of Conrad's *Lord Jim* in *The Political Unconscious* provides a suitable example of a kind of reading against the grain that a postcolonial interpretation demands, when faced with a reading that attempts to sublate the specific "interruption," or the interstices, through which the colonial text utters its interrogations, its contrapuntal critique. Reading Conrad's narrative and ideological contradictions "as a canceled realism . . . like a Hegelian *Aufhebung*" (266), Jameson represents the fundamental ambivalences of the ethical (honor/guilt) and the aesthetic (premodern/postmodern) as the allegorical restitution of the socially concrete subtext of late nineteenth-century rationalization and reification. What his brilliant allegory of late capitalism fails to represent sufficiently is the specifically colonial address of the narrative aporia contained in the ambivalent, obsessive repetition of the phrase "He was one of us" as the major trope of social and psychic identification throughout the text. The repetition of "He was one of us" reveals the fragile margins of the concepts of Western civility and cultural community put under colonial stress; Jim is reclaimed at the moment when he is in danger of being cast out, or made outcaste, manifestly "not one of us." Such a discursive ambivalence at the very heart of the issue of honor and duty in the colonial service represents the liminality, if not the end, of the masculinist, heroic ideal (and ideology) of a healthy imperial Englishness—those pink bits on the map that Conrad believed were genuinely salvaged by being the preserve of English colonization, which served the larger idea, and ideal, of Western civil society.

Such problematic issues are activated within the terms and traditions of postcolonial critique as it reinscribes the cultural relations between spheres of social antagonism. Current debates in postmodernism question the cunning of modernity—its historical ironies, its disjunctive temporalities, its paradoxes of progress, its representational aporia. It would profoundly change the values, and judgments, of such interrogations, if they were open to the argument that metropolitan histories of civitas cannot be conceived without evoking the savage colonial antecedents of the ideals of civility. It also suggests, by implication, that the language of rights and obligations, so central to the modern myth of a people, must be questioned on the basis of the anomalous and discriminatory legal and cultural status assigned to migrant, diasporic, and refugee populations. Inevitably, they find themselves on the frontiers between cultures and nations, often on the other side of the law.

The postcolonial perspective forces us to rethink the profound limitations of a consensual and collusive "liberal" sense of cultural community. It insists that cultural and political identity are constructed through a process of alterity. Questions of race and cultural difference overlay issues of sexuality and gender and overdetermine the social alliances of class and democratic socialism. The time for "assimilating" minorities to holistic and organic notions of cultural value has dramatically passed. The very language of cultural community needs to be rethought from a postcolonial perspective, in a move similar to the profound shift in the language of sexuality, the self, and cultural community, effected by feminists in the 1970s and the gay community in the 1980s.

Culture becomes as much an uncomfortable, disturbing practice of survival and supplementarity—between art and politics, past and present, the public and the private—as its resplendent being is a moment of pleasure, enlightenment, or liberation. It is from such narrative positions that the postcolonial prerogative seeks to affirm and extend a new collaborative dimension, both within the margins of the nation-space and across boundaries between nations and peoples. My use of poststructuralist theory emerges from this postcolonial contramodernity. I attempt to represent a certain defeat, or even an impossibility, of the "West" in its authorization of the "idea" of colonization. Driven by the subaltern history of the margins of modernity—rather than by the failures of logocentricism—I have tried, in some small measure, to revise the known, to rename the postmodern from the position of the postcolonial.

## New Times

The enunciative position of contemporary cultural studies is both complex and problematic. It attempts to institutionalize a range of transgressive discourses whose strategies are elaborated around nonequivalent sites of representation where a history of discrimination and misrepresentation is common among, say, women, blacks, homosexuals, and Third World migrants. However, the "signs" that construct such histories and identities—gender, race, homophobia, postwar diaspora, refugees, the international division of labor, and so on—not only differ in content but often produce incompatible systems of signification and engage distinct forms of social subjectivity. To provide a social imaginary that is based on the articulation of differential, even disjunctive, moments of history and culture, contemporary critics resort to the peculiar temporality of the language metaphor. It is as if the arbitrariness of the sign, the indeterminacy of writing, the splitting of the subject of enunciation, these theoretical concepts, produce the most useful descriptions of the formation of "postmodern" cultural subjects and their strategies of ideological identification.

Cornel West enacts "a measure of *synechdochical* thinking" (my emphasis) as he attempts to talk of the problems of address in the context of a black, radical, "practicalist" culture:

> A tremendous articulateness is syncopated with the African drumbeat . . . into an American postmodernist product: there is no subject expressing originary anguish here but a fragmented subject, pulling from past and present, innovatively producing a heterogeneous product. . . . [I]t is part and parcel of the subversive energies of black underclass youth, energies that are forced to take a cultural mode of articulation. . . .                              ("Interview" 280–81)

Stuart Hall, writing from the perspective of the fragmented, marginalized, racially discriminated against members of a post-Thatcherite underclass, questions the sententiousness of Left orthodoxy where

> we go on thinking a unilinear and irreversible political logic, driven by some abstract entity that we call the economic or capital unfolding to its pre-ordained end.                              (273)

Earlier in his book, he uses the linguistic sign as a metaphor for a more differential and contingent political logic of ideology:

> [T]he ideological sign is always multi-accentual, and Janus-faced—that is, it can be discursively rearticulated to construct new meanings, connect with different social practices, and position social subjects differently. . . . Like other symbolic or discursive formations, [ideology] is connective across different positions, between apparently dissimilar, sometimes contradictory, ideas. Its "unity" is always in quotation marks and always complex, a suturing together of elements which have no necessary or eternal "belongingness." It is always, in that sense, organized around arbitrary and not natural closures.    (9–10)

The "language" metaphor raises the question of cultural difference and incommensurability, not the consensual, ethnocentric notion of the pluralistic existence of cultural diversity. It represents the temporality of cultural meaning as "multi-accentual," "discursively rearticulated." It is a time of the cultural sign that unsettles the liberal ethic of tolerance and the pluralist framework of multiculturalism. Increasingly, the issue of cultural difference emerges at points of social crises, and the questions of identity that it raises are agonistic; identity is claimed either from a position of marginality or in an attempt at gaining the center: in both senses, ex-centric. In Britain today this is certainly true of the experimental art and film emerging from the Left, associated with the postcolonial experience of migration and diaspora and articulated in the cultural exploration of new ethnicities.

Cultural causality faced with the attenuated temporality of the contingent does not simply change the rules and ratios of representation; it transforms the temporal structure of culture's significations. The authority and authenticity of customary, traditional practices—culture's relation to the historic past—is not dehistoricized in Hall's language metaphor. Those anchoring moments are revalued as a form of anteriority—a before that has no a prior(ity)—whose causality is effective because it returns to displace the present, to make it disjunctive. This kind of disjunctive temporality is of the utmost importance for the politics of cultural difference. It creates a signifying time for the inscription of cultural incommensurability where differences cannot be sublated or totalized because "they somehow occupy the same space" (C. Taylor 145). It is this liminal form of cultural identification that is relevant to Charles Taylor's proposal for a "minimal rationality" as the basis for nonethnocentric, transcultural judgments. The effect of cultural incommensurability is that it "takes us beyond merely *formal criteria of rationality*, and points us toward the human *activity of articulation* which gives the value of rationality its sense" (151; emphasis added).

Minimal rationality, as the process of the activity of articulation embodied in the language metaphor, alters the subject of culture from an epistemological function to an enunciative practice. If culture as epistemology focuses on function and intention, then culture as enunciation focuses on signification and institutionalization; if the epistemological tends toward a reflection of its empirical referent or object, the enunciative attempts repeatedly to reinscribe and relocate the political claim to cultural priority and hierarchy (high/low, ours/theirs) in the social institution of the signifying activity. The epistemological is locked into the hermeneutic circle, in the description of cultural elements as they tend toward a totality. The enunciative is a more dialogic process that attempts to track displacements and realignments that are the effects of cultural antagonisms and articulations—subverting the rationale of the hegemonic moment and relocating alternative, hybrid sites of cultural negotiation.

My shift from the cultural as an epistemological object to culture as an enactive, enunciatory site opens up possibilities for other "times" of cultural meaning (retroactive, prefigurative) and other narrative spaces (phantasmic, metaphorical). My purpose in specifying the enunciative present in the articulation of culture is to provide a process by which objectified others may be turned into subjects of their history and experience. My theoretical argument has a descriptive history in recent work in literary and cultural studies by African American and black British writers. Hortense Spillers, for instance, evokes the field of "enunciative possibility" to reconstitute the narrative of slavery:

> [A]s many times as we re-open slavery's closure we are hurtled rapidly forward into the dizzying motions of a symbolic enterprise, and it becomes increasingly clear that the cultural synthesis we call "slavery" was never homogenous in its practices and conceptions, nor unitary in the faces it has yielded.    (29)

Deborah McDowell, in her reading of Sherley Anne Williams's *Dessa Rose*, argues that it is the temporality of the enunciatory " 'present' and its discourses . . . in heterogeneous and messy array," opened up in the narrative, that enables the book to wrestle vigorously with "the critique of the subject and the critique of binary oppositions . . . with questions of the politics and problematics of language and representation" ("Negotiations" 147). Paul Gilroy writes of the dialogic, performative "community" of black music—rap, dub, scratching—as a way of constituting an open sense of black collectivity in the shifting, changing beat of the present (see ch. 5). More recently, Houston A. Baker, Jr., has made a spirited argument against "high cultural" sententiousness and for the "very, very sound game of rap (music)," which comes through vibrantly in the title of his essay "Hybridity, the Rap Race, and Pedagogy for the 1990s." In his perceptive introduction to an anthology of black feminist criticism, Henry Louis Gates, Jr., describes the contestations and negotiations of black feminists as empowering cultural and textual strategies precisely because the critical position they occupy is free of the "inverted" polarities of a "counter-politics of exclusion":

> They have never been obsessed with arriving at any singular self-image; or legislating who may or may not speak on the subject; or policing boundaries between "us" and "them."    (*Reading* 8)

What is striking about the theoretical focus on the enunciatory present as a liberatory discursive strategy is its proposal that emergent cultural identifications are articulated at the liminal edge of identity—in that arbitrary closure, that "unity . . . in quotation marks" (Hall) that the language metaphor so clearly enacts. Postcolonial and black critiques propose forms of contestatory subjectivities that are empowered in the act of erasing the politics of binary opposition—the inverted polarities of a counterpolitics (Gates). There is an attempt to construct a theory of the social imaginary that requires no subject expressing originary anguish (West), no singular self-image (Gates), no necessary or eternal belongingness (Hall). The contingent and the liminal become the times and the spaces for the historical representation of the subjects of cultural difference in a postcolonial criticism where the dialectic of culture and identification is neither binary nor sublatory.

It is the ambivalence enacted in the enunciative present—disjunctive and multiaccentual—that produces the objective of postmodern political desire, what Hall calls "arbitrary closure," *like the signifier*. But this arbitrary closure is also the cultural space for opening up new forms of identification that may confuse the continuity of historical temporalities, confound the ordering of cultural symbols, traumatize tradition. The African drumbeat syncopating heterogenous black American postmodernism, the arbitrary but strategic logic of politics—these moments contest the sententious "conclusion" of the discipline of culture history.

We cannot understand what is being proposed for "new times" within postmodernism—politics at the site of cultural enunciation, cultural signs spoken at the margins of social identity and antagonism—if we do not briefly explore the paradoxes of the language metaphor. In each of the illustrations I've provided, the language metaphor opens up a space where a theoretical disclosure is used to move beyond theory; a form of cultural experience and identity is envisaged in a theoretical description that does not set up a theory-practice polarity, nor does theory become "prior" to the contingency of social experience. This "beyond theory" is itself a liminal form of signification that creates a space for the contingent, indeterminate articulation of social "experience" that is particularly important for envisaging emergent cultural identities. But it is a representation of "experience" without the transparent reality of empiricism and outside the intentional mastery of the "author." Nevertheless, it is a representation of social experience as the contingency of history—the indeterminacy that makes subversion and revision possible—that is profoundly concerned with questions of cultural "authorization."

To evoke this "beyond theory," I turn to Roland Barthes's exploration of the cultural space "outside the sentence." In *The Pleasure of the Text* I find a subtle suggestion that beyond theory you do not simply encounter its opposition, theory/practice, but an "outside" that places the articulation of the two—theory and practice, language and politics—in a productive, supplementary relation: "a non-dialectical middle, a structure of jointed predication, which cannot itself be comprehended by the predicates it distributes. . . . Not that this inability . . . shows a lack of power; rather this inability is constitutive of the very possibility of the logic of identity . . ." (Gasché, *Tain* 210).

## *Outside the Sentence*

Half-asleep on his banquette in a bar, of which Tangiers is the exemplary site, Barthes attempts to "enumerate the stereophony of languages within earshot": music, conversations, chairs, glasses, Arabic, French.[1] Suddenly the inner speech of the writer turns into the exorbitant space of the Moroccan souk:

> [T]hrough me passed words, syntagms, bits of formulae and no sentence formed, as though that were the law of such a language. This speech at once very cultural and very savage, was above all lexical, sporadic; it set up in me, through its apparent flow, a definitive discontinuity: this non-sentence was in no way something that could not have acceded to the sentence, that might have been before the sentence; it was: what is . . . *outside the sentence.*
> 
> (*Pleasure* 49; emphasis added)

At this point, Barthes writes, all linguistics that gives an exorbitant dignity to predicative syntax fell away. In its wake it becomes possible to subvert the "power of completion which defines sentence mastery and marks, as with a supreme, dearly won, conquered *savoir faire*, the agents of the sentence" (*Pleasure* 50). The hierarchy and the subordinations of the sentence are replaced by the definitive discontinuity of the text, and what emerges is a form of writing that Barthes describes as "writing aloud":

> a text of pulsional incidents, the language lined with flesh, a text where we can hear the grain of the throat . . . a whole carnal stereophony: the articulation of the tongue, not the meaning of language.    (*Pleasure* 66–67)

Why return to the semiotician's daydream? Why begin with "theory" as story, as narrative and anecdote, rather than with the history or method? Beginning with the semiotic project—enumerating all the languages within earshot—evokes memories of the seminal influence of semiotics within our contemporary critical discourse. To that end, this *petit récit* rehearses some of the major themes of contemporary theory prefigured in the practice of semiotics—the author as an enunciative space; the formation of textuality after the fall of linguistics; the agonism between the sentence of predicative syntax and the discontinuous subject of discourse; the disjunction between the lexical and the grammatical dramatized in the liberty (perhaps libertinism) of the signifier.

To encounter Barthes's daydream is to acknowledge the formative contribution of semiotics to those influential concepts—sign, text, limit text, idiolect, *écriture*—that have become all the more important since they have passed into the unconscious of our critical trade. When Barthes attempts to produce, with his suggestive, erratic brilliance, a space for the pleasure of the text somewhere between "the political policeman and the psychoanalytical policeman"—that is, between "futility and/or guilt, pleasure is either idle or vain, a class notion or an illusion" (*Pleasure* 57)—what memories he evokes of the attempts, in the late 1970s and mid-1980s, to hold fast the political line while the poetic line struggled to free itself from its post-Althusserian arrest. What guilt, what pleasure.

To thematize theory is, for the moment, beside the point. To reduce this weird and wonderful daydream of the semiotic pedagogue, somewhat in his cups, to just another repetition of the theoretical litany of the death of the author would be reductive in the extreme. For the daydream takes semiotics by surprise; it turns pedagogy into the exploration of its own limits. If you seek simply the sententious or the exegetical, you will not grasp the hybrid moment outside the sentence—not quite experience, not yet concept; part dream, part analysis; neither signifier nor signified; in the intermediate space between theory and practice that disrupts the disciplinary semiological demand to enumerate all the languages within earshot. The daydream is supplementary, not alternative, to acting in the real world, Freud reminds us; the structure of fantasy narrates the subject of daydream as the articulation of incommensurable temporalities, disavowed wishes, and discontinuous scenarios. The meaning of fantasy does not emerge in the predicative or propositional value we might attach to being outside the sentence. Rather, the performative structure of the text reveals a temporality of discourse that I believe is significant. It opens up a narrative strategy for the emergence and negotiation of those agencies of the marginal, minority, subaltern, or diasporic that incite us to think through—and beyond—theory.

What is caught anecdotally "outside the sentence," in Barthes's concept, is that problematic space—performative rather than experiential, nonsententious but no less theoretical—of which poststructuralist theory speaks in its many varied voices. In spite of the fall of a predictable, predicative linguistics, the space of the nonsentence is not a negative ontology: not *before* the sentence but something that *could have* acceded to the sentence and yet was *outside* it. This discourse is indeed one of indeterminism, unexpectability, one that is neither "pure" contingency or negativity nor endless deferral. "Outside the sentence" is not to be opposed to the inner voice; the nonsentence does not relate to the sentence as a polarity. The timeless capture that stages such epistemological "confrontations," in Richard Rorty's term, is now interrupted and interrogated in the doubleness of writing—"at once very cultural and very savage," "as though that were the law of such a language" (Barthes, *Pleasure* 49). This disturbs what Derrida calls the occidental stereotomy, the ontological, circumscribing space between subject and object, inside and outside ("My Chances" 25). It is the question of agency, as it emerges in relation to the indeterminate and the contingent, that I want to explore outside the sentence and its circumscribing spaces. However, I want to preserve, at all times, that menacing sense in which the nonsentence is contiguous with the sentence, near but different, not simply its anarchic disruption.

## Tangiers or Casablanca?

What we encounter outside the sentence, beyond the occidental stereotomy, is what I shall call the "temporality" of Tangiers. It is a structure of temporality that will emerge only slowly and indirectly, as time goes by, as they say in Moroccan bars, whether in Tangiers or Casablanca. There is, however, an instructive difference between Casablanca and Tangiers. In Casablanca the passage of time preserves the identity of language; the possibility of naming over time is fixed in the repetition:

> You must remember this
> a kiss is still a kiss
> a sigh is but a sigh
> the fundamental things apply
> As time goes by. . . .
>    (*Casablanca*)

"Play it again, Sam," which is perhaps the Western world's most celebrated demand for repetition, is still an invocation to similitude, a return to the eternal verities.

In Tangiers, as time goes by, it produces an iterative temporality that erases the occidental spaces of language—inside/outside, past/present, those foundationalist epistemological positions of Western empiricism and historicism. Tangiers opens up disjunctive, incommensurable relations of spacing and temporality *within* the sign—an "internal difference of the so-called ultimate element (*stoikheion*, trait, letter, seminal mark)" (Derrida, "My Chances" 10). The nonsentence is not before (either as the past or a priori) or inside (either as depth or presence) but outside (both spatially and temporally ex-centric, interruptive, in-between, on the borderlines, turning inside outside). In each of these inscriptions there is a doubling and a splitting of the temporal and spatial dimensions in the very act of signification. What emerges in this agonistic, ambivalent form of speech—"at once very cultural and very savage"—is a question about the subject of discourse and the agency of the letter: Can there be a social subject of the "nonsentence"? Is it possible to conceive of historical agency in that disjunctive, indeterminate moment of discourse outside the sentence? Is the whole thing no more than a theoretical fantasy that reduces any form of political critique to a daydream?

These apprehensions about the agency of the aporetic and the ambivalent become more acute when political claims are made for their strategic action. This is precisely Terry Eagleton's recent position, in his critique of the libertarian pessimism of poststructuralism:

> [It is] libertarian because something of the old model of expression/repression lingers on in the dream of an entirely free-floating signifier, an infinite textual productivity, an existence blessedly free from the shackles of truth, meaning and sociality. Pessimistic, because whatever blocks such creativity—law, meaning, power, closure—is acknowledged to be built into it, in a sceptical recognition of the imbrication of authority and desire. . . .
>
> (*Ideology of the Aesthetic* 387)

The agency implicit in this discourse is objectified in a structure of the negotiation of meaning that is not a free-floating time lack but a *time lag*—a contingent moment—in the signification of closure. Tangiers, the "sign" of the "nonsentence," turns retroactively, at the end of Barthes's essay, into a form of discourse that he names "writing aloud." The time lag between the event of the sign (Tangiers) and its discursive eventuality (writing aloud) exemplifies a process where intentionality is negotiated retrospectively. (For a brilliant reading of this process in Lacan, see Forrester, *Seductions* 207–10.) The sign finds its closure retroactively in a discourse that it anticipates in the semiotic fantasy: there is a contiguity, a coextensivity, between Tangiers (as sign) and writing aloud (discursive formation), in that writing aloud is the mode of inscription of which Tangiers is a sign. There is no strict causality between Tangiers as the beginning of predication and writing aloud as the end or closure; but there is no free-floating signifier or an infinity of textual productivity. There is the more complex possibility of negotiating meaning and agency through the time lag in between the sign (Tangiers) and its initiation of a discourse or narrative, where the relation of theory to practice is part of what Derrida termed "jointed predication." In this sense, closure comes to be effected in the contingent moment of repetition, "an overlap without equivalence: *fort: da*" (*Post Card* 321).

The temporality of Tangiers is a lesson in reading the agency of the social text as ambivalent and catachrestic. Gayatri Spivak has usefully described the "negotiation" of the postcolonial position "in terms of reversing, displacing and seizing the apparatus of value-coding," constituting a catachrestic space: words or concepts wrested from their proper meaning, "a concept-metaphor without an adequate referent" that perverts its embedded context.

Spivak continues, "Claiming catachresis from a space that one cannot not want to inhabit [the sentence, sententious], yet must criticize [from outside the sentence] is then, the deconstructive predicament of the postcolonial" ("Post-structuralism" 225, 227, 228).

This Derridean position is close to the conceptual predicament outside the sentence. I have attempted to provide the discursive temporality, or time lag, which is crucial to the process by which this turning around—of tropes, ideologies, concept metaphors—comes to be textualized and specified in postcolonial agency: the moment when the "bar" of the occidental sterotomy is turned into the coextensive, contingent boundaries of relocation and reinscription: the catachrestic gesture. The insistent issue in any such move is the nature of the negotiatory agent realized through the time lag. How does agency come to be specified and individuated, outside the discourses of individualism? How does the time lag signify individuation as a position that is an effect of the "intersub-jective": contiguous with the social and yet contingent, indeterminate, in relation to it?[2]

Writing aloud, for Barthes, is neither the "expressive" function of language as authorial intention or generic determination nor meaning personified (*Pleasure* 66–67).[3] It is similar to the *actio* repressed by classical rhetoric, and it is the "corporeal exteriorization of discourse." It is the art of guiding one's body into discourse, in such a way that the subject's accession to, and erasure in, the signifier as individuated is paradoxically accompanied by its remainder, an afterbirth, a double. Its noise—"crackle, grate, cut"—makes vocal and visible, across the flow of the sentence's communicative code, the struggle involved in the insertion of agency—wound and bow, death and life—into discourse. In Lacanian terms, which are appropriate here, this "noise" is the "leftover" after the *capittonage*, or positioning, of the signifier for the subject. The Lacanian "voice" that speaks outside the sentence is itself the voice of an interrogative, calculative agency: "*Che vuoi?* You are telling me that, but what do you want with it, what are you aiming at?" (For a clear, recent explanation of this process, see Zizek 104–11.) What speaks in the place of this question, Jacques Lacan writes, is a "third locus which is neither my speech nor my interlocutor" (*Ecrits* 173).

The time lag opens up this negotiatory space between putting the question to the subject and the subject's repetition "around" the neither/nor of the third locus. This constitutes the return of the subject as agent, as the interrogative agency in the catachrestic position. Such a disjunctive space of temporality is the locus of symbolic identification that structures the intersub-jective realm—the realm of otherness and the social—where "we identify ourselves with the other precisely at a point at which he is inimitable, at the point which eludes resemblance" (Zizek 109). My contention, elaborated in my writings on postcolonial discourse (see *The Location of Culture*) in terms of mimicry, hybridity, sly civility, is that this liminal moment of identification—eluding resemblance—produces a subversive strategy of subaltern agency that negotiates its own authority through a process of iterative "unpicking" and incommensurable, insurgent relinking. It singularizes the "totality" of authority by suggesting that agency requires a grounding, but it does not require a totalization of those grounds; it requires movement and maneuver, but it does not require a temporality of continuity or accumulation; it requires direction and contingent closure but not teleology and holism. (For elaboration of these concepts, see Bhabha, "Commitment" and "DissemiNation.")

The individuation of the agent occurs in a moment of displacement. It is a pulsional incident, the split-second movement when the process of the subject's designation—its fixity—opens up beside it, uncannily *Abseits*, a supplementary space of contingency. In this "return" of the subject, thrown back across the distance of the signified, outside the sentence, the agent emerges as a form of retroactivity, *Nachträglichkeit*. It is not agency as itself (transcendent, transparent) or in itself (unitary, organic, autonomous). As a result of its own splitting in the time lag of signification, the moment of the subject's individuation emerges as an effect of the intersubjective—as the return of the subject as agent. This means that those elements of social "consciousness" imperative for agency—deliberative, individuated action and specificity in analysis—can now be thought outside that epistemology that insists on the subject as always prior to the social or on the knowledge of the social as necessarily subsuming or sublating the particular "difference" in the transcendent homogeneity of the general. The iterative and contingent that marks this intersubjective relation can never be libertarian or free-floating, as Eagleton claims, because the agent, constituted in the subject's return, is in the dialogic position of calculation, negotiation, interrogation: *Che vuoi*?

## Agent without a Cause?

Something of this genealogy of postcolonial agency has already been encountered in my expositions of the ambivalent and the multivalent in the language metaphor at work in West's "synechdochical thinking" about black American cultural hybridity and Hall's notion of "politics like a language." The implications of this line of thinking were productively realized in the work of Spillers, McDowell, Baker, Gates, and Gilroy, all of whom emphasize the importance of the creative heterogeneity of the enunciatory "present" that liberates the discourse of emancipation from binary closures. I want to give contingency another turn—through the Barthesian fantasy—by throwing the last line of the text, its conclusion, together with an earlier moment when Barthes speaks suggestively of closure as agency. Once again, we have an overlap without equivalence. For the notion of a nonteleological and a nondialectical form of closure has often been considered the most problematic issue for the postmodern agent without a cause:

> [Writing aloud] succeed[s] in shifting the signified a great distance and in throwing, so to speak, the anonymous body of the actor into my ear. . . . And this body of bliss is also *my historical subject*; for it is at the *conclusion* of a very complex process of biographical, historical, sociological, neurotic elements . . . that I control the contradictory interplay of [cultural] pleasure and [non-cultural] bliss that I write myself as a subject at present out of place.
>
> *(Pleasure* 62, 67; emphasis added)

The contingency of the subject as agent is articulated in a double dimension, a dramatic action. The signified is distanced; the resulting time lag opens up the space between the lexical and the grammatical, between enunciation and enounced, in between the anchoring of signifiers. Then, suddenly, this in-between spatial dimension, this distancing, converts itself into the temporality of the "throw" that iteratively (re)turns the subject as a moment of conclusion and control: a historically or contextually specific subject. How are we to think of the control or conclusion in the context of contingency? We need, not surprisingly, to invoke both meanings of *contingency* and then to repeat the difference of the one in the other. Recall my suggestion to interrupt the occidental stereotomy—inside/outside, space/time—and to think, outside the sentence, at once very cultural and very savage.

The contingent is contiguity, metonymy, the touching of spatial boundaries at a tangent, and, at the same time, the contingent is the temporality of the indeterminate and the undecidable. It is the kinetic tension that holds these together and apart within discourse. They represent the repetition of the one in or as the other, in a structure of "abyssal overlapping" (a Derridean term), which enables us to conceive of strategic closure and control for the agent. Representing social contradiction or antagonism in this doubling discourse of contingency—where the spatial dimension of contiguity is reiterated in the temporality of the indeterminate—cannot be dismissed as the arcane practice of the undecidable or aporetic. The importance of the problematic of contingency for historical discourse is evident in Ranajit Guha's attempt to represent the specificity of rebel consciousness (see "Dominance").

Guha's argument reveals the need for such a double and disjunctive sense of the contingent, although his own reading of the concept, in terms of the "universal-contingent" couple, is more Hegelian in its elaboration ("Dominance" 230). Rebel consciousness is inscribed in two major narratives. In bourgeois-nationalist historiography, it is seen as "pure spontaneity pitted against the will of the State as embodied in the Raj." The will of the rebels is either denied or subsumed in the individualized capacity of its leaders, who frequently belong to the elite gentry. Radical historiography failed to specify rebel consciousness because its continuist narrative ranged "peasant revolts as a succession of events ranged along a direct line of descent ... as a heritage." In assimilating all moments of rebel consciousness to the "highest moment of the series—indeed to an Ideal Consciousness"—these historians "are ill-equipped to cope with contradictions which are indeed the stuff history is made of" ("Prose" 39).

Guha's elaborations of rebel contradiction as consciousness are strongly suggestive of agency as the activity of the contingent. What I have described as the return of the subject is present in his account of rebel consciousness as self-alienated. My suggestion that the problematic of contingency strategically allows for a spatial contiguity—solidarity, collectivite action—to be (re)articulated in the moment of indeterminancy is, reading between the lines, very close to his sense of the strategic alliances at work in the contradictory and hybrid sites, and symbols, of peasant revolt. What historiography fails to grasp is indeed agency at the point of the "combination of sectarianism and militancy ..., [specifically] the *ambiguity* of such phenomena ..."; causality as the "time" of indeterminate articulation: "the *swift* transformation of class struggle into communal strife and vice versa in our countryside ..."; and ambivalence at the point of "individuation" as an intersubjective affect:

> Blinded by the glare of a perfect and immaculate consciousness the historian sees nothing ... but solidarity in rebel behaviour and fails to notice its Other, namely, betrayal. ... He underestimates the brakes put on [insurgency as a *generalized* movement] by localism and territoriality.          (40)

Finally, as if to provide an emblem for my notion of agency in the apparatus of contingency—its hybrid figuring of space and time—Guha, quoting Sunil Sen's *Agrarian Struggle in Bengal* beautifully describes the "ambiguity of such phenomena" as the hybridized signs and sites during the Tebhaga movement in Dinajpur:

> Muslim peasants [came] to the Kisan Sabha "sometimes inscribing a hammer and a sickle on the Muslim League flag" and young maulavis "[recited] melodious verses from the Koran" at village meetings "as they condemned the jotedari system and the practice of charging high interest rates."          (39)

## The Social Text: Bakhtin and Arendt

The contingent conditions of agency also take us to the heart of Mikhail M. Bakhtin's important attempt, in speech genres, to designate the enunciative

454     POSTCOLONIAL CRITICISM

subject of heteroglossia and dialogism (see *Speech* 90–95). As with Guha, my reading will be catachrestic: reading between the lines, taking neither him at his word nor me fully at mine. In focusing on how the chain of speech communication comes to be constituted (93), I deal with Bakhtin's attempt to individuate social agency as an aftereffect of the intersubjective. My cross-hatched matrix of contingency—as spatial difference and temporal distance, to turn the terms somewhat—enables us to see how Bakhtin provides a knowledge of the transformation of social discourse while displacing the originating subject and the causal and continuist progress of discourse:

> The object, as it were, has already been articulated, disputed, elucidated and evaluated in various ways. . . . The speaker is not the biblical Adam . . . as simplistic ideas about communication as a logical-psychological basis for the sentence suggest. (93)

Bakhtin's use of the metaphor of the chain of communication picks up the sense of contingency as contiguity, while the question of the "link" immediately raises the issue of contingency as the indeterminate. Bakhtin's displacement of the author as agent results from his acknowledgment of the "complex, multiplanar" structure of the speech genre that exists in that kinetic tension in between the two forces of contingency. The spatial boundaries of the object of utterance are contiguous in the assimilation of the other's speech; but the allusion to another's utterance produces a dialogical turn, a moment of indeterminancy in the act of "addressivity" (Bakhtin's concept) that gives rise within the chain of speech communion to "unmediated responsive reactions and dialogic reverberations" (94).

Although Bakhtin acknowledges this double movement in the chain of the utterance, there is a sense in which he disavows its effectivity at the point of the enunciation of discursive agency. He displaces this conceptual problem that concerns the performativity of the speech act—its enunciative modalities of time and space—to an empiricist acknowledgment of the "area of human activity and everyday life to which the given utterance is related" (93). It is not that the social context does not localize the utterance; it is simply that the process of specification and individuation must also be inscribed within Bakhtin's theory, as the modality through which the speech genre comes to recognize the specific as a signifying limit, a discursive boundary.

There are moments when Bakhtin obliquely touches on the tense doubling of the contingent that I have described. When he talks of the "dialogic overtones" that permeate the agency of utterance—"many half-concealed or completely concealed words of others with varying degrees of foreignness"— his metaphors hint at the iterative intersubjective temporality in which the agency is realized "outside" the author:

> [T]he utterance appears to be furrowed with distant and barely audible echoes of changes of speech subjects and dialogic overtones, greatly weakened utterance boundaries that are completely permeable to the author's expression. The utterance proves to be a very complex and multiplanar phenomenon if considered not in isolation and with respect to its author . . . but as a link in the chain of communication. . . .     (93)

Through this landscape of echoes and ambivalent boundaries, framed in passing, furrowed horizons, the agent who is "not Adam," time-lagged, emerges fleetingly, as return or repetition, into the social realm of discourse.

Agency, as the return of the subject, as "not Adam," has a more directly political history in Hannah Arendt's portrayal of the troubled narrative of social causality. According to Arendt, the notorious uncertainty of all political matters arises from the fact that the disclosure of *who*—the agent as individuation—is contiguous with the *what* of the intersubjective realm. This contiguous relation between *who* and *what* cannot be transcended but must be accepted as a form of indeterminism and doubling. The *who* of agency bears no mimetic immediacy or adequacy of representation. It can only be signified outside the sentence in that sporadic, ambivalent temporality that inhabits the notorious unreliability of ancient oracles who "neither reveal nor hide in words but give manifest signs" (*Human Condition* 185; see also 175–95). The unreliability of signs introduces a perplexity in the social text:

> The perplexity is that in any series of events that together form a story with a unique meaning we can at best isolate the agent who set the whole process into motion; and although this agent frequently remains the subject, the "hero" of the story, we can never point unequivocally to him as the author of its outcome.     (185)

This is the structure of the intersubjective space between agents, what Arendt terms human "inter-est." It is this public sphere of language and action that must become at once the theater and the screen for the manifestation of the capacities of human agency. Tangiers-like, the event and its eventuality are separated; the narrative time lag makes the *who* and the *what* contingent, splitting them, so that the agent remains the subject, in suspension, outside the sentence. The agent who "causes" the narrative becomes part of the interest, the intersubjective realm, only because we cannot point unequivocally to that agent at the point of outcome. It is the contingency that constitutes individuation—in the return of the subject as agent—that protects the interest of the intersubjective realm. Individuation—unlike the individual—is not before the social but outside it; it can accede to the social but is not equivalent to it: it is properly contingent to the social, in both senses of the word. Remember the space outside the sentence.

The contingency of closure socializes the agent as a collective "effect" in the distancing of the author. Between the cause and its intentionality falls the shadow. Can we then unquestionably propose that a story has a unique meaning in the first place? To what end does the series of events tend if the author of the outcome is not unequivocally the author of the cause? Does it not suggest that agency arises in the return of the subject, from the interruption of the series of events as a kind of interrogation and reinscription of before and after? Where the two touch is there not that kinetic tension between the contingent as the contiguous and the indeterminate? Is it not from there that agency speaks and acts: *Che vuoi*?

These questions are provoked by Arendt's brilliant suggestiveness, for her writing symptomatically performs the perplexities she evokes. Having brought close together the unique meaning and the causal agent, she says that the "invisible actor" is an "invention arising from a mental perplexity" corresponding to no real experience (184). It is this distancing of the signified, this anxious phantasm or simulacrum—in the place of the author—that, according to Arendt, indicates most clearly the political nature of history. The sign of the political is, moreover, not invested in "the character of the story itself but only [in] the *mode* in which it came into existence" (186). So it is the realm of representation and the process of signification that constitutes the space of the political. What is temporal in the mode of existence of the political? Here Arendt resorts to a form of repetition to resolve the ambivalence of her argument. The "reification" of the agent can only occur, she writes, through "a kind of repetition, the imitation of mimesis, which according to Aristotle prevails in all arts but is actually appropriate to the drama" (187).

This repetition of the agent, reified in the liberal vision of togetherness, is quite different from my sense of the contingent agency for our postcolonial age. The reasons for this are not difficult to find. Arendt's belief in the revelatory qualities of Aristotelian mimesis is grounded in a notion of community, or the public sphere, that is largely consensual: "where people are *with* others and neither for nor against them—that is sheer human togetherness" (180). When people are passionately for or against one another, then human togetherness is lost as they deny the fullness of Aristotelian mimetic time. Arendt's form of social mimesis does not deal with social marginality as a product of the liberal state, which can, if articulated, reveal the limitations of its common sense (inter-est) of society from the perspective of minorities or the marginalized. Social violence is, for Arendt, the denial of the disclosure of agency, the point at which "speech becomes 'mere talk,' simply one more means towards the end" (180).

My concern is with other, incommensurable articulations of human togetherness, as they are related to cultural difference and discrimination. For instance, human togetherness may come to represent the forces of hegemonic authority; or a solidarity founded in victimization and suffering may, implacably, sometimes violently, become bound against oppression; or a subaltern or minority agency may attempt to interrogate and rearticulate the "inter-est" of society that marginalizes its interests. These discourses of cultural dissent and social antagonism cannot find their agents in Arendt's Aristotelian mimesis. In the process I've described as the return of the subject, there is an agency that seeks revision and reinscription: the attempt to renegotiate the third locus, the intersubjective realm. The repetition of the iterative, the activity of the time lag, is not so much arbitrary as interruptive, a closure that is not conclusion but a liminal interrogation outside the sentence.

In "Where Is Speech? Where Is Language?" Lacan describes this moment of negotiation from within the "metaphoricity" of language while making a laconic reference to the ordering of symbols in the realm of social discourse:

> It is the temporal element . . . or the temporal break . . . the intervention of a scansion permitting the intervention of something which can take on meaning for a subject. . . . There is in fact a reality of signs within which there exists a world of truth entirely deprived of subjectivity, and that, on the other hand there has been a historical development of subjectivity manifestly directed towards the rediscovery of truth which lies in the order of symbols.
>
> (284–85)

The process of reinscription and negotiation—the insertion or intervention of something that takes on new meaning—happens in the temporal break in between the sign, deprived of subjectivity, in the realm of the intersubjective. Through this time lag—the temporal break in representation—emerges the process of agency both as a historical development and as the narrative agency of historical discourse. What comes out so clearly in Lacan's genealogy of the subject is that the agent's intentionality, which seems "manifestly directed" toward the truth of the order of symbols in the social imaginary, is also an effect of the rediscovery of the world of truth denied subjectivity (because it is intersubjective) at the level of the sign. It is in the contingent tension that sign and symbol overlap and are indeterminately articulated through the "temporal break." Where the sign deprived of the subject—intersubjectivity—returns as subjectivity directed toward the rediscovery of truth, then a (re)ordering of symbols becomes possible in the sphere of the social. When the sign ceases the synchronous flow of the symbol, it also seizes the power to elaborate—through the time lag—new and hybrid agencies and articulations. This is the moment for revisions.

## *Revisions*

The concept of reinscription and negotiation that I am elaborating must not be confused with the powers of "redescription" that have become the hallmark of the liberal ironist or neopragmatist. I do not offer a critique of this influential nonfoundationalist position here except to point to the obvious differences of approach. Rorty's conception of the representation of difference in social discourse is the consensual overlapping of "final vocabularies" that allow imaginative identification with the other so long as certain words— *"kindness, decency, dignity"*—are held in common (*Contingency* 92, 93). However, as he says, the liberal ironist can never elaborate an empowering strategy. Just how disempowering his views are for the non-Western other, how steeped in a Western ethnocentrism, is seen, appropriately for a nonfoundationalist, in a footnote.

Rorty suggests that

> liberal society already contains the institutions for its own improvement [and that] Western social and political thought may have had the last conceptual revolution it needs in J. S. Mill's suggestion that governments should optimize the balance between leaving people's private lives alone and preventing suffering. (63)

Appended to this is the footnote where liberal ironists suddenly lose their powers of redescription:

> This is not to say that the world has had the last political revolution it needs. It is hard to imagine the diminution of cruelty in countries like South Africa, Paraguay, and Albania without violent revolution.... But in such countries raw courage (like that of the leaders of COSATU or the signers of Charta 77) is the relevant virtue, not the sort of reflective acumen which makes contributions to social theory. (63n21)

This is where Rorty's conversation stops, but we must force the dialogue to acknowledge postcolonial social and cultural theory that reveals the limits of liberalism in the postcolonial perspective: "Bourgeois culture hits its historical limit in colonialism," writes Guha sententiously ("Dominance" 277), and, almost as if to speak outside the sentence, Veena Das reinscribes Guha's thought into the affective language of a metaphor and the body: "Subaltern rebellions can only provide a night-time of love.... Yet perhaps in capturing this defiance the historian has given us a means of constructing the objects of such power as *subjects*" (277; emphasis added).

In her excellent essay "Subaltern as Perspective," Das demands a historiography of the subaltern that displaces the paradigm of social action as defined primarily by rational action. She seeks a form of discourse where affective and iterative writing develops its own language. History as a writing that constructs the moment of defiance emerges in the "magma of significations," for the "representational closure which presents itself when we encounter thought in objectified forms is now ripped open. Instead we see this order interrogated" (313). In an argument that demands an enunciative temporality remarkably close to my notion of the time lag that circulates at the point of the sign's seizure/caesura of symbolic synchronicity, Das locates the moment of transgression in the splitting of the discursive present: A greater attention is required to locate transgressive agency in "the splitting of the various types of speech produced into statements of referential truth in the indicative present" (316).

This emphasis on the disjunctive present of utterance enables the historian to get away from defining subaltern consciousness as binary, as having positive or negative dimensions. It allows the articulation of subaltern agency to emerge as relocation and reinscription. In the seizure of the sign, as I've argued, there is neither dialectical sublation nor the empty signifier: there is a contestation of the given symbols of authority that shift the terrains of antagonism. The synchronicity in the social ordering of symbols is challenged within its own terms, but the grounds of engagement have been displaced in a supplementary movement that exceeds those terms. This is the historical movement of hybridity as camouflage, as a contesting, antagonistic agency functioning in the time lag of sign/symbol, which is a space in between the rules of engagement. It is this theoretical form of political agency I've attempted to develop that Das beautifully fleshes out in a historical argument:

> It is the nature of the conflict within which a caste or tribe is locked which may provide the characteristics of the historical moment; to assume that we may know a priori the mentalities of castes or communities is to take an essentialist perspective which the evidence produced in the very volumes of *Subaltern Studies* would not support.     (320)

Is the contingent structure of agency not similar to what Frantz Fanon describes as the knowledge of the practice of action?[4] Fanon argues that the primitive Manichaeanism of the settler—black and white, Arab and Christian—breaks down in the present of struggle for independence. Polarities come to be replaced with truths that are only partial, limited, and unstable. Each "local ebb of the tide reviews the political question from the standpoint of all political networks." The leaders should stand firmly against those within the movement who tend to think that "shades of meaning constitute dangers and drive wedges into the solid block of popular opinion" (*Wretched* 117–18). What

Das and Fanon both describe is the potentiality of agency constituted through the strategic use of historical contingency.

The form of agency that I've attempted to describe through the cut and thrust of sign and symbol, the signifying conditions of contingency, the nighttime of love, returns to interrogate that most audacious dialectic of modernity provided by contemporary theory—Foucault's "Man and His Doubles." Foucault's productive influence on postcolonial scholars, from Australia to India, has not been unqualified, particularly in his construction of modernity. Mitchell Dean, writing in the Melbourne journal *Thesis Eleven*, remarks that the identity of the West's modernity obsessively remains "the most general horizon under which all of Foucault's actual historical analyses are landmarked" (49). And for this very reason, Partha Chatterjee argues that Foucault's genealogy of power has limited uses in the developing world. The combination of modern and archaic regimes of power produces unexpected forms of disciplinarity and governmentality that make Foucault's epistemes inappropriate, even obsolete (Spivak, *In Other Worlds* 209).

But could Foucault's text, which bears such an attenuated relation to Western modernity, be free of that epistemic displacement—through the (post)colonial formation—that constitutes the West's sense of itself as progressive, civil, modern? Does the disavowal of colonialism turn Foucault's "sign" of the West into the symptom of an obsessional modernity? Can the colonial moment ever not be contingent—the contiguous *as* indeterminancy—to Foucault's argument?

At the magisterial end of *The Order of Things*, when the section on history confronts its uncanny doubles—the countersciences of anthropology and psychoanalysis—the argument begins to unravel. It happens at a symptomatic moment when the representation of cultural difference attenuates the sense of history as the embedding, domesticating "homeland" of the human sciences. For the finitude of history—its moment of doubling—participates in the conditionality of the contingent. An incommensurable doubleness ensues between history as the "homeland" of the human sciences—its cultural area, its chronological or geographical boundaries—and the claims of historicism to universalism. At that point, "the subject of knowledge becomes the nexus of different times, foreign to it and heterogeneous in respect to one another" (369). In that contingent doubling of history and nineteenth-century historicism the time lag in the discourse enables the return of historical agency:

> Since *time* comes to him from somewhere other than himself he constitutes himself as a subject of history only by the superimposition of ... the history of things, the history of words. ... But this relation of simple passivity is immediately reversed ... for he too has a right to a development quite as positive as that of beings and things, one no less autonomous.     (369)

As a result the *heimlich* historical subject that arises in the nineteenth century cannot stop constituting the *unheimlich* knowledge of itself by compulsively relating one cultural episode to another in an infinitely repetitious series of events that are metonymic and indeterminate. The grand narratives of nineteenth-century historicism on which its claims to universalism were founded—evolutionism, utilitarianism, evangelism—were also, in another textual and territorial time space, the technologies of colonial and imperialist governance. It is the "rationalism" of these ideologies of progress that increasingly comes to be eroded in the encounter with the contingency of cultural difference. Elsewhere I have explored this historical process, perfectly caught in the picturesque words of a desperate missionary in the early nineteenth century as the colonial predicament of "sly civility" (see "Sly Civility"). The result of this colonial encounter, its antagonisms and ambivalences, has a major effect on what Foucault beautifully describes as the "slenderness of the narrative" of history in that era most renowned for its historicizing (and colonizing) of the world and the word (*Order* 371).

History now "takes place on the outer limits of the object and subject," Foucault writes (372), and it is to probe the uncanny unconscious of history's doubling that he resorts to anthropology and psychoanalysis. In these disciplines the cultural unconscious is spoken in the slenderness of narrative—ambivalence, catachresis, contingency, iteration, abyssal overlapping. In the agonistic temporal break that articulates the cultural symbol to the psychic sign, we shall discover the postcolonial symptom of Foucault's discourse. Writing of the history of anthropology as the "counterdiscourse" to modernity—as the possibility of a human science *post*modernism—Foucault says:

> There is a certain position in the Western *ratio* that was constituted in its history and provides a foundation for the relation it can have with all other societies, *even with the society in which it historically appeared.*
>
> (377; emphasis added)

In a massive forgetting, Foucault fails to name that "certain position" and its historical constitution. By disavowing it, however, he names it in a negation in the next breath: "Obviously this does not mean that the colonizing situation is indispensable to ethnology."

Are we demanding, from the postcolonial position, that Foucault should rehistoricize colonialism as the missing moment in the dialectic of modernity? Do we want him to "complete" his argument by appropriating ours? Definitely not. I suggest that the postcolonial is metaleptically present in his text in that moment of contingency that allows the contiguity of his argument—thought following thought—to progress. Then, suddenly, at the point of its closure, a curious indeterminacy enters the chain of discourse. This becomes the space for a new discursive temporality, another place of enunciation that will not allow the argument to expand, to include and sublate what is said in opposition to it. We could call this the catachrestic moment in all critical elaboration or the incommensurable time/space of contingency in all forms of closure.

In this spirit of conclusion, I want to suggest a departure for the postcolonial text in the Foucauldian forgetting. In talking of psychoanalysis Foucault is able to see how knowledge and power come together in the enunciative "present" of transference: the "calm violence"—as he calls it—of a relationship that constitutes the discourse. By disavowing the colonial moment as an enunciative present in the historical and epistemological condition of Western modernity, Foucault can say little about the transferential relation between the West and its colonial history. He disavows precisely the colonial text as the foundation for the relation the Western ratio can have "even with the society in which it historically appeared" (*Order* 377).

Reading from this perspective we can see that, in insistently spatializing the "time" of history, Foucault constitutes a doubling that is strangely collusive with its dispersal, equivalent to its equivocation, and uncannily self-constituting, despite its game of "double and splits." Read from the transferential perspective, the Western ratio of (post)modernity encounters itself contingently, in the liminality of cultural difference. If we introduce this transferential perspective where the Western ratio returns to itself from the time lag of the colonial relation, then we see how modernity and postmodernity are constituted from the marginal perspective of cultural difference. They encounter themselves contingently at the point at which the internal difference of their own societies are reiterated in terms of the difference of the other, the alterity of the postcolonial site. At this point of self-alienation postcolonial agency returns, in a spirit of calm violence, to interrogate Foucault's fluent doubling of the figures of modernity.

What it reveals is not some buried concept but a truth about the symptom of Foucault's thinking, the style of discourse and narrative that objectifies his concepts. It reveals the reason for Foucault's desire to anxiously play with the folds of Western modernity, fraying the finitudes of human beings, obsessively undoing and doing up the threads of that "slender narrative" of nineteenth-century historicism. This nervous narrative illustrates and attenuates his own argument; like the slender thread of history, it refuses to be woven in, menacingly hanging loose from the margins. What stops the narrative thread from breaking is Foucault's concern to introduce, at the nexus of his doubling, the idea that "the man who appears at the beginning of the nineteenth century is dehistoricized" (369).

The dehistoricized authority of "Man and His Doubles" produces, in the same historical period, those forces of normalization and naturalization that create a modern Western disciplinary society. The invisible power that is invested in this dehistoricized figure of Man is gained at the cost of those "others"—women, natives, the colonized, the indentured and enslaved—who, at the same time but in other spaces, were becoming the peoples without a history.

### Notes

[1] I wrote this section in response to Stephen Greenblatt's musing question, put in a bar in Cambridge, Massachusetts: "What happens in that partial, passing moment in between the chain of signifiers?" As it turns out, Cambridge is not that far from Tangiers.

[2] In an interview, Spivak also talks of the "irreducible lag-effect" that is not "what is behind the sign system or after it, which the sign system can't keep up with as the 'real thing'—but you must take into account that what you are tapping in terms of cultural self-representation in order to mobilize, or what you are noticing the other side as tapping, also in order to mobilize, must also work with the lag-effect, so that the real task of the political activist is *persistently* to undo the lag-effect . . ." (qtd. in Harasym 125). I have argued for a related temporality of political intervention in "The Commitment to Theory."

[3] Mine is a tendentious exploration and reconstitution of Barthes's concept, often read against the grain of Barthes's celebratory, situationist *detournement*. It is not an exposition, as I have made clear repeatedly throughout the essay.

[4] I have changed the order of Fanon's argument to give an efficient summary of it.

## Selected Bibliography

Anderson, Benedict. *Imagined Communities: Reflections on the Origin and Spread of Nationalism*. London: Verso, 1983.
  Anderson's volume focuses on the discursive and historical conditions that create the affective and imaginary identifications of nationhood in the modern world.

Barker, Francis, et al., eds. *Europe and Its Others*. Proc. of Essex Conf. on the Sociology of Literature. July 1984. 2 vols. Colchester: U of Essex, 1985.
  Covering a wide range of literary and historical subjects from diverse methodological perspectives, this collection contains some of the founding essays of postcolonial criticism.

Bennington, Geoff, Rachel Bowlby, and Robert Young, eds. *Colonialism*. Spec. issue of *Oxford Literary Review* 9 (1987): 2–158.

Bhabha, Homi K., ed. *Nation and Narration*. New York: Routledge, 1991.

Investigating the political aesthetic of "nationness," these essays explore the cultural forms in which the social life (and death) of the nation is articulated in a range of textual and discursive genres.

Fanon, Frantz. *Black Skin, White Masks*. Trans. Charles Markmann. New York: Grove, 1967.
Fanon's inspired work addresses the psychic and cultural dimensions of the perverse "body" of racialized discourse in both the colonial and the metropolitan worlds.

——. *The Wretched of the Earth*. Trans. Constance Farrington. Harmondsworth, Eng.: Penguin, 1969.
An extension and transformation of the ideas expressed in *Black Skin*, this volume deals with the problems of culture and community within conditions of political insurgency and the struggle against imperialism.

Gates, Henry Louis, Jr., ed. *"Race," Writing, and Difference*. Chicago: U of Chicago P, 1986.
These essays describe the cultural representations through which the concept of race and the practice of racism create forms of cultural domination.

Gilroy, Paul. *There Ain't No Black in the Union Jack*. London: Hutchinson, 1987.
Both Gilroy and Hall (see below) rethink concepts of culture, community, and counterhegemonic politics in terms of contemporary metropolitan racism and its "nationalist" context.

Guha, Ranajit, and Gayatri C. Spivak, eds. *Selected Subaltern Studies*. New York: Oxford UP, 1988.
The authors in this collection rewrite the Indian colonial past, and the postcolonial present, in a tension with contemporary theories of historiography. The volume also attempts a more general discussion of the concepts of the specific and the local in historical narrative.

Hall, Stuart. *The Hard Road to Renewal*. London: Verso, 1988.

JanMohamed, Abdul R., and David Lloyd, eds. *The Nature and Context of Minority Discourse*. New York: Oxford UP, 1991.
Challenging the centrality of the canon, this volume attempts to construct a category of communal discourse that represents the condition of minorities but contests their "marginal" status.

Mohanty, Chandra Talpade, Ann Russo, and Lourdes Torres, eds. *Third World Women and the Politics of Feminism*. Bloomington: Indiana UP, 1991.
As the title suggests, this work focuses on women's resistance to domination in a transnational context.

Nandy, Ashis. *The Intimate Enemy: Loss and Recovery of Self under Colonialism*. New York: Oxford UP, 1983.

A contemporary Indian social scientist addresses psychological issues involved in constructing a nonnationalist cultural identity in the postcolonial era.

Said, Edward. *After the Last Sky: Palestinian Lives*. New York: Pantheon, 1986.

Although Said's *Orientalism* inaugurated the postcolonial field, this textual testimony of the Palestinian diaspora, its historical ironies, and cultural dilemmas explores aspects of exile, migration, displacement, and the problems of constructing a narrative of cultural authority and authenticity.

Sangari, Kumkum, and Sudesh Vaid, eds. *Recasting Women in India: Essays in Colonial History*. New Brunswick: Rutgers UP, 1990.

The essays in this volume redefine postcolonial cultural criticism from the feminist perspective, usefully placed outside the locale of the Western academy and its institutions.

Spivak, Gayatri Chakravorty. *In Other Worlds: Essays in Cultural Politics*. New York: Methuen, 1987.

This work examines the colonial and postcolonial texts from the Marxist-feminist perspective in a deconstructive spirit.

Young, Robert, ed. *Neocolonialism*. Spec. issue of *Oxford Literary Review* 13 (1991): 2–265.

This issue tracks the changing terrain of the postcolonial enterprise.

———. *White Mythologies: Writing, History, and the West*. London: Routledge, 1990.

Young's illustrative exploration of the limits of historicism as a discourse of Western cultural authority provides a genealogy for the postcolonial enterprise.

# $C$ omposition Studies

## RICHARD MARIUS

The story of English composition in today's college and university should be the dream text of a deconstructionist, for the discipline pulsates with opposites, good and bad news, and plain contradictions. An optimistic tone pervades the discipline, but I find myself among the pessimists. I maintain that, against the background of the present *practical* state of the discipline, all the research going on in composition and rhetoric matters not at all. I can think of no book or article devoted to research or theory that has made a particle of difference in the general teaching of composition for the past twenty or thirty years—and I can think of a great many commonly held assumptions in the discipline that are supported by no major research at all.

One cannot therefore consider in any realistic way the state of scholarship in composition without calling attention to the woeful condition of the discipline itself that renders all the scholarship merely ornamental. Composition remains overwhelmingly practical, and the most important books are not about theory or research; the most important books are textbooks. The working conditions of the discipline make them conservative and closed to such research as does go on.

Theory and research do exist. Composition specialists regularly publish articles in journals like *College Composition and Communication* and the *Journal of Advanced Composition*. *College English* was once considered a journal for composition, but in recent years it has become largely devoted to literary essays and to poetry. A number of books—many of them collections of essays by composition specialists—intended for the composition teacher pour from the presses.[1] Many are anecdotal, including essays by writers on how they write. The English language itself maintains its vitality despite the lament of purists—common for the last two centuries—that it is in collapse. The cultural significance of historical attitudes towards "correct English" has come under serious scrutiny in the past decade, providing teachers of composition with some perspective on attitudes toward language in the wider educated society.[2] We are not limited to the popular "stylists" William Safire, Edwin Newman, and John Simon in understanding what is happening to our language. In short, composition has a modern literature, and of course it has the ancient tradition of rhetoric to which it is heir. The teacher of writing can call on Aristotle, Quintilian, Cicero, along with modern authorities, to bolster the notion that the discipline has substance. And some composition specialists even do so.[3]

The status of the profession itself seems to be improving slightly. The Conference on College Composition and Communication draws five or six thousand teachers to its annual convention in March, and the status of writing program director has been elevated in many schools. Some universities are turning out composition specialists with doctorates in rhetoric. While such news is encouraging, deep fissures crack and grumble just beneath the surface of this green landscape. We have surprisingly little research that provides statistics about writing programs. But longtime directors of writing programs can recite, in the automatic cadences of an old priest reciting the litany of a funeral, the difficulties they encounter.

The critical, intractable problem is that the teaching of composition in four-year schools is still relegated to part-time, adjunct faculty whose pay is lousy, whose institutional loyalty is nil, and whose shifting ranks make it almost impossible for any writing program to develop a stable and trustworthy core of mentors who can provide close and continuing support for younger members of the staff. Worse, most writing teachers in large universities are graduate students, and most of them, however dedicated, think of themselves as doing time in the writing program so they can advance to their *real* careers— teaching literature.

The departments that consider composition a career for adults are most likely to be in two-year colleges. There, hard-working faculty members toil year after year, often teaching four and five sections of composition every semester, sometimes with twenty-five or thirty-five students in a section; forced to work sixty hours a week or more, they have little time to publish in journals or to keep up with the literature in the field. All this they do for scandalously low wages. The two-year college teachers are heroes of the academic world, but they are often scorned and neglected both within academe and outside.

What do directors of writing programs then do to earn their keep? Do we convey the scholarship of the discipline to our teachers? Well, we try. But we have practical duties that get in the way of the theories. We are always soliciting applications, reading dossiers, interviewing candidates, training staff members as their time and ours permit, evaluating teachers, telling one or two or three people that they are not doing well enough to be given another one-year contract, telling one or two or three people that they are doing brilliantly but that the institution will not let them stay beyond a fixed term—or that if they can stay, they are locked into a fixed wage scale that will be equal for all others in their lowly ranks and that they will receive no special benefits for excellence or special punishment for mediocrity. Naturally, in this litigious age, the director of a writing program will be threatened with lawsuits by those who he or she decides are not good enough to continue. None of this includes the teacher who gets a "real" job two weeks before school begins and must be replaced from a pool made more shallow by the Darwinian law that ensures that the best people already have jobs in September. Nor have we yet mentioned the stress of dealing with the inevitable mistakes one makes in hiring so many people—mistakes that, among other things, mean that every three or four years most directors must deal with a teacher who in a quiet or an extreme way goes crazy.

What do research and theory matter under these conditions? How can the discipline take root in such shifting sands? The books and the articles are there, and the hard-working director can distill them and present them to a staff, and some of this lore may rub off on teachers and make a difference in the classroom. In our program we have regular seminars for our teachers, analyzing assignments, papers, comments by teachers on student work, and the goals of our various courses. Our small senior staff visits classes and evaluates teaching. We work hard to interest teachers in the literature of the discipline. Like all other leaders of composition programs, we find that task difficult. I do not recall meeting a young teacher in, say, history or literature or philosophy or religion who had no interest in the most important literature in the discipline. But I have run into only a handful of part-time writing teachers very much interested in the literature of composition.

Some of that literature, of course, is dismally written—a continuing shame to teachers of writing and one that now and then draws acerbic comment (see Erlanger). The poor writing in the field reflects a schism within composition itself: Are writing teachers technicians or humanists? We ask for a writing sample from candidates seeking jobs with us. I sometimes don't know whether to laugh or to cry over horrors I see in dossiers—the confusions, the jargon, the opacity of prose written by some who have earned advanced degrees in composition and intend to spend their lives teaching it.

The most important literature for writing teachers is not theoretical or historical; writing teachers depend on textbooks, and it is in the textbooks that we gain the most accurate idea of what is *really* going on in the field. There seem to be thousands of them. They flow into any writing program like Noah's flood, threatening to swamp whole offices.

The reason for the numbers is simple. The total market for textbooks about writing is well over a million copies a year. No one knows the exact figure, but editors in high places have told me that they think one million is far too low. A textbook that may sell 10,000 copies a year makes a tidy little profit; a handbook that sells 100,000 copies a year makes a small fortune. So, anyone who teaches writing, knows the discipline, and can turn an acceptable sentence finds acquisitions editors couching at the door.

Textbooks focus on what works in the classroom. The composition teacher—usually untrained in rhetoric and hardly supervised—is out there in the jungle, fighting for his or her life against the onslaught of too many students and too little time. The textbooks become handbooks for survival.

What is the result? One I mentioned: the more intellectual studies in rhetoric and composition are shunted aside. Most composition teachers read hardly anything about the history of rhetoric, the rhetorical analysis of texts, the search for an implied author behind texts, even the analysis of published prose of the sort that Francis Christensen pioneered more than two decades ago or the more recent effort of Robert Scholes to work out, in *Textual Power*, linkage between deconstructionist theory and classroom teaching of writing.

At meetings of the CCCC and at the composition sessions of the MLA, those writing about composition theory enjoy pride of place. In consequence, the field of composition has experienced a rift not unlike that existing between the theorists and the more traditional faculty members in literature. Howard B. Tinberg, a brilliant writer teaching in a two-year college, comments that "the low esteem with which classroom instruction is held among theorists and scholars in the field is the most serious problem confronting composition today" (38).

The results are similar to those in literature. The theorists are much talked about and draw crowds at meetings. But classroom teachers have to be interested in what works, and most are not theoretically inclined. The textbooks are ruled by this practical demand and by another major consideration—teacher expectations. Teachers will not buy a textbook radically different from the textbooks they have always taught, even if the textbooks embody the latest theory. For example, teachers want paragraphs defined by the "topic sentence"—after all, since Alexander Bain defined the paragraph in 1866, composition teachers have been teaching topic sentences. We know that many paragraphs lack topic sentences and that the concept is often confusing. But when I suggested to a now-departed editor of one of my textbooks a few years ago that we approach the paragraph in a more empirical way, he demurred. "If we don't have topic sentences, teachers will not buy our books," he said.

For the same reason, the most popular writing textbooks come packed with all the grammar that can be bound between two covers. It is not that students need such heavy dosages of grammar; the most critical problems in grammar encountered by most college students could probably be covered in a three-page handout. Mina Shaughnessy taught us years ago that the best way to correct students' grammar is to classify their errors so that, for example, we do not assume that every mistake in the use of a past participle is a different one. Instead, we are seeing one error that appears in different guises. Our most useful approach is to work on one of those errors at a time by asking students to revise it away.

As best I can tell, Shaughnessy's admirable findings have been largely ignored. The thick sections in writing handbooks on every imaginable problem in grammar are there not for students but for the comfort of teachers. No matter what research says about the futility of teaching writing by imposing grammar drills, grammar exercises thrive both in high school and in most colleges.

Marketing therefore pulls composition textbooks—and perhaps other textbooks as well—into a rough consensus that is hard for research to crack. The same editor who objected to my heresy about paragraphs told me that the secret of a successful textbook is that about eighty percent of its content agrees with the best-sellers in the field. The best-sellers contain complicated models of paragraphs based on various kinds of topic sentences—topic sentences at the beginning, in the middle, at the end, funnel sentences, and so forth. No matter that one will rarely find a descriptive or narrative paragraph with anything that resembles a topic sentence and that many expository paragraphs lack them, too. Topic sentences sell, and there they are, like dinosaurs at the dinner table.

Without arguing that the textbooks are exactly alike (there is that other twenty percent my former textbook editor mentioned), I believe that a rough consensus of assumptions dominates most of them.

The first is that most writing assigned in composition courses is auto-biographical. Robert J. Connors, one of the brightest historians of composition, has examined the radical difference between the personal writing common today in the composition classroom and the rhetorical tradition of Aristotle and Cicero. In the ancient world, Connors says, orators had to establish an *ethos*, a standing, an authority by having contributed something to the civic community. Only then did orators have the right to call attention to their own experiences (166–67).

No more. "From the 1890's through today," Connors says, "personal writing assignments have remained central to the teaching of composition. Almost every writing course includes personal writing, most start with it, and many concentrate on it" (177). One has only to skim over the handbooks and most other texts to verify Connors's pronouncement.

Why is this so? The fundamental reason, I think, is that we are all aware that students write best about subjects they are familiar with. Students are interested in themselves, and the prevailing wisdom holds that they know more about themselves than they do about anything else. Most college teachers I know lament how little their students read, how small their interest is in the world outside.[4] When I teach freshmen, I regularly ask how many of them read a daily newspaper. Over the years, on the average, three or four hands will go up in a group of fifteen students.

Allan Bloom and others of his gloomy persuasion see this student generation in hopeless decadence, eroticism, narcissism, and nihilism, compared with a glorious golden age that produced intellectual giants like *them* (see esp. *Closing of the American Mind* 227–40).

But remember that Connors reports that the drift of composition toward the personal began in the late nineteenth century and has continued to this day. I have read a fair number of Harvard student papers in composition from the entire nineteenth century. I am prepared to argue that those written earlier in the century, whether they are personal essays or not, are better than those we find in the 1890s.

What happened? The establishment of English literature departments in the second half of the last century meant that distinguished professors taught English literature—not composition, not even rhetoric. As religious orthodoxy lost its hold on the educated, literature professors found in Shakespeare and Milton—staples in their curricula—the source of moral uplift and cohesion necessary for the stability of society and for the formation of common values among the elite who directed it. No one can read the surviving lectures of Harvard's Barrett Wendell on Shakespeare (Wendell insisted on writing "Shakespere") without seeing a secular priest in action, teaching his charges how to get along in polite society.

When literature became a bible and its professors priests, composition inevitably took an inferior position. No one had much faith that students had anything to say worth the bother of asking a high priest of literature to read it. Not surprisingly, students who were expected to be boring usually were. In 1963, Wayne C. Booth set forth the problems of teaching freshman composition, in a speech he called "Boring from Within: The Art of the Freshman Essay." He recounted the dreary story of the high school English teacher who told students that nothing they said in their papers would make a difference. They were to be graded simply on the spelling and grammatical errors they made on their weekly themes. The consequence was predictable. No wonder that Booth could say, "Our students bore us, even when they take a seemingly lively controversial tone, because they have nothing to say, to us or to anybody else."

A contributing cause to the impoverishment of the student mind was the death of rhetoric as a discipline in the late nineteenth century. By then rhetoric seemed to have become an artifice unneeded by a democratic society, in which ordinary people wanted plain truth and believed themselves able to make sense of it without embellishments.

The discipline had also become trivial, its intricate classifications disconnected from substance. Losing its powerful organizing force for discourse, rhetoric had sunk into self-centered elaborations. Even as early as 1663, Samuel Butler had written in *Hudibras*:

All a rhetorician's rules
Teach nothing but to name his tools.
(4)

By the late nineteenth century, Butler's view had won the field, and "rhetoric" was on its way to becoming a pejorative term.

The death of rhetoric just as literature was becoming an established discipline within universities was a calamity for English composition—one more reason to make composition inferior. Without rhetoric to define their task, composition teachers were told by their superiors, the literature people, that their job was to teach the "rules" and to "correct" student papers.

Lacking any grounding in rhetoric, composition teachers had no tools to analyze the thought and development of student papers or to help students say something intelligent and worthwhile. The writing teacher assigned "themes" and expected them to be trivial and filled with "mistakes" that the teacher could mark, proving that he or she was doing something useful.

I do not mean to mock or denigrate all the goals of this attitude. For in one of the paradoxes of human life, this sorry state of affairs was partly a consequence of a grand ideal—public education for all. The public school system reached out to classes of people who for centuries had been condemned by ignorance to the loom and the plow, the stove and the threshing floor, the cottage industry and the mill. Unfortunately, the values of this mass education were shaped and ossified by class consciousness and an Anglo-Saxon Protestantism appalled by immigration that brought millions of central and east Europeans and some Asians to the United States.

Public education set out to anglicize the newcomers, to tell them what literature was best for them and to help them speak and write English without embarrassment. Most immigrants agreed about the means if not the ends because English was the language of power. Multitudes of immigrants believed (like my Greek father) that correct English was the rite of passage into this wondrous new tribe called "American." George Bernard Shaw's *Pygmalion* transformed Eliza Doolittle from Cockney guttersnipe to great lady by giving her the right grammar and the right accent. Why could English teachers not accomplish a similar miracle for the polyglot and polymorphous students who packed their classrooms?

Diction and grammar distinguished the decent and the decorous who "belonged" from the great unwashed who did not. Knowing the right grammar was a little like knowing the right fork to use at dinner—and it surely is no accident that rule books about grammar and books about etiquette proliferated at the same time. But if teaching composition students how to be correct was the goal, what they wrote did not matter.

Under these conditions, composition became what it remains—the domain of beginners in the profession, graduate students or young faculty members, or, finally, the part-time adjunct so common today. And why not? If the goal of composition is to mark errors, any modestly educated person can do that. Young teachers, working intimately with students and much more concerned than senior faculty members that students like them or at any rate respect them, found that students resisted least when they wrote about themselves. And so the practice has continued, and the textbooks have followed along. As Connors has demonstrated, the assumption of the textbooks is that students must at least begin with a personal essay. Some go further to assume that writing is therapy and that therefore personal writing is the only writing that *really* counts.[5]

At the heart of the emphasis on personal writing is the assumption that the development of fluency and confidence in autobiographical writing will lead to fluency and competence in the analytical writing students will do elsewhere in college and in life. The textbooks are agreed in the inevitability of progress from the autobiographical to more detached projects in research—though no research either supports or refutes this view. All handbooks have a mandatory section on the term paper, or, as it is frequently called now, the "library paper" or "research paper," always placed in a later chapter, which invariably includes a "model term paper." The primary aim of these papers is to teach students to use the library, to look up sources, and to incorporate them in proper footnote and bibliographic forms in their final drafts.

An unspoken assumption rules this arrangement. It is that the other papers students write in the composition course will be *without* notes, *without* the quotation from other sources. That is, *except* for the term paper, students will be writing on their own, off the tops of their heads, even when they make an argument. Anyone who has read one of the dreary student papers on abortion or capital punishment that seem to come from a student sausage machine knows that most of them assume that no one has ever written on these subjects before. Students use sources only in the term paper, and it is commonly a pastiche. Connors describes the situation well: "Library research, often unconnected to any writing purpose beyond amassing brute facts for regurgitation into a 'research paper,' became very popular around 1920 and has remained a staple in writing courses ever since" (178).

The consequences are dismal. Every August, I read about seventy or eighty portfolios of writing from transfer students to Harvard who come from colleges and universities all over the nation. My job is to decide whether these students should be exempt from our required freshman writing course, and most papers I read are the standard term papers of the composition course. Every year more than half these papers fall into a category that I call "model airplane." These are papers whose writing resembles what kids do when they buy a model airplane in a hobby shop. They come home and glue it together on their dining room tables, following directions and seeking to create a model that looks like the picture on the box. The student writers exhibit no originality, no creativity, no sustained, rational discourse that explains or builds a careful argument. Their only contribution is to fit the pieces of research together—usually throwing out any evidence that contradicts their "thesis." Often their sources are newspapers and magazines such as *Time* or *Newsweek*, and they have more the form of an encyclopedia article than a thoughtful essay. It looks like research, but it is only cut and paste from secondary sources. Most textbooks in the field do not teach students to do anything else.

The dichotomy here is striking. In their personal writing in the composition course, students are told to establish an individual voice, to let readers know that a real human being stands behind the text, to tell a story that only they can tell. But then they are assigned a term paper, and they produce a lifeless stuffed beast that stares off the pages through the glass eyes of its footnotes. The model papers reproduced in most textbooks teach by example that such a dichotomy is just fine.

Another major assumption of the textbooks is that students must be taught and led through a step-by-step writing process. The emphasis on process arises from the commonsense notion that few writers produce a good finished product in a first draft. Writers study, organize, write, rewrite, give their work to friends, study it again themselves, and rewrite yet again—and perhaps again and again. The notion of writing process swept the textbooks about fifteen years ago—and it is all to the good. Handbooks have bloomed with subject trees, mapping exercises, listing, sample drafts, and other devices intended to lead students from invention of a subject to a final draft. At times in the past decade at the CCCC convention, the term *writing process* has been waved over sessions as though it were a mantra or a spell, destined by repetition to do magic.

An experienced writer must ask why the notion of process took so long to arrive in the teaching of composition when writers have long taken it for granted. The answer, I think, goes back to the central thesis of this essay, the inferior place of composition in the academy. Writing teachers work so hard and under such adverse conditions that few of them have time to write anything. Some do write; some even write brilliantly. But the fine composition specialists who publish anything write textbooks or essays about composition—not essays for general consumption. And as others have pointed out, many of these works are dismally written. Composition teachers scarcely know the world of the professional writer, even the professional academic writer.

But there is one quality that seems to me to be sorely missing in this talk about process. Writing process makes final sense only if there is an ideal out there, a goal, an end that shapes the steps of the process. The goal requires some consensus on what the product of the freshman writing course should be. It is just this consensus that is entirely lacking in the discipline. In consequence, the writing process movement runs the risk of resembling the mad architect who thinks that construction is the all-important task but who has no idea of what the building will look like in the end.

What can we do? I feel pessimistic at this moment that we can do much of anything about the fundamental problem I have pointed out in the beginning of this essay—the lowly professional position of the discipline of composition, dependent as it is on a shifting, part-time staff in the four-year schools and on desperately overworked teachers in the two-year colleges. The political climate in this country stands solidly against any notion that the American people should sacrifice to improve education, from kindergarten through graduate school. We sacrifice only to protect oil fields. Education is left to scavenge at back doors.

I do not believe that we should go gently into that good night of public indifference, however. I believe we should make nuisances of ourselves, that we should be rude and loud and demanding in getting the plight of the writing teacher before the public and before administrators in higher education. What miracles they expect of us! How patronizing are those faculty members in our institutions when they tell us how firmly they support our labors, even as they let our adjuncts toil twice as hard as assistant professors for thousands of dollars less money.

But we need to reform our own house, too. Above all, we need some consensus on the product to which our much-repeated talk about process leads. Writing is obviously many, many things, and no writing program—especially no freshman writing program offering a required course—can teach all kinds of writing. We must locate our writing programs solidly in the curricula of which we are a part, especially liberal arts curricula, where writing programs have their natural home.

I suggest that we agree to teach students how to explain texts, especially texts about ideas. Get rid of autobiographical writing in the freshman composition course. I have spent a great deal of my life teaching history and English literature, having students write as many papers in a term as they are assigned in almost any writing class. If the texts are interesting and if the students are interested in them, and if the teacher is helpful, they find ideas in those texts and expound on them without having to wade through a demeaning apprenticeship of writing about themselves.

In a recent book, Howard Gardner has called attention to research done at Johns Hopkins and MIT "that students who receive honor grades in college-level physics courses are frequently unable to solve basic problems and questions encountered in a form slightly different from that on which they have been formally instructed and tested" (3). I would be willing to bet my faculty status that similar research in other fields would reveal the same unflattering results.

A college writing program should not be engaged in teaching students to understand their psyches or to write articles to be published in a wine connoisseur's magazine. It should be directed to having them give close readings of a manageable number of texts, writing drafts about those texts until they emerge with some understanding of what they are reading.

At Harvard, we are experimenting with "theme courses," writing seminars based on a small number of texts grouped around a narrow theme that allows students to study thoroughly a few leading ideas—a few texts from black women writers, a few texts from important civil rights cases, a few texts from Shakespeare, a few texts from some aspect of the Vietnam War. Give students some choice about the courses where they will fulfill the writing requirement, and give them something to write about besides their grandmothers or their souls or "a turning point in my life."

Assign about four essays a term but require multiple drafts of each, each to be read by the teacher and commented on for its qualities of thought and expression. Keep the drafts going until students can quote sources easily, support their own thoughts with arguments based on evidence, and shape the whole into an essay that observes the conventions for that genre of writing. In short, teach for students' understanding of texts and for their ability to convey their understanding to readers.

Autobiographical writing demeans our profession. While our colleagues in history, literature, and the other liberal arts are asking for writing about the world out there, we often look like a crowd of amateur therapists delivering dime-store psychology to adolescents. Our discipline then becomes trivial in the eyes of the larger faculty.

Limit the texts that students read and write about in a writing course. A hundred pages of source material provides more than enough for a semester of composition if those pages are well chosen. Give students too many sources, and they will write what I once heard Ken Macrorie call "Engfish," falsely authoritative papers about subjects that quickly become too much for them. Eliminate the term paper, with its legions of secondary sources and its phony thesis. Require a few sources for every paper, but be sure that students understand something important about each of those sources.

Teach rhetoric. Teach it to our teachers; teach it to our students. Give them some sense of what we do when we write, of the implied author lurking between the lines, the unstated purposes and contradictions that can often be deconstructed from texts, the assumptions that writers may or may not make explicit in their words. In short, teach students and instructors alike to be good readers and to understand the shape of written discourse. Teach the topics and the tropes. Teach the syllogism and the enthymeme.

Continually explore textual possibilities for student writing. What texts can shape a writing course and attract students? Can we perhaps open the curriculum to texts that interest students even if they do not represent the higher literature so beloved by traditionalists? Can we not find myriads of texts in history, philosophy, religion, and other disciplines to make the basis of a writing course? And can we not draw graduate students and others from those various disciplines to teach those texts with at least enough authority to help students write intelligently about them? We have recently installed a course in writing about horror. We are watching to see what happens to it.

Arrange discussions between members of the composition faculty and faculty members who require writing in other disciplines in the university. We have a lot to teach each other.

Conduct research that will follow students through college, to see what good or ill the composition course does for them. The largest gap in our research in composition lies right here; we do not know, finally, whether a composition course does any good. True, we do not know what a college education does for most people who partake of it except to certify to employers that graduates can operate in a disciplined way through a long and complicated task. But it seems especially shocking to me that we lack any major study that follows students through their academic careers and into later life to see what effect the composition course has on their writing.

My general argument in this article is bound to offend just about everybody. It is that the voluminous research in composition has had little effect on the discipline as a whole. Research is overshadowed by the overwhelmingly practical nature of our discipline and the crushingly inferior status that composition occupies in academe. The miserable working conditions of most composition teachers mean that they cling to textbooks and ignore other writing about composition. We need studies of the effects that composition courses have on students, but we have almost none.

The solutions that I suggest for our problems are largely practical. They are aimed at giving us some coherence among ourselves and some cohesion with the faculty members in other disciplines who should be our colleagues in helping students understand the education they are getting. Such proposals provide a foundation on which research may be built.

But above all, we must labor to make the discipline of composition more professional, more established within colleges and universities. Otherwise the entire discipline will continue to be fragmented and its theory and research of little avail.

## Notes

[1]Recent worthwhile books include M. Schwartz, ed., *Writer's Craft, Teacher's Art*; Bogel and Gottschalk, eds. *Teaching Prose*; Connors, Ede, and Lunsford, eds., *Essays on Classical Rhetoric and Modern Discourse*; McQuade, ed., *The Territory of Language*; Bartholomae and Petrosky, *Facts, Artifacts, and Counterfacts*; Lindemann, *A Rhetoric for Writing Teachers*; and Waldrep, ed., *Writers on Writing*.

[2]See especially Daniels, *Famous Last Words*, and the delightful book *Grammar and Good Taste*, by Baron.

[3]The standard text joining ancient and modern rhetoric is Corbett, *Classical Rhetoric for the Modern Student*.

[4]For an amusing but sorrowing anecdotal reflection on this problem, see "What, *Me* Read?" by my colleague Sven Birkerts.

[5]I hope I do not do Peter Elbow an injustice by saying that this is the message I get from his popular book *Writing without Teachers*. In many sessions at various meetings where I have heard Elbow speak, he has often said that he does indeed prize academic writing, good arguments and exposition, and even literary criticism. But somehow these affirmations are never convincing to me; and the adoring crowds who cram lecture halls to hear him seem to respond with the warmest enthusiasm to his sarcastic baiting and bashing of academic writers.

## Selected Bibliography

Baron, Dennis E. *Grammar and Good Taste: Reforming the American Language.* New Haven: Yale UP, 1982.

Bartholomae, David, and Anthony R. Petrosky. *Facts, Artifacts, and Counterfacts: Theory and Method for a Reading and Writing Course.* Upper Montclair: Boynton, 1986.

An excellent work on a problem often taken for granted—how to make students good readers as we try to make them good writers. The focus here is on the basic writer—once called the writer in need of remedial work.

Bogel, Frederic V., and Katherine K. Gottschalk, eds. *Teaching Prose: A Guide for Writing Instructors.* New York: Norton, 1984.

A splendid collection of essays dealing with every aspect of the teaching of composition.

Christensen, Francis. *Notes toward a New Rhetoric: Nine Essays For Teachers.* Ed. Bonniejean Christensen. 2nd ed. New York: Harper, 1978.

Connors, Robert J. "Personal Writing Assignments." *College Composition and Communication* 38 (1987): 166–83.

Connors, Robert J., Lisa S. Ede, and Andrea A. Lunsford, eds. *Essays on*

*Classical Rhetoric and Modern Discourse.* Carbondale: Southern Illinois UP, 1984.

One of the best guides to joining classical rhetoric to modern teaching. The collection of learned essays by experts is valuable for teachers but not always written with verve.

Corbett, Edward P. J. *Classical Rhetoric for the Modern Student.* 3rd ed. New York: Oxford UP, 1990.

Technically a textbook with readings, but a work that every writing teacher should know by heart. Written by the genial Nestor of the profession, the volume was somewhat simplified after the second edition.

Corbett, Edward P. J., James L. Golden, and Goodwin F. Berquist, eds. *Essays on the Rhetoric of the Western World.* Dubuque: Kendall, 1990.

Fine historical studies with emphasis on the application of rhetoric to various intellectual pursuits. The first essay in the collection, "Where Do English Departments Come From?" is essential to anyone teaching composition—or English literature.

Daniels, Harvey A. *Famous Last Words: The American Language Crisis Reconsidered.* Carbondale: Southern Illinois UP, 1983.

Intelligent and often very funny defense of the vitality of our language against the academic Chicken Littles of the world for whom the linguistic skies are always falling.

Elbow, Peter. *Writing without Teachers.* New York: Oxford UP, 1973.

Perhaps the most influential book in the writing-process movement, sharing its virtues and its flaws. Elbow developed the concept of "free writing," but his book looks at times as if the title might better have been "Writing as Therapy."

Emig, Janet. *The Composing Processes of Twelfth Graders.* Urbana: NCTE, 1971.

One of the first solid pieces of research on a practical topic in composition, done by a canny observer.

Erlanger, Rachel. "Johnny's Teacher Can't Write Either." *New York Times* 12 June 1991: A27.

Gardner, Howard. *The Unschooled Mind: How Children Think and How Schools Should Teach.* New York: Basic, 1991.

A clear, quietly passionate book on how children learn, how the schools are failing them, and how we can teach better—with much emphasis on the importance of the teaching of writing as a means of learning.

Graves, Richard L., ed. *Rhetoric and Composition: A Sourcebook for Teachers and Writers.* Upper Montclair: Boynton, 1984.

An excellent collection of essays, most with a practical bent, by major figures in the field such as James M. McCrimmon, Donald Murray, Nancy Sommers, Winston Weathers.

Lindemann, Erika. *A Rhetoric for Writing Teachers.* 1982. 2nd ed. New York: Oxford UP, 1987.
Very much the classic in the field, including every aspect of teaching composition, from a survey of theories of cognition to the teaching of revision. Lindemann summarizes vast scholarship but, alas, writes poorly.

McQuade, Donald A., ed. *The Territory of Language: Linguistics, Stylistics, and the Teaching of Composition.* Carbondale: Southern Illinois UP, 1986.
Intellectual, generally well written, and cogent efforts to join linguistics to the teaching of composition. The work includes research on many of the most gnawing problems of the discipline.

Scholes, Robert. *Textual Power: Literary Theory and the Teaching of English.* New Haven: Yale UP, 1985.
A wise book by one of the masters of literature and writing. How do we make students critics, and how do we apply some of the insights of modern criticism to the teaching of writing?

Schwartz, Mimi, ed. *Writer's Craft, Teacher's Art: Teaching What We Know.* Portsmouth: Boynton, 1991.
Essays by teachers of writing on the way they teach, the problems they confront, and the major issues in the profession.

Shaughnessy, Mina P. *Errors and Expectations: A Guide for the Teaching of Basic Writing.* New York: Oxford UP, 1977.
A discussion of how to comment on papers in a university with an open-admissions policy. If any single book is a "classic" in the field of composition, this is it.

Sommers, Nancy. "Responding to Student Writing." *College Composition and Communication* 33 (1982): 148–56.
A classic work, showing that a lousy student paper is often the teacher's fault.

Tinberg, Howard B. " 'An Enlargement of Observations': More on Theory Building in the Composition Classroom." *College Composition and Communication* 42 (1991): 36–44.
A witty piece about the gulf between those who expound theory and those who may teach five sections of composition a term.

Waldrep, Tom, ed. *Writers on Writing.* 2 vols. New York: Random, 1988.
From writing instructors, insights on how they go about practicing what they teach.

White, Edward M. *Teaching and Assessing Writing.* San Francisco: Jossey-Bass, 1986.

A book that may save a writing teacher's life. White treats almost every aspect of teaching composition—including ways to handle the vast paper load most teachers face by the use of holistic scoring—and does so with uncommon common sense.

# *C*omposition and Literary Studies

## DONALD MCQUADE

Before his mysterious disappearance and probable death in 1974, Oscar Zeta Acosta, the rotund lawyer and activist with a gargantuan appetite for food, drugs, and life on the edge and the model for Hunter S. Thompson's "Dr. Gonzo" in *Fear and Loathing in Las Vegas*, completed a remarkably engaging and candid two-part account of coming of age as a Chicano in San Francisco, East Los Angeles, and on the road in the psychedelic sixties. In the first of these books, *The Autobiography of a Brown Buffalo*, Acosta explores the difficulties of searching for personal and cultural identity in a society fragmenting around him by focusing on the familial tensions that erupt when his parents try to erase what is distinctively Mexican in themselves and in their children (see also Acosta, *Revolt*). By insisting that their children adapt themselves to the possibilities of the "better life" imagined for them by the dominant Anglo culture, Acosta's parents succeed only at instilling a sense of insecurity and fraudulence in their son. Trying to negotiate the spaces between two worlds, he cannot settle into the dignity of either culture.

In the book's final episode, Acosta, struggling to contend with the difficulties of living in a world of divided identities, imagines himself addressing a group of like-minded revolutionaries:

> Ladies and gentlemen . . . My name is Oscar Acosta. My father is an Indian from the mountains of Durango. Although I cannot speak his language . . . you see, Spanish is the language of our conquerors, English is the language of our conquerors. . . . No one ever asked me or my brother if we wanted to be American citizens. We are all citizens by default. They stole our land and made us half-slaves. They destroyed our gods and made us bow down to a dead man who's been strung up for 2000 years. . . . Now what we need is, first, to give ourselves a new name. We need a new identity. A name and a language all our own. (*Autobiography* 198; ellipses in original)

Acosta proposes that they call themselves the "Brown Buffalo People," which invokes not only "the roots in [their] Mexican past, [their] Aztec ancestry" but also "the animal that everyone slaughtered" (198). Having come to terms with his fabricated—and circumscribed—identity by the end of the book, Acosta expresses his final recognition in language that at once frees him from the burden of what he had regarded to be a personal defect and underscores his conviction that his circumstances are the necessary outcome of the historical predicament of being trapped between two worlds:

> What I see now, on this rainy day in January 1968, what is clear to me after this sojourn is that I am neither a Mexican nor an American. I am neither a Catholic nor a Protestant. I am a Chicano by ancestry and a Brown Buffalo by choice.                                                                                    (199)

By ending with an act of self-assertion—rendered from the inside out—Acosta is able finally to author his own dream, of becoming "Zeta, the world famous Chicano Lawyer who helped to start the last revolution . . ." (199). Yet his assertion of individual identity remains unvalidated, a freedom unrealized in, or connected to, anything more tangible than what he calls a "plan."

Although Acosta's crisis is clearly a more severe human predicament than the problems of institutional self-definition confronting teachers of writing, there are nevertheless several useful points of comparison to draw here. An account of what has transpired in composition studies over the past few decades would follow a narrative line roughly similar to Acosta's, highlighting many of the same issues about insecurity, multiple identities, authority, and self-determination, as well as featuring similar Nietzschean acts of self-assertion and ongoing struggles for intellectual and cultural substantiation. The stories practitioners tell about their attempts to assert an independent intellectual identity for composition studies are replete with memorable reports of skeptical, paternalistic, condescending, and occasionally even hostile responses —terms remarkably consistent with Acosta's description of the resistances he faced as he attempted to construct an identity distinct from that imposed on him by history and circumstance. In addition, Acosta's predicament is directly, rather than analogically, relevant both to the predicaments many composition students face in writing courses and especially to the point that composition studies continues to be both the initial and a principal academic site of the everyday struggles of many minority students with such issues as race, class, and ethnic identity and power as they attempt, in Acosta's terms, to claim "a name and a language." Acosta's story is telling for composition studies in yet another way: it is ultimately about redefining an identity through deconstructing and restaging the power that silently constructs it.

Virtually every area of intellectual inquiry has been marked in recent years by various crises in identity and vision as well as in subjects and methods of inquiry. In biology and anthropology, for example, the traditional boundaries of research and pedagogy have been radically redrawn. But what distinguishes the story of composition studies from those of other intellectual areas in recent decades is that academic power and politics have more often been exercised *on* than *in* it. Situated marginally as the necessary "other" along the borders of literature, literary criticism, and rhetoric, composition studies remains one of the most contested territories in the topography of contemporary American academic culture. Viewed from the outside, composition has become—and increasingly so in the past two decades—at once the locus and the currency for the political struggles in the humanities over human and institutional resources. Composition continues to underwrite the costs of doing the "major" work of more established disciplines, despite being granted little respect for the "service" it provides. Viewed from the inside, composition studies has become a burgeoning area in which impressive advances in scholarship and pedagogy rub up against individual and institutional issues of power, race, ethnicity, class, and gender at the beginning of virtually every instructional hour. At stake in the recent history of composition studies as an area of intellectual inquiry is the outcome not only of ongoing individual efforts to establish the dignity of—and to earn recognition for—research and teaching in composition but also of continuing debates, conducted in administrative offices and departmental corridors, about authority over managing its institutional and instructional capital, its budget and curriculum. In this respect, composition studies remains one of the few academic disciplines in which outsiders insist on naming and authorizing its activities, without accepting the intellectual responsibility—and the institutional consequences—for doing so.

Traditionally defined by others in terms of what it is not and, until recently, most often regulated by those not conversant in either its research methodologies or its pedagogical values, composition studies remains an academic borderland with a fractured history, an intellectual arena in which different traditions, languages, sets of practice, and political values compete daily for the attention and the loyalty (often expressed as continued enrollments) of hundreds, and often thousands, of undergraduates on every campus in this country.[1] Despite recent efforts in the academy to ascribe to it a syncretic, suturing function, composition is still widely perceived as a wound between two domains, a laceration whose edges touch literary criticism and rhetoric—historically marginal to the intellectual interests of both and yet currently central to the institutional needs of each.

In this essay I recount some of the main lines of that story as well as highlight the readily observable features and the more nuanced shadings marking the academic boundaries that encompass composition studies. As with all such stories, this one is told from a particular point of view: from the perspective of someone who still carries two academic passports. Trained in literary history and criticism, I came to work in composition studies by happenstance in the early 1970s—on the first day of open admissions in the City University of New York. Recruited to teach American literature, I was immediately assigned to what senior faculty members regarded as an equally, if not more, important duty: to serve alongside other young colleagues as, to invoke the prevailing metaphors of those years, "the shock troops" on "the front line" of institutional defense against the "onslaught" of ill-prepared students admitted to the university under the politically contentious terms of its open admissions policy, which guaranteed a tuition-free place in the university to every resident of New York City who graduated from an accredited high school. Viewed from either side of the desk, instruction in composition in that context involved much more than "a raid on the inarticulate"; it never ceased to be at once terrifying and exhilarating, an unnerving combination of constantly taking risks—of examining and putting into daily practice previously untested assumptions about the nature and significance of such basic, and enabling, acts as writing and reading—and of acting on the ethical and pedagogical imperatives that are the consequences of a commitment to the principles of a literate democracy. Through their interactions with faculty members, the students in open admissions reinvented the professional lives and interests of their instructors, who had been trained in traditional graduate programs in literature. From that time forward, I have been preoccupied with and sustained by these dual interests in composition and literature—and in their intersections.

Unlike the most recent generation of scholars and teachers who have been trained as specialists in composition, scholars and teachers who have produced much of its latest research and who have laid claim to the integrity and independence of its disciplinary boundaries, I have spent much of my professional life exploring the interstices between composition and literary studies. And, much like others who cross borders, I continue to grapple with the lingering effects of a double, if not a divided, identity—the legacy my students have left me. Yet, like Acosta, I seek to claim neither status nor sympathy for myself as a victim; I seek simply to make clear who I am by training, by experience, and by choice—to recount "what I see now," "what is clear to me" from the perspective of what has been more than a twenty-year "sojourn" on *both* sides of the border between composition and literary studies. In doing so, I seek to remind myself and others that intellectual lives—mediated through such issues as access and class—are often at stake in posting the boundaries that define a discipline, recognizing the Foucauldian reverberations of that term (see *Discipline*). When I view composition studies—and the faculty members and students who work in it—from either side of its borders, from either inside or outside the area, I see a conceptual territory where everything seems possible and yet circumscribed.

In discussing composition's relations with literary studies and rhetoric in terms of circumscription, I mean to suggest here a good deal more than a post-Derridean acknowledgment of a theoretical point about writing would allow. In this sense, this essay sets out to be more than an exercise in academic

topography. By surveying the most influential scholarship in composition studies over the past few decades, I intend to explore this notion of circumscription—for both faculty members and students—not only by mapping the
intellectual and institutional demarcations between and among composition,
literature, literary criticism, and rhetoric but also by examining the sociocultural assumptions and the implications of the practices that govern student and
faculty migrations across what historically have been—and in many parts
of the profession continue to be—clearly drawn and insistently maintained
boundaries.

This essay provides neither the occasion nor the space to document
fully the centuries-old territorial conflicts between literary studies and rhetoric—often about dominion over composition. Patricia Bizzell and Bruce Herzberg provide, with remarkable clarity and insight, a historical perspective on
these tensions in *The Rhetorical Tradition*.[2] Let me simply highlight here a few
significant points in the bifurcated history of the intellectual and institutional
relations between rhetoric and literary studies, points that create a context
within which to understand and appreciate the advances in composition research and pedagogy in recent decades. Viewed from this perspective, composition serves as the common thread in (the material basis for) the distinctive
pedagogical designs of each discipline.

## Composition versus Belles Lettres: A Class Distinction

Traditionally, the study and practice of rhetoric was associated with
civic oratory and with the writing of history, poetry, and literary criticism.
From the Renaissance through the eighteenth century, readers of literature
regularly drew on the principles of classical rhetoric—and especially on those
promulgated by Aristotle, Cicero, and Quintilian—to form their critical judgments. Interest in applying the rules of classical eloquence to the reading of
literature increased on both sides of the Channel throughout this period.
Sparked by the work of Corneille, Racine, Molière, and La Fontaine, cultural
nationalism surged under the reign of Louis XIV and peaked in the establishment of the French Academy. In a similar vein, in the work of the most influential Augustan writers—including, for example, Pope and Swift—literature,
and especially satire, served to raise civic consciousness by promoting national
pride and virtuousness through instruction that pleased. However, the publication and widespread practice of the principles expounded in George Campbell's
*Philosophy of Rhetoric* (1776) and especially Hugh Blair's *Lectures on Rhetoric
and Belles-Lettres* (1783) shifted the grounds of rhetoric from the study of
persuasion (the strategies used to express thought) to the study of thought

itself (the psychology of its production) and to the moral qualities of the taste associated with it. At the same time that these books were gaining increased influence and Blair's principles and practices were being widely adopted in textbook form in American schools and colleges, other important educational reforms were taking root—particularly those that affected women, increased literacy rates among the working classes, and substituted composition in the vernacular for drill in Latin. These factors gradually converged to undermine the primacy of the classical rhetorical tradition in nineteenth-century Europe and the United States. As education became less the intellectual property of the elite and more a practical and political tool to train an increasingly industrialized work force, the historical links between and among rhetoric, literature, and literary criticism began to weaken.

Bizzell and Herzberg trace the historical separation of rhetoric and literature to an even more specific distinction, drawn in the early nineteenth century by Coleridge and others, between "the *active* concerns of rhetoric and the *contemplative* ones of literature" (639). By the mid-nineteenth century, the British began to formalize this distinction by dividing instruction in rhetoric from belles lettres, and American universities (led by Johns Hopkins and Harvard) did much the same. Because of the terms of this separation, composition eventually emerged as a branch of rhetoric, which in turn came to be promoted, largely through the influence of such works as Henry Day's *Elements of the Art of Rhetoric* (1858), as "the art of discourse" or, more often, the "faculty of communicating thoughts" (qtd. in Bizzell and Herzberg 864). In such circumstances, composition assumed a derivative identity, what Bizzell and Herzberg identify as its "connective rather than creative" function (663). The opposition between "connective" and "creative" is similar to the distinctions Coleridge draws between "active" and "contemplative" and between "imagination" and "reason"; the opposition is also reminiscent of the difference in Kant's use of *der verstand* (understanding) and *die vernunft* (reason). The seeming balance of such oppositions suggests a continuum, a continuous, level plane. Yet, when examined more carefully, each binary reveals a hierarchical relation.

Historically, hierarchical metaphors have characterized the work of composition: "service," "lower-division," "basic skills," "required course," and the like. These terms suggest that composition functions at a lower level of ability, purpose, and seriousness, as though composition were fundamentally inferior to either rhetoric (as Blair conceived it) or belles lettres. In this sense, composition is characterized as concrete and practical rather than abstract and theoretical, as operational rather than speculative, as circumspect rather than imaginative. Consider, for example, the implications of the association of composition with the word *practical*: it emphasizes the prudence, the efficiency, and the economy of an act, an agent, or a solution—the *workability*, say, of an idea or a plan, which, in turn, depends on the extent to which the plan is managed properly. In practice and effect, composition remains a matter of work, of training and managing labor-intensive skills. Because it is still often described in terms of the service or the product it provides, rather than the process or the production it involves, composition remains distinct from either rhetoric or belles lettres in the capacity, rank, and authority associated with—and permitted to—it.

The shared emphasis on creativity and authority in belles lettres and rhetoric continued to be emphasized well into the nineteenth century in such influential treatises as Alexander Bain's *English Composition and Rhetoric* (1866). Bain identified poetry as one of the principal modes for discourse—the others were description, narration, exposition, and persuasion—and established paragraph unity as the central measure of effective composition. Bain's followers dropped poetry from his list of modes but used his account of the others and of paragraph unity to establish standards of organization and performance in composition—prototypes that, well over a century later, continue to dominate the patterns of reading and writing assigned in many college composition courses.

By the end of the nineteenth century, the institutional pressures to establish instructional independence for rhetoric and belles lettres intensified. During this same period, the rapid increase in scientific and technological information prompted rhetoricians to downplay persuasion and to promote exposition as the most effective means to manage the new knowledge, a service to which composition was soon dedicated. Adams Sherman Hill, one of the most prominent rhetoricians of the period, blurred the instructional boundaries as well as the hierarchical distinction between rhetoric and composition when he defined rhetoric as "the art of efficient communication." Hill combined Bain's attention to the modes of discourse and paragraph unity with a prescriptive approach to teaching the "mechanics" of communication—to applying accurately the rules of grammar and usage (qtd. in Bizzell and Herzberg 881).[3] In this sense, Hill's functional approach to composition constituted an early academic version of Frederick Winslow Taylor's principles of scientific management and a further step deeper into the divided politics of academic class relations.

Taylor's notions of time management and efficiency, so influential in American corporate enterprise's plans to increase the productivity of blue-collar workers, also infiltrated middle-class reading habits. Those with little time and patience to read full-length books could purchase *Reader's Digest* (founded in 1922) or subscribe to the Book-of-the-Month Club (1926). Readily consumable condensations of political and business affairs appeared in such aptly named weekly magazines as *Time* (founded in 1923), *Fortune* (1933), and *Life* (1936). So, too, the nation's most popular mass market magazines stepped up the number of features aimed at satisfying the increasingly specialized interests of different readers. In this sense, popular magazines were quickly becoming the intellectual version of a department store or supermarket. The shifts in the contents of popular American magazines also reflected the diminished status of the essay as a literary genre. In search of "better" ways to live, many readers lacked the time and curiosity to ponder a writer's eloquent reflections on the self or the world. In the consumer culture of the period, most popular magazines substantially reduced the number of literary essays they published, reserving more and more space for up-to-date information about the world and offering advice about managing the complexities of mass-produced, faster-paced lives. (Matthew Arnold called journalism "literature in a hurry.") In such circumstances, recipe replaced reflection, and reading for information replaced reading for pleasure. In a provocative review entitled "The Modern Essay," Virginia Woolf provides an essayist's point of view on this problem: "To write weekly, to write daily for busy people catching trains in the morning or for tired people coming home in the evening, is a heart-breaking task for men who know good writing from bad" (219). Woolf's critique is presented, however, from the vantage point of an upper class that obviously had a stake in preserving such distinctions in taste. Instruction in writing quickly adapted to the cultural technocracy that emerged in the first few decades of the century. One example of the functional rather than creative role assigned to composition can be seen in a pronounced shift in the writer's point of view—from the confident observations of an intensely resolute "I" to the safety of a voice protected by generalization, by what Woolf calls "a common greyness" (220). Stretched thin by the syntactical effort to control information by generalizing about it, the essay in particular—and composition in general—surrendered its major distinguishing feature: the presence of a strong, unequivocal, individual voice.

The pressures of specialization and information management as well as the addition of new subjects reduced the presence and narrowed the scope of composition and rhetoric in the early-twentieth-century college curriculum. The traditional concerns of rhetoric gradually resurfaced in other departments, and the newly formed speech departments assumed responsibility for its history, methods, and theories.[4] During this same period, English departments resumed teaching writing and accentuated the service dimensions of instruction in composition. The titles of several widely used textbooks highlight the practical function and the managerial responsibility assigned to composition in the early twentieth century, and insisted on ever since: John F. Genung's *Practical Elements of Rhetoric* (1886), John H. Nason's *Efficient Composition* (1917), and John B. Opdyke's *Working Composition* (1917), and the like. The distinction embedded in these titles between "practical" writing and literature also reflects American society's demand for literate workers and consumers, as well as the desire of one class to distinguish their interests and tastes from those of other classes. (The dichotomy between composition and belles lettres also relegated "creative writing" to the category of surplus, excess, or luxury— as opposed to necessary or functional. Viewed from another angle, composition is *value extracted*, creative writing *value added*.) Such titles not only underscore the values assigned to composition in the curriculum but also point up the more focused attention and values *within* composition pedagogy and practice and *on* new assertions about, and technologies for, communication and control of information. Attention to technique becomes a defining feature of different specializations—within and beyond the academy.

The emphasis on specialization proved equally applicable to scholarship, and especially within departments of English literature, where the essay was quickly adapted to serve as the principal form for academic writing. Within the context of the increasing professionalization and specialization of literary studies, the status of the essay was reduced further—from being a *primary* form *of* literature to its continuing standing as a *secondary* source, as a commentary *on* literature. The grounds for instruction in writing shifted accordingly. English departments exercised greater authority over instruction in written composition, reduced its importance as an emerging subject of independent study, and put its instructional energies in the service of literary criticism. Students were soon required to produce models of correctness—in spelling, punctuation, syntax, grammar, and expression—that displayed the products of rigorously controlled analyses of literature drawn from a designated list of standard authors. This managerial version of instruction in composition soon became a required course in the first-year college curriculum. And, as tradition would have it, the idea that nonfiction prose operates in the service of literature continues to dominate institutional definitions of their relationship.

The reduction in the literary status of nonfiction as well as the more managerial focus of textbooks in composition established the basis for what has become an enormously important—but still-unexamined—assumption in American colleges and universities: that there is an irrevocable distinction between composition and literature. Virtually every article I have read in recent English studies—whether written by someone identified as having a special interest in literature or in composition—continues either to presuppose unwittingly or to insist doggedly that "literature" should be identified and discussed in terms of talent, composition in terms of skill. Even so rigorous and radical a theorist as Paul de Man, for example, announcing his focus on "the study of tropes and figures," feels compelled to add that this "is how the term *rhetoric* is used here, and not in the derived sense of comment or of eloquence or of persuasion," ("Semilogy" 6). For virtually everyone concerned, literature involves "major" texts and ways of reading intrinsically autonomous artistic objects that demand sophisticated powers of analysis and synthesis. Often those who specialize in literary theory and criticism consider the work of those who have an abiding professional interest in composition theory, research, and pedagogy as impoverished in both subjects for and methods of analysis. Given such assumptions, literature is aesthetic, composition merely utilitarian. Literature specialists teach "elective" courses in upper-division "major" programs; composition teachers "service" courses in fulfillment of lower-division general-education requirements. Within such class strictures, literature remains elegant and elite, composition commonplace and déclassé. In this sense, literature excludes, or precludes, composition. In the midst of the current debates about what constitutes the "literary," literature continues to be defined *against* composition, in much the same ways in which the boundaries of "class," "taste," and "culture" are drawn. Yet there may well be a paradoxical dimension of this resistance to inclusion: it may be desirable for the emotional economy of English studies to have an internal stranger like composition—in order to preserve for literature the sense of the prestige of its own activities.

Until quite recently, English departments quietly but insistently maintained this subservient relation between literature and composition by making writing about canonical literature the focal point of composition instruction. Few departments heeded the calls of such progressive educators as John Dewey to devote greater attention to writing beyond the curriculum and to view it as a means to provide the wave of immigrants in early-twentieth-century America with the communicative skills needed not only to function in the workplace but also to contribute to the nation's cultural life. In *Literature as Exploration* (1938), Louise Rosenblatt did succeed—however modestly, in the face of what was rather formidable opposition—in broadening the range of acceptable responses to literature by encouraging young readers to learn more about themselves through writing about the dialogical nature of their experiences with literature. Rosenblatt's efforts to renegotiate the terms of the relation between the reader and literature roughly coincided with equally enduring and radical reformulations of rhetorical theory—as well as with reinvigorated applications of rhetorical analysis—during the period between the two wars.

The work of I. A. Richards and Kenneth Burke created the prospect of building new, and more productive, links between and among literature, literary criticism, and rhetoric and provided the terms for redrawing the intersections of each with composition. Richards and Burke each used rhetoric to articulate a new theory of—and practice for—literary criticism. In *The Meaning of Meaning* (1923), coauthored with C. K. Ogden, Richards laid the groundwork for directing literary criticism away from the philological, historical, and biographical analyses of his predecessors. Then a philosopher of language, Richards argued that acts of interpretation determine meaning in context, not the inherent properties and the significance of words. In *The Philosophy of Rhetoric* (1936) Richards positioned rhetoric at the center of this theory of meaning, defining it as "how words work in discourse" and as "the study of misunderstanding and its remedies" (3, 6). He had already put these two precepts into practice in *Practical Criticism* (1929), in which he reported on an experiment he conducted with his students; he asked them to interpret several poems about which they were provided with no additional information. Richards's classification and analysis of their responses—as well as his accounts of their misreadings—soon served as the procedural basis for New Criticism, what would become the dominant form of literary criticism well into the 1960s.[5]

In many respects, Burke established an even more radical position on the relations between literature and rhetoric. In *Counter-statement* (1931) he declared that because literature used language to move readers, it constituted a form of persuasion and therefore could—and should—be governed by rhetorical theory and practice. Burke developed and extended this argument in *A Grammar of Motives* (1945) and *A Rhetoric of Motives* (1950), in which he applied it to virtually all forms of discourse: oral as well as written, popular as well as canonical, social as well as scientific and philosophical. Burke's definition of rhetoric as the "art of persuasion, or a study of the means of persuasion available for any given situation" (qtd. in Bizzell and Herzberg 1034) and his identification of motivation behind all discourse made virtually every form of communication a proper subject for rhetorical inquiry. Composition studies might well have flourished immediately under Burke's charge and tutelage, and especially under the aegis of his rhetorical literary criticism, but his influence was not evident—in any durable way—in composition research and pedagogy until the 1960s, and then somewhat obliquely, initially through the publication of Wayne C. Booth's controversial study *The Rhetoric of Fiction* (1961), which asserted that great works of literature had distinctive and discernible persuasive agendas embedded in them. Burke's theories also resurfaced later in the development of reader-response criticism and deconstruction, as well as in more recent applications of Marxist theory to literature.[6]

English departments remained indifferent to the revival of rhetoric—and more specifically to the work of Burke—in the years immediately before and after the Second World War, principally because rhetoric was still widely regarded as a province of speech departments, whose curriculum focused on public speaking and thereby reinforced rhetoric's newly accentuated identity as a preprofessional skill. Yet the widespread adoption of the principles and procedures of New Criticism (along with its values and assumptions) in the years before—and the decades after—the Second World War might well be the most important obstacle in what has been, until recently, the halting process of self-identification for composition studies, the ongoing effort to articulate an intellectual foundation on which to build an independent professional status for those with scholarly and pedagogical interests in the work of words. New Criticism institutionalized within the university curriculum the hierarchical distinction between the aesthetic standards of "literature" and the practical concerns of "composition" and made operative within the academy the class differentiation implicit in the word *practical*.

The assumption among the most celebrated practitioners of New Criticism has been adopted by both their successors and detractors—namely, that the purpose of composition is to serve the more privileged interests of literature. In effect, or so the argument goes, the writing produced in college composition courses does not warrant, nor could it sustain, attention to its aesthetic features. For example, in *Understanding Poetry* Cleanth Brooks and Robert Penn Warren set out to highlight what they call the "fundamental resemblances" between poetry and other forms of discourse—"for only by an understanding of the resemblances can one appreciate the meaning of the differences" (1). They move even more quickly to emphasize the distinctions between the aesthetic properties of poetry, its "nonpractical functions," and the information produced by the "practical man" (2). In the process, Brooks and Warren repeatedly underscore composition's subservient relation to literature, discussing the latter in nearly reverential terms while addressing the former in a rather patronizing tone. Nowhere in their analyses does the slightest attention to student writing surface. (In contrast, Richards's sustained attention to student writing has endeared him to many who teach composition.) In this respect, there is a painful irony evident in a method of literary criticism devoted to celebrating both the distinctive voice and tone of each writer and the aesthetic and moral values of literature; its proponents seem to ignore the efforts of inexperienced writers to articulate an appreciable sense of their state(s) of consciousness in terms that express the individuality and integrity of their visions and voices. Yet Brooks and Warren, placing a formalist premium on the autonomous, self-referential nature of "real" literature, could hardly be expected to treat the writing that students submitted as literary. A student's essay would not be regarded as literary precisely because it is manifestly "about" something and because it usually recommends, if not urges, its readers to articulate a position, adopt a belief, or display an attitude. For the New Critics, however, "real" literature (*Hamlet*, for example) asks nothing of its readers other than that they see it as an aesthetic object. This fundamentally Kantian view of art as an occasion for desireless contemplation still lurks at—or near—the center of our collective aesthetics. And it is within the context of New Criticism that recent composition studies began a slow, but steady, process of self-articulation.

New Criticism did have, however, at least a few salubrious effects on the teaching of writing: in contrast to Woolf, the New Critics encouraged a more democratic view of literature, one that treated literature not only as a matter of taste but also as a subject that could be learned and appreciated by applying the tools and concepts they provided. Yet in this respect, many of the tools used in the practice of New Criticism (for example, "substitution") were devices drawn from the instructional repertoire of writing teachers. As Robert Scholes and others have recently argued, New Criticism helped democratize reading and demonstrate that reading and interpretation are forms of writing. New Criticism also focused considerable attention on the linguistic and stylistic complexities of the literature it promoted. Such emphasis on the intricacy of language and meaning would eventually serve well those interested in exploring how students generated meaning through compositional choices, although it was assumed that those choices—and the texts within which they were positioned—did not warrant the attention of anyone except the student who wrote them and the instructor who read them. Because of the marginalized status and the privacy of the writing students produced within the context of New Criticism, it is not at all surprising that the instructional relation between language and thought was treated principally in formulaic or mechanical terms. In effect, writing became—literally and figuratively—a discipline, a matter of drills. In this sense, the recent history of composition studies might be characterized as an untiring effort to free writing as a discipline from the limitations of the "disciplinary" behavior imposed on it.

The diminished stature ascribed to composition during the period of the ascendancy—and domination—of New Criticism became evident soon after the National Council of Teachers of English commissioned Richard R. Braddock, Richard Lloyd-Jones, and Lowell Schoer, under the supervision and with the assistance of the NCTE Committee on the State of Knowledge about Composition, to conduct a comprehensive survey of research on composition. Their report, published in 1963 as *Research in Written Composition*, featured few notable landmarks, although the volume did articulate—as well as exemplify—standards of excellence for the research it advocated.[7] Given the lack of professional standing ascribed to composition studies in the early 1960s, the NCTE report contained few surprises. But it did confirm a regrettable tradition within English studies: the tendency to divide itself along academic class lines.

Sharply drawn class distinctions continue to circumscribe the institutional relations between literature and composition studies. For example, composition instruction, and the research and concepts that infused it, have long been relegated to the marginal precincts of freshman composition, housed, and often literally so, in the basement of many English departments. Teachers of composition would eventually be depicted—and treated—in terms comparable to those used to regulate the entrance of immigrants into American life: they were paid low wages and granted few, if any, benefits to do work that others were at least reluctant, if not altogether unwilling, to perform. Much like their students, composition instructors traditionally were assigned to specific composition classes because of what they *lacked*—graduate students lacking in degrees, professorial faculty members lacking in scholarly productivity. Metaphors from the work of such manual laborers as gardeners and janitors surfaced frequently in descriptions of the activities—and the results—expected of writing teachers: planting, cultivating, and pruning; cleaning up, repairing, and polishing. More recently, composition instructors have been given the even more marginal identity of migrant workers—undocumented aliens, border crossers hired to cultivate, pick, and prepare the best in each year's new crop for delivery to more privileged people. (For examples and analyses of such metaphors, see Braddock, Lloyd-Jones, and Schoer; Irmscher; and McQuade, "Case.") In practice, composition studies remains at once labor-intensive and service-oriented.

Because composition studies has traditionally been defined in such negative terms, it is not difficult to understand why so many of our colleagues respond to the allure of literature and seek the academic status associated with it. In one sense, the hierarchical relationship between composition and literature might be viewed as an example of what Alfred North Whitehead, in *Science and the Modern World*, identifies as the fallacy of simple location: the nature of something is equivalent to its place. Applied to the fundamental language (*rank, title, position, tenure, promotion, increment, class*, and the like) and considerations (thoughtfulness in dealing with students, curriculum decisions, salaries, benefits, professional status) of English studies, this line of thinking has informed many of the expectations, performances, and attitudes of those who were—and are—assigned to teach writing. In this respect, it comes as no surprise to note that an important measure of one's professional standing is how quickly one can remove oneself from the burdensome responsibilities of teaching composition and other lower-division courses. The still-operative assumption in many parts of the profession is that the higher one is on the ladder of English studies, the lower the service load one carries each semester. Given this rationale, the reward for ascending to the status of a "distinguished professor" at a "prestigious university" may very well be not having to teach at all.

Institutional stereotypes and myths about composition studies, and about the faculty members and students engaged in its activities, remain difficult to dismantle, despite the extraordinary and often radical advances in scholarship and pedagogy that have marked the discipline over the past quarter-century—from correcting the products students produce to respecting the idiosyncrasies of the various composing processes in which they are engaged, from emphasizing mastery of grammatical rules to establishing practiced confidence and fluency, from requiring students to repeat prescriptive and formulaic exercises to encouraging them to explore the self-expressive potential of writing, from applying "closed" systems of practice based on universals (for example, the five-paragraph theme) to advocating open, relativized approaches to intellectual authority (individual authorship) over subjects and forms, from following precepts to developing percepts as the basis for writing effectively.

Despite the lingering institutional and professional prejudice with which it must contend, composition studies has been transformed over the past few decades from a world in which faculty members and students were at the receiving end of experience to one in which they are closer to its origins, from a world in which people are named and a presence is constructed for them to one in which they seek to shape their own identities and, like Acosta, to create "a name and a language all our own."

## *Composition Studies: Shaping an Identity*

The first appreciable effects of the efforts of those engaged in composition studies to create—from the inside out—a new name and a language for themselves and to identify the distinctive features of their work surfaced during the mid-1960s. By the end of the decade, an ever-increasing and visible number of college and university faculty had chosen to focus their research and scholarly interests on writing and had helped devise an agenda for composition studies that initially could be characterized at least in principle by what Acosta called the "last revolution." Developments in composition research appeared with greater frequency in such journals as *College English* and *College Composition and Communication*; researchers and practitioners started building on and arguing with each other's work in print.[8] The impact of these advances on classroom practice, however, remained uncertain. Yet one point quickly became clear enough: although composition studies had begun to articulate "a new identity" and a "plan" for shaping its own future, the hierarchical power relationship between composition and literature would remain the same—one of professional subservience.

A conference on the teaching of English held at Dartmouth College in 1966 might well be regarded as the occasion that signaled substantive changes in the development and direction of composition studies. Jointly sponsored by the Modern Language Association and the National Council of Teachers of English, these extended conversations involved teachers and scholars from all levels of education and from both sides of the Atlantic, brought together to discuss the state—as well as the future—of English studies. A major outgrowth of the conference appeared in the increasing attention given to the self-expressive purposes of writing. In the years following the Dartmouth meeting, the role of students in the composition curriculum gradually became far more active, their writing more expressive. Composition instruction shifted from repetitive exercises that produced standardized essays with interchangeable parts to a focus on writing as a tool for learning—about oneself and about the world.

The pace of the movement toward a student-centered curriculum accelerated in the late 1960s, largely as a result of the widespread adoption of the instructional principles and practices unfolded by James Moffett in *Teaching the Universe of Discourse* and the curricular application of the research of James Britton and his British colleagues, published in 1975 as *The Development of Writing Abilities (11–18)*. From their analysis of nearly two thousand essays written by British youngsters, Britton and his colleagues named three general categories of writing: *transactional* (communication of information), *poetic* (creation of aesthetic objects), and *expressive* (exploration of ideas and their relation to feelings, intentions, and other forms of knowledge). They argued persuasively that the greater use of expressive writing in the curriculum invites students to participate more energetically and satisfyingly in authoring their own education, in contrast to the insipid, self-protective prose produced in standardized forms of transactional writing, what Ken Macrorie, in *Telling Writing*, dubbed "Engfish."

A surge of first-rate research and scholarship on student writing charged the listless state of composition pedagogy in the late 1960s and early 1970s. Francis Christensen converted his research on the sentence and paragraph structure of professional writers into sound pedagogical advice for teachers seeking innovative ways to improve student writing. Published initially in the late 1960s and reprinted in his *Notes toward a New Rhetoric*, Christensen's articles demonstrated that students could practice what professional writers regularly produced—"cumulative sentences," in which words and phrases are added to modify and to make more complex the main clause through differing levels of abstraction. (In this sense, the structure of paragraphs resembles the cumulative structure of sentences.) James Kinneavy extended Christensen's attention to the shapes of prose in a seminal article entitled "The Basic Aims of Discourse," which became the conceptual core of his still-influential study of composition *A Theory of Discourse*. Kinneavy identified four main types of writing: *referential* (emphasizes the subject), *persuasive* (the effect on the reader), *literary* (the language used), and *expressive* (the writer). Kinneavy's taxonomy of discourse helped establish a firm theoretical footing for composition instruction, widened its range, and clarified its varied purposes.

Building on this solid conceptual base, other researchers and practitioners helped create a new identity for composition studies by shifting the emphasis in its research and pedagogy from correctness to self-articulation and fluency. Macrorie energized instructional practice by challenging the assumptions of an inert, standardized curriculum and posting an ethics of composition. In *Telling Writing* he declared that students would improve their writing if they concentrated on telling the truth about their own experiences. The book provided a detailed pedagogy for instructors to draw on as they helped students express themselves more unequivocally and forcefully, a pedagogy that encouraged students to move from writing regularly in a journal to formulating larger meanings through developing confidence in reading and writing more critically. In 1973, Peter Elbow published *Writing without Teachers*, the most influential—and enduring—challenge to what had been the long-standing tradition of training young writers to display predictable forms of correctness. Elbow urged those who had not determined exactly what they wanted to say before writing to resist editing prematurely; he provided a helpful introduction to "freewriting," a sustained form of nonstop writing that eventually would create an intellectual gravitational field for an essay. Through the process of creating multiple drafts and working in small groups to satisfy the expectations of oneself, fellow writers, and specific genres, young writers could create, Elbow argued, productive, teacherless conditions for writing and reading.

The concepts and instructional practices developed by Moffett, Britton, Christensen, Kinneavy, Macrorie, Elbow, and others were published as a reaction, at least in part, to the traditional emphasis on models and correctness in composition pedagogy. They challenged the prevailing assumptions in the most widely used college textbooks and handbooks on writing during the 1960s, decades-old prescriptive guides to composition that presumed that students had already done a great deal of writing in secondary school but had failed to do it properly—that is, they had not measured up to the standards established for them. Much like the dozens of competitors it outsold, the *Harbrace College Handbook* (which remains the all-time best-selling handbook in composition courses) treated grammar in sociocultural terms: a grammatical mistake was regarded as the failure of a particular voice to meet the demands of a specific social context. As a result, good grammar was often viewed as a matter of good manners, a sign of taste and class distinction. While people sometimes talked as if a grammar didn't exist, grammarians sometimes wrote, as several of the handbooks of the 1960s illustrated, as if people didn't talk. Yet, curiously enough, instruction in writing during the 1960s rarely seemed to funnel or convert the energies and extravagances of conversation, the risk and daring of talk, into the dynamics of composition. Instead, producing models of exemplary behavior in prose remained the aim as well as the habit of much daily instructional practice.

Another aspect of correctness characterized instruction in composition well into the 1970s. Students learned quite early in their academic careers to temper strong expressions of their convictions in order to suit the sensibility of a polite audience. (The specific prohibition, in many schools, of the personal pronoun *I* is another version of this restriction.) In taking the edge off, in rounding out their opinions and judgments, student writers were expected to smooth over conflict, to make it appear as consensus. In effect, composition instruction had been designed to minimize confrontation and to maximize moderation. In "The Politics of Syntax," Jonathan Kozol made a similar point about elementary and secondary school instruction: "The syntax of the school becomes thereby not just a syntax of enforced consensus, but also a syntax of benevolent ideals. The level of pain to which we are permitted access is the level proper to a person who is not in pain—or else who has been trained not to believe that other people are." "There are many adjectives of pity," Kozol noted, "but few verbs of rage, within the dialogue of social justice as defined by text or teacher in the U.S. public schools" (24–25). Surely those of us who taught during the 1960s and 1970s can recall how much of the writing our students produced was toneless, how much of it omitted details and point of view, how much of it sounded voiceless.

Perhaps the most significant development in the collective endeavor to establish an identity and a language for composition research and pedagogy over the past few decades can be traced to the remarkable effort, led by Janet Emig, to demystify the process of composition. Emig studied the writing of eight high school seniors, each of whom composed three essays aloud. Her attention to the intricacies of production, published in 1971 as *The Composing Processes of Twelfth Graders*, provided fresh terms and a new direction for composition studies—away from the products and toward the processes of writing. Emig found that the students' writing could be classified as either reflexive (informal writing focusing on the writer's experience, in multiple drafts, and with the writer as its primary audience) or extensive (more formal prose focusing on information, in fewer drafts, and with the teacher as the primary audience). In the foreword to her study, Emig's work was characterized as "an audacious venture into relatively unexplored territory," for which she was "forced to chart her own course" (v). More than two decades later, the groundwork as well as the bearing Emig established for scholarship in composition studies remains exemplary in every humanistic sense.

Emig's leading composition studies away from analyzing models of excellence toward exploring the "mess" of writing—from an emphasis on thought to thinking—coincided roughly with the development of reliable information about, as well as instructional guides to, various stages of the composing process. As a result of Gordon Rohman's pioneering work on "pre-writing," invention became a much more important—and frequently practiced—aspect of what came to be better understood as the recursive nature of the composing process. Other metaphors were created to describe various dimensions of the composing process, the most prominent of which was the particle-wave-field paradigm described by Richard E. Young, Alton L. Becker, and Kenneth L. Pike. Drawing on scholarship in psychology and linguistics, Young, Becker, and Pike developed a college textbook for writing instruction, *Rhetoric, Discovery, and Change*, which, from all accounts, was rarely used by students in undergraduate courses but remained an influential study among instructors and graduate students interested in the principles of teaching invention and persuasion. The clarity and authority with which these, and other, similarly accomplished researchers and teachers presented their findings underscored the increasing confidence of composition scholars to articulate agendas as well as to venture across disciplinary borders in search of productive professional exchanges.

In their eminently useful *Bedford Bibliography for Teachers of Writing*, Bizzell and Herzberg trace the appearance of terminology from cognitive psychology and psycholinguistics in composition studies back to the early 1970s, when composition researchers deliberately changed the language used to describe composition from the "writing process" to the "composing process." "The significance of this shift," Bizzell and Herzberg explain, was to accentuate the new emphasis in composition studies "on the cognitive activities involved in writing. 'Composing' . . . is what goes on in the writer's head and then is recorded in writing" (5). In *A Conceptual Theory of Rhetoric*, Frank D'Angelo drew on linguistics and cognitive science to demonstrate that rhetorical patterns parallel conceptual structures. Yet the most significant—and still provocative—example of the purposeful adaptation of cognitive science to explanations of the composing process appeared several years later. In "A Cognitive Process Theory of Writing," Linda S. Flower and John R. Hayes developed a "protocol analysis" for examining the choices students make while writing. Flower and Hayes designated three essential elements of the composing process: the *task environment* (external conditions), the *writer's long-term memory* (including knowledge of how to write as well as information about the subject at hand), and the *writing process* as it occurs in the mind. They proceeded to identify three stages in the composing process: the *planning stage* (generating and organizing), the *translating stage* (putting thoughts to paper), and the *reviewing stage* (evaluating and revising).

The diction Flower and Hayes use to highlight the sequential relation between the planning and translating phases of the composing process endorses a well-rooted idea about the relation between thinking and writing. Traceable to classical rhetoric, this venerable idea has dominated virtually all composition instruction ever since: thinking is an internalized, deeply engaging activity, and writing is its external, finished expression. What remains essentially unchallenged in this notion, however, is the hierarchical relation embedded in descriptions of the nature and sequence of these activities. The language we routinely use reinforces this distinction: we speak of our difficulties in "expressing an idea" or "putting our thoughts on paper." The assumption remains that our thoughts exist in some formidable way, in some higher state, before they exist in (that is, before we begin translating them into) words.

Even if we were to grant this assumption, a related question remains unanswered: Do we really know what we want to say before we actually say it? This issue began to capture the attention of cognitive psychologists, psycholinguists, and composition researchers. Flower and Hayes address the question, but take it up only in their account of the third phase of the composing process—the reviewing stage, in which writers evaluate and revise their compositions. While this question continues to elicit research and speculation from those concerned with the relation between mental and verbal behavior, few scholars either within or beyond composition studies seem to have tackled the problem from a more practical point of view: What would be the results if writers assumed that thinking were not a more valued activity than writing but one that could proceed simultaneously with writing? In other words, what would happen if teachers and writers resisted the current sequential and hierarchical connections between thinking and writing by instead thinking in writing? In this respect, consider the wisdom of Gertrude Stein's advice about making meaning in composition: "You will write if you will write without thinking of the results in terms of a result, but think of the writing in terms of discovery, which is to say that creation must take place between the pen and the paper, not before in a thought or afterwards in a recasting. Yes, before in a thought, but not in careful thinking" (38). Stein's attention to the complex link between thinking and writing, process and product, principle and practice, as well as to the discovery of meaning in composing, also characterizes the exemplary research that substantiated an autonomous academic identity for composition studies in recent years.

Mina P. Shaughnessy's research on basic writing remapped the territory of composition studies and provided the English profession with what remains its most incisive and influential analysis of the texts student writers produce. Published as *Errors and Expectations*, Shaughnessy's study of the logic of the errors that marked the placement examinations of nearly three thousand students admitted to the City University of New York under the auspices of its open admissions policy revealed systematic gaps in their knowledge of the traditional structures for composition. Yet she also discovered, in her analysis of the writing samples of these unpracticed writers, patterns in their adaptations of these unfamiliar writing conventions. At the same time, *Errors and Expectations* demonstrated Shaughnessy's extraordinary sensitivity to the pressures and confusions confronting basic writers each time they set out to compose:

> One senses the struggle to fashion out of the fragments of past instruction a system that will relieve the writer of the task of deciding what to do in each instance where alternative forms or conventions stick in the mind. But the task seems too demanding and the rewards too stingy for someone who can step out of a classroom and in a moment be in the thick of conversation with friends.                                    (10)

Shaughnessy argued eloquently—and convincingly—that teachers of writing ought to create frequent opportunities for basic writers to establish more practiced authority over the principles that inform academic writing rather than to continue drilling them in grammatical constructions.

In a curious way, as I trust this passage suggests, Shaughnessy was also sensitive to the pressures and confusions that confronted teachers of writing and, more generally, composition studies in the mid-1970s. Consider, for example, her use of such phrases as "the struggle to fashion out of the fragments of past instruction," "the task of deciding what to do in each instance where alternative forms or conventions stick in the mind," and "the task seems too demanding and the rewards too stingy." These terms strike me as being at least equally applicable to the difficulties of teaching writing during the early years of its development as an independent and respected discipline. In this sense, many students and faculty members who were engaged in composition studies at the time *Errors and Expectations* was published could be said to have established similar goals for themselves—what Shaughnessy describes as efforts "to move across the territory of language as if they had a map and not as if they were being forced to make their way across a mine field" (10).

*Errors and Expectations* remains our profession's most humanistic introduction to the challenges and satisfactions—for students and faculty members—of thinking about basic writing. The book also strengthened and stretched—from the inside out—the reach of research and teaching in composition studies by drawing on the findings of other disciplines in the face of rapidly and radically changing undergraduate demographics: many more students of color; many more first-generation college students; many more from lower- and middle-class working families; many more passive learners, students who were more spectators to educational experiences than participants, more unengaged than their label "disadvantaged" suggested. *Errors and Expectations* addressed directly—and encouragingly—such issues as the linguistic and sociocultural identities and resources of these students as well as the teaching materials and strategies needed to respond adequately to their backgrounds and interests. By creating a vocabulary and a set of metaphors to talk about and to these students, Shaughnessy better prepared teachers of writing to provide these students access to the conventions and expectations of academic discourse. In every sense, *Errors and Expectations* exemplified the professional dignity of scholarship and research in composition, underscored what is at stake in that work, established a scholarly standard for it, and set a direction for a great deal of the scholarship and practice that followed it.

At the time of Shaughnessy's death, in 1978, composition studies had already done much to articulate—and in several instances to refine—a new, and self-determined, agenda for research and pedagogy, one in which scholarly achievement overshadowed the expectations generated by any externally imposed "plan" or identity. Yet much more remained to be accomplished: debates over principles and priorities needed to occur. And from all accounts, many composition researchers and practitioners were eager to begin such discussions and to enter into them with a shared commitment to pursuing "process," an approach to composition studies that depended on at least a willingness, and perhaps even a firm resolve, to recognize and respect difference—in all of its racial, cultural, professional, and compositional reverberations.

By the early 1980s, the findings of numerous research projects on the various ways in which writers compose were widely circulated and gradually adapted to classroom practice. The most notable of these were Sondra Perl's "Understanding Composing" and Nancy Sommers's "Revision Strategies of Student Writers and Experienced Adult Writers," published in the same issue (December 1980) of *College Composition and Communication*. Both articles described—and demonstrated—the recursive nature of the writing process, and Sommers's established the terms of our understanding of what writers do when they revise and of the way revising, as a recursive activity, differs in substantive ways from correcting and editing. Sommers concluded that student writers revise "locally," adding, deleting, or rearranging words and phrases. Experienced writers, however, revise in "global" terms, reworking form and adding, deleting, or rearranging sentences and paragraphs to establish greater control over their prose as well as to accommodate the knowledge and expectations of their readers.

Shaughnessy's commitment to helping basic writers gain access to academic discourse soon became the focal point for the work of a new generation of composition scholars. The most significant publications on this subject emerged from the work of Patricia Bizzell, David Bartholomae, and Mike Rose. In the first of these, "Cognition, Convention, and Certainty," Bizzell extended and enriched Shaughnessy's findings by identifying—and characterizing—the two principal theoretical lines informing recent composition research, with special attention to the ways in which these theories describe the difficulties students face as they write. The "inner-directed theorists" (such as Flower and Hayes) focused, Bizzell explained, on the internal and "universal, fundamental structures of thought and language" and on the strategies students can employ to develop the cognitive skills that enable them to write. Bizzell argued that the separation of thinking from writing in the inner-directed model overemphasizes the students' deficiencies and ignores the knowledge and sensitivity to context they bring to composing activities. In contrast, the "outer-directed theorists" concentrate on "the social processes whereby language-learning and thinking capacities are shaped by particular communities. . . . The staple activity of outer-directed writing instruction will be analysis of the conventions of particular discourse communities." In their attention to the dialectical relation between language and thought in such matters as convention, the outer-directed theorists regard students' unfamiliarity with the conventions of particular discourse communities as the principal cause of their compositional difficulties. The solution to this dilemma would be to "demystify the conventions of the academic discourse community" (218) by teaching those traditional forms in composition courses.

In "Inventing the University" Bartholomae assessed the interpretive conventions and authoritative personas that inexperienced writers must master in order to sound like experts in their academic writing. In effect, Bartholomae's essay analyzed the errors basic writers make as they struggle to approximate "the commonplaces, set phrases, rituals and gestures, habits of mind, tricks of persuasion, obligatory conclusions and necessary connections" that mark the discourse of knowledge and power in academic communities (146). This essay served as part of the conceptual foundation for *Facts, Artifacts, and Counterfacts* in which Bartholomae and Anthony R. Petrosky posited a theory as well as a curriculum for integrating reading, writing, and critical thinking—based on the conviction that the most effective way to help students develop the intellectual abilities required for academic work is to engage them in extended conversations with some of the most powerful voices of academic culture.

In the wake of Shaughnessy's work and in many instances inspired by it, writing researchers and teachers began to change the professional identity of composition studies in substantive terms—from being subject *to* literary studies to becoming a subject *for* scholarly inquiry and speculation in its own right. Rose's work stands out among the most notable of many efforts to create an independent identity for composition studies. In "The Language of Exclusion" he demonstrated that the terms used to portray writing instruction (*error, skill, remediation, illiteracy*, and the like) underscore the marginal position of composition in the academy and relegate the faculty members and students engaged in its activities to the status of second-class citizens in what should be a democratic, egalitarian community of inquiry. Challenging the assumptions embedded in such terminology, Rose called for a more respectful view of the enabling work of composition studies, one that more accurately—and responsibly—describes the teaching and learning of writing. He extended his analysis of basic writing in "Remedial Writing Courses." In *Lives on the Boundary* Rose unpacked—and expanded on—the argument of this essay in a series of compelling vignettes from his own life both as an "underprepared" student and as a teacher of those identified in such debilitating terms.

## *Composition Studies: Interdisciplinary Approaches*

Recognizing the necessity to understand the specific needs and resources of inexperienced writers prompted many composition researchers, scholars, and practitioners to broaden the scope of their thinking about writing by drawing on the work of other disciplines. In this respect, Shaughnessy's scholarship had an additional indelible impact on composition studies: it encouraged and authorized interdisciplinary work by creating a standard for the results of such inquiry. Although grounded in literary studies, her work reached far beyond it for applicable speculation and knowledge. The work of M. L. J. Abercrombie provides one example. Shaughnessy adapted to the instructional purposes of writing teachers the principles outlined in Abercrombie's *Anatomy of Judgment*, which described the curricular efforts to improve the diagnostic skills of medical students in England. Shaughnessy found Abercrombie's work on the collaborative techniques of small-group diagnoses and decisions "useful to the writing teacher in pointing up the social aspects of thinking, the conditions under which people are most likely to get ideas." In the company of an ever-widening circle of colleagues, Shaughnessy read broadly in such areas as anthropology, psychology, language acquisition, educational and literacy studies—as well as the work of, among others, Christensen, Elbow, Emig, Kinneavy, and Moffett—to understand the composing process and the situation of the language learner. She appended an annotated list of these "borrowings," as she called them, to *Errors and Expectations* as a "place" where others could "begin in a field where almost everything remains to be done" (298).

A sense of urgency characterized the development of composition studies—in both intellectual and institutional terms. In such circumstances, drawing on the most productive research in other disciplines was not a luxury but an intellectual and practical necessity, especially in view of the rapidly changing demographics of undergraduate education. Composition scholars and practitioners frequently crossed the borders of other disciplines in search of productive conversation and research that might assist them in their own work. For example, Ann E. Berthoff helped sharpen the terms and strengthen the quality of the debate over principles and practice in composition studies by viewing the teaching of writing in philosophical terms. In *The Making of Meaning* and *The Sense of Learning*, Berthoff drew on the work of, among others, William James, Charles Sanders Peirce, I. A. Richards (especially *Philosophy of Rhetoric*), and Susanne K. Langer (particularly *Philosophy in a New Key*) to engage in what she characterized as "casual harangues and serious polemic" on such matters as "the role of the teacher as researcher, the definition of pedagogy, theories of meaning and meaning-making, the nature of perception, images of composing, models of process, writing across the curriculum, and writing as a way of knowing and a mode of learning" (*Making* v). Teachers of writing could assess their interest in particular principles soon enough: How well did each yield appreciable results? How well did it work to improve student writing?

Classroom applications of literacy studies offer another example of the relation of composition studies to the work of other disciplines. With the publication of *Pedagogy of the Oppressed* and *Cultural Action for Freedom*, Paulo Freire became a presence in composition studies and, more specifically, in discussions of literacy issues within the context of political oppression. Freire's argument—that it is not education that shapes society but society that shapes education to accommodate the interests of those in control—had a major impact both on subsequent literacy studies and on strategies for developing a set of cultural practices (what he calls "critical consciousness") to teach writing, practices designed to promote emancipatory and democratic change. To note but two of numerous examples of Freire's influence: Berthoff explores Freire's concept of a "pedagogy of knowing" in *The Sense of Learning*; Ira Schor presents thirteen curricular applications of Freire's principles in *Freire for the Classroom*.

In a strikingly different approach to literacy issues, the anthropologist and linguist Shirley Brice Heath has provided numerous insightful readings of the sociocultural contexts for composition. Her study of the socially constructed patterns of oral and written language use in three Carolina communities, *Ways with Words*, enriched our understanding of the cultural circumstances within which writers function; it set a direction, tone, and standard of excellence for subsequent discussions of the interdisciplinary dimensions of "literacy," a highly contested and problematic term both within the academy and in the public discourse about education. Other studies of literacy, including the work of the psychologists Sylvia Scribner and Michael Cole, reflected, in turn, the influence of Lev Vygotsky's *Thought and Language*, which explored the cognitive processes and social conditions that govern the link between thought and language. The multiple perspectives brought to bear on the recent controversy within composition studies over the orality-literacy dichotomy highlights another example of what has increasingly become the interdisciplinary nature of composition theory, scholarship, and pedagogy. (For an insightful discussion of this topic, see the Fall–Winter 1986 issue of *Pre/Text*, esp. Daniell's article, "Against the Great Leap Theory." See also Ong; Brandt; and Lunsford, Moglen, and Slevin.)

Productive dialogue with colleagues in other disciplines soon carried over into collaborative activities in the classroom, which became a site—and eventually a center—for research on and applications of small-group learning. In "The Brooklyn Plan: Attaining Intellectual Growth through Peer-Group Tutoring," Kenneth A. Bruffee articulated an early version of what became an influential idea about making meaning through negotiation and agreement in writing courses. He refined the rationale for this approach in "Collaborative Learning and the 'Conversation of Mankind,'" in which he drew on the work of William G. Perry in *Intellectual and Ethical Development in the College Years*, Stanley Fish in *Is There a Text in This Class?* and especially Richard

Rorty in *Philosophy and the Mirror of Nature* to argue that knowledge is socially constructed through "conversation" in a discourse community and that students can develop knowledge through various forms of collaborative learning. In "The Structure of Knowledge and the Future of Liberal Education," Bruffee challenged the long-standing assumption that knowledge is best secured by individual effort in a fundamentally hierarchical educational system. Citing the contributions of Einstein, the physicist Werner Karl Heisenberg, and the mathematician Kurt Gödel, he asserted that, because knowledge can be generated—and disseminated—through social activities, education ought to provide more opportunities for students to engage in such collaborative activities as peer-editing and what came to be known as "writing across the curriculum."[9]

The principles underpinning the pedagogical forms of collaboration developed within and for the composition curriculum were later extended to new concepts of peer interaction and cooperation. The most significant changes in the curriculum included a workshop approach to teaching writing, made most prominently by Donald M. Murray. In *A Writer Teaches Writing* this Pulitzer Prize–winning journalist and teacher provided a wealth of sensible—and classroom-tested—advice on virtually every aspect of teaching writing: from offering an insightful overview of the writing process to designing syllabi and responding effectively to student writing. An outgrowth of the workshop approach, such instructional support services as writing centers established a conceptual and an operational base—as well as an institutional identity—of their own. More recent advances in the instructional uses of computers and compositional networks also reflect commitments to collaborative principles. (See Holdstein; Holdstein and Selfe. Selfe edits *Computers and Composition*, a journal published three times a year by Michigan Technological University.)

Extending the collaborative uses of writing into the discourse conventions of other disciplines reinforced the conceptual and instructional links between composition and the research taking place in those areas. The early applications of the principles of writing across the curriculum derive principally from the work of Britton and his colleagues, whose curriculum project, directed by Nancy Martin, is described in *Writing and Learning across the Curriculum 11–16*. In this country, the writing-across-the-curriculum movement received its earliest—and most articulate—advocacy in the work of Elaine Maimon and her colleagues at Beaver College, as well as in the programmatic initiatives encouraged by Toby Fulwiler, Art Young, and their colleagues at Michigan Technological University. In numerous articles, textbooks, and collections of essays, Maimon, Fulwiler, and many others led a concerted effort not only to resituate the composing process within the discourse conventions of disciplines other than English but also to shift the instructional uses of writing—from serving as an instrument to measure student mastery of course content to functioning as a means to encourage and enrich learning.

## The Professionalization of Composition Studies

By the early 1990s, composition studies had developed into one of the most interdisciplinary areas of humanistic scholarship and inquiry. The next several years offer composition studies myriad opportunities to consolidate the remarkable achievements of the past few decades. Evidence of the increased interest in—and professionalization of—writing research and classroom practice is everywhere to be seen. The Teaching of Writing Division now contains the second largest membership roll in the Modern Language Association. The Conference on College Composition and Communication (CCCC), the national organization dedicated specifically to serving the professional interests and needs of teachers of writing, has enjoyed sustained growth in membership throughout the past quarter-century, and attendance at its annual meeting has risen steadily and substantially. The CCCC can now boast that it enjoys the highest percentage of membership attendance at its annual meeting of any professional organization in the humanities. (The nearly four thousand participants in the 1990 meeting in Chicago constituted more than fifty percent of CCCC's total individual membership.) It is not surprising that with such an active membership, the ratio of proposal acceptance to rejection for the CCCC convention program (approximately 1:9) now ranks at, or very near, the top of the list of the most competitive in the humanities.

There has also been an impressive increase in the number and quality of bibliographies, publishing enterprises, graduate programs, and journals devoted to research and scholarship in composition. The first major effort to create a reasonably comprehensive bibliography for composition studies was led by Gary Tate, who edited *Teaching Composition: Ten Bibliographic Essays* (1976), revised and enlarged in 1987 as *Teaching Composition: Twelve Bibliographic Essays*. Virtually single-handedly, Richard L. Larson prepared an annotated bibliography of books and articles related to composition and published several annual installments in *College Composition and Communication*. Erika Lindemann has coordinated the publication of three volumes in the *Longman Bibliography of Composition and Rhetoric*, an invaluable scholarly tool now published for CCCC by Southern Illinois University Press and edited by Gail Hawisher and Cynthia Selfe. Bizzell and Herzberg have recently prepared the third edition of *The Bedford Bibliography for Teachers of Writing*, a remarkably full, informative, and yet compact guide to the important work "for those who wish to extend their knowledge in this prospering discipline, knowledge that is essential for teaching English in colleges today" (iii). During the past decade, first-rate graduate programs in composition studies—including those at the University of Pittsburgh, Ohio State, University of Southern California, New Hampshire, Rensselaer Polytechnic, and Texas—have flourished, along with such research facilities and teacher networks as the National Center for the Study of Writing and Literacy and the National Writing Project, both housed at the University of California, Berkeley. So, too, the number of monographs published, promoted, and sold by Oxford University Press, Southern Illinois University Press, Random House, Prentice-Hall, Peter Lang, NCTE, and the MLA has risen dramatically. There is clearly no shortage of outstanding—and significant—manuscripts on virtually every aspect of composition studies.

In addition to such major periodicals as *College Composition and Communication* and *College English*, each with impressive records of publishing much of the important work in composition studies, several newer journals—among others, *Pre/Text, Rhetoric Review*, and *Written Communication*—have provided attractive professional venues for disseminating the high-quality research and speculation that continues to emerge from every part of the nation. In addition, more specialized periodicals—such as the *Journal of Basic Writing, Journal of Advanced Composition, Computers and Composition, WPA: Writing Program Administration*, and the *Writing Center Journal*—have earned wide readerships. The pages of these periodicals highlight the ongoing professional debate over long-standing as well as more recent issues and concerns in composition studies, including research on the composing process, basic writing, the history of rhetoric, the relations of composition with literature and rhetoric, and such relatively new areas of inquiry as feminist and cultural studies, computers and composition, and writing across the curriculum. In their contributions to these journals, scholars and teachers respond imaginatively and responsibly to changing student demographics, develop strategies for retaining minority students, and grapple with the need for equitable terms and conditions of employment, especially for those of our colleagues who are hired to teach part-time.[10] These various publishing venues for productive work in composition celebrate the results of intellectual risk taking and demonstrate that access, excellence, and diversity are fully compatible—in principle and in practice.

Composition studies has continued to broaden and deepen gradually rather than rapidly shift the focus of its professional interests. Its recent scholarship and pedagogy have demonstrated, for example, far greater sensitivity to issues of race, class, gender, and ideology than in earlier years. The work of James Berlin on the contested history of writing instruction; Linda Brodkey on authority and the construction of the self ("On the Subjects"); Joseph Harris on the conflicting voices within discourse communities; Susan Miller on rescuing instruction from its dependence on canonical, "major" texts; Patricia Harkin and John Schilb on the discursive formation of knowledge in postmodern class-rooms; Judith Summerfield and Geoffrey Summerfield on the social contexts for composition—as well as collections of essays edited by John Bullock and John Trimbur on the politics of writing instruction and by Cynthia Caywood and Gillian Overing on the relations of feminist scholarship and composition studies—represent a few of the many insightful views of issues that confront teachers and students of writing each time they open or close the door to their classroom or office. In this sense, composition studies had continued to build (by aggregation rather than substitution) on the advances in its collective thinking—from product to process to the social and material conditions and contexts for composition. Because pedagogical visions routinely collide with ethical, political, and cultural values in the daily activities of composition studies, its classrooms may well be best situated, as Gerald Graff, in *Professing Literature*, urges, to teach the conflicts. (For a differing view of the stakes involved in teaching the conflicts, see Fish, "Common Touch.") Whether composition teachers make creative use of the methodological and cultural controversies that polarize departments, the classes they teach will continue to function as the dynamic locus as well as the final arbiter of the intellectual risks they take and of the principles, practices, and values they profess and teach.

## Again and Still: Composition versus Literature

I have drawn a distinction between "professing" and "teaching" here to underscore what remains the fundamental difference in the ways in which many of our colleagues in English gauge progress and reform in literary as opposed to composition studies. Progress and reform are most visible in a changed curriculum for literary studies and in a different pedagogy for composition.[11] Yet I would like to reexamine this distinction and note that it blurs another important difference—between a curriculum for literary studies that is conceptually and operationally professor-centered (a literature curriculum conceived for individual exercise of initiative and power) and a curriculum *and* a pedagogy for composition studies that are, in principle and practice, necessarily student-centered (a curriculum and a pedagogy conceived as training in skills for powerlessness—for adaptive rather than originative behavior). It may be the class difference embedded in this distinction between an emphasis on faculty rather than on students—whatever the similarities or differences in their socioeconomic status—that is at the bottom of the muffled rift in English studies in American higher education, "muffled" because issues of class are ones that we as professionals, and the nation as a whole, find it difficult to acknowledge.

In any case, I would like to suggest that the institutional and intellectual resources traditionally vested in the distinction between emphasizing curriculum and emphasizing pedagogy lie at the root of the historical—and the current—tensions between literary studies and composition. This uneasy relation has been exacerbated in recent years by the increasing pressure exerted by institutional authorities on the budgets, working conditions, enrollments, and professional dignity and terms of advancement imposed on each. The issue of the institutional legitimacy of writing centers and student support services will not be readily acceded to by all readers of this volume; in times of reduced budgets many faculty members view the activities these units provide as expendable. These tensions erupted into controversy when Maxine Hairston called public attention to them in her Chair's Address at the 1985 CCCC convention. Her remarks, published subsequently in *College Composition and Communication*, invoked the language of troubled domestic relations and marital disputes: teachers of composition are relegated to the inferior positions of battered wives, victims of unrequited love, abused domestics, and minorities treated arrogantly and imperiously.

Likening the circumstances of teachers of writing to those in the histories of women and minorities, Hairston urges that writing teachers "must pay attention to what our inner selves tell us, find our own values and listen to our own voices—values and voices that are not against someone else, but for ourselves" (278). After considering several equally unattractive options, however, Hairston recommends that teachers of writing separate and in fact divorce themselves from what she calls "the patriarchal hierarchy of English departments" and act on "our most radical option . . . to petition to split the composition and rhetoric program from the English department and form a department of rhetoric" (280). "Perhaps we should even consider," she notes, "joining with speech communication and journalism to form a new and vital department of language and communication, and once more make humanism and rhetoric relevant in our modern society" (281). To this day, the dispute remains unresolved. While the terms of the divorce have yet to be litigated and the prospects of reconciliation remain dim, the resentments and resistances on both sides—only occasionally and begrudgingly acknowledged—continue to smolder.

A few years earlier, several prominent figures from the worlds of composition, literature, and rhetoric—including Frederick Crews, J. Hillis Miller, Walter J. Ong, Wayne Booth, Robert Scholes, and Elaine Maimon—conducted an informative and provocative conversation in print (gathered under the title *Composition and Literature: Bridging the Gap*, edited by Winifred Bryan Horner) in which they explored the conceptual and pedagogical ties between composition and literature. In that same year, Richard Lanham made a compelling case, in *Literacy and the Survival of Humanism*, for the need to reconcile the study of literature and composition through a focus on the principles and practices of humanistic inquiry they share. Seeking to "keep the teaching of literature and the teaching of composition in some kind of humane relationship with each other" (ix), Lanham drew on the "post-Darwinian synthesis" in the biological and social sciences to create a curriculum for literature and composition at the University of California, Los Angeles, that works from "the inside out," as "a training in self-conscious motive, and not, as with a list of set texts that 'guarantee' liberation, from the outside in" (9).

Marie Ponsot and Rosemary Deen, working at the same time but in a rather different institutional setting (City University of New York), made the notion of proceeding pedagogically from the inside out not only possible but quite plausible. In *Beat Not the Poor Desk* Ponsot and Deen provided an engaging introduction to a remarkably successful, error-free pedagogy that makes writing the primary activity in the composition classroom and the literary elements of student writing one of the principal aims of reading. Ponsot and Deen's classroom-tested inductive approach to teaching composition and literature emphasizes prolific writing and reading, as well as abundant practice in such literary structures as the fable and parable, as a means to appreciate and practice the various shapes of exposition. In a more poststructuralist vein, Scholes assesses, in *Textual Power*, what concepts of textuality offer to teachers and students of literature and composition. He argues for a shift from a canon-based curriculum to one in textual studies, a move that focuses on the notion of textual power—as it emerges in the reader's struggle with the text and the writer's struggle with the world.

The work of Northrop Frye provided an important precedent for the admirable efforts of Lanham and Scholes, and especially Ponsot and Deen, to "bridge the gap" between composition and literature. In a series of six radio broadcasts for the Canadian Broadcasting Corporation entitled "The Massey Lectures" and later published as *The Educated Imagination*, Frye explored the "values" and "uses" of literature in what was then labeled "a new scientific age." In the fifth of these lectures, Frye presented a refreshingly incisive view of the relations between literature and composition as well as a provocative critique of our profession's traditional efforts to lead students from mastery of compositional skills to practiced knowledge of "classic" works of literature and the rigors of literary analysis:

> In every properly taught subject, we start at the center and work outwards. To try to teach literature by starting with the applied use of words, or "effective communication," as it's often called, then gradually work into literature through the more documentary forms of prose fiction and finally into poetry, seems to me a futile procedure. If literature is to be properly taught, we have to start at its center, which is poetry, then work outward to literary prose, then

outward from there to the applied languages of business and professions and ordinary life. Poetry is the most direct and simple means of expressing oneself in words: the most primitive nations have poetry, but only quite well developed civilizations can produce good prose.                                            (121)

Most, if not all, of us who teach composition and literature endorse, routinely, a set of pedagogical assumptions and practices that work from the outside in—from, in effect, composition to literature. Most English departments provide students with intense and extended instruction in the "basic skills" of writing and reading, with the hope that such instruction will encourage, if not inspire, these students to study literature. Frye advocates a pedagogy that would reverse that emphasis—one that would encourage students to move from literature out to what he calls "literary prose" and the "applied languages."

In choosing to invoke this provocative statement from a distinguished literary critic whose work, lamentably, seems to be moving closer to the periphery, if not settling into the shadows of current literary debate, I do not endorse the distinction he draws between "literature" and the "applied arts." My intention is simply to underscore the benefits—for students and faculty members—of inverting the relation between composition and literature, of remapping the continuum to include student writing. Such an approach, however, does not solve the problem: the fundamentally hierarchical link between literature and composition persists. Whether Frye situates literature at the center or at the edges of humanistic inquiry and pedagogy, he assumes that literature occupies a position irrevocably superior to that of composition. Much as was the case with "active" and "contemplative," "creative" and "connective," a hierarchical distinction informs the continuum between such binary terms as *literature* and *composition*, particularly student writing.

As the passage from Frye highlights, addressing the hierarchical relation between literature and composition can no longer be simply a matter of drawing, or redrawing, boundaries but must also involve an effort to reconceptualize the fundamental features of each—reimagining *each* from the inside out. By examining both composition and literature from the inside out, we may discover what they have in common. Doing so offers English studies perhaps its best opportunity to recognize, for example, that these two seemingly disparate worlds share a human desire—the stubborn itch to think in writing in enduring ways.

At the same time, we need to resist any inclination to gloss over or homogenize the differences between composition and literature, much in the manner, and no doubt with what would be the same deleterious effects, as, say, the term *Hispanic*, as an institutional and governmental category, erases the distinctions between and among the cultures and behaviors of Mexicans, Puerto Ricans, and Venezuelans. As Catharine Stimpson reminds us in her

1990 presidential address to the MLA, "We must refuse to reduce complex intellectual movements to single words and then to belittle the movements through ritualistic evocations of the words. Obvious examples are the misuse of *feminist* and *theory*. Once the example might have been *comp*" ("On Difference" 409). In this sense, composition studies literalizes the concept of—as well as the clash over—difference and cultural otherness. In the process, composition studies converts multiplicity into an epistemology.

In order to recognize similarities and to acknowledge the differences between composition and literature, we may well need, as Acosta reminds us, a new name and a new language. Reexamining—and perhaps reconfiguring— the borders between and among composition, literary criticism, and rhetoric might well begin with an effort to demystify the very terms used to chart these intersections. Consider, for example, the pedagogical and institutional implications of the prevailing metaphor in postsecondary education: "fields" of knowledge. While "fields" in principle is no doubt intended to suggest intellectual expanses, cognitive terrain to be charted and cultivated, in practice it more often works negatively to suggest boundaries, enclosures, intellectual barriers—boxed knowledge. This metaphor supports, finally, an isolated, insulated view of scholarship, pedagogy, and learning.

Within each field, conversation is basically possible between what William Carlos Williams called "specialists in a certain pen" (*Embodiment* 46). Consider how the conversations within different disciplines are becoming increasingly difficult as the language of each becomes increasingly specialized, self-referential, and virtually enclosed. The situation proves especially problematic for students, who in many instances must master the vocabulary and nuances of such languages *before* they can talk to their instructors about their work. And, in the light of the proliferation of specialized languages, many students have neither the time, the intellectual energy, nor the coping strategies to do so. Talking to faculty members and student majors in disciplines different from our own may well resemble, as Maimon has noted, the potential awkwardness and embarrassment of talking to strangers. The community of inquiry that should constitute a college or a university has become increasingly fragmented, atomistic, and often contentious intellectual cells. Under such circumstances it is not surprising that undergraduates often talk about their time to degree in the language of prisons ("How long do you have to go?" "When do you get out?" "What time are you free?") and illness ("What do you have this semester?"), as though their courses were sentences and diseases they had to learn to endure.

The metaphor of "fields," when applied to knowledge, may also bear in it terms of inferiority, if not intimidation. The word might carry the suggestion that students—and faculty members—view themselves as incomplete, and perhaps even inadequate. Implicit in the metaphor is the myth that scholarship will lead us eventually to a time when we will understand everything about an area. But a field of knowledge is not a static area but rather a dynamic locus—a focus—in which the processes of change, growth, and development are ever present. In this respect, knowledge of a field does not exist at the end of scholarship, at the end of an education, but infuses every aspect of it. If knowledge is a process, an ongoing activity, then our conceptions of both fields of learning and our places in them will be characterized by mysteries, doubts, and uncertainties. Knowledge is not an escape from ignorance—as if knowledge were an enclosed field whose fence we had to climb over in order to arrive at knowing. It is, instead, a getting to (an acquisitiveness) as well as a positing (a reading of experience). "Knowledge" is, finally, like "education," "composition," "literature," and "culture," a noun in process—a process of establishing relations, of mapping interconnections, of crossing borders, of constantly redrawing boundaries (see also McDermott; Miles). We need equally processive—rather than "boxed"—language to think productively about such activities. We need to view "field" as a locus, as a site for growth and cultivation (from the medieval Latin *cultivare*). To do so, we need to recover the experience (and hence the metaphors) of *primary production*. Literature and composition are primary forms of cultural production. Positional and spatial metaphors inhibit and complicate such discussion.

Teachers of composition and literature have an ethical obligation to students to resist metaphors and definitions of literature that grant privileged status to certain texts and perforce exclude others. We ought no longer to accept definitions of literature that are based on exclusivity, on deliberate acts of omission. In this respect, I agree with Terry Eagleton's observation in *Literary Theory*: "When I use the words 'literary' and 'literature,'" he explains, "I place them under an invisible crossing-out mark, to indicate that these terms will not really do but that we have no better ones at the moment" (11). Eagleton's comment recalls a similar observation by Rorty, who argues, in *Philosophy and the Mirror of Nature*, that critics should assume no general or a priori truths about the nature of literature and language. Teachers of writing need to participate more vigorously in the crucial debates about what constitutes literature. The relative absence of the voices of composition teachers in these spirited discussions tacitly endorses, however inadvertently, the fundamental academic class distinction between composition and literature, between writing and belles lettres.

Let me offer two democratic propositions to balance the belief in the hierarchical position of literature: an act of composition constitutes one of the most important forms of nonviolent individual empowerment in late twentieth-century America; the essay is the most egalitarian form of literature we have. If the essay represents our most democratic form of literature, then it is also the most democratic in terms of its subject matter, structure, and readership.

It seems, however, that it is precisely because anyone can write an essay that it has been so effectively removed from the twentieth-century literary canon. Since the early decades of the twentieth century, the essay has been relegated to the marginalized position as a secondary source. A related proposition now seems appropriate: we need to reclaim for literature *and* composition the essay's identity as a primary form of literature—both in principle and in editorial and classroom practice. As soon as the essay as a primary form of composition and literature has been reaffirmed, then those of us who teach composition and literature can relax into the knowledge that all of what we teach deserves the same respectful attention previously reserved for literature.

An even more radical redefinition of what constitutes the literary now seems in order: it must account for—and include—student writing. I would recommend that composition teachers approach the writing their students do with the same attitude(s) with which they respond to literature. There are several decided advantages to doing so. Literary study is informed by an enormously important assumption: no one does it wrong. That assumption does not preclude the judgment, however, that some writers are more accomplished than others, but it does suggest that, in the world of literature, right and wrong are not as important as the sustained ability of a writer's performance with language. In effect, I am recommending that teachers of composition and literature identify for their students as soon as feasible the continuum from composition to literature—not in hierarchical terms but through descriptions of the processes involved—and that students be encouraged to locate, however provisionally, their own work along the continuum of composition and literature. I'd also recommend that students be encouraged as early as possible to recognize, explore, and develop those features of their writing that connect both ends of the continuum.

The crisis in the class-bound hierarchical relation between composition and literature is not simply an issue of self-representation, of how one's voice and self are prefabricated subjects, but also a matter of survival—of individual voices. In this respect, our culture cannot bear the literal and figurative disappearance of such distinctive voices as that of Acosta. And given the socioeconomic, political, and cultural deprivation that haunts so many dimensions of contemporary American life, the risks seem more urgent—and the stakes higher—than ever before. As the competition for decreasing institutional resources intensifies in the leaner years ahead, teaching and scholarship in composition studies will figure prominently in the debates about budgetary priorities, about what colleges and universities can "afford." I trust that I am not exaggerating when I note that "service" traditionally absorbs the brunt of fiscal reductions. In the conservative "retrenchment" that looms before us, composition teachers and scholars must be alert to the dangers of arguing from the other side—that their work is exceptional. Viewed from that perspective, the discoveries in, about, and of composition might be ascribed, ironically, the status of expendable student-indulging "luxuries." Without encouraging and actively assisting all of our students to write and read prolifically and to understand the nature of their own productivity and authority in relation to these acts—as their contributions to public, civic, and productive aspects of verbal culture—we may find ourselves, along with our students, in far more harrowing circumstances, struggling to express our individual and collective identities in what Freire calls the "culture of silence."[12]

### Notes

[1]For an incisive account of the similarly divided world of contemporary art and of the border crossings in it, see Gomez-Pena, "Documented/Undocumented."

[2]For additional bibliographic references for primary and secondary sources on the history of the relations of literature and rhetoric, see *Historical Rhetoric* and *The Present State of Scholarship in Historical and Contemporary Rhetoric*, both edited by Horner.

[3]Berlin and Inkster analyze the principles—as well as the consequences—of privileging instruction in exposition, in "Current-Traditional Rhetoric: Paradigm and Practice."

[4]For an account of the history of speech communication as an academic discipline, see *Speech Communication in the 20th Century*, ed. Benson. Graff offers an insightful history of literary studies in *Professing Literature*. Berlin provides an engaging history of writing pedagogy in *Writing Instruction in Nineteenth-Century American Colleges* and *Rhetoric and Reality*.

[5]There are striking parallels between the efforts to make writing more efficient and the development of both New Criticism and analytic philosophy, which received one of its earliest—and most important—cumulative expressions in Ayer's *Language, Truth, and Logic*. This movement toward positivism and principles of verification aimed at making philosophy more efficient in both its focus and its procedures. For example, in the years following World War II, Ayer, Wittgenstein, and Bertrand Russell articulated a far more efficient vision of ordinary language, in which each sentence remains important to the extent that it can be broken down into particular sense data. Failing that, all other sentences are emotive, and therefore poetic. Whatever the intentions of its founders, New Criticism might be viewed as the literary counterpart of analytic philosophy. Both eliminate context, regarding it as a basic encumbrance on analysis. So, too, it strikes me as no mere coincidence that the rise of quantitative analysis in the social sciences, and especially in social and political analysis, also surfaces during this period.

[6]The work of Bakhtin, less well known then, and more influential now, addressed many of the same issues, but without any attention to their rhetorical origins or consequences. See *Marxism and the Philosophy of Language*.

[7]In 1967, NCTE began publishing *Research in the Teaching of English*. This report, published quarterly, presents findings on a wide range of topics in composition and in a variety of settings.

[8]Throughout the essay, I have resisted applying the word *theory* to composition studies, principally because the term is imbued with class distinctions that capitalize on a genteel value system, one that privileges the aesthetic and the general.

[9]For a comprehensive treatment of one aspect of the instructional consequences of the principles of collaborative learning, see Gere.

[10]The issue of creating professional and equitable terms and conditions for employment for part-time teachers of writing gained national attention with the publication of the "Wyoming Resolution," drafted by Robertson, Crowley, and Lentricchia. This resolution, passed unanimously at the 1987 business meeting of CCCC, coincided with the creation of the Committee on Professional Standards for Quality Education. The committee published an initial report entitled "CCCC Initiatives on the Wyoming Conference Resolution: A Draft Report." A revised version was published as the CCCC Executive Committee's "Statement of Principles and Standards for the Postsecondary Teaching of Writing." More recently, the Committee on Professional Standards published an update on its work: "A Progress Report from the CCCC Committee on Professional Standards." The committee found support for its work in the report issued by the MLA Commission on Writing and Literature, which developed helpful guidelines for assessing scholarship and service in composition studies. See "Report of the Commission on Writing and Literature."

[11]I am indebted to Steven Mailloux for drawing this incisive distinction during a public conversation at the MLA-sponsored ADE Summer Seminar at Claremont College, 1991.

[12]For their encouragement and assistance in preparing various drafts of this essay, I would like to thank Mitchell Breitwieser, Anne Middleton, Miles Myers, and Kathleen Moran.

## Selected Bibliography

Bartholomae, David. "Inventing the University." *When a Writer Can't Write: Studies in Writer's Block and Other Composing Process Problems*. Ed. Mike Rose. New York: Guilford, 1985. 134–66.

Berthoff, Ann E. *The Making of Meaning: Metaphors, Models, and Maxims for Writing Teachers*. Upper Montclair: Boynton, 1981.

Bizzell, Patricia. "Cognition, Convention, and Certainty: What We Need to Know about Writing." *Pre/Text* 3 (1982): 213–43.

Bizzell, Patricia, and Bruce Herzberg, eds. *The Rhetorical Tradition*. Boston: Bedford, 1990.

Britton, James, et al. *The Development of Writing Abilities (11–18)*. London: Macmillan, 1975.

Bruffee, Kenneth A. "The Brooklyn Plan: Attaining Intellectual Growth through Peer-Group Tutoring." *Liberal Education* 64 (1978): 447–69.

Christensen, Francis. *Notes toward a New Rhetoric: Nine Essays for Teachers*. Ed. Bonniejean Christensen. 2nd ed. New York: Harper, 1978.

Elbow, Peter. *Writing without Teachers*. New York: Oxford UP, 1973.

Emig, Janet. *The Composing Processes of Twelfth Graders*. Urbana: NCTE, 1971.

Flower, Linda S., and John R. Hayes. "A Cognitive Process Theory of Writing." *College Composition and Communication* 32 (1981): 365–87.

Freire, Paulo. *Pedagogy of the Oppressed*. Trans. Myra Bergman Ramos. New York: Seabury, 1968.

Frye, Northrop. *The Educated Imagination*. Bloomington: Indiana UP, 1964.

Heath, Shirley Brice. *Ways with Words: Language, Life, and Work in Communities and Classrooms*. New York: Cambridge UP, 1983.

Kinneavy, James L. *A Theory of Discourse*. 1971. New York: Norton, 1980.

Lanham, Richard A. *Literacy and the Survival of Humanism*. New Haven: Yale UP, 1983.

Moffett, James. *Teaching the Universe of Discourse*. Boston: Houghton, 1968.

Murray, Donald M. *A Writer Teaches Writing*. 2nd ed. Boston: Houghton, 1985.

Perl, Sondra. "Understanding Composing." *College Composition and Communication* 31 (1980): 363–69.

Ponsot, Marie, and Rosemary Deen. *Beat Not the Poor Desk*. Upper Montclair: Boynton, 1982.

Rose, Mike. "The Language of Exclusion: Writing Instruction at the University." *College English* 47 (1985): 341–59.

———. *Lives on the Boundary: The Struggles and Achievements of America's Underprepared*. New York: Free, 1989.

Scholes, Robert. *Textual Power: Literary Theory and the Teaching of English*. New Haven: Yale UP, 1985.

Shaughnessy, Mina P. *Errors and Expectations: A Guide for the Teacher of Basic Writing*. New York: Oxford UP, 1977.

Sommers, Nancy. "Revision Strategies of Student Writers and Experienced Adult Writers." *College Composition and Communication* 31 (1980): 378–88.

Tate, Gary, ed. *Teaching Composition: Twelve Bibliographic Essays*. Fort Worth: Texas Christian UP, 1987.

Young, Richard E., Alton L. Becker, and Kenneth L. Pike. *Rhetoric, Discovery, and Change*. New York: Harcourt, 1970.

# Notes on Contributors

**John Bender** is a professor of English and comparative literature at Stanford University. He is the author of *Spenser and Literary Pictorialism* and *Imagining the Penitentiary: Fiction and the Architecture of Mind in Eighteenth-Century England* and a coeditor of *The Ends of Rhetoric* and *Chronotypes: The Construction of Time*.

**Homi K. Bhabha** lectures in English literature and literary theory at the University of Sussex. He is the author of *The Location of Culture* and numerous essays on postcolonial theory and criticism and the editor of *Nation and Narration*.

**Walter Cohen** is a professor of comparative literature at Cornell University and the author of *Drama of a Nation: Public Theater in Renaissance England and Spain*.

**Deborah Esch** is an associate professor of English at the University of Toronto. She is the author of *The Senses of the Past* and a coeditor of Jacques Derrida's *Negotiations* and *Institutions of Philosophy*.

**Frances Ferguson** is a professor of English and humanities at Johns Hopkins University. She is the author of *Wordsworth: Language as Counter-spirit* and *Solitude and the Sublime: Romanticism and the Aesthetics of Individuation*.

**Philip Fisher** is a professor of English at Harvard University. He is the author, most recently, of *Making and Effacing Art: Modern American Art in a Culture of Museums* and *Hard Facts: Setting and Form in the American Novel* and the editor of *The New American Studies: Essays from Representions*.

**Henry Louis Gates, Jr.**, is a professor of humanities at Harvard University. He is the author of *Figures in Black: Words, Signs, and the "Racial" Self*; *The Signifying Monkey: A Theory of African American Literary Criticism*; and *Loose Canons*.

**Gerald Graff** is a professor of English and education at the University of Chicago. He is the author, most recently, of *Professing Literature: An Institutional History* and *Beyond the Culture Wars*.

**Stephen Greenblatt** is a professor of English at the University of California, Berkeley. His books include *Renaissance Self-Fashioning: From More to Shakespeare*; *Shakespearean Negotiations: The Circulation of Social Energy in Renaissance England*; *Learning to Curse: Essays in Early Modern Culture*; and, most recently, *Marvelous Possessions: The Wonder of the New World*.

**Giles Gunn** is a professor of English at the University of California, Santa Barbara. He is the author of *F. O. Matthiessen: The Critical Achievement*;

*The Interpretation of Otherness: Literature, Religion, and the American Imagination*; *The Culture of Criticism and the Criticism of Culture*; and, most recently, *Thinking across the American Grain: Ideology, Intellect, and the New Pragmatism*.

**William Kerrigan** is a professor of English at the University of Massachusetts, Amherst. He is the author of *The Prophetic Milton* and *The Sacred Complex: On the Psychogenesis of* Paradise Lost and coauthor of *The Idea of the Renaissance*.

**George Levine** is a professor of English and the director of the Center for the Critical Analysis of Contemporary Culture at Rutgers University, New Brunswick. He is the author of *The Boundaries of Fiction: Carlyle, Macaulay, Newman*; *The Realistic Imagination: English Fiction from* Frankenstein *to* Lady Chatterley; and, most recently, *Darwin and the Novelists: Patterns of Science in Victorian Fiction*.

**Leah S. Marcus** is a professor of English at the University of Texas, Austin. Her books include *Childhood and Cultural Despair*; *The Politics of Mirth: Jonson, Herrick, Milton, Marvell, and the Defense of Old Holiday Pastimes*; and *Puzzling Shakespeare: Local Reading and Its Discontents*.

**Richard Marius** has directed the expository writing program at Harvard University since 1978. He is the author of the biographies *Luther* and *Thomas More*, three writing textbooks, and three novels, which include *The Coming of Rain, Bound for the Promised Land*, and, most recently, *After the War*.

**Donald McQuade**, a professor of English at the University of California, Berkeley, has published widely on composition as well as on American literature and culture. His books include *Popular Writing in America*; *Edsels, Luckies, and Frigidaires: Advertising the American Way*; *Student Writers at Work*; *The Territory of Language: Linguistics, Stylistics, and the Teaching of Composition*; and *Thinking in Writing*. He is also the general editor of *The Harper American Literature*.

**Anne Middleton**, a professor of English at the University of California, Berkeley, has published essays on Chaucer and Langland. She is currently preparing a book on Langland, vernacular authorship, and the category of the literary.

**Louis Montrose** is a professor of English literature and chair of the Department of Literature at the University of California, San Diego. He has published extensively on Elizabethan culture and on theory and method in the historical analysis of literature.

**Marjorie Perloff** is a professor of humanities at Stanford University. Her books include *The Poetics of Indeterminacy: Rimbaud to Cage*; *The Dance* *of the Intellect*; *The Futurist Moment: Avant-Garde, Avant-Guerre, and the Language of Rupture*; *Poetic License: Studies in Modernist and Postmodernist Lyric*; and, most recently, *Radical Artifice: Writing Poetry in the Age of Media*.

**Bruce Robbins** is a professor of English and comparative literature at Rutgers University, New Brunswick. He is the author of *The Servant's Hand: English Fiction from Below* and the editor of *Intellectuals: Aesthetics, Politics, Academics* and *The Phantom Public Sphere*.

**John Carlos Rowe** teaches United States literature and culture at the University of California, Irvine, where he is a member of the Critical Theory Institute. He is the author of *Henry Adams and Henry James: The Emergence of a Modern Consciousness*; *Through the Custom-House: Nineteenth-Century American Fiction and Modern Theory*; and *The Theoretical Dimensions of Henry James*. He is a coeditor, with Rick Berg, of *The Vietnam War and American Culture*.

**Eve Kosofsky Sedgwick** is a professor of English at Duke University and the author of *Between Men: English Literature and Male Homosocial Desire* and *Epistemology of the Closet*.

**Meredith Skura** is a professor of English at Rice University. She is the author of *The Literary Use of the Psychoanalytic Process* and the forthcoming *Shakespeare the Actor and the Purposes of Playing*.

**Catharine R. Stimpson** is University Professor at Rutgers University, New Brunswick. Her many works include *Women's Studies in the United States*; *Reflections: Women's Self-Image in Contemporary Photography*; and *Where the Meanings Are: Feminism and Cultural Spaces*.

**Cecelia Tichi** is a professor of English at Vanderbilt University. She is the author of *New World, New Earth: Environmental Reform in American Literature from the Puritans through Whitman*; *Shifting Gears: Technology, Literature, Culture in Modernist America*; and, most recently, *Electronic Hearth: Creating an American Television Culture*.

# $\mathcal{W}$orks Cited

Abel, Elizabeth, ed. *Writing and Sexual Difference*. Chicago: U of Chicago P, 1982.

Abercrombie, M. L. J. *The Anatomy of Judgment: An Investigation into the Processes of Perception and Reasoning*. New York: Basic, 1960.

Abrams, M. H. "English Romanticism: The Spirit of the Age." Gleckner and Enscoe 314–30.

———. "Structure and Style in the Greater Romantic Lyric." *From Sensibility to Romanticism*. Ed. Frederick W. Hilles and Harold Bloom. New York: Oxford UP, 1965. 527–60.

Acosta, Oscar Zeta. *The Autobiography of a Brown Buffalo*. 1972. New York: Random, 1989.

———. *The Revolt of the Cockroach People*. San Francisco: Straight Arrow, 1973.

Adams, Hazard, and Leroy Searle, eds. *Critical Theory since 1965*. Tallahassee: Florida State UP, 1986.

Adams, Henry. *The Education of Henry Adams*. Boston: Massachusetts Hist. Soc., 1918.

Adams, M. Ray. *Studies in the Literary Backgrounds of English Radicalism*. Lancaster: Franklin and Marshall Coll., 1947.

Adelman, Janet. " 'Anger's My Meat': Feeding and Dependency in *Coriolanus*." *Shakespeare: Pattern of Excelling Nature*. Ed. David Bevington and Jay L. Halio. Cranbury: Associated UP, 1978. 108–24.

Adorno, Rolena. *Guaman Poma: Writing and Resistance in Colonial Peru*. Austin: U of Texas P, 1986.

Adorno, Theodor W. *Philosophy of Modern Music*. Trans. Anne G. Mitchell. New York: Continuum, 1973.

———. *Prisms*. Trans. Samuel Weber and Shierry Weber. London: Neville, 1967.

Aers, David. *Community, Gender, and Individual Identity: English Writing, 1360–1430*. London: Routledge, 1988.

———. "*Piers Plowman*: Poverty, Work, and Community." *Community* 20–72.

———. "Rewriting the Middle Ages: Some Suggestions." *Journal of Medieval and Renaissance Studies* 18 (1988): 221–40.

Aers, David, Jonathan Cook, and David Punter. *Romanticism and Ideology: Studies in English Writing, 1765–1830*. London: Routledge, 1981.

Alcoff, Linda. "Cultural Feminism versus Post-structuralism: The Identity Crisis in Feminist Theory." *Signs* 13 (1988): 405–36.

Alford, John. "The Grammatical Metaphor: A Survey of Its Use in the Middle Ages." *Speculum* 57 (1982): 728–60.

Allen, Judson. *The Ethnical Poetic of the Later Middle Ages*. Toronto: U of Toronto P, 1982.

——. *The Friar as Critic: Literary Attitudes in the Later Middle Ages.* Nashville: Vanderbilt UP, 1971.

Allen, Michael J. B., and Kenneth Muir, eds. *Shakespeare's Plays in Quarto: A Facsimile Edition of Copies Primarily from the Henry E. Huntington Library.* Berkeley: U of California P, 1981.

Alpers, Svetlana. *The Art of Describing: Dutch Art in the Seventeenth Century.* Chicago: U of Chicago P, 1983.

Alter, Robert. *The Pleasures of Reading in an Ideological Age.* New York: Simon, 1989.

Althusser, Louis. *Essays on Ideology.* London: Verso, 1984.

——. *For Marx.* Trans. Ben Brewster. London: NLB, 1977.

——. *Lenin and Philosophy and Other Essays.* Trans. Ben Brewster. New York: Monthly Rev., 1971.

Anderson, Benedict. *Imagined Communities: Reflections on the Origin and Spread of Nationalism.* London: Verso, 1983.

Anderson, Perry. *In the Tracks of Historical Materialism.* Chicago: U of Chicago P, 1984.

Appiah, Kwame Anthony. "The Conservation of 'Race.'" *Black American Literature Forum* 23 (1989): 37–60.

——. "Out of Africa: Topologies of Nativism." *Yale Journal of Criticism* 2 (1988): 153–78.

——. "Race." *Critical Terms for Literary Study.* Ed. Frank Lentricchia and Thomas McLaughlin. Chicago: U of Chicago P, 1990. 274–87.

Arac, Jonathan. "F. O. Matthiessen: Authorizing an American Renaissance." Michaels and Pease 90–112.

Arac, Jonathan, Wlad Godzich, and Wallace Martin, eds. *The Yale Critics: Deconstruction in America.* Minneapolis: U of Minnesota P, 1983.

Arac, Jonathan, and Barbara Johnson, eds. *Consequences of Theory: Selected Papers from the English Institute, 1987–88.* Baltimore: Johns Hopkins UP, 1991.

Arendt, Hannah. *The Human Condition.* Chicago: U of Chicago P, 1958.

——. *The Origins of Totalitarianism.* New York: Harcourt, 1951.

Ariès, Philippe. *Centuries of Childhood: A Social History of Family Life.* Trans. Robert Baldick. New York: Vintage, 1962.

Armstrong, Nancy. *Desire and Domestic Fiction: A Political History of the Novel.* New York: Oxford UP, 1987.

——. "Introduction: Literature as Women's History." *Genre* 19 (1986): 347–69.

Armstrong, Nancy, and Leonard Tennenhouse, eds. *The Ideology of Conduct: Essays in Literature and the History of Sexuality.* New York: Methuen, 1987.

——. *The Imaginary Puritan: Literature and the Origins of Personal Life.* Berkeley: U of California P, 1991.

Arnold, Matthew. *The Complete Prose Works of Matthew Arnold.* Ed. R. H. Super. 11 vols. Ann Arbor: U of Michigan P, 1960–77.

——. "Doing as One Likes." *Complete Prose Works* 5: 115–36.

———. "The Study of Poetry." *Complete Prose Works* 9: 161–88.

———. "Sweetness and Light." *Complete Prose Works* 5: 90–114.

Aronowitz, Stanley. *The Crisis in Historical Materialism: Class, Politics, and Culture in Marxist Theory.* New York: Praeger, 1981.

Asad, Talal. "Anthropological Conceptions of Religion: Reflections on Geertz." *Man* 18 (1983): 237–59.

Aston, T. H., and C. H. E. Philpin, eds. *The Brenner Debate: Agrarian Class Structure and Economic Development in Pre-industrial Europe.* Cambridge: Cambridge UP, 1985.

Auden, W. H. "D. H. Lawrence." *The Dyer's Hand and Other Essays.* New York: Vintage, 1968. 277–95.

Auerbach, Nina. *Communities of Women: An Idea in Fiction.* Cambridge: Harvard UP, 1978.

———. *Woman and the Demon.* Cambridge: Harvard UP, 1982.

Averill, James. *Wordsworth and the Poetry of Human Suffering.* Ithaca: Cornell UP, 1980.

Awkward, Michael. "Appropriative Gestures: Theory and Afro-American Literary Criticism." Kauffman 238–46.

Ayer, A. J. *Language, Truth, and Logic.* London: Gollancz, 1936.

Bain, Alexander. *English Composition and Rhetoric: A Manual.* American ed., rev. 1866. New York: Appleton, 1980.

Baker, Houston, Jr. *Blues, Ideology, and Afro-American Literature: A Vernacular Theory.* Chicago: U of Chicago P, 1984.

———. "Figurations for a New American Literary History." Bercovitch and Jehlen 145–71.

———. *Hybridity, the Rap Race, and the Pedagogy of the 1990s.* New York: Meridian, 1990.

———. *Modernism and the Harlem Renaissance.* Chicago: U of Chicago P, 1987.

Bakhtin, Mikhail M. *The Dialogic Imagination: Four Essays.* 1975. Trans. Caryl Emerson and Michael Holquist. Austin: U of Texas P, 1981.

———. *Marxism and the Philosophy of Language.* 1929. New York: Seminar, 1973.

———. *Rabelais and His World.* Trans. Helene Iswolsky. Cambridge: MIT P, 1968.

———. *Speech, Genres, and Other Late Essays.* Trans. Vern W. McGee. Ed. Caryl Emerson and Michael Holquist. Austin: U of Texas P, 1986.

Bal, Mieke, ed. *Psychopoetics—Theory.* Spec. issue of *Poetics* 13 (1984): 301–420.

Baldick, Chris. *The Social Mission of English Criticism, 1848–1932.* Oxford: Clarendon–Oxford UP, 1983.

Baldwin, James. *Notes of a Native Son.* Boston: Beacon, 1955.

Baraka, Imamu Amiri, and Larry Neal, eds. *Black Fire.* New York: Morrow, 1968.

Barber, C. L. *Creating Elizabethan Tragedy: The Theater of Marlowe and Kyd.* Ed. Richard P. Wheeler. Chicago: U of Chicago P, 1988.

——. *Shakespeare's Festive Comedy: A Study in Dramatic Form and Its Relation to Social Custom.* 1959. New York: Meridian, 1963.

Barker, Arthur. *Milton and the Puritan Dilemma.* Toronto: U of Toronto P, 1942.

Barker, Francis. *The Tremulous Private Body: Essays on Subjection.* New York: Methuen, 1984.

Barker, Francis, et al., eds. *Europe and Its Others.* Proc. of Essex Conf. on the Sociology of Literature. July 1984. 2 vols. Colchester: U of Essex, 1985.

Barnes, Djuna. "Recruiting for Metachorie: Mme. Valentine de Saint-Point Talks of Her Church of Music." *Interviews.* Ed. Alyce Barry. Fwd. Douglas Messerli. Washington: Sun, 1985. 223–35.

Baron, Dennis. *Grammar and Good Taste: Reforming the American Language.* New Haven: Yale UP, 1982.

Barrell, John. *The Political Theory of Painting from Reynolds to Hazlitt.* New Haven: Yale UP, 1986.

Barricelli, Jean-Pierre, and Joseph Gibaldi, eds. *Interrelations of Literature.* New York: MLA, 1982.

Barth, John. *The Friday Book: Essays and Other Non-fiction.* New York: Putnam, 1984.

——. *Lost in the Funhouse: Fiction for Print, Tape, Live Voice.* Garden City: Doubleday, 1968.

Barthes, Roland. "The Death of the Author." *Image-Music-Text.* Trans. Stephen Heath. New York: Hill, 1977. 142–48.

——. "From Work to Text." *Textual Strategies: Perspectives in Post-structuralist Criticism.* Ed. Josué V. Harari. Ithaca: Cornell UP, 1979. 73–81.

——. *A Lover's Discourse: Fragments.* Trans. Richard Howard. New York: Hill, 1978.

——. *The Pleasure of the Text.* Trans. Richard Miller. New York: Hill, 1975.

Bartholomae, David. "Inventing the University." *When a Writer Can't Write: Studies in Writer's Block and Other Composing Process Problems.* Ed. Mike Rose. New York: Guilford, 1985. 134–66.

Bartholomae, David, and Anthony R. Petrosky. *Facts, Artifacts, and Counterfacts: Theory and Method for a Reading and Writing Course.* Upper Montclair: Boynton, 1986.

Bartlett, Neil. *Who Was That Man? A Present for Mr. Oscar Wilde.* London: Serpent's Tail, 1988.

Bate, Walter Jackson. "The Crisis in English Studies." *Harvard Magazine* Sept.–Oct. 1982: 46–53.

Baudrillard, Jean. *Forget Foucault.* New York: Semiotext(e), 1987.

Bayley, John. *The Romantic Survival: A Study in Poetic Evolution.* 1957. London: Chatto, 1969.

Baym, Nina. "Early Histories of American Literature: A Chapter in the Institution of New England." *American Literary History* 1 (1989): 459–88.

——. "The Madwoman and Her Languages: Why I Don't Do Feminist Theory." Benstock, *Feminist Issues* 45–61.

————. *Novels, Readers, and Reviewers: Responses to Fiction in Antebellum America.* Ithaca: Cornell UP, 1984.

————. *Women's Fiction: A Guide to Novels by and about Women in America, 1820–1870.* Ithaca: Cornell UP, 1978.

Beauvoir, Simone de. *The Second Sex.* Trans. and ed. H. M. Parshley. New York: Knopf, 1953.

Beckett, Samuel. *Proust.* New York: Grove, 1931.

Beer, Gillian. *Darwin's Plots: Evolutionary Narrative in Darwin, George Eliot, and Nineteenth-Century Fiction.* London: Routledge, 1983.

Beilin, Elaine V. *Redeeming Eve: Women Writers of the English Renaissance.* Princeton: Princeton UP, 1987.

Bell, Michael Davitt. *The Development of American Romance: The Sacrifice of Relation.* Chicago: U of Chicago P, 1986.

Bellah, Robert N., Richard Madsen, William M. Sullivan, Ann Swidler, and Steven M. Tipton. *Habits of the Heart: Individualism and Commitment in American Life.* 1985. New York: Harper, 1986.

Bender, John. *Imagining the Penitentiary: Fiction and the Architecture of Mind in Eighteenth-Century England.* Chicago: U of Chicago P, 1987.

————. *Spenser and Literary Pictorialism.* Princeton: Princeton UP, 1972.

Benjamin, Walter. *Illuminations.* Ed. Hannah Arendt. Trans. Harry Zohn. New York: Schocken, 1969.

————. "The Image of Proust." *Illuminations* 201–15.

Bennett, Paula. "The Pea That Duty Locks: Clitoral Imagery in Emily Dickinson." MLA Convention. Washington, 27 Dec. 1989. Rpt. as "The Pea That Duty Locks: Lesbian and Feminist-Heterosexual Readings of Emily Dickinson's Poetry." *Lesbian Texts and Contexts: Radical Revisions.* Ed. Karla Jay and Joanne Glasgow. New York: New York UP, 1990. 104–25.

Bennett, Tony. "Texts in History: The Determinations of Readings and Their Texts." *Post-structuralism and the Question of History.* Ed. Derek Attridge, Geoff Bennington, and Robert Young. Cambridge: Cambridge UP, 1987. 63–81.

Bennett, William J. *Our Children and Our Country: Improving America's Schools and Affirming the Common Culture.* New York: Simon, 1988.

————. *To Reclaim a Legacy: A Report on the Humanities in Higher Education.* Washington: NEH, 1984.

Bennington, Geoff, Rachel Bowlby, and Robert Young, eds. *Colonialism.* Spec. issue of *Oxford Literary Review* 9 (1987): 2–158.

Benson, Thomas, ed. *Speech Communication in the Twentieth Century.* Carbondale: Southern Illinois UP, 1985.

Benstock, Shari, ed. *Feminist Issues in Literary Scholarship.* Bloomington: Indiana UP, 1987.

————. *Women of the Left Bank: Paris, 1900–1940.* Austin: U of Texas P, 1986.

Bentley, G. E. *The Professions of Dramatist and Player in Shakespeare's Time, 1590–1642*. Rev. ed. Princeton: Princeton UP, 1986.

Bercovitch, Sacvan. *The American Jeremiad*. Madison: U of Wisconsin P, 1978.

———. "Horologicals to Chronometricals: The Rhetoric of the Jeremiad." *Literary Monographs*. Vol. 3. Ed. Eric Rothstein. Madison: U of Wisconsin P, 1970. 1–124.

———. *The Office of the* Scarlet Letter. Baltimore: Johns Hopkins UP, 1991.

———. "The Problem of Ideology in American Literary History." *Critical Inquiry* 12 (1986): 631–53.

———. *Puritan Origins of the American Self*. New Haven: Yale UP, 1975.

———, ed. *Reconstructing American Literary History*. Harvard English Studies 13. Cambridge: Harvard UP, 1986.

Bercovitch, Sacvan, and Myra Jehlen, eds. *Ideology and Classic American Literature*. New York: Cambridge UP, 1986.

Bergeron, David, ed. *Pageants and Entertainments of Anthony Munday: A Critical Edition*. New York: Garland, 1985.

Berlin, James A. *Rhetoric and Reality: Writing Instruction in American Colleges, 1900–1985*. Carbondale: Southern Illinois UP, 1987.

———. *Writing Instruction in Nineteenth-Century American Colleges*. Carbondale: Southern Illinois UP, 1984.

Berlin, James A., and Robert P. Inkster. "Current-Traditional Rhetoric: Paradigm and Practice." *Freshman English News* 8 (1980): 13–14.

Berman, Russell A. "Modernism, Fascism, and the Institution of Literature." Chefdor, Quinones, and Wachtel 94–102.

Bernstein, Charles. *Content's Dream: Essays, 1975–1984*. Los Angeles: Sun, 1984.

———. "Thought's Measure." *Content's Dream* 61–88.

———. "Undone Business." *Content's Dream* 321–39.

Bersani, Leo. "Is the Rectum a Grave?" Crimp 197–222.

Berthoff, Ann E. *The Making of Meaning: Metaphors, Models, and Maxims for Writing Teachers*. Upper Montclair: Boynton, 1981.

———. *The Sense of Learning*. Portsmouth: Heinemann, 1990.

Bethurum, Dorothy, ed. *Critical Approaches to Medieval Literature: Selected Papers from the English Institute, 1958–1959*. New York: Columbia UP, 1960.

Bewell, Alan. *Wordsworth and the Enlightenment: Nature, Man, and Society in the Experimental Poetry*. New Haven: Yale UP, 1989.

Bhabha, Homi. "The Commitment to Theory." *New Formations* 5 (Summer 1988): 5–23. Rpt. in *Questions of the Third Cinema*. Ed. J. Pines and P. Willemen. London: British Film Inst., 1989. 111–32.

———. "DissemiNation: Time, Narrative, and the Margins of the Modern Nation." *Nation and Narration* 291–320.

———. *The Location of Culture*. London: Routledge, forthcoming.

———, ed. *Nation and Narration*. New York: Routledge, 1991.

———. "Sly Civility." *October* 34 (1985): 71–80.

Bialostosky, Don. *Making Tales: The Poetics of Wordsworth's Narrative Experiments.* Chicago: U of Chicago P, 1984.

Biersack, Aletta. "Local Knowledge, Local History: Geertz and Beyond." Hunt, *New Cultural History* 72–96.

Birkerts, Sven. "What, Me Read? The Difficulties of Teaching Writing to Students Who Don't Read for Pleasure." *Harvard Magazine* Sept.–Oct. 1989: 35.

Bishop, John. *Joyce's Book of the Dark:* Finnegans Wake. Madison: U of Wisconsin P, 1986.

Bizzell, Patricia. "Cognition, Convention, and Certainty: What We Need to Know about Writing." *Pre/Text* 3 (1982): 213–43.

Bizzell, Patricia, and Bruce Herzberg. *The Bedford Bibliography for Teachers of Writing.* 3rd ed. Boston: Bedford, 1991.

———, eds. *The Rhetorical Tradition.* Boston: Bedford, 1990.

Blair, Hugh. *Lectures on Rhetoric and Belles-Lettres.* 1783. Ed. Harold Harding. Carbondale: Southern Illinois UP, 1965.

Blayney, Peter W. M. *The First Folio of Shakespeare.* Washington: Folger Lib., 1991.

Bloch, R. Howard. *Etymologies and Genealogies: A Literary Anthropology of the French Middle Ages.* Chicago: U of Chicago P, 1983.

———. *Medieval French Literature and Law.* Berkeley: U of California P, 1977.

———. "Naturalism, Nationalism, Medievalism." *Romanic Review* 76 (1985): 342–60.

Bloom, Allan. *The Closing of the American Mind: How Higher Education Has Failed Democracy and Impoverished the Souls of Today's Students.* New York: Simon, 1987.

Bloom, Harold. *The Anxiety of Influence: A Theory of Poetry.* New York: Oxford UP, 1973.

———. *A Map of Misreading.* New York: Oxford UP, 1975.

———. *The Ringers in the Tower.* Chicago: U of Chicago P, 1971.

———. *Romanticism and Consciousness: Essays in Criticism.* New York: Norton, 1970.

———. "The Sorrows of American Jewish Poetry." *Figures of Capable Imagination.* New York: Seabury, 1976. 247–62.

———. *The Visionary Company.* Ithaca: Cornell UP, 1961.

———. *Wallace Stevens: The Poems of Our Climate.* Ithaca: Cornell UP, 1977.

———. *Yeats.* New York: Oxford UP, 1970.

Bloom, Harold, Paul de Man, Jacques Derrida, Geoffrey Hartman, and J. Hillis Miller. *Deconstruction and Criticism.* New York: Seabury, 1979.

Bloomfield, Morton. Rev. of *On Four Modern Humanists,* ed. Arthur R. Evans, Jr. *Romance Philology* 24 (1970–71): 506–10.

———. *Piers Plowman as Fourteenth-Century Apocalypse.* New Brunswick: Rutgers UP, 1962.

———. "Symbolism in Medieval Literature." *Modern Philology* 61 (1958): 73–81.

Bogel, Frederic V., and Katherine K. Gottschalk, eds. *Teaching Prose: A Guide for Writing Instructors*. New York: Norton, 1984.

Bonaparte, Marie. *The Life and Works of Edgar Allan Poe*. 1933. London: Imago, 1949.

Bond, Donald F., ed. *The Spectator*. 5 vols. Oxford: Clarendon–Oxford UP, 1965.

Boone, Joseph A., and Michael Cadden, eds. *Engendering Men: The Question of Male Feminist Criticism*. New York: Routledge, 1990.

Boose, Lynda E. "The Family in Shakespeare Studies; or, Studies in the Family of Shakespeareans; or, The Politics of Politics." *Renaissance Quarterly* 40 (1987): 707–42.

Booth, Wayne C. "Boring from Within: The Art of the Freshman Essay." *The Norton Reader*. 7th ed. Ed. Arthur M. Eastman et al. New York: Norton, 1988. 332–43.

———. *The Company We Keep*. Berkeley: U of California P, 1988.

———. *The Rhetoric of Fiction*. Chicago: U of Chicago P, 1961.

Boskin, Joseph. *Sambo: The Rise and Demise of an American Jester*. New York: Oxford UP, 1986.

Bosse, Henrich. *Autorschaft ist Werkherrschaft: Über die Entstehung des Urheberrechts aus dem Geist der Goethezeit*. Paderborn: Schoningh, 1981.

Boswell, John. *Christianity, Social Tolerance, and Homosexuality: Gay People in Western Europe from the Beginning of the Christian Era to the Fourteenth Century*. Chicago: U of Chicago P, 1980.

Bourdieu, Pierre. *Ce que parler veut dire: L'économie des échanges linguistiques*. Paris: Fayard, 1981.

———. *Outline of a Theory of Practice*. Trans. Richard Nice. Cambridge: Cambridge UP, 1977.

Bowie, Malcolm. "Jacques Lacan." *Structuralism and Since: From Lévi-Strauss to Derrida*. Ed. John Sturrock. New York: Oxford UP, 1979. 116–53.

Bradbury, Malcolm. *The Modern World: The Great Writers*. New York: Viking, 1988.

Braddock, Richard R., Richard Lloyd-Jones, and Lowell Schoer. *Research in Written Composition*. Urbana: NCTE, 1963.

Braden, Gordon. *The Classics and English Renaissance Poetry*. New Haven: Yale UP, 1978.

Bradley, Scully, Richard Croom Beatty, and E. Hudson Long, eds. *The American Tradition in Literature*. 3rd ed. New York: Norton, 1967.

Brandt, Deborah. *Literacy as Involvement: The Acts of Writers, Readers, and Texts*. Carbondale: Southern Illinois UP, 1990.

Brantlinger, Patrick. *Crusoe's Footprints: Cultural Studies in Britain and America*. New York: Routledge, 1990.

Bray, Alan. *Homosexuality in Renaissance England*. London: Gay Men's, 1982.

Bredvold, Louis I. "The Gloom of the Tory Satirists." *Pope and His Contemporaries: Essays Presented to George Sherburn*. Ed. James L. Clifford and Louis A. Landa. Oxford: Clarendon–Oxford UP, 1949. 1–19. Rpt. in *Eighteenth-Century*

*Literature: Modern Essays in Criticism.* Ed. James L. Clifford. New York: Oxford UP, 1959.

Breitwieser, Mitchell. *American Puritanism and the Defence of Mourning: Religion, Grief, and Ethnology in Mary White Rowlandson's Captivity Narrative.* Madison: U of Wisconsin P, 1990.

Briggs, Asa. *Victorian Cities.* New York: Harper, 1965.

———. *Victorian People.* Chicago: U of Chicago P, 1955.

———. *Victorian Things.* Chicago: U of Chicago P, 1989.

Brink, Jean R. "Who Fashioned Edmund Spenser? The Textual History of Complaints." *Studies in Philology* 88 (1991): 53–68.

Brion-Guerry, L. *L'année 1913: Les formes esthétiques de l'œuvre d'art à la veille de la première querre mondiale.* 3 vols. Paris: Klincksieck, 1971–73.

Brisman, Leslie. *Milton's Poetry of Choice and Its Romantic Heirs.* Ithaca: Cornell UP, 1973.

———. *Romantic Origins.* Ithaca: Cornell UP, 1978.

Britton, James, et al. *The Development of Writing Abilities (11–18).* London: Macmillan, 1975.

Brodkey, Linda. *Academic Writing as Social Practice.* Philadelphia: Temple UP, 1987.

———. "On the Subjects of Class and Gender in 'The Literacy Letters.' " *College English* 51 (1989): 125–41.

Brooks, Cleanth. *Modern Poetry and the Tradition.* Rev. ed. New York: Oxford, 1965.

———. *The Well Wrought Urn: Studies in the Structure of Poetry.* 1947. London: Dobson, 1949.

Brooks, Cleanth, and Robert Penn Warren. *Understanding Poetry.* 3rd ed. New York: Holt, 1960.

Brooks, David. "From Western Lit to Westerns as Lit." *Wall Street Journal* 2 Feb. 1988: 36.

Brower, Reuben. *The Fields of Light: An Experiment in Critical Reading.* New York: Oxford UP, 1951.

Brown, Marshall. *Preromanticism.* Stanford: Stanford UP, 1991.

Brown, Patricia Leigh. "A City Built for Rock 'n' Roll." *New York Times* 5 Oct. 1989: C1+.

Bruffee, Kenneth A. "The Brooklyn Plan: Attaining Intellectual Growth through Peer-Group Tutoring." *Liberal Education* 64 (1978): 447–69.

———. "Collaborative Learning and the 'Conversation of Mankind.' " *College English* 46 (1984): 635–52.

———. "The Structure of Knowledge and the Future of Liberal Education." *Liberal Education* 67 (1981): 177–86.

Bruss, Elizabeth. *Beautiful Theories: The Spectacle of Discourse in Contemporary Criticism.* Baltimore: Johns Hopkins UP, 1982.

Buckley, Jerome Hamilton. *The Victorian Temper.* Cambridge: Harvard UP, 1951.

Budick, Sanford. *The Dividing Muse: Images of Sacred Disjunction in Milton's Poetry.* New Haven: Yale UP, 1985.

Buell, Lawrence. *New England Literary Culture: From Revolution through Renaissance.* New York: Cambridge UP, 1986.

Bullen, J. B., ed. *The Sun Is God: Painting, Literature, and Mythology in the Nineteenth Century.* Oxford; Clarendon–Oxford UP, 1989.

Bullock, John, and John Trimbur, eds. *The Politics of Writing Instruction.* Portsmouth: Heinemann, 1990.

Burckhardt, Jacob. *The Civilization of the Renaissance in Italy.* Trans. S. G. C. Middlemore. 2 vols. New York: Harper, 1958.

Burgan, Mary. "Women in Academe in the '90s: Back to the Future, Part II." *Change* Mar.–Apr. 1990: 74–76.

Bürger, Peter. *Theory of the Avant-Garde.* Trans. Michael Shaw. Minneapolis: U of Minnesota P, 1984.

Burke, Kenneth. *Counter-statement.* 1931. Berkeley: U of California P, 1968.

———. *A Grammar of Motives.* 1945. Berkeley: U of California P, 1969.

———. *A Rhetoric of Motives.* 1950. Berkeley: U of California P, 1969.

Burrow, J. W. *Evolution and Society: A Study in Victorian Social Theory.* Cambridge: Cambridge UP, 1966.

Burrow, John A. "The Alterity of Medieval Literature." *New Literary History* 10 (1979): 377–83.

———. *Ricardian Poetry.* New Haven: Yale UP, 1971.

Butler, Judith. *Gender Trouble: Feminism and the Subversion of Identity.* New York: Routledge, 1989.

Butler, Marilyn. *Romantics, Rebels, and Reactionaries: English Literature and Its Background, 1760–1830.* New York: Oxford UP, 1982.

Butler, Samuel. *Hudibras.* Ed. John Wilders. Oxford: Clarendon–Oxford UP, 1967.

Bynum, Caroline Walker. *Holy Feast and Holy Fast: The Religious Significance of Food to Medieval Women.* Berkeley: U of California P, 1987.

———. *Jesus as Mother.* Berkeley: U of California P, 1982.

———. "Women's Stories, Women's Symbols: A Critique of Victor Turner's Theory of Liminality." *Anthropology and the Study of Religions.* Ed. Frank E. Reynolds and Robert Moore. Chicago: U of Chicago P, 1984. 105–25. Rpt. in *Fragmentation and Redemption: Essays on Gender and the Human Body in Medieval Religion.* By Bynum. New York: Zone, 1991. 27–51.

Cain, William E. *F. O. Matthiessen and the Politics of Criticism.* Madison: U of Wisconsin P, 1988.

Calinescu, Matei. *Five Faces of Modernity: Modernism, Avant-Garde, Decadence, Kitsch, Postmodernism.* Durham: Duke UP, 1987.

Callaghan, Dympna. *Woman and Gender in Renaissance Tragedy.* Atlantic Highlands: Humanities, 1989.

Campbell, George. *Philosophy of Rhetoric.* 1776. Ed. Lloyd Bitzer. Carbondale: Southern Illinois UP, 1963.

Canup, John. *Out of the Wilderness: The Emergence of an American Identity in Colonial New England.* Middletown: Wesleyan UP, 1990.

Carby, Hazel V. *Reconstructing Womanhood: The Emergence of the Afro-American Woman Novelist.* New York: Oxford UP, 1987.

Carey, John. *John Donne: Life, Mind, and Art.* New York: Oxford UP, 1981.

Carnochan, W. B. *Gibbon's Solitude: The Inward World of the Historian.* Stanford: Stanford UP, 1987.

Carruthers, Mary. *The Search for St. Truth.* Evanston: Northwestern UP, 1973.

*Casablanca.* Dir. Michael Curtiz. Prod. Hal B. Wallis. Warner, 1942.

Case, Sue-Ellen. "Toward a Butch-Femme Aesthetic." *Making a Spectacle: Feminist Essays on Contemporary Women's Theatre.* Ed. Lynda Hart. Ann Arbor: U of Michigan P, 1989. 282–99.

Caserio, Robert. *Plot, Story, and the Novel: From Dickens and Poe to the Modern Period.* Princeton: Princeton UP, 1979.

Casillo, Robert. *The Genealogy of Demons: Anti-Semitism, Fascism, and the Myths of Ezra Pound.* Evanston: Northwestern UP, 1988.

Castle, Terry. *Masquerade and Civilization in Eighteenth-Century English Culture and Fiction.* Stanford: Stanford UP, 1986.

Cavell, Stanley. *The Claim of Reason.* Oxford: Oxford UP, 1979.

——. *In Quest of the Ordinary.* Chicago: U of Chicago P, 1988.

——. *Pursuits of Happiness.* Cambridge: Harvard UP, 1981.

——. *The Senses of Walden.* New York: Viking, 1972.

Caywood, Cynthia, and Gillian Overing, eds. *Teaching Writing: Pedagogy, Gender, and Equity.* Albany: State U of New York P, 1987.

Chamberlain, Mariam, ed. *Women in Academe: Progress and Prospects.* New York: Sage, 1988.

Chandler, James. *Wordsworth's Second Nature: A Study of the Poetry and Politics.* Chicago: U of Chicago P, 1984.

Chase, Cynthia. *Decomposing Figures: Rhetorical Readings in the Romantic Tradition.* Baltimore: Johns Hopkins UP, 1986.

——. "The Decomposition of the Elephants: Double-Reading *Daniel Deronda.*" *PMLA* 92 (1978): 215–27.

——. "'Transference' as Trope and Persuasion." Rimmon-Kenan 211–32.

——. "The Witty Butcher's Wife: Freud, Lacan, and the Conversion of Resistance to Theory." *MLN* 102 (1987): 989–1013.

Chase, Richard Volney. *The American Novel and Its Tradition.* Garden City: Doubleday, 1957.

Chefdor, Monique, Ricardo Quinones, and Albert Wachtel, eds. *Modernism: Challenges and Perspectives.* Urbana: U of Illinois P, 1986.

Cheney, Lynne V. *American Memory: A Report on the Humanities in the Nation's Public Schools*. Washington: NEH, 1987.

———. *Humanities in America: A Report to the President, the Congress, and the American People*. Washington: NEH, 1988.

Christ, Carol. *Victorian and Modern Poetics*. Chicago: U of Chicago P, 1984.

Christensen, Francis. *Notes toward a New Rhetoric: Nine Essays for Teachers*. Ed. Bonniejean Christensen. 2nd ed. New York: Harper, 1978.

Christensen, Jerome. *Coleridge's Blessed Machine of Language*. Ithaca: Cornell UP, 1981.

———. *Practicing Enlightenment: Hume and the Formation of a Literary Career*. Madison: U of Wisconsin P, 1987.

Christian, Barbara. *Black Women Novelists: The Development of a Tradition, 1892–1976*. New York: Greenwood, 1980.

———. "The Race for Theory." *Cultural Critique* 6 (1987): 67–79. Rpt. in Kauffman 225–37.

Claridge, Laura, and Elizabeth Langland, eds. *Out of Bounds: Male Writers and Gender(ed) Criticism*. Amherst: U of Massachusetts P, 1990.

Clark, G. Kitson. *The Making of Victorian England*. Cambridge: Harvard UP, 1962.

Clifford, James. *The Predicament of Culture: Twentieth-Century Ethnography, Literature, and Art*. Cambridge: Harvard UP, 1988.

Clifford, James, and George E. Marcus, eds. *Writing Culture: The Poetics and Politics of Ethnography*. Berkeley: U of California P, 1986.

Coen, Stanley J. Introduction. *Essays on the Relationship of Author and Reader*. Spec. issue of *Psychoanalysis and Contemporary Thought* 5.1 (1982): 3–15.

Cohen, Ed. "Legislating the Norm." *Displacing Homophobia*. Ed. Ronald R. Butters, John M. Clum, and Michael Moon. Durham: Duke UP, 1990. 182–217.

Cohen, Ralph, ed. *The Future of Literary Theory*. New York: Routledge, 1989.

———, ed. *Psychology and Literature: Some Contemporary Dimensions*. Spec. issue of *New Literary History* 12 (1980): 1–218.

Cohen, Walter. "Political Criticism of Shakespeare." Howard and O'Connor 18–46.

Coletti, Theresa. "Reading REED: History and the Records of Early English Drama." L. Patterson, *Literary Practice* 248–84.

Colish, Marcia. *The Mirror of Language: A Study in the Medieval Theory of Language*. New Haven: Yale UP, 1968.

Collins, Jim. *Uncommon Cultures: Popular Culture and Post-modernism*. New York: Routledge, 1989.

Conference on College Composition and Communication. Committee on Professional Standards. "CCCC Initiatives on the Wyoming Conference Resolution: A Draft Report." *College Composition and Communication* 40 (1989): 61–72.

———. "A Progress Report from the CCCC Committee on Professional Standards." *College Composition and Communication* 42 (1991): 330–44.

Conference on College Composition and Communication. Executive Committee. "Statement of Principles and Standards for the Postsecondary Teaching of Writing." *College Composition and Communication* 40 (1990): 329–36.

Connor, Steven. *Postmodernist Culture: An Introduction to Theories of the Contemporary.* Oxford: Blackwell, 1989.

Connors, Robert J. "Personal Writing Assignments." *College Composition and Communication* 38 (1987): 166–83.

Connors, Robert J., Lisa S. Ede, and Andrea A. Lunsford, eds. *Essays on Classical Rhetoric and Modern Discourse.* Carbondale: Southern Illinois UP, 1984.

Cooper, A. M. "Psychoanalysis at One Hundred Years: Beginnings of Maturity." *Journal of the American Psychoanalytic Association* 32 (1984): 245–67.

Corbett, Edward P. J. *Classical Rhetoric for the Modern Student.* 3rd ed. New York: Oxford UP, 1990.

Corbett, Edward P. J., James L. Golden, and Goodwin F. Berquist, eds. *Essays on the Rhetoric of the Western World.* Dubuque: Kendall, 1990.

Crapanzano, Vincent. "Hermes's Dilemma: The Masking of Subversion in Ethnographic Description." Clifford and Marcus 50–76.

Crews, Frederick. *Out of My System: Psychoanalysis, Ideology, and Critical Method.* New York: Oxford UP, 1975.

Crimp, Douglas, ed. *AIDS: Cultural Analysis, Cultural Activism.* Cambridge: MIT P, 1988.

Culler, Jonathan. "Literary Criticism and the American University." *Framing the Sign: Criticism and Its Institutions.* Norman: U of Oklahoma P, 1988. 3–40.

———. *On Deconstruction: Theory and Criticism after Structuralism.* Ithaca: Cornell UP, 1982.

Curran, Stuart. *Poetic Form and British Romanticism.* New York: Oxford UP, 1986.

Dale, Peter Allan. *In Pursuit of a Scientific Culture: Science, Art, and Society in the Victorian Age.* Madison: U of Wisconsin P, 1989.

d'Alembert, Jean le Rond. *Preliminary Discourse to the Encyclopedia of Diderot.* Ed. and trans. Richard N. Schwab. Indianapolis: Bobbs, 1963.

Daly, Mary, with Jane Caputi. *Webster's First New Intergalactic Wickedary of the English Language.* Boston: Beacon, 1987.

Damrosch, Leo. *Fictions of Reality in the Age of Hume and Johnson.* Madison: U of Wisconsin P, 1989.

D'Angelo, Frank. *A Conceptual Theory of Rhetoric.* Cambridge: Winthrop, 1975.

Daniell, Beth. "Against the Great Leap Theory of Literacy." *Pre/Text* 7 (1986): 181–93.

Daniels, Harvey A. *Famous Last Words: The American Language Crisis Reconsidered.* Carbondale: Southern Illinois UP, 1983.

Das, Veena. "Subaltern as Perspective." *Subaltern Studies.* Vol. 6. Ed. Ranajit Guha. New Delhi: Oxford UP, 1989. 310–24.

Dauber, Kenneth. *The Idea of Authorship in America.* Madison: U of Wisconsin P, 1990.

Davidson, Cathy N. *Revolution and the Word: The Rise of the Novel in America*. New York: Oxford UP, 1986.

Davie, Donald. *Ezra Pound: Poet and Sculptor*. New York: Oxford UP, 1964.

———. *Pound*. London: Fontana-Collins, 1975.

Davis, Natalie Zemon. *Society and Culture in Early Modern France*. Stanford: Stanford UP, 1975.

Davis, Richard Beale. *Intellectual Life in the Colonial South, 1585–1763*. 3 vols. Knoxville: U of Tennessee P, 1978.

Davis, Robert Con, ed. *Lacan and Narration: The Psychoanalytic Difference in Narrative Theory*. Baltimore: Johns Hopkins UP, 1983.

Day, Henry. *Elements of the Art of Rhetoric*. New York: Scribner's, 1858. Rev. and rpt. as *The Art of Discourse*. 1867.

Dean, Mitchell. "Foucault's Obsession with Western Modernity." *Thesis Eleven* 14 (1986): 45–61.

De Bolla, Peter. *The Discourse of the Sublime: Readings in History, Aesthetics, and the Subject*. New York: Blackwell, 1989.

de Grazia, Margreta. "The Ideological Textual Apparatus: Shakespeare's *Sonnets* in 1780." Prospectus for new ed. of the *Sonnets*.

———. *Shakespeare Verbatim: The Reproduction of Authenticity and the 1790 Apparatus*. Oxford: Clarendon–Oxford UP, 1991.

Delany, Paul, and George P. Landow, eds. *Hypermedia and Literary Studies*. Cambridge: MIT P, 1991.

DeLaura, David. *Hebrew and Hellene in Victorian England: Newman, Arnold, and Pater*. Austin: U of Texas P, 1969.

de Lauretis, Teresa, ed. *Feminist Studies/Critical Studies*. Bloomington: Indiana UP, 1986.

———. "Sexual Indifference and Lesbian Representation." *Theatre Journal* 40 (1988): 155–77.

Delbanco, Andrew. *The Puritan Ordeal*. Cambridge: Harvard UP, 1989.

Deleuze, Gilles, and Félix Guattari. *Anti-Oedipus: Capitalism and Schizophrenia*. Trans. Robert Hurley et al. Minneapolis: U of Minnesota P, 1982.

de Man, Paul. *Aesthetic Ideology*. Ed. Andrzej Warminski. Minneapolis: U of Minnesota P, forthcoming.

———. *Allegories of Reading: Figural Language in Rousseau, Nietzsche, Rilke, and Proust*. New Haven: Yale UP, 1979.

———. *Blindness and Insight: Essays in the Rhetoric of Contemporary Criticism*. New York: Oxford UP, 1971. 2nd ed. Minneapolis: U of Minnesota P, 1983.

———. "Excuses." *Allegories* 278–301.

———. "Intentional Structure of the Romantic Nature Image." *Romanticism and Consciousness: Essays in Criticism*. Ed. Harold Bloom. New York: Norton, 1970. 65–77.

———. "Literary History and Literary Modernity." *Blindness and Insight* (2nd ed.) 142–65.

———. "Pascal's Allegory of Persuasion." *Allegory and Representation.* Ed. Stephen J. Greenblatt. Baltimore: Johns Hopkins UP, 1981. 1–25.

———. "Phenomenality and Materiality in Kant." *Hermeneutics: Questions and Prospects.* Ed. Gary Shapiro and Alan Sica. Amherst: U of Massachusetts P, 1984. 121–44.

———. "The Resistance to Theory." *Resistance* 3–20.

———. *The Resistance to Theory.* Minneapolis: U of Minnesota P, 1986.

———. *The Rhetoric of Romanticism.* New York: Columbia UP, 1984.

———. "Semiology and Rhetoric." *Allegories* 3–20.

———. "Wordsworth and the Victorians." *Rhetoric* 83–92.

Derrida, Jacques. "But, beyond . . . : Open Letter to Anne McClinstock and Rob Nixon." Trans. Peggy Kamuf. *Critical Inquiry* 13 (1986): 155–70.

———. "The Conflict of Faculties: A *Mochlos.*" Trans. Cynthia Chase, Jonathan Culler, and Irving Wohlfarth. *Institutions of Philosophy.* Ed. Deborah Esch and Thomas Keenan. Cambridge: Harvard UP, 1991.

———. "Deconstruction in America." Interview with James Creech, Peggy Kamuf, and Jane Todd. *Critical Exchange* 17 (Winter 1985): 1–33.

———. *Dissemination.* Trans. Barbara Johnson. Chicago: U of Chicago P, 1981.

———. *Glas.* Paris: Galilée, 1974. Trans. John P. Leavey and Richard Rand. Lincoln: U of Nebraska P, 1986.

———. "In Discussion with Christopher Norris." *Deconstruction II.* New York: St. Martin's, 1989. 7–11.

———. "The Laws of Reflection: Nelson Mandela, in Admiration." *For Nelson Mandela.* Ed. Derrida and Mustapha Tlili. New York: Holt, 1987. 13–42.

———. "Letter to a Japanese Friend." *Derrida and Différance.* Ed. David Wood and Robert Bransconi. Coventry: Parousia, 1985. 107–27.

———. *Margins of Philosophy.* Trans. Alan Bass. Chicago: U of Chicago P, 1982.

———. *Memoires for Paul de Man.* Trans. Cecile Lindsay, Jonathan Culler, and Eduardo Cadava. New York: Columbia UP, 1986.

———. "My Chances/Mes Chances." *Taking Chances: Derrida, Psychoanalysis, Literature.* Ed. Joseph H. Smith and William Kerrigan. Baltimore: Johns Hopkins UP, 1984. 1–32.

———. *Negotiations.* Ed. Deborah Esch and Thomas Keenan. Minneapolis: U of Minnesota P, forthcoming.

———. *Of Grammatology.* Trans. Gayatri C. Spivak. Baltimore: Johns Hopkins UP, 1976.

———. *Positions.* Trans. Alan Bass. Chicago: U of Chicago P, 1982.

———. *The Post Card: From Socrates to Freud and Beyond.* Trans. Alan Bass. Chicago: U of Chicago P, 1987.

——. "The Principle of Reason: The University in the Eyes of Its Pupils." Trans. Catherine Porter and Edward P. Morris. *Diacritics* 13.3 (1983): 3–20.

——. "Some Statements and Truisms about Neo-logisms, Newisms, Postisms, Parasitisms, and Other Small Seisisms." *The States of "Theory."* New York: Columbia UP, 1990. 63–94.

——. "Structure, Sign, and Play in the Discourse of the Human Sciences." Donato and Macksey 247–72.

——. *The Truth in Painting.* Trans. Geoff Bennington and Ian McLeod. Chicago: U of Chicago P, 1987.

——. *Writing and Difference.* Trans. Alan Bass. Chicago: U of Chicago P, 1978.

diBattista, Maria. *Virginia Woolf's Major Novels: The Fables of Anon.* New Haven: Yale UP, 1980.

Dickinson, Emily. *The Complete Poems of Emily Dickinson.* Ed. Thomas H. Johnson. Boston: Little, 1960.

Dimock, Wai-chee. *Empire for Liberty: Melville and the Poetics of Individualism.* Princeton: Princeton UP, 1989.

Docherty, Thomas. *John Donne Undone.* London: Methuen, 1986.

Dollimore, Jonathan. "Homophobia and Sexual Difference." *Oxford Literary Review* 8.1–1 (1986).

——. *Radical Tragedy: Religion, Ideology, and Power in the Drama of Shakespeare and His Contemporaries.* Chicago: U of Chicago P, 1984.

Dollimore, Jonathan, and Alan Sinfield. "Culture and Textuality: Debating Cultural Materialism." *Textual Practice* 4 (1990): 91–100.

——, eds. *Political Shakespeare: New Essays in Cultural Materialism.* Ithaca: Cornell UP, 1985.

Donaldson, E. Talbot, ed. *Chaucer's Poetry: An Anthology for the Modern Reader.* New York: Ronald, 1975.

Donato, Eugenio. "The Two Languages of Criticism." Donato and Macksey 89–97.

Donato, Eugenio, and Richard Macksey, eds. *The Languages of Criticism and the Sciences of Man: The Structuralist Controversy.* Baltimore: Johns Hopkins UP, 1970.

Donoghue, Denis. "The Joy of Texts." Rev. of *The Pleasures of Reading in an Ideological Age,* by Robert Alter. *New Republic* 26 June 1989: 36–38.

Doody, Margaret Anne. *The Daring Muse: Augustan Poetry Reconsidered.* Cambridge: Cambridge UP, 1985.

Douglas, Alfred. "Two Loves." *Chameleon* 1.1 (1894): 26–28.

Douglas, Ann. *The Feminization of American Culture.* New York: Knopf, 1977.

Dowling, Linda. *Language and Decadence in the Victorian Fin de Siècle.* Princeton: Princeton UP, 1986.

Dowling, William. *Language and Logos in Boswell's* Life of Johnson. Princeton: Princeton UP, 1981.

Draine, Betsy. "Refusing the Wisdom of Solomon: Some Recent Feminist Literary Theory." *Signs* 15 (1989): 144–70.

Drakakis, John, ed. *Alternative Shakespeares.* London: Methuen, 1985.

D'Souza, Dinesh. *Illiberal Education: The Politics of Race and Sex on Campus.* New York: Free, 1991.

Duby, Georges. *The Three Orders: Feudal Society Imagined.* Trans. Arthur Goldhammer. Chicago: U of Chicago P, 1980.

Dyer, Richard. "Seen to Be Believed: Some Problems in the Representation of Gay People as Typical." *Studies in Visual Communication* 9.2 (1983): 2–19.

Eagleton, Terry. "Escape into the Ineffable." *Times Literary Supplement* 24–30 Nov. 1989: 1291–92.

———. *Ideology: An Introduction.* London: Verso, 1991.

———. *The Ideology of the Aesthetic.* Oxford: Blackwell, 1990.

———. *Literary Theory: An Introduction.* Minneapolis: U of Minnesota P, 1983.

Eaves, Morris, and Michael Fischer, eds. *Romanticism and Contemporary Criticism.* Ithaca: Cornell UP, 1986.

Egerton, Sarah Fyge Field. "The Emulation." *First Feminists: British Women Writers, 1578–1799.* Ed. Moira Ferguson. Bloomington: Indiana UP, 1985. 170.

Eichner, Hans. "The Rise of Modern Science and the Genesis of Romanticism." *PMLA* 97 (1982): 8–30.

Eisenstein, Elizabeth. *The Printing Press as an Agent of Change.* 2 vols. Cambridge: Cambridge UP, 1979.

Eisenstein, Hester, and Alice Jardine. *The Future of Difference.* Boston: Hall, 1980.

Elbow, Peter. *Writing without Teachers.* New York: Oxford UP, 1973.

Eliot, T. S. *On Poetry and Poets.* London: Faber, 1957.

———. *Selected Essays.* Rev. ed. New York: Harcourt, 1964.

———. "Tradition and the Individual Talent." *Selected Essays* 3–11.

———. *The Use of Poetry and the Use of Criticism: Studies in the Relation of Criticism to Poetry in England.* London: Faber, 1933.

Elliot, Emory, ed. *The Columbia Literary History of the United States.* New York: Columbia UP, 1986.

Ellison, Julie. *Delicate Subjects: Romanticism, Gender, and the Ethics of Understanding.* Ithaca: Cornell UP, 1990.

Ellmann, Mary. *Thinking about Women.* New York: Harcourt, 1968.

Ellmann, Richard. *The Identity of Yeats.* 2nd ed. New York: Oxford UP, 1964.

Ellmann, Richard, and Charles Feidelson, Jr., eds. *The Modern Tradition: Backgrounds of Modern Literature.* New York: Oxford UP, 1965.

Emerson, Ralph Waldo. "Napoleon." *The Selected Writings of Ralph Waldo Emerson.* Ed. Brooks Atkinson. New York: Modern Library, 1940.

Emig, Janet. *The Composing Processes of Twelfth Graders.* Urbana: NCTE, 1971.

Enck, John. "John Barth: An Interview." *Contemporary Literature* 6 (1965): 3–14.

Ende, Stuart A. *Keats and the Sublime.* New Haven: Yale UP, 1976.

Epstein, Julia. *The Iron Pen: Frances Burney and the Politics of Women's Writing.* Madison: U of Wisconsin P, 1989.

Epstein, William H. "Counter-intelligence: Cold-War Criticism and Eighteenth-Century Studies." *ELH* 57 (1990): 63–99.

Erickson, Peter. "Rewriting the Renaissance, Rewriting Ourselves." *Shakespeare Quarterly* 38 (1987): 327–37.

Erickson, Robert A. *Mother Midnight: Birth, Sex, and Fate in the Eighteenth-Century Novel.* New York: AMS, 1987.

Erlanger, Rachel. "Johnny's Teacher Can't Write Either." *New York Times* 12 June 1991: A27.

Ettelbrick, Paula L. "Gay Marriage: A Must or a Bust? Since When Was Marriage the Path to Liberation?" *Out/Look: National Lesbian and Gay Quarterly* 6 (1989): 9+.

Eysteinsson, Astradur. *The Concept of Modernism.* Ithaca: Cornell UP, 1990.

Faderman, Lilian. *Surpassing the Love of Man.* New York: Morrow, 1982.

Fanon, Frantz. *Black Skin, White Masks.* Trans. Charles Markmann. New York: Grove, 1967.

———. *The Wretched of the Earth.* Trans. Constance Farrington. Harmondsworth, Eng.: Penguin, 1969.

Febvre, Lucien. "Frontière: The Word and the Concept." *A New Kind of History.* Ed. Peter Burke. Trans. K. Folca. London: Routledge, 1973. 208–18.

Feidelson, Charles, Jr. *Symbolism and American Literature.* Chicago: U of Chicago P, 1953.

Feldstein, Richard, and Henry Sussman, eds. *Psychoanalysis and. . . .* New York: Routledge, 1990.

Felman, Shoshana, ed. *Jacques Lacan and the Adventure of Insight.* Cambridge: Harvard UP, 1987.

———. *Literature and Psychoanalysis: The Question of Reading: Otherwise.* Spec. issue of *Yale French Studies* 55–56 (1978): 3–508. Baltimore: Johns Hopkins UP, 1982.

———. "To Open the Question." *Literature* 5–10.

———. "Turning the Screw of Interpretation." *Literature* 94–207.

*Feminist Readings: French Texts/American Contexts.* Spec. issue of *Yale French Studies* 62 (1981): 3–352.

Ferguson, Frances. *Solitude and the Sublime: Romanticism and the Aesthetics of Individuation.* New York: Routledge, forthcoming.

———. *Wordsworth: Language as Counter-spirit.* New Haven: Yale UP, 1977.

Ferguson, Margaret W., Maureen Quilligan, and Nancy J. Vickers, eds. *Rewriting the Renaissance: The Discourses of Sexual Difference in Early Modern Europe.* Chicago: U of Chicago P, 1986.

Ferguson, Margaret W., and Barry Weller, eds. *Mariam.* By Elizabeth Carey. Berkeley: U of California P, forthcoming.

Ferguson, Robert A. *Law and Letters in American Culture*. Cambridge: Harvard UP, 1984.

Fiedler, Leslie, and Houston A. Baker, Jr., eds. *Opening Up the Canon: Selected Papers from the English Institute, 1979*. Baltimore: Johns Hopkins UP, 1981.

Findlay, Len. "Otherwise Engaged: Postmodernism and the Resistance to History." *English Studies in Canada* 14.4 (1988): 383–99.

Fineman, Joel. "The History of the Anecdote: Fiction and Fiction." Veeser 49–76.

Fischer, David Hackett. *Albion's Seed: Four British Folkways in America*. New York: Oxford UP, 1989.

Fish, Stanley E. "Authors-Readers: Jonson's Community of the Same." *Representations* 7 (1984): 26–58.

———. "The Common Touch; or, One Size Fits All." *The Politics of Liberal Education*. Ed. Darryl J. Gless and Barbara Herrnstein Smith. Durham: Duke UP, 1992. 241–66.

———. *Is There a Text in This Class?* Cambridge: Harvard UP, 1980.

———. *The Living Temple: George Herbert and Catechizing*. Berkeley: U of California P, 1978.

———. *Surprised by Sin: The Reader in* Paradise Lost. London: Macmillan, 1967.

Fisher, Dexter, ed. *Minority Language and Literature: Retrospective and Perspective*. New York: MLA, 1977.

———, ed. *The Third Woman: Minority Women Writers in the United States*. Boston: Houghton, 1981.

Fisher, Dexter, and Robert B. Stepto, eds. *Afro-American Literature: The Reconstruction of Instruction*. New York: MLA, 1979.

Fisher, Philip. *Hard Facts: Setting and Form in the American Novel*. New York: Oxford UP, 1987.

Fite, David. *Harold Bloom: The Rhetoric of Romantic Vision*. Amherst: U of Massachusetts P, 1985.

Fliegelman, Jay. *Prodigals and Pilgrims: The American Revolution against Patriarchal Authority, 1750–1800*. New York: Cambridge UP, 1982.

Flieger, Jerry Aline. *The Purloined Punchline: Freud's Comic Theory and the Postmodern Text*. Baltimore: Johns Hopkins UP, 1991.

Flower, Linda S., and John R. Hayes. "A Cognitive Process Theory of Writing." *College Composition and Communication* 32 (1981): 365–87.

Flynn, Elizabeth A., and Patrocinio Schweickart, eds. *Gender and Reading: Essays on Readers, Texts, and Contexts*. Baltimore: Johns Hopkins UP, 1986.

Forrester, John. "Psychoanalysis or Literature?" *French Studies* 35 (1981): 170–79.

———. *The Seductions of Psychoanalysis*. Cambridge: Cambridge UP, 1990.

Foster, Hal, ed. *The Anti-aesthetic: Essays on Postmodern Culture*. Port Townsend: Bay, 1983.

Foucault, Michel. *Discipline and Punish*. Trans. Alan Sheridan. New York: Vintage, 1979.

———. "The Discourse on Language." *The Archaeology of Knowledge*. Trans. Alan Sheridan. New York: Pantheon, 1972. 215–37.

———. *The History of Sexuality: An Introduction*. Trans. Robert Hurley. New York: Pantheon, 1978. Vol. 1 of *The History of Sexuality*. 3 vols. 1978–86.

———. *Madness and Civilization: A History of Insanity in the Age of Reason*. Trans. Richard Howard. 1965. New York: Vintage, 1973.

———. "Man and His Doubles." *Order* 303–43.

———. *The Order of Things: An Archaeology of the Human Sciences*. Trans. Alan Sheridan. London: Tavistock, 1970.

———. *Power/Knowledge: Selected Interviews and Other Writings, 1972–1977*. New York: Pantheon, 1980.

———. "What Is an Author?" Trans. Josué V. Harari. *Foucault Reader*. Ed. Paul Rabinow. New York: Pantheon, 1979. 101–20.

Fox-Genovese, Elizabeth. "Literary Criticism and the Politics of New Historicism." Veeser 213–24.

Fradenburg, Louise. "Narrative and Capital in Late-Medieval Scotland." L. Patterson, *Literary Practice* 285–333.

Frank, Joseph. "Spatial Form in Modern Literature." 1949. *The Widening Gyre: Crisis and Mastery in Modern Literature*. Bloomington: Indiana UP, 1968. 3–62.

Freire, Paulo. *Cultural Action for Freedom*. Cambridge: Center for the Study of Development and Social Change, 1970.

———. *Pedagogy of the Oppressed*. Trans. Myra Bergman Ramos. New York: Seabury, 1970.

Freud, Sigmund. *The Complete Psychological Works of Sigmund Freud: Standard Edition*. Ed. James Strachey. 24 vols. London: Hogarth, 1953–74.

———. "The Ego and the Id." 1923. *Works*, vol. 14.

———. "Five Lectures on Psychoanalysis." 1910. *Works*, vol. 11.

———. "Fragment of an Analysis of a Case of Hysteria." 1905. *Works* 7: 7–122.

———. "Instincts and Their Vicissitudes." 1915. *Works*, vol. 14.

———. *The Interpretation of Dreams*. 1900. *Works*, vols. 4–5.

Fried, Michael. "Courbet's Femininity." *Courbet Reconsidered*. Ed. Sarah Fraunce and Linda Nochlin. New Haven: Yale UP, 1988. 43–53.

Frosh, Stephen. *The Politics of Psychoanalysis: An Introduction to Freudian and Post-Freudian Theory*. New Haven: Yale UP, 1987.

Froula, Christine. "When Eve Reads Milton: Undoing Canonical Economy." *Critical Inquiry* 10 (1983): 321–47.

Fry, Paul H. *The Poet's Calling in the English Ode*. New Haven: Yale UP, 1980.

Frye, Marilyn. *The Politics of Reality: Essays in Feminist Theory*. Trumansburg: Crossing, 1983.

Frye, Northrop. *Anatomy of Criticism*. Princeton: Princeton UP, 1957.

———. *The Educated Imagination*. Bloomington: Indiana UP, 1964.

Fulwiler, Toby. "The Argument for Writing across the Curriculum." *Writing across the Disciplines*. Ed. Art Young and Fulwiler. Upper Montclair: Boynton, 1986.

Fulwiler, Toby, and Art Young, eds. *Programs That Work: Models and Methods for Writing across the Curriculum*. Portsmouth: Heinemann, 1990.

Fumerton, Patricia. *Cultural Aesthetics: Renaissance Literature and the Practice of Social Ornament*. Chicago: U of Chicago P, 1991.

Fuss, Diana. *Essentially Speaking: Feminism, Nature, and Difference*. New York: Routledge, 1989.

Gadamer, Hans-Georg. *Philosophical Hermeneutics*. Trans. David E. Linge. Berkeley: U of California P, 1976.

Gallagher, Catherine. *The Industrial Reformation of English Fiction, 1832–1867*. Chicago: U of Chicago P, 1985.

———. "Marxism and the New Historicism." Veeser 37–48.

Gallop, Jane. *The Daughter's Seduction: Feminism and Psychoanalysis*. Ithaca: Cornell UP, 1982.

———. *Reading Lacan*. Ithaca: Cornell UP, 1985.

Gallop, Jane, and Carolyn Burke. "Psychoanalysis and Feminism in France." Eisenstein and Jardine 106–21.

Galperin, William. *Revision and Authority in Wordsworth: The Interpretation of a Career*. Philadelphia: U of Pennsylvania P, 1989.

Garber, Marjorie, ed. *Cannibals, Witches, and Divorce: Estranging the Renaissance*. Baltimore: Johns Hopkins UP, 1985.

———. *Shakespeare's Ghost Writers: Literature as Uncanny Causality*. New York: Methuen, 1987.

Gardner, Howard. *The Unschooled Mind: How Children Think and How Schools Should Teach*. New York: Basic, 1991.

Garis, Robert. *The Dickens Theatre: A Reassessment of the Novels*. New York: Oxford UP, 1965.

Garner, Shirley Nelson, Claire Kahane, and Madelon Sprengnether, eds. *The (M)Other Tongue: Essays in Feminist Psychoanalytic Interpretation*. Ithaca: Cornell UP, 1985.

Garrett, Peter K. *The Victorian Multiplot Novel: Studies in Dialogic Form*. New Haven: Yale UP, 1980.

Gasché, Rodolphe. Introduction. Warminski, *Readings in Interpretation* ix–xxvi.

———. *The Tain of the Mirror*. Cambridge: Harvard UP, 1986.

Gates, Henry Louis, Jr., ed. *Black Literature and Literary Theory*. New York: Methuen, 1984.

———. "Critical Remarks." *Anatomy of Racism*. Ed. David A. Goldberg. Minneapolis: U of Minnesota P, 1990. 319–29.

———, ed. *"Race," Writing, and Difference*. Chicago: U of Chicago P, 1986.

———, ed. *Reading Black, Reading Feminist: A Critical Anthology*. New York: NAL, 1990.

——. *The Signifying Monkey: A Theory of African-American Literary Criticism.* New York: Oxford UP, 1988.

Gay, Peter. *The Enlightenment: A Comprehensive Anthology.* New York: Simon, 1973.

Gayle, Addison, ed. *The Black Aesthetic.* Garden City: Doubleday, 1971.

Geertz, Clifford. "Deep Play: Notes on the Balinese Cockfight." *Interpretation* 412–53.

——. *The Interpretation of Cultures: Selected Essays.* New York: Basic, 1973.

——. *Local Knowledge: Further Essays in Interpretive Anthropology.* New York: Basic, 1983.

——. *Negara: The Theatre State in Nineteenth-Century Bali.* Princeton: Princeton UP, 1980.

Geismar, Maxwell. Introduction. *Soul on Ice.* By Eldridge Cleaver. New York: Dell, 1968.

Gelpi, Albert. *A Coherent Splendor: The American Poetic Renaissance, 1910–1950.* Cambridge: Cambridge UP, 1987.

Genung, John F. *The Practical Elements of Rhetoric.* Boston: Ginn, 1886.

Gere, Anne Ruggles. *Writing Groups: History, Theory, and Implications.* Carbondale: Southern Illinois UP, 1987.

Gibaldi, Joseph, ed. *Introduction to Scholarship in Modern Languages and Literatures.* New York: MLA, 1981.

Gibbon, Edward. *Miscellaneous Works.* Ed. John Sheffield. 2nd ed. 5 vols. London, 1814.

Giddens, Anthony. *Central Problems in Social Theory: Action, Structure, and Contradiction in Social Analysis.* Berkeley: U of California P, 1979.

——. *The Class Structure of the Advanced Societies.* London: Hutchinson, 1973.

——. *The Consequences of Modernity.* Stanford: Stanford UP, 1990.

Gilbert, Sandra M. "The American Sexual Poetics of Walt Whitman and Emily Dickinson." Bercovitch, *Reconstructing* 123–54.

Gilbert, Sandra M., and Susan Gubar. *The Madwoman in the Attic: The Woman Writer and the Nineteenth-Century Literary Imagination.* New Haven: Yale UP, 1979.

——. "The Mirror and the Vamp: Reflections on Feminist Criticism." R. Cohen, *Future* 144–66.

——. *No Man's Land: The Place of the Woman Writer in the Twentieth Century.* 2 vols. to date. New Haven: Yale UP, 1988–9. Vol. 1.: *The War of the Words.* Vol. 2: *Sexchanges.*

——, eds. *Norton Anthology of Literature by Women: The Tradition in English.* New York: Norton, 1985.

——. "Review Essay: A Revisionary Company." *Novel* 10 (1977): 158–66.

Gilmore, Michael T. *American Romanticism and the Marketplace.* Chicago: U of Chicago P, 1985.

Gilroy, Paul. *There Ain't No Black in the Union Jack.* London: Hutchinson, 1987.

Gilsdorf, Aletha Joy Bourne. "The Puritan Apocalypse: New England Eschatology in the Seventeenth Century." Diss. Yale U, 1965.

Girard, René. *Violence and the Sacred*. Trans. Patrick Gregory. Baltimore: Johns Hopkins UP, 1977.

Giroux, Henry A., ed. *Postmodernism, Feminism, and Cultural Politics: Redrawing Educational Boundaries*. Albany: State U of New York P, 1991.

Gleckner, Robert F., and Gerald E. Enscoe, eds. *Romanticism: Points of View*. Englewood Cliffs: Prentice, 1970.

Godzich, Wlad. "The Culture of Illiteracy." *Enclitic* 15–16 (1984): 27–35.

———. Foreword. *Heterologies: Discourses on the Other*. By Michel de Certeau. Trans. Brian Massumi. Minneapolis: U of Minnesota P, 1986. vii–xxi.

———. "The Tiger on the Paper Mat." De Man, *Resistance* ix–xviii.

Godzich, Wlad, and Jeffrey Kittay. *The Emergence of Prose*. Minneapolis: U of Minnesota P, 1987.

Goldberg, Jonathan. *James I and the Politics of Literature: Jonson, Donne, and Their Contemporaries*. Baltimore: Johns Hopkins UP, 1983.

———. "The Politics of Renaissance Literature: A Review Essay." *ELH* 49 (1982): 514–42.

———. "Textual Properties." *Shakespeare Quarterly* 37 (1986): 213–17.

———. *Voice Terminal Echo: Postmodernism and English Renaissance Texts*. New York: Methuen, 1986.

Golding, Sue. "James Dean: The Almost-Perfect Lesbian Hermaphrodite." *On Our Backs* (Winter 1988): 18–19, 39–44.

Goldstein, Laurence. *The Flying Machine and Modern Literature*. Bloomington: Indiana UP, 1986.

Gomez-Pena, Guillermo. "Documented/Undocumented." *The Graywolf Annual Five: Multi-cultural Literacy*. Ed. Rick Simonson and Scott Walker. Saint Paul: Graywolf, 1988. 127–34.

Goodheart, Eugene. "Against Coercion." Messer-Davidow 179–85.

Gornick, Vivian, and B. K. Moran. *Woman in Sexist Society: Studies in Power and Powerlessness*. New York: Basic, 1971.

Gossin, Pamela. *Literary Resolutions of Scientific Revolutions: Astronomy and the Literary Imaginations of Donne, Swift, and Hardy*. Diss. U of Wisconsin, 1989.

Grady, Hugh. *The Modernist Shakespeare: Critical Texts in a Material World*. New York: Oxford UP, 1991.

Graff, Gerald. *Professing Literature: An Institutional History*. Chicago: U of Chicago P, 1987.

———. "The Promise of American Literature Studies." *Professing* 209–25.

Graff, Gerald, and Michael Warner, eds. *The Origins of Literary Studies in America: A Documentary Anthology*. New York: Routledge, 1989.

Grahn, Judy. *Another Mother Tongue: Gay Words, Gay Worlds*. Boston: Beacon, 1984.

Gramsci, Antonio. *Selections from the Prison Notebooks*. Ed. and trans. Quintin Hoare and Geoffrey Nowell Smith. New York: International, 1971.

Graves, Richard L., ed. *Rhetoric and Composition: A Sourcebook for Teachers and Writers*. Upper Montclair: Boynton, 1984.

Green, D. H. "Orality and Reading: The State of Research in Medieval Studies." *Speculum* 65 (1990): 267–80.

Green, Richard Firth. *Poets and Princepleasers*. Toronto: U of Toronto P, 1980.

Greenblatt, Stephen J. Introduction. *The Forms of Power and the Power of Forms in the Renaissance*. Spec. issue of *Genre* 15.1–2 (1982): 3–6.

———. "Invisible Bullets: Renaissance Authority and Its Subversion." Dollimore and Sinfield, *Political Shakespeare* 18–47.

———. *Marvelous Possessions: The Wonder of the New World*. Chicago: U of Chicago P, 1991.

———. *Renaissance Self-Fashioning: From More to Shakespeare*. Chicago: U of Chicago P, 1980.

———, ed. *Representing the English Renaissance*. Berkeley: U of California P, 1988.

———. *Shakespearean Negotiations: The Circulation of Social Energy in Renaissance England*. Berkeley: U of California P, 1988.

———. "Towards a Poetics of Culture." *Southern Review* [Australia] 20 (1987): 3–15. Rpt. in Veeser 1–14.

Greene, Gayle, and Coppélia Kahn, eds. *Making a Difference: Feminist Literary Criticism*. New York: Methuen, 1985.

Greene, Thomas M. "The Poetics of Discovery: A Reading of Donne's Elegy 19." *Yale Journal of Criticism* 2 (1989): 129–43.

Gross, John J. *The Rise and Fall of the Man of Letters: A Study of the Idiosyncratic and the Humane in Modern Literature*. New York: Macmillan, 1969.

Grossberg, Lawrence, Cary Nelson, and Paula Treichler, eds. *Cultural Studies*. New York: Routledge, 1991.

Guha, Ranajit. "Dominance without Hegemony and Its Historiography." *Subaltern Studies*. Vol. 6. Ed. Guha. New Delhi: Oxford UP, 1989. 210–309.

———. "The Prose of Counter-insurgency." *Subaltern Studies*. Vol. 2. Ed. Guha. New Delhi: Oxford UP, 1983. 1–42.

Guha, Ranajit, and Gayatri C. Spivak, eds. *Selected Subaltern Studies*. New York: Oxford UP, 1988.

Guibbory, Achsah. *The Map of Time: Seventeenth-Century English Literature and Ideas of Pattern in History*. Urbana: U of Illinois P, 1986.

Guillory, John. "Canonical and Non-canonical: A Critique of the Current Debate." *ELH* 54 (1987): 483–527.

———. *Poetic Authority: Spenser, Milton, and Literary History*. New York: Columbia UP, 1983.

Gunew, Sneja. "Framing Marginalia: Distinguishing the Textual Politics of the Marginal Voice." *Southern Review* 10 (1985): 142–56.

Gunn, Daniel. *Psychoanalysis and Fiction: An Exploration of Literary and Psychoanalytic Borders*. Cambridge: Cambridge UP, 1988.

Gunn, Giles. *The Culture of Criticism and the Criticism of Culture*. New York: Oxford UP, 1987.

————. *F. O. Matthiessen: The Critical Achievement*. Seattle: U of Washington P, 1975.

————. "The Kingdoms of Theory and the New Historicism in America." *Yale Review* 76 (1987): 207–36.

————. *Thinking across the American Grain: Ideology, Intellect, and the New Pragmatism*. Chicago: U of Chicago P, 1992.

Gura, Philip P. *A Glimpse of Sion's Glory: Puritan Radicalism in New England, 1620–1660*. Middletown: Wesleyan UP, 1984.

Habermas, Jürgen. *Legitimation Crisis*. Trans. Thomas McCarthy. Boston: Beacon, 1975.

————. *The Philosophical Discourse of Modernity: Twelve Lectures*. Trans. Frederick G. Lawrence. Cambridge: MIT P, 1987.

Hairston, Maxine. "Breaking Our Bonds and Reaffirming Our Connections." *College Composition and Communication* 36 (1985): 272–83.

Hall, Stuart. *The Hard Road to Renewal*. London: Verso, 1988.

Hall, Stuart, Dorothy Hobson, Andrew Lowe, and Paul Willis, eds. *Culture, Media, Language: Working Papers in Cultural Studies, 1972–79*. London: Unwin, 1980.

Haller, William. *The Rise of Puritanism*. New York: Columbia UP, 1938.

Halley, Janet E. "The Politics of the Closet: Towards Equal Protection for Gay, Lesbian, and Bisexual Identity." *UCLA Law Review* 36.5 (1989): 915–76.

Halperin, David M. *One Hundred Years of Homosexuality and Other Essays on Greek Love*. New York: Routledge, 1989.

Hannay, Margaret P., ed. *Silent but for the Word: Tudor Women as Patrons, Translators, and Writers of Religious Works*. Kent: Kent State UP, 1985.

————. *Philip's Phoenix: Mary Sidney, Countess of Pembroke*. New York: Oxford UP, 1990.

Harasym, S., ed. *The Postcolonial Critic*. New York: Routledge, 1990.

Hardy, Barbara. *The Appropriate Form*. London: Athlone, 1964.

————. *The Novels of George Eliot*. London: Athlone, 1959.

Harkin, Patricia, and John Schilb, eds. *Contending with Words: Composition and Rhetoric in a Postmodern Age*. New York: MLA, 1991.

Harris, Joseph. "The Idea of Community in the Study of Writing." *College Composition and Communication* 40 (1989): 11–22.

Harrison, John A. *The Reactionaries: A Study of the Anti-democratic Intelligentsia*. New York: Schocken, 1966.

Hartman, Geoffrey H. *The Fate of Reading and Other Essays*. Chicago: U of Chicago P, 1975.

————. "I. A. Richards and the Dream of Communication." *Fate* 20–40.

————, ed. *Psychoanalysis and the Question of the Text*. Baltimore: Johns Hopkins UP, 1978.

———. "Romanticism and Anti-Self-Consciousness." *Beyond Formalism: Literary Essays 1958–1970*. New Haven: Yale UP, 1970. 298–310.

———. *Wordsworth's Poetry, 1787–1814*. 2nd ed. New Haven: Yale UP, 1971.

Hassan, Ihab. *The Dismemberment of Orpheus: Toward a Postmodern Literature*. 2nd ed. Madison: U of Wisconsin P, 1982.

———. *The Postmodern Turn: Essays in Postmodern Theory and Culture*. Columbus: Ohio State UP, 1987.

Hawkes, Terence. *That Shakespeherian Rag: Essays on a Critical Process*. New York: Methuen, 1986.

Hawthorne, Nathaniel. *The Scarlet Letter*. Boston: Houghton, 1883.

Hayles, N. Katherine. *The Cosmic Web: Scientific Field Models and Literary Strategies in the Twentieth Century*. Ithaca: Cornell UP, 1984.

Heath, Shirley Brice. *Ways with Words: Language, Life, and Work in Communities and Classrooms*. New York: Cambridge UP, 1983.

Hedrick, Beth. *The Love of Matter: Occultism and Authority in Seventeenth-Century Literature*. In progress.

Heidegger, Martin. *The Question Concerning Technology and Other Essays*. Trans. William Lovitt. New York: Harper, 1977.

Heilbrun, Carolyn G. "Bringing the Spirit Back to English Studies." Showalter, *New Feminist Criticism* 21–28.

———. "The Character of Hamlet's Mother." *Hamlet's Mother and Other Women*. New York: Columbia UP, 1990. 1–17.

———. "The Politics of Mind: Women, Tradition, and the University." *Papers on Language and Literature* 24 (1988): 231–44.

———. *Toward a Recognition of Androgyny*. New York: Knopf, 1973.

Heimann, Paula. "The Dynamics of Transference Interpretation." *International Journal of Psychoanalysis* 37 (1956): 303–10.

Heinzelman, Susan Sage. "Hard Cases, Easy Cases, and Weird Cases: Canon Formation in Law and Literature." *Mosaic* 21.2–3 (1988): 59–72.

Heisch, Allison, ed. *The Speeches of Queen Elizabeth I*. Madison: U of Wisconsin P, forthcoming.

Hejinian, Lyn. "Two Stein Talks: (1) Language and Realism, (2) Grammar and Landscape." *Temblor* 3 (1986): 128–39.

Helgerson, Richard. *Self-Crowned Laureates: Spenser, Jonson, Milton, and the Literary System*. Berkeley: U of California P, 1983.

Helsinger, Elizabeth, Robin Lauterbach Sheets, and William Veeder, eds. *The Woman Question: Society and Literature in Britain and America, 1837–1883*. 3 vols. New York: Garland, 1989.

Herbert, T. Walter, Jr. "Nathaniel Hawthorne, Una Hawthorne, and *The Scarlet Letter*: Interactive Selfhoods and the Cultural Construction of Gender." *PMLA* 103 (1988): 285–95.

Hertz, Neil. *The End of the Line: Essays on Psychoanalysis and the Sublime.* New York: Columbia UP, 1985.

Hester, M. Thomas. *Kinde Pitty and Brave Scorn: John Donne's Satyres.* Durham: Duke UP, 1982.

Higham, John, ed. *Ethnic Leadership in America.* Baltimore: Johns Hopkins UP, 1978.

Hill, Adams Sherman. *Principles of Rhetoric.* 1878. Rev. ed. New York: American, 1893.

Hill, Christopher. *Milton and the English Revolution.* 1977. New York: Viking, 1978.

Himmelfarb, Gertrude. *The New History and the Old: Critical Essays and Reappraisals.* Cambridge: Harvard UP, 1987.

Hinman, Charlton, ed. *The First Folio of Shakespeare.* New York: Norton, 1968.

*History and. . . .* Spec. issue of *New Literary History* 21 (1990): 239–432.

Hoffman, Daniel. *Form and Fable in American Fiction.* 1961. New York: Oxford UP, 1965.

Hoffman, Frederick J. *Freudianism and the Literary Mind.* Baton Rouge: Louisiana State UP, 1945.

Hogan, Patrick Colm, and Lalita Pandit, eds. *Criticism and Lacan: Essays and Dialogue on Language, Structure, and the Unconscious.* Athens: U of Georgia P, 1990.

Hogle, Jerrold E. *Shelley's Process: Radical Transference and the Development of His Major Works.* New York: Oxford UP, 1988.

Hohendahl, Peter Uwe. *The Institution of Criticism.* Ithaca: Cornell UP, 1982.

Holdstein, Deborah. *On Composition and Computers.* New York: MLA, 1987.

Holdstein, Deborah, and Cynthia L. Selfe. *Computers and Writing: Theory, Research, Practice.* New York: MLA, 1990.

Holland, Norman. *The Dynamics of Literary Response.* New York: Norton, 1968.

———. *Five Readers Reading.* New Haven: Yale UP, 1975.

———. *The I.* New Haven: Yale UP, 1985.

———. "Re-covering 'The Purloined Letter': Reading as a Personal Transaction." Muller and Richardson 307–22.

Hollibaugh, Amber, and Cherríe Moraga. "What We're Rollin' Around in Bed With." *Heresies* 12.3 (1981): 58–62.

Holloway, John. *The Victorian Sage.* London: Macmillan, 1953.

Holstun, James. "Ranting at the New Historicism." *English Literary Renaissance* 19 (1989): 189–225.

Homans, Margaret. *Bearing the Word: Language and Female Experience in Nineteenth-Century Women's Writing.* Chicago: U of Chicago P, 1986.

———. *Women Writers and Poetic Identity.* Princeton: Princeton UP, 1980.

Horkheimer, Max, and Theodor W. Adorno. *Dialectic of Enlightenment.* 1944. Trans. John Cumming. New York: Herder, 1972.

Horner, Winifred Bryan, ed. *Composition and Literature: Bridging the Gap.* Chicago: U of Chicago P, 1983.

——, ed. *Historical Rhetoric: An Annotated Bibliography of Selected Sources in English*. Boston: Hall, 1980.

——, ed. *The Present State of Scholarship in Historical and Contemporary Rhetoric*. Columbia: U of Missouri P, 1983.

Houghton, Walter. *The Victorian Frame of Mind, 1830–1870*. New Haven: Yale UP, 1957.

Howard, Jean E., and Marion F. O'Connor. *Shakespeare Reproduced: The Text in History and Ideology*. New York: Methuen, 1987.

Howard, June. "Feminist Differings: Recent Surveys of Feminist Literary Theory and Criticism." *Feminist Studies* 14 (1988): 167–90.

Howard, Leon. *The Connecticut Wits*. Chicago: U of Chicago P, 1943.

——. *Literature and the American Tradition*. Garden City: Doubleday, 1960.

Howe, Irving, ed. *The Idea of the Modern in Literature and the Arts*. New York: Horizon, 1967.

——. *A Margin of Hope: An Intellectual Autobiography*. New York: Harcourt, 1982.

——. "What Should We Be Teaching?" *Dissent* (Fall 1988): 477–79.

Huber, Bettina J. "Women in the Modern Languages, 1970–1990." *Profession 90*. New York: MLA, 1990. 58–73.

Hudson, Anne. *The Premature Reformation: Wycliffite Texts and Lollard History*. Oxford: Clarendon–Oxford UP, 1988.

Hull, Gloria T., Patricia Bell, and Barbara Smith. *All the Women Are White, All the Blacks Are Men, But Some of Us Are Brave: Black Women's Studies*. Old Westbury: Feminist, 1982.

Hull, Suzanne W. *Chaste, Silent, and Obedient: English Books for Women, 1475–1640*. San Marino: Huntington Lib., 1982.

Hunt, Lynn. "History as Gesture; or, The Scandal of History." Arac and Johnson 91–107.

——, ed. *The New Cultural History*. Berkeley: U of California P, 1989.

Hunter, J. Paul. *Before Novels: The Cultural Contexts of Eighteenth-Century English Fiction*. New York: Norton, 1990.

Hutcheon, Linda. *A Poetics of Postmodernism: History, Theory, and Fiction*. New York: Routledge, 1988.

——. *A Politics of Postmodernism*. New York: Routledge, 1989.

Huyssen, Andreas. *After the Great Divide: Modernism, Mass Culture, Postmodernism*. Bloomington: Indiana UP, 1986.

Hyman, Stanley Edgar. *The Armed Vision: A Study in the Methods of Modern Literary Criticism*. New York: Vintage, 1955.

Irigaray, Luce. *This Sex Which Is Not One*. Trans. Catherine Porter, with Carolyn Burke. Ithaca: Cornell UP, 1985.

Irmscher, William F. *Teaching Expository Writing*. New York: Holt, 1979.

Jacobus, Mary. *Reading Woman: Essays in Feminist Criticism*. New York: Columbia UP, 1986.

———. *Romanticism, Writing, and Sexual Difference: Essays on* The Prelude. Oxford: Clarendon–Oxford UP, 1990.

———. *Tradition and Experiment in Wordsworth's* Lyrical Ballads *(1798)*. Oxford: Clarendon–Oxford UP, 1966.

Jacoby, Russell. *The Last Intellectuals: American Culture in the Age of Academe*. New York: Basic, 1987.

James, Henry. *The Ambassadors*. New York: Harper, 1903.

James, Mervyn. "Ritual, Drama, and the Social Body in the Late Medieval English Town." *Past and Present* 98 (1983): 3–29.

Jameson, Fredric. *Fables of Aggression: Wyndham Lewis, the Modernist as Fascist*. Berkeley: U of California P, 1979.

———. Foreword. *Caliban and Other Essays*. By Roberto Retamar. Trans. E. Baker. Minneapolis: U of Minnesota P, 1989. vii–xii.

———. *Marxism and Form: Twentieth-Century Dialectical Theories of Literature*. Princeton: Princeton UP, 1971.

———. "Marxism and Historicism." *New Literary History* 1 (1979): 41–72.

———. "Modernism and Its Repressed: Or, Robbe-Grillet as Anti-colonialist." *The Ideologies of Theory: Essays, 1971–1986*. Minneapolis: U of Minnesota P, 1988. 167–80.

———. *The Political Unconscious: Narrative as a Socially Symbolic Act*. Ithaca: Cornell UP, 1981.

———. "Postmodernism; or, The Cultural Logic of Late Capitalism." *New Left Review* 146 (1984): 59–92. Rpt. in *Postmodernism* 1–54.

———. *Postmodernism; or, The Cultural Logic of Late Capitalism*. Durham: Duke UP, 1991.

JanMohamed, Abdul R., and David Lloyd, eds. *The Nature and Context of Minority Discourse*. New York: Oxford UP, 1991.

Jann, Rosemary. *The Art and Science of Victorian History*. Athens: Ohio State UP, 1985.

Jardine, Alice A. *Gynesis: Configurations of Woman and Modernity*. Ithaca: Cornell UP, 1985.

Jardine, Alice A., and Paul Smith, eds. *Men in Feminism*. New York: Methuen, 1987.

Jay, Martin. *The Dialectical Imagination: A History of the Frankfurt School and the Institute of Social Research*. Boston: Little, 1973.

Jehlen, Myra. *American Incarnation: The Individual, the Nation, and the Continent*. Cambridge: Harvard UP, 1986.

———. "Archimedes and the Paradox of Feminist Criticism." *Signs* 6 (1981): 575–601.

Johnson, Barbara. *The Critical Difference: Essays in the Contemporary Rhetoric of Reading*. Baltimore: Johns Hopkins UP, 1980.

———. "The Frame of Reference: Poe, Lacan, Derrida." Felman, *Literature* 457–505.

———. *A World of Difference*. Baltimore: Johns Hopkins UP, 1987.

Johnston, Kenneth R. *Wordsworth and "The Recluse."* New Haven: Yale UP, 1984.

Johnston, Kenneth R., and Gene Ruoff. *The Age of William Wordsworth: Critical Essays on the Romantic Tradition.* New Brunswick: Rutgers UP, 1987.

Johnston, Kenneth R., et al. *Romantic Revolutions: Criticism and Theory.* Bloomington: Indiana UP, 1990.

Jordan, Cynthia. *Second Stories: The Politics of Language, Form, and Gender in Early American Fictions.* Chapel Hill: U of North Carolina P, 1989.

Jordan, Frank, ed. *The English Romantic Poets: A Review of Research and Criticism.* 3rd rev. ed. and 4th ed. New York: MLA, 1972, 1985.

Jordan, Robert M. *Chaucer and the Shape of Creation: The Aesthetic Possibilities of Inorganic Structure.* Cambridge: Harvard UP, 1967.

Jordanova, Ludmilla. "Natural Facts: A Historical Perspective on Science and Sexuality." *Nature, Culture, and Gender.* Ed. Carol P. MacCormack and Marilyn Strathern. Cambridge: Cambridge UP, 1980. 42–69.

———. "Naturalizing the Family: Literature and the Bio-medical Sciences in the Late Eighteenth Century." *Languages of Nature: Critical Essays on Science and Literature.* Ed. Jordanova. New Brunswick: Rutgers UP, 1986. 86–116.

———. *Sexual Visions: Images of Gender in Science and Medicine between the Eighteenth and Twentieth Centuries.* Madison: U of Wisconsin P, 1989.

Kahn, Coppélia. *Man's Estate: Masculine Identity in Shakespeare.* Berkeley: U of California P, 1981.

Kamuf, Peggy. "Pieces of Resistance." *Reading de Man Reading.* Ed. Lindsay Waters and Wlad Godzich. Minneapolis: U of Minnesota P, 1989. 136–54.

Kane, George, and E. Talbot Donaldson, eds. Piers Plowman: *The B Version.* London: Athlone, 1975.

Kant, Immanuel. *Critique of Judgment.* Trans. J. H. Bernard. New York: Hafner, 1966.

———. "What Is Enlightenment?" *On History.* By Kant. Ed. and trans. Lewis White Beck. Indianapolis: Bobbs, 1957. 3–10.

Kaplan, E. Ann, ed. *Psychoanalysis and Cinema.* New York: Routledge, 1990.

Kaplan, Morton, and Robert Kloss. *The Unspoken Motive: A Guide to Psychoanalytic Literary Criticism.* New York: Free, 1973.

Kaplan, Sydney Janet. "Review Essay: Literary Criticism." *Signs* 4 (1979): 514–27.

Kasson, Joy S. *Marble Queens and Captives: Women in Nineteenth-Century American Sculpture.* New Haven: Yale UP, 1990.

Katz, Jonathan Ned. *Gay/Lesbian Almanac: A New Documentary.* New York: Harper, 1983.

Kauffman, Linda, ed. *Gender and Theory: Dialogues on Feminist Criticism.* Oxford: Blackwell, 1989.

Kazin, Alfred. *On Native Grounds: An Interpretation of Modern American Prose Literature.* New York: Reynal, 1942.

Keach, William. *Shelley's Style.* New York: Routledge, 1985.

Keesing, Roger M. "Anthropology as Interpretive Quest." *Current Anthropology* 28 (1987): 161–76.

Kelley, Theresa M. *Wordsworth's Revisionary Aesthetics*. New York: Cambridge UP, 1988.

Kellner, Hans. *Language and Historical Representation: Getting the Story Crooked*. Madison: U of Wisconsin P, 1989.

Kelly[-Gadol], Joan. "Did Women Have a Renaissance?" *Becoming Visible: Women in European History*. Ed. Renate Bridenthal and Claudia Koonz. Boston: Houghton, 1977. 139–61.

Kelsall, M., et al., eds. *Literature and Criticism: A New Century Guide*. Beckenham: Croom, 1990.

Kendrick, Christopher. *Milton: A Study in Ideology and Form*. London: Methuen, 1986.

Kenner, Hugh. *Dublin's Joyce*. 1956. New York: Columbia UP, 1987.

———. *A Homemade World: The American Modernist Writers*. 1975. Baltimore: Johns Hopkins UP, 1989.

———. *Joyce's Voices*. Berkeley: U of California P, 1978.

———. *The Poetry of Ezra Pound*. 1951. Lincoln: U of Nebraska P, 1985.

———. *The Pound Era*. Berkeley: U of California P, 1971.

———. *A Reader's Guide to Samuel Beckett*. New York: Farrar, 1973.

———. *Samuel Beckett: A Critical Study*. Berkeley: U of California P, 1974.

———. *A Sinking Island: The Modern English Writers*. 1988. Baltimore: Johns Hopkins UP, 1989.

———. *The Stoic Comedians: Flaubert, Joyce, and Beckett*. Berkeley: U of California P, 1974.

———. *Ulysses*. London: Allen, 1980.

Kerber, Linda. *Federalists in Dissent: Imagery and Ideology in Jeffersonian America*. Ithaca: Cornell UP, 1970.

Kermode, Frank. *Romantic Image*. 1957. New York: Vintage, 1964.

———. *The Sense of an Ending: Studies in the Theory of Fiction*. New York: Oxford UP, 1967.

Kerrigan, William. Introduction. Smith and Kerrigan ix–xxvii.

———. *The Sacred Complex: On the Psychogenesis of Paradise Lost*. Cambridge: Harvard UP, 1983.

Kerrigan, William, and Gordon Braden. *The Idea of the Renaissance*. Baltimore: Johns Hopkins UP, 1989.

Kettle, Arnold. *An Introduction to the English Novel*. London: Hutchinson U Lib., 1959.

Kibbey, Ann. *The Interpretation of Material Shapes in Puritanism: A Study of Rhetoric, Prejudice, and Violence*. New York: Cambridge UP, 1986.

King, Katie. "The Situation of Lesbianism as Feminism's Magical Sign: Contests for Meaning and the US Women's Movement, 1968–72." *Feminist Critiques of Popular Culture*. Ed. Paula Treichler and Ellen Wartella. Spec. issue of *Communication* 9 (1986): 65–91.

Kinneavy, James L. "The Basic Aims of Discourse." *College Composition and Communication* 20 (1969): 297–304.

———. *A Theory of Discourse.* 1971. New York: Norton, 1980.

Klancher, Jon P. *The Making of English Reading Audiences, 1790–1832.* Madison: U of Wisconsin P, 1987.

Knapp, John. "A Response to Mieke Bal's *Psychopoetics.*" *Style* 21.2 (1987): 259–80.

Knapp, Steven. "The Concrete Universal." Unpublished essay.

———. *Personification and the Sublime: Milton to Coleridge.* Cambridge: Harvard UP, 1985.

Knights, L. C. *Drama and Society in the Age of Jonson.* London: Chatto, 1937.

Knoepflmacher, U. C., and G. B. Tennyson, eds. *Nature and the Victorian Imagination.* Berkeley: U of California P, 1977.

Kohut, Heinz. *How Does Analysis Cure?* Ed. Arnold Goldberg. Chicago: U of Chicago P, 1984.

———. *The Search for Self: Selected Writings of Heinz Kohut, 1950–1978.* Ed. Paul H. Ornstein. 2 vols. New York: International UP, 1978.

———. *Self Psychology and the Humanities: Reflections on a New Psychoanalytic Approach.* Ed. Charles B. Strozier. New York: Norton, 1985.

Kolodny, Annette. "Dancing through the Minefield: Some Observations on the Theory, Practice, and Politics of a Feminist Literary Criticism." Showalter, *New Feminist Criticism* 144–67.

———. *The Land before Her: Fantasy and Experience of the American Frontiers, 1630–1860.* Chapel Hill: U of North Carolina P, 1984.

———. *The Lay of the Land: Metaphor and Experience in American Life and Letters.* Chapel Hill: U of North Carolina P, 1975.

———. "Review Essay: Literary Criticism." *Signs* 2 (1976): 404–21.

Kolve, V. A. *Chaucer and the Imagery of Narrative: The First Five Canterbury Tales.* Stanford: Stanford UP, 1984.

———. *The Play Called Corpus Christi.* Stanford: Stanford UP, 1966.

Koselleck, Reinhart. *Future's Past: On the Semantics of Historical Time.* Trans. Keith Tribe. Cambridge: MIT P, 1985.

Kozol, Jonathan. "The Politics of Syntax." *English Journal* 64 (1975): 22–27.

Kramarae, Cheris, and Paula A. Treichler. *A Feminist Dictionary.* Boston: Pandora, 1985.

Krieger, Murray, ed. *The Aims of Representation.* New York: Columbia UP, 1987.

Kris, Ernst. *Psychoanalytic Explorations in Art.* 1952. New York: Schocken, 1964.

Kucich, John. "Narrative Theory as History: A Review of Problems in Victorian Fiction Studies." *Victorian Studies* 28 (1985): 657–75.

Kurtzweil, Edith, and William Philips, eds. *Literature and Psychoanalysis.* New York: Columbia UP, 1983.

Lacan, Jacques. "Agency of the Letter in the Unconscious." *Ecrits* 146–78.

——. "Desire and the Interpretation of Desire in *Hamlet*." *Yale French Studies* 55–56 (1977): 11–52.

——. *Ecrits*. Trans. Alan Sheridan. London: Tavistock, 1977.

——. *The Four Fundamental Concepts of Psycho-analysis*. Ed. Jacques-Alain Miller. Trans. Alan Sheridan. London: Hogarth, 1977.

——. "The Freudian Thing; or, The Meaning of the Return to Freud in Psychoanalysis." *Ecrits* 114–45.

——. *The Seminars of Jacques Lacan, 1954–55*. Ed. Jacques-Alain Miller. Trans. Sylvana Tomaselli. Cambridge: Cambridge UP, 1988.

——. "Where Is Speech? Where Is Language?" *Seminars* 277–93.

LaCapra, Dominick. "Rethinking Intellectual History and Reading Texts." *Rethinking Intellectual History*. Ithaca: Cornell UP, 1983. 23–71.

——. *Soundings in Critical Theory*. Ithaca: Cornell UP, 1989.

Laclau, Ernesto, and Chantal Mouffe. *Hegemony and Socialist Strategy: Towards a Radical Democratic Politics*. Trans. Winston Moore and Paul Cammack. London: Verso, 1985.

Lamb, Mary Ellen. *Gender and Authorship in the Sidney Circle*. Madison: U of Wisconsin P, 1990.

Landes, Joan. *Women and the Public Sphere in the Age of the French Revolution*. Ithaca: Cornell UP, 1988.

Landry, Donna. *The Muses of Resistance: Laboring-Class Women's Poetry in Britain, 1739–1796*. Cambridge: Cambridge UP, 1990.

Lang, Amy Schrager. "Introduction to *The Captivity and Restoration of Mrs. Mary Rowlandson*." *Journeys in New Worlds: Early American Women's Narratives*. Ed. Daniel B. Shea. Madison: U of Wisconsin P, 1990. 13–26.

——. *Prophetic Woman: Anne Hutchinson and the Problem of Dissent in the Literature of New England*. Berkeley: U of California P, 1987.

Langbaum, Robert. *The Poetry of Experience: The Dramatic Monologue in Modern Literary Tradition*. New York: Norton, 1957.

Langer, Susanne K. *Philosophy in a New Key*. Cambridge: Harvard UP, 1957.

Lanham, Richard A. *Literacy and the Survival of Humanism*. New Haven: Yale UP, 1983.

Lanser, Susan S. "Feminist Criticism, 'The Yellow Wallpaper,' and the Politics of Color in America." *Feminist Studies* 15 (1989): 415–41.

Lanser, Susan S., and Evelyn T. Beck. "[Why] Are There No Great Women Critics? And What Difference Does It Make?" *The Prism of Sex: Essays in the Sociology of Knowledge*. Ed. Julia A. Sherman and Beck. Madison: U of Wisconsin P, 1979. 79–91.

Laplanche, Jean. *Life and Death in Psychoanalysis*. Trans. Jeffrey Mehlman. Baltimore: Johns Hopkins UP, 1976.

Lardner, James. "War of the Words." *Washington Post* 6 Mar. 1983: G1+.

Larson, Richard L. "Selected Bibliography of Research and Writing about the Teaching of Composition." *College Composition and Communication* 26–30 (May 1975–79).

———. "Selected Bibliography of Scholarship on Composition and Rhetoric." *College Composition and Communication* 38–39 (Oct. 1987–88).

Lauter, Paul, et al., eds. *The Heath Anthology of American Literature*. Lexington: Heath, 1990.

Lawlor, John. "The Imaginative Unity of *Piers Plowman*." *Review of English Studies* ns 8 (1957): 241–61.

Lawrence, D. H. "The Future of the Novel: Surgery for the Novel—or a Bomb." Lawrence, *Study* 149–55.

———. *The Letters of D. H. Lawrence*. Ed. George Zytaruk and James Boulton. 4 vols. to date. Cambridge: Cambridge UP, 1980–.

———. *Studies in Classic American Literature*. 1923. New York: Viking, 1961.

———. "Study of Thomas Hardy." *Study* 1–128.

———. *Study of Thomas Hardy and Other Essays*. Ed. Bruce Steele. Cambridge: Cambridge UP, 1985.

Leavis, F. R. *English Literature in Our Time and the University*. London: Chatto, 1967.

———. *The Great Tradition*. New York: Stewart, 1948.

———, ed. *Mill on Bentham and Coleridge*. New York: Stewart, 1950.

———. *New Bearings in English Poetry: A Study of the Contemporary Situation*. 1932. London: Chatto, 1954.

Leavy, Stanley. Rev. of *Ecrits: A Selection*, by Jacques Lacan. *New York Times* 2 Oct. 1977: 10+.

Leclaire, Serge. "Jerome; or, Death in the Life of the Obsessed." Schneiderman 94–113.

Lentricchia, Frank. *After the New Criticism*. Chicago: U of Chicago P, 1980.

———. *Criticism and Social Change*. Chicago: U of Chicago P, 1983.

———. "Foucault's Legacy." Veeser 231–42.

Le Roy Ladurie, Emmanuel. *Carnival in Romans*. Trans. Mary Feeney. New York: Braziller, 1979.

Lesser, Simon O. *The Whispered Meanings: Selected Essays of Simon O. Lesser*. Ed. Robert Sprich and Richard W. Noland. Amherst: U of Massachusetts P, 1977.

Levenson, Jill, ed. *Romeo and Juliet*. New York: Oxford UP, forthcoming.

Levenson, Michael H. *A Genealogy of Modernism: A Study of English Literary Doctrine, 1908–1922*. Cambridge: Cambridge UP, 1984.

Levine, George. *The Boundaries of Fiction: Carlyle, Macaulay, Newman*. Princeton: Princeton UP, 1968.

———. *Darwin and the Novelists: Patterns of Science in Victorian Fiction*. Cambridge: Harvard UP, 1988.

———. *The Realistic Imagination: English Fiction from* Frankenstein *to* Lady Chatterley. Chicago: U of Chicago P, 1981.

Levine, George, and William Madden, eds. *The Art of Victorian Prose*. New York: Oxford UP, 1968.

Levine, Robert S. *Conspiracy and Romance: Studies in Brockden Brown, Cooper, Hawthorne, and Melville*. New York: Cambridge UP, 1989.

Levinson, Marjorie. *Keats's Life of Allegory: The Origins of a Style*. Oxford: Blackwell, 1988.

———. *The Romantic Fragment Poem*. Chapel Hill: U of North Carolina P, 1986.

———. *Wordsworth's Great Period Poems*. Cambridge: Cambridge UP, 1986.

Levinson, Marjorie, Marilyn Butler, Jerome McGann, and Paul Hamilton. *Rethinking Historicism: Critical Readings in Romantic History*. Oxford: Blackwell, 1989.

Lewis, R. W. B. *The American Adam: Innocence, Tragedy, and Tradition in the Nineteenth Century*. Chicago: U of Chicago P, 1955.

Lindemann, Erika. *CCCC Bibliography of Composition and Rhetoric: 1989*. Carbondale: Southern Illinois UP, 1991.

———, ed. *Longman Bibliography of Composition and Rhetoric: 1984–1985* and *1986*. New York: Longman, 1987, 1988.

———. *A Rhetoric for Writing Teachers*. 1982. 2nd ed. New York: Oxford UP, 1987.

Liu, Alan. "The Power of Formalism: The New Historicism." *ELH* 56 (1989): 721–71.

———. *Wordsworth: The Sense of History*. Stanford: Stanford UP, 1989.

Lloyd-Jones, Richard, and Andrea A. Lunsford, eds. *The English Coalition Conference: Democracy through Language*. Urbana: NCTE, 1989.

Locke, John. *An Essay Concerning Human Understanding*. Ed. Alexander Campbell Fraser. 2 vols. New York: Dover, 1959.

Lockridge, Laurence S. *The Ethics of Romanticism*. Cambridge: Cambridge UP, 1989.

Loewald, Hans. "Psychoanalytic Theory and the Psychoanalytic Process." *Psychoanalytic Study of the Child* 25 (1970): 45–68.

Loewenstein, Joseph. "The Script in the Marketplace." *Representations* 12 (1985): 101–14.

Lorde, Audre. *Sister Outsider: Essays and Speeches*. Trumansburg: Crossing, 1984.

Lovejoy, Arthur O. "On the Discrimination of Romanticisms." 1924. Gleckner and Enscoe 66–81.

Lukács, Georg. *History and Class Consciousness: Studies in Marxist Dialectics*. 1923. Trans. Rodney Livingstone. Cambridge: MIT P, 1971.

Lunsford, Andrea A., Helene Moglen, and James Slevin, eds. *The Right to Literacy*. New York: MLA, 1990.

Lyotard, Jean-François. *The Postmodern Condition: A Report on Knowledge*. Trans. Geoff Bennington and Brian Massumi. Minneapolis: U of Minnesota P, 1984.

Mabbott, Thomas Ollive. "Text of 'The Purloined Letter,' with Notes." Muller and Richardson 3–27.

Macdonell, Diane. *Theories of Discourse*. Oxford: Blackwell, 1986.

Macfarlane, Alan. *The Origins of English Individualism: The Family, Property, and Social Transition*. Cambridge: Cambridge UP, 1978.

Machiavelli, Niccolò. The Prince *and the Discourses*. Ed. Max Lerner. New York: Modern Lib., 1950.

MacIntyre, Alasdair. *After Virtue*. London: Duckworth, 1981.

Mack, Maynard. *Collected in Himself: Essays Critical, Biographical, and Bibliographical on Pope and Some of His Contemporaries*. Newark: U of Delaware P, 1982.

MacKinnon, Catharine A. "Feminism, Marxism, Method, and the State: An Agenda for Theory." *Signs* 7 (1982): 515–44.

———. "Feminism, Marxism, Method, and the State: Toward a Feminist Jurisprudence." *Signs* 8 (1983): 635–58.

Macrorie, Ken. *Telling Writing*. Rochelle Park: Hayden, 1970.

Mailloux, Steven. *Interpretive Conventions: The Reader in the Study of American Fiction*. Ithaca: Cornell UP, 1982.

Maimon, Elaine. "Cinderella to Hercules: Demythologizing Writing across the Curriculum." *Journal of Basic Writing* 2 (1980): 3–11.

———. "Talking to Strangers." *College Composition and Communication* 30 (1979): 364–69.

———. "Writing in All the Arts and Sciences: Getting Started and Gaining Momentum." *WPA: Writing Program Administration* 4 (1981): 9–13.

Mallin, Eric. *The End of Troy: Shakespeare at Mid-Career*. Forthcoming.

Mann, Michael. "The Social Cohesion of Liberal Democracy." *American Sociological Review* 35 (1970): 423–39.

Mann, Paul. *The Theory Death of the Avant-Garde*. Bloomington: Indiana UP, 1991.

Manning, Peter J. *Reading Romantics: Texts and Contexts*. New York: Oxford UP, 1990.

Marcus, George E., and Michael J. Fischer, eds. *Anthropology as Cultural Critique: An Experimental Moment in the Human Sciences*. Chicago: U of Chicago P, 1986.

Marcus, Jane, ed. *Virginia Woolf: A Feminist Slant*. Lincoln: U of Nebraska P, 1983.

———, ed. *Virginia Woolf and Bloomsbury: A Centenary Celebration*. Bloomington: Indiana UP, 1985.

Marcus, Leah S. *Puzzling Shakespeare: Local Reading and Its Discontents*. Chicago: U of Chicago P, 1988.

Marcuse, Herbert. *One-Dimensional Man: Studies in the Ideology of Advanced Industrial Society*. Boston: Beacon, 1964.

Marks, Elaine, and Isabelle de Courtivron, eds. *New French Feminisms: An Anthology*. New York: Schocken, 1981.

Marotti, Arthur. *John Donne, Coterie Poet*. Madison: U of Wisconsin P, 1986.

———. *Manuscript, Print, and the English Renaissance Lyric*. In progress.

Marr, David. *American Worlds since Emerson*. Amherst: U of Massachusetts P, 1987.

Marshall, David. *The Figure of the Theater: Shaftesbury, Defoe, Adam Smith, and George Eliot*. New York: Columbia UP, 1986.

Martin, Loy. *Browning's Dramatic Monologues and the Post-Romantic Subject*. Baltimore: Johns Hopkins UP, 1985.

Martin, Nancy, et al. *Writing and Learning across the Curriculum 11–16*. London: Ward Lock, 1976.

Martin, Wendy. *An American Triptych: Anne Bradstreet, Emily Dickinson, Adrienne Rich*. Chapel Hill: U of North Carolina P, 1984.

Marx, Karl, and Friedrich Engels. *The Marx-Engels Reader*. Ed. Robert C. Tucker. 2nd ed. New York: Norton, 1978.

Marx, Leo. *The Machine in the Garden: Technology and the Pastoral Ideal in America*. New York: Oxford UP, 1964.

Matthiessen, F. O. *The Achievement of T. S. Eliot: An Essay on the Nature of Poetry*. 1935, 1947. 3rd ed. New York: Oxford UP, 1959.

———. *American Renaissance: Art and Expression in the Age of Emerson and Whitman*. New York: Oxford UP, 1941.

Maus, Katharine. *Ben Jonson and the Roman Frame of Mind*. Princeton: Princeton UP, 1984.

McCanles, Michael. "The Authentic Discourse of the Renaissance." *Diacritics* 10 (1980): 77–87.

McCarthy, Thomas. *The Critical Theory of Jürgen Habermas*. Cambridge: MIT P, 1978.

———. "Translator's Introduction." Habermas, *Legitimation Crisis* vii–xxiv.

McColley, Diane Kelsey. "Milton and the Sexes." *Cambridge Companion to Milton*. Ed. Dennis Danielson. Cambridge: Cambridge UP, 1989. 147–66.

———. *Milton's Eve*. Urbana: U of Illinois P, 1983.

McColley, Grant. Paradise Lost: *An Account of Its Growth and Major Origins*. Chicago: Packard, 1940.

McDermott, John J. "Cultural Literacy." *Streams of Experience: Reflections on the History and Philosophy of American Culture*. Amherst: U of Massachusetts P, 1986. 185–90.

McDowell, Deborah E. "Negotiations between Tenses: Witnessing Slavery after Freedom—*Dessa Rose*." McDowell and Rampersad 144–63.

———. "New Directions for Black Feminist Criticism." Showalter, *New Feminist Criticism* 186–99.

McDowell, Deborah E., and Arnold Rampersad, eds. *Slavery and the Literary Imagination*. Baltimore: Johns Hopkins UP, 1989.

McEuen, Kathryn. *Classical Influence upon the Tribe of Ben*. Cedar Rapids: Torch, 1939.

McFarland, Thomas. *Originality and Imagination*. Baltimore: Johns Hopkins UP, 1985.

———. *Romanticism and the Forms of Ruin: Wordsworth, Coleridge, and Modalities of Fragmentation*. Princeton: Princeton UP, 1981.

McFarlane, K. B. *John Wycliffe and the Beginnings of Nonconformity*. London: English UP, 1952.

McGann, Jerome J. *The Beauty of Inflections: Literary Investigations in Historical Method and Theory*. Oxford: Clarendon–Oxford UP, 1985.

——. "Christina Rossetti's Poems: A New Edition and a Revaluation." *Victorian Studies* 23 (1980): 237–54.

——. *A Critique of Modern Textual Criticism.* Chicago: U of Chicago P, 1983.

——, ed. *Historical Studies and Literary Criticism.* Madison: U of Wisconsin P, 1985.

——. *Romantic Ideology.* Chicago: U of Chicago P, 1983.

——. *Social Values and Poetic Acts: The Theoretical Judgment of Literary Work.* Cambridge: Harvard UP, 1988.

——. *Swinburne: An Experiment in Criticism.* Chicago: U of Chicago P, 1972.

McKay, Nellie. "Response." Messer-Davidow 161–67.

McKenzie, D. F. *Bibliography and the Sociology of Texts.* London: British Lib., 1986.

McKeon, Michael. *The Origins of the English Novel, 1600–1740.* Baltimore: Johns Hopkins UP, 1987.

McLeod, Randall. "UN *Editing* Shak-speare." *Substance* 33–34 (1982): 26–55.

McLuskie, Kathleen. *Renaissance Dramatists.* Atlantic Highlands: Humanities, 1989.

McQuade, Donald A. "The Case of the Migrant Workers." *WPA: Writing Program Administration* 5 (1981): 29–35.

——, ed. *The Territory of Language: Linguistics, Stylistics, and the Teaching of Composition.* Carbondale: Southern Illinois UP, 1986.

McQuade, Donald, et al., eds. *The Harper American Literature.* New York: Harper, 1986.

McWilliams, John P. *Hawthorne, Melville, and the American Character.* New York: Cambridge UP, 1984.

——. *Political Justice in a Republic.* Berkeley: U of California P, 1972.

Mellor, Anne K. *English Romantic Irony.* Cambridge: Harvard UP, 1980.

——, ed. *Romanticism and Feminism.* Bloomington: Indiana UP, 1988.

Meltzer, Françoise, ed. *The Trial(s) of Psychoanalysis.* Spec. issue of *Critical Inquiry* 13 (1987): 215–414.

Melville, Herman. "Bartleby the Scrivener." *Selected Writings of Herman Melville.* New York: Random, 1952. 3–47.

——. *The Confidence-Man: His Masquerade.* New York: Grove, 1955.

——. *Pierre; or, The Ambiguities.* New York: Grove, 1957.

Messer-Davidow, Ellen. "The Philosophical Bases of Feminist Literary Criticisms." With comments by Joan Hartman, Cary Nelson, Ruth Hubbard, Gerald Graff, Patricia Clark Smith, Amy Ling, Nellie McKay, Jane Tompkins, Eugene Goodheart. *New Literary History* 19 (1987): 63–195.

Michaels, Walter Benn. *The Gold Standard and the Logic of Naturalism.* Berkeley: U of California P, 1987.

Michaels, Walter Benn, and Donald E. Pease, eds. *The American Renaissance Reconsidered: Selected Papers from the English Institute, 1982–83.* Baltimore: Johns Hopkins UP, 1985.

Middlekauff, Robert. *The Mathers: Three Generations of Puritan Intellectuals, 1596–1728.* New York: Oxford UP, 1971.

Middleton, Anne. "Introduction: The Critical Heritage." *A Companion to* Piers Plowman. Ed. John A. Alford. Berkeley: U of California P, 1988. 1–25.

Miles, Josephine. *Fields of Learning.* Berkeley: Oyez, 1968.

Miller, D. A. *Narrative and Its Discontents: Problems of Closure in the Traditional Novel.* Princeton: Princeton UP, 1981.

———. *The Novel and the Police.* Berkeley: U of California P, 1988.

Miller, J. Hillis. *Charles Dickens: The World of His Novels.* Cambridge: Harvard UP, 1959.

———. *The Disappearance of God: Five Nineteenth-Century Writers.* Cambridge: Harvard UP, 1963.

———. *Fiction and Repetition: Seven English Novels.* Cambridge: Harvard UP, 1982.

———. *The Form of Victorian Fiction.* Notre Dame: U of Notre Dame P, 1968.

———. *The Linguistic Moment: From Wordsworth to Stevens.* Princeton: Princeton UP, 1985.

———. "Narrative and History." *ELH* 41 (1974): 455–73.

———. "Optic and Semiotic in *Middlemarch.*" *The Worlds of Victorian Fiction.* Ed. J. H. Buckley. Cambridge: Harvard UP, 1975. 125–45.

———. *Poets of Reality: Six Twentieth-Century Writers.* 1965. New York: Atheneum, 1969.

———. "Presidential Address 1986. The Triumph of Theory, the Resistance to Reading, and the Question of the Material Base." *PMLA* 102 (1987): 281–91.

Miller, Jane. *Women Writing about Men.* New York: Pantheon, 1986.

Miller, Nancy K. *Subject to Change: Reading Feminist Writing.* New York: Columbia UP, 1988.

Miller, Perry. *Errand into the Wilderness.* Cambridge: Harvard UP, 1956.

———. *The New England Mind.* 2 vols. Vol. 1: *The Seventeenth Century.* 1936. Vol. 2: *From Colony to Province.* 1953. Boston: Beacon, 1953.

Miller, Susan. *Rescuing the Subject: A Critical Introduction to Rhetoric and the Writer.* Carbondale: Southern Illinois UP, 1989.

Millett, Kate. Personal Communication. 26 Mar. 1990.

———. *Sexual Politics.* 1970. New York: Ballantine, 1978.

Milton, John. *Complete Poems and Major Prose.* Ed. Merritt Y. Hughes. Indianapolis: Bobbs, 1957.

Minnis, A. J. *Medieval Theory of Authorship: Scholastic Literary Attitudes in the Later Middle Ages.* London: Scolar, 1984.

*Misogyny, Misandry, and Misanthropy.* Spec. issue of *Representations* 20 (1987): 1–228.

Mitchell, W. J. T. *Blake's Composite Art: A Study of the Illuminated Poetry.* Princeton: Princeton UP, 1978.

MLA Commission on Writing and Literature. "Report of the Commission on Writing and Literature." *Profession 88.* New York: MLA, 1988.

Modiano, Raimonda. *Coleridge and the Concept of Nature*. Tallahassee: Florida State UP, 1985.

Moers, Ellen. *Literary Women: The Great Writers*. 1976. New York: Oxford UP, 1985.

Moffett, James. *Teaching the Universe of Discourse*. Boston: Houghton, 1968.

Mohanty, Chandra Talpade, Ann Russo, and Lourdes Torres, eds. *Third World Women and the Politics of Feminism*. Bloomington: Indiana UP, 1991.

Moi, Toril. *Sexual/Textual Politics: Feminist Literary Theory*. New York: Methuen, 1985.

Montrose, Louis. " 'Eliza, Queene of Shepheardes' and the Pastoral of Power." *English Literary Renaissance* 10 (1980): 153–82.

——. "Of Gentlemen and Shepherds: The Politics of Elizabethan Pastoral Form." *ELH* 50 (1983): 415–59.

——. " 'The Place of a Brother' in *As You Like It*: Social Process and Comic Form." *Shakespeare Quarterly* 32 (1981): 28–54.

——. "The Purpose of Playing: Reflections on a Shakespearean Anthropology." *Helios* ns 7 (1980): 51–74.

——. "Renaissance Literary Studies and the Subject of History." *English Literary Renaissance* 16 (1986): 5–12.

——. " 'Shaping Fantasies': Figurations of Gender and Power in Elizabethan Culture." *Representations* 2 (1983): 61–94.

Moraga, Cherríe. *Loving in the War Years: Lo que nunca paso por sus labios*. Boston: South End, 1983.

Morton, A. L., ed. *Freedom in Arms: A Selection of Leveller Writings*. New York: International, 1975.

Mulhern, Frances. *The Moment of "Scrutiny."* London: NLB, 1979.

Mullan, John. *Sentiment and Sociability: The Language of Feeling in the Eighteenth Century*. Oxford: Clarendon–Oxford UP, 1988.

Mullaney, Steven. "Lying like the Truth: Riddle, Representation, and Treason in Renaissance England." *ELH* 47 (1980): 32–48.

——. *The Place of the Stage: License, Play, and Power in Renaissance England*. Chicago: U of Chicago P, 1988.

——. "Strange Things, Gross Terms, Curious Customs: The Rehearsal of Cultures in the Late Renaissance." *Representations* 3 (1983): 40–67.

Muller, John P., and William J. Richardson, eds. *The Purloined Poe: Lacon, Derrida, and Psychoanalytic Reading*. Baltimore: Johns Hopkins UP, 1988.

Mulvey, Laura. "Visual Pleasure and Narrative Cinema." *Screen* 16.3 (1975): 6–18.

Murray, Donald M. *A Writer Teaches Writing*. 2nd ed. Boston: Houghton, 1985.

Murray, K. M. Elizabeth. *Caught in the Web of Words: James Murray and the Oxford English Dictionary*. Oxford: Oxford UP, 1979.

Muscatine, Charles. *Chaucer and the French Tradition*. Berkeley: U of California P, 1957.

——. "The Locus of Action in Medieval Narrative." *Romance Philology* 17 (1963): 115–22.

Nandy, Ashis. *The Intimate Enemy: Loss and Recovery of Self under Colonialism.* New York: Oxford UP, 1983.

Nason, John H. *Efficient Composition.* New York: New York UP, 1917.

Neely, Carol T. "Constructing the Subject: Feminist Practice and New Renaissance Discourses." *English Literary Renaissance* 18 (1988): 5–18.

———. "Feminist Criticism in Motion." *For Alma Mater: Theory and Practice in Feminist Scholarship.* Ed. Paula Treichler, Cheris Kramarae, and Beth Stafford. Urbana: U of Illinois P, 1985. 69–90.

Neff, Emery. *Carlyle.* New York: Norton, 1932.

———. *Carlyle and Mill: An Introduction to Victorian Thought.* New York: Columbia UP, 1926.

Nelson, Cary. "Feminism, Language, and Philosophy." Messer-Davidow 117–28.

———. *Repression and Recovery: Modern American Poetry and the Politics of Cultural Memory, 1910–1945.* Madison: U of Wisconsin P, 1989.

Nelson, Cary, and Lawrence Grossberg, eds. *Marxism and the Interpretation of Culture.* Urbana: U of Illinois P, 1988.

Nestle, Joan. "Butch-Fem Relationships." *Heresies* 2.3 (1981): 21–24.

Newman, Charles. *The Post-modern Aura: The Act of Fiction in an Age of Inflation.* Evanston: Northwestern UP, 1985.

Newman, Karen. *Fashioning Femininity and English Renaissance Drama.* Chicago: U of Chicago P, 1991.

Newton, Esther. "The Mythic Mannish Lesbian: Radclyffe Hall and the New Woman." *The Lesbian Issue: Essays from Signs.* Ed. Estelle B. Freedman et al. Chicago: U of Chicago P, 1985. 7–25.

Newton, Judith. "History as Usual?: Feminism and the 'New Historicism.'" *Cultural Critique* 9 (1988): 87–121.

Nichols, Stephen, ed. *The New Philology.* Spec. issue of *Speculum* 65.1 (1990): 1–266.

———. "Philology in a Manuscript Culture." *New Philology* 1–10.

Nicholson, Linda, ed. *Feminism/Postmodernism.* New York: Routledge, 1989.

Nietzsche, Friedrich. The Birth of Tragedy *and* The Genealogy of Morals. Trans. Francis Golffing. New York: Doubleday, 1956.

Norbrook, David. *Poetry and Politics in the English Renaissance.* London: Routledge, 1984.

Nussbaum, Felicity. *The Autobiographical Subject: Gender and Ideology in Eighteenth-Century England.* Baltimore: Johns Hopkins UP, 1989.

Nussbaum, Felicity, and Laura Brown, eds. *The New Eighteenth Century: Theory, Politics, English Literature.* New York: Methuen, 1987.

Nyquist, Mary, and Margaret W. Ferguson. *Re-membering Milton: Essays on the Texts and Traditions.* New York: Methuen, 1987.

Oakeshott, Michael, ed. *Leviathan.* By Thomas Hobbes. Oxford: Blackwell, 1957.

O'Gorman, Edmundo. *The Invention of America: An Inquiry into the Historical Nature of the New World and the Meaning of Its History.* Westport: Greenwood, 1972.

Oliphant, Dave, and Robin Bradford, eds. *New Directions in Textual Studies*. Austin: Ransom Center, U of Texas, 1990.

Olsen, Tillie. "Women Who Are Writers in Our Century: One Out of Twelve." *College English* 34 (1972): 6–17.

Ong, Walter J. *Orality and Literacy: The Technologizing of the Word*. New York: Methuen, 1982.

Opdyke, John B. *Working Composition*. Boston: Heath, 1917.

Orgel, Stephen. "The Authentic Shakespeare." *Representations* 21 (1988): 1–25.

——, ed. *The Complete Masques*. By Ben Jonson. New Haven: Yale UP, 1969.

——. *The Illusion of Power: Political Theater in the English Renaissance*. Berkeley: U of California P, 1975.

——. "Nobody's Perfect; or, Why Did the English Stage Take Boys for Women?" *South Atlantic Quarterly* 88 (1989): 7–29.

Orgel, Stephen, and Roy Strong, eds. *Inigo Jones: The Theatre of the Stuart Court*. 2 vols. Berkeley: U of California P, 1973.

Ottaway, David B. "U.S. Alerted to Embassy Bugs in '79." *Washington Post* 23 Apr. 1987: A1+.

Ozick, Cynthia. "Science and Letters: God's Work—and Ours." *New York Times Book Review* 27 Sept. 1987: 3+.

Panofsky, Erwin. *Meaning in the Visual Arts*. New York: Anchor-Doubleday, 1955.

Paradis, James, and Thomas Postlewait, eds. *Victorian Science and Victorian Values*. New Brunswick: Rutgers UP, 1981.

Parker, Patricia. *Literary Fat Ladies: Rhetoric, Gender, Property*. New York: Methuen, 1987.

Parker, Reeve. *Coleridge's Meditative Art*. Ithaca: Cornell UP, 1975.

Parkes, Malcolm B. "The Influence of the Concepts of *Ordinatio* and *Compilatio* on the Development of the Book." *Medieval Learning and Literature: Essays Presented to R. W. Hunt*. Ed. J. J. G. Alexander and M. T. Gibson. Oxford: Oxford UP, 1975. 115–41.

Parry, Graham. *The Golden Age Restor'd: The Culture of the Stuart Court, 1603–42*. New York: St. Martin's, 1981.

Patterson, Annabel. *Censorship and Interpretation: The Conditions of Writing and Reading in Early Modern England*. Madison: U of Wisconsin P, 1984.

Patterson, Lee, ed. *Literary Practice and Social Change in Britain, 1380–1530*. The New Historicism: Studies in Cultural Poetics 8. Berkeley: U of California P, 1990.

——. *Negotiating the Past: The Historical Understanding of Medieval Literature*. Madison: U of Wisconsin P, 1987.

——. " 'No man his reson herde': Peasant Consciousness, Chaucer's Miller, and the Structure of the *Canterbury Tales*." *Literary Practice* 113–55.

——. "On the Margin: Postmodernism, Ironic History, and Medieval Studies." Nichols, *New Philology* 87–108.

Paulson, Ronald. *Breaking and Remaking: Aesthetic Practice in England, 1700–1820*. New Brunswick: Rutgers UP, 1989.

Payne, Robert. *The Key of Remembrance*. New Haven: Yale UP, 1963.

Pease, Donald E. "*Moby Dick* and the Cold War." Michaels and Pease 113–55.

———. *Visionary Compacts: American Renaissance Writings in Cultural Context*. Madison: U of Wisconsin Press, 1987.

Pebworth, Ted-Larry, and Ernest W. Sullivan II. "Rational Presentation of Multiple Textual Traditions." *Papers of the Bibliographical Society of America* 83 (1989): 43–60.

Pêcheux, Michel. *Language, Semantics, and Ideology: Stating the Obvious*. New York: St. Martin's, 1982.

Pechter, Edward. "The New Historicism and Its Discontents: Politicizing Renaissance Drama." *PMLA* 102 (1987): 292–303.

Pecora, Vincent P. "The Limits of Local Knowledge." Veeser 243–76.

Pequigney, Joseph. *Such Is My Love: A Study of Shakespeare's Sonnets*. Chicago: U of Chicago P, 1985.

Perl, Sondra. "Understanding Composing." *College Composition and Communication* 31 (1980): 363–69.

Perloff, Marjorie. *The Dance of the Intellect: Studies in the Poetry of the Pound Tradition*. Cambridge: Cambridge UP, 1985.

———. *The Futurist Moment: Avant-Garde, Avant-Guerre, and the Language of Rupture*. Chicago: U of Chicago P, 1986.

———. *The Poetics of Indeterminacy: Rimbaud to Cage*. Princeton: Princeton UP, 1981.

Perry, William G. *Intellectual and Ethical Development in the College Years*. New York: Holt, 1970.

Pinch, Adela. "Female Chatter: Meter, Masochism, and the *Lyrical Ballads*." *ELH* 55 (1988): 835–52.

Poggioli, Renato. *The Theory of the Avant-Garde*. Trans. Gerald Fitzgerald. 1962. Cambridge: Harvard UP, 1968.

Poirier, Richard. *The Performing Self: Compositions and Decompositions in the Languages of Contemporary Life*. New York: Oxford UP, 1971.

———. "The Politics of Self-Parody." *Partisan Review* 35 (1968): 339–53.

———. *The Renewal of Literature: Emersonian Reflections*. New York: Random, 1987.

———. *Robert Frost: The Work of Knowing*. New York: Oxford UP, 1977.

Pollak, Ellen. *The Poetics of Sexual Myth: Gender and Ideology in the Verse of Swift and Pope*. Chicago: U of Chicago P, 1985.

Ponsot, Marie, and Rosemary Deen. *Beat Not the Poor Desk*. Upper Montclair: Boynton, 1982.

Poovey, Mary. *Uneven Developments: The Ideological Work of Gender in Mid-Victorian England*. Chicago: U of Chicago P, 1988.

Porte, Joel, ed. *Emerson: Prospect and Retrospect*. Harvard English Studies 10. Cambridge: Harvard UP, 1982.

Porter, Carolyn. "Are We Being Historical Yet?" *South Atlantic Quarterly* 87 (1988): 743–86.

———. "History and Literature: 'After the New Historicism.'" *New Literary History* 21 (1990): 253–72.

———. "Reification and American Literature." Bercovitch and Jehlen 188–217.

———. *Seeing and Being: The Plight of the Participant Observer in Emerson, James, Adams, and Faulkner.* Middletown: Wesleyan UP, 1981.

Poster, Mark. *The Mode of Information: Poststructuralism and Social Context.* Chicago: U of Chicago P, 1990.

Postman, Neal. *Amusing Ourselves to Death: Public Discourse in the Age of Show Business.* New York: Penguin, 1985.

Pound, Ezra. "A Retrospect." 1918. *The Literary Essays of Ezra Pound.* Ed. T. S. Eliot. London: Faber, 1954. 3–14.

Pythian-Adams, Charles. "Ceremony and the Citizen: The Communal Year at Coventry 1450–1550." *Crisis and Order in English Towns, 1500–1700.* Ed. Peter Clark and Paul Slack. Toronto: U of Toronto P, 1972. 57–85.

———. *Desolation of a City: Coventry and the Urban Crisis of the Late Middle Ages.* Cambridge: Cambridge UP, 1979.

Quint, David. *Epic and Empire.* Princeton: Princeton UP, forthcoming.

Rajan, Balachandra. *The Form of the Unfinished: English Poetics from Spenser to Pound.* Princeton: Princeton UP, 1985.

Rajan, Tillotama. *Dark Interpreter: The Discourse of Romanticism.* Ithaca: Cornell UP, 1980.

———. *The Supplement of Reading: Figures of Understanding in Romantic Theory and Practice.* Ithaca: Cornell UP, 1990.

Rampersad, Arnold. *The Life of Langston Hughes.* New York: Oxford UP, 1986.

Rapaport, Herman. "*Effi Briest* and *La Chose Freudienne.*" Hogan and Pandit 223–47.

Rebhorn, Wayne A. *Foxes and Lions: Machiavelli's Confidence Men.* Ithaca: Cornell UP, 1988.

Reed, Adolph, Jr., ed. *Race, Politics, and Culture.* New York: Greenwood, 1986.

Reed, Arden, ed. *Romanticism and Language.* Ithaca: Cornell UP, 1984.

Register, Cheri. "American Feminist Literary Criticism: A Bibliographical Introduction." *Feminist Literary Criticism: Explorations in Theory.* Ed. Josephine Donovan. Lexington: UP of Kentucky, 1975. 1–28.

———. "Review Essay: Literary Criticism." *Signs* 6 (1980): 268–82.

Reguero, Helen. *The Limits of Imagination: Wordsworth, Yeats, and Stevens.* Ithaca: Cornell UP, 1976.

Reynolds, David S. *Beneath the American Renaissance: The Subversive Imagination in the Age of Emerson and Melville.* New York: Knopf, 1988.

Rich, Adrienne. "Compulsory Heterosexuality and Lesbian Existence." *Women, Sex, and Sexuality.* Ed. Catharine R. Stimpson and Ethel Spector Person. Chicago: U of Chicago P, 1980. 62–91.

———. *On Lies, Secrets, and Silence: Selected Prose, 1966–1978.* New York: Norton, 1979.

———. "When We Dead Awaken: Writing as Re-vision." *College English* 34 (1972): 18–30.

Richards, I. A. *The Philosophy of Rhetoric.* 1936. New York: Oxford UP, 1965.

———. *Practical Criticism: A Study of Literary Judgment.* 1929. New York: Harcourt, 1960.

Richards, I. A., and C. K. Ogden. *The Meaning of Meaning.* 1923. San Diego: Harcourt, 1989.

Richardson, Robert D. *Henry Thoreau: A Life of the Mind.* Berkeley: U of California P, 1986.

Richetti, John. *Philosophical Writing: Locke, Berkeley, Hume.* Cambridge: Harvard UP, 1983.

Ricoeur, Paul. *Freud and Philosophy: An Essay on Interpretation.* Trans. Denis Savage. New Haven: Yale UP, 1970.

Rieff, Philip. "The Impossible Culture." *Salmagundi* 58–59 (1982–83): 406–26.

Riggs, David. *Ben Jonson: A Life.* Cambridge: Harvard UP, 1989.

Rimbaud, Arthur. "Une saison en enfer." *Oeuvres.* Ed. Suzanne Bernard. Paris: Garnier, 1980. 211–41.

Rimmon-Kenan, Shlomith, ed. *Discourse in Psychoanalysis and Literature.* London: Methuen, 1987.

Robbins, Bruce. "Power and Pantheons: Literary Tradition in Some Literary Journals." *Literature and History* 8.2 (1982): 147–58.

Roberts, Josephine A., ed. *The Countess of Montgomerie's Urania.* By Mary Wroth. 2 vols. In progress.

———, ed. *The Poems of Lady Mary Wroth.* Baton Rouge: Louisiana State UP, 1983.

Robertson, D. W. *A Preface to Chaucer.* Princeton: Princeton UP, 1962.

Robertson, Linda R., Sharon Crowley, and Frank Lentricchia. "The Wyoming Conference Resolution Opposing Unfair Salaries and Working Conditions for Post-secondary Teachers of Writing." *College English* 49 (1987): 274–80.

Robinson, Jeffrey. *The Walk: Notes on a Romantic Image.* Norman: U of Oklahoma P, 1989.

Robinson, Lillian S. *Sex, Class, and Culture.* 1978. New York: Methuen, 1986.

Roe, Nicholas. *Wordsworth and Coleridge: The Radical Years.* Oxford: Clarendon–Oxford UP, 1988.

Rogers, Katharine M. *The Troublesome Helpmate: A History of Misogyny in Literature.* Seattle: U of Washington P, 1966.

Rogin, Michael Paul. *Subversive Genealogy: The Politics and Art of Herman Melville.* Berkeley: U of California P, 1979.

Rohman, Gordon. "Pre-writing: The Stage of Discovery in the Writing Process." *College Composition and Communication* 16 (1965): 106–12.

Roland, Alan, ed. *Psychoanalysis, Creativity, and Literature: A French-American Inquiry.* New York: Columbia UP, 1978.

Rorty, Richard. *Consequence of Pragmatism.* Minneapolis: U of Minnesota P, 1982.

———. *Contingency, Irony, and Solidarity.* Cambridge: Cambridge UP, 1989.

———. *Philosophy and the Mirror of Nature.* Princeton: Princeton UP, 1979.

Rose, Mark. *The Author as Proprietor.* Cambridge: Harvard UP, 1992.

———. "The Author as Proprietor: *Donaldson v. Becket* and the Genealogy of Modern Authorship." *Representations* 23 (1988): 51–85.

Rose, Mary Beth. *The Expense of Spirit: Love and Sexuality in Renaissance Drama.* Ithaca: Cornell UP, 1988.

———, ed. *Women in the Middle Ages and the Renaissance: Literary and Historical Perspectives.* Syracuse: Syracuse UP, 1986.

Rose, Mike. "The Language of Exclusion: Writing Instruction at the University." *College English* 47 (1985): 341–59.

———. *Lives on the Boundary: The Struggles and Achievements of America's Underprepared.* New York: Free, 1989.

———. "Remedial Writing Courses: A Critique and a Proposal." *College English* 45 (1983): 109–28.

Rose, Phyllis. *Woman of Letters: A Life of Virginia Woolf.* New York: Oxford UP, 1978.

Rosen, Victor. "The Relevance of 'Style' to Certain Aspects of Defence and the Synthetic Function of the Ego." *International Journal of Psychoanalysis* 42 (1961): 447–57.

Rosenberg, Rosalind. *Beyond Separate Spheres: Intellectual Roots of Modern Feminism.* New Haven: Yale UP, 1982.

Rosenblatt, Louise M. *Literature as Exploration.* 1938. New York: MLA, 1983.

Ross, Andrew. *No Respect: Intellectuals and Popular Culture.* New York: Routledge, 1989.

Ross, Marlon B. *The Contours of Masculine Desire: Romanticism and the Rise of Women's Poetry.* New York: Oxford UP, 1989.

Rousseau, G. S., and Roy Porter. *Exoticism in the Enlightenment.* Manchester: Manchester UP, 1990.

———. *Sexual Underworlds of the Enlightenment.* Chapel Hill: U of North Carolina P, 1988.

Rowe, John Carlos. "From Documentary to Docudrama: Vietnam on Television in the 1980s." *Genre* 21 (1988): 451–77.

Rubin, Gayle. "Thinking Sex: Notes for a Radical Theory of the Politics of Sexuality." Vance 267–319.

———. "The Traffic in Women: Notes on the 'Political Economy' of Sex." *Toward an Anthropology of Women.* Ed. Rayna R. Reiter. New York: Monthly Review, 1975. 157–210.

Ruland, Richard, and Malcolm Bradbury. *From Puritanism to Postmodernism.* London: Routledge, 1991.

Rumrich, John Peter. *Matter of Glory: A New Preface to* Paradise Lost. Pittsburgh: U of Pittsburgh P, 1987.

——. *Uninventing Milton.* In progress.

Sahlins, Marshall. *Culture and Practical Reason.* Chicago: U of Chicago P, 1975.

——. *Islands of History.* Chicago: U of Chicago P, 1985.

Sahlins, Peter. "Natural Frontiers Revisited: France's Boundaries since the Seventeenth Century." *American Historical Review* 95 (1990): 1423–51.

Said, Edward. *After the Last Sky: Palestinian Lives.* New York: Pantheon, 1986.

——. *Beginnings.* New York: Columbia UP, 1975.

——. "Opponents, Audiences, Constituencies, and Community." *Critical Inquiry* 9 (1982): 1–26.

——. "Third World Intellectuals and Metropolitan Culture." *Raritan* 9.3 (1990): 27–50.

——. *The World, the Text, and the Critic.* Cambridge: Harvard UP, 1983.

Sánchez, Marta Ester. *Contemporary Chicana Poetry: A Critical Approach to an Emerging Literature.* Berkeley: U of California P, 1985.

Sangari, Kumkum, and Sudesh Vaid, eds. *Recasting Women in India: Essays in Colonial History.* New Brunswick: Rutgers UP, 1990.

Sartre, Jean-Paul. *Critique of Dialectical Reason: Theory of Practical Ensembles.* Trans. Alan Sheridan-Smith. Vol. 1. London: NLB, 1976.

——. *Imagination: A Psychological Critique.* Trans. Forrest Williams. Ann Arbor: U of Michigan P, 1972.

Schenck, Celeste M. "All of a Piece: Women's Poetry and Autobiography." *Life/lines: Theorizing Women's Autobiography.* Ed. Bella Brodzki and Schenck. Ithaca: Cornell UP, 1988. 281–305.

*Schlesinger Library on the History of Women in America, Radcliffe College.* Spec. issue of *Schlesinger Library's Current Periodicals* 14 (Oct. 1989).

Schneiderman, Daniel, ed. *Returning to Freud: Clinical Psychoanalysis in the School of Lacan.* New Haven: Yale UP, 1980.

Scholes, Robert. *Protocols of Reading.* New Haven: Yale UP, 1989.

——. *Textual Power: Literary Theory and the Teaching of English.* New Haven: Yale UP, 1985.

Schor, Ira. *Freire for the Classroom: A Sourcebook for Liberatory Teaching.* Portsmouth: Heinemann, 1987.

Schor, Naomi. "Female Paranoia: The Case for Psychoanalytic Feminist Criticism." *Yale French Studies* 62 (1981): 204–19.

——. "For a Restricted Thematic." Eisenstein and Jardine 167–92.

Schwartz, Mimi, ed. *Writer's Craft, Teacher's Art: Teaching What We Know.* Portsmouth: Boynton, 1991.

Schwartz, Regina M. *Remembering and Repeating: Biblical Creation in* Paradise Lost. Cambridge: Cambridge UP, 1988.

Schwartz, Sanford. *The Matrix of Modernism: Pound, Eliot, and Early Twentieth-Century Thought.* Princeton: Princeton UP, 1985.

Scott, Bonnie Kime, ed. *The Gender of Modernism: A Critical Anthology.* Bloomington: Indiana UP, 1990.

Scribner, Sylvia, and Michael Cole. *The Psychology of Literacy.* Cambridge: Harvard UP, 1981.

Scrivener, Michael Henry. *Radical Shelley: The Philosophical Anarchism and Utopian Thought of Percy Bysshe Shelley.* Princeton: Princeton UP, 1982.

Scruton, Roger. *Kant.* New York: Oxford UP, 1982.

"Security at the American Embassy in Moscow and the United States–Soviet Embassy Exchange Agreements." *Hearings before the Subcommittee of International Operations of the Committee on Foreign Affairs, House of Representatives* 22 Apr. 1987. Washington: GPO, 1988. 35–127.

Sedgwick, Eve Kosofsky. *Between Men: English Literature and Male Homosocial Desire.* New York: Columbia UP, 1985.

——. *Epistemology of the Closet.* Berkeley: U of California P, 1990.

——. "Jane Austen and the Masturbating Girl." *Critical Inquiry* 17 (1991): 818–37.

Seidel, Michael. *Exile and the Narrative Imagination.* New Haven: Yale UP, 1986.

Sen, Sunil. *Agrarian Struggle in Bengal, 1946–47.* New Delhi: Oxford UP, 1972.

Shaffer, E. S. *'Kubla Khan' and* The Fall of Jerusalem: *The Mythological School in Biblical Criticism and Secular Literature, 1770–1880.* Cambridge: Cambridge UP, 1975.

Shankman, Paul. "The Thick and the Thin: On the Interpretive Theoretical Program of Clifford Geertz." *Current Anthropology* 25 (1984): 262–79.

Shaughnessy, Mina P. *Errors and Expectations: A Guide for the Teacher of Basic Writing.* New York: Oxford UP, 1977.

Shoaf, R. A. *Milton, Poet of Duality: A Study of Semiosis in the Poetry and the Prose.* New Haven: Yale UP, 1985.

Showalter, Elaine. "A Criticism of Our Own: Autonomy and Assimilation in Afro-American and Feminist Literary Theory." R. Cohen, *Future* 347–69.

——. "Feminist Criticism in the Wilderness." *New Feminist Criticism* 243–70.

——. *A Literature of Their Own: British Women Novelists from Brontë to Lessing.* Princeton: Princeton UP, 1977.

——, ed. *The New Feminist Criticism: Essays on Women, Literature, and Theory.* New York: Pantheon, 1985.

——. "Review Essay: Literary Criticism." *Signs* 1 (1975): 435–60.

——. "Toward a Feminist Poetics." *New Feminist Criticism* 125–43.

——. "Women's Time, Women's Space: Writing the History of Feminist Criticism." Benstock, *Feminist Issues* 30–44.

Shulman, Robert. *Social Criticism and Nineteenth-Century American Fictions.* Columbia: U of Missouri P, 1987.

Shuttleworth, Sally. *George Eliot and Nineteenth-Century Science: The Make-Believe of a Beginning*. Cambridge: Cambridge UP, 1984.

Simpson, David. *Irony and Authority in Romantic Poetry*. London: Macmillan, 1979.

———. "Literary Criticism and the Return to 'History.'" *Critical Inquiry* 14 (1988): 721–47.

———. *Wordsworth and the Figurings of the Real*. Atlantic Highlands: Humanities, 1982.

———. *Wordsworth's Historical Imagination: The Poetry of Displacement*. New York: Methuen, 1987.

Simpson, Lewis P. *The Dispossessed Garden: Pastoral and History in Southern Literature*. Athens: U of Georgia P, 1975.

Siskin, Clifford. *The Historicity of Romantic Discourse*. New York: Oxford UP, 1988.

Skinner, Quentin. "Meaning and Understanding in the History of Ideas." *History and Theory* 8 (1969): 3–53.

Skura, Meredith. *The Literary Use of the Psychoanalytic Process*. New Haven: Yale UP, 1981.

Slatin, John M. "Text and Hypertext: Reflections on the Role of the Computer in Teaching Modern American Poetry." *Humanities and the Computer: New Directions*. Ed. David S. Miall. Oxford: Clarendon–Oxford UP, 1990. 123–35.

Slemon, Stephen. "Cultural Alterity and Colonial Discourse." *Southern Review* 20 (1987): 102–07.

Slotkin, Richard. *Regeneration through Violence: The Mythology of the American Frontier*. Middletown: Wesleyan UP, 1973.

Smith, Barbara K., ed. *Home Girls: A Black Feminist Anthology*. New York: Kitchen Table, 1983.

———. "Toward a Black Feminist Criticism." Showalter, *New Feminist Criticism* 168–85.

Smith, Bruce R. *Homosexual Desire in Shakespeare's England: A Cultural Poetics*. Chicago: U of Chicago P, 1991.

Smith, Henry Nash. "Symbol and Idea in *Virgin Land*." Bercovitch and Jehlen 21–35.

———. *Virgin Land: The American West as Symbol and Myth*. Cambridge: Harvard UP, 1950.

Smith, Joseph H., and William Kerrigan, eds. *Interpreting Lacan*. Psychiatry and the Humanities 6. New Haven: Yale UP, 1983.

Smith, Paul. *Discerning the Subject*. Minneapolis: U of Minnesota P, 1988.

Sollors, Werner. *Amiri Baraka/Leroi Jones: The Quest for a "Populist Modernism."* New York: Columbia UP, 1978.

———. *Beyond Ethnicity: Consent and Descent in American Culture*. New York: Oxford UP, 1986.

Solomon, Barbara Miller. *In the Company of Educated Women*. New Haven: Yale UP, 1985.

Sommers, Nancy. "Responding to Student Writing." *College Composition and Communication* 33 (1982): 148–56.

——. "Revision Strategies of Student Writers and Experienced Adult Writers." *College Composition and Communication* 31 (1980): 378–88.

Sperry, Stuart M. *Shelley's Major Verse: The Narrative and Dramatic Poetry.* Cambridge: Harvard UP, 1988.

Spiegel, Gabrielle. "History, Historicism, and the Social Logic of the Text in the Middle Ages." Nichols, *New Philology* 59–86.

Spiller, Robert, et al. *Literary History of the United States.* 1949. New York: Macmillan, 1953.

Spillers, Hortense. "Changing the Letter." McDowell and Rampersad 25–61.

Spillers, Hortense, and Marjorie Pryse, eds. *Conjuring: Black Women, Black Fiction, and Literary Tradition.* Bloomington: Indiana UP, 1985.

Spivak, Gayatri Chakravorty. "French Feminism in an International Frame." Spec. issue of *Yale French Studies* 62 (1981): 154–84.

——. *In Other Worlds: Essays in Cultural Politics.* New York: Methuen, 1987.

——. "The Letter as Cutting Edge." Felman, *Literature* 208–26.

——. "Poststructuralism, Marginality, Postcolonialism, and Value." *Literary Theory Today.* Ed. P. Collier and H. Gaya Ryan. Cambridge: Polity, 1990. 219–44.

Stallybrass, Peter, and Allon White. *The Politics and Poetics of Transgression.* Ithaca: Cornell UP, 1986.

Stanton, Domna C. "Autogynography: Is the Subject Different?" *The Female Autograph.* Ed. Stanton. New York: New York Literary Forum, 1984. 5–22.

Stein, Gertrude. *How Writing Is Written.* Ed. Robert B. Haas. Los Angeles: Black Sparrow, 1974.

Stepto, Robert. "Distrust of the Reader in Afro-American Narratives." Bercovitch, *Reconstructing* 300–22.

——. *From behind the Veil: A Study of Afro-American Narrative.* Urbana: U of Illinois P, 1979.

Stimpson, Catharine R. "Knowing Women." Marjorie Smart Memorial Lecture. *Women in Higher Education.* Ed. D. R. Jones and S. L. Davies. Armidale: Univ. of New England [Australia], 1990. 11–47.

——. "Presidential Address 1990. On Differences." *PMLA* 106 (1991): 402–11.

——. "Woolf's Room, Our Project." R. Cohen, *Future* 129–43.

Stock, Brian. "*Antiqui* or *Moderni?*" *New Literary History* 10 (1979): 391–400.

——. *The Implications of Literacy.* Princeton: Princeton UP, 1983.

——. "The Middle Ages as Subject and Object: Romantic Attitudes and Academic Medievalism." *New Literary History* 5 (1974): 527–47.

Stocking, George W., Jr. "Matthew Arnold, E. B. Tylor, and the Uses of Invention." *Race, Culture, and Evolution: Essays in the History of Anthropology.* Chicago: U of Chicago P, 1968. 69–90.

Stoddard, Thomas B. "Gay Marriage: A Must or a Bust? Why Gay People Should Seek the Right to Marry." *Out/look: National Lesbian and Gay Quarterly* 6 (1989): 9–13.

Stone, Lawrence. *The Family, Sex, and Marriage in England, 1500–1800.* New York: Harper, 1977.

Strier, Richard. *Love Known: Theology and Experience in George Herbert's Poetry.* Chicago: U of Chicago P, 1983.

Sukenick, Ronald. *The Death of the Novel and Other Stories.* New York: Dial, 1969.

Summerfield, Judith, and Geoffrey Summerfield. *Texts and Contexts: A Contribution to the Theory and Practice of Teaching Composition.* New York: Random, 1986.

Sundquist, Eric J. "*Benito Cereno* and New World Slavery." Bercovitch, *Reconstructing* 93–122.

Svendsen, Kester. *Milton and Science.* Cambridge: Harvard UP, 1956.

Swann, Jim. "Giving New Depth to the Surface: Psychoanalysis, Literature, and Society." *Psychoanalytic Review* 62 (1975): 5–28.

Tannenbaum, Leslie. *Biblical Tradition in Blake's Early Prophecies: The Great Code of Art.* Princeton: Princeton UP, 1982.

Tashjian, Dickran. *Skyscraper Primitives: Dada and the American Avant-Garde, 1910–1925.* Middletown: Wesleyan UP, 1975.

Tate, Gary, ed. *Teaching Composition: Twelve Bibliographic Essays.* Fort Worth: Texas Christian UP, 1987.

Taylor, Charles. *Philosophy and the Human Sciences.* Cambridge: Cambridge UP, 1985.

Taylor, Frederick Winslow. *Principles of Scientific Management.* New York: Harper, 1911.

Taylor, Gary, and Michael Warren, eds. *The Division of the Kingdoms: Shakespeare's Two Versions of King Lear.* Oxford: Clarendon–Oxford UP, 1983.

Tennenhouse, Leonard. *Power on Display: The Politics of Shakespeare's Genres.* New York: Methuen, 1986.

Thomas, Keith. *Religion and the Decline of Magic: Studies in Popular Beliefs in Sixteenth- and Seventeenth-Century England.* 1971. Harmondsworth, Eng.: Penguin, 1973.

Thompson, E. P. *The Making of the English Working Class.* New York: Viking, 1963.

——. *The Poverty of Theory.* London: Merlin, 1978.

Thompson, Hunter S. *Fear and Loathing in Las Vegas.* San Francisco: Straight Arrow, 1972.

Thompson, John B. *Studies in the Theory of Ideology.* Berkeley: U of California P, 1984.

Tichi, Cecelia. *New World, New Earth: Environmental Reform in American Literature from the Puritans through Whitman.* New Haven: Yale UP, 1979.

——. *Shifting Gears: Technology, Literature, Culture in Modernist America.* Chapel Hill: U of North Carolina P, 1987.

Tillyard, E. M. W. *The Elizabethan World Picture: A Study of the Idea of Order in the Age of Shakespeare, Donne, and Milton.* London: Chatto, 1943.

Tinberg, Howard B. " 'An Enlargement of Observations': More on Theory Building in the

Composition Classroom." *College Composition and Communication* 42 (1991): 36–44.

Todd, Janet M. *The Sign of Angellica: Women, Writing, and Fiction, 1660–1800.* London: Virago, 1989.

Todorov, Tzvetan. *The Conquest of America: The Question of the Other.* Trans. Richard Howard. New York: Harper, 1984.

———. *Theories of the Symbol.* Trans. Catherine Porter. 1977. Ithaca: Cornell UP, 1982.

Tomlinson, Charles. *Some Americans: A Personal Record.* Berkeley: U of California P, 1981.

Tompkins, Jane. *Sensational Designs: The Cultural Work of American Fiction, 1790–1860.* New York: Oxford UP, 1985.

Trachtenberg, Alan. *Reading American Photographs: Images as History, Mathew Brady to Walker Evans.* New York: Hill, 1989.

Trilling, Lionel. *Beyond Culture: Essays on Literature and Learning.* New York: Viking, 1965.

———. "Freud and Literature." *The Liberal Imagination: Essays on Literature and Society.* Garden City: Doubleday, 1953. 32–54.

Trollope, Anthony. *Barchester Towers.* London: Oxford UP, 1960.

Trousdale, Marion. "A Trip through the Divided Kingdoms." *Shakespeare Quarterly* 37 (1986): 218–23.

Trumbach, Randolph, ed. *Sodomy Trials: Seven Documents.* New York: Garland, 1986.

Tucker, Herbert. *Browning's Beginnings: The Art of Disclosure.* Minneapolis: U of Minnesota P, 1980.

———. *Tennyson and the Doom of Romanticism.* Cambridge: Harvard UP, 1987.

Turner, Frederick Jackson. "The Significance of the Frontier in American History." *The Frontier in American History.* New York: Holt, 1920. 1–38.

Turner, James Grantham. *One Flesh: Paradisal Marriage and Sexual Relations in the Age of Milton.* Oxford: Clarendon–Oxford UP, 1987.

Tuve, Rosemond. *Allegorical Imagery.* Princeton: Princeton UP, 1966.

Tuveson, Ernest Lee. *Millennium and Utopia: A Study in the Background of the Idea of Progress.* Berkeley: U of California P, 1949.

Ulmer, Gregory L. *Applied Grammatology: Post(e)-Pedagogy from Jacques Derrida to Joseph Beuys.* Baltimore: Johns Hopkins UP, 1984.

Underdown, David. *Revel, Riot, and Rebellion: Popular Politics and Culture in England, 1603–1660.* Oxford: Clarendon–Oxford UP, 1985.

Urkowitz, Steven. *Shakespeare's Revision of* King Lear. Princeton: Princeton UP, 1980.

Vale, Juliet. *Edward III and Chivalry.* Woodbridge: Boydell, 1982.

Vale, Malcolm. *War and Chivalry.* London: Duckworth, 1981.

Vance, Carole S., ed. *Pleasure and Danger: Exploring Female Sexuality.* Boston: Routledge, 1984.

Veeser, H. Aram, ed. *The New Historicism.* New York: Routledge, 1989.

Vendler, Helen. *The Odes of John Keats.* Cambridge: Harvard UP, 1983.

———. *Part of Nature, Part of Us: Modern American Poets.* Cambridge: Harvard UP, 1980.

Vicinus, Martha. *The Industrial Muse: A Study of Nineteenth-Century British Working-Class Literature.* New York: Barnes, 1975.

———, ed. *Suffer and Be Still: Women in the Victorian Age.* Bloomington: Indiana UP, 1973.

———, ed. *A Widening Sphere: Changing Roles of Victorian Women.* Bloomington: Indiana UP, 1977.

Vickers, Brian, ed. *Occult and Scientific Mentalities in the Renaissance.* Cambridge: Cambridge UP, 1984.

Vygotsky, Lev. *Thought and Language.* Trans. Eugenia Hanfman and Gertrude Vakar. Cambridge: MIT P, 1962.

Wagner, Roy. *The Invention of Culture.* Rev. ed. Chicago: U of Chicago P, 1981.

Waldrep, Tom, ed. *Writers on Writing.* 2 vols. New York: Random, 1988.

Walker, Julia M., ed. *Milton and the Idea of Woman.* Urbana: U of Illinois P, 1988.

Wall, Cheryl, ed. *Changing Our Own Words: Essays on Criticism, Theory, and Writing by Black Women.* New Brunswick: Rutgers UP, 1989.

Wallace, David. "Carving Up Time and the World: Medieval-Renaissance Turf Wars: Historiography and Personal History." Working Papers 11. Milwaukee: U of Wisconsin, Center for Twentieth-Century Studies, 1990–91. 1–24.

Waller, Marguerite. "Academic Tootsie: The Denial of Difference and the Difference It Makes." *Diacritics* 17 (1987): 2–20.

Wallerstein, Robert S. "One Psychoanalysis or Many?" *International Journal of Psychoanalysis* 69 (1988): 5–21.

Walters, Ronald G. "Signs of the Times: Clifford Geertz and Historians." *Social Research* 47 (1980): 537–56.

Warminski, Andrzej. "Deconstruction in America/Heidegger Reading Hölderlin." *Critical Exchange* 17 (Winter 1985): 45–59.

———. *Readings in Interpretation: Hölderlin, Hegel, Heidegger.* Minneapolis: U of Minnesota P, 1987.

Warner, Michael. *The Letters of the Republic: Publication and the Public Sphere in Eighteenth-Century America.* Cambridge: Harvard UP, 1990.

Warner, William B. *Reading* Clarissa: *The Struggles of Interpretation.* New Haven: Yale UP, 1979.

Warren, Joyce W. *The American Narcissus: Individualism and Women in Nineteenth-Century American Fiction.* 1984. New Brunswick: Rutgers UP, 1989.

Warren, Michael, ed. *The Complete* King Lear, *1608–1623.* Berkeley: U of California P, 1989.

Washington, Mary Helen, ed. *Black-Eyed Susan: Classic Stories by and about Black Women.* Garden City: Anchor-Doubleday, 1975.

Watney, Simon. "The Spectacle of AIDS." Crimp 71–86.

Watt, Ian. *Conrad in the Nineteenth Century.* Berkeley: U of California P, 1979.

Wayne, Don E. "New Historicism." *Literature and Criticism: A New Century Guide*. Ed. Kelsall et al. London: Routledge, 1990.

——. *Penshurst: The Semiotics of Place and the Poetics of History*. Madison: U of Wisconsin P, 1984.

——. "Power, Politics, and the Shakespearean Text." Howard and O'Connor 47–67.

Weber, Donald. "Historicizing the Errand." *American Literary History* 2 (1990): 101–18.

Weber, Samuel. *Institution and Interpretation*. Minneapolis: U of Minnesota P, 1987.

——. Introduction. *Demarcating the Disciplines*. Minneapolis: U of Minnesota P, 1986. ix–xii.

——. *Return to Freud: Jacques Lacan's Dislocation of Psychoanalysis*. Trans. Michael Levine. Cambridge: Cambridge UP, 1991.

*Webster's New Collegiate Dictionary*. Springfield: Merriam, 1980.

Weeks, Jeffrey. *Sexuality and Its Discontents: Meanings, Myths, and Modern Sexualities*. London: Routledge, 1985.

Weimann, Robert. *Structure and Society in Literary History: Studies in the History and Theory of Historical Studies*. Rev. ed. Baltimore: Johns Hopkins UP, 1984.

Weiskel, Thomas. *The Romantic Sublime: Studies in the Structure and Psychology of Transcendence*. Baltimore: Johns Hopkins UP, 1976.

Wellbery, David E. *Lessing's* Laocoön. Cambridge: Cambridge UP, 1984.

Wellek, René. "The Concept of Romanticism in Literary History." 1949. Gleckner and Enscoe 181–205.

——. "Destroying Literary Studies." *New Criterion* Dec. 1983: 1–8.

——. "Periods and Movements in Literary History." *English Institute Annal 1940*. New York: Columbia UP, 1941. 73–93.

Wells, Stanley, and Gary Taylor, eds. *William Shakespeare: A Textual Companion*. Oxford: Clarendon–Oxford UP, 1987.

——, eds. *William Shakespeare: The Complete Works*. Oxford: Clarendon–Oxford UP, 1986.

Welsh, Alexander. *George Eliot and Blackmail*. Cambridge: Harvard UP, 1985.

Wendell, Barrett. *William Shakespere*. New York: Scribner's, 1901.

West, Cornel. "Interview with Cornel West." *Universal Abandon*. Ed. Andrew Ross. Edinburgh: Edinburgh UP, 1988. 269–82.

——. "Theory, Pragmatisms, and Politics." Arac and Johnson 22–38.

Whigham, Frank. *Ambition and Privilege: The Social Tropes of Elizabethan Courtesy Theory*. Berkeley: U of California P, 1984.

White, Edward M. *Teaching and Assessing Writing*. San Francisco: Jossey-Bass, 1986.

White, Hayden. *The Content of Form: Narrative Discourse and Historical Representation*. Baltimore: Johns Hopkins UP, 1987.

——. *Metahistory: The Historical Imagination in Nineteenth-Century Europe*. Baltimore: Johns Hopkins UP, 1973.

——. "New Historicism: A Comment." Veeser 293–302.

——. *Tropics of Discourse*. Baltimore: John Hopkins UP, 1978.

Whitehead, Alfred North. *Science and the Modern World*. 1925. New York: Macmillan, 1953.

Wilden, Anthony. "Lacan and the Discourse of the Other." *The Language of the Self: The Function of Language in Psychoanalysis*. By Jacques Lacan. Trans. Wilden. Baltimore: Johns Hopkins UP, 1965. 157–311.

——. *System and Structure: Essays in Communication and Exchange*. London: Tavistock, 1972.

Will, George. "Literary Politics." *Newsweek* 22 Apr. 1991: 72.

Willey, Basil. *More Nineteenth Century Studies*. London: Chatto, 1956.

——. *Nineteenth Century Studies*. London: Chatto, 1949.

Williams, Raymond. *The Country and the City*. New York: Oxford UP, 1973.

——. *Culture*. London: Fontana, 1981.

——. *Culture and Society, 1780–1950*. Garden City: Doubleday, 1958.

——. "Distance." *What I Came to Say*. London: Hutchinson, 1989. 36–43.

——. *Marxism and Literature*. Oxford: Oxford UP, 1977.

——. *Politics and Letters*. New York: Schocken, 1979.

——. *The Politics of Modernism: Against the New Conformists*. Ed. Tony Pinkney. London: Verso, 1989.

——. *Television: Technology and Cultural Form*. London: Fontana, 1974.

Williams, William Carlos. *The Embodiment of Knowledge*. New York: New Directions, 1974.

——. *Imaginations*. Ed. Webster Schott. New York: New Directions, 1970.

——. *Spring and All*. *Imaginations* 85–151.

Wilson, Edmund. *Axel's Castle: A Study in the Imaginative Literature of 1870–1930*. 1931. New York: Scribner's, 1969.

——. "The Two Scrooges." *Eight Essays*. New York: Doubleday, 1954. 11–91.

Wilson, Katharina M., ed. *Women Writers of the Renaissance and Reformation*. Athens: U of Georgia P, 1987.

Wimsatt, W. K., Jr., and Monroe C. Beardsley. "The Intentional Fallacy." *The Verbal Icon*. Lexington: U of Kentucky P, 1954. 3–18.

Winnicott, D. W. "The Theory of the Parent-Infant Relationship." *International Journal of Psychoanalysis* 41 (1960): 585–95.

——. "Transitional Objects and Transitional Phenomena." *International Journal of Psychoanalysis* 34 (1953): 89–94.

Winnow, Jackie. "Lesbians Working on AIDS: Assessing the Impact on Health Care for Women." *Out/look: National Lesbian and Gay Quarterly* 5 (1989): 10–18.

Wittig, Monique, and Sande Zeig. *Lesbian Peoples: Material for a Dictionary*. New York: Avon, 1979.

Wittreich, Joseph. *Feminist Milton*. Ithaca: Cornell UP, 1987.

Wojciehowski, Dolora. *Old Masters, New Subjects: Renaissance and Postmodern Theories of Will*. Stanford: Stanford UP, 1992.

Wolfe, Don M. *Milton in the Puritan Revolution*. New York: Nelson, 1941.

Wolfson, Susan. *The Questioning Presence: Wordsworth, Keats, and the Interrogative Mode in Romantic Poetry*. Ithaca: Cornell UP, 1986.

Wood, Gordon S. "Struggle over the Puritans." *New York Review of Books* 9 Nov. 1989: 26+.

Woodbridge, Linda. *Women and the English Renaissance: Literature and the Nature of Womankind, 1540–1620*. Urbana: U of Illinois P, 1984.

Woodward, Kathleen, ed. *The Myths of Information: Technology and Postindustrial Culture*. Madison: Coda, 1980.

Woodward, Kenneth L., et al. "A New Look at Lit Crit." *Newsweek* 22 June 1981: 80–83.

Woolf, Virginia. "The Modern Essay." *The Common Reader: First Series*. 1923. New York: Harcourt, 1953.

——. "Modern Fiction." *Virginia Woolf Reader* 283–91.

——. "Mr. Bennett and Mrs. Brown." *Virginia Woolf Reader* 192–212.

——. *A Room of One's Own*. 1929. New York: Harvest-Harcourt, 1963.

——. *The Virginia Woolf Reader*. Ed. Mitchell A. Leaska. San Diego: Harcourt, 1984.

Wright, Elizabeth. "Another Look at Lacan and Literary Criticism." *New Literary History* 19 (1988): 617–27.

——. "The New Psychoanalysis and Literary Criticism: A Reading of Hawthorne and Melville." *Poetics Today* 3 (1982): 89–95.

——. *Psychoanalytic Criticism: Theory in Practice*. London: Metheun, 1984.

Yaeger, Patricia. *Honey-Mad Women: Emancipatory Strategies in Women's Writing*. New York: Columbia UP, 1988.

Yeats, William Butler, ed. *The Oxford Book of Modern Verse, 1892–1935*. Oxford: Clarendon–Oxford UP, 1936.

Yellin, Jean Fagan. *The Intricate Knot: Black Figures in American Literature, 1776–1863*. New York: New York UP, 1972.

Yingling, Thomas E. *Hart Crane and the Homosexual Text: New Thresholds, New Anatomies*. Chicago: U of Chicago P, 1990.

Young, G. M. *Victorian England: Portrait of an Age*. Oxford: Oxford UP, 1936.

Young, Richard E., Alton L. Becker, and Kenneth L. Pike. *Rhetoric, Discovery, and Change*. New York: Harcourt, 1970.

Young, Robert, ed. *Neocolonialism*. Spec. issue of *Oxford Literary Review* 13 (1991): 2–265.

——. *White Mythologies: Writing, History, and the West*. London: Routledge, 1990.

Zizek, Slavoj. *The Sublime Object of Ideology*. London: Verso, 1989.

Zumthor, Paul. *Speaking of the Middle Ages*. Lincoln: U of Nebraska P, 1986.

Zwerdling, Alex. *Virginia Woolf and the Real World*. Berkeley: U of California P, 1986.

# $\mathcal{I}$ndex